LOOKING UNTO

CHRIST

IN EVERY THOUGHT

LOOKING UNTO CHRIST IN EVERY THOUGHT

Defeating Fear, Doubt and Discouragement

Dennis R Deaton

Rooftop Publishing
Sandy, Utah

Library of Congress Cataloging-in-Publication

Name: Deaton, Dennis R, author.
Title: Looking Unto Christ in Every Thought / Dennis R Deaton

Description: Sandy, Utah: Rooftop Publishing, [2021] Includes bibliographical references and index.

Summary: "Author Dennis R Deaton sets forth guidelines to accurately diagnose Satan's discouraging deceptions, and assist faithful disciples of Jesus Christ to stand firm against doubt, fear, and discouragement." Provided by publisher.

Identifiers:
Library of Congress Control Number: 2021921549
ISBN 978-1-7335863-6-8 (hardback)
ISBN 978-1-7335863-9-9 (softcover)
ISBN 978-1-7335863-7-5 (audio)
ISBN 978-1-7335863-8-2 (ebook)

Subjects: Faith in Jesus Christ – The Church of Jesus Christ of Latter-day Saints. | Prayer – The Church of Jesus Christ of Latter-day Saints. | God's promises – The Church of Jesus Christ of Latter-day Saints-Doctrines.

Classification: LLCN-2021921549

Cover Artist: Danny R. Hahlbohm, ©2021 Danny Hahlbohm, inspired-art.com

Dedication

Dedicated to you—the intelligence of spirit—that you may look unto Christ in every thought and doubt not or fear not. That you may talk of Christ, rejoice in Christ, preach of Christ, prophesy of Christ, and look to him for a remission of your sins. That you may yield to the enticings of the Holy Spirit, and put off the natural man and become a saint through the Atonement of Christ the Lord.

Table of Contents

Preface

I hadn't planned to write another book.

Having written five already, one of which won awards, I was fairly certain I had crossed that canyon, never to go back and look down into the maw of the beast again. Writing a book is a daunting task, requiring hours of thought, research and fact-checking—and that's only the beginning. Interspersed are near-incessant mental battles of self-questioning, coupled with seemingly endless bouts of writer's block.[1]

On the threshold of a comfortable retirement, I was ready to devote heart and soul, and the bulk of my time, to my calling in the Church—the most wonderful calling I could conceive of holding—a stake patriarch. The office of patriarch is unique among all others in the Melchizedek Priesthood. It entails no leadership, counseling, teaching or administrative duties. Its main requirement is essentially its only requirement: Live worthy enough to obtain Heavenly Father's mind and will through the Spirit of prophecy and revelation on a regular and continuous basis in behalf of another person who will be basing the majority of his or her most crucial life decisions on what is written on paper above your signature. Piece of cake, right?

Humbled and grateful beyond expression, I was seeking to magnify my calling, rejoicing in its rigors, striving to live up to and embody them. Everything moved along quite smoothly until the fall of 2019. Over a period of a few months, I felt occasional whispers urging me to write a book for members of The Church of Jesus Christ of Latter-day Saints in which I would distill my life's work, writings

---

1 For those who think Joseph Smith, or any other person, wrote the Book of Mormon or any tome remotely like it, without the aid of the Library of Congress, a search engine on the internet, a word processor, and intellectually equipped with nothing more than a rudimentary grade-school education, my response is, "try it." And do it, with little or no income, while being driven from residence to residence by disdainful neighbors and vicious persecutors before you reach age twenty-five.

and church experience into a book dealing with the adversary's meddlings and interferences with our thoughts. The impressions came softly at first. Regretfully, I admit I questioned whether they were of the Lord, something I thought I'd learned *not* to do as a patriarch.

In November 2019, I was jolted by a prompting so firm it felt like a chastisement to the point of being a voice in my mind. "If you're not going to write it, I'll get somebody else to do it." My soul still hurts a bit when I think of this experience. I feel remorse that the Lord had to be so direct in order for me to take action.

Many of us have moments when, looking back, we realize we were being prepared for something without knowing what it was or that we were being prepared for it. I believe such to be the case with this book. I now see so many places and ways the truths I am striving to convey in this book would have been of tremendous benefit to me had I recognized them earlier.

Background

As background, I grew up in the Salt Lake Valley, was baptized in the Salt Lake Tabernacle, and endowed and married in the Salt Lake Temple. My parents were wonderful role models in so many ways; yet, due to my father's discomfort with religion, we were what is now called a "less active family." My parents certainly were not *against* the Church, but we seldom attended as a family. In my teen years I usually went to church alone and was active in Aaronic Priesthood quorum and scouting activities. There was no scripture reading (we didn't even have scriptures in our home), no family home evenings, no family prayers before bed.

As I grew older, I recognized many of my peers had a greater knowledge of the scriptures. Feeling behind and somewhat deprived, I became determined to catch up. In high school, I bought my own scriptures and attended and graduated from seminary. By the time I entered the mission field, I was much better versed in the standard works and had a sound understanding of the gospel. While on my mission, I was blessed to associate with elders who had extensive knowledge they had gained from reading the *Teachings of the Prophet Joseph Smith,* compiled by Joseph Fielding Smith. I wrote my mother and asked her to send me a copy, which she did. I devoured the book. For me, it opened up a whole new perspective about the reality of personal revelation. Near the end of my mission, I had an experience I will never forget. It was the first time the Spirit connected two doctrinal wires in a new and meaningful way in my mind. "Click." It almost felt like a mild electrical shock as the two ideas came together. I still savor the feeling of light and excitement I felt at that time. I had received a *revelation!* Yeh, *me*!

After my mission I pursued my goal of going to dental school and I obtained my doctorate six years later. Despite the demands of school, I consistently made ample time for scripture study and continued to grow in my knowledge of the gospel as more "clicks" came. My appreciation for the Prophet Joseph Smith grew deeper. My love for Heavenly Father and for my Savior Jesus Christ burgeoned—I felt they knew me and wanted me to keep learning more about how to communicate with them. My desire to teach the gospel grew commensurately, and I wound up teaching an early morning institute class at the College of Eastern Utah in Price, my wife Susan's hometown. I had also set up a successful dental practice there.

However, a few years and a number of clicks later, I started feeling restless about my life and couldn't quite put my finger on why. Something was missing; it had nothing to do with doctrine, the meaning and purpose of life, or my testimony. All of that was solidly in place. I enjoyed my profession and serving in callings in the Church. Susan and I had a lovely home, good friends, and an income sufficient that she could live her dream of being a stay-at-home mother of a good-sized family of children. We were enjoying the life we had always dreamed of. Still, I was restless; something was incomplete.

Ironic as it may seem, in view of my calling as a patriarch, I had not received my patriarchal blessing. I had never even *heard* of patriarchal blessings until I arrived in the mission field. Upon returning from my mission, I immediately met Susan, we fell in love, were married in the temple and, shortly thereafter, headed to dental school. Everything just kept falling into place, and the thought of obtaining a patriarchal blessing never entered my mind, until I became afflicted with this chronic restlessness.

At Susan's suggestion, I finally sought and received my patriarchal blessing. In it I learned that dentistry was but a steppingstone. My life's calling was to be a teacher; I possessed a gift to explain complex scriptures and doctrines so others could understand them. I was further promised that through my life's work I would associate with many people and initiate programs that would help others learn the truths of the gospel, and that I would be instrumental in spreading these truths to all nations.

Within a few years of receiving my patriarchal blessing, I co-founded a corporate training company, and was the chief designer of the human development curriculum based on principles of the restored gospel. This organization and its teachings have positively impacted the lives of tens of thousands of people across the world.

Designed under frequent and continuous guidance of the Spirit, this unique brand of individual development and leadership training focused on one central premise: *"We alter our destiny by altering our thoughts."* The restlessness I experienced prior to my patriarchal blessing has been quenched and I have channeled my energy over the past three decades to studying, pondering, seeking and receiving inspiration and divine guidance to help people understand the workings of their minds and the power of their thoughts.

Whereas I started out learning to express gospel principles in a vocabulary that made sense in business settings, in *Looking Unto Christ in Every Thought,* I am now putting the message and vocabulary back into its original context. In this book, I blend the full spectrum of my life's study and teachings—uniting insights I've gained through my professional experience with what I've learned through continuous scripture study and church service.

Of myself, I simply say, "I strive to be a devout Latter-day Saint and disciple of the Lord Jesus Christ, serving Him with all my might, mind, and strength." As far back as I can remember I have had a testimony of the restored gospel of Jesus Christ and the mission of the Prophet Joseph Smith. I was born with it. As I am of no particular stature in or out of the Church, this book is not to be regarded as a pronouncement of official doctrine of The Church of Jesus Christ of Latter-day Saints. I alone am responsible for its content, its shortcomings and its flaws. And, if any good comes of it, may the praise, honor and glory be to the Father and the Son forever and ever. Amen.

Introduction

As members of The Church of Jesus Christ of Latter-day Saints, our Father in Heaven offers us promises so grand and glorious that we have a hard time comprehending them, let alone living up to them. For most of us, it's even a considerable stretch to believe we can obtain these privileges at some future point in the realms ahead, much less in this life. Yet, it's about these very tentative, self-doubting thoughts this book is written.

Despite how many times we've heard Joseph's testimony of what happened when he asked in faith, *nothing wavering*, we struggle to believe the same promise actually, truly, applies to us as well.

Even as we read "If *any of you* lack wisdom …" and "giveth to *all men* liberally and upbraideth not" (James 1:5, emphasis added), we entertain thoughts like, "Oh, that could never apply to me. Things like that are way out of my league, they're only for foreordained prophets and apostles. I'm not worthy enough. I have too many faults and have committed too many sins." If you have never in your life entertained such thoughts, then this book is not for you. If, on the other hand, versions or variations on those thoughts show up with some frequency, then this book has a great deal to offer you.

The two primary purposes of this book are to alert you and make you more aware of Satan's tactics and how prevalent they are and to provide you with viable ways to unmask the liar within and repel his nefarious devices.

Make no mistake about it. We are in a war—a conflict far more sinister and consequential than the horrible physical versions waged among the children of men. The casualties and fatalities of manmade wars are limited to the physical body and the brief span of mortal existence. The war waged by Lucifer against us has *eternal* consequences. By accurately diagnosing Satan's discouraging deceptions, we are able to forthrightly confront them; and can exercise intentional, powerful faith in the Lord Jesus Christ, who is mighty to save and who will empower *all* who put their unqualified trust in Him. It is to this end this book is dedicated. I earnestly believe that by looking unto Christ—exercising faith in Him manifest through obedience to the laws and ordinances of His gospel—each of us can "be saved from our enemies, and from the hand of all those who hate us" (JST Luke 1:70).

How the Book is Organized

Looking Unto Christ in Every Thought: Defeating Fear, Doubt and Discouragement is divided into four sections. In Section One, *Building on a Firm Foundation,* we will follow the logic of the Prophet Joseph Smith that "It is necessary for us to have an understanding of God himself. … If men do not comprehend the character of God, they do not comprehend themselves."[1] Chapters One through Four establish a doctrinal foundation for obtaining God's promises by studying what the Prophet taught about 1) who God is; 2) who we are; 3) the fundamental truth about the use of our agency; and 4) the premises upon which our eternal progression rests.

In Section Two, *Principles of Mind Management*, we focus on a crucial skill of true disciples—mental discipline. How much we make of our opportunities in mortality hinges on how we choose to use our agency or, put more clearly, the thoughts we choose to dwell upon and the ones we choose to reject.

Our judgment and state of immortality will be determined by what we have become through the Atonement of Christ, evidenced by the works, words, and thoughts we chose while in our mortal state (Alma 12:14). We literally become the product of our thoughts (Proverbs 23:7). Chapters Five through Ten cover the principles and laws that govern our mental powers and how to leverage them.

If all the above were not enough of a challenge, we must also grapple with the reality that we have an archenemy of our souls who is unleashing every evil scheme, stratagem,

1 Joseph Smith, Jr., *Teachings of the Prophet Joseph Smith,* (Salt Lake City: Deseret Book Company, 1976), 343.

and tactic devisable to deter, discourage, and defeat us. Section Three, *Recognizing and Defeating Satan's Ploys,* takes direct aim at developing skills to both diagnose and defeat Satan's ploys. So cunning and diabolical are these assaults—their instigation so stealthily devised—we are largely unaware of how constantly and insidiously they are working upon us. In Chapters 11 through 21, we explore specific strategies of the devil and learn ways to reject and defeat each one of them.

In culmination, Section Four, *Looking Unto Christ in Every Thought,* Chapters 22 through 28, we devote attention to the crowning jewels—the supernal promises extended to each of us through the Atonement of Jesus Christ. We live in the times when "The visions and blessings of old are returning and angels are coming to visit the earth," as sung at the dedication of the Kirtland Temple. Such spiritual privileges pertain as equally to members of The Church of Jesus Christ of Latter-day Saints today as they did to the early saints in Kirtland, for the Christ we worship is no respecter of persons (D&C 1:35). He remains everlastingly the same unchangeable God—the same yesterday, and today, and forever (Hebrews 13:8).

In truth, the ultimate true witness, guide and teacher whose mission it is to lead us to the Father and the Son and to testify of their divinity and holiness is the Holy Ghost, the third member of the Godhead. With a fervent prayer in my heart, I invite you to read, study, and pray over each chapter and hearken to the voice of the Spirit as He tailors the concepts to you and your current challenges and responsibilities. I suggest you jot notes in the margins or in a journal as the Spirit speaks to you. What you discover will be more precious than rubies.

By definition, a disciple is one who undertakes a discipline, which implies a certain amount of rigor and concerted effort. By pausing to pray and ponder, the Holy Ghost will increase your personal understanding and help you know how to apply it. Your extra effort and focused mind will allow the Holy Ghost to add "revelation upon revelation, knowledge upon knowledge, that thou mayest know the mysteries and peaceable things—that which bringeth joy, that which bringeth life eternal" (D&C 42:61).

Writing this book has been a soul-stretching experience for me, spiced with many sweet moments of flowing inspiration as the Spirit guided my writings. May your experience of reading this book be as fruitful.

SECTION ONE

Building on a Firm Foundation

"True doctrine, understood, changes attitudes and behavior. The study of the doctrines of the gospel will improve behavior quicker than a study of behavior will improve behavior."

— Boyd K. Packer, "Do Not Fear," *Ensign*, May 2004, 79.

CHAPTER 1

Who God Is

"They've got to understand who God is! They've got to know how much love He has for them—how beloved they truly are to Him! They don't know His character or His attributes—that He's a *loving, caring* God—who cares about *them*—who *really, really cares about them!*"

Those words coming over the phone were spoken by my brother-in-law, a retired physician, who now spends much of his time working with brilliant, faithful, talented Latter-day Saints—most of them are recently returned missionaries brimming with eternal potential. There was an unmistakable and unusual mixture of emotion in his voice. On one hand he was overjoyed at the success many of them were experiencing. Intermingled was also a heart-touching plaintive tone—a pathos—almost a plea in behalf of others who were still struggling. Dr. Dan, as he's often referred to, is a missionary volunteer working in the Church's addiction recovery program.

We had often spoken about the work he was doing and the deep satisfaction he felt in doing it. "We help them understand the power of the Atonement of Jesus Christ, especially the enabling power of Christ. When they come to realize how readily the Lord will impart His grace—the power they need to overcome their addiction—the success rate is phenomenal. They break free! They get their life back based on truth. Amazingly, most of them within a year find their eternal companion and are married in the temple." Elation always permeated his words.

Today's call was not all that different except for the emphasis he placed on what he considered to be the key to the whole process. His heart was heavy for those who had not yet had their breakthrough, and he knew the reason why. It came down to a satanic lie they held in their belief system that they had not yet been able to dispel. Tragically, these returned missionaries are not the only ones. Lucifer has succeeded in convincing a large number of God's children of the deadly heresy that God is a harsh, judgmental being who is slow to forgive and quick to condemn. Then the next phase of the evil arsenic gets personal:

> *"You don't have what it takes. You'll never make it. You have to be perfect in order to please Him. Look how many times you've tried, and every time you've failed. The gospel might work for others, but it won't work for you. You're worthless and hopeless. Besides, you've already messed your life up so badly there's no way forward for you. You've blown your chance. When are you going to stop kidding yourself? You're a joke and a hypocrite. You may as well pack it in, give up, and quit."*

This diatribe laden with lies about God and about you is Satan's most prominent weapon to undermine your spiritual confidence and destroy your faith in Christ and your loving, merciful Heavenly Father.

The word "gospel" means good news; and one of its foremost pieces of good news is this: the truth, which is more powerful than lies, will ultimately prevail. When we do not just hear but really *believe* and *act on* the truth, the Lord's words will be proven valid for each of us. What He said to His early disciples, He is saying to you and me, "And ye shall know the truth, and the truth shall make you free" (John 8:32).

The Truth about Heavenly Father

The scriptures testify that God is "merciful and gracious, longsuffering and abundant in goodness and truth" (Exodus 34:6), and "slow to anger and plenteous in mercy" (Psalms 103:6–8). "God is love. … Herein is love, not that we loved God, but that *he loved us,* and sent his Son to be the propitiation for our sins" (1 John 4:8–10, emphasis added). "God so loved the world that he gave his only begotten Son, that whosoever believeth in him should not perish, but have everlasting life. For God sent not his Son into the world to condemn the world; but that the world through him might be saved" (John 3:16–17).

God is *not* a condemning God. The Prophet Joseph Smith said, "Our Heavenly Father is more liberal in His views, and boundless in His mercies and blessings, than we are ready to believe or receive."[1] Who would know better than Joseph Smith just how approachable and eager to impart wisdom God is? He is this dispensation's foremost witness that God giveth to *all* men *liberally, without upbraiding, scolding or chastising.*

How touching is Enoch's personal testimony of this truth. He was *shocked* to see God weeping over the transgressions of His children. Enoch could hardly fathom how such sorrow can be possible. Expressing his dismay directly to God, "… seeing thou are holy … and naught but peace, justice, and truth is the habitation of thy throne; and mercy shall go before thy face and have no end," Enoch poses his semi-stunned query, "How is it thou canst weep?" (Moses 7:29–31). Then comes the deeply touching and highly revealing insight into the character and true nature of our Heavenly Father. God responds,

> *Behold these thy brethren; they are the workmanship of mine own hands, and I gave unto them their knowledge, in the day I created them; and in the Garden of Eden, gave I unto man his agency; and unto thy brethren*

1 Smith, *Teachings of the Prophet Joseph Smith*, 257.

> *have I said, and also given commandment, that they should love one another, and that they should choose me, their Father; but behold, they are without affection, and they hate their own blood (Moses 7:32–33).*

A heart-broken Heavenly Father, who loves His children far more than even the most kindly, loving, earthly parent, is essentially saying, "These are *my children.* And look what they are doing to themselves and to each other—all because they won't turn to me so I can help them, lift them, heal them and exalt them. How can I *not* weep?"

Heavenly Father is anything but aloof and unapproachable. Far from haughty and harsh, He is gentle and kind *and humble.* How tender is Moroni's testimony of this truth. Having had a personal conversation that emphatically confirmed how loving and open God is, Moroni shares: "And then shall ye know that I have seen Jesus, and that he hath talked with me face to face, and that *he told me in plain humility,* even as a man telleth another in mine own language, concerning these things" (Ether 12:39, emphasis added). How can we not be moved when we envision Moroni's description of Christ, the Eternal God, speaking *in plain humility* with him? Does this account not shatter the wall of lies Satan casts up to deceive us and undermine our faith in our loving, compassionate Father? Are we not all prodigals who, having wandered from our heavenly home, are yearning to come back to our Father and be warmly welcomed? If "yes" is your answer, then please, please remember what happened when the prodigal son had "come to himself" and turned back toward his father. "But when he was yet a great way off, his father saw him, and had compassion, and ran, and fell on his neck, and kissed him" (Luke 15:20). If we will walk toward him, He will run toward us and greet us with an embrace indescribable in earthly terms. This is not just poetic metaphor. Such an experience is not just for the elite spiritual athletes we call apostles and prophets (which is yet another lie sown by the devil). It is available to all, for our God is no respecter of persons. Give special attention to how Moroni closes his account of his personal visit with the Lord.

> *And now, I would commend you to seek this Jesus of whom the prophets and apostles have written, that the grace of God the Father, and also the Lord Jesus Christ, and the Holy Ghost, which beareth record of them, may be and abide in you forever. Amen. (Ether 12:41).*

God Knew We Wouldn't Progress Perfectly

God knew we wouldn't progress perfectly, and He planned for it. Go back to the image in your mind of a loving father running towards his wayward son. Even as the son was begging for his freedom to spend his inheritance any way he wished, this father had a pretty good idea of how things would turn out for his son. Undoubtedly, the father held onto the hope that the son would remember his unflagging love and would return home once the son had learned his lesson. Now humbled and repentant, the son *did* head back to his father, hoping to be accepted, if only as a hired servant. And, the son's hope was vindicated, beyond his expectations. Can you imagine the exhilaration the son must have experienced when he saw his father *running* towards him? The son's realization that his father's love had never wavered, despite his misdeeds and poor choices, must have brought overwhelming joy and momentous relief. Is there not a tender longing in all our hearts for just such a confirmation?

Happily, Heavenly Father's unwavering love for His children is one of the most precious pieces of "good news" embedded in the gospel of Jesus Christ. The scriptures, prophets and Holy Spirit all testify that we too, in spite of our many imperfections, can count on God's never-wavering love. Let us put our doubts aside, and rely on the love of the Father and the merits of His Son to learn what we came here to learn, overcome what we came here to overcome, and pursue our course up the covenant path until we receive the loving embrace of our Heavenly Father welcoming us back home.

The parable offers more to us than reassurance of God's ever-constant love for us. Similar to the father in the parable, our loving Heavenly Father knew we lacked experience in choosing good over evil, and we would have to learn lessons the hard way. Our Father knew none of us, save His Only Begotten, could progress perfectly, which is why His whole plan is referred to as the Plan of *Salvation.* He knew every one of us would need to be *saved*—saved from ignorance, pride, bad decisions, omissions and sins. He knew we would all struggle with mastering our mortal bodies and there would be many slips and falls as we learn how to govern these marvelous but unruly tabernacles. He is not shocked or surprised or even disappointed when we stumble. He planned for it. He organized His entire plan around us blowing our inheritance. Amazingly, God is not angry with us when we sin. He's only angry when his children sin *and won't repent.* It's not our sins that disappoint him—it's our refusal to reach out to Him for the help we need in order to overcome the flesh and keep the commandments.

Divine help is the crux of the plan: None of us can or are expected to do it all on our own. In order to return to the Father, we have to turn to the Son. No matter how determined and committed we might be, none of us can do it alone, on our own power. The more we grit our teeth, resolve and bear down, and try to do it on our own, the more we realize how insufficient our strength actually is. Sooner or later we all come to realize we need the Savior, the One with all power, both in heaven and on earth. If we will come unto Him, put our trust in Him, and rely on Him, He will bestow upon us His grace—His enabling power—infusing us with spiritual strength to put off the natural man and become a saint through the power of His Atonement. This glorious truth is stated clearly in the Book of Ether:

> *And if men come unto me I will show unto them their weakness. I give unto men weakness that they may be humble; and my grace is sufficient for all men that humble themselves before me; for if they humble themselves before me, and have faith in me, then will I make weak things become strong unto them (Ether 12:27).*

So, please underscore the following:

1) Yes, here in mortality you are in a battle for your very soul.

2) Yes, you are up against a vicious, cunning foe—the very embodiment of evil—Lucifer, the Arch-Antichrist.

3) Yes, you are wrestling with and trying to school an unruly, mortal tabernacle with tendencies that must be controlled and taught to be obedient.

4) And yet, as Elder Boyd K. Packer declared, "… there is no habit, no addiction, no rebellion, no transgression, no apostasy, no crime exempted from the promise of complete forgiveness. This is the promise of the Atonement of Christ."[2]

5) And yet, "though your sins be as scarlet, they shall be as white as snow" (Isaiah 1:18).

6) And yet, you can lift up your head and be of good cheer; and put on the brightness of hope, for, "In the world ye shall have tribulation: but be of good cheer; I [Christ] have overcome the world" (John 16:33).

7) And yet, through faith in Jesus Christ and trust in your Heavenly Father's love and power, you will come to know personally that Christ's

---

2 Packer, "The Brilliant Morning of Forgiveness," *Ensign,* November 1995, 20.

enabling power is more than sufficient for you and everyone else who will come unto Christ humbly seeking to be perfected in Him.

These seven core truths are a big part of the good news about Heavenly Father's loving plan for His children. None of us begins with perfect faith. We are here to grow in faith by exercising imperfect faith to the extent we are able each step of the way. If we truly humble ourselves and put our growing faith in Christ, our submissiveness and deep humility are enough to obtain the grace of Christ which is the power of God unto salvation bestowed upon all who earnestly seek Him.

Witnesses of Heavenly Father's Love and of His Power

During the earthly ministry of the Lord, He was approached by a desperate father whose son had been possessed of a devil since birth. To confirm how evil and heartless Satan can be, read the account in Mark 9, which tells of the unabated cruelty inflicted upon the son. The father had some belief in Jesus, or he would not have requested a miracle. Yet, his faith was not perfect. "Jesus said unto him, If thou canst believe, all things are possible to him that believeth. And straightway the father of the child cried out, and said with tears, Lord, I believe; help thou mine unbelief" (Mark 9:23–24). Though there was much room for growth in the man's faith, the lack thereof did not prevent the miracle. Christ rebuked the devil within and it departed.

This heartening account should "help" our unbelief and bolster it. Does it not give us all a little more impetus to keep approaching the Father and the Son exercising as much faith as we have at that moment? We cannot do more. And, the Lord does not require more than we have. He just requests a full and honest offering of *all we do have*. Heavenly Father does not put any limits on us. Only we do that. I love the Savior's words to the heart-broken father, "… all things are possible to him that believeth" (Mark 9:23). I think of them often as a way to keep forging ahead.

None of us know how far we can go. Perhaps you might be inspired as I have been with the experience of a young missionary. Yes, he became an ordained apostle of the Lord, but Elder Orson F. Whitney did not know how far he could go at the time. He was just striving to do his best to be a good missionary when he had a dream that dramatically focused and energized his life. He wrote:

> *I seemed to be in the Garden of Gethsemane, a witness of the Savior's agony. . . . Standing behind a tree in the foreground, I beheld Jesus, with Peter, James, and John, as they came through a little wicket gate at my right. Leaving the three Apostles there, after telling them to kneel and pray, the Son of God passed over to the other side, where He also knelt and prayed … "Oh my Father, if it be possible, let this cup pass from me; nevertheless not as I will but as Thou wilt." As He prayed the tears streamed down His face, which was toward me. I was so moved at the sight that I also wept, out of pure sympathy. My whole heart went out to Him; I loved Him with all my soul, and longed to be with Him as I longed for nothing else.*
>
> *Presently He arose and walked to where those Apostles were kneeling—fast asleep! He shook them gently, awoke them, and in a tone of tender reproach, untinctured by the least show of anger or impatience, asked them plaintively if they could not watch with Him one hour.…*
>
> *All at once the circumstance seemed to change. … Instead of before, it was after the crucifixion, and the Savior, with those three Apostles, now stood together in a group at my left. They were about to depart and ascend into Heaven. I could endure it no longer. I ran from behind the tree, fell at His feet, clasped Him around the knees, and begged Him to take me with Him.*

I shall never forget the kind and gentle manner in which He stooped, raised me up and embraced me. It was so vivid, so real. I felt the very warmth of His body, as He held me in His arms and said in the tenderest tones: "No, my son; those have finished their work; they can go with me; but you must stay and finish yours." Still I clung to Him. Gazing up into His face—for He was taller than I—I besought Him fervently: "Well, promise me that I will come to you at the last." Smiling sweetly, He said: "That will depend entirely upon yourself." I awoke with a sob in my throat, and it was morning."[3]

This sacred dream teaches many things, not the least of which is how loving the Father and Son truly are, and how much they want us to know of their love and feel it in this life. How much of their love we experience "will depend entirely upon ourselves."

3 Orson F. Whitney, *Through Memory's Halls: The Life Story of Orson F. Whitney, as Told by Himself* (Independence, MO: Zion's Printing and Publishing, 1930), 81–83. Cited by Spencer W. Kimball, *Faith Precedes the Miracle,* (Salt Lake City: Deseret Book Company, 1969), 26–27.

CHAPTER 2

Knowing Yourself: An Eternal, Independent, Self-Governing Being

Now that you know who God is, it is imperative you know who you are. In the glorious doctrinal masterpiece, The King Follett Discourse, the Prophet Joseph Smith said, "If we start right, it is easy to go right all the time; but if we start wrong, we may go wrong, and it will be a hard matter to get right."[1] To truly worship God, which is to emulate and be like Him, Joseph reasoned, we must know Him (what kind of a being God is) and know ourselves (what kind of beings we are). To know who we are, Joseph wants us to know about beginnings. He knows, and knows that we know, that the first verse in the Bible reads, "In the beginning God created the heaven and the earth" (Gen. 1:1). What beginning? The beginning of *everything*?—the beginning of time, space, and the universe?—the beginning of God Himself? Certainly not. For God is eternal. He had no beginning and will have no end and is, as Enoch said, "from all eternity to all eternity" (Moses 7:29). The "beginning" spoken of in Genesis 1:1 refers to the creation of this earth and its associated atmospheric envelope.

---

1 Smith, *Teachings of the Prophet Joseph Smith*, 343.

In this discourse, Joseph is not focused on the earth; he wants us to know who God is and who we are. To do so, he takes us back to "the morn of creation":

> *I intend to edify you with the simple truths from heaven. In the first place, I wish to go back to the beginning—to the morn of creation. … It is necessary for us to have an understanding of God himself in the beginning. … If men do not comprehend the character of God, they do not comprehend themselves. I want to go back to the beginning, and so lift your minds into a more lofty sphere and a more exalted understanding than what the human mind generally aspires to.*[2]

Though we can scarcely wrap our mortal minds around the vast concept of eternity or something always existing—having no beginning and no end—Joseph wants us to do our best to grasp that concept. He wants us to not only understand that God is an eternal, self-existent being, he wants us to understand that the same truth applies to us. Of all the stunning eternal truths taught by the Prophet Joseph Smith, none outranks his teachings about who we are and how we relate to our Father in Heaven. When it comes to conscious beings, the first startling truth is: In the beginning there was no beginning. All the conscious beings we refer to—in whatever state of progression they may be—Gods, angels, unembodied spirits, disembodied spirits, mortal men, women and children—as *conscious thinking individuals*, none had a beginning.

Speaking of man's essential identity, the Prophet states:

> *The soul—the mind of man—the immortal spirit. Where did it come from? All learned men and doctors of divinity say that God created it in the beginning; but it is not so: the very idea lessens man in my estimation. … We say that God himself is a self-existent being. Who*

2 Smith, *Teachings of the Prophet Joseph Smith*, 342–343.

told you so? It is correct enough; but how did it get into your heads? Who told you that man did not exist in like manner upon the same principles? Man does exist upon the same principles.[3]

Throughout this discourse, Joseph equates several terms: the soul, the mind of man, the immortal spirit, the mind, the intelligence, the intelligence of spirits. Keep in mind Joseph was declaring these momentous truths while standing on his feet, speaking under the power of the Spirit, with no prepared notes. As you have probably experienced yourself, when bearing your testimony or speaking from the heart, there are times when you sense what the Spirit is prompting you to say, but you struggle to find just the right words to say it.

It is obvious Joseph senses some limitation in the English vocabulary of his day. In endeavoring to put across a correct understanding of man's primordial identity, no single word seems to quite capture and express the meaning he wants us to grasp. Clearly, we should have no doubt Joseph knew that all of God's children are His literally begotten spirit sons and daughters. Joseph is taking us a step further by teaching that the essential identity of each of God's spirit children was not created. He refers to that essential identity as the "intelligence of spirits"[4]—the conscious thinking being—the unique, self-existent, individual personality we refer to as "me." Joseph reasoned, "Is it logical to say that the intelligence of spirits is immortal, and yet that it had a beginning? The intelligence of spirits had no beginning, neither will it have an end."[5] In an earlier address, Joseph taught, "The spirit of man is not a created being; it existed from all eternity and will exist to eternity."[6] President Joseph Fielding Smith clarifies the vocabulary:

In saying "the spirit of man is not created" the Prophet without any doubt had in mind the intelligence as explained in the Doctrine and

3 Smith, *Teachings of the Prophet Joseph Smith,* 351.
4 Ibid., 343.
5 Ibid., 353, emphasis added.
6 Ibid., 158.

> *Covenants, Sec. 93:29: "Man was also in the beginning with God. Intelligence, or the light of truth, was not created or made, neither indeed can be." From this we gather that the intelligence in man was not created, but the Prophet taught very clearly that man is in very deed the offspring of God, and that the spirits of men were born in the spirit world the children of God.*[7]

Each of us carries an innate awareness of self. We recognize an inner, personal identity—the "me" located inside our body—which is separate and distinct from everything else outside our body—including the vastness of space itself, as far in all directions as our mortal minds can project. There is "me" inside, and everything else is "out there."

To describe this self-existent entity, Joseph adapted the word "intelligence," giving it a new definition. Heretofore the word "intelligence" referred to a characteristic or an attribute of the mind. In this discourse, he used it as a *synonym* for the mind. What you and I refer to as our "mind" is what Joseph called our "intelligence." Because this intelligence is now housed in a spirit body, it can also be referred to as our "intelligence of spirit," which Joseph also called "the mind of man." He goes on to say, "The mind or intelligence which man possesses is co-equal [co-eternal] with God himself."[8]

Joseph also taught that intelligences can acquire and increase in intelligence, using the word intelligence as an attribute of the mind. The latter sense refers to the amount or degree of knowledge a being—an intelligence—can possess. In the next statement, notice how Joseph uses the word intelligence in three separate ways:

> *The first principles of man are self-existent with God. God himself, finding he was in the midst of spirits and glory, because he was more*

7 Smith, *Teachings of the Prophet Joseph Smith,* 158 (footnote).
8 Ibid., 352–353.

> **intelligent**, *saw proper to institute laws whereby the rest could have a privilege to advance like himself. The relationship we have with God places us in a situation to advance in knowledge. He has power to institute laws to instruct the weaker* **intelligences**, *that they may be exalted with himself, so that they might have one glory upon another, and all that knowledge, power, glory, and* **intelligence**, *which is requisite in order to save them in the world of spirits.*[9]

First, in the phrase "because he was more intelligent" he used it as an adjective: indicating the degree of mental capacity a mind possesses. Second, in the phrase "laws to instruct the weaker intelligences," he used it as a noun: an individual being or personality. Third, in the phrase "knowledge, power, glory, and intelligence" he referred to the truth and light a being acquires and possesses by keeping God's commandments (D&C 93:28, 36).

With this vital clarification in terms, we are now prepared to go where the Prophet wanted to take us and bask in the light of unparalleled glorious truths.

> *I am dwelling on the immortality of the spirit of man. Is it logical to say that the intelligence of spirits is immortal, and yet that it had a beginning? The intelligence of spirits had no beginning, neither will it have an end. That is good logic. That which has a beginning may have an end. There never was a time when there were not spirits; for they are co-equal (co-eternal) with our Father in heaven.*[10]

> *As the Lord liveth, if it [the intelligence] had a beginning, it will have an end. … God never had the power to create the spirit of man at all. … God himself could not create himself. Intelligence is eternal and exists upon a self-existent principle … and there is no creation about it.*[11]

9 Smith, *Teachings of the Prophet Joseph Smith,* 354, emphasis added.
10 Ibid., 353.
11 Ibid., 354.

Further bolstering the key point that our individual intelligence was not created, is the revelation given to the Prophet in May of 1833:

> *Man was also in the beginning with God. Intelligence, or the light of truth,* was not created or made, neither indeed can be. … *Behold,* here is the agency of *man***,** *and here is the condemnation of man; because that which was from the beginning is plainly manifest unto them, and they receive not the light (D&C 93:29–31, emphasis added).*

This is one of the most precious and potent passages in our standard works. Consider carefully its significance and implications. You are an uncreated, self-aware, self-governing intelligence possessing certain inherent qualities that make you an individual intelligent being. As an intelligence, you exist as an independent thinker of thoughts in whatever sphere God may place you, be that the spirit world, mortality, or immortality. You always have been, and you ever will be, independent and free to think whatever thoughts you want to think.

The next notable characteristic of the intelligence is its capability of instant self-assessment. We can think about our thinking, right in the process of thinking; and we can examine and weigh the value of those thoughts. This ability leads us to recognize the next significant characteristic of the intelligence: It has the independent ability to make decisions about what it's thinking. In other words, the intelligence is constantly *making choices.* It can choose to stay with its current thought or switch to another. As an independent, self-governing intelligence, you are not only the thinker of your thoughts, you are also the sole judge of their value. Every thought you dwell on represents a choice on your part. Only you make the choice of which thoughts you'll entertain and which you'll reject.

This is your foremost characteristic, your ultimate freedom, and your sole responsibility. "Behold, here is the agency of man, and here is the condemnation of man" (D&C 93:31). You and you alone make the choices that determine, spiritually and temporally, if, when, how far, and how fast you progress. You—the intelligence of spirit within—are the chooser within. It has always been that way and it will always be that way.

CHAPTER 3

Knowing Yourself: A Beloved Son or Daughter of Heavenly Parents

How great the wisdom and the foresight of "The Family: A Proclamation to the World." Pronounced by President Gordon B. Hinckley on September 23, 1995, it constitutes a pearl of great price to a generation searching to find itself and understand its identity, purpose and destiny. "All human beings — male and female—are created in the image of God. Each is a beloved spirit son or daughter of heavenly parents, and, as such, each has a divine nature and destiny."[1] This inspired sentence is rich with reassuring truths. Every being who is, ever was, and ever will be born on this earth can draw spiritual strength and confidence from the supernal truth that he or she is a literal child of heavenly parents. Sweet and soothing are the words of Eliza R. Snow, who reasoned with sublimely pure logic that if there is a Heavenly Father, there must surely be a Heavenly Mother.[2]

One truth leading to another, we thereby learn that each individual intelligence had an actual birth as a spirit. In a truth appropriately veiled

---

1 Gordon B. Hinckley, "The Family: A Proclamation to the World," *Ensign,* November 1995.

2 "O My Father," *Hymns of the Church of Jesus Christ of Latter-day Saints,* (Salt Lake City: The Church of Jesus Christ of Latter-day Saints, 1985) (revised in 2002), no. 292.

because of its sacredness, we are led to understand what that means. As that which is temporal is in the likeness of that which is spiritual, through an expression of divine love between our Heavenly Parents our individual intelligence was tabernacled in a spirit body, becoming thereby in the truest sense a begotten spirit daughter or son of God. Through this birth, the state of the intelligence is forever changed, improved and amplified. Now inseparably integrated into a spirit body, the intelligence is the literal offspring of immortal, exalted parents. As such, each spirit is as immortal as his or her parents and will never die. In other words, the intelligence can never be separated from its spirit body. Consistent with the law of heredity, at conception, children inherit the capacity to develop the same characteristics, faculties and powers of their parents. However, as an uncreated individual entity it has always existed, and in that sense is co-eternal with God. At birth, the newly embodied intelligence enters a vastly augmented level of existence referred to as his or her "first estate." The amplified possibilities gained in the transition from an intelligence to a spirit being are of such a magnitude that it makes the term "quantum leap" a feeble metaphor.

Once endowed with a spirit body, each spirit child is nurtured and educated by loving celestial parents. Although innately unique, each spirit is provided equal and maximum opportunity for growth, expression, experience and progress according to the exercise of his or her agency. In light of the scripture, "And I, God, created man in mine own image, in the image of mine Only Begotten created I him; male and female created I them," (Moses 2:27) we know a spirit body is in the likeness of a physical body—two arms, two legs, one nose, one mouth. When Jesus walked on the stormy Sea of Galilee, the disciples saw a human figure and immediately concluded it was a "*spirit*."[3] The most explicit testimony of the nature of our spirits is the Lord's

3 Matt. 14:26, emphasis added.

conversation with the brother of Jared in which He says: "Behold, this body, which ye now behold, is the body of my spirit; and man have I created after the body of my spirit" (Ether 3:16). President Joseph F. Smith confirmed,

> *God created man in His own image. This is just as true of the spirit as it is of the body, which is only the clothing of the spirit, its complement; the two together constituting the soul. The spirit of man is in the form of man, and the spirits of all creatures are in the likeness of their bodies. This was plainly taught by the Prophet Joseph Smith.*[4]

The Magnitude of Our Potential

Recognizing the divine significance of the likeness between the spiritual and the temporal now leads us to priceless insights. In mortality, at conception we receive a marvelous chromosomal inheritance. The genetic codes of our earthly parents first split in half. A copy of each parent's genome unites and the two become one. We, their offspring, are thus endowed with the physical characteristics and attributes of our parents. As President Lorenzo Snow taught, the same principle of inheritance applies to us as spirit children of our heavenly parents.

> *We were born in the image of God our Father; he begot us like unto himself. There is the nature of deity in the composition of our spiritual organization; in our spiritual birth our Father transmitted to us the capabilities, powers and faculties which he himself possessed, as much so as the child on its mother's bosom possesses, although in an undeveloped state, the faculties, powers and susceptibilities of its parent.*[5]

As our spiritual parents are glorified exalted beings possessing the powers to create and procreate, as part of our spiritual genetic inheritance,

---

4 *Teachings of the Presidents of the Church: Joseph F. Smith,* (Salt Lake City: The Church of Jesus Christ of Latter-day Saints), [35744], 335.

5 Lorenzo Snow, *Journal of Discourses,* (London: Latter-day Saints Book Depot), 14:302.

we acquire the same divine potentials as they. These capacities are literally embedded in our individual spirit's DNA. Every one of God's offspring has the potential to be one with the Gods as one of the Gods.

"As man is now, God once was; as God is man may be,"[6] is the hallmark teaching of President Lorenzo Snow. Expanding on this doctrine, President Snow said,

> *Through a continual course of progression, our Heavenly Father [and Mother] has received exaltation and glory, and He points out the same path; and inasmuch as He is clothed with power, authority, and glory, He says, "Walk ye up and come in possession of the same glory and happiness that I possess" … and we are perfectly assured that, inasmuch as we are faithful, we shall eventually come in possession of everything that the mind of man can conceive of—everything that heart can desire."*[7]

For many Christians of other denominations, this truth is so magnificent and startling they have a hard time accepting it. Many think the very idea is blasphemous, even though the Apostle Paul, whom they highly revere, testifies: "Let this mind be in you, which was also in Christ Jesus: Who, being in the form of God, thought it not robbery to be equal with God" (Phil. 2:5–6).

Worded as though written to the Apostle Paul, his fellow servant in Christ, President Snow penned this inspiring poem:

Dear Brother:
Hast thou not been unwisely bold,
Man's destiny to thus unfold?
To raise, promote such high desire,
Such vast ambition thus inspire?

---

6 Lorenzo Snow, *The Teachings of Lorenzo Snow,* (Salt Lake City: Bookcraft, 1996), 1.

7 Lorenzo Snow, *Journal of Discourses,* 5:313.

Still, 'tis no phantom that we trace
Man's ultimatum in life's race;
This royal path has long been trod
By righteous men, each now a God:
As Abra'm, Isaac, Jacob, too,
First babes, then men—to gods they grew.
As man now is, our God once was;
Ah, well, that taught by you, dear Paul,
Though much amazed, we see it all;
Our Father God, has ope'd our eyes,
We cannot view it otherwise.
The boy, like to his father grown,
Has but attained unto his own;
To grow to sire from state of son,
Is not 'gainst Nature's course to run.
A son of God, like God to be,
Would not be robbing Deity;
And he who has this hope within,
Will purify himself from sin.[8]

As the Gods Are Eternal, So Is the Plan

Inasmuch as our Heavenly Parents were once as we are now, logic says that They too have followed the same eternal plan that Jesus followed and we now follow. Again, the Prophet Joseph Smith opened the eyes of our understanding:

> *These are incomprehensible ideas to some, but they are simple. It is the first principle of the Gospel to know for a certainty the Character*

8 *The Teachings of Lorenzo Snow*, 8–9.

> *of God, and to know that we may converse with him as one man converses with another, and that he was once a man like us; yea, that God himself, the Father of us all, dwelt on an earth, the same as Jesus Christ himself did; and I will show it from the Bible.*[9]

Adding upon this illuminating truth, the Prophet explained:

> *If Jesus Christ was the Son of God, and John discovered that God the Father of Jesus Christ had a Father, you may suppose that He had a Father also. Where was there ever a son without a father? And where was there ever a father without first being a son? ... I despise the idea of being scared to death at such a doctrine, for the Bible is full of it.*[10]

In explaining what is meant by the terms "heirs of God and joint heirs with Jesus Christ," the Prophet declares: "What is it? To inherit the same power, the same glory and the same exaltation, until you arrive at the station of a God, and ascend the throne of eternal power, the same as those who have gone before."[11]

The God we worship—our Heavenly Parents—have previously exercised their agency and followed the same Eternal Plan of the Father to arrive at the divine and holy station they now occupy and enjoy. President Joseph F. Smith said, "We are precisely in the same condition and under the same circumstance that God our Heavenly Father was when He was passing through this or a similar ordeal."[12] Thus we come to realize the inspired refrain "Come follow me" does in fact "extend to holier spheres … as wider fields expand to view." And that "we must the onward path pursue … and follow him unceasingly, whate'er our lot or sphere may be."[13]

---

9 Smith, *Teachings of the Prophet Joseph Smith,* 345.
10 Ibid., 373.
11 Ibid,, 347.
12 Joseph F. Smith, *Journal of Discourses,* 25:58.
13 "Come Follow Me," *Hymns,* no. 116.

The Central and Crucial Role of Agency

Whereas many people who believe in Christ reject the glorious truth "as man is now, God once was; as God is man may be," it has become so commonplace among members of the Church, that some think of this truth as a given—a "fait accompli." It is not. Membership in the Church, even active membership, is a good start, but alone far from sufficient.

In the natural world, given the right conditions, a sunflower seed inevitably grows up to be a mature sunflower plant—that one single seed yielding a harvest of dozens of seeds. A German shepherd puppy inevitably grows up to be a full-grown adult German shepherd dog. The genetic codes within the sunflower seed and the puppy drive the growth and maturation process, and agency has nothing whatever to do with the eventual outcome.

Unlike the plant and animal creations of God, our maturation to the adult stature of our Heavenly Parents is not automatic nor inevitable. Although we have been endowed with their celestial *capacities*—a gift beyond measurement—whether or not those capacities are developed and come to full fruition depends on the use of our agency. What we do with our spiritual genetic endowment is entirely up to us.

Knowing of such magnificent possibilities is one thing, undertaking the rigors of the ascent is another. Loving our Heavenly Father enough to submit our will to His, take upon us the yoke of Christ and deny ourselves of all ungodliness involves ongoing choices and actions. Nowhere in the Father's eternal plan is obedience mandated or compelled. From start to finish, progression is up to the individual. Whether or not we grow, progress and develop any of the divine attributes rests on how we use our agency, as affirmed by President Henry B. Eyring: "Greater holiness will not come simply by *asking* for it. It will come by *doing what is needed* for God to change

14 Henry B. Eyring, "Holiness and the Plan of Happiness," *Ensign,* November 2019, 103, emphasis added.

us."[14] And, Elder Bruce C. Hafen said, "We can have eternal life if we want it, but only if there is nothing else we want more."[15]

If we are apathetic, indolent or rebellious, we reap the corresponding harvest. "But wo unto him that has the law given, yea, that has all the commandments of God, like unto us, and that transgresseth them, and that wasteth the days of his probation, for awful is his state" (2 Nephi 9:27).

Mormon in the Book of Helaman wrote,

> *And now remember, remember, my brethren, that whosoever perisheth, perisheth unto himself; and whosoever doeth iniquity, doeth it unto himself; for behold, ye are free; ye are permitted to act for yourselves; for behold, God hath given unto you a knowledge and he hath made you free (Helaman 14:30).*

On the other hand, the scriptures testify that if we choose to strive with all our might, mind, and strength to realize our celestially endowed potential, we can, through the Atonement of Jesus Christ, become "perfect even as our Father in Heaven is perfect" (Matt . 5:48), and truly and wholly be like the Savior.

---

15 Bruce C.Hafen, "The Atonement: All for All," *Ensign,* May 2004, 98.

CHAPTER 4

The Crux of Responsibility

In the early years of the church Christ founded, as prophesied by the apostle Paul, many false prophets and even false christs infiltrated the ranks of the early Christians, "not sparing the flock" (Acts 20:28–30). For their evil and selfish purposes which were no doubt inspired by Satan, they spread all manner of distortions and false doctrines throughout the church, corrupting the gospel taught by the Savior. Peter also warned of "false prophets also among the people, even as there shall be false teachers among you, who privily shall bring in damnable heresies, even denying the Lord that bought them, and bring upon themselves swift destruction" (2 Peter 2:1).

Consequently and tragically, the pristine words of truth written under the inspiration of the Holy Ghost were ransacked and many of the plain and precious truths they once contained were removed. Over the ensuing centuries, the loss of these vital truths caused people who wanted to find the truth and come unto Christ to stumble, and the churches they founded were based on incorrect assumptions and incomplete doctrines.

Paramount among the plain and precious truths that were lost were the doctrines related to premortal life. Although traces of these essential truths remain in portions of the New Testament, the teachings regarding premortal life were aggressively expunged. The truths about our true nature as uncreated, self-existent beings, our birth as spirit children of Heavenly Parents, a plan of happiness, and foreordained missions and family organizations were branded blasphemous heresies by the early church fathers, and punishments were meted out to those who believed and taught them.[1] The original church, along with its saving truths, doctrines, and priesthood powers, was lost.

The Book of Mormon plainly reveals that Satan was behind all of this for quite obvious reasons. The adversary knew how essential and potent those truths would be in unmasking him, the father of all lies, and his devious ploys. Worse yet for him, they would empower God's children with the ability to recognize, resist, and reject him and his minions along with all of his evil designs.

Knowing the war in heaven was all about agency, we should not be surprised that the corruption of the gospel would center on shrouding the truth about individual agency. Withholding the plain and precious truth that we are uncreated, self-existent, self-governing beings would be among the foremost truths Satan would want to conceal because that realization puts the responsibility for all the choices made by those intelligent beings where it actually belongs—squarely on their own shoulders. That truth puts the responsibility completely and entirely on the individual. We—each of us—are individually and personally responsible for every choice we make.

That single, salient truth removes the foundation for the multitude of excuses, rationalizations and evasions the adversary wants to plant in our heads. He knows the seductive power of blaming. He knows the futility of rationalizing. He knows how fruitless it is for us to point fingers and shift

1 Hugh Nibley, "A Strange Thing in the Land: The Return of the Book of Enoch," *Enoch the Prophet, The Collected Works of Hugh Nibley*, (Salt Lake City: Deseret Book Company, 1986), 2:95–98.

responsibility. He knows it, but he doesn't want us to know it. When we recognize we are only hurting and hampering ourselves when we plunge headlong into the mire of non-responsibility, after a while and with a little effort, we stop shifting responsibility and we start owning it, which is precisely why Satan doesn't want us to know the truth.

As long as we choose to dodge responsibility, placing it everywhere but with ourselves, we don't repent or improve. If we insist on waiting for everyone else to get their acts together and repent, the days of our probation fly by and, before we know it, the summer is past and the harvest is ended and we've squandered our existence. It happens so softly and subtly. We buy into the fallacy because shifting responsibility is by far the easiest and seemingly the least painful way to get by in life. Believing our failings are not our fault and there's nothing we have to do about them or, indeed, anything we *can* do about them is seductively enticing.

At the crux of the doctrine of personal responsibility, we find Satan's prime target for assigning blame: God. If people do not know their true identity as choosers of their own thoughts—a power they innately possess and wielded even before becoming a begotten spirit son or daughter of God—they almost have no other choice than to see God as the responsible party. "If God created me," they reason, "then the way I am is the result of His choices not mine. God is responsible and the one to blame for who I am and what I do, not me. I simply cannot help it. I am who I am because God made me this way" is a common self-justification in our day, but it's not a new one.

Although they may not realize it, Christian theologians who hold that God created mankind out of nothing and each of his children come into being only at the time of their mortal birth, paint themselves into a similar contradictory corner. The tenet of mainstream Christianity holds that God, of His own free will and choice, decided to create the spirits and the bodies of all His children and place them on an earth, which

He also created out of nothing. Being a perfect God, that would mean each of His children is precisely as He preferred and deemed proper. And where does that idea put the responsibility for the actions and outcomes of each of those beings? On Him. All of the moral responsibility for the actions of every person born on this earth then falls on God. Following that logic, one has to conclude God created Hitler to be Hitler, Gandhi to be Gandhi, Mother Teresa to be Mother Teresa. And it doesn't stop there. The next logical step is that all of the rest of us are exactly predetermined to be who we are, making the idea of agency null and void. Under that ideology, we humans are essentially nothing more than preset and predestined automatons that God created to perform precisely as He programmed from the beginning. Such doctrine even implies a certain degree of perverseness in the character of God, because it implies that He wanted to witness the continuous stream of mayhem caused by mankind's frailties and follies. Furthermore, this idea makes the premise of mortal probation utterly meaningless. It totally contradicts the sense and necessity of an eventual judgment. What value would there be in assessing the accountability of individuals if there were no independent responsibility for making choices? Why would God even go through the sham of rewarding some individuals for doing good and punishing others for doing bad, if those individuals were fundamentally nothing more than pre-programmed beings devoid of actual agency? Clearly, such doctrine flies in the face of all reason, logic and sense.

Rather than being blamed, our Father in Heaven should be blessed—honored for the generosity and wisdom of His great plan of happiness, providing intelligences who were organized before the world was with the opportunity for growth and development without limit. "For the earth is full, and there is enough and to spare; yea, I prepared all things, and have given unto the children of men to be agents unto themselves" (D&C 104:17).

The Devil Can't Make You Do It

Years ago, TV comedian Flip Wilson rose to popularity on a famed punch line—a phony excuse for bad behavior—"the devil made me do it." His line always produced chuckles as the audience saw through the flimsy explanation of why his character, Geraldine Jones, continually succumbed to buying yet another dress on sale.

Temptations may come from outside sources but we, and we alone, determine what we'll do with them. The Prophet Joseph Smith taught this point.

> *[Joseph] then observed that Satan was generally blamed for the evils which we did, but if he was the cause of all our wickedness, men could not be condemned. The devil could not compel mankind to do evil; all was voluntary. … God would not exert any compulsory means, and the devil could not; and such ideas as were entertained on these subjects by many were absurd.*[2]

Although we live in a generation when many people refuse to accept responsibility for their conduct or character, the actual source of our shortcomings comes down to the choices we make. Ideas and impulses are continually presented from outside sources, but we alone decide whether we'll embrace or reject them. Elder Neal A. Maxwell said, "Of course our genes, circumstances, and environments matter very much, and they shape us significantly. Yet there remains an inner zone in which we are sovereign, unless we abdicate. In this zone lies the essence of our individuality and our personal accountability."[3] We are the responsible party. Until we fully acknowledge our sole responsibility for our outcomes, not much will ever change in our lives, no matter what other tactics or tools we may try.

---

2 Smith, *Teachings of the Prophet Joseph Smith,* 187, emphasis added.
3 Neal A. Maxwell, "According to the Desires of [Our] Hearts," *Ensign*, November 1996, 21–22.

Elder Maxwell pointed out that even the intensity and duration of our temptations are a function of our choices. "Remember, brothers and sisters, it is our own desires which determine the sizing and the attractiveness of various temptations. We set our thermostats as to temptations."[4] Some people balk at that idea and say, "It's not my fault if the media keeps throwing all these alluring temptations at me." True, we may not be able to curb the media's penchant for casting enticing images at us, but we do control how long they linger. When a dessert commercial invites me to break my commitment to cut back on sweets, I'm still in the driver's seat. The temptation lasts only as long as I allow my mind to dwell on that particular image. If I choose to focus on the dessert and imagine its tastes and textures beguiling my palate, the intensity of the temptation grows. On the other hand, if I reject the invitation and focus my attention on something else, the temptation is essentially ended the moment I direct my thoughts to that other subject. As an old country sage pointed out, "You can't keep a bird from landing on your head, but you don't have to let it build a nest there."

If doing wrong were not an enticement, then choosing right over wrong would have no value, and making the right choice would have no power. Human history is saturated with examples of women and men who were tempted to take a lower road but who refused to do so. In their minds they weighed the options and chose the higher payoff. Take for example Joseph, son of Jacob, who was not born with the right to be the firstborn heir of Israel but who lived worthy of it. Despite being repeatedly enticed by Potiphar's wife to commit adultery, he maintained his moral purity, saying to her, "There is none greater in this house than I; neither hath he [her husband] kept back anything from me … how then can I do this great wickedness, and sin against God?" (Genesis 39:9) Even with this refusal, Zuliekha did not relent and devised a scheme of

4 Maxwell, "According to the Desires of [Our] Hearts," *Ensign*, November 1996, 21–22.

entrapment, which failed because Joseph fled from the scene with her latching on to his garment as he made his escape (Gen 39:11–12. Notably, Joseph's faithfulness was not immediately rewarded. He even wound up in prison on false charges because of her accusations, but he did not curse God or even doubt Him. Neither did he murmur. Rather, Joseph meekly bore his afflictions, patiently waiting on Jehovah to deliver him. In contrast, Rueben, Jacob's firstborn son of Leah, his first wife, fell from his birthright position. Presented with far less enticement than Joseph, Rueben committed sexual sin within his father's household and lost the birthright. Consequently, the birthright went to the virtuous Joseph, the firstborn son of the second wife.

Another tragic figure in the Old Testament is King David, who from his rooftop witnessed an enticing scene below. As his eyes fell upon Bathsheba, another man's wife, he did not curb his first impulses, undoubtedly fanned by Lucifer's suggestions. Rather than rejecting the temptation by leaving the scene as Joseph did, he dwelt upon it to the point he acted on it. Then, one sin leading to another, David instigated the murder of Bathsheba's husband, Uriah, and reaped the whirlwind, falling from his highly favored status with the Lord. Months of tears and remorse of conscience could have been averted had David redirected his thoughts in that moment on the rooftop. It was certainly within David's power to do so. He had demonstrated extraordinary discipline and self-control at other times. He could surely have done it again, but he didn't. Nothing in the scenario was beyond his power to resist.

There are other tragic examples in both scriptural and secular history. The pattern is the same—temptation was presented, the thinker weighed the options and chose immediate gratification in lieu of eventual greatness. In all of those cases, Satan played a role but he was not the determinant. He could only allure, tempt and entice. In every case, the chooser made the choice.

So we can't blame God and we can't blame Satan. Who's left? As the famed comic strip "Pogo" pointed out, "We have met the enemy, and he is us!"[5] And as late-night TV host Jack Paar said, "Looking back, my life so far seems like one long obstacle race, with me as the chief obstacle."[6]

Personal Responsibility: The Law Upon Which All Blessings Are Predicated

A correct understanding of our agency and personal responsibility for our choices is key to unlocking the answers to the deepest, most perplexing questions we wrestle with. A lack of understanding of this one doctrine leads to many becoming lost and confused about who they are and their ability to rise above the ploys of the adversary. It is imperative we see the responsibility-dodging, no-fault philosophy of the world as the "wide gate" and "broad way" that leads to destruction (Matt 7:13). Actually, in our generation, it's gone from being a path to a super-highway. Elder Neal A. Maxwell declared:

> *Mostly, brothers and sisters, we become the victims of our own wrong desires. Moreover, we live in an age when many simply refuse to feel responsible for themselves. Thus, a crystal-clear understanding of the doctrines pertaining to desire is so vital because of the spreading effluent oozing out of so many unjustified excuses by so many. This is like a sludge which is sweeping society along toward "the gulf of misery and endless wo." … Like it or not, therefore, reality requires that we acknowledge our responsibility for our desires. … It is up to us. God will facilitate, but He will not force.*[7]

---

5 Walt Kelly, www.abebooks.com/signed-first-edition/Pogo-Met-Enemy-Kelly-Walt-New/11434418087/bd, November 1, 1987.

6 Jack Paar, *I Kid You Not,* (New York: Pocket Books, Inc., 1960), 229.

7 Maxwell, "According to the Desires of [Our] Hearts," *Ensign*, November 1996, 21–22, emphasis added.

It is up to us! God lovingly beckons and supports, but He will not force. Each intelligence is innately free to think and choose what she or he desires to think. Elder Dale G. Renlund summed up the central purpose of mortal probation when he said, "Our Heavenly Father's goal in parenting is not to have His children *do* what is right; it is to have His children *choose* to do what is right and ultimately become like Him."[8] Because we have the ability to think about and evaluate our thoughts, right in the process of thinking them, who but us can be responsible for those choices and their consequences? God constantly invites, blesses, and proffers grace. Satan constantly entices, tempts, and tantalizes. But neither God nor the devil is *making* you or me do anything. Everything we do is a choice and every choice is up to us. We seldom sing hymn 240 in our meetings, but it's in our hymnbooks for a reason. It teaches an important truth:

> *Know this that every man is free, To choose his life and what he'll be; For this eternal truth is giv'n; That God will force no man to heav'n.*
>
> *He'll call, persuade, direct aright, And bless with wisdom, love, and light, In nameless ways be good and kind, But never force the human mind.*[9]

The Book of Mormon is replete with this doctrine. Rejecting, rebelling, and turning away from the Lord are all consistently described as choices, as are hearkening, heeding, and turning back to the Lord. The purpose of our mortal existence rests upon our freedom of choice and how we wield it—the very thing we fought for in premortal life. All those who signed up for Satan's plan forfeited their participation in the pending mortal experience and were denied a body. If we look down and see a body below our chin, then it's prima facie evidence that we willingly chose to enter mortality

8 Renlund, "Choose Ye This Day," *Ensign,* November 2018, 105, emphasis added.
9 "Know This, That Every Soul Is Free," *Hymns,* no. 240.

to make choices between right and wrong. We knew we would have to teach our at-first unruly bodies to obey the principles and laws we accepted before we were permitted to have a body. Elder Dale G. Renlund plainly declared this doctrine:

> *God established a plan. … Personal choice was—and is—vital to this plan, which we learned about in our premortal existence. We accepted the plan and chose to come to earth. … Agency allows us to choose to get on the path, or not. It allows us to get off, or not. Just as we cannot be forced to obey, we cannot be forced to disobey. No one can, without our cooperation, take us off the path.*[10]

The doctrinal truths regarding agency are plainly set forth by apostles and prophets, ancient and modern. In the Articles of Faith of The Church of Jesus Christ, we read: "We believe that men will be punished for their own sins and not for Adam's transgression." We also believe men will be punished for their own sins and not Lucifer's temptations.

10 Renlund, "Choose You This Day," *Ensign*, November 2018, 105–106.

SECTION TWO

Principles of Mind Management

"The greatest mystery a man ever learned, is to know how to control the human mind, and bring every faculty and power of the same in subjection to Jesus Christ; this is the greatest mystery we have to learn while in these tabernacles of clay."

— President Brigham Young, *Journal of Discourses* 1:46, April 9, 1852.

CHAPTER 5

The Agency to Choose, The Power to Create

It is one thing to know we are independent, self-governing, thinking beings, free to choose and act for ourselves, but quite another to grasp the huge ramifications of this truth. Throughout this book we will expand our appreciation and application of it. In everyday context, we generally refer to our intelligence of spirit as our "mind" and the workings of our intelligence as our "thoughts." In this book we will keep with these usages, knowing as we do, that our mind is the self-aware thinker of thoughts—the intelligence of spirit—clothed in a mortal body.

Your mind is self-governing and independent. No one can bind your mind and make you think thoughts you don't wish to think or choose attitudes you don't want to adopt. Each person is completely independent in that internal sphere, and that inalienable ability is the essence of our agency. So sacred is our capacity to think independently, God Himself will never infringe upon it. If He were to exercise control or compulsion upon the minds of His children, God would cease to be God, having violated the most fundamental of all heavenly laws. Thus, you and I are free to use our agency to think what we want to think and refuse to think what we don't. Even in the most coercive environments, human beings retain this God-granted prerogative.

In a poignant example, Dr. Viktor Frankl recounts his experience and observations while a prisoner in Auschwitz in his classic book, *Man's Search for Meaning*. Austrian by nationality and a respected psychiatrist by profession, Frankl was also Jewish by faith and lineage. During World War II, Frankl, along with members of his family, was shipped in a loathsome boxcar to Auschwitz. There he experienced the full brunt of the nightmare we call the Holocaust. The Nazis took away every piece of personal property, the clothes they were wearing—even the gold crowns off their teeth. They took away every human right, except one: each individual's ability to think freely. An avid student of human behavior, Frankl became part of one of the most gruesome laboratories on human behavior in modern times. Accordingly, his observations carry great meaning for all of us. Living in that unspeakably brutal, demeaning environment, Frankl observed a broad spectrum of reactions and behaviors among his fellow prisoners. Understandably, some of them were stricken with overwhelming fear and were paralyzed by it. Others grew sullen and withdrawn. Some became angry and bitter and grew more selfish; and some managed to stay hopeful and perseverant.

Frankl observed what happened when prisoners, after hanging on for a number of months, made the choice to abandon hope and simply give up. He described it as a pivotal moment. The day they cast aside their hopes and "ceased living for the future" marked the beginning of the end for them. It was as though they had signed their own death certificate. They invariably began to decline mentally, spiritually, and physically. An underlying illness would suddenly overtake them. In a matter of hours, they died.[1]

1 Victor E. Frankl, *Man's Search for Meaning*, (New York: Simon & Schuster, 1984), 78–82.

Within himself, Frankl began to discover how much control he had over his personal experience in the camp. For example, while shoveling rocks on an icy cold morning, he could feel the sublime joy of a beautiful sunrise and feel gratitude to God. Even though his wife was not actually present, and had perished without him knowing it, Frankl found he could bring his wife's love to him and feel her encouragement by simply focusing on a cherished memory.

Summarizing a major conclusion from his experience in the camp, Frankl wrote,

> *Everything can be taken from man but one thing: the last of the human freedoms—to choose one's attitude in any given set of circumstances, to choose one's own way. In the final analysis, it becomes clear that the sort of person the prisoner became was the result of an inner decision and not the result of camp influence alone.*[2]

In whatever environment or circumstance, his conclusion holds true: Who we become is the result of what we think. All of our outcomes are the result of our inner decisions. Even for the poor souls in Auschwitz, it was not the Nazis, the barbed wire fences, the guard dogs, nor any of the other atrocious circumstances that determined their reactions or responses and the consequences of them. The determinant was their inner decisions. Frankl explained, "Fundamentally, therefore, any man can, even under such circumstances, decide what shall become of him mentally and spiritually."[3] Frankl was not saying he believed mankind saves itself spiritually. He was saying our level of spirituality is in our own hands. We can either cultivate spirituality or we can reject and shun it—a truth that is confirmed in 2 Nephi 2:27:

---

2 Frankl, *Man's Search for Meaning,* 75.

3 Ibid., 75.

> *Wherefore, men are free according to the flesh; and all things are given them which are expedient unto man. And they are free to choose liberty and eternal life, through the great Mediator of all men, or to choose captivity and death, according to the captivity and power of the devil; for he seeketh that all men might be miserable like unto himself.*

Notice Nephi's emphasis on the freedom to choose, a theme echoed by his brother Jacob: "Therefore, cheer up your hearts, and remember that ye are free to act for yourselves—to choose the way of everlasting death or the way of eternal life" (2 Ne 10:23). It is also worthy to note that "cheering up one's heart" and "remembering" are matters of agency; we are not compelled but are free to choose to do either, neither, or both.

Learning to govern our thoughts and purify our hearts is more than a mere sidebar on the screen of our earthly priorities; it is the main theme—the very essence of our mortal probation. When our life is weighed in the balance, it will be the sum of our thoughts, just as it says in the proverb, "As a man thinketh in his heart, so is he" (Prov 23:7). President George Albert Smith shared his personal discovery of this truth:

> *As a child, thirteen years of age, I went to school at the Brigham Young Academy. … Dr. Maeser one day stood up and said: "Not only will you be held accountable for the things you do, but you will be held responsible for the very thoughts you think."*
>
> *Being a boy, not in the habit of controlling my thoughts very much, it was quite a puzzle to me what I was to do, and it worried me. In fact, it stuck to me just like a burr. About a week or ten days after that it suddenly came to me what he meant. … Why of course you'll be held accountable for your thoughts, because when your life is completed in mortality, it will be the sum of your thoughts.*[4]

---

4 Cited in Ezra Taft Benson, "Think on Christ," *Ensign*, April 1984, 10.

President Spencer W. Kimball stated,

> *The relationship of character to thought cannot be too strongly emphasized. How could a person possibly become what he is not thinking? Nor is any thought, when persistently entertained, too small to have an effect. The "divinity that shapes our ends" is indeed in ourselves.*[5]

Factors versus Determinants

Several years ago, I became fascinated by the compelling accounts of people who battled great adversity and overcame major setbacks. I wanted to understand their thought processes and conclusions. I wanted to gain the same skills they exhibited, sensing that sooner or later I would have to use them myself. (It turned out I was right.) The first thing I learned was that some had great support systems. I also discovered some of them did not. Some of them had horrible upbringings and, at the time of their catastrophic event, had no support from family, friends, or co-workers. So I crossed "upbringing" and "support system" off the list of determinants. Support systems are important and valuable factors, but in the end that's all they are—factors. They are not determinants.

The same went for education, social environment, race, gender, religion, nationality, age, sexual orientation, financial status, political philosophy, and birth order. All were factors, some more influential than others. Yet, even which factors were influential and how much each played into the equation were markedly varied, scattered all over the board. Even DNA, long held as the ultimate determinant, especially in the scientific community, turned out to not be as automatic and absolute as once believed. It too can now be regarded as a factor, because a fairly

5 Spencer W. Kimball, *Miracle of Forgiveness,* (Salt Lake City: Deseret Book Company, 1973), 104–105.

new wing of science, epigenetics, has established clearly that your DNA is not your destiny.

It turns out there is one and only one determinant. That one determinant held true in every case. It was the key for every single person who overcame their catastrophic event and moved on to live a productive life and accomplish respectable, sometimes even stunning, things. Some of them knew, sensed or discovered the determinant right away. Others took longer. Yet, when all the dust cleared, for all of them, it came down to a crystal-clear realization of the power they held to determine how things would turn out for them in the end.

As an excellent illustration, I refer you to a TED talk by Amy Purdy.[6] I point to it for two reasons: it's delightfully engaging and inspiring, and it reprises a beloved and familiar theme. The details of Amy's story are unique to her, but the plot is familiar. The majority of heartwarming movies we cherish or books we reread time and again all tell essentially the same story. Sympathetic characters, who we quickly come to like and identify with, start out with a good life with lots of promise. And then disaster strikes. Their world is turned upside down and the future appears hopelessly bleak. Their first attempts to turn things around fail, making the situation even more dismal. They (key word coming up next) *almost* give up and quit—but then, for some reason or another, they decide to give it one last shot. They summon their last dab of courage and go for it. Their last shot kind of works, and the door of hope creaks open just a tad. So they try again, and things improve even more. So, they keep on trying. And trying. And then (get your handkerchief ready), they get their one big shot for victory and vindication, and they nail it! And the crowd goes wild! In my marriage, the next part is where my wife, Susan, with total emotional control, smiles and puts her arm around her husband who's sobbing like a sap and hands him a tissue.

---

6 Amy Purdy, "Living Beyond Limits," Ted.com/talks/amy_purdy_living_beyond_limits/transcript.

We love these stories. Though we've heard them dozens of times, we never get tired of them. Why? Because they resonate with some template inside us—a familiar theme—perhaps a metaphor of our journey through life. We will come back to this point later in the book.

In her TED talk, Amy Purdy, tells her story in a positive, humble way, beginning with the thought-provoking question, "If your life were a book and you were the author, how would you want your story to go?"[7] She then takes us back to her carefree days as a young, newly graduated massage therapist who dreamed of traveling the world, snowboarding her way through life—independent and free. That dream comes crashing down when she is hit with bacterial meningitis. Within a matter of weeks, she loses both kidneys, her spleen, and both legs below the knees. Trying to bounce back, she is presented with two ugly, ill-fitting artificial legs that caused excruciating pain just strapping them on to her stumps, let alone walking. The prospects of being so limited by those bulky limbs dashed her hopes of mobility and snowboarding, sending her into a downward spiral. She went to bed, curled up, and dropped out of life. She described herself at that point as being, "completely, mentally, emotionally, and physically broken." She remained that way for days. Eventually she came to grips with the fact that nothing was going to change unless and until she "created a new Amy." And that's what she did. She describes visualizing herself, in sensory detail, carving down the slopes on her snowboard, wind in her face, feeling the beat of her racing heart, as if it were happening in that very moment.

I call this level of visualization "visioneering."[8]

Amy recounts many inspiring and humorous steps along the way to co-founding a successful non-profit organization, Adaptive Action Sports,

7 Purdy, Ted.com/talks/amy_purdy_living_beyond_limits, 0:04.

8 Dennis R Deaton, *The Book on Mind Management,* (Mesa: Quma Learning Systems, Inc., 1994), 137–142.

that makes innovative equipment for the disabled. She also won two back-to-back gold medals, making her the highest ranking adaptive female snowboarder in the world.

Amy Purdy's discovery that she could "create a new Amy" is exhilarating because way down deep the Spirit is telling us we can do it too. One of the greatest blessings we derive from our knowledge of the Atonement of Jesus Christ is that it's never too late to change. No matter how far we've wandered from the covenant path and messed things up, each of us can change and get better. The gospel word for "continuous change" and "improvement" is repentance, which we often associate with overcoming grievous sin. In truth, repentance means changing how we think.[9] The call from the prophets to repent daily doesn't mean we go running into the bishop's office twice a day. It means we keep making choices instead of excuses and continue forward on the path of continuous change. Through the Atonement of Christ and a working relationship with our Heavenly Father, we are gradually transformed and become like Him.

Many people who overcome a major crisis or setback look back on it as a godsend because through that experience they learned they could do their version of "creating a new Amy." Some believe they couldn't have learned what they did in any other way. Through the bone-jolting experiences that abruptly interrupted their own agendas, they had to stop and deal with something so significant it required their full attention. This new reality prompted them to reconsider and revise their views about themselves and what life is all about. Having to deal with such a catastrophic wake up call, they are able to learn one of the greatest epiphanies of all epiphanies: Each of us gets to *create our own life!*

This epiphany begins with realizing we are not our circumstances or conditions or limitations or even our bodies. We each have a body, but we

---

9 See Russell M. Nelson, "We Can Do Better and Be Better," *Ensign*, May 2019, 67–69.

are not our body. We have feelings, but we are not our feelings. We have emotions, but we are not our emotions. Ultimately, we are the selector—the chooser—of our feelings and emotions. Like Amy, you get to choose how you *feel* about your current challenges. You decide the emotional energy you bring to those situations. This realization leads to another even more stunning truth. If you are the chooser of your emotions, along with their corresponding reactions and consequences, then you are actually the *creator* of your emotions and reactions.

President David O. McKay said it succinctly, "Man is the creator of his own happiness."[10] He elaborated, "Man's success or failure, happiness or misery, depends upon what he seeks and what he chooses. What a man is, what a nation is, may largely be determined by his or its dominant quest. It is a tragic thing to carry through life a low concept of this quest."[11]

Hence, each of us is in charge of how everything turns out in our life. Every day, through our varied experiences of daily living, we get to *choose* who we'll be, and how we'll be, in each and all of those situations. Each one presents us with the choice to cower, cope, or conquer. Once we realize we are choosers and creators of our feelings and emotions, we hold the key to unlocking every dilemma, solving every problem, and improving every facet of our character. A popular podcaster April Price declares this golden insight at the beginning of each episode of her podcast, *The 100% Awesome Podcast*.[12] She says, "You might not know it, but every result in your life is one hundred percent because of the thoughts you think. And that, my friends, is one hundred percent awesome."

In the seminars and training sessions I teach, I am often explaining these concepts to people who do not have the background of the restored

10 David O. McKay, *Secrets of a Happy Life,* (Salt Lake City: Bookcraft, 1967), 171.

11 David O. McKay, *Gospel Ideals,* (Salt Lake City: The Improvement Era, 1953), 491.

12 April Price, host. "Re-ranking Your Awesome Brain," *aprilpricecoaching.com, The 100% Awesome Podcast,* Episode 1, May 8, 2019.

gospel of Jesus Christ. Frequently, I share contrasting examples of two people who have experienced almost identical challenges but who end up with dramatically different results. Sometimes it's two people who failed to get into medical school; or two people who lost their jobs and whose career tracks were demolished; or two who experienced difficult, ugly divorces; or two with terminal cancer; or two who lost loved ones under heart-rending circumstances. After describing each of the cases and the dramatically different outcomes, I ask the question: "So, what makes the telling difference? Why do some people flounder while others rise to the occasion?" I usually get a variety of answers, such as support systems, upbringing, genetics and financial advantages. Quite often the first answer is "attitude." In response, I say to them, "To a degree 'attitude' is an accurate answer. Without question, attitudes are huge drivers in how we react or respond, and how we experience our experiences. But attitude is not quite the bottom line."

Do you see why I say that? When we talk about attitudes being the drivers, it's as though we are giving an attitude a mind of its own. So, I push back on attitude being the determinant, and I ask the participants why I might do that. Almost always someone will get closer to the bull's eye with, "Because an attitude is a choice!" Then I say, "Yes! It's a choice, but we're not done yet. If it's a choice, then there must be a chooser! And, who or what is the chooser? It's you and it's me—the thinkers of thoughts inside our bodies. And that being the case, it means that an *attitude is a creation*. We create our attitudes and a whole lot more in our minds!" At that moment, I often see a lot of people having an aha moment and thereby I receive my real paycheck for the day.

Moment by moment, thought by thought, you author your own script. Whether you do it actively or passively, you are ultimately the cause determining which effects occur. People are victims of circumstance only if they believe they are and take a passive approach, letting their lives become subject to outside forces. People can make dramatic, stunning changes by simply deciding they've had enough of their current self and situation and decide to take charge of a change. In many cases the effects are amazingly rapid.

As we cast aside old doubts and fears, we trigger new creative ideas that energize every aspect of our lives—from the very next sequence of thoughts to the physical energy in our bodies. We come to realize the potential we are now acting on has been there all along, and so have the opportunities. They have been staring us in the face for quite some time. We just couldn't see them until we decided to open our minds to a higher thought. It's in that moment we validate an incredibly important truth: We see that it has *only* been our thoughts that have been holding us back all along!

When we fully accept how directly everything from our circumstances to our character corresponds to the thoughts we choose and the images we hold in our minds, that realization stands tall among the most significant revelations we can ever receive.

The Need for a Savior

There is not one result in your life that does not depend on the states of mind you choose. Honestly, I do not think it's taking the point too far to say that we can overcome any obstacle, bear any hardship, and become all we are capable of becoming through the wise and proper exercise of our agency.

"But" you may say, "it sounds like you are negating the need for a Savior. Don't you know we can't save ourselves? Aren't you forgetting no one can be saved except through the mercy and merits and grace of Jesus Christ—that He is the truth, the life, and the way? My answer is a wholehearted and resounding, *YES!* I believe these truths! I know they are true; and I continually and earnestly strive to love the Savior, live His gospel and keep my covenants. And, in doing so here is what I have found. If I grow and how much I grow is still *always* up to me! Christ stands at the door and knocks, but I have to make up my mind to open the door and let Him in. I know faith is the first principle of the gospel and it's a gift from God.[13] But He doesn't bestow that gift wholesale. It is bestowed incrementally as I turn my thoughts to Him and choose to exert my faith through *my thoughts*!

The scholarly apostle Orson Pratt said, "Faith is not an abstract principle, separate and distinct from the mind, but *it is a certain condition or state of the mind itself.*"[14] Pow! Bang! Boom! I can't, don't, or won't repent until I come to realize how my prideful rationalizations and self-deceptions (all hatched in my mind)—prevent me from taking full responsibility for my sins and omissions. I can come to Christ, supplicating for His grace to have the courage to confess and forsake my sins, only *through my thoughts.* I can't, don't, or won't keep my covenants without a full, all-out, *mental* effort. I can only offer a broken heart and contrite spirit—the ultimate sacrifice I must offer the Lord in similitude of His ultimate sacrifice for me—when I present the profoundly submissive *state of mind* of a little child and *choose* to offer my all in service and devotion to Him who is mighty to save.

The Savior has given His all to work out the infinite atonement. He wants my all in return. Ultimately, the highest and wisest use of my agency is to come unto Christ, look to Him in every thought, and willfully submit with all my mental, emotional, physical and spiritual faculties to follow the covenant path of unqualified, unconditional discipleship. No one else can do it for me. There is no salvation by proxy for the living.

Each one of us has to *make up our minds* to have no other gods before Him and to come unto Christ with all our might, mind and strength (2 Nephi 25:29). No lazy, half-hearted, feeble-minded effort will do. We're

13 "Faith is a gift of God bestowed as a reward for personal righteousness. It is always given when righteousness is present, and the greater the measure of obedience to God's laws the greater will be the endowment of faith." Bruce R. McConkie, *Mormon Doctrine,* (Salt Lake City: Deseret Book Company, 1966), 264.

14 Orson Pratt, *The True Faith,* (Liverpool, England, 1856), 1, emphasis added.

the only ones who can decide to take control of our mortal, easily tempted, frequently distracted mind and worship the only true God and Jesus Christ whom Heavenly Father has sent. Thus on that basis I submit to you this declaration:

> *The consummate truth of life is that we alter our destiny by altering our thoughts. The mind is our most crucial determinant, our crowning asset, our ultimate arena of battle. If we will master the power of our minds, we may do or be whatsoever we will.*[15]

It all begins and it all depends on your mind.

---

15 Deaton, *The Book on Mind Management,* 1994, 4.

CHAPTER 6

Minding the Mind

Brigham Young declared, "The greatest mystery a man ever learned, is to know how to control the human mind, and bring every faculty and power of the same in subjection to Jesus Christ; this is the greatest mystery we have to learn while in these tabernacles of clay."[1] Remember, when we talk about the mind, we are *not* talking about the brain. Although our intelligence, now housed in our mortal body, occupies roughly the same space as our brains, an important distinction must be made between the two.

The intelligence of spirit we call the mind is much more than the brain. Your brain is the governing organ—the information-collection and control center of your mortal body. Scientifically, we are only scratching the surface of understanding its marvels. Yet one distinction is paramount: mind and brain are not synonymous. Up until recently, in the opinion of science, the human mind was simply the resulting phenomenon or manifestation of brain activity. Supposedly everything going on in our heads—our thoughts, consciousness, personality, sense of humor, and individual idiosyncrasies—were merely the end product of the neuroanatomy and biochemistry of the

1 Brigham Young, *Journal of Discourses,* 1:46.

brain.[2] Human beings were simply physical machines that just happen to think. Confining themselves to the study of the gray matter and the white matter, neuroscientists completely disregarded the most essential matter—each human's unique, self-governing individuality. Still today, there are many in the scientific community who scoff at the idea that the mind is not only separate, distinct and independent from the brain, but also superior to it.[3]

The mind is so much more than the product of the electrochemical workings of neural tissue. Our mind, not our brain is our identity and personality—our essence. The brain is the organic cloak, a garment, worn by the mind and used to further its progress. The brain has no individual identity, awareness or intentionality of its own. It's just meat. Marvelous as it is when animated by an intelligent spirit, in and of itself it is nothing more than an intricate configuration of neurons and glial cells positioned on the top of your spinal cord. When inhabited by a spirit, the brain sends and receives electro-chemical signals to and from the rest of an equally amazing system of nerves and nodes, which in turn trigger and govern the countless activities within our bodies. Conversely, when the spirit leaves the body, the brain, along with the rest of the body, is just dust returning to dust.

My purpose in making this distinction is to emphasize the truth of not only who we are but *what* we are in order to clarify our understanding of our mortal state. Knowing that it is our mind, not our mortal brain, that is making the choices that determine our results is key to exerting control where control will succeed. Mind is the specific, intelligent entity each of us recognizes as our inner essence of self—the individual, personal, self-aware being of intelligence, which in the deepest sense, is the essential "me" within.

2 Sir Francis Crick, *The Astonishing Hypothesis: The Scientific Search for the Soul,* (New York: Touchstone, 1994), 3.

3 Deaton, *The Book on Mind Management,* 18–19.

Each of us has a clear, ever-present, conscious awareness of what is "me" and "not me," of what is "in here" versus "out there."

Where the "You" Resides

When we think about the location of our consciousness, we recognize it as being located in the upper third of our heads. A few years ago, when I had the opportunity to talk with a class of fourth graders, I invited one of them to come up to the front of the room. I asked the boy, "When you think about you—you as a person—can you point to where you are?" If you are visualizing this scene in your mind, I suspect you're imagining the boy being a bit hesitant to answer, not sure of what in the world I was asking. So I took a moment to help him understand what I meant by "the you." Once he and his classmates understood what I meant, I asked him, "Where is that 'you' located? Where is it inside your body?" I then pointed to his foot. "Does it feel like 'you' are down there in your foot?" After a brief pause, he shook his head and said, "No." I pointed to his knee and asked, "Are you there in your knee?" Catching on to my drift, he promptly and confidently said, "No." When I pointed to his heart and asked the question, he paused to think about it carefully. Then, again with a smile on his face, he said, "No." I then asked him, without pointing to any part of his body at all, "So where is the 'you?'" As the realization hit him, he pointed to his forehead and with a twinkle of awareness in his eye, he said, "Here!" Your mind and your brain have a close working relationship, but they are not synonymous.

Mind is the intelligence of spirit, the sentient entity that exists, and is totally capable of thought—separate from the body. A number of people have had near-death experiences. These people describe death as an out-of-body experience. Some have actually watched, from the viewpoint of an outside spectator, paramedics working on their body. Though outside their body (which includes the brain), their unique personal identity remains intact, exactly the same as when in the body. They were not obliterated when their heart stopped beating and their brain waves ceased. Neither was their consciousness radically revised or altered. As a conscious, feeling entity they are the same, in the body and out. They still love who they loved, feel as they felt, and think as they thought. In every way they continue to completely identify with who they have been and still are. They remain themselves. In other words, it is possible to be "out of your body" and even "out of this world," but you can never be "out of your mind." You are it, and it is you.

What About My Heart?

We frequently think of our brain as the seat of our thoughts and our heart as the seat of our emotions. Just as our brain is just meat, our heart is just a muscular pump. The mortal heart is a truly amazing workhorse. When healthy, it dutifully and continually moves our blood into the lungs, where it is oxygenated and then pushed out by the heart into the rest of the body. Blood being the life of the mortal body, the vital role of the heart is beyond essential yet easily taken for granted. For our purposes here, without taking anything away from the heart's central life-sustaining role, it does lack one rather important property: It doesn't think. It can sense signals from the nervous and hormonal systems and responds to them, but it has no conscious awareness and cannot think. I hear your question: "What's your point?"

My point is that whenever the scriptures, or any of us talk about the heart, we are talking about the inner workings of our individual intelligence of spirit—our mind. When the scriptures refer to the "thoughts of our hearts," they are not speaking literally but figuratively. "Praying with full purpose of heart" and asking "with a sincere heart, with real intent" are beautiful phrases as powerful and purposeful as they are poetic; and they refer to focused thoughts.

Not all thoughts and feelings are of the same magnitude. Some are silly and superficial; others are extremely deep and sacred. When we speak of profound sentiments and ideas, it is altogether appropriate for us to refer to them as "coming from the heart," rather than the mind. Whether we speak of "thoughts in our mind" or "thoughts in our heart," we understand they are one and the same.

The Mind Designs and Redesigns the Brain

Our brains are not permanently set in their ways. The anatomy and circuitry of our brains are constantly being altered and reconfigured to perform better. What governs this continuous ongoing reconfiguration? The thoughts we select and repeat in our minds. A single fleeting thought is carried by a spontaneously formed circuit of brain cells, called neurons; and each thought leaves a slight imprint of its course. As we repeat or dwell on a given thought, the neuronal connections in that circuit branch out and become more durable and interconnected with each repetition. Neurons that fire together wire together, which means patterns in our thoughts become patterns in our brains. Our brains wire and re-wire themselves in direct response to our most-used thought patterns. Dr. Jeffrey M. Schwartz, a psychiatrist and authority in neuroplasticity, wrote: "Neuroplasticity refers to the ability of neurons to forge new connections, to blaze new paths through the cortex, even to assume new roles. In short, neuroplasticity means rewiring of the brain."[4] In other words, according to Dr. Schwartz, *we are in charge of the rewiring!*

> *Conscious thoughts and volitions can, and do, play a powerful causal role in the world, including influencing the activity in the brain. … Willed mental activity can clearly and systematically alter brain*

4 Jeffrey M. Schwartz, *The Mind and the Brain*, (New York: HarperCollins Publishers, 2002), 15, emphasis added.

> *function. The exertion of willful mental effort generates physical force that has the power to change how the brain works and even its physical structure. The result is directed neuroplasticity.*[5]

It's not just figurative or poetic when we say, "as a man thinketh, so is he." In the most literal of terms, the thoughts we willfully, or even idly, dwell on are shaping who we are, just as the prophets have told us all along. Paul warned the Galatians, "God is not mocked: for whatsoever a man soweth, that shall he also reap. For he that soweth to his flesh shall of the flesh reap corruption; but he that soweth to the Spirit shall of the Spirit reap life everlasting" (Gal. 6:7–8).

President David O. McKay said, "The thought in your mind at this moment is contributing, however infinitesimally, almost imperceptibly to the shaping of your soul, even to the lineaments of your countenance ... even passing and idle thoughts leave their impression."[6] The knowledge that our thoughts have the power to actually transform our brains, for better or worse, is both sobering and energizing. Think of the opportunities we forfeit when we ignore the prophetic warnings and allow our thoughts to take the course of least resistance, wandering onto subjects that cause the alarm of our conscience to go off. It's just as the prophet Alma said, if we don't govern our thoughts well, "our thoughts will also condemn us" (Alma 12:14). More ominous still are the mind-numbing trances we fall into when we allow ourselves to stare hour after hour at TVs, computers and smartphones. It's not just the insipid drivel we often choose to view. Through deliberately manipulated content, modern Gadiantons are conniving behind the scenes shaping neuronal circuits to get gain, tailored to each person's specific choices and weaknesses. Without us even being

5 Schwartz, *The Mind and the Brain,* 16–18, emphasis added.
6 Kimball, *Miracle of Forgiveness,* 105.

aware, the circuits of our brains are *literally* being rewired in ways to suit Lucifer's ends at the expense of our souls.[7]

An Inspiring Perspective

I believe most people would be shocked and amazed by what we can attain when we discipline and elevate our thoughts! I am not just taking about positive mental attitude. Recall the words of the Prophet Joseph Smith cited earlier; "All the minds and spirits that God ever sent into the world *are susceptible of enlargement.*"[8] At first blush, we think we understand the idea: All of God's children can learn. I believe the Prophet's statement goes beyond that. Consider the last four words "are susceptible of enlargement"—particularly the last word. What does "enlargement" mean? My thesaurus says, "increased, augmentation, doubling, tripling, quadrupling, amplification, magnification." What is capable of being enlarged? *It's the mind —the intelligence*—the thinking part of your ageless spirit. Joseph isn't just talking about the *amount of knowledge* the intelligence can store being enlarged (although that's certainly true). He's saying *the intelligence itself* can be increased, augmented, amplified, and magnified!

The next thunderbolt is equally electrifying. Joseph said this truth applies to each of us—"*all* the minds and spirits that God ever sent into the world!" We're all innately capable of becoming smarter, wiser, kinder and more like God! No one is left out. We all have the opportunity and capacity to increase the intelligence of our intelligence, which means not just getting smarter. It means increasing in all dimensions and aspects of our character—all of this made possible through the Atonement of Jesus Christ in Heavenly Father's great plan of happiness. And, again, what we do with this possibility, and how far we take it is a matter of agency. I pray that a sense of wonder and rejoicing is enlivening your soul as you read this.

---

7 *The Social Dilemma,* Netflix documentary.

8 Smith, *Teachings of the Prophet Joseph Smith,* 354, emphasis added.

There aren't many ideas more appealing, temporally or spiritually, than the idea we can become not only more knowledgeable but more intelligent and smarter. Allow me to let you in on a little secret, if you ever get in the mood to write a best-selling book. Do you know what the second most popular topic for a non-fiction book in the self-help genre is? Books that hold out the promise that the readers can think better, increase their IQ, be as creative as Leonardo da Vinci, and by unleashing their creative genius become as rich as Bill Gates and Jeff Bezos combined. (Of course, the *most* popular self-help topic is the one where you can become attractively thinner and look like a supermodel without eating salad.) Levity aside, as you seek, ponder, pray, and fast—you qualify for the Lord's promise to "receive revelation upon revelation, knowledge upon knowledge" (D&C 42:61) and also the promise recorded in the Book of Mormon to receive more.

> *Thus saith the Lord God: I will give unto the children of men line upon line, precept upon precept, here a little and there a little; and blessed are those who hearken unto my precepts, and lend an ear unto my counsel, for they shall learn wisdom; for unto him that receiveth I will give more; and from them that shall say, We have enough, from them shall be taken away even that which they have (2 Ne 28:30).*

The more knowledge or skill we gain in a given field or art, the more the brain develops and expands its capacity to suit the specific demand. That principle of neuroplasticity holds true whether the knowledge or skill is factual, practical, physical or spiritual. For example, the brain of a virtuoso violinist will be larger and more intricate in the area that controls the dexterity of the left hand. The violinist's hours of effort and focused repetition to master the fingering have driven changes in her brain to support and facilitate her musicality. Her brain has obediently changed according to her chosen desire. This is emblematic of what happens on a deeper level. Every principle of truth we learn and every godly attribute we incorporate into our character enlarges our mind. You thus enlarge the intelligence of your intelligence. "For intelligence cleaveth unto intelligence; wisdom receiveth wisdom; truth embraceth truth … light cleaveth unto light" (D&C 88:40). Elder Neal A. Maxwell affirms:

> *Those attributes and skills are portable. They are never obsolete and will be much needed in the next world. How often have you and I pondered just what it is, therefore, that will rise with us in the resurrection? Our intelligence will rise with us—meaning not simply our IQ, but our capacity to receive and apply truth. Our talents, attributes and skills will rise with us. Certainly, also, our capacity to learn and our degree of self-discipline; and our capacity to work.*[9]

The intelligence we call mind is capable of enlargement, continuous improvement and boundless progression. In fact, you hunger for that growth. Inherently embedded in all of us churns a deep inner drive to learn, grow, expand and improve. The extent of this advancement has no bounds. Unlimited potential is not a hollow superlative; it is an accurate description of your eternal birthright as a child of God.

9 Maxwell, "Grounded, Rooted, Established, and Settled," BYU Devotional Address, September 15, 1981.

CHAPTER 7

Laws of the Mind

"The Winds of Fate," by Ella Wheeler Wilcox is well worth pondering. Consider its first stanza:

One ship drives east, and another drives west
With the selfsame winds that blow;
'Tis the set of the sails
And not the gales
That tells them the way to go.[1]

"The set of the sails" I see as a metaphor for taking charge of our thought processes. The destination is not determined by the direction the wind may or may not be blowing. No matter the direction of the wind, skilled sailors can reach their desired destination using a technique called tacking. With any science, the more laws we know and the better we know them, the higher the likelihood of success.

The fundamental laws of the mortal mind are not complicated, but their ramifications are enormous, and we are going to consider each one

1 Ella Wheeler Wilcox, *World Voices*, (New York: Hearst's International Library Company, 1916), "The Winds of Fate".

of them. In their most succinct form, these four laws are: 1) The Mind Must Think; 2) The Mind Thinks Boundlessly; 3) The Mind Thinks Exclusively; and 4) The Mind Drives the Body. As we understand and apply these laws, we amplify our prospects for growth and development in mortality. Heavenly Father's great plan of happiness extends tremendous opportunities to each of us, limited only by how we choose to use our agency to think and to act!

Law No. 1: The Mind Must Think

Every waking minute your mind is in a constant state of activity. You can guide your mind, speed it up, slow it down, and even bring it to a virtual stillness—but you cannot entirely stop it. Mental activity is synonymous with life itself, because mental activity is the essence of your intelligence which is now cloaked in a body. In mortality, when the brain waves go flat, a person is pronounced dead because the spirit has departed the body. Rene' Descartes captured the very essence of this truth in succinct terms: "Cogito, ergo sum. I think, therefore I am."[2]

Ramifications of Law No. 1

We think, and with those thoughts we *create*. By the thoughts we think, we create the quality of life we experience and the person we become. The impact of our thoughts goes beyond influencing, shaping, or guiding. By our mental choices, you and I determine how we experience mortality and how much we make of it, thus crafting the inner world we live in. We establish our own happiness or misery, abundance or scarcity, bondage or freedom. In the foremost example of the law of cause and effect, we harvest in life, only and exactly, what we sow in our minds.

---

2 https://www.britannica.com/topic/cogito-ergo-sum.

Since your mind is in a constant state of activity, the planting and corresponding harvesting are always going on. You are continuously generating a never-ending flow of causes, thus producing an endless yield of effects. If you take a passive approach to managing your thoughts, it doesn't stop the planting or the harvesting; it simply means you relinquish control of your outcomes. The scriptures warn us of the consequences of such indifference (see Alma 12:14). When we do not actively and responsibly manage our mind, we allow the world and other outside forces to intervene and determine our outcomes. Learning to recognize worldly and satanic influences and repel them is of paramount importance.

At this very instant, you are reaping the consequences of your mental choices. You have been where your thoughts have led you. You now stand where your thoughts have brought you. And you will only go as high and as far as your thoughts will take you. Once we truly see that our thoughts are the *cause* of all our *effects*, and that we have total control over that causative force, we own the equivalent to the "lapis philosophorum,"—the legendary alchemist's stone capable of turning lead into gold.

Each of us possesses the distinctive ability to monitor and evaluate our thoughts. As you will see later on, our ability for instant self-analysis allows us to have the upper hand in the battle with the adversary. It is crucial we respect and cultivate the ability to choose in order to resume control when our thoughts wander or come under the influence of Satan. When we cede control and succumb to his ploys, we allow ourselves to become subject to the will of the devil (D&C 29:40). If we continue down such a path, we diminish our ability to choose righteously and endanger our agency to the point we can actually lose it (Alma 34:35), which was Lucifer's aim from the beginning. Being led captive at Satan's will and subject to satanic power beyond our control is a chilling thought but nonetheless true (Moses 4:3–4). Note the warning words of Elder Neal A. Maxwell:

> *To the extent that we are not willing to be led by the Lord, we will be driven by our appetites, or we will be greatly preoccupied with the lesser things of the day. … Ironically, if the Master is a stranger to us, then we will merely end up serving other masters. The sovereignty of these other masters is real, even if it sometimes is subtle, for they do call their cadence.*[3]

The fact that your mind must, by its very nature, think also means that you are always in the game! There are no spectators. None of us gets to sit on the bench and watch. Like it or not, we are constantly in the game. You're on the court playing the game right now. You have chosen to use this time to read and provoke yourself to think about something worthwhile. As you continue to fill your mind with productive thoughts, your choices will bear good fruit.

Law No. 2: The Mind Thinks Boundlessly

Not only is your mind in a constant state of activity, but it is also virtually boundless in its capabilities. You have limitless imaginative and creative abilities. You can think, imagine, and dream of anything. Don't pass over that lightly. Think of what a marvelous capacity you possess to dream, invent, and create at will. There are no inherent ceilings or boundaries. You can turn knowledge and perceptions upside down. You can take facts and data and mold them into ingenious new meanings and purposes. Sifting and selecting, keeping or discarding, your mind moves through vast volumes of input every waking hour. At any given moment you have the ability to construct new combinations of thought. You can assemble commonplace facts into stunningly clever associations, breaking into new territory. You can entertain anything from the whimsical to the technical,

3 Maxwell, "Swallowed Up in the Will of the Father," *Ensign,* November 1995.

the mundane to the spiritual. Thinking in new ways is a challenge for all of us. It may not be easy, but it is definitely possible.

The free-flowing river of thoughts takes the course of least resistance, unless we choose otherwise. Environment, culture, and education all play crucial roles in forming a framework for our thoughts, and often we allow this framework to become rigid, reducing our openness to new ideas and mental constructs. But, since these frameworks are acquired, they can also be adjusted. You can put your mind to work and break out of molds if you so direct it. Your boundaries, borders, or ceilings are not inherent.

A second sense in which your mind thinks boundlessly is that it is ungovernable by any other force. No outside force can make you think thoughts against your will. You can be enticed, but no one can dictate your thought processes unless you relinquish control. Over the years people have wondered about brain washing and the ability to control another's thoughts. The consensus among authorities is that people can be coerced to a point of submission. The instigators so torture the body or humiliate the personality that the person surrenders or feigns a submission in order to escape the painful treatment. But even that proves the point. The individual must submit, and without that internal surrender outside ideas cannot be one-sidedly imposed. Nothing external can override conscious will. You are uniquely independent in that internal realm.

Ramifications of Law No. 2

A practical ramification of this law helps us avoid common rationalizations prevalent in everyday situations. One simple example is the statement, "Rude drivers make me mad." If no person or circumstance can usurp control of our thoughts, then what others do or say cannot be responsible for how we react or feel. The episodes of life that happen "out there" have no hard-wired connection to what happens "in here." There is a critical separation. What happens externally is only an event, not a cause. What happens externally is what happens externally—and what happens internally amounts to a decision. Outside events are essentially neutral. They are not "good" or "bad" until we interpret them and give them meaning. In this case "rude" is a value judgment (which may or may not have basis) which evokes a corresponding emotion. We are mad all right, but nobody *made* us mad. Getting mad is a choice; and a big part of our testing in mortality is to learn to take responsibility for our demeanor and respond with forbearance and grace rather than anger and resentment. Neal A. Maxwell points this out:

> *Built into the seemingly ordinary experiences of life are opportunities for us to acquire the eternal attributes—love, mercy, meekness, patience, submissiveness and to develop and sharpen such skills as how to communicate, motivate, delegate and manage our time and talents and our thoughts in accordance with eternal priorities.*[4]

Albert Schweitzer articulated a similar idea: "Man must cease attributing his problems to his environment and learn again to exercise his will."[5]

Law No. 3: The Mind Thinks Exclusively

The third law means the mind thinks one thought at a time. It doesn't matter how busy you are, how great your demands, or how high your IQ, your conscious mind can focus and concentrate on only one thought at any given moment. Scientists call this property lateral or peripheral inhibition. Although your mind can flit from idea to idea at such blazing rates of speed you have the impression you are entertaining simultaneous thoughts, such is not the case. Your conscious mind maintains an exclusive stage. Only one player can perform there at any given moment, and you have full control over which player it is. Any thought that dwells on center stage

4 Maxwell, "Grounded, Rooted, Established, and Settled.
5 https://www.goodreads.com/quotes/Schweitzer.

and becomes dominant in your mind, represents a preference on your part. Choose it well. Thoughts that dwell on center stage are directives to the body to be brought into reality. Every dominant thought propels you to fulfill or complete it.

At one time I thought of this trait of single-mindedness as an unfortunate limitation. "Wouldn't it be wonderful if I could focus on multiple topics at the same time?" "I could talk on the phone, balance my checkbook, read a book, and write a book all at the same time." Think of it, on Saturdays, you could work and relax simultaneously. In truth, our one-track mind is a notable advantage. If we shift from a passive approach to mind management and be more selective about what we dwell on, we make more progress temporally and spiritually.

Ramifications of Law No. 3

Fear and doubt cannot exist in the same mind with confidence and faith. They have to be exchanged for one another. If you are plagued with worry, you are not managing your mind. You are allowing your imagination to follow a negative track. I know this from personal experience. I used to be a world-class worrier. If there had ever been an Olympic event in worrying, I would have been the gold medalist; I could out-worry anyone. On a fairly regular basis, I'd find myself mired in a 3:15 a.m. the-world-is-coming-to-an-end mental movie. You may have had one or two of your own. At 3:15 in the morning, we wake up, body rested, mind alert. We wonder, "Why am I not sleeping? Something must be wrong." Dread now creeps into the room like an eerie fog. We go back and relive a litany of bad experiences—failures, klutzy mistakes, an argument we had with someone years ago. We put ourselves right back into the scene. Formulating a clever retort, we say to ourselves, "Ooh, I wish I would have said that to him. That would have really gotten him." Then we think of our bills and about the next recession lurking around the corner. Maybe our business will fail … maybe we'll be laid off … the national debt looming larger by the minute. Soon we picture starving people in the streets. Our family is among them. We all look like emaciated refugees. And on it goes. For two hours, we toss and turn, tying the sheets in knots and our stomachs as well.

I have come to validate, at least to my own satisfaction, that such experiences are self-permitted; and we don't have to go there. When we feel negative players moving onto center stage, we can firmly refuse to entertain them. We can shift focus and put our attention on better subjects. One of my "safety valves" is to ask myself, "Dennis, what do you want to make happen? What would you like to see take place in the next six months? Where do you want to be with your business? Where do you want to be spiritually?" Constructing a mental picture of where I want to be in six months—what I want to make happen—does not allow me to marinate in negative experiences of the past. In summary, when afflicted with nightmares, picture what you want, not what you fear.

Law No. 4: The Mind Drives The Body

The body is a dependent entity, a functionary of the mind. The body, with the brain as its governing organ, does nothing independent of the mind. The mind wills, the brain directs, and the body acts. Every feat, every action, every conscious movement is initiated by the mind—and the brain-body complex responds to bring ideas into physical reality. The mind is independent; the body is dependent.

Granted, a remarkable synergism exists between mind and body. A principle of direct reciprocity governs this relationship. Under the influence of positive mental energy, the body benefits, operating more efficiently and effectively. Balanced, homeostatic harmony among the physical systems results and all systems integrate and function better. In such a state, the body reciprocates benefits back to the mind and enhances the powers of the mind. We think better because we feel better;

and we feel better because we think better; and the converse holds just as true—simple as that.

In this classic interdependent relationship, the body affects the mind, and the mind affects the body, but mind takes precedence—especially when it comes to behavior. When the mind fully commits, the body has no choice in the matter. It must comply. The body may resist or complain, but in the final analysis, the mind overrules the body. Over the course of his career, Davis Phinney, a world-class cyclist and former Olympian, won nearly every major bicycle event in North America. Internationally, he also proved himself, winning stages in the most prestigious of all biking competitions, the Tour de France. One of his reflections underscores the point:

> *After training hard, your body reaches a different plateau and it's a neat state to be in. You get to the edge of physical breakdown, of totally blowing out, then you recover and go on. The key is to cut off your body from the neck down. There are times when you think you can't turn the pedals anymore, but you know just ahead you'll get a little break. It does get bad sometimes. I mean, I cry a lot during races … but I keep hustling because I know I'll feel better in a while.*[6]

Davis knows if he lets the mind rule, his body will respond. If he maintains focus on his end goal (what he wants), his body will follow and ultimately become stronger and more powerful.

Ramifications of Law No. 4

The body solicits, but the mind decides. The mind should listen to the body and exercise wisdom and judgment. Pain and fatigue need to be respected, but they do not govern human behavior. Ultimately, it is the mind that determines outcomes. The human will is what rules. When you

6 Used with permission. Granted by the Davis Phinney Foundation, September 30, 2020.

decide to press on and overcome, despite the pain, your body eventually must come around and obey. The ability to bring the body into compliance to noble vision constitutes greatness.

Every goal and every act—heroic or menial—begins as a thought. When even a fleeting thought becomes a center of attention—a dominant thought—the body faithfully responds. The physical body is an awesome, intricate, God-given instrument that brings focused thought into the physical world. In the final analysis, *behavior is the mind driving the body in fulfillment of dominant thought.*

Behavior is an effect; thoughts are the cause. Whatever we do, we do first in our mind. Our battles with temptations are won or lost in the form of decisions about the focal points we choose to dwell on moment by moment. Both the good and bad we do come from the self-same source—the thoughts and desires we select and nurture in our minds—as affirmed by Paul: "To be carnally minded is death; but to be spiritually minded is life and peace" (Rom. 8:6). And Nephi taught: "Men are free according to the flesh... and they are free to choose liberty and eternal life...or to choose captivity and death" (2 Nephi 2:27).

Who Do You Think You Are?

In one of my seminars, a woman named Tari shared her personal experience of the impact of how her dominant thoughts shaped who she had become. She explained that through her sophomore year of high school, she thought of herself as an ultra-shy wallflower. Consequently, she came to be viewed that same way by her classmates. "I was so frightened and unsure of myself," she said, "I'd actually figure out ways of getting to my classes so as to run into the fewest people. When I would get to class, I'd avoid eye contact and rarely engage in conversations. I was so afraid of saying something the kids would think was stupid, I just withdrew. I wasn't very happy, but I didn't know what to do about it."

At the beginning of her junior year, her father came home from work with what he believed was going to be bad news. He said, "Tari, I've been transferred. We're moving out of the state. You're going to have to pull out of school and make new friends." "Truth was," she said, "in a weird sort of way, I was kind of relieved. Contrary to the old adage that you never get a second chance to make a first impression, I felt I kind of did! I was going to a new place, where nobody knew me or how I'd been in the past. There was no reputation to live up to, or in my case, to live 'down to.'"

So, she decided to turn over a proverbial new leaf. When she walked into school in her new location, she summoned a pint of courage and made a promise to herself—one that changed the direction of her life. "I made myself get out of my shell," she said. "I made myself start greeting people, smiling and nodding as I walked through the hallways. When I got to class, I'd try to start a conversation and follow up on it the next day. At first it was scary, and I felt totally awkward, but even after the first day I felt better about myself and happier. Every day it got a little easier, and eventually I became quite confident and had a great group of friends. In my senior year, people actually encouraged me to run for class office, and to my amazement I won!"

What were the factors determining Tari, the outgoing extrovert, and Tari, the shy frightened introvert? Her thought processes. Tari's life-changing breakthrough came when she entertained and accepted one momentous thought: that she had the absolute freedom to be who she wanted to be. Nobody was *making* her play the wallflower role. As strange as it may seem, she was choosing it. And, if she was choosing that persona, she could set it aside and choose another—one that would produce more happiness.

Both versions of Tari were a creation. She wasn't innately a shy person or an outgoing person. She, like all of us, is inherently a totally independent thinker of thoughts. Both renditions of Tari were manifestations of the habitual thoughts she was choosing at the time. The more she fostered one pattern of thought, the more automatic it became, and the more it seemed to be her very identity. But it wasn't. She always had the choice to be one way or the other. None of Heavenly Father's children have permanently fixed demeanors and attitudes, eternally cast in unalterable dispositions and set ways. We are all works in progress. The excuse "I *am* who I am, and I can't be anything else" is erroneous and self-limiting because that view denies the whole premise of eternal progression and the reality that through faith in Christ and repentance, we can one day attain the same attributes and perfections as our Heavenly Parents.

The Owner/Victim Choice

Aware of it or not, each of us not only chooses the apps that run in our minds, we also select the fundamental operating system on which they run. In the Book of Mormon we are taught that there are essentially two operating platforms: To act or to be acted upon (2 Nephi 2:26). To sharpen your grasp of these two operating systems, consider them as two contrasting mindsets or patterns of thinking—owner thinking (to act) and victim thinking (being acted upon).

By divine design, throughout the course of our lives, we all encounter bumps in the road. Some amount to mild irritations; others are bone-jolting adversities. At these disruptive moments, we make a decision: We choose whether to respond as an owner or react as a victim. Each option, owner or victim, has its consequence and produces a result. The cumulative impact of these owner or victim choices cannot be overstated, for it is in those moments that we decide whether we will act or be acted upon.

I am not using the terms "owner" and "victim" as identities or classifications or "types of people." They describe two fundamental patterns of thought—two contrasting ways of interpreting situations, characterizing oneself, and viewing the world. Notably, we can (and do) change from one mindset to the other in a fraction of a second. You can be in a meeting and be solidly in the owner mindset, taking responsibility and focusing on solving problems. As you leave the meeting, you get a call from your upset teenage daughter who accuses you of making her late for volleyball practice. Immediately, you slip into victim mode, believing the thought that "if you were a better mother and more organized, you wouldn't allow things like this to happen."

So, when we use the term "owner" in this way we're talking about taking responsibility for who we are and how we act. When we think in owner terms, we tend to live more independent of circumstance. The ups and downs of the day don't define who we are; neither do they dictate our mood or demeanor. When something goes awry, owners can be disappointed and frustrated, but they don't have to find someone to blame. In the owner mindset, we tend to focus our thinking on what to do—what options we have and what actions we can take. In this mindset we aren't incessantly cheerful every minute of the day. When owners fall short of a goal, we are disappointed. When we suffer losses, we grieve. Looking for what we can learn and appreciate, we also heal and go on. We do not hang on to our grief or prolong the suffering.

From an ownership point of view, we understand life is not easy, and we don't expect it to be. We keep in mind that we are here to learn to be optimistic and full of faith, come what may, according to the Lord's individual plan for us. That doesn't mean we go looking for obstacles or hoping things will get hard; but, at the same time, we are seldom surprised by trouble. In the face of adversity, we stand on our foundation of faith and look unto Christ for revelation and strength to overcome our obstacles.

In the owner mindset, we recognize the hand of the Lord in both the blessings and the trials of life—and submit to the Lord's timing in all things. We carry a sense of gratitude for the downs as well as the ups. We maintain a positive outlook knowing we may not control the winds in life, but we do regulate our own sails. When the gales blow against us, we learn to seek the Lord's guidance and tack into the headwind. When we do, and we finally reach our intended port, the headwinds of adversity leave behind an unexpected windfall. Our gratitude to the Lord and the joy and satisfaction we feel are much greater for those excursions than for the tailwind-aided pleasure cruises. The joy of victory is always proportionate to the degree of difficulty and opposition.

Mastering your mind—bringing your thoughts into complete alignment and unity with the mind of the Father—is the greatest of all quests. For that is the essence of what our Lord and Savior Jesus Christ did to become one with the Father. The Prophet Joseph declared, "And he [the Son] being the Only Begotten of the Father … having overcome, received a fullness of the glory of the Father, possessing the same mind with the Father … the Father and the Son possessing the same mind, the same wisdom, glory, power, and fullness."[7] In such light, we glimpse a deeper understanding of Christ's hallowed words, "Come follow Me." According to Heavenly Father's great plan to bring to pass our immortality and eternal life, the ultimate purpose of our existence is to learn the principles of mind mastery, so we become one with the Father and the Son.

---

7 Joseph Smith, Jr., *Lectures on Faith,* (Salt Lake City: Deseret Book Company, 1985), Lecture Fifth, 2.

CHAPTER 8

Ground Rules of the Battle

As part of His great plan of happiness, Heavenly Father has established ground rules for our earthly conflict between good and evil. The battle exists for one central purpose: God is providing His children a practical hands-on classroom to experience the tugs and pulls of the world, including the temptations of Satan, so we can use our agency to develop righteousness. To do so, there must be real choices with corresponding consequences. Millions of God's children have wandered in darkness and stumbled in the absence of correct knowledge of the purpose of mortality. Without this understanding, people cannot understand why—if there is a loving God—mortal life could be fraught with so much evil, sorrow, injustice and pain. Through Lehi's teachings in the Book of Mormon we learn *why* there must be opposition in all things: If there is no possibility of sin, there can be no righteousness, which by definition, is to choose good over evil in the presence of evil, not the absence of evil. Mark the words of Elder Bruce R. McConkie:

> *Men must have a choice; they must be able to choose; there must be opposites; they must have agency; they must be free to worship the Lord or to follow Satan. All this is imperative. It is inherent in the whole*

> *plan of salvation. And unless men have the agency to choose to do good and work righteousness—and, in fact, do so—they cannot be saved. There is no other way.*[1]

Righteousness is manifested and developed by resisting evil, particularly when it comes disguised as something pleasurable and desirable.

Ground Rule No. 1: There Must Needs Be Opposition

In a vision, Abraham learned Heavenly Father's purpose for creating the earth: to be the place where God's children could make choices in order to attain "glory added upon their heads forever and ever" (Abraham 3:26). Through the exercise of their agency, they would have to show they were willing to "do all things whatsoever the Lord their God shall command them" (Abraham 3:22–25). "All things" and "whatsoever" imply a broad range of choices of varying degrees and magnitudes—everything from stark extremes between good and evil, and some where the distinction between good and evil would be more difficult to discern. Whatever the case, it is clear there would have to be opposition in *all things*, because an opposite cannot exist in the absence of a polar counterpart. Without bitter, there can be no conception of sweet. Without sorrow, there can be no sense of joy. Without vice, virtue has no meaning. And, in order to have meaning, a law must have both a reward and a penalty attached; otherwise, the law is moot. "For it must needs be, that there is an opposition in all things. If not so … righteousness could not be brought to pass, neither wickedness, neither holiness nor misery, neither good nor bad "(2 Ne. 2:11).

Ground Rule No. 2: Therefore There Must Be an Adversary

Polar opposites, such as "good and evil" or "concrete and abstract" can exist as generalized ideas in our minds—detached and impersonal. The

---

1 Bruce R. McConkie, *The Mortal Messiah*, (Salt Lake City: Deseret Book Company, 1979), Vol. 1, 406.

same is true of the terms "God" and "love." When it comes to real-life meaning, the difference between concrete and abstract is huge. "Romance" is abstract; "passionate kissing" is concrete. Heavenly Father and Jesus Christ are real beings, not abstract concepts, who invite us to have a real, not intellectual, relationship with Them—during mortal life and beyond. Their work and their glory is to bring to pass our everlasting, personal, and permanent relationship with Them—eternal life.

Hence, in accordance with the first ground rule: "it must needs be, that there must be opposition in all things" (2 Ne. 2:11), just as there must be a Christ who epitomizes and promotes good, there must also be a Satan or anti-Christ who epitomizes and promotes evil. President Dallin H. Oaks, declared:

> *God created this earth as a place where his beloved spirit children could be born into mortality to receive a physical body and to have the opportunity for eternal progress by making righteous choices. To be meaningful, mortal choices have to be made between contesting forces of good and evil. There had to be opposition; and therefore an adversary who was cast out because of rebellion was allowed to tempt God's children to act contrary to God's plan.*[2]

Elder Bruce R. McConkie wrote:

> *If there is a God, there is also a devil. It is the Lord who invites and entices men, by his Spirit—the light of Christ—to choose the right; it is the devil who invites and entices men to choose evil works rather than good. The enticements of the devil are temptation, and temptation is, and "must needs be," an essential part of the plan of salvation. … Hence, there is—and must be—a devil, and he is the father of lies and of wickedness … continuing the war that commenced in heaven.*[3]

---

2 Dallin H. Oaks, "Truth and the Plan," *Ensign,* November 2018, 26.
3 McConkie, *The Mortal Messiah,* Vol. 1, 407–408.

So, the battle lines are drawn. The battle is fierce and the stakes are eternally high. The antichrist, Lucifer, is relentless and determined to defeat you, me and all of Heavenly Father's children. But, as the Lord Jesus Christ said to Peter, He also says to us, "Behold, Satan hath desired to have you, that he may sift you as wheat: But I have prayed for thee, that thy faith fail not: and when thou art converted, strengthen thy brethren" (Luke 22:32).

Ground Rule No. 3: The Battle Must Be Fair

Despite the ferocity and cunning of our adversary, Christ urges His disciples to "Be of good cheer, and do not fear, for I the Lord am with you, and will stand by you" (D&C 68:6); and "In this world ye shall have tribulation: but be of good cheer; I have overcome the world" (John 16:33). Because the Father and the Son are far more powerful than our enemy, all things we encounter in our mortal probations "shall work together for good to them that walk uprightly" (D&C 100:15; 90:24) When we contemplate the infinite power and boundless love of our Heavenly Father, we realize a deeply reassuring truth. In order for us to experience and learn from evil and not be overwhelmed by it, Heavenly Father has designed this probationary state so the elements of the battle are stacked in our favor. That's the good news and the third ground rule: *The battle has to be fair.* Now, hold on, don't bail out on this idea just yet. Being a parent myself, I know all parents are faced with a child's complaint, "This isn't fair." Frequently our response is, "Well, sooner or later, you're going to learn life isn't fair. It wasn't meant to be fair. So buck up, kiddo, and deal with it."

So, here's my explanation for the seeming contradiction. Satan, as we all know, is a very powerful and evil being, as Joseph Smith found out dramatically in the Sacred Grove.

> *I kneeled down and began to offer up the desires of my heart to God. I had scarcely done so, when immediately I was seized upon by some power which entirely overcame me, and had such an astonishing*

> *influence over me as to bind my tongue so that I could not speak. Thick darkness gathered around me, and it seemed to me for a time as if I were doomed to sudden destruction. But, exerting all my powers to call upon God to deliver me out of the power of this enemy which had seized upon me, and at the very moment when I was ready to sink into despair and abandon myself to destruction—not to an imaginary ruin, but to the power of some actual being from the unseen world, who had such marvelous power as I had never before felt in any being. (Joseph Smith History 1:15–16, emphasis added.)*

Satan knows what's at stake at this crucial moment in mortal history. If he can stop Joseph and squelch the Restoration before the bud even starts, he would score the winning run in the final dispensation of the World Series of Mortality. Neither Satan nor Heavenly Father is messing around here; they're playing the ultimate game of hardball at this moment of moments. Satan was intent on literally destroying Joseph and would have, but for one thing. Heavenly Father would not allow him to go that far. In the measure of Lucifer's powers, both temporal and spiritual, he was powerful enough to overwhelm the boy Joseph and end his life. But God's love for Joseph and, more importantly, His *justice* would not allow such an overwhelmingly uneven disparity of power to prevail. It just would not be fair.

This same principle and reasoning applies, thankfully, to you and me. Lucifer has sufficient power to overwhelm any of us. He could exert such mental and physical power over us we wouldn't stand a chance. But, if he did so, the whole purpose of a probation, where we are free to exercise our agency to choose between good and evil, would be annihilated.

We have an apt example in Job. Heavenly Father allows Satan sufficient leeway to inflict all kinds of havoc on Job's property, his family and his body—but he is not permitted to take Job's life (Job 1:12; 2:6). As He did with Job and with Joseph, God sets the limits for our trials and testing commensurate with our spiritual strength. The measure of our tests cannot exceed our ability to resist or bear them. The Apostle Paul taught, "There hath no temptation taken you but such as is common to man: but God is faithful, who will not suffer you to be tempted above that ye are able; but will with the temptation also make a way to escape, that ye may be able to bear it" (1 Corinthians 10:13). Lucifer has the power to utterly overwhelm any of us but, due to the atonement and power of Jesus Christ, Satan's power is checked. He can only go so far and cannot exceed each individual's power to withstand. Why? It wouldn't be fair.

Ground Rule No. 4: The Curriculum is Personally Tailored

For the testing and proving to be meaningful and just for each of us, there must be a personally customized curriculum. What value would there be in testing a kindergartener on calculus or a physics professor on arithmetic? Elder Neal A. Maxwell taught, "I believe with all my heart that because God loves us there are some particularized challenges that he will deliver to each of us. He will customize the curriculum for each of us in order to teach us the things we most need to know. He will set before us in life what we need, not always what we like."[4] It seems fairly obvious that in premortal life Nephi had grown to higher spiritual stature than you or me. What would be our ceiling would be Nephi's floor. In order for Nephi to progress and for his mortal probation to have any meaning, he would need to face challenges, temptations, and afflictions suited to his station, and greater than ours, which he obviously did.

This principle of individually adapted testing applies to all of God's children. No one can be tested beyond his or her capacity to endure in this life. We may be tested to the ultimate limit of our current ability, but, in no case, ever beyond it. In Heavenly Father's wisdom, each of us experiences exactly what we need and in the proportion we need it.

---

4 Maxwell, "But For a Small Moment," BYU Devotional Address, September 1, 1974.

Three Significant Advantages

The Great Plan of Happiness is *Heavenly Father's* plan; and it's an *eternal* plan—enacted in instances without number—worlds without end. Through it He brings to pass the immortality and eternal life of His children. Its ultimate success is astronomical. Without violating the laws of justice or infringing on our agency, our Heavenly Father assists and promotes our agency by extending advantages in our favor. Here are three of them:

1. We Have Total Control Over Our Thoughts

According to God's plan, your mind and will are completely your own. "There remains an inner zone in which we are sovereign, unless we abdicate," says Elder Maxwell.[5] We can yield our wills to either Satan or the Lord, or even to other beings. But no one can compel us to yield it. Even so, we are up against a powerful, formidable foe. Sheri Dew, a former counselor in the Relief Society general presidency, said, "No one knows better than God what we're up against. No one understands better how powerful Satan is. … Yet, that is precisely why you gain power every time you resist him." Rather than intimidating or discouraging us, Sister Dew is pointing out what a tremendous source of motivation the truth can be. "Now here's the really stunning reality," she declared, "we can either be influenced in a dramatic way by the power of Satan, which is pretty pervasive in the world today. Or we can be influenced in a dramatic way by the power of God. The devil cannot make us do anything. The only power he has over us is the power that we give him by intentionally, willfully sinning."[6]

The war in heaven was about power. The essence of our struggle in mortality is also all about power—and how much power we will possess as we leave this sphere and enter the realm ahead. God allows Satan to act

5 Maxwell, "According to the Desires of [Our] Hearts," *Ensign,* November 1996, 21–22.
6 Sheri Dew, *God Wants a Powerful People,* (Salt Lake City: Deseret Book Audio Library, 2004), Track 6.

on us, so we have the opportunity to resist and act against him. Each and every time we reject a satanic enticement, we gain power proportionate to the enticement. Though both God and Satan whisper, entice, prompt, and present ideas to our minds, we have the right and ability to choose whom we will follow and obey. Whatever the situation or circumstance, you are always the chooser.

2. We Have Control Over Our Personal Battlefield

Recall two points made earlier:

1) The only thing over which we have absolute control is our thoughts.

2) The only thing *we need* to control is our thoughts.

This second point gives us the basis to battle and defeat the adversary. The scope of the battle is narrowed so as to be manageable, and we're not spread too thin. The battlefield is discrete and defined. We can't and we don't have to control circumstances, events, or other people. Learning to focus only on what we can control gives us more power to determine the outcomes of our choices. All the rest of the stuff—the cares and concerns weighing us down—we leave in the hands of the author of the Plan who will take care of everything else. Fretting over things we can't control—the junk we let plague our minds—never has nor ever will bring a solution. It just siphons our energy.

3. We Have a Body and Satan Doesn't

The Prophet Joseph Smith taught, "All beings who have bodies have power over those who have not. The devil has no power over us only as we permit him. The moment we revolt at anything which comes from God, the devil takes power."[7] Possessing a body, in which the Holy Spirit

7 Smith, *Teachings of the Prophet Joseph Smith,* 181.

can dwell, you have power Satan doesn't have. He forfeited his privilege of having a body, thereby losing a tremendous amount of light he once possessed. And he has power over us only as we lose light by rejecting God's laws and counsel. Disobedience and rebellion repel the Spirit and open the door for Satan's influence to fill the void. Literally.

Your body actually functions as a shield and a protection to your spirit here in mortality. While it is true many of Satan's ploys center on afflicting your body and urging you to misuse its most ennobling faculties, you still retain the upper hand. Through the pathway of your mind, you retain the ability to resist Satan and repent and return to the God of light and grace, thus subduing and refining your mortal appetites. President Brigham Young taught, "The body is framed for the tabernacle or house in which the spirit has to dwell. This tabernacle is formed expressly to hold its spirit *and shield it. … The spirit must overcome the body in the flesh*, and the flesh become subject to the spirit in all things."[8]

When you put your body in motion, taking action and accomplishing worthwhile things, you leverage power over Satan, interrupting and shutting him down. You may have already noticed this effect. Walking, mowing the lawn, folding laundry, biking, ironing clothes, weeding the garden produce a feeling of well-being and set the stage for receiving revelation and promptings of the Spirit. Even if your physical activity level wouldn't impress anyone at the gym, your brain is supplied with more oxygen which energizes your brain, as the Spirit feeds your mind and fosters inspiration that invigorates your soul.

The blessings promised in the Word of Wisdom pertain to both body and spirit. We "receive health in the navel and marrow to the bones … run and not be weary and walk and not faint;" *and* will "find wisdom and great treasures of knowledge, even hidden treasures" (D&C 89:18–20). In

---

8 Young, *Journal of Discourses,* 9:139, emphasis added.

a remarkable spiritual synergy, taking proper care of your tabernacle blesses your intelligence as well as its earthly abode.

Concluding Questions

The trying and testing of mortality is not based on any single, once-and-for-all choice; rather, a continuum of small, simple choices—dozens of which are made each day—determine whom we serve now and hereafter. Both Christ and Satan are doing everything in their respective power to invite us to their side. The decision would seem to be a simple matter—a mere repeat of the choices made in premortal life—for no one granted the privilege of a mortal body, along with this probationary opportunity, chose to follow Satan. The poignant questions now are:

- What choices are you making now?
- To whose voice are you listening most?
- And unto whom do you look and list to obey?

CHAPTER 9

The War in Heaven in Our Heads

Now we get to the heart and heat of the battle. The colossal clash, which John the Revelator called the "war in heaven" is a ferocious conflict centered on our agency. Driven by deep-seated pride, Lucifer, rebelled against the Father and His Plan of Redemption. When the Father said, "Whom shall I send?" His Beloved and Chosen from the beginning said, "Here am I, send me." Lucifer said, "Here am I send me." When Elohim said, "I will send the first," Lucifer refused to sustain the Father and His plan and endeavored to convince others to do the same as he, and many did (Abraham 3:27–28). In fact, the "many" amounted to a staggering number—a third of the hosts of heaven. All of these spirit children made the same egregious error as Lucifer; they used their agency to rebel rather than sustain and uphold. Instead, they turned away from their creator and, choosing to follow Lucifer rather than God, became subject to the will and power of the one they chose to follow. War ensued and the rebels "were thrust down and thus came the devil and his angels" (D&C 29:36–37). John the Revelator reveals additional details:

> *And there was war in heaven: Michael and his angels fought against the dragon; and the dragon fought and his angels, And prevailed not; neither was their place found any more in heaven. And the great dragon was cast out, that old serpent, called the Devil, and Satan, which deceiveth the whole world: he was cast out into the earth, and his angels were cast out with him (Rev 12:7–9).*

Moses also testifies, "he [Lucifer] became Satan, yea even the devil, the father of lies, to deceive and to blind men, and to lead them captive at his will" (Moses 4:4).

Satan, along with those who followed him, became devils by choosing to use their agency to turn away and rebel against the Father (2 Ne. 9:9). Rebellion was the essence of the War in Heaven, and the essence of the continuation of the war here on earth. Every person who obtains a body on this earth obtains that blessing because they refused to rebel and chose to sustain the Father's plan and His Beloved Son. The Prophet Joseph Smith taught, "At the first organization in heaven we were all present, and saw the Savior chosen and appointed and the plan of salvation made, and we sanctioned it."[1]

The war that started in heaven is far from over. Satan's enmity towards God has not abated; if anything it has intensified. And his tactics haven't changed either; he is still hell-bent on convincing Heavenly Father's children to use their agency to rebel against Him and turn away, which then makes them subject to Satan, captive at his will (Moses 4:4). He now vents his rage and venom upon the inhabitants of the earth. "Woe to the inhabiters of the earth and of the sea! for the devil is come down unto you, having great wrath, because he knoweth that he hath but a short time" (Revelation 12:12). You and I are still in Satan's vicious crosshairs. He aims to go beyond thwarting our

1 Smith, *Teachings of the Prophet Joseph Smith,* 181.

progress and making us miserable like unto himself, he seeks to destroy our agency, take over our bodies, and obliterate all hope of obtaining eternal life (Mark 5:1–13). And how exactly does he accomplish these evil objectives? In mortality, he does it the very same way he did in heaven. Note carefully the Father's words: "And also a third part of the hosts of heaven turned he away from me *because of their agency*!" (D&C 29:36, emphasis added). Hear it, O mankind! How did Lucifer get a third of the hosts of heaven to rebel against the Father and follow him? *Through their agency.* How is he endeavoring to sift you and me as wheat? By carefully enticing us to misuse, even pervert, *how we exercise our agency*. He cannot abruptly seize control and take over. You and I must be complicit in the matter. He grooms us, courting our compliance one small choice at a time.

It is one thing to stumble and sin—and another to sin and refuse to repent. Sin is to turn away from God. If we take responsibility for our sins and turn back to the Father, looking unto Christ and relying on his mercy and merits, we are welcomed back with open arms. To prevent us from turning back to the Father, Satan attempts to separate us from God, seducing us to deny responsibility for our acts and place blame on Him. "God doesn't love you," "His laws are too strict," "The commandments are outdated," are but a few of the Satanic lies through which "the devil cheateth [our] souls, and leadeth [us] away carefully down to hell" (2 Ne. 28:21). Though Satan's falsehoods are the antithesis of truth, the more we listen to them, the more we tend to believe them. Our participation allows Satan to get us to *use our agency to forfeit our agency* and cede our will to him. Could anything be more ingeniously diabolical?

Precisely how Satan instigates his insidious warfare and how we can defend ourselves and defeat him is a primary purpose of this book. We will unmask Satan's most effective form of warfare—a ploy so devilish and subtle, for the most part, we are not even aware it's happening.

The War in Our Heads

The key to gaining leverage over the adversary is understanding that *we are not alone in our heads.* Not all the thoughts inside your mind are generated by your own intelligence of spirit. Plato said, "Thinking is the soul talking to itself." This is true, but it's not the only one talking. There are in fact two other voices present. There is the voice of the Spirit (1 Ne 4:18; D&C 84:46) and the voice of the Adversary—the "liar from the beginning" (D&C 93:25). We teach even our little ones that Heavenly Father speaks to us through a "still small voice" which is not an audible voice; it's a voice we hear in our minds. Satan, the great counterfeiter, uses the very same methodology and has honed it to a fine art. He has mastered the skill of inserting his thoughts into our minds with such stealth we think the thoughts are our own. In later chapters, we will focus on how to hearken to the voice of the Spirit. For now, we will concentrate on battling Satan's efforts to smother and supplant both our own voice and the voice of the Lord.

Myriad are the scriptural references to Satan's interference with our thoughts. He plants his thoughts, putting his intrusions so subtly into our minds, we scarcely recognize the intervention. I cite but a few:

- But Peter said, Ananias, why hath Satan filled thine heart to lie to the Holy Ghost, and to keep back part of the price of the land? (Acts 5:3)
- And behold, others he flattereth away, and telleth them there is no hell; and he saith unto them: I am no devil, for there is none—and thus he whispereth in their ears, until he grasps them with his awful chains, from whence there is no deliverance (2 Ne. 28:22).
- For Satan putteth it into their hearts to anger against you (D&C 63:28).

Similarly, we have also been warned by the leaders of the Church:

- "We should be on guard always to resist Satan's advances. He has power to place thoughts in our minds and to whisper to us in unspoken impressions to entice us to satisfy our appetites or desires and in various other ways he plays upon our weaknesses and desires."[2] –President Joseph Fielding Smith
- "It is Satan who puts hopeless thoughts into the hearts of those who have made mistakes."[3] –Sister Julie B. Beck
- "He (Lucifer) is the one who tells us we are not adequate, the one who tells us we are not good enough, the one who tells us there is no recovery from a mistake. He is the ultimate bully, the one who kicks us when we are down."[4] –Elder Dale G. Renlund

To Be Enticed Is Not a Sin

We are here in mortality to learn to use our agency to choose to do good and be good when we are immersed in enticements to do otherwise. This point seems so patently obvious to us, it hardly needs emphasis. Yet, in the arena of our daily battle, it is a different matter. The enticings of the evil one are often far from obvious, making it easy to succumb to them. *"How can that be?"* we wonder. In the scriptures we are taught "the Spirit giveth light to every man that cometh into the world" (D&C 84:46). Haven't we all got a conscience—a guide and an early warning system to alert us? We do but, oh, the subtlety of our adversary! He deceives us into believing his thoughts are our thoughts. Then he berates us for thinking a thought, which was not ours in the first place, endeavoring to make us feel guilty and convince us to proceed with acting on it. Critical

2 Joseph Fielding Smith, *Answers to Gospel Questions,* (Salt Lake City: Deseret Book Company, 1960), Vol. 3, 81.
3 Julie B. Beck, "Remembering, Repenting and Changing", *Young Women's General Meeting,* March 24, 2007.
4 Renlund, "Choose Ye This Day", *Ensign,* November 2018, 105.

to navigating this mental labyrinth is understanding that being enticed is not a sin.

Experiencing an evil or impure impulse—an overture injected into our minds by the adversary—does not mean we are unclean in our thoughts. Initially, it is a temptation and only a temptation. In mortality, we cannot stop the perpetual influx of enticements and temptations. It is the crux of our mortal test. Temptations become sins only if we accept and dwell on them. If you entertain them, add to them, or even "savor" them, then, yes, you are committing sin in your head, as the Lord plainly taught (Matt 5:28; 3 Ne. 12:28). However, if you catch and identify them for what they are—Satan's tawdry attempts to get you to sin—and promptly shift your thinking, refusing to dwell on them, you have not sinned. If fact, the opposite is true; you have actually increased in righteousness. Lehi taught that the very definition of righteousness is to be exposed to temptation but not succumb to it (2 Ne 2:13). Each time you unmask one of Satan's ploys and reject it, you achieve a small but significant moral victory and add another drop of oil to your lamp of righteousness.

Without this insight, we also become vulnerable to another satanic ploy, which Satan throws on top of the first temptation. Once he's convinced you and me that we're the one who spawned the temptation, he berates us and then compounds his assault by suggesting we may as well continue since we've already sinned in our minds.

The Temptations of Christ

No being who ever has lived, or ever will draw mortal breath on this planet, endured greater temptations or weathered fiercer storms of satanic assault than our Beloved Lord and Savior Jesus Christ, particularly in Gethsemane and on Calvary. Yea, the very grandeur of His peerlessly sinless life derives its significance for us sin-prone mortals from one singular truth: Jesus knew firsthand exactly and completely what we face and battle. He knows it because He suffered it all himself—personally, deeply, totally. "Our Lord, as a mortal, was subject to the same laws of trial and testing that govern all mortals," wrote Elder Bruce R. McConkie. Satan wants to bury this vital truth, so he can get us to think Christ was so superior to us in every way he could not possibly relate to our mortal experience and be compassionately touched by our pain and struggles. Countering that falsehood, Elder McConkie wrote, "[Christ] lived and breathed as all men do. … He was hungry, cold, tired, sick, and afflicted, as all men are. … He was a man, a mortal man, a son of Adam, and God his Father saw fit to let him live as other men live, experience as they experience, sorrow and suffer as they do, and overcome as they must."[5]

It is hard for us to picture the Lord as having mortal characteristics. Because Christ had no striking physical appearance that would indicate His inward greatness, let alone divinity, Judas Iscariot had to identify Jesus to the arresting mob by a kiss on the cheek. Yet, it's the Savior's authentic mortality that helps us understand why the people of Nazareth, having seen him grow up in their midst, had such a difficult time accepting Him as the Messiah (Matt 13:54–58). Even at least two of His half-brothers, James and Jude, sons of Mary and Joseph, did not believe Jesus was the Messiah *until after* His resurrection (John 7:1–10). It was then that they recognized His divinity, converted and held positions of authority in the primitive church.

The actuality of the Savior's mortal qualities should in no way diminish the stature of the Lord's perfection and righteousness; rather, it should dramatically enhance it. If He was more like us than we commonly suppose, does it not amplify our respect for Him, His ministry, miracles and atoning sacrifice and deepen our sense of awe and reverence for who He is and what He accomplished? Moreover, doesn't this realization

---

5 McConkie, *The Mortal Messiah,* Vol. 1, 5–6.

markedly strengthen our hopes of being able to accept His invitation to "come follow me?"

No one knew more about temptation and what it takes to resist it than our Lord. Consider C. S. Lewis' inspired insight:

> *No man knows how bad he is till he has tried very hard to be good. A silly idea is current that good people do not know what temptation means. This is an obvious lie. Only those who try to resist temptation know how strong it is. … A man who gives in to temptation after five minutes simply does not know what it would have been like an hour later. … We never find out the strength of the evil impulse inside us until we try to fight it: and Christ, because He was the only man who never yielded to temptation, is also the only man who knows to the full what temptation means—the only complete realist.*[6]

Christ Was the Ideal Example, Not the Exception, to the Law of Temptation

Jesus Christ could not be the Savior of the world, the Truth, the Life and the Way, if He were given special treatment. The notion that Jesus was like the rich kid up the block whose daddy gave him everything is a repugnant falsehood perpetuated by the adversary to undermine the greatness of Christ's character and the majesty of His Atonement. How glorious is the truth that from His own personal experience, He understands our mortal plight because He experienced it all to the utmost degree himself. He could not rightfully claim to be the greatest of all (D&C 19) —greater even than father Abraham, whose test is revered as the ultimate of tests, unless he had surpassed it. As we ponder this doctrine, a thunderbolt of priceless enlightenment strengthens our faith in the Lord Jesus Christ. When we glimpse the immense satanic pressure to sin the adversary heaped upon

6 C. S. Lewis, *Mere Christianity*, (New York: HarperCollins Publishers, 1952), 142.

the Lord in His mortal state, we not only gain deeper love and respect for Him, but it also strengthens our resolve to resist Satan's temptations. It is little wonder that in the ordinance of the sacrament we twice covenant "to always remember." Facing the tsunami of temptation Satan hurled at the Lord in the final make-or-break moments in Gethsemane, our Savior neither succumbed, nor wavered, nor rationalized. He faced it all—the full onslaught of temptation and contradiction—perfectly. Yea, He resisted even unto blood. (Heb 12:4).

Praise be to the prophets, particularly those of the latter days, whose teachings and testimonies part the sacred veil protecting these glorious truths from the profane. The effulgent rays of the Book of Mormon in particular impart a correct understanding of Christ's experience with temptation. Consider the awe-inspiring wallop of awareness we gain by knowing Jesus was tested to the utmost degree in mortality yet remained without sin.

> *And lo, he shall suffer temptations, and pain of body, hunger, thirst, and fatigue,* even more than man can suffer, except it be unto death; *for behold, blood cometh from every pore, so great shall be his anguish for the wickedness and the abominations of his people (Mosiah 3:7, emphasis added).*

He endured such exquisite suffering to open the way and strengthen us with His grace, a gift he willingly gives because "it behoved him to be made like unto his brethren. … For in that he himself hath suffered being tempted, he is able to succor them that are tempted" (Heb. 2:17–18). Could He, in the truest sense, know what it's like to be in our shoes unless He had triumphed against the full extremity of temptation, above and beyond what all others have endured? How else and how better could He demonstrate to us it is possible to live without sin? "For we have not an high priest which cannot be touched with the feeling of our infirmities; but was in all points tempted like as we are, yet without sin" (Heb. 4:15).

Like Us, Christ's Victories Were Internal

Like us, Jesus fought His battles with Satan in the arena of His thoughts. Not even those very close to Him, and in His immediate presence, were able to tell from His outward appearance what battles He waged in His mind. This is especially evident at the last supper. The evangelists, in fact, mention Jesus telling his disciples, "My soul is exceeding sorrowful, even unto death," something they had not apparently recognized by His outward expression. His thoughts, like our own, were His and His alone. Only the Father, who knows the thoughts, intents, and desires of all His children, knows the details. Precisely how our Savior dealt with them we do not know. What we know is "He suffered temptations, but gave no heed to them" (D&C 20:22). And of Christ's conflict with the arch-tempter we can be absolutely certain: He never lost a battle, and He decisively won the war.

CHAPTER 10

Prevalence of Satanic Thoughts

We are all aware Satan tempts us to commit sin. Almost automatically, when we think of sins and temptations our minds turn to the Ten Commandments, particularly do not murder, commit adultery, steal, lie, or covet. Rightly, we usually label any urges from the adversary to commit those sins as satanic thoughts.

During His mortal ministry, the Lord made it clear that impure thoughts defile us. When the Pharisees got all tangled up in their picky interpretations of the Jewish law about cleanliness and washing hands before eating, Jesus instructed them: "There is nothing from without [outside] a man, that entering into him can defile him." With or without unwashed hands, what we take in and consume in the form of physical intake does not make us unclean spiritually. "But," he said, "the things which come *out of* him, those are they that defile the man" (Mark 7:15). When His disciples needed clarification, the Lord said, "Are ye so without understanding also? Do ye not perceive, that whatsoever thing from without entereth into the man, it cannot defile him" because it doesn't dwell in his mind to be acted upon but into his stomach and is expelled (Mark 7:18–19). Then comes the key that unlocks the meaning of His parable, "For from within, out of the heart of men, *proceed evil thoughts*, adulteries, fornications, murders, thefts, covetousness, wickedness, deceit, lasciviousness, an evil eye, blasphemy, pride, foolishness. All these evil things come from within and defile the man" (Mark 7:19–23).

In teaching the higher law to his disciples, the Lord emphatically taught the importance of governing and taking charge of one's thoughts. What is conceived in the mind has a direct connection to emotions, actions and results. Speaking specifically of adultery, the Lord warned his disciples to dispel adulterous thoughts. "He that looketh upon a woman to lust after her ..."—in other words, he who elaborates and dwells on imagery of an adulterous act and contemplates the steps of committing the sin—"hath committed adultery already in his heart" (3 Ne. 12:28). Such choices offend the Spirit and weaken resolve, increasing the power of the temptation and the likelihood of succumbing to it. Lucifer does all he can to beguile us into dwelling on impure scenarios because all human actions are first pre-created in the mind before they are created physically.

Other Thoughts Are Also Satanic

Without discounting the gravity of major sins one iota, I submit that Satan's efforts to lure us into committing major sins is but the proverbial tip of the iceberg of satanic ploys. He has other prevalent and frequent strategies he unleashes on us that are just as potentially injurious as the ones he uses to tempt us to commit major sins—but these tactics are far more diabolically disguised.

Hear it, O ye ends of the earth! Any thought that tears you down; diminishes your sense of worth; questions your identity as a child of God; or urges you to doubt, belittle, or berate yourself, is *not* coming from you (your intelligence of spirit); and it is most certainly not coming from a divine source. It is coming from the depths of the infernal pit, from Lucifer and the household of Satan on the dark side of the veil.

Any thought that diminishes a person's value is a satanic thought. Any thought that urges you to be critical, judgmental or negative in any way about yourself or others is a satanic thought. Any thought that sows doubt about the reality of God, Heavenly Father's love for you, Christ's desire or ability to lift, empower and save you from Lucifer's grasp is a satanic thought. Any thought that discourages you from praying, studying the scriptures, attending sacrament meeting, worshiping in the temple, or magnifying your calling as a minister is a satanic thought. Any thoughts that foster discouragement, depression, despondency, dejection or despair are satanic thoughts. Any thoughts that encourage you to shirk, dodge, minimize or rationalize your responsibility for your actions, reactions, sins of commission, and sins of omission—preventing you from repenting and progressing—are assuredly satanic thoughts. Like Amulek, I cannot list all the ways Satan wants to intervene and tamper with your thinking, knock you off course, or halt your progress, but there are many and they are constant.

Any thought that discourages you or holds you back from improving in order to draw closer to God, your spouse, your loved ones, your neighbors, or your ward members is a satanic thought. Any thought that leads to impatience, petty judgments, and unkind characterizations of others—clerks at the store, people in line ahead of you, or slow drivers in front of you—comes from your adversary. Any thought that fosters division and separation from your fellowman, that induces you to be selfish, prideful, or disdainful is a satanic thought. Any thought that perpetuates ill feelings, promotes negative emotions—sadness, misery, loneliness, depression, prolonged guilt, or anxiety is a satanic thought. Any thought that inclines you to postpone or forego a righteous impulse or an act of kindness or compassionate service is a satanic thought. Any thought that tells you that change, or repentance, or losing weight, or returning to school, or retraining for a better paying job is not possible or realistic is a satanic thought. Any thought that urges you to withhold gratitude, appreciation, or love is likewise of evil origin.

Anytime you get the urge to honk your horn in frustration, curse, swear, criticize or look down on another person, you're experiencing a satanic thought. Any self-pitying thought that encourages you to feel sorry for yourself, pout, whine, murmur, think your lot is hard, or be self-indulgent is being prompted by the enemy of your soul; and so are thoughts that incite fault-finding, blaming, or impugning another person's character or motives. Any thought that urges you to hold onto a grudge, nurture a wound, plot revenge, or search on the internet for a hit man is a satanic thought.

Any thought that keeps you from reaching out to others, giving someone the benefit of the doubt, cutting them some slack, forgiving, forgetting, relinquishing or releasing hatred is a satanic thought. Any thought that justifies you taking offense, holding resentment toward your stake president or bishop, and keeps you from enjoying association and sociality with your ward or stake members, that stops you from partaking of the sacrament because so-and-so might be at church is a satanic thought. Any thought telling you it's all right to take advantage of your neighbor, get something for nothing, cut corners when it comes to keeping the commandments is a satanic thought. If the virtues that qualify you for doing the work of the Lord are faith, hope, charity, with an eye single to the glory of God, then any thoughts that counter those virtues and engender the opposite qualities—faithlessness, hopelessness, withholding love and service, selfishness, pride, self-exaltation and vanity—are clearly satanic thoughts.

In fact, any thought that results in you being ornery, out of sorts, touchy, spiteful, cross, unhappy, grouchy, grumpy, dopey or sneezy are not coming from the mirror on the wall or the actions of others. They are reactions Lucifer is urging you to exhibit to mar any occasion or situation, including standing in line at "the happiest place on earth." He delights in spurring you to do anything to spoil the moment, take you out of the moment, keep you from focusing on the moment and being fully present in conversations. Whenever you are feeling contentious, easily irritated, or annoyed you are experiencing the influence of Lucifer's efforts to ruin your day and put a dent in your relationships.

Satan tries to make you believe it is difficult to hear and feel the Spirit and how unlikely it is that you're receiving promptings from the Spirit. He is a master at keeping you from praying, questioning whether you are worthy to pray, distracting you as you pray, and doubting you'll ever get an answer when you pray. He sows the belief that it's almost impossible to receive answers to prayers—that only prophets and their wives get prompt answers to their prayers.

Satan is a genius in getting you to take your commitments to extremes so you will run out of gas and question why you're doing things that nobody notices or appreciates. He loves to tell you that your works are insufficient and he delights in pointing out your many flaws and imperfections. He rejoices in dishing out judgment on how you could have done everything so much better. He's an expert at getting you to believe you're never doing enough or doing it well enough. He rejoices in convincing you that, if you can't live the gospel with perfection, God will not be pleased or find you acceptable. Similarly, he likes to remind you of how overloaded and busy you already are, so you won't accept callings or volunteer for assignments. Or, if you do, he urges you to put things off to the last minute, so the joy of service you might obtain is smothered by the frenzy you feel.

Any thought that irritates you, irks you, upsets you, or provokes you to resentment is of Satan's instigation. Any thought that prevents you from pursuing lofty goals, trying something new or hard, working through setbacks, overcoming obstacles and persisting, is sown by the adversary. When you do undertake a new challenge, any impression telling you it'll never work, it's all futile and you'd better just give up before you embarrass yourself is a satanic missive.

Cleverest of all his insidious ploys is to convince you that none of this kind of thinking has anything whatsoever to do with him. "For there is no devil," he whispers (2 Ne. 28:22). He sells that lie because he wants you to accept responsibility for the thoughts *he authored and planted* in your head. Once you believe the initial thought was yours, not his, he compounds his attack by getting you to berate yourself for having thought that negative thought. His final assault occurs when you eventually realize that berating yourself doesn't cure anything; it only makes you more miserable. He then tries to get you to beat yourself up for beating yourself up.

Looking Forward

The prevalence of satanic interference may surprise and unsettle you. My intent is not to disturb you but to alleviate the burden of a major misconception a good many people carry—that the sudden presence of an unkind or impure thought in their mind is a sin. Note it, please! To be *enticed* by the devil *is not* a sin. Being presented with an evil impulse—a proposition injected into your mind by the adversary—does not mean you are unclean in your thoughts. You are *not* responsible for the satanic thoughts that pop into your mind; you *are only responsible for what you do with them.*

The intent of this chapter is to increase your awareness of the adversary's insidious ploys and how subtle and prevalent they actually are. If not alerted to this reality, you are at a severe disadvantage in the "war in heaven" going on in your head. You simply can't win the war if you don't know the real enemy or how he's attacking you. Once you become aware of Satan's methods and near-constant tamperings with your thoughts, you can detect his evil tactics and turn the tables on him. In the coming chapters, we will examine the specifics of Satan's ploys in more depth and how to counter them. Then we will examine how we can live closer to the Spirit and draw upon the power of our Lord and Savior Jesus Christ to obtain the glorious promises freely offered by the Father to all who will come unto Christ and look to Him in every thought.

As you foil the adversary's traps, and draw closer to your Savior, you will experience more control over your thoughts, your emotions, your actions and your outcomes. Your confidence will grow and fear will diminish. Hope will supplant doubt. Clarity and certainty will cut through confusion and falsehoods. You will feel better about yourself and not only have more love to offer but more room in your soul to receive it.

SECTION THREE

Recognizing and Defeating Satan's Ploys

"Wherefore, men are free according to the flesh; and all things are given them which are expedient unto man. And they are free to choose liberty and eternal life, through the great Mediator of all men, or to choose captivity and death, according to the captivity and power of the devil; for he seeketh that all men might be miserable like unto himself."

— 2 Nephi 2:27

CHAPTER 11

The Biggest Lies You Will Ever Hear Are in Your Head

The biggest lies you'll ever hear are in your head, masquerading as your own thoughts. Like Alma, I wish with great energy "that I were an angel, and could … speak with the trump of God, with a voice to shake the earth" (Alma 29:1). I wish that every man, woman and child could recognize how prevalent and incessant the voice of the adversary is in our lives. It affects every facet of our lives—our moods, our thoughts about events, circumstances, and other people. Most diabolically of all, he is relentless in his attacks on our beliefs about ourselves.

Like most vital insights, my realizations about Satan's warfare came gradually, line upon line, precept upon precept, here a little and there a little—until one day I was thrown headlong into a crash course of experiential awakening. It amounted to being the most gut-wrenching experience of my life—one I will ever be grateful for. Because my part of the story is only one component, to protect other's privacy I will offer no details. I hope it is enough for me to say that it was through this experience that I became acquainted with a book, *Life Without Ed,* by Jenni Schaefer with Thom Rutledge—a book I never dreamed I would ever need or read. Coming when and how it did was a gift from God. It is a courageously told experience of Jenni's battle with and victory over her eating disorder. Its subtitle, *How One Woman Declared Independence from her Eating Disorder,* is sufficient to set the stage.

Thom Rutledge, Jenni's therapist, has helped many persons with eating disorders recover and live free of this deeply personal battle with the adversary. The key breakthrough in the therapy occurs when the person is able to recognize the truth already mentioned—that we are not alone in our heads. Thom teaches clients to personify the disease, giving it—him—a name and to think of him as an evil dictator who is exerting malevolent control over them. Once they can identify him and his coercive tactics, they are able to confront him and defeat him. Since they are dealing with an Eating Disorder they call their opponent "Ed." Jenni writes, "The first step in breaking free from Ed was learning how to distinguish between the two of us. I had to determine which thoughts came from Ed and which ones belonged to me. Next I had to learn to disagree with and disobey Ed."[1]

Detect, Disagree, Disobey

Just as we have been instructed to liken the scriptures unto ourselves, we can all benefit from likening Jenni Schaefer's experience with our own. I know from personal experience the tremendous leverage we gain over Satan when we

1) learn to detect his voice and distinguish his voice from our own;
2) confront his lies and bullying and disagree with his lies; and

1 Jenni Schaefer with Thom Rutledge, *Life Without Ed,* (New York: McGraw-Hill, 2004), 1.

3) disobey him and refuse to submit our will to his.

Detecting

Once we recognize Lucifer's intent and tactics, we can better discern his voice. The Lord taught his disciples how to detect false prophets and recognize them as servants of Satan. At the same time, He taught us how to discern the devil when he's tampering with our thoughts. He said, "Ye shall know them by their fruits," (Matt 7:16). In other words, when a thought passes through our mind, we can ask ourselves, "If I retain this thought, where will it lead and what outcomes will it produce?" Elder David A. Bednar helps us recognize the marked contrast between the fruits of the devil and the fruits of the Spirit:

> *Lucifer labors to make the sons and daughters of God confused and unhappy and to hinder their eternal progression. The overarching intent of the father of lies is that all of us would become "miserable like unto himself." Lucifer wants us ultimately to be alone in the dark and without hope.*[2]

Lucifer wants us to be 1) alone; 2) in the dark; 3) without hope; 4) confused; 5) unhappy; 6) hindered in our progression; and 7) miserable. These are the fruits of the devil.

The fruits of the Savior are the categorical opposites: 1) sweet union and communion not only with Him and the Father but also with everyone we love; 2) light and celestial glory; 3) hope; 4) knowledgeable and confident about who we are; 5) happiness; 6) steady progress to full conversion; 7) an abundant fullness of joy! These are the fruits of the Lord.

This stark contrast begs the question, "Who in their right mind would choose the fruits of the devil over the fruits of Christ?" The obvious answer

---

2 David A. Bednar, "We Believe in Being Chaste," *Ensign,* May 2013, 43.

is "no one!" No one in his or her right mind would do that. So, how does Satan pull off such a massive deception? With sophistry and stealth, he suffuses his thoughts into ours—so carefully we hardly recognize the difference between his thoughts and our own. Ever so softly and gradually, Satan transitions us from our "right mind" into one so commingled with his thoughts it becomes difficult to distinguish the difference. Then, not discerning his distortions, we find ourselves suffering the fruits of the devil cited above and at a loss as to what lies at the root of our misery or what to do about it. If we don't get to the actual source of the problem, we cannot counter its effects.

Thanks be to God for the Book of Mormon and, on this specific topic, for the prophet Moroni (Moroni 7:12–17). He saw our day and witnessed our plight—the results of Satan's deceptive clouding and confusing of our thoughts and the consequent fruits we would suffer. Using the Lord's "by-their-fruits-ye-shall-know-them" principle, in six monumentally insightful verses, Moroni offers us the inspired counsel needed to take charge of our thoughts and be "in our right minds:"

First, reasoning in terms so simple a child can understand, Moroni clarifies which fruits come from which source, "all things which are good cometh of God; and that which is evil cometh of the devil." He then emphasizes Satan's persistent efforts: "the devil is an enemy unto God, and fighteth against him *continually*, and inviteth and enticeth to sin, and to do that which is evil *continually.*" After assuring us that God invites and entices us "to do good continually," Moroni warns us to pay attention in order to not be deceived. He counsels us to watch carefully how we judge—what we choose to approve and what we choose to condemn. "Take heed," he warns "that ye do not judge that which is evil to be of God, or that which is good and of God to be of the devil." Then, he gives us the key to the vault. "I show unto you the way to judge, for every thing [thought] which inviteth to do good and to persuade to believe in Christ, is sent forth by the power and gift of Christ; wherefore ye may know *with a perfect knowledge,* it is of God." And by contrast, the opposite proves equally accurate: "But whatsoever thing [thought] persuadeth men to do evil, and believe not in Christ, and deny him, and serve not God, then ye may know *with a perfect knowledge* it is of the devil" (Moroni 7:12–17, emphasis added).

Any thought that strengthens our confidence and our resolve to love the Lord our God with all our might, mind, and strength, and to serve Him and our neighbor in the name of Jesus Christ is of God. We should not discount or delay acting on such thoughts. Conversely, any thought that distances us from God; lessens our view of ourselves; or urges us to disregard or disrespect others; or impedes us from enjoying the gifts of the Spirit is to be cast out of our mind as promptly as possible.

"Easier said than done," you say. "It's not as simple and easy as you make it sound, Dennis." Granted. I agree, at least in part. I will hold with Moroni that it is plain. I also agree that just because a thing is plain and seemingly simple, doesn't make it easy. Detecting Satan is not easy. If it were, we wouldn't see all the pain, suffering, injustice and misery that abounds. Yet, I hasten to say, though it may not be easy (at first), neither is it arduous or impossible. So let's get practical and specific.

Personify the Opponent

As a first step, I recommend following the approach Thom Rutledge taught Jenni Schaefer—personify the opponent. Personifying gives us the distinct advantage of dealing with the adversary head on, directly and forcefully. Go ahead, chose your epithet—Satan, the Spook, the Devil. I have used all of those and still do. One of my mission presidents, Hartman Rector, Jr., a general authority, called him "Ol' Scratch." In my seminars, when people are not comfortable using scriptural or religious terminology, I have suggested another name. Rarely have I found a person who does not relate to some kind of internal negative voice. They relate to the idea of negative self-talk or the doubter in their head—the naysayer kindling doubts, stoking fears, and holding them back from doing their best, or throwing water on their dreams and goals.

Personally, I don't care much for the term "negative self-talk" because it completely misses the point. It is talk—and it's certainly negative—but it's *not you*, the self, that's doing the talking. It's another skeptical unfriendly entity. So I started labeling this negative voice the Skeptic Inside, which works fine until you convert it to an acronym SI, like Ed for Eating Disorder. So in my training courses, I call the doubter the SKeptic Against Me or SKAM. I'll pause while you roll your eyes. Actually, the double entendre has some value. What is a scam after all? It's a scheme or ploy to rob you of your wealth. That's what SKAM is doing. He's trying to rob you of your value and wealth, in every way possible. This acronym works for a lot of people, but if it doesn't feel right for you, make up your own.

What makes SKAM's ploys so insidious and hard to detect is now quite obvious. The voice we're talking about isn't actually an audible voice; it's more of an impression. As with promptings of the Holy Ghost or whisperings of the Spirit, we feel or sense them, rather than hear them. Over time, without realizing it, we get so accustomed to SKAM's whisperings we have a hard time recognizing them and realizing they're not our own thoughts or voice at all. It takes a bit of elevated awareness and concentration to pull back the curtain on the evil wizard behind the curtain. Yet, that's all it takes—just a little self-awareness and practice.

Four Characteristics for Detection

Here are four characteristics to help you detect a satanic thought or impression:

1) It tears down rather than builds. It belittles—you, others, correct principles and worthy causes. It judges harshly. It causes division and separation—pushing people away rather than attracting them. It promotes ill will and unkind feelings.

2) It is bossy, coercive and strict. It wants to be in control. Jenni Schaefer shares this example:

Ed: I can't believe that you are going to eat lunch today.
Jenni: My friends are taking me out. I have no choice.
Ed: When it comes to ordering from the menu, I'm in charge.
Jenni (nodding head): Of course.
Ed: We'll just play with the food and hide it under napkins.
Jenni: Okay.[3]

3) It feels dark. It may take a little longer to actually feel the voice. But just as the whisperings of the Spirit impart light and hope and a sense of peace, SKAM's voice imparts doubt, discomfort and depression. It feels dark because it is dark—coming from a dark being.

4) It uses *second person* grammar. You, instead of I. "You are worthless. You're never going to be able to do this. You are going to make a fool of yourself. They're just trying to use you." Without doubt, this is the most telling characteristic of the four. Start looking for "You phrases" in your head and you'll soon catch on to SKAM and his coercive efforts.

Knowing Satan's voice is disguised as our own thoughts, we are able to elevate our vigilance, determination and effectiveness in the battle of thoughts. Through experience we learn to recognize the difference between Satan's voice and our own. Once we get fairly good at detecting him, we can disagree with him and then disobey him.

An excellent example of learning to detect, disagree and disobey the adversary was given in a sacrament meeting I attended:

---

3 Schaefer and Rutledge, *Life Without Ed,* xxiii

Lana's Experience

I want to tell you how excited I was to be called to speak this morning. I love when you're given the blessing to speak. I remember a time when I felt a lot differently about speaking in public. I avoided even saying a prayer at church, to the point where I would arrive just a little late to my classes and leave a little early, just in case I was called on. This was because I had a learning disability when I was young and Satan used that to keep me down. For years I had a speech problem and my mom was the only one who could understand me. Kids at school would tease me relentlessly. Even at church, when I would be asked to pray in primary, they would laugh at my attempts. I often wondered why my parents had me if I was so stupid. I felt like such a mistake. Somehow Satan's voice became louder than my Savior's. I heard his words in my mind loudly, "You're so stupid; you can't even talk; you can't read; you are nothing."

Over the years, my speech became better through speech therapy, but my mind never heard anything different than self-doubt. You're stupid. You can't do anything right. My mind was like a tape recorder, repeating all of the negative words I had ever heard, and some Satan coined all on his own, knowing exactly what would cripple me the most.

When I was sixteen, we had new missionaries coming to our ward. My dad was bishop at the time, so we were always feeding them. I was hoping for some really cute ones. However, on Sunday an older couple entered our ward as our missionaries. The McBrides were all about teaching adults how to read better.

What a blessing it turned out to be. They taught me how to read and the world became so much brighter. I could understand the words that I read for the first time. My confidence grew. It took time for Satan's words to leave me, but I learned I could replace them with the Savior's words.

At times Satan's words creep back in, but I know his voice right away, because I know my Savior's voice better.[4]

Lana's experience shows how coercive and mean SKAM really is. Note the shaming and the name calling he employed. There was not one wisp of pity extended, just repeated bashing. Satan is relentless and preys upon even the young and defenseless. He goes for the jugular and rejoices in knocking us down, pummeling us and keeping us down. And he will keep us there until we realize we can stand up and refute him.

Never Suppress a Generous Thought

Another frequent ploy SKAM uses is to intercept or counter a good deed by getting us to second guess or doubt ourselves even when, or maybe *especially* when, we receive a righteous prompting and go to act upon it. Common to all of us is the experience of receiving an impulse or prompting to do something good or nice for someone, and then foregoing it. Why do we dismiss it or procrastinate it into oblivion? We fail to recognize SKAM's delicately instigated subversion. Rather than identifying it as SKAM appealing to our lazy mortal side, we go along with it, instead of just acting and following through on the original prompting.

Sister Bonnie D. Parkin, former general president of the Relief Society, shared a classic example. As you read, see if it seems familiar.

My daughter-in-law's mother, Susan, was a wonderful seamstress. President Kimball lived in their ward. One Sunday, Susan noticed that he had a new suit. Her father had recently returned from a trip

4 Used with permission, Lana Russell, excerpts from sacrament meeting talk, 2019.

to New York and had brought her some exquisite silk fabric. Susan thought that fabric would make a handsome tie to go with President Kimball's new suit. So on Monday she made the tie. She wrapped it in tissue paper and walked up the block to President Kimball's home.

On her way to the front door, she suddenly stopped and thought, "Who am I to make a tie for the prophet? He probably has plenty of them." Deciding she had made a mistake, she turned to leave.

Just then Sister Kimball opened the front door and said, "Oh, Susan!"

Stumbling all over herself, Susan said, "I saw President Kimball in his new suit on Sunday. Dad just brought me some silk from New York … and so I made him a tie."

Before Susan could continue, Sister Kimball stopped her, took hold of her shoulders, and said: *"Susan, never suppress a generous thought."*[5]

Whether Susan herself came up with the idea of making the tie, or it was a prompting of the Spirit, I can tell you one thing for sure: The thought that came into her mind as she walked up to the door was so typical of SKAM and his tone, there can be little doubt where it came from. Notice that the thought came suddenly to her mind out of the blue. "On her way to the front door, she suddenly stopped and thought …. " I suggest Susan didn't stop and think. The "thought" was actually imposed on her—something she felt or "heard" rather than thought. Then notice how SKAM gets Susan to question herself and think she was somehow unworthy to deliver the gift. "Who am I to make a tie for the prophet? He probably has plenty of them." Had Susan been more aware of SKAM's tone and tactics, my guess is that the actual thought was "Who are *you* to make a tie for the prophet?" The end result—again, a

5 Bonnie D. Parkin, "Personal Ministry: Sacred and Precious", *BYU Devotional,* February 13, 2007.

classic sign the thought came from the adversary—was that Susan started feeling embarrassed, possibly even ashamed, for "being so presumptuous as to think that she was worthy enough to give a gift to the prophet." I further suggest you have also felt prompted to do something—go to the temple, call or text your ministering sister or family, visit a shut-in—and then allowed some sort of rationalization to stop you. I can recall many of my own such experiences.

The Parable of the Stranded Goat

I have a favorite running trail. Not long ago, as I was running along this path, I saw some baby goats in a fenced yard. One of the little goats was up on top of an eight-foot block wall; a few of his little friends gathered below him on my side of the wall. As I approached, the little goats started bleating at me. You might not know this about me, but it happens that I speak goat. (To be honest, I didn't know it myself until this moment.) As I kept my running pace, the kids turned and looked right at me and started pleading with their eyes and frantic little bleats. "Help our little friend! He's stuck on the wall. He can't get down. Please help our little friend!"

I knew exactly what they wanted, but rather than setting aside something I thought was highly important (which it wasn't) and act on it, I went for the junk SKAM threw at me. *"This is crazy. Get a grip on yourself, Dennis. That's a goat. It has hooves and teeth, and it might bite. Who knows what could happen? That wall is high, you're not even sure you could reach the goat if you tried. What if the owners see you and think you're a baby kid-napper? Someone else will get him down. Someone who likes goats, or knows about goats, or isn't afraid of goats, or isn't possibly allergic to goats, or who has a degree in animal husbandry with an emphasis on goat rescue."*

One of the little goats started running back and forth, desperately expressing his anxiety. He looked at me, then looked up at his friend, looked back at me, and then bleated his cry for help. "Help our little friend!" It was so clear what he wanted and what he was expressing, I didn't even have to speak fluent goat to get it. I *almost* started toward him.

But then SKAM jumped in again: *"That's not even your goat. This is not your problem or area of expertise. Those sharp hooves and teeth can do damage. When exactly did you have your last tetanus shot? You're just out for a nice peaceful run, minding your own business. Surely someone else will help. Plus, you're on pace to run a sub-ten-minute-mile here."* And so I kept going. I finished my run, got my heartrate up, did my daily cardio, got my endorphins pumping, and crossed "exercise" off my list. But I couldn't shake the image of that little baby goat in trouble. In fact, every time I run past that spot, I wonder how he got down, how long he was up there, and who finally came to his rescue. Or did he leap off the wall and injure himself? I'm still haunted by the memory even though I have found a new running path. It was a missed opportunity. I was too busy entertaining selfish thoughts, too busy with my own agenda. (A ten-minute mile, people!) How many other opportunities have I side-stepped or shirked because I allowed SKAM's petty points to play long enough in my head to convince me that somebody else would take care of the problem.

Victim Mode

A subtle and important distinction has become apparent to me. SKAM is most effective when I am in victim mode, framing a situation as being only about my needs. Instead, when I am thinking outside myself, praying in the morning to be able recognize an opportunity to get past myself and to act immediately on something—anything—that would help someone else, everything else in my day goes better. And, even if it doesn't make the six o'clock news, each time I detect, disagree and disobey a selfish thought, I take a step away from SKAM and a step closer to Christ and that is more than enough.

CHAPTER 12

A Diagram of Human Behavior

While studying the medical sciences, I learned the importance of the law of cause and effect. You can't successfully treat an effect if you don't know the cause. I dove into my studies with excitement, eager to learn everything I could about the human body and what makes it tick (and sometimes tic). Text books were helpful but I found the real learning took place when I visualized or experienced what the words were describing. The way to learn the anatomy of the body was to dissect a cadaver or two. The way to defeat a bacterium is to learn its characteristics through performing experiments in the microbiology lab. I also learned if I couldn't have a physical example or experience, the next best thing was a diagram. When it comes to human behavior, since we can't physically see what's going on inside the mind, a diagram will have to do.

The power of the diagram I am about to share may not knock you off your chair at first; nevertheless, I believe as you use it, the day will come when you will wonder how you ever got along without it. As we've already established, all human behavior begins in the mind—everything from the tones of our voices and our body language to our feelings, actions, and reactions come from our thoughts. Although this idea sounds reassuringly simple and correct, putting it into practice is more difficult. Why? Because we're living life amid a hailstorm of circumstances and events. Stuff flies at us incessantly and at warp speed. We hardly have time to process one event, when another one hits. The onslaught of happenings is relentless and at times bewildering. Every waking minute we are either coming from, in the middle of, or on our way to the next event. So, for a moment, let's slow down and diagram what's going on.

Stages in a Diagram of Human Behavior

Stage 1: Events

Life is happening—events and situations occur. It is critical to understand that all events and situations are absolutely neutral until they are interpreted. Each event is neither good nor bad—it just is. Data gathered by the senses—hearing, touch, taste, smell and sight—are sent to the brain for the mind to interpret. And that is Stage 2.

Stage 2: Thoughts/Interpretations

At amazing speed, the mind sorts through all kinds of thought options and makes sense of the data, interpreting the event and what it means.

Stage 3: Feelings/Emotions

The interpretation generates a feeling or an emotion corresponding to the thought.

Stage 4: Behavior—Actions, Reactions, Inaction

Feelings and emotions drive behavior—actions, reactions or inaction *corresponding to the feeling.*

Stage 5: Results/Outcomes

Then, consistent with the Law of the Harvest, our actions and reactions act upon the event or circumstance and determine our outcomes. It is not just important; *it is imperative* to note that you are in control of the results and outcomes—from start to finish. Not only do you make the choice at Stage 2—the interpretation—you retain the ability to evaluate the process that follows. You can revise or modify the flow anywhere along the way—at either Stage 3 or 4, or both.

A Diagram of Human Behavior

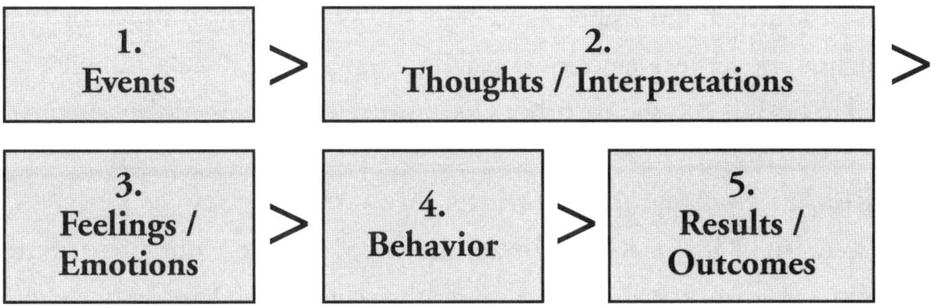

Now, let's look at a simple example. A father came home after a hard day at work and found that his five-year old had emptied the entire toys-and-games closet, strewing parts and pieces of Lego sets and jigsaw puzzles wall-to-wall in the family room, contrary to the family rule of "only one toy at a time." The father immediately reacted, emoting frustration and saying things like, "You make me so mad"—sentiments that were not really meant and which were immediately regretted. The reaction occurred almost automatically as though it were a hard-wired circuit. But it wasn't. Between the event and the emotion there was a choice. An interpretation was made. At first, the statement, "you make me mad" placed blame on the child. But the child could not *make* the father mad—it was the father's own interpretation of the situation that produced the emotion and the corresponding behavior that followed.

The diagram helps us gain clarity about this and many other everyday scenarios. To better understand the key points, we will start with the result stage and work backwards. The result (Stage 5) was an injured relationship.

The behavior or action (4) that produced the result was the parent's reaction, which was driven by (3) an emotion—some combination of anger, frustration, and exasperation. What were these emotions based on? The *event*? Nope. As the diagram shows, there is *no direct connection between events and emotions.* The event did not determine the emotion. Did the emotion arise on its own through some mystical form of spontaneous combustion? Was it imposed by atmospheric or even cosmic conditions? It is vital we all acknowledge the actual source of our feelings and emotions. Every feeling is preceded by a thought. The father's emotional reaction was triggered by a thought he selected in his mind—and that thought ultimately determined the outcome.

The Role of Events and Situations

It's common for us to add in another step. We are wont to attribute everything from our feelings to our results to outside elements—events, situations and other people. This idea comes from the adversary. In fact, if it's not his favorite ploy, it's certainly one of his most effective, and the diagram helps us see why. This ploy seduces us into shifting responsibility from our self, the thinker of thoughts, to something outside ourself. Once SKAM gets us to shift responsibility from the thoughts in our mind, and attribute the cause to outside events, he has set us to work on the wrong battle. Rather than the issue being about him and us, he's made it be about an infinite number of outside factors, over which we have little or no control—creating confusion and misdirection of our efforts. It's a brilliant ploy he uses incessantly.

When an email you're expecting doesn't show up in your inbox as soon as you want it, SKAM immediately jumps into the interpretation business and injects a value judgment and forecasts an outcome. Something like, *"Drat! This is a catastrophe. Now you won't be able to get your report finished by noon. It's going to throw your whole schedule into chaos. You may even have to work late and miss Amy's birthday party. She's only going to turn eleven once, you know. She'll resent it for the rest of her life. Even years of therapy will not repair the damage. You and your daughter will never be close. All because the jerks over in finance can't send a simple email response to your request."* An interpretation along such lines is sure to evoke frustration, which will quickly kindle anger and generate an action. In this case, it could be an irate phone call to a co-worker or an email reminder typed in ALL CAPS! You can compose your own prediction of the results.

SKAM is ever eager to insert interpretations that someone or something else is at fault. Why? Because it opens the door to victim thinking with all its telltale side effects—finger-pointing, blaming, resenting and accusing others—or even God, all of which creates division. Convincing us we have been unfairly acted upon by events and other people, SKAM tells us we are powerless to do anything about it. In addition to generating antipathy towards others, he swindles us into a major case of inaction as we marinate in the misery of blame and self-pity. The perfect result for SKAM is the worst for us. Unless we stop moping and take action, we get zero improvement of the results and everything remains as it is.

An Incorrect Model

The adversary has succeeded in convincing many of us that circumstances, events and other people are the source of our woes. It's all about "what happened to you," rather than "what were you thinking" or "what meaning have you given to what happened?" To make real and steady progress, spiritually or temporally, we must solidify this very important point about events in our thinking. It's not just important, it's crucial. Events never *cause* thoughts. Events never *cause* feelings. Events are neutral and mean nothing until they are *interpreted* and *assigned* a meaning.

Let's go back to our example. Just before the parent's interpretation there *was* a situation—a certain set of circumstances—a hard day for the parent, some household rules, a five-year-old playing in a room, and an array of scattered toys. Put all of them together, and what does all that mean? Nothing—absolutely nothing. It's just an event—a batch of data. *Neutral* data. As an event unfolds, in our minds we are habit-prone to quickly assign a meaning to it. We seldom just observe it. We do this with or without SKAM's help. Almost instantaneously a judgment forms in our heads, giving the data some kind of moral value—good or bad, right or wrong, pleasing or displeasing. But it is crucial we are clear on this point: The meaning and value judgments are all interpretations—mental creations—a set of *chosen* thoughts or line of thinking.

Meaning is *always* in "the eye (mind) of the beholder." Situations and events have no inherent value until we assign one. Events are neutral. They are not good or bad. They are just props on the stage with no pre-determined plot. Hence, 1) We are never justified in placing blame for our feelings on events or other people. 2) We are responsible for our responses—our moods and emotions. 3) We are responsible for our behavior—actions, reactions and inaction. Thus, 4) We are ultimately responsible for the end results.

Whether or not we learn the spiritual lessons from our earthly experiences to hone and acquire the attributes of Christ is up to us. Even in small moments, like being stuck in traffic, we have the opportunity to show Him how much we love Him and want to be like Him by responding the way He would. So, yes, in seemingly inconsequential, even trivial events or moments in life, and especially in major trials where certain realities will not be changed or taken out of our way, we are reaping exactly what we sow. So in that sense, *we are responsible for every result in our life.* Yep, all of them.

To deceive us, SKAM does his utmost to obscure the reality of our full responsibility. He stirs up a smoke screen—a mist of darkness—to induce us to see ourselves as innocent victims, perpetually acted upon by outside forces beyond our control, with absolutely no ability to do anything about them. When we really understand how deftly SKAM is misdirecting our attention to something we can do nothing about, we have to step back and admit the ploy is downright … well, satanic.

A Second Look at the Diagram

In mortal probation, at Stage 1, a steady stream of *neutral* events and situations is ongoing. At Stage 2, the mind is poised and ready to render interpretations. Now comes the crunch. Almost always, before we've fully had a chance to process the incoming data independently, we receive help.

Expanded Diagram

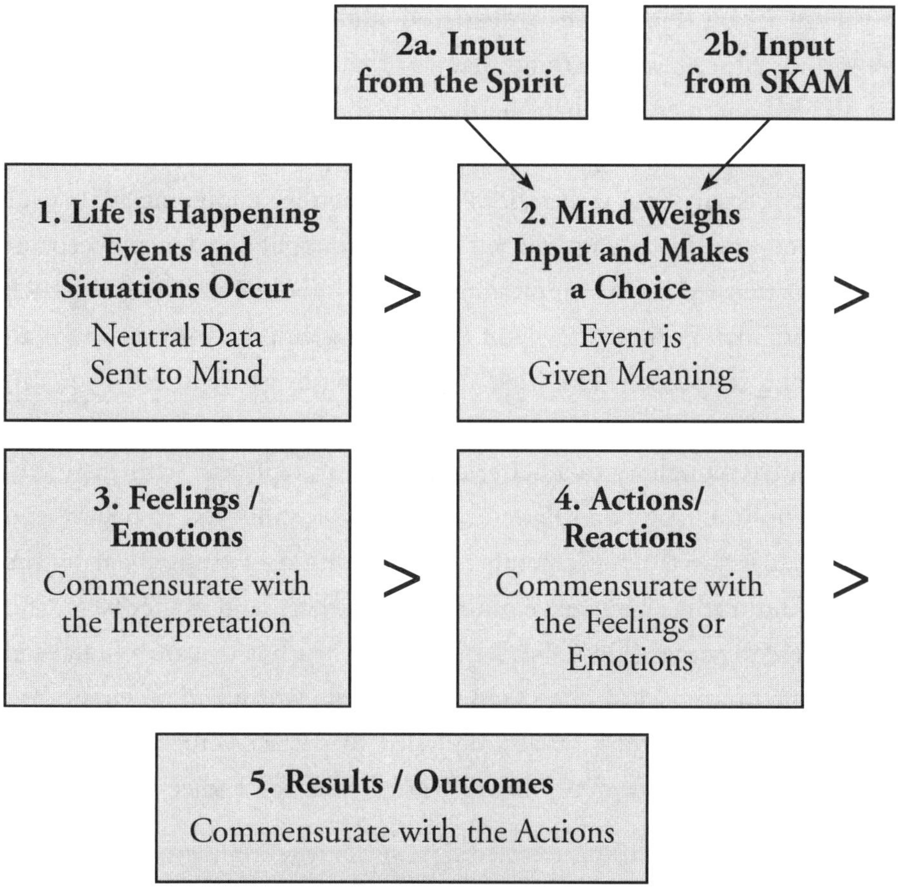

Born with the Light of Christ (conscience) and the additional influence of the Holy Ghost, we feel, more than hear, a still small voice giving us input, as shown on an expanded version of the diagram (Stage 2a).

This kindly light invites us to be generous, good, kind and to make a righteous choice. Simultaneously, there being a need for opposition in all things, we get "help" from SKAM and his spirit minions (Stage 2b). Ever ready to smother or supplant a good deed, SKAM immediately injects a contrary alternative. With the increased awareness you are gaining, you are better able to detect and counter SKAM's intervention at Stage 2 and go with the prompting of the Spirit.

Even if you don't catch it then, you still have ample opportunity to thwart his efforts. Keep in mind that it's often easier to recognize the *effect* of SKAM's intervention than the thought that precipitates it. When you recognize feelings of anger, resentment, sadness or anxiousness, you can be pretty certain SKAM has been playing a role, tampering with your interpretations. By asking yourself, "What thought did I just accept or dwell on that led to this unpleasant feeling?" you are able to trace back to the originating thought. Upon finding that culprit, you can make an assessment. If you don't like what you're feeling or where it leads, you can refuse to hang on to it. You can rid yourself of it by choosing to replace the negative thought with a better one. You can replace it with the truth. You are not the faulty and flawed being SKAM wants you to believe you are. What is the truth? Remember, the definition of truth given by the Lord: "And truth is knowledge of things as they are, and as they were, and as they are to come" (D&C 93: 24). And, the truth is you are a literal son or daughter of the Most High God with infinite worth and potential. You are simply in a learning process designed to perfect your character and attributes to such a degree you will be one with the Father and the Son. That's who you really are, and that's the truth!

Places to Intercept SKAM

If, at first, you are not able to intercept SKAM's lies at Stage 2, you've just passed the normal test. The truth is most of us learn to detect SKAM's ploys more readily at Stage 3—the Feelings and Emotions Stage. As you become ever more aware that your feelings are triggered by your thoughts, you will get better at interrupting SKAM's ploys at Stage 2. Making the choice to replace rather than suppress a negative characterization of yourself will allow your true self to emerge and grow stronger. More importantly you will discover how much control you actually have over how you feel at any given time, about anything or anyone. And the good news just keeps coming. As you take charge of how you feel and gain more control over your emotions, your behavior improves, just as suggested in the diagram. Since your actions are consistent with your feelings and emotions, better emotional control generates a corresponding improvement in how you relate to your current situations and challenges.

Maintaining Perspective

Lest we get too smug with the idea that we're only a week or so away from total emotional perfection, let's make sure we stay tethered to reality. Despite what skills we possess and how much we practice them, there are going to be times when SKAM's ploys work. He hits the right note, we buy into his tune and we get ornery, upset and hard to live with. As we've established before, we always retain the ability to choose how we will act. All is not lost if we get to Stage 4 riding the tidal wave of frustration. We're still responsible and still the chooser. Sometimes it's all we can do to stifle our anger and keep from blowing our stack. Even at that point, we have the power to resist the urge to kick a hole in the wall. And, when we slam on the brakes just before we go careening off the emotional cliff, we have still scored a victory and thwarted the enemy of our soul. Always keep in mind that however wobbly and imperfect your path to the Action Stage may be, if you end up doing what's right, your results will still match your actions and be counted for righteousness. Then, just as surely as day follows night, your results and outcomes, Stage 5, will follow and correspond to your actions in Stage 4, and you will find you have a lot more say about how things turn out in your life. You will still have tests. You will still experience sorrow and pain. Life will not suddenly turn into the best version of Disneyland imaginable. However, you will be a better, stronger, more loving disciple of Jesus Christ, making the many small choices that contribute to a healthier, happier life—and you will grow steadily closer to Christ as you grow steadily to be like Christ.

CHAPTER 13

Making It Real

We may not be able to recognize an audible voice, but we can certainly increase our ability to recognize the *effects* of Satan's influence upon us. If we get better at noticing and acknowledging a negative feeling when it hits, it may not be all we can do with it, but it's a great start. Often, we just go with whatever mood we happen to be feeling at the moment—enjoying or suffering its effects without recognizing we have choice in the matter. When we become aware of a negative mood or feeling, we can evaluate it; and, if we don't want to feel that way, we can choose something else. A new feeling, mood, or mindset is only one thought away. This is especially valuable when we're suddenly hit out of nowhere with a thought to judge, find fault, or dislike someone or something. We can be pretty sure such harsh, critical thoughts are coming from the adversary.

As a child of a loving Heavenly Father, it's not in your spiritual nature to be judgmental and hypercritical. You came into this world as a loving, innocent being with a clean slate. "Every spirit of man was innocent in the beginning; and God having redeemed man from the fall, men became again, in their infant state, innocent before God" (D&C 93:38). It's in mortality that we become subject to the forces of evil and take on judgmental tendencies and antisocial character traits. Nelson Mandela pointed this out; "No one is born hating another person because of the color of his skin, or his background or his religion. People learn to hate, and if they can learn to hate, they can be taught to love, for love comes more naturally to the human heart than its opposite."[1]

I suspect you might have had experiences where a sudden, inexplicable dislike for something or someone comes over you for no reason. For example, you may be sitting in your usual pew in the chapel, feeling at peace, reverently preparing to partake of the sacrament. You notice a person you've never met before who takes a seat not far from you. Almost instantly conflicting thoughts occur. Your first thought may be, *"Oh, a new person. After the meeting, I'll introduce myself and welcome him."* If it's not your first thought, it may have already been diverted by another thought—a judgmental one. *"I wonder where he came from. Reminds me of a guy I hated in high school. Kind of a weird tie, too. I wouldn't be caught dead wearing a tie like that to church."* At that point you're well on your way to withholding your greeting by telling yourself somebody else will probably welcome him.

Picture the diagram with the two additional input sources that represent SKAM and the Spirit. You don't have to be Sherlock Holmes to know which one spawned which thought. It's obvious what's going on and how we should act and what we should do. In real life, however, it's not so obvious—and, unless you're the ward mission leader, you may have a fairly low batting average in stifling SKAM and making a friendly introduction to visitors and new members. Any resistance to welcoming a new person is likely coming from the opposition. Remember, Lucifer is all about separating, dividing, and withholding love, wanting us to end up being alone and friendless. Otherwise, why in the world would we ever put off the Spirit or our own inclination to be friendly and not go up to

1 Nelson Mandela, *Long Walk to Freedom,* (Boston, New York, London: Little, Brown and Company, 1994), 622.

someone and extend a warm welcome? And why do we instantaneously make snap judgments to dislike someone based on nothing more than an initial impression? You've likely also had the opposite experience. Initially being averse to greeting someone for no real reason, eventually getting to know that person, becoming good friends, and saturating a box of Kleenex when they move out of the ward. So, theory aside, what's a disciple of Christ to do? My experience tells me the best thing is to shut down the debate in your head right from the start. Call SKAM out, let him know you're not buying in, strike up a conversation with the person, and see what comes of it.

Before we consider another example, let's be clear about one thing. In no way are we justified in blaming SKAM for our shallow behavior. He's not *making us* do or be anything. He's only *tempting us* to be indifferent and self-centered. It's always up to us whether we yield to the enticings of the Holy Spirit or to the enticing from the dark side. SKAM can sure make victim thinking seem justified, but he cannot force our responses against our will. We have to accept his urgings and choose to play along. Ever and always, we are the chooser—the responsible party.

More Real Stuff

Staying with the work of making the learning real, let's explore another example. While you are talking with a good friend, she shares some positive news about a mutual acquaintance. Someone else's success should be good news, right? How often do you take it that way? How often, within the blink of an eye do you feel a little miffed about what you just heard? Do you suddenly get the urge to make a sarcastic remark or brood over the news for rest of the day? If you can relate to these symptoms, what do you do? First, acknowledge what you're actually feeling. Instead of marinating in it, identify it. Admit, "I'm *feeling* jealous." That's a key step; don't dismiss it. If you can name it, you can tame it. And if I were your mental edge coach, I'd then say,

Dennis: "Good. I'm glad you're owning that feeling. What else are you feeling?"

You: "Well, I'm feeling kind of miserable too."

D: "Good. I like how you're phrasing that. You're not personifying the feeling. You're not turning it into an identity by saying, 'I am jealous,' or 'I am miserable.' Feelings are just feelings. They're not traits or facets of your personality that are permanently encoded. They're quite transient actually; they can come and go in an instant. So, what do you know about feelings?"

Y: "Well, I'm beginning to understand that it's pretty normal to have all kinds of feelings. I can feel happy one minute and miserable the next."

D: "Right—and I like how you're saying that also. It's okay to say you can be happy or sad; but it's actually more accurate to say you're feeling happy or sad. What else?"

Y: "It's okay to have feelings. There's nothing wrong or bad about feeling bad. There's nothing sinful about feeling disappointed or lonely or even angry, for that matter. It's all a part of normal life."

D: "So where do you want to go from here? Do we need to talk about the situation that ticked you off?"

Y: "Nice try, Dennis, you almost got me with that one. I would have fallen for your trick question a few weeks ago, but I like what I've learned. Working with the diagram, I've learned that events and situations can't make me be anything or feel anything. They're just neutral."

D: "Awesome. So, given that you have a huge spectrum of feelings to choose from, do we need to talk about why you chose to feel jealous?"

Y: "Well, again the diagram helps. I didn't exactly choose to feel jealous, per se. I must have chosen a thought, or bought into a thought, that triggered the feeling of jealousy."

D: "Outstanding. So can you trace back to uncover which thought in your mind triggered the jealousy?

Y: "Well, maybe. You might have to give me a minute but, if I understand the diagram correctly, it may not matter. Because, if I ever want to feel something different than I'm feeling, all I have to do is select a new thought. So, it's not actually necessary I figure out exactly which thought I had so I can replace it specifically. I can just start where I am and ask myself, 'how do I want to feel right now?' Right?"

D: "Exactly."

The Gap

Mortality is the classroom where we get to learn and practice the skills we will carry forward with us. "Whatever principle of intelligence we attain unto in this life, it will rise with us in the resurrection. And if a person gains more knowledge and intelligence in this life through his diligence and obedience than another, he will have so much the advantage in the world to come" (D&C 130:18–19). To consistently respond rather than reflexively react to events and situations is a skill of infinite value. To develop this skill, we must learn to pay attention to our decision points at Stage 2, the Interpretation Stage in the diagram where we make the choices. Between stimulus and response there is a split-second pause or gap between the time an event occurs and our *almost* instantaneous reaction to it. That small gap is a big deal.

Suppose you receive an e-mail from your boss informing you of an abrupt change in your schedule. If the e-mail isn't worded to your liking, your first thought might be you're being treated unfairly which then produces a sudden surge of resentment. Decision point: If you choose to go with your first reaction and go with the resentment, then the veins in your neck start bulging, the arteries constrict, your heartrate speeds up, and your blood pressure goes sky high. You excuse yourself from responsibility, telling yourself that your boss is at fault. However, the truth remains that at the decision point you could have taken ownership and opted for a different interpretation of the email which would have altered the stream of ensuing physical effects within your body. Between the stimulus (e-mail) and the response (what happens in your body) you have a decision point—a moment of choice. It's there, in that gap where the juice in life, sweet or sour, is squeezed.

To Panic or Not to Panic

I have a friend who owns a Harley-Davidson motorcycle. He loves to ride it at high speed on Arizona's Superstition Freeway, without a helmet. (Aside from that, he's a very intelligent human being.) Frequently, he carves time out of his busy schedule to climb on his Harley and race over black asphalt at shocking rates of speed. Saguaro cacti and Palo Verde trees seem to whiz by on the periphery, and molecules of nitrogen and oxygen whip through his hair. In his mind all of that sensory data is configured as a joyride. He's having a ball. He throws his head back, laughing and cackling. If he has any pent-up frustrations, he blasts those out into the stratosphere. During his thirty-minute joyride, the pharmacy inside his body releases a variety of very beneficial substances, including Interleuken-2 an immuno-accelerant that enables the body to guard itself from all sorts of threats. With its help, my friend's body is better prepared to defeat cancer, fight infections and deflect recurrences of things it's been exposed to in the past. In effect, he has inoculated himself with greater health and vitality.

In contrast, sometimes he invites me to join him on one of these *joyrides.* I do so with a fair amount of apprehension. At the time, it doesn't seem like my trepidation is a choice on my part, but it is. I picture myself speeding over the same asphalt, having about the same molecules of nitrogen and oxygen whipping through my *helmet*. While my friend is shouting and laughing all I am able to think about are all the catastrophes I am narrowly escaping. I'm picturing what a pair of Levis, along with the skin and muscles within them, will look like after they've scraped across a hundred yards of asphalt or what my face and helmet might look like as a grill ornament on an eighteen-wheeler. Concerned for my physical well-being I have flashes of panic, even moments when I wish I had invested in a box of Depends (if you get my drift). The pharmacy inside my body reflects my fear and panic. Instead of producing Interleukin-2, my body has been pumping out copious amounts of stress hormones, including cortisol, a potent immuno-suppressant.

You can see where I'm leading you. It's not the motorcycle, asphalt, or molecules of nitrogen in the atmosphere that makes the telling difference. It's the mental creation, the configuration of thoughts. One person's joy is another person's panic. Both are mental constructs formed in the interpretative gap.

Minding the Gap

Without awareness, the gap between stimulus and response seems to vanish altogether. When that happens, our responses become fairly automatic—just a series of conditioned responses to the routine flow of repeated stimuli, and we unwittingly become victims of our habits. However, when we are mindful of the gap and pause, we widen the gap and make room for choices. We then see a spectrum of options—and usually make a better choice. Being aware of our ability to choose, and making thoughtful choices, constitutes the essence of mental discipline. Enhancing our mental discipline is not as difficult as we may think. We can view discipline as "too hard" and "not worth the pain," or we can look at it as a soul-stretching invitation to pay the price for something that is ultimately priceless—the realization of our true eternal potential.

Retraining ourselves to see the value and the possibilities that arise out of adverse circumstances is another reward that comes from looking at discipline as a way to grow. Doing so might not be our natural tendency, for the "natural man is an enemy to God," but minding the gap is the best way to put off our natural tendencies and become saints through the Atonement of Christ (Mosiah 3:19).

Opening Up Options

When we encounter a setback or loss, we can learn to recognize and resist the immediate victim thoughts SKAM flashes into our gap such as, "*Oh, no. Here we go again. Why does stuff like this always happen to me?*" We can learn to widen the mental interpretative gap and find better options. It can be as simple as saying, "Whoa, slow down for a second. Here's a decision point. Breathe through your nose and make a choice."

To illustrate: One of my clients, I'll call him Charlie, was in turmoil about being passed over for a job promotion. He liked his work and the people he worked with; even so, upon learning the news, he became irate. In the coaching session, he was still steaming and on the verge of quitting his job. Our dialogue went something like this:

Charlie: The main reason I want to quit is I want to tell Phil (the boss) exactly where he can stuff his car keys. Even though I'd be out of a job, it'd be worth it. I've been so loyal to this guy, and this is the thanks I get.

Dennis: Keep in mind, SKAM wants to separate us from other people to promote misery. He constantly sows seeds of misunderstanding to create distance and bad feelings, especially in relationships with high potential for doing good. So look carefully at whether you're buying into one of his traps. He loves to sell you on how terribly you've been mistreated and disrespected because it lights the fuse to self-serving overreactions that may feel good in the moment, but later we regret. So let's slow down and use the diagram. What is Stage 1?

C: Phil chose somebody less qualified than me for team leader in my section.

D: That sounds more like an interpretation or negative judgment than an event. Remember the key point of the diagram: Events are neutral. Try again.

C: Ok. Phil chose Biff Wonnacott to be the new team leader in my section.

D: If that fact were announced on CNN tonight, how many people in America would be incited to riot or hire a hit man to do bodily harm to Phil?

C: (Chuckles).

D: So, let's go back to the diagram, and walk through the key points. What is the source of any feeling—whether it be revenge or elation?

C: A thought. Every feeling is preceded and precipitated by a thought.

D: Right. Whose thought?

C: Well, ultimately, it's my choice, but in the gap, I get input from other sources—the Spirit and the Spook. And, by the feelings and emotions they evoke, I can distinguish pretty fast which is which.

D: Yes, and here's another tool to add to that. When you recognize SKAM is coming at you, especially when he's urging you to do something driven by strong emotions, ask yourself, "What is SKAM trying to accomplish? What's his motive for trying to get me to feel this feeling and act on this emotion?"

C: I used something like that the other day. I was getting upset with my wife and I could kind of sense SKAM was trying to escalate things. So, I said to myself, "No way. I'm not going to fall for that, and I didn't."

D: Excellent. And what did you do after that?

C: I put my arms around her, kissed her, and told her I loved her and how grateful I am she's my eternal companion.

D: Now, apply this approach to the situation with your boss. What's SKAM's motive for stoking your resentment?

C: He wants to divide me and the boss and break up the team.

D: When you look at it through that lens, wouldn't you say that SKAM must have a sense that you and the team you're with have a high potential for success?

C: Well, I never thought of it that way, but, yes, I can kind of see that now.

D: So where does that lead you?

A discussion ensued about how to show more appreciation for *everybody* on the team and things went forward from there.

In a later conversation when I asked my client about his perspectives now, he said, "One of the best parts of becoming more aware of SKAM's tricks and traps is the satisfaction that comes from side-stepping them. It's been so helpful to keep in mind that events are neutral. They're not positive or negative until I make a choice about how to look at them. Rather than go with my knee-jerk reaction like I used to do, I now see that so-called impulse was spurred by the devil—and recognizing that helps me pay attention to what the Spirit is inviting me to do."

Showing Forth More Love

It may not hold true in all instances but, more often than not, when we sense tension between ourselves and another person, the Spirit is inviting us to show more kindness and patience. Rather than assuming the worst, the Spirit is inviting us to give others the benefit of the doubt and assume good intentions. In gospel terms it's called "love unfeigned." In the workplace it can be called "respect and appreciation." Even at times when "moved upon by the Holy Ghost," and words of admonition or correction are needed, the words must be couched in genuine love, showing forth an increase of love toward the person we have reproved, lest he perceives us to be his enemy (D&C 121:43). In the Broadway musical, Camelot, King Arthur goes to Merlin for marital advice, and the answer he receives is wise, and beautifully encapsulated in three words, "Just love her."

My wife and I have a good friend who was called to be the matron in a temple. When she received this calling, she was humbled and very concerned about the responsibilities of that role. She fretted about her inability to recall the names of hundreds of temple workers with whom she wanted to have a genuine rapport. As her doubt and worry increased, she made her concerns a matter of prayer and was comforted to hear this calming reassurance: "I know their names. You just need to love them."

One could argue that Satan's most ardent motive is to get us to withhold love. SKAM makes up all sorts of fallacies—most of them malicious fiction—about the motives and character of other people. It's never complimentary. It's always critical. Why? Because judging repels and love attracts. Love, the greatest unifying force in the universe, has a marvelous transforming power in both time and eternity. So, if all else fails, remember this: When you're not sure how to respond, love is always the best option. "Charity never faileth."

Sudden Attacks

I had a conversation with another client, whom I will call Jane, that further illustrates the power of love.

Jane: Sometimes I will be doing fine and all of a sudden, I will get a feeling of dread or uneasiness—something kind of out of the blue. Sometimes I have a thought and then I feel the emotion that immediately follows it. But sometimes it seems like the emotion just shows up on its own. If I have a feeling and I don't even know why I'm having that, what's going on there?

Dennis: You're not alone. I suspect it happens to all of us—quite often, in fact. I bet your sudden feeling wasn't even associated with what you were doing at that moment or anything at all. It just showed up out of nowhere.

J: Yes, the feeling was totally unrelated to what was happening.

D: Sometimes there's no logic to it all and that's a telltale sign where it's coming from. For instance, you're driving down the street minding your own business, thinking what a beautiful day it is and how great it is to be alive. You're light-hearted and happy. Those blissful moments really irk SKAM. He just hates to see you basking in positive feelings. He's jealous of your joy, so he'll pull something out of the blue, whether it pertains to the moment or not, and he'll throw it into your mind just to spoil the moment.

To do that, he'll often dig up an old memory. There's no reason that memory should flash into your mind at that moment, so you might attribute it to a random pulse of your memory. But is that really logical? Why would your memory do that? Furthermore, have you also noticed it's never something pleasant? If it were just random activity in your memory, why wouldn't you have about an equal number of positive memories? It's almost never a memory of when you did someone a favor or lifted someone's burden or when you did something really well. It's almost always an embarrassing moment, a hurtful misunderstanding, a bad financial decision, an argument you had with someone years ago, or a time when you failed. It's always something to which SKAM can attach a little venom so it stings a bit and stirs up regret or anguish. Am I right?

J: Come to think about it, yes. It's always something negative and upsetting.

D: I've always been intrigued by the Apostle Paul's term "fiery dart" (Eph 6:16). It's an apt description of this ploy we're talking about. The word "dart" in modern English evokes a mental picture of a small, pointed projectile people in English pubs throw at a target. In the original biblical Greek, the word translates better as javelin, spear, or arrow. Up until the 20th century, fiery darts—flaming arrows—were fearsome weapons. With little risk to the archer, the fiery darts could be launched from a distance to set roofs, buildings, and even gun powder stockades ablaze. Paul's vivid metaphor captures the terror that comes from a fear-producing weapon that strikes with peace-destroying effects.

So SKAM notices you're feeling cheerful and calm—and he can't stand it. Out of utter maliciousness, he'll jab you in the heart with a thought and attach a jolt of pain to go along with it.

J: What do I do about them when these darts hit?

D: Based on what you've learned, what do you think you could do?

J: Well, first, it kind of irritates me that SKAM goes around ruining my happy moments and even spoiling simple joys. Right now, I might be feeling just a tiny bit like Jesus felt when he cleansed the temple. I feel like putting my foot down. Instead of allowing these sudden attacks to linger and put up with them, I want to reject SKAM directly and firmly.

Quenching the Darts

In the chapters ahead we will discuss in detail a variety of ways to battle Satan's schemes and defeat him. In this chapter we have described two types of satanic ploys: SKAM jumping into the Interpretation Stage, and injecting a negative thought into an event, disrupting your happiness. Consider Dina Rossell's experience.

I was backpacking in the Eastern High Sierras with my husband Todd. The hike was hard, but it was also fun and the surroundings were beautiful. Usually when we backpack, we have a huge group, but with Covid-19 restrictions, this time it was just me and Todd. I loved it, and I loved our time together, laughing, talking reminiscing. We finally got to where we were going to camp for the next three nights. We found a beautiful spot next to a lovely alpine lake at about 11,000 feet elevation. It's quiet up there. You don't see very many people. It was amazing. It's very rare my husband and I have time alone, and I was looking forward not only to the time together but the majestic scenery of the Sierras.

That night, I suddenly became overwhelmed with worry about our twenty-three-year-old son. As a mom, I know Satan likes to work on me and give me anxiety about my family. Why do I always listen to him? You can't call and check on anyone when you are at 11,000 feet. There is no cell reception at that altitude. So I said a prayer to my Heavenly Father and I asked Him to watch over my son. I also asked the Lord to bring me comfort and to keep me calm. I wanted to know that my family would be okay while I was gone, so I could enjoy

> *this time with my husband. That may seem silly. But I'm a mom, and moms often worry. Many of my prayers are to alleviate fears and concerns for my children, and there's often no rational reason to worry. I know it's Satan trying to distract me and get in the way. But I also know my Heavenly Father loves me. I know He answers my prayers. He immediately sent me a calm feeling of peace and reassurance that all would be well at home. I am so grateful for that small little moment. It was important to me and Heavenly Father knew it. I felt his love in that moment.*[2]

Any time a thought or a feeling attempts to rob you of happiness, spoil the moment, create turmoil, ruin your peace, it almost always comes from SKAM. Earlier in the chapter a new matron in the temple gained peace and confidence by making her uneasiness of mind a matter of prayer. Dina Rossell was able to chase away a perturbing thought and calm her troubled mind by offering a heartfelt prayer. In both cases each of these women looked to the Lord in their thoughts about their thoughts, and the Lord promptly answered. How sweet and significant the words, "Look unto me in every thought; doubt not, fear not" (D&C 6:36).

Developing Response-Ability

In mortality, we become conditioned to go directly from stimulus to *reaction* with little or no forethought, whereas a *response* requires consideration. Sometimes it seems as though there's no time for a *choice* anywhere along the sequence. Something happens and, bam, we go from interpretation to emotion to reaction in less than a blink of the eye—in a seemingly unavoidable case of a stimulus generating an automatic set response. In those moments, SKAM immediately shifts our attention from what we can do to intercept the reaction by telling us we had no

---

2 Personal correspondence. Used with permission.

choice because it wasn't our fault. Our reaction, he suggests, was caused by some outside source—generally another person. He wants to divert our attention from our role in the matter, by urging us to dive headlong into finger-pointing and wishing everybody else would grow up and change. He must laugh at our frustration every time we think we can actually blame somebody else into improving our behavior—or their behavior sufficient to improve our outcomes.

Developing the "response-ability" of a calm, patient, emotionally stable disciple of Christ is no small undertaking, nevertheless this skill is central to our becoming true disciples of the Lord Jesus Christ. Despite all the hatred, rejection and persecution he endured, no murmuring word or railing accusation escaped His tongue. He remained focused on doing the will of the Father in all things and overcoming the world. At the last supper, the Lord reassured His inner circle of their eventual triumph as He announced His own: "In the world ye shall have tribulation: but be of good cheer; I have overcome the world" (John 16:33).

Moreover, the sacramental covenant to "always remember Him" brings us to a deep state of humility and reverence as we consider the magnitude and grandeur of His personal composure and self-restraint especially manifest in the events from Gethsemane to Calvary. Upon entering the Garden of Gethsemane, the Lord revealed what he was feeling to Peter, James and John as He "began to be sorrowful and very heavy. … 'My soul is exceeding sorrowful, even unto death'" (Matthew 26:37–38). Then walking a short distance away from them, He commenced to experience the agonies required of the Father, "which suffering caused myself, even God, the greatest of all, to tremble because of pain, and to bleed at every pore, and to suffer both body and spirit—and would that I might not drink the bitter cup, and shrink" (D&C 19:18). While having endured the agony just described, He returned to His apostles and instead of finding them praying for Him, He finds them asleep. Although disappointed, He responded with no irritation, only a compassionate, "Sleep on now, and take your rest: behold the hour is at hand, and the Son of man is betrayed into the hands of sinners" (Matthew 26:45).

The ultimate evidence of the Lord's consummate composure and of having overcome the world is then manifest. He endured all the indignities human disdain and hatred could inflict, along with the added physical pain of beatings and scourging compounded by the complex of physical tortures associated with crucifixion. While thus afflicted and burdened, the infinite agonies introduced in Gethsemane are then unleashed in full measure during the final hours on the cross. Amid the confluence of all these sources of exquisite suffering, our magnificent Savior and Redeemer completed His foreordained mission with a divine manifestation of meekness, strength and composure only a God could display.

As lofty and challenging as the goal of becoming like Christ may seem to be for us in this state of mortality, it is nonetheless the request and promise the Lord extends to us in the words "come follow me." He does so with the intent to bless, sustain and empower us to step-by-step, follow in His footsteps, beginning wherever each one of us may be at this moment. Being able to choose, rather than react, especially in extreme circumstances is the essence of what is meant by, "overcoming the world" and what the Lord invites us to do. And the rewards for doing so are immeasurable and eternal (Rev. 2:7, 11, 17, 26; 3:12, 21).

CHAPTER 14

Five Effective Tactics

Armed with truth, we are able to detect the telltale fruits of Lucifer's deceptions. With knowledge of and obedience to the truth, we can confront SKAM directly and prepare ourselves to obtain spiritual power beyond ourselves—the enabling grace of the Lord Jesus Christ.

New Testament accounts of how the Lord dealt with Satan instruct us, for He is the way. After Christ's forty-day fast in the wilderness, Satan came to tempt Him (Luke 4:2). It's a one-on-one encounter. Each temptation was an invitation that appealed to Christ's mortal nature. Each was designed to evoke desire (an ardent feeling) by presenting a mental image (thought) that begs for gratification (action). In each case, the Lord firmly rebuffs Satan's ploy, refusing to entertain any of Satan's proposals (thoughts), even for a moment. Notice how he does it.

Recognizing immediately where Satan wants to lead His thoughts, the Savior confronts Satan personally and directly. No pause, no hesitation. Christ counters the ploys by turning them around on the adversary, disagreeing with Satan's premises and rejecting his invitations. "Turn stones into bread to my satisfy physical hunger? Far above the physical bread, I choose the manna from the Father and will 'live by every word that proceedeth out of the mouth of God'" (Matt. 4:2–4). "Cast myself off the temple to verify my Father's love? I know who I am and whose I am. I will follow the admonitions in the scriptures and will not tempt my God" (Luke 4:9–11). "Worship you, Satan, to possess the glory of the world? Seriously? I've had enough of your fallacies. Get thee hence, Satan: for it is written, Thou shalt worship the Lord thy God, and him only shalt thou serve" (Luke 4:7–13).

Five Effective Tactics for Battling Satan's Ploys:

1. Personify the opponent: Make the battle direct and personal. Apply what you've learned. Put a name on your opponent—the enemy of your soul—so you can face him directly and confront his sly schemes head on. Like a clever magician, SKAM tries to hide behind the façade of misdirection. Whispering in your ears, he directs focus and blame on you, on outside events and on other people, rather than on himself. Note Nephi's warning, "And he saith unto them: I am no devil, for there is none—and thus he whispereth in their ears" (2 Ne. 28:22). He's been getting away with his nasty little sneak attacks on you for years. Well, the sham is over. You have always known his intent; now you are getting crystal clear on his methodology and his point of attack.

In World War II the turning point in the War in the Pacific was the Battle of Midway. Thanks to the brilliant work of a little-known code breaker, Joe Rochefort, the U.S. Navy was able to foil and repel the enemy's plan to establish control of the Pacific. Rochefort was able to predict down to the day, hour and direction how the attack on Midway would unfold. Armed with this accurate knowledge, the U.S. Navy was able to deliver a devastating blow on the Japanese Imperial Navy. After this victory, the momentum swung to the Allies favor and stayed with them to the end of the war.

We can liken this example to our war with the adversary. Knowledge is power. Knowledge of correct doctrine is the most powerful of all, especially in dealing with Lucifer and his unseen forces, just as the Prophet Joseph Smith taught us:

> *A man is saved no faster than he gets knowledge, for if he does not get knowledge, he will be brought into captivity by some evil power in the other world, as evil spirits will have more knowledge, and consequently more power than many men who are on the earth.*[1]

Armed with accurate knowledge you too can deliver a devastating blow to Satan and his navy. And, it's high time, isn't it? We all need to follow Nephi's example and say to ourselves, "Awake, my soul! No longer droop in sin. Rejoice, O my heart, and give place no more for the enemy of my soul" (2 Ne. 4:28).

2. Stop listening. Start talking back. For the sake of example, put yourself into this familiar scenario. It's Sunday morning, the Sabbath Day. As you are waking up, SKAM injects his noise, "Oh, wouldn't it be so nice to just lie here and lounge around for a few hours? You know, you actually deserve some R&R. A little more sleep would do you good, and you'd be off to a stronger start on Monday. Besides, you're not going to get that much out of church anyway. All the hassle of getting up and getting the kids ready for church isn't worth it. You're just going to hear the same things over again—stuff you've heard a thousand times before. And, you're doing a pretty good job on most of it anyway." Tell me you haven't been there and heard his diatribe in several different forms. There's the one about going to the temple; one about ministering to a ward member; one about keeping your commitment to *study*, not just read, the Book of Mormon; one about paying tithing or a generous fast offering; one about fasting on fast Sunday. While this list is far from exhaustive, it is certainly exhausting to contemplate.

---

1 Smith, *Teachings of the Prophet Joseph Smith,* 217.

Once you recognize the pattern, it almost becomes comical. You make a personal commitment to go the temple on Wednesday evening. Like Joe Rochefort, you can just about predict what's coming next. Starting Wednesday morning, bright and early, and continuing throughout the day, you will be bombarded with a steady stream of mishaps, "urgent" necessities, extenuating circumstances, and oxen in the mire—all potential excuses to help you see it's not only too inconvenient, but categorically impossible, for you to make it to the temple.

Notice, that all of the noise playing in your head is posing as your own thoughts, but is it? Are you really *saying* all that to yourself or are *you listening to it?* At first it might seem like your own thoughts, but when you pause and examine, you become aware that it's not your thoughts at all. You can verify this because you can actually talk back to it, while it's rattling along in your mind. Once you recognize this, stop listening and talk back!

I have used this tactic countless times and have taught it to others. It works more consistently than Tylenol relieves a headache. The next time SKAM starts telling you on the Sabbath Day what a nice comfy bed you have, try something like, "Okay, SKAM, you can skip the rest of your script. I get it. You don't want me to go to church today. Since you're a liar and working to thwart me, I'm going to assume there's actually a fairly important and valuable reason you don't want me to go today. Even if nothing spectacular happens, it doesn't matter. Because I will have, at the very least, been obedient. I will have chosen to do what the Lord wants me to do and disobeyed what you want me to do. And, if that's all that takes place, that will be more than enough. As small and insignificant as going or not going to church may seem, it's being obedient to small and simple things that adds up, puts oil in my lamp, draws me one step closer to the Savior, and one step farther from you."

A response like that has never failed to produce a feeling of light, warmth, energy and joy inside me that lasts for hours. And, since one of

SKAM's biggest goals is to make God's children miserable, I get a kick out of knowing I can turn the tables on SKAM and make him miserable instead. In the math of battling Satan, your joy equals his misery.

3. Counter with a 180-Degree Reversal

You can take the idea just described one step further. You can really get under Satan's skin, if he had any, by turning the tables on SKAM and going the extra mile in disobeying his ploys. I'm not a boxer (and I can prove it), but I do know that counter-punching—immediately attacking after you've received a blow—is a potent tactic, one that catches your opponent off guard and compromises his balance. In the case of SKAM enticing you to stay home from church, you can add power to your response with something like this: "Oh, so you don't want me to go to church. Well, I tell you what. I'm not just going to church—I'm going to make the most of every minute. I'm not just going to sit there and vegetate. I'm going to look for opportunities to make a difference. I'm going to look for people who might be feeling a little downcast or lonely. I'm going to greet them, shake their hand, put my arm around them, and tell them I'm glad to see them. (Because I will be.) I'm going to ask them how they're doing, and I'll take the time to listen and care about what they're saying. I'm going to look for an opportunity to make a meaningful comment in the lesson—maybe even bear my testimony about something being taught. If there's a service project or request for volunteer work, I'll accept and work it into my schedule. And I'll pray for the speakers, the teachers and the ward leaders and listen carefully for promptings of what actions I can take to be obedient and honor the counsel given by my leaders."

As you respond to Satan's ploys with this kind of energy, you are likely to get fewer of them and you will discover or rediscover places where you have grown complacent and lazy and see where a bit of repentance is in order. Reward enough.

4. Take Action

You may have already noticed how the first three tactics connect and build one upon the next. You will find them to be very effective—but only if you keep your word and follow through consistently on your promises—particularly the ones you make in your counterpunch. Otherwise, you are just boasting, which offends the Spirt. Rather than "putting off the natural man and becoming a saint through the Atonement of Jesus Christ," you will be aiding and abetting SKAM. Accordingly, as you sincerely act upon your counterpunch promises, you increase the enabling power Christ promises to give you to become His begotten son or daughter. You will be keeping the law upon which such great blessings are predicated by elevating and amplifying your discipleship. James testified, "Blessed is the man that resisteth temptation: for when he is tried, he shall receive the crown of life, which the Lord hath promised to them that love him" (JST James 1:12).

Taking action is a powerful tactic for "putting off the natural man" (Mosiah 3:19) and combatting Satan's influence in your life. You can't just say what you're going to do, you absolutely must act and fulfill as James enjoined. "But be ye doers of the word and not hearers only, deceiving your own selves" (James 1:22). And note the tremendous declaration James adds, "God resisteth the proud, but giveth grace unto the humble. Submit yourselves therefore to God. *Resist the devil, and he will flee from you"* (James 4:6–7, emphasis added).

Whenever you resist the devil, he flees because you are empowered by the Holy Spirit. Still clear in my memory is a simple yet vivid experience I had as a deacon-age youth. I was walking home alone from a youth activity when I came across a wallet lying on the asphalt. I picked it up and discovered it had money in it but don't recall how much. I didn't stop to count it. I can't remember a distinct temptation or anything like that, but I can't imagine SKAM passing up an opportunity to throw one at me. I immediately recognized the name on the ID inside—Brother McRae—a member of the ward. I bounded up the steps of his front porch and rang the doorbell. He hadn't even realized his wallet was missing. He offered no reward—just a sincere thanks for my gesture, and in another few seconds I was resuming my walk home.

The reason I remember this small moment so well is what happened after. As I continued homeward, I was suddenly showered (the best way I can describe it) with the most wonderful warm, peaceful, joyful feeling, engulfing me head to toe. I felt *wonderful.* I can't remember how long it lasted, but I do remember the feeling was similar to my experience of sitting in the backseat of my parent's car on the way home from the Salt Lake Tabernacle after my baptism. I remember saying over and over to my parents, "I feel so clean. I feel so clean."

We all have the simple everyday interferences when SKAM tries to keep us from performing small acts of kindness and service. Sometimes, however, both the issue and the stakes are much higher. Sometimes we contemplate making big changes like whether or not to relocate to a new city, change careers, or take on a new leadership responsibility. Like you, I have been in those moments of decision, standing in the middle of a crossroads fraught with uncertainty and risk. Often what adds to the weight of the choice is the clear understanding that it isn't just about how it affects you. Other people will be impacted as well. Their lives will be disrupted too. As Latter-day Saints, we know what to do in such times; we fast and pray. Sometimes we seek counsel from priesthood leaders, wise and experienced family members and friends. My experience has been that the Lord does not always answer the first prayer. Or the second. Sometimes the silence seems deafening.

Other experiences, somewhat similar in nature, but not nearly as disruptive or risky also occur. Perhaps you are asked to take on a new task or assignment at work, a calling to work in the temple, or a family crisis throws unexpected demands on your shoulders—something for which you feel unprepared and unqualified. It could even be an opportunity to speak, sing or perform before a large audience. Or it could be a challenge you take on by choice that will stretch you way out of your comfort zone. In any of these situations, where you are venturing into the unknown, SKAM will go into hyper-drive and pull out all the stops to undermine your confidence and stop you from growing. Knowing that the biggest lies you will ever hear are in your own head, masquerading as your own thoughts will prove to be invaluable.

When, not if, SKAM starts telling you that you can't do something, you don't have to believe him. You can harness his ploy and use it to bolster your resolve to act on the idea or accept the opportunity, daunting as it may first appear to be. You can turn the tables on SKAM once again and draw power from the whole experience, start to finish. First, you need to recognize—up front and clearly—that if SKAM is saying you can't do something it is absolute evidence that you *can.* Otherwise, he wouldn't waste his efforts trying to discourage you. If it's an automatic, slam-dunk surety you're destined to fail, wouldn't he just let you proceed—perhaps even encourage you to venture—knowing you're going to fall flat on your face? Wouldn't he just get out of your way and enjoy witnessing your comical fiasco? With your knowledge of Satan's ploys, you can actually turn his frantic rants to stop you to your advantage. Pause and think. Aren't his efforts a backdoor confirmation that you're not only *capable* but *highly likely* to succeed?

If your venture is going to be hard, he also knows you'll need to rely on the Lord to accomplish it and doing so will bring you closer to Him and strengthen your relationship. You will come to know firsthand that the tender mercies and miracles that occur as you tackle something with divine aid are *not* coincidences. Standing tall will give you the strength, confidence, and added skills to go on to do something even greater. Moreover, all along the way, you will likely be blessing the lives of a number of others. All of these positive experiences will rankle Lucifer all the more. So, no wonder he's going to come at you hard with all of the fallacies about how weak and inept and undeserving you are. Seeing these satanic attempts to thwart you in their true light actually becomes reassuring and motivating. Isn't knowledge wonderful, powerful and exciting!

5. Depersonalize your role!

Don't be shocked when SKAM comes at you with fiery darts *about you.* For one, you've already heard most of it before. "You're about to make a fool of yourself. You're going to embarrass yourself. You're not only going to look stupid, you're going to prove it before the whole world. You'll never recover. People will snicker at you the rest of your life." When you hear that familiar lecture, you are ready to unleash tactic number 5 and tell SKAM, "*It's not about me at all.*" Being your own mental coach, ask yourself, "Is there even a remote possibility my going for this goal would end up helping just one other person? Is it faintly possible I could be a catalyst for demolishing a major roadblock or solving a problem another person has wrestled with for years? Could I be an answer to someone else's prayer?" If you would honestly have to answer these questions with, "Yes, I suppose it's possible," then, my friend, this is *not about you.* It's about the people you can help—even if it's only one solitary person. And the follow-up question is this, "If it's possible that it could help one person, isn't it reasonable you might—just might—help more than one, maybe even several people?" If the answer is "Yes," then again, it's definitely not about you, it's about who knows how many other people—perhaps even hundreds. Once you can shift your thinking to realize it's never been just about you, then the inspired words of Marianne Williamson will give you something to really think about and digest.

> *Our deepest fear is not that we are inadequate. Our deepest fear is that we are powerful beyond measure. It is our light, not our darkness that most frightens us. We ask ourselves, 'Who am I to be brilliant, gorgeous, talented, fabulous?' Actually, who are you not to be? You are a child*

> *of God. You playing small does not serve the world. There is nothing enlightened about shrinking so that other people won't feel insecure around you. We are all meant to shine, as children do. We were born to make manifest the glory of God that is within us. It's not just in some of us; it's in everyone. And as we let our own light shine, we unconsciously give other people permission to do the same. As we are liberated from our own fear, our presence automatically liberates others.*[2]

In the grand plan of our Heavenly Father, He is weaving the threads of our lives and many others together, creating an intricate, gorgeous tapestry. In His divinely designed celestial work of art, none of us are accomplishing any of this on our own, nor for our own selfish interests. Heavenly Father works through other people to bless our lives and works through us to bless theirs.

As effective as the other four tactics are, I believe the fifth is the most significant. By negating Satan's ploys, you gain a firsthand knowledge—even a perfect knowledge—that Gabriel's counsel to Mary is true and applies to you and every one of Heavenly Father's children, "Fear not, Mary, for with God nothing is impossible." So, tell Lucifer you are not going to be intimidated, or talked out of your opportunity to make a magnificent leap forward in your own development. Take your best shot at helping who-knows-how-many other people to do or be more in their lives. And whether it's millions or few, it doesn't matter, because it's always up to the Lord anyway. It's not your ballgame; it's His and you're one of His valuable players. Yes, you can choose to sit on the bench if you want. Yes, you can, of course, also play it safe and cozy if you wish. But how much greater will be your joy when you throw ego and embarrassment to the wind and go for something that will require a major stretch and find out that all you've got is *still* not enough. In those courageous moments, you will find the

2 Marianne Williamson, *A Return to Love,* (New York: HarperCollins Publishers, 1992), 190.

Lord, the author of your faith, with an out-stretched hand and a mighty arm, there to finish your faith. It's only when you get to an extremity that you allow the Savior to reach into your life more deeply than you have ever allowed Him before. When you're snug and comfy, you don't need a savior. (At least you don't think so.) It's when you try walking on boisterous waters that you call on Him with enough intensity to find Him and gain assurance of His ever-vigilant presence. In light of the humiliation and hostility He had to endure, it seems a small price to risk a little embarrassment or a bit of persecution to show Him how much you really want to be like Him and will do anything it takes to draw closer to Him.

CHAPTER 15

Halting Between Opinions

Having pulled back the curtain on the wicked wizard and exposing the range and prevalence of his manipulations, let's zero in on one of Satan's most prominent schemes—sowing confusion to befuddle our minds.

The scriptures describe two separate and competitive societies battling for authority. One is called Zion, whose citizens are pure in heart (D&C 97:21) and remarkably united (Moses 7:18). They are of one heart and one mind—and there are no poor among them because they are all industrious and self-reliant (Moses 7:18; D&C 42:42; 68:30; 75:28–29). An apt symbol for Zion and the traits of a Zion people is associated with Deseret, the Jaredite word for honeybee (Ether 2:3)—a hive created by a united group of diligent co-workers.

The other society is Babylon, which represents worldly exploitation, and the insatiable lust for riches. Babylon is characterized by selfishness, greed and materialism—the pursuit of wealth in order to get gain by oppressing others. This society is all about ranking, castes, and social status. A great and spacious building has many floors. One wonders how much arrogance and enmity towards others, including God, one must have to own an apartment on the penthouse floor—the level from which one can look down on everyone else.

The King of Zion is Jesus Christ—the Prince of Peace, the Lamb of God—He is the truth, the life, and the way. He is The Word, the example, the embodiment, the perfect illustration. His ways are openness, plainness and clarity—the antithesis of ambiguity.

The King of Babylon, on the other hand, is Lucifer—the "liar from the beginning" (D&C 93:25). He fosters works of darkness done in darkness. He abhors truth and plainness and seeks to create division and spread antipathy among God's children through misinformation, half-truths and lies. The Hebrew word for Babylon is Babel and means "*confusion* of voices."[1]

The Day of Confusion

We live in the times of confusion prophesied by Isaiah, the great prophet who aptly described our day. He saw a time when people would "call evil good, and good evil, [and] put darkness for light, and light for darkness" (Isa 5:20). Clearly, Lucifer has succeeded in creating confusion and spreading enmity upon the earth about many moral issues—the definition of life, gender, marriage, and religious freedom. Beyond such larger issues, we are even inundated in contradictory information about simple everyday matters. When someone encourages us "to eat healthy" does anyone know with certainty what in today's world that means? Are eggs good for you or not? What about oils and fats? Does wheat heal or harm? Which kinds of vitamin supplements *cause* cancer rather than cure it? Names for dietary plans have become identities. Are you vegan? Paleo? Or, Mitochondrial? (Personally, I've become a nutritional schizophrenic: I'm a paleo-vegan-Siamese ketotarian who skips the entire egg and just eats the shells.)

1 https://www.studylight.org/dictionaries/eng/hbd/b/babel.html.

"Hey, Have You Noticed that Blemish on Your Forehead?"

On a serious note, one of SKAM's modern ploys focuses on distorting correct principles relating to caring for one's personal appearance. Even being "neat and comely" (Alma 1:27), is taken to extremes. Today satanically promoted perfectionism over physical appearance runs rampant in our society, inflicting more personal damage than any virus. From nutrition to exercise to grooming to fashion, obsession over outward appearance drains checking accounts as people try in vain to remedy some discrepancy between their body and the manipulated images on magazine covers. It is heart-rending to consider how much anxiety and self-loathing results from attempting to achieve standards that have been intentionally distorted and are physically unattainable. It's Satan's perfect storm.

What does Lucifer accomplish by spreading this tidal wave of falsehoods and conflicting pseudo-facts? For one thing, he keeps us out of action. Mired in the quest to keep up with every newscast, podcast and forecast, we spend precious time plowing through streams of posts, many of which are from questionable and even anonymous sources. Within minutes we shift from being the searcher to becoming the follower. Link after link, the hands on the clock are ticking as we click to yet another opinion untainted by facts. The second casualty is our mental state. Trying to discern truth amid tumults of opinion overloads our neuronal circuits and our brains become fatigued. Boggled by confusion, we become unsettled and indecisive. The final casualty is our emotional state. Consistent with Stage 2, saturating our minds with strident, deceptively slanted doctrines of men does not produce uplifting feelings of hope and optimism. Rather, soaking in a brine of animosity, we become burdened with feelings of anxiety, frustration, and anger. Consider carefully your sources of information and monitor your feelings both during and after imbibing. Do you feel uplifted and closer to the Spirit or downcast and depressed? That question is a litmus test for discerning the source of what you've been ingesting. Put another way, if you're feeling happy and pretty good about your life, and you want to get over it, just spend two hours surfing conspiracy theories on the internet.

Making Good Decisions

Centuries ago, the prophet Elijah issued a wake-up message to the children of Israel: "How long halt ye between two opinions? if the Lord be God, follow him: but if Baal, then follow him" (1 Kings 18:21). Apparently, the tactic of promoting indecision worked on ancient Israel about as well as it does on modern Israel today. Satan gets many of us to halt between worshipping the Father in the name of the Son by confusing us with so many tantalizing diversions and distractions. While most of these choices are not egregiously evil per se, they nonetheless divert our attention from the weightier matters of our probation, and distract us from making a full, all-out commitment to serve God with *all* our might, mind, and strength.

Sowing confusion, SKAM gets us to be indecisive, halting between multiple opinions, by convincing us that each decision has one and only one right choice. He implies dire, irreversible consequences if we don't make the correct one. "You better get this right," he chides. "Important things hang in the balance here—time, money, image. If you don't get this right, you'll look like a fool. They'll revoke your birth certificate and make you leave the planet."

My good friend, Steve Chandler, and I have been colleagues in human development training for a number of years. Steve's rise to become the most prolific author in the self-help genre is a tremendous story in its own. With a sophisticated wit, he teaches serious points through a unique brand of dry humor. From his book, *Crazy Good*, he illustrates the trap of indecisiveness even over trivial matters.

> *Trying to decide things can take you right out of the flow of life. Whereas choosing moves things right along. I am at the bookstore and*

I have just bought two books. There is a long line of people behind me and the counter lady is asking me whether I want my receipt with me or whether I want her to put it in the bag with the books.

"I don't know," I say trying to decide which makes more sense.

She looks at me and raises her eyebrows. I look back at her.

I say, "What do you suggest?"

"Sir, it's up to you."

"Well, what is the downside of my just putting it in my pocket? Will someone be inspecting the bag?"

"No, sir," she says. "So I'll just give it to you, then." And she holds the receipt out for me to take.

"Wait a minute," I say, pulling my hand away. "I'm thinking the bag might be a better place for me to have it. Right? But really I'm not certain of that."

"Sir, please . . ."

"Do you mind if I call my wife? She knows about these kinds of things and it will just take a second."

"Would you please step out of line?"

"Yes sure. But should I leave the receipt with you until I decide where I'm going to put it? Or should I hold it? What do you think, maybe give it to another customer to hold for us until I reach my wife? Her phone seems to be busy."

I get home later and notice that I can't find the receipt anywhere.[2]

---

2 Steve Chandler, *Crazy Good,* (Anna Maria, FL: Maurice Bassett, 2015), 21–22.

In many cases, "turning right or left at Oak Street" has no significant bearing on an outcome. You can reach the destination and the variation in which route is of little moment. In such cases, it is ridiculous to equivocate. We just make a decision and go.

Learning by Doing Our Best

In seminars, I've been asked, "What is the mindset behind the inordinate fixation on avoiding "the wrong decision?" My answer is, "Our unwillingness to take responsibility for our outcomes—thinking that in the end we have little to say about how things turn out." This thinking runs contrary to one of the main things we are here to learn. In this probationary state, we are to learn principles and acquire skills in the likeness of our Heavenly Parents. Hence, God expects us to use our wits to work out many things on our own, using our agency to make decisions and learn to exercise good judgment. As a part of that, like it or not, we are allowed to make poor decisions and dumb mistakes—even permitted to commit grievous sins. As the maxim goes, "good decisions come from experience; and experience comes from bad decisions." Hence, Heavenly Father will even allow us to make the same mistake over and over, if that's what it takes for us to finally learn the lesson. A good friend of mine put it this way: "If I am dumb enough to keep learning the same lesson over and over, God will let me."

Knowing that great power comes from submitting our will to the will of the Father, Brigham Young explained that God will not always or immediately manifest His will to us, requiring us to develop judgment through experience. Additionally, Brigham gave counsel on how to proceed, "If I do not know the will of my Father, and what He requires of me in a certain transaction, if I ask Him to give me wisdom concerning any requirement in life, or in regard to my own course … and get no answer from Him, and then do the very best that my judgement will teach me,

He is bound to own and honor that transaction, and He will do so to all intents and purposes."[3] Embracing this teaching will help us move forward in confidence.

Making the Decision Be The Right One

When making big decisions, we are often hesitant in moving forward because the stakes seem so high, for ourselves and others we love. We agonize over the decisions, wanting to know for certain how the movie will turn out, as though we're merely a passive observer in the audience. In reality, we are co-authors with the Father in writing the scripts for our mortal movies, and need to see ourselves as *the principal determinant*—the one who has the responsibility for making the initial decision *and also* for doing all in our power to make the decision turn out "right."

The Lord wants us to develop the faith in Him and in ourselves to *create the outcome* we want. SKAM seeks to deceive us by selling us on the fallacy that *the decision itself* somehow has all the power. He wants us to believe the chooser has no responsibility for how things turn out beyond the initial decision. According to SKAM, once the decision is made, the die is cast and the machinery is set in motion and cannot be stopped or altered. Everything will just proceed onto its predetermined conclusion. That fatalistic perspective is another satanic fallacy.

As choosers and creative beings, we have a lot to say about whether a decision—even a major decision—turns out to be a "good one" or not. We are in charge of the decision all along the way, from the initial choice on through to the finish. Ultimately, we're the one who determines whether or not the decision was a "good one" by our additional decisions and actions, and also, when things don't go as planned, how we look at the outcome and what we learned from the entire process. Heavenly

---

3 Young, *Journal of Discourses,* Vol. 3, 205.

Father wants us to make decisions and learn from them. In the eternal scope of things, the "good-est" thing that could happen might be for the original idea to struggle mightily and even fail. Haven't we all heard successful people say they learned more from their initial failures than from their successes?

Understanding Our Part in the Lord's Will

One of the highest priorities in our earthly learning curve is to learn to own our decisions as we grow in faith by doing all in our power while trusting in the Lord. Sometimes we have to "be diligent; and know that He is God." Sometimes we have to *persist* in taking responsibility for fulfilling the law upon which our desired outcome is predicated. Knowing that it is Heavenly Father's *will* that we learn and grow, we have to be careful to not ascribe initial failures to His will, evading our personal responsibility in the equation. It might be that the successful outcome we seek is in fact His will, but we haven't as yet fulfilled the law upon which success is predicated. Rather than taking responsibility to work harder and pray harder, we often shirk and say, "It must not have been the Lord's will."

Elder Gene R. Cook cautioned us about this tendency to put the responsibility on the Lord rather than on ourselves. Referring to instances when things don't turn out as hoped, he points out, "It's either that it's not [God's] will or that we have fallen short. And, it's been my experience, that *it's mostly the latter*—that we have not paid the price, thus the heavens could not respond." Then he elaborates,

> *And I'd like to say to you as soberly as I can, brothers and sisters, that around the church when things don't work out people are quick to say, 'well it must not have been the will of the Lord because it didn't happen.' Now, when somebody says that, what they're really doing is*

> *doubting. They're putting the responsibility with Him, as if it was his mood somehow. My experience with good members is the reason for the lack of answers to our prayers is not so much lack of worthiness or … that you can't measure up, nearly as much as … not persisting and really pleading with the Lord for the answer. That's where most of it lies.*[4]

We do well to remember the Lord's frequent phrase "According to *your* faith…" (Matt. 9:29; D&C 8:11) and His reminder "according to men's faith it shall be done unto them," (D&C 52:20). With these words, He is teaching us where the responsibility lies.

"If Only I Hadn't . . ."

Satan's ploy of delaying decisions until we know for certain whether or not they are "good" has a first cousin. I refer to second guessing. SKAM must smile ear to ear when, after having finally made a decision, we waste precious time looking back, re-examining it. Can anything be more useless in our drive to making the decision turn out well? Ruing and regretting are like immersing ourselves in a tub of water filled with leeches—allowing nagging doubts and regrets to suck the lifeblood out of us. Perhaps you think my simile is overly dramatic. You may be right. It may only be for my own benefit. It has taken me a number of years to catch onto this ploy and get past it. For me the actual phrasing of the ploy was "If only I hadn't …" Often it was coupled with the sudden attack ploy mentioned in Chapter 13, Making it Real. I'd be cruising along feeling fine when out of nowhere would come a memory of some disaster from my past. Frequently it would be a financial decision that had not gone well. Bam! The memory would hit and like an ingrained chain reaction, the words would come into my head, "If only I hadn't …" and I'd rehearse and regret the decision. I am

4 Gene R. Cook, *Receiving Answers to Prayers,* Audio CD, (Salt Lake City: Deseret Book Company, 1996).

embarrassed to admit how often and how long this tactic worked on me. As my understanding of Satan's methods increased, I was able to shut it down by asking, "What did I learn from that experience?" and "Where do I want to go from here?" Engaging in this way, I'm able to put my mind to work on an action to take rather than stew on something I can no longer act on. This approach has worked well for me. Try it and see what happens.

CHAPTER 16

The Subtle Deception of Distraction

Heavenly Father sent a cadre of remarkable minds—genuine geniuses—into the world during the latter part of the eighteenth century. We call them the Founding Fathers. Under the tutelage and guidance of the Spirit of the Lord, these brilliant minds forged the sacred founding documents of the greatest democracy ever to grace this planet. They did it through focused thinking, pondering, as well as fierce and open debate. These founding documents have been templates for the majority of the democracies and republics that followed.

Highly significant is *the way* Heavenly Father brought all of this about. He could have just sent an angel down in the middle of one of the assemblages of the Continental Congress and said, "All right boys, here you go" and presented them with the Declaration of Independence, the Constitution, and the Bill of Rights. Neither in the founding of this nation, nor in the founding of His Church did he simply deliver the final product. He always worked with and through His children in their imperfect state because the eternal rewards He wants them to attain cannot be bestowed. They are developed and obtained through faith and works—and great works require more than puny effort; they require the degree of effort and dedication proportionate to the greatness of the desired or needed outcome.

As Nephi knew, no matter how daunting the task, Father always prepares a way and provides the sustaining revelation and grace to accomplish the righteous things He prompts His children to do, and that includes you and me (1 Ne 3:7). He provides His children with the conditions and opportunities to think, ponder, labor, and wrestle with challenges. He allows us to grow and stretch through hard mental and physical work. He wants us to build up nations, families, businesses, and even His true Church and kingdom—so through those efforts we can develop the characteristics and stature of the Son of God. We are to use our intelligence to the extent of our capability in order to further expand and hone our intelligence. He wants us to use our minds in order to amplify our minds!

In the divine wisdom of God, the ends are the means, and the means are the ends. The striving and struggling to achieve the *ends*—the building up of the kingdom of God on earth—serve as the *means* whereby His children develop the faith and attributes necessary to dwell in His presence. Thus, the development of the faith and attributes—the *means* by which the kingdom is built—are the actual *ends* Heavenly Father had in mind in order to bring to pass the immortality and eternal life of His children.

The Gift of Genius

Among the brightest of the geniuses comprising America's Founding Fathers stood Alexander Hamilton. Many of Hamilton's peers held him to be the most intelligent of their group. Note what he says about genius:

> *Men give me credit for genius. All the genius I have lies in this; when I have a subject in hand, I study it profoundly. Day and night it is before me. My mind becomes pervaded with it. Then the effort that I have*

made is what people are pleased to call the fruit of genius. It is the fruit of labor and thought.[1]

In the context of describing exceptional human proficiencies the word *gift* is often misunderstood. Many think "having a gift" means the talent was merely bestowed—granted without the slightest effort on the part of the recipient. Such a notion runs counter to the revealed word of God—"There is a law irrevocably decreed in heaven upon which *all* blessings are predicated" (D&C 130:20, emphasis added). Note that Hamilton did not deny having a gift, but he described how much effort he had to devote in order to obtain the superlative insights that came to him. Even if your mission is to be a major player in the founding of a great nation, you cannot simply "wish upon a star." You still have to pay the price.

In mortality, our mind thinks exclusively, meaning we're able to focus on only one thought at any given moment.[2] That narrowed field of focus does not apply to celestial beings, and we sometimes yearn for the ability to multi-task. Yet, that restriction serves an absolutely vital and indispensable purpose in the development of our faith and spirituality. Each of us must learn to control and leverage this property and resist Satan's attempts to fragment our attention.

One of the most overlooked powers we can develop is a lengthy attention span. Alexander Hamilton received inspiration from on high during, and as a result of, his prolonged, focused concentration. In the Church we are encouraged to study things out in our minds, meditate, ponder, and pray with full purpose and real intent. Whenever we are totally focused on a worthwhile endeavor, we feel happy, confident and composed. There are at least two reasons why: We have totally blocked out SKAM's noise and

1 Alexander Hamilton, "Alexander Hamilton Quotes", *Quotes.net,* STAND4 LLC, 2020. Web. 27 Oct 2020, <https://www.quotes.net/53508.

2 See chapter seven.

distractions, and we are drawing closer to and receiving approval of the Spirit. In that single-minded undistracted state, we often receive revelation and answers to prayers. Brigham Young delivered timeless counsel on the rewards of focused attention:

> *If a congregation wish to … receive an increase of wisdom and knowledge, their minds must be intent on the subject before them. They must not suffer their thoughts to be roaming over the earth; they must not permit their minds to be scanning and traversing their everyday duties and avocations. If they do, they are not blessed with that store of knowledge they otherwise might obtain through paying that attention necessary to enable them to clearly understand.*

Without discounting the challenge involved, he highlighted the rewarding payoff: "It is a masterwork to school our minds so as at all times to exercise complete power over them. If the people would so educate themselves as to control their thinking powers, they would derive a great advantage from it. They could improve much faster than they now do."[3]

The Law of Attention

Vitally important is the innate ability of the intelligence to choose what to focus and dwell on. A journalist once asked me for a concise summary of the essence of mental discipline and mind management. I said, "Managing one's attention." If asked the same question today, I would give the same answer, but with even more certainty and emphasis. I now call it the Law of Focused Attention, which is: *At any given moment, the field of our focused attention is the scope and extent of our universe.* When you are totally engrossed in one activity—reading a story to your grandchild, preparing a talk, repairing a leaky faucet, or sitting in your easy chair

3 Young, *Journal of Discourses,* Vol 6, 93–94.

listening to a symphony—each of those totally-focused experiences are the height, breadth and depth of your world at that moment. The state of the economy, the strife in the Middle East, how messy your garage may be, don't interfere. For all intents and purposes, they are totally non-existent. And, when you're totally present—when you're in the moment and only that moment—even time itself seems to disappear.

The power of focused attention pertains to both temporal and spiritual endeavors. "Only through focus can you do world-class things," avowed Bill Gates, "no matter how capable you are. My success … is that I have focused in on a few things."[4] Famed success coach Zig Ziglar warned, "I don't care how much power, brilliance or energy you have, if you don't harness it and focus it on a specific target and hold it there you're never going to accomplish as much as your ability warrants."[5] Correct principles have an interesting way of showing up in a variety of applications. You may not be a body-builder, but you can still gain value from Arnold Schwarzenegger's use of focused attention in becoming the greatest bodybuilder of his generation.

> *While you're doing an exercise, if you concentrate and visualize your muscles growing while commanding and demanding them to grow, the results will come much faster. The mental picture you form of what you want to be and what you want to accomplish can greatly aid your progress toward attaining those goals. … Every repetition of every set was done with intense concentration.*[6]

Schwarzenegger's use of mental imagery bears strong resemblance to the "eye of faith" described by Moroni: "And there were many whose faith

---

4 Bill Gates, "One-on-One with Bill Gates," Scott Eason, CNBC.com, August 29, 2007.

5 Zig Ziglar, *See You at the Top*, (Greta, LA: Pelican Publishing Company, 1975, 2010), 166.

6 Arnold Schwarzenegger, https://www.muscleandfitness.com/features/active-lifestyle/arnold-schwarzeneggers-muscle-building-mental-strategy.

was so exceedingly strong, even before Christ came, who could not be kept from within the veil, *but truly saw with their eyes the things which they had beheld with an eye of faith*, and they were glad" (Ether 12:19, emphasis added)! Researcher and author, Sharon Begley, sheds more light on the power and potential of focused attention and its effects on our brain and our memory.

> *Attention must be paid. Even without knowing exactly how mind influences brain, neuroscientists have evidence that it somehow involves paying attention.... for instance, millions of neurons are registering the images of the letters on this page, as well as the white space between the letters ... you are not really seeing the white spaces, because you are not paying attention to them as you are the black lines and curves. Without attention, information that our senses take in—what we see, hear, feel, smell, and taste—literally does not register in the mind. ... What you see is determined by what you pay attention to.*[7]

As we gain appreciation for the law of focused attention, our personal vision of ourselves also grows. The Spirit warms our soul, urging us to believe in higher things for ourselves. Seeing us from the eternal possibilities as God sees us, modern apostles beckon us to strive harder to develop our concentration and the powers of our minds. Apostle Orson Hyde spoke boldly of the mind and what can be accomplished by concentrating its powers:

> *When Moses was leading the children of Israel out of Egypt, they murmured because they had no water to drink. He was grieved with them, but he had power to concentrate his mind. And what power was there in that mind? He smote the rock, and out gushed the water. Did his rod have power to split the rock? No; but the concentration of his*

---

7 Sharon Begley, *Train Your Mind, Change Your Brain,* (New York: HarperCollins Publishers, 2002), 156–157.

mind on that rock did. There was a power in it to split the rock and bring out water to the thirsty thousands.[8]

He equated Moses' "concentration of his mind" with the power of faith, describing the exercise of faith as "a concentrated effort of mind." He further declared:

The mind is armed with almighty power; and if we could concentrate its powers, and overcome the power of the Devil, we could remove that mountain as easily as to heal a sick person. It requires only faith as a grain of mustard seed, or a concentrated effort of mind.

Then, Elder Hyde comes directly to the essence of this chapter.

Let the mind be concentrated, and it possesses almighty power. It is the agent of the Almighty clothed with mortal tabernacles, and we must learn to discipline it, and bring it to bear on one point, and not allow the Devil to interfere and confuse it, nor divert it from the great object we have in view.[9]

Visioneering: A State of Mind and a Way of Concentrating the Mind

Concentrating our mind and exercising our faith are closely related and go hand in glove, opening up huge possibilities for each of us, temporally and spiritually. To explain what I mean, let me suggest an additional term for your vocabulary: Visioneering.

Visioneering describes both a state of mind and a way of using the mind; and far surpasses cursory visualization. As a jet is to a kite, a Formula One race car to a bicycle, so the principle of *visioneering the future as though it were the present,* ranks as the primary component of the creative process,

8 Orson Hyde, *Journal of Discourses,* Vol. 7, 152–153.
9 Hyde, *Journal of Discourses,* Vol. 7, 153.

a form of spiritual creation. In the Book of Ether, we find precious truths found nowhere else in our standard works, such as an expanded reference to "seeing with an eye of faith" (Ether 12:19). After presenting a sort of Lehite spiritual Hall of Fame—a list of those on the American continent who experienced mighty miracles through faith, including the moving account of the Brother of Jared piercing the veil, Moroni shares a pearl of great price. "And there *were many* whose faith was so exceedingly strong, even before Christ came, who could not be kept from within the veil, but truly saw with their eyes *the things which they had beheld with an eye of faith*, and they were glad" [10] (Ether 12:19). Note there were *many* who had envisioned stunning spiritual experiences in their mind's eye before they came to be in reality. These spiritual attainments were first experienced as imagery in the mind, and were developed and held in such vivid detail, that all doubt was erased, and the powers of heaven could not be stayed. They *had* to come into being. Let he that hath eyes to see, let him see.

The value of visioneering appears in the fifth chapter of Alma in the Book of Mormon. Likening the scriptures unto ourselves, Alma asks us to picture ourselves standing before the throne of judgment with the purest of judges smiling down upon us in glorious perfection. If you take a moment to actually do that, then you will appreciate what Alma was doing to jolt his brethren out of their state of complacency. Picturing yourself literally standing before God in an unclean, unsanctified state, you sense in a deep and poignant way that in that moment no one would dare feign purity and worthiness. The full humbling and motivating power of Alma's warning to thoroughly and honestly repent becomes operative and apparent *only if* we slow down and vividly project ourselves forward in time and sincerely "prehearse" that experience. In fact, let us do that. As Alma walks us through a series of introspective questions,[11] we can accept his words and endeavor

10 "And they were glad" has got to be one of the "All Time Understatements in History."

11 See Alma 5:14–24.

to actually experience—see, hear, and feel—the future that he testifies will surely be a reality one day. In verse 14, Alma asks us to carefully consider the penetrating question, "Have ye spiritually been born of God?" To help us introspect more deeply, he helps us understand what is meant by the scriptural term "born of God" here in the flesh. In the scriptures, there are two designations for the spirit children of God. Those born into this state of mortality, thereby being cut off from the presence of God, are called "the sons of men," "the daughters of men" and "the children of men." When mortals, faithfully and fully comply with the principles and ordinances of the gospel of Jesus Christ, and *actually receive* the Holy Ghost who sanctifies their souls,[12] they become new creatures. Such devoted ones are then referred to as "the children of Christ, his sons, and his daughters,"[13] and they are no longer the children of men. This understanding helps us to appreciate the weight and magnitude of Alma's penetrating question, "Have ye spiritually been born of God?" along with his two follow-up questions, "Have ye received his image in your countenance?" and "Have ye experienced this mighty change in your hearts?" We now understand that Alma is not using figurative language; he is speaking literally.

That Alma expects us to delve deeply into a concerted spiritual exploration, not just skim the surface, is evident by yet another question, "Do you *look forward with an eye of faith* and *view* this mortal body raised in immortality … to stand before God to be judged …." Plainly, he is urging us to take his plea seriously, with real intent, and to use our ability to project ourselves forward in time (visioneering) and put ourselves into a pre-hearsal of that most telling of moments.

If you are "likening the scriptures unto yourself," and pausing for a moment not only to picture but also put yourself in the moment—seeing, hearing and feeling—the surroundings, the Holy Being, clothed in brilliant

12 Mosiah 27: 24–26.
13 Mosiah 5:7.

white, with radiant celestial glory beaming from His smiling face, then you are going where Alma wants you to go and experiencing what he invites you to experience. And the rest of his guided visioneering will have significantly more impact and value for you.

"I say unto you," he continues, "can you *imagine* to yourselves [literally envision in your mind] that ye *hear the voice of the Lord*, saying unto you, in that day: Come unto me ye blessed, for behold, your works have been the works of righteousness upon the face of the earth?" Notice, he is asking you to involve other senses, not just the visual. He wants you to be so "in the moment" that you *hear the voice of the Lord* utter the blessed commendation.

Next Alma urges us to envision a very different encounter with God: "Or do ye *imagine to yourselves* that ye can lie unto the Lord in that day, and say—Lord, our works have been righteous works upon the face of the earth—and that he will save you? Or … can ye imagine yourselves brought before the tribunal of God with your souls filled with guilt and remorse, having a remembrance of all your guilt, yea, a perfect remembrance of all your wickedness, yea, a remembrance that ye have set at defiance the commandments of God?"[14] If you pause to accept Alma's recommendation, you will undoubtedly sense the utter desolation you would feel and how utterly wrong it would be to attempt to lie your way through such an interview. Alma repeatedly invites us to "look up" and "look forward," and he asks us "how will any of you feel," in order to get a true picture of where we stand spiritually. He asks, "Are your garments stained with blood and all manner of filthiness?" knowing the question will have an awakening effect on his readers in response to such a stirring vision.

You might even choose to picture being in the congregation Alma was addressing. As you engage in his "conference address," it is not all that

---

14 Alma 5:14–24.

difficult to picture Alma and the tone of his delivery. I doubt he delivered his words in harsh, judgmental tones. Given he experienced a dramatic and painful conversion himself, he was likely filled with overflowing compassion for those he called his beloved brethren. I imagine him articulating these introspective questions with a lump in his throat, tears welling up in his eyes, and his voice quavering.

Concentrate on What Matters Most—Eternally

You can do just about anything, but you cannot do everything. There's just not enough time to do it all. This limitation is by divine design. As a divinely planned litmus test of our values and where our heart lies, Heavenly Father offers a field of unlimited possibilities. There is no end to the useful and righteous ways we could spend our time, let alone the equally infinite list of evil and selfish ways. Why? Because it forces us to make choices. By our choices we manifest our true desires and level of commitment. How we choose to spend our time puts our true priorities and values on display and will be the essence of our judgment. Consider Elder Richard G. Scott's warning: "Part of that testing here is to have so many seemingly interesting things to do that we can forget the main purposes for being here. Satan works very hard so that the essential things won't happen."[15] And what is the test? Our use of our agency in the matrix of time shows clearly who or what we worship. Rather than skimming the two questions he poses, may I suggest taking a moment to prayerfully ponder and record your thoughts as prompted by the Holy Ghost: "Study the things you do in your discretionary time, that time you are free to control. Do you find that it is centered in those things that are of highest priority and of greatest importance? Or do you unconsciously, consistently fill it with trivia and activities that are not of enduring value nor help you

15 Scott, Richard G., "Jesus Christ, Our Redeemer." *Ensign,* May 1997, 54.

accomplish the purpose for which you came to earth?"[16] Elder Scott goes on to counsel us to take a look at the broader landscape of our life in light of the eternal rewards at stake. "Think of the long view of life, not just what's going to happen today or tomorrow. Don't give up what you most want in life for something you think you want now."[17]

Now comes the golden nugget embedded in his message. Are you just socially and culturally engaged in the Church? Or are you living your life so the doctrines of the priesthood (applying to both men and women) are distilling upon your soul as the dews of heaven? It may be revealing to consider that "dews" are the *daily doses* of moisture bestowed from above. "The essential things must be accomplished during your testing period on earth," counsels the apostle. "They must have first priority. They must not be sacrificed for lesser things, even though they are good and worthwhile accomplishments. Be wise and don't let good things crowd out those that are essential. What *are* the essential ones? *They are related to doctrine.*"[18]

Sealing his message of earnest counsel, spoken in the tone of a plea, Elder Scott utters a voice of warning: "Whether you intend to or not, when you live as though the Savior and His teachings are only one of many other important priorities in your life, you are clearly on the road to disappointment and likely on the path to tragedy."[19]

Loving God With All Our Heart, Mind, Might and Strength

To Moses on Sinai, Jehovah said "For I the Lord God am a jealous God," (Exo. 20:5) as part of what is dubbed the Law of Moses. This law was given by the God of Abraham, Isaac, and Jacob as a schoolmaster to bring a wayward people back to the path they had left. The heart of this

16 Scott, "Jesus Christ, Our Redeemer," *Ensign*, May 1997, 58.
17 Ibid., 58.
18 Ibid., 54, emphasis added.
19 Ibid., 58.

preparatory gospel was the Decalogue—the Ten Commandments. The first of the ten is "Thou shalt have no other Gods before me" (Exo. 20:3). Nothing is to take priority over our love for and worship of our God. Our Savior, the selfsame being who gave the Decalogue to Moses, taught the same truth during His mortal ministry: "Thou shalt love the Lord thy God with all thy heart, and with all thy soul, and with all thy mind. This is the first and great commandment" (Matt. 22:37–38).

Why is loving God above all others and above all else the first and great commandment in both the preparatory gospel and the higher law Christ taught? Elder Dieter F. Uchtdorf answers the question plainly.

> *God the Eternal Father did not give that first great commandment because He needs us to love Him. His power and glory are not diminished should we disregard, deny, or even defile His name. … No, God does not need us to love Him. But oh, how we need to love God! For what we love determines what we seek. What we seek determines what we think and do. What we think and do determines who we are—and who we will become.*[20]

Should we be amazed then that one of Lucifer's primary objectives would be to divert us from focusing on God and get us to divide our love and attention into fragmented pieces? Should we be surprised that God forewarned us about how Satan would go about his deceptive diversions? Upon declaring the first commandment, Jehovah gives the second, which is actually an adjunct to the first, rather than a separate commandment. God cautions us and explains what might get in the way of us keeping the first. He warns us to not get distracted by idols and false gods—especially and specifically *images of our own making*. Pointedly, God enjoins us to beware of bowing down to them—having them set before our faces,

20 Dieter F. Uchtdorf, "The Love of God," *Ensign*, November 2009, 21–22.

holding them in our hands, staring at them hour after hour. The Lord doesn't just urge us, He commands us *to make unto ourselves* no graven images.[21] We may look down upon the idol worshipers of the past. Yet, if we were to count the hours this generation spends staring at screens filled with images, one could make a fairly strong case that we are the most idolatrous generation ever to walk this planet. Like the Pied Piper, SKAM lulls us into a stupor of thought as he leads us away from our eternal values and goals, substituting counterfeits, usurpers of time and attention, and air-brushed streams of tantalizing images. With a little twist here and a temptation there, he induces us to bow down and serve to-do lists and schedules, not to mention tweets, texts, posts, and likes on social media. Today, it is so easy to be "online and up to date" with the world, while being "offline and out of touch" with our Heavenly Father.

Elder Joseph B. Wirthlin warned of this trap:

> *I fear that some members of the Lord's Church "live far beneath our privileges" with regard to the gift of the Holy Ghost. Some are distracted by the things of the world that block out the influence of the Holy Ghost, preventing them from recognizing spiritual promptings. This is a noisy and busy world that we live in. Remember that being busy is not necessarily being spiritual. If we are not careful, the things of this world can crowd out the things of the Spirit. Some are spiritually deadened and past feeling because of their choices to commit sin. Others simply hover in spiritual complacency with no desire to rise above themselves and commune with the Infinite. If they would open their hearts to the refining influence of this unspeakable gift of the Holy Ghost, a glorious new spiritual dimension would come to light. Their eyes would gaze upon a vista scarcely imaginable. They could know for*

21 A graven image is a "carved" man-made idol—often self-made and sometimes handheld.

themselves things of the Spirit that are choice, precious, and capable of enlarging the soul, expanding the mind, and filling the heart with inexpressible joy.[22]

Specifically calling our attention to the "unspeakable gift of the Holy Ghost," Elder Wirthlin points to glorious blessings we forfeit by allowing our priorities to drift from the essentials alluded to earlier by Elder Scott. What could be more essential for us than to prayerfully evaluate our priorities? And what could be more valuable than seeking the Lord's continuous revelation in refining them as we progress?

But *One* Thing is Needful: The Mary and Martha Principle

Since you can think only one thought at a time, you can also do only one thing at a time—and, as the Lord taught Martha and all His disciples, each choice has eternal consequences.

But Martha was cumbered about much serving, and came to him, and said, Lord, dost thou not care that my sister hath left me to serve alone? bid her therefore that she help me. And Jesus answered and said unto her, Martha, Martha, thou art careful and troubled about many things: But one thing is needful: and Mary hath chosen that good part, which shall not be taken away from her (Luke 10:40–42).

One thing is needful for each of us at any given time. Many things can be good and some can be better. But only one thing can be best. Of all possible choices at that once-in-a-lifetime moment in the home of Simon the Leper, did not Mary's choice represent the best? Was it not the "one needful thing"—the best of all possible options at that moment? For those who believe God can make more of their lives than they can, they constantly seek to know their "one needful thing." Fasting and praying to know the

22 Joseph B. Wirthlin, "The Unspeakable Gift," *Ensign*, May 2003, 26.

Lord's will for them becomes their way of life. Through personal revelation they gain keen awareness of what is needful and what is a distraction. And they focus. Not many worthy practices for Sabbath Day worship surpasses seeking Heavenly Father's answer to the question, "At this time, Father, what is the one needful thing for me to focus on right now?"

CHAPTER 17

Avoiding Division and Contention

Zion is both a society and a city. Perfecting and purifying the people comes first. When the people become Zion—the pure in heart (D&C 97:21), they build a city called Zion. Note the sequence in the description of Enoch's Zion:

> *And the Lord blessed the land, and they were blessed upon the mountains, and upon the high places, and did flourish.*
>
> *And the Lord called his people Zion, because they were of one heart and one mind, and dwelt in righteousness; and there was no poor among them.*
>
> *And Enoch continued his preaching in righteousness unto the people of God. And it came to pass in his days, that he built a city that was called the City of Holiness, even ZION (Moses 7:17–19).*

No doubt the City of Enoch was glorious. What greater evidence could there be than the inhabitants and their city—gardens, cows, and carrots—being translated and taken up to dwell in the presence of the Lord. Despite the grandeur of this event, we have only the scant details recorded in the passage above. In the Book of Mormon, we find a description of the Nephites who established Zion following the appearance of the Lord. Let us consider carefully the verses in 4 Nephi; "[T]he people were all converted unto the Lord … both Nephites and Lamanites, and there were no contentions and disputations among them, and every man did deal justly one with another" (4 Ne 1:2). Note Mormon's emphasis on one particular quality: "no contentions and disputations among them." Of all the attributes they surely possessed that could have been mentioned—faith, virtue, knowledge, temperance, patience, brotherly kindness, godliness, charity, humility, diligence—the first is "no contentions and disputations among them." A few verses later, we read, "And it came to pass that there was no contention among all the people, in all the land; but there were mighty miracles wrought among the disciples of Jesus" (4 Ne 1:13). Mormon, knowing his words were meant for the people in the latter days, again puts particular emphasis on the absence of contention, connecting it with the working of mighty miracles. Verse 15 reads, "And it came to pass that there was no contention in the land, because of the love of God which did dwell in the hearts of the people." Here Mormon links the lack of contention with the indwelling love of God—charity—the pure love of Christ. Verse 16 reads, "There were no envyings, nor strifes, nor tumults, nor whoredoms, nor lyings, nor murders, nor any manner of lasciviousness; and surely there could not be a happier people among all the people who had been created by the hand of God." How wonderful; and how different from the worldwide contention we know today—the complete antithesis.

Along with all the emphasis on the absence of contention, Mormon set forth another key attribute of the people. There were no cliques, factions, or denominations. There was no division among the people. They were of one heart and one mind—one in Christ: "There were no robbers, nor murderers, neither were there Lamanites, nor any manner of -ites; but they were in one, the children of Christ, and heirs to the kingdom of God. And how blessed were they! For the Lord did bless them in all their doings… and there was no contention in all the land" (4 Ne 1:17–18).

Whatever the will and work of the Father and the Son may be, the exact opposite is the will and work of the adversary, affirmed and encapsulated in one of his names, the anti-Christ. As the name clearly denotes the anti-Christ is adamantly against anything and everything Christ represents, embodies and stands for. If Christ's mission is to build up Zion, the anti-Christ's mission is to prevent it or tear it down. If Christ promotes peace, Lucifer promotes contention. If Christ promotes benevolence and brotherly kindness, Lucifer sows hatred and hostility. If Christ inspires oneness and agreement, Lucifer fosters division and separation. If Christ encourages gathering and uniting, Lucifer causes dispersion and isolation.

Among the more prominent lines of thinking Satan seeks to germinate are unkind, antipathetic, anti-social thoughts that impede and disrupt loving relationships. Any and all thoughts that lead to anger and bad feelings towards others are of satanic origin. So are any thoughts that lead to animosity, envy, hatred, jealousy, impatience, censure, resentment or judgment. Any lines of thinking that lead to or cause division, separation, contention, disagreement, disputation or strife are satanic devilish thoughts.

The following scriptures clearly warn us of Satan's intent and tactics:

> *For verily, verily I say unto you, he that hath the spirit of contention is not of me, but is of the devil, who is the father of contention, and he stirreth up the hearts of men to contend with anger, one with another (3 Ne. 11:29).*

> *Verily, verily, I say unto you, that Satan has great hold upon their hearts; he stirreth them up to iniquity against that which is good. … Yea, he stirreth up their hearts to anger against this work (D&C 10:20, 24).*

> *And now behold, my son, I fear lest the Lamanites shall destroy this people; for they do not repent, and Satan stirreth them up continually to anger one with another (Moroni 9:3).*[1]

How Satan Sows Seeds of Animosity and Hatred

Lucifer kept the Lamanites constantly stirred up to anger against the Nephites by convincing them they were victims. Here is the story he planted in their heads: "*Your fathers, Laman and Lemuel, were the elder sons of Lehi and righteous men who were entitled to be the heirs of their father's wealth and earthly estate. Their younger brother was a schemer and a scoundrel. The evil Nephi concocted and executed a plan to rob your fathers of their birthright and their inheritance, and he succeeded. He dragged them out into the wilderness and ....* " The more the adversary was able to get them to view their history from the standpoint of being innocent victims, the angrier they became.

The interesting thing about victim thinking is the reversal that takes place in the mind of the victim thinker. When people feel they have been wronged by unfair forces beyond their control, they initially get defensive. As they foment on the perceived injustice and unfairness of their situation, they collect evidence of all the ways they have been mistreated and wronged. Once SKAM gets them percolating on this line of thinking, he can then spin a monologue of half-truths and exaggerations that shifts them from defensive to offensive. SKAM further urges, "*It's not fair, and you don't have to take it any longer. You need to stand up for yourself. Toughen up. Get angry. Strike back. Make them pay for all they've done to you.*"

When we think like victims, we tend to take the bumps and jolts of life as personal affronts. From that perspective, disappointing events don't just happen, they seem to happen *to* us or upon us. In victim mode, the

1 See also 2 Ne. 28:19; Alma 27:12; Mosiah 23:15; 3 Ne. 11:29; D&C 136:23.

tendency is to then find a scapegoat—someone to blame and resent. The sly part of Satan's ploy is that in order for the thinker to play the part of a victim, there has to be another player in the drama. There has to be a villain! Villainizing other people is a classic satanic strategy—a sure way to create contention, animosity, hostility and eventually violence—everything antithetical to the characteristics of Zion.

This satanic maneuver plays out on many levels and in many arenas. We see it at the heart of geo-political tension that often turns into armed conflicts and wars. It has reached epidemic proportions in national and state politics and is employed as a prime way of getting votes. Look no further than the prevalence of the distorted negative campaign ads in the media. Contention is a prominent dynamic in occupational, familial and marital discord as well. In all of these settings, victim thinking shows up as blaming, fault-finding, and deflecting responsibility. Whenever anything is one hundred percent another person's fault, you know for sure you're in victim mode, toiling under the influence of the anti-Christ.

Blaming is a Dangerous Habit

Blaming and shifting responsibility are as addictive and destructive as cocaine. Blaming can become so habitual we're not even consciously aware of how often we use it. Let me give you a specific example. Being offended is a form of blaming. When we say, "Someone offended me," we're placing the responsibility for our emotions on the other person. The Diagram shows this to be an erroneous premise. No one can *make* you mad. Your anger comes from the victim thoughts proposed by SKAM and accepted and amplified by you.

Elder David A. Bednar delivered a clear message about victim thinking and the consequences of seeing ourselves as an effect rather than a cause. He first states that being offended is a choice.

> *When we believe or say we have been offended, we usually mean we feel insulted, mistreated, snubbed, or disrespected. And certainly clumsy, embarrassing, unprincipled, and mean-spirited things do occur in our interactions with other people that would allow us to take offense. However, it ultimately is impossible for another person to offend you or to offend me. Indeed, believing that another person offended us is fundamentally false. To be offended is a* choice *we make; it is not a* condition *inflicted or imposed upon us by someone or something else.*[2]

Then he illustrates the significant consequences that ensue when we choose a victim mentality and take offense.

> *Let me make sure I understand what has happened to you. Because someone at church offended you, you have not been blessed by the ordinance of the sacrament. You have withdrawn yourself from the constant companionship of the Holy Ghost. Because someone at church offended you, you have cut yourself off from priesthood ordinances and the holy temple. You have discontinued your opportunity to serve others and to learn and grow. And you are leaving barriers that will impede the spiritual progress of your children, your children's children, and the generations that will follow.*[3]

Our hearts have to go out to those who make this error in judgment. They have allowed Lucifer to deceive them into thinking their disengagement and withdrawal somehow hurts the perceived offender. In actuality, however, like so many of Satan's tactics, victim thinking is designed to backfire and wound the choosers and rob them of joy and blessings.

The most startling example of the tragic effects of taking offense is Judas Iscariot:

---

2 Bednar, "And Nothing Shall Offend Them," *Ensign*, November 2006, 90.

3 Ibid., 89.

> *Nevertheless, Judas Iscariot, even one of the twelve, went unto the chief priests, to betray Jesus unto them, for he turned away from him and was offended because of his words. And when the chief priests heard of him, they were glad, and promised to give him money (JST Mark 14:31).*

Never Suppress a Peace-Making Thought

A married couple had an argument over what seemed at the moment to be a major issue. Words were exchanged. IQs were questioned. Judgments about who is actually "the stubborn one" in the marriage were levied. A Cold War ensued. Both went about their routine activities in the home with icy efficiency, each endeavoring to avoid eye-to-eye, much less physical contact, at all costs. Meanwhile, SKAM was having a field day manipulating their thoughts and stoking their individual pride. If we could plant a listening device into their inner world of thoughts, it might sound something like this: "I don't need to apologize—this isn't my fault. I didn't start this. Besides I'm always the one who apologizes first. I deserve to be apologized to for once." When we get into those lines of thinking we offend and repel the Spirit. Negative feelings result and, though we may not recognize it right away, our own spirit is wounded. We feel empty, unloved, and disconsolate. These feelings trigger an escalation of antipathetic and selfish thoughts. "I don't deserve this kind of treatment. This whole thing is not working out. I never should have gotten into this situation. I feel like walking out this door and never coming back." Notice, that "walking out this door" is not a *feeling* at all. It's actually another one of SKAM's thought injections that he's disguising as a "feeling." In reality it's his suggestion about what action he'd like us to take. Running out, fleeing an uncomfortable situation, is a poor "solution," which is, of course, exactly why Satan wants you to fall for it. It only promotes greater separation and division—distancing you all the more from the one you love, preventing you from coming back together and working things out. Simultaneously, he is endeavoring to separate and distance you from God. When you're entertaining these kinds of thoughts and fanning these kinds of negative emotions, the last thing you feel like doing is praying. So, again, when you come to terms with SKAM's actual motive and objective, what is the solution? Disobey him. Do exactly the opposite. Consciously choose to stop dwelling on how unfairly you've been treated. Stop spending mental energy recruiting and bringing back all of your past grievances which SKAM will happily research and supply you with the longer you wallow in victim thinking.

SKAM wants you to refrain from making an apology and saying "I'm sorry. It was my fault." So, what's the first thing to do? Set aside your pride and break the ice barrier between you and your spouse with a sincere, "Honey, let's cut this out. I apologize. I'm sorry. I know I could've done better. Honestly, I'm sorry. I love you. I hate the feelings that come when I'm separated from you. Can we talk this over and work out a better way?"

Let me share the reflection of someone who applied this suggestion:

> *When I stop for a second and think about where those thoughts lead, it's always to the same place: a continuation of the contention. He wants me to believe that I am owed something, like an apology, and, not having received one, I am justified in not doing what I know is right. It is the victim mentality you describe. I remember hearing a man say that he admires those who are able to apologize first even when they know it is not their fault. What a revelation: apologizing is a trait to be admired, not feared. Why am I so afraid of being the one to apologize first? Why don't I race to be that person? The only reason I can think of is because Spook tells me there's something wrong with that.*[4]

4 Personal confidential correspondence, used with permission. Name withheld.

The Antidote for Division

As the Lord contrasted His higher law with the lesser or preparatory law, He pointed to a set of particular virtues now known as the Beatitudes. To each He appended a specific blessing—a particular holy reward. Such emphasis indicates how much He desires His true disciples to pay attention, seek for and cultivate those attributes. Not surprisingly, the Prince of Peace stressed peace-making as one of the higher virtues. "And blessed are all the peacemakers, for they shall be called the children of God" (3 Ne. 12:9).

One principle stands supreme in countering the division and contention the adversary is implanting in the hearts of people across the world. No other act can produce more healing, relief, and cleansing. The divine principle that can cure discord among brethren, heal wounded souls, and bring peace to any relationship on any scale is *forgiveness.*

When people are not of one mind and one heart it is generally because selfishness and pride have separated the parties. The cure is unilateral forgiveness, not waiting for the other party to change or request it. Elder Dieter F. Uchtdorf taught:

> *The people around us are not perfect. People do things that annoy, disappoint, and anger. In this mortal life it will always be that way. Nevertheless, we must let go of our grievances. Part of the purpose of mortality is to learn how to let go of such things. That is the Lord's way. Remember, heaven is filled with those who have this in common: They are forgiven. And they forgive. Lay your burden at the Savior's feet. Let go of judgment. Allow Christ's Atonement to change and heal your heart. … The merciful will obtain mercy.*[5]

Nothing will bring greater joy and peace to the one who forgives, irrespective of whether the other party deserves or acknowledges or even

5 Uchtdorf, "The Merciful Shall Obtain Mercy," *Ensign,* May 2012, 77.

accepts the act and expression of forgiveness. The forgiver always receives an outpouring of the Spirit; sometimes it's more than an outpouring, it's more like a flood.

Forgiving One Who Dissembled

The beloved hymn, "Now Let Us Rejoice," was written by William W. Phelps, who composed many cherished and oft-sung latter-day anthems. The second verse begins, "We'll love one another and never dissemble, but cease to do evil and ever be one." Shockingly, later on W.W. Phelps did dissemble. After being excommunicated for improper financial dealings in Far West, he became a bitter enemy of the Prophet Joseph Smith and the Church. William's testimony in court against Joseph and others led to their incarceration.[6] Joseph and his fellow prisoners suffered in Liberty Jail during the frigid Missouri winter from December 1, 1838 to April 6, 1839. It was also partly on Phelps' testimony that Lilburn W. Boggs, governor of Missouri, issued the infamous "extermination order" driving the saints out of the state, destitute and homeless, leaving trails of blood in the snow.

In 1840, a repentant Phelps wrote to the Prophet pleading for Joseph's forgiveness and permission to be re-baptized.[7] Being as mortal as the next man, it would not have been surprising had the prophet denied, or at least delayed his response for several months or a year or two. One could have reasoned the prolonged separation would do William some good and make sure he learned his lesson. The response of the Prophet was prompt and heartfelt. He wrote back,

> *It is true, that we have suffered much in consequence of your behavior—the cup of gall, already enough for mortals to drink, was indeed filled*

6 Joseph Smith, Jr., *History of the Church,* Vol. 3, (Salt Lake City: Deseret Book Company, 1970), 359.

7 Smith, *History of the Church,* Vol. 4, 141–142.

> *to overflowing when you turned against us. … However, the cup has been drunk, the will of our Father has been done, and we are yet alive, for which we thank the Lord.… Believing your confession to be real, and your repentance genuine, I shall be happy once again to give you the right hand of fellowship, and rejoice over the returning prodigal. … Come on, dear brother, since the war is past, for friends at first, are friends again at last.*[8]

Shortly after the Prophet Joseph Smith was martyred, William W. Phelps, receiving inspiration from on high, composed "Praise to the Man," the soul-stirring hymn that never fails to rouse and edify the hearts of all who love the one who communed with Jehovah.

8 Smith, Vol. 4, 163–164.

CHAPTER 18

Vanquishing Fear

Fear and doubt cannot coexist in the same mind with confidence and faith. They have to be exchanged for one another. So taught the Prophet Joseph Smith:

> *Where doubt and uncertainty are, there faith is not, nor can it be. For doubt and faith do not exist in the same person at the same time; so that persons whose minds are under doubts and fears cannot have unshaken confidence; and where unshaken confidence is not, there faith is weak."*[1]

If no two thoughts can occupy your mind at the same time, it means by choosing one thought you are deselecting and blocking all other thoughts.

Bouts of fear are common to all of us. Some people are afflicted more than others, but no one is entirely exempt. If you are bedeviled with fear and doubt, it is time to increase your commitment to shift from a passive state to an active one. You don't have to erase them or unthink them; and you can go well beyond trying to simply ignore them. The most

1 Smith, *Lectures on Faith,* Lecture Sixth, 12.

effective approach is to override and replace them by firmly redirecting your attention to things of the Spirit. Redirecting your focus becomes much easier and effective when you recognize where the negatives are coming from, who is behind them all, and why he's trying to deceive you. It makes sense, therefore, to delve a little deeper into the satanic strategy of inflicting fear.

The Anatomy of Fear

Fear is a state of mind with an emotional wallop attached. It acts so immediately—the onset of fear is so rapid—it's as though there's no interpretative gap at all. One moment we're calm and serene, minding our own business, and in the blink of an eye, zap!—out of nowhere we get hit with a taser-like jolt of fear. The impulse goes from thought to emotion to physical impact so rapidly our bodies are thrust into defense mode before our minds have a chance to be aware of it, let alone make a conscious choice. Biologically, this rapid response serves a worthwhile purpose. When a physical threat is perceived, instantaneous reaction triggers a fight-or-flee response for defensive purposes. It is an essential survival mechanism for our protection. Satan also uses it as a weapon against us.

Lucifer has the power to inflict fear and he uses it liberally. President Gordon B. Hinckley taught, "Fear comes not of God, but rather … from the adversary."[2] Elder M. Russell Ballard said, "Doubt and fear are tools of Satan."[3] Elder John A. Widtsoe said, "Fear is the devil's first and chief tool."[4] Why? What satanic purpose does injecting God's children with fear serve and why is it so frequently smeared upon us? Fear is one of Satan's most potent and prevalent ploys because it is

2 *Teachings of Presidents of the Church: Gordon B. Hinckley,* (Church of Jesus Christ of Latter-day Saints), 338

3 M. Russell Ballard, "Pure Testimony", *Ensign,* November 2004.

4 John A. Widtsoe, *Conference Report,* (Church of Jesus Christ of Latter-day Saints, April 1950), 127.

so effective at impeding our progress. Fear *stops us from taking action.* Elder F. Enzio Busche was the first general authority of the Church called from his native Germany. When taught by the missionaries, his wife, Jutta, accepted the good news of the gospel quite readily. Brother Busche, however, struggled mightily with fear as Satan tried to prevent him from being baptized.

> *One of the powers the adversary has is to fill us with fear. I was sometimes in complete panic as I thought about becoming a member of the LDS church. I was tortured with wondering what my parents would say, what my customers would think, and how my children might feel later on in their lives. I worried about continuing to achieve a good livelihood if I were considered an outcast in German society. How could I withdraw from all the influential circles of which I was a part? My feelings of panic were so acute that there were periods when I hated the time that the missionaries came because I was not innocent anymore. I could no longer say that I did not know the truth. I hated the predicament in which I found myself, and I almost wished I had never listened to the missionaries in the first place."*[5]

Could the prevalence of fear in our minds possibly be because it works so well? Is there any other emotion that grips us and chokes the air out of our will quite as effectively? Were we to actually calculate all the times fear has stopped us from pursuing a goal or kept us from learning a new skill, I believe the sum would be staggering. How much of our greatness has fear stolen over the years? How much will it continue to rob us in the future? Emily Dickinson urges us to consider such questions.

---

5 F. Enzio Busche, *Yearning for the Living God,* (Salt Lake City: Deseret Book Company, 2004), 78.

We never know how high we are
Till we are called to rise;
And then, if we are true to plan,
Our statures touch the skies—

The Heroism we recite
Would be a daily thing,
Did not ourselves the Cubits warp
For fear to be a King—[6]

We Can Override Fear

Although we seldom think of them as such, fear and doubt are states of mind—meaning we have the power to choose whether they go or stay. Like any other thoughts, we have the ability to examine them and make the choice to put up with them or reject and replace them. Again, it comes down to choice. This incontrovertible right to choose puts us in charge. When rightly viewed, this truth is extremely empowering. None of us are victims, powerless to change our ways or outcomes. The circumstances in which we are born and the events that take place over the course of our lives influence our decisions and actions greatly. Yet, in the final analysis, they do not *determine* them. You are free to interpret your past and your present any way you want. Whatever circumstances you face right now do not determine how you experience them. One of my favorite comic strips is "Family Circle," created by Bil Keane. One strip shows the mother greeting her ten-year old daughter Dolly coming through the front door after attending a birthday party. Thel (the Mom) asks, "How was the party?" Dolly replies, "Terrible! Worst one ever." Before she can find out why, Jeffy the younger brother comes through the door, and Thel asks him

6 Emily Dickinson, *The Complete Poems of Emily Dickinson,* (Boston, New York, London: Little, Brown and Company, 1960), Poem 1176.

the same question, "How was the party?" Jeffy responds enthusiastically, "It was awesome! Tommy threw up all over his birthday cake." Moral of the Story: The quality of a party is in the eye of the interpreter. We decide how we look at and interpret events, even *future* events. The basis of a lot of our most gripping fears is the interpretation of something that has not even happened as yet.

Frequently, SKAM implants the idea that the future is a threatening, scary place, full of catastrophes because it allows our imaginations (along with his help) to abide in fear. "Terrible things beyond your control are going to happen" is one of his favorite themes because he doesn't have to provide any evidence to prove his dire assertions. And we let him get away with it because we seldom pause to check his track record. I don't know about you, but in my head SKAM is a horrible forecaster of upcoming economic disasters. He has predicted 114 of the last three recessions. Nevertheless, I've gone along with many of his predictions of imminent disaster, and spent too many restless nights, tossing and turning in dread and fear.

And the Same Applies to Worry

Worry is sort of the warm-up act to fear, a milder form of panic, but often more prevalent and pernicious. To induce us to worry, Satan first gets us to think that a given situation is cosmically catastrophic, overblowing the damages and consequences to a degree rivaling Godzilla ravaging Tokyo in a class B horror flick. He then follows it up with the insinuation that we are powerless to do anything whatsoever about it, leading us to believe that the best thing to do is to fret and stew over it. What an ingenious no-win and no-way-out trap! Selling us on the fallacy that we can't do anything while convincing us that worrying will serve some useful purpose (which it doesn't and never will) he locks us into a continuous negative feedback loop. It's like a mental NASCAR circuit where we just go around and around the same oval and never get anywhere. Like its big brother, fear, worry locks us in a futile mental state that aids and abets inaction. Rather than making plans about what we can do to remedy a situation and take action, we get short-circuited into worry. In fact, the vise-like jaws of the worry trap rests on the fact that in many cases there *is* nothing we can do about it. It's SKAM's perfect no-win game instigated to get us to waste time, dissipate our energy and make ourselves miserable.

For instance, SKAM urges us to worry about who's going to win the next election, which way the futures markets are going to turn, and how long the drought in the West is going to last. Those may be legitimate concerns, but the point is that our fretting over them has no impact at all on how those things turn out. Yet that fact won't stop SKAM from trying to convince us otherwise. "If you worry long and hard enough," he says, "you can prevent all this mayhem from happening. Your worry will save the world! Go for it! You'll be written up in history books and they'll make a movie out of your life. Dennis saved the world because he worried all of life's threats into utter submission and ground them to powder by the overwhelming power of his fretting prowess. (I'm trying to get you to chuckle a bit, so together we can see what an ineffective option it is for us to choose worry as a solution to anything.) I hope you see the point. Worry is likely the most fruitless mental pattern we entertain in our heads. It never solves or improves anything. It only wastes time and leads to our becoming grumpy and hard to live with. Moreover, worry simultaneously impairs our ability to be in the moment and enjoy the good things happening around us. We are so wrapped up in our no-win circuit, there is no room in our one-track mind to think of anything or anyone else.

A Lesson from Bridge of Spies

The futility of worrying is well illustrated in the movie *Bridge of Spies*, a true story about how a lawyer, James B. Donovan, negotiated a prisoner exchange during the Cold War. Donovan represented a convicted Soviet KGB spy, Rudolf Abel, who is in a no-win situation. Being convicted of espionage by the United States, he is due to be executed—so the exchange would seem to be a lifesaver. However, as it turns out, the USSR wants him back so they can execute him on unproven allegations that he has divulged some of their secrets. As Donovan explains the gravity of Abel's situation, he notices that Abel is unruffled and calm.

> *D: Let's start here. If you are firm in your resolve not to cooperate with the U.S. Government …*
>
> *A: (Interrupting) I am.*
>
> *D: Then do not talk to anyone else about your case inside of government or out. Except to me, to the extent that you trust me. I have a mandate to serve you. Nobody else does. Quite frankly, everyone else has a vested interest in sending you to the electric chair.*
>
> *A: (Calmly) All right.*
>
> *D: You don't seem alarmed.*
>
> *A: (Shrugging his shoulders slightly). Would it help?*[7]

So, plain and simple, right there is a strong antidote for worry. "Would it help?" is the perfect question to ask ourselves. We don't need an app or a digital algorithm to curb and conquer worry. We need to step up and take responsibility for allowing our thoughts to go round and round on the gerbil wheel. Ask yourself, "Is this helping? Is this fixing or even mildly improving the situation?" If not, take charge and shift your thoughts to positive action you can take on something totally unrelated to the worry topic you're stuck in. Action—positive physical activity—is a proven way

---

7 *Bridge of Spies,* directed by Steven Spielberg (2015), Touchstone Pictures.

of breaking the spell. The old saw, "Don't just sit there, do something" is actually quite effective. If you can't think of something constructive on your own, drop to your knees or just bow your head, and ask, "Heavenly Father, who needs my help right now? Who needs to hear a kind word of encouragement? What action would you have me take to shake this darkness and help build thy kingdom in some small way?" Then, do it. As you will see in the case of casting out fear, expressing Heavenly Father's love to someone through service is a powerful way to supplant worry and defeat the adversary's purposes.

Origin of Fear

Fear, worry, and doubt are mental states imposed on us by the enemy of our souls like the most insistent drug dealer. Most of us would not question in the least that the Holy Spirit is constantly urging us to think and act in ways that promote happiness through spiritual striving and faith. Many of us, however, are less certain about the origin of fear and states of mind that undermine happiness, spiritual growth and faith. That uncertainty leaves us vulnerable to the effects of fear and we find it more difficult to vanquish. By their fruits ye shall know their origins. Fear is an insidious ploy inflicted upon us by the devil, rather than an inherent flaw in our spirit. As long as we think of fear as a personal defect in our character, we are far less effective in countering it. As long as we think it's about us and not him, Lucifer can hide out and compound the pain and damage using his favorite one-two punch. After imposing his thought on us, he then chides and belittles us for thinking it. With fear, the worst part is he also attaches a bit of emotional and physical poison to the thought so it stings as he injects it, and we feel it in our body as well as our mind. Medical studies on the effects of fear have shown that it damages certain parts of the brain like the hippocampus, an important part of the limbic system, which regulates emotion, learning, memory and (take note) *motivation.* Fear also weakens the immune system, opening the door to other physical maladies. As mortals we experience a wide variety of fears—heights, flying, failure, illnesses, poverty, rejection and ridicule, as well as spiders, sharks and snakes. Some of us have both a fear of speaking in sacrament meeting and a fear of asking people to speak in sacrament meeting. Though our fears may be different, no one is exempt from experiencing bouts with the adversary; and learning to defeat him is an invaluable skill.

If You Can Recognize It, You Can Rebut It

As we become more aware of the prevalence of Satan's tactics, the better we get at recognizing them for what they are and realize we don't have to sit back and take it any longer. When you stop to analyze those negative episodes, you realize *fear comes upon you.* It doesn't come *from* you. Often, the feeling comes *before* the thought or simultaneous with the thought, which is a sign that fear is not *coming from* your mind, it's *coming to* your mind—a telling sign you're being *acted upon.* The next time you are afflicted with a bout of fear or worry, take careful notice of your mental posture at that moment. Likely, you'll recognize you're in a passive posture—not *generating* the fear-producing thoughts; it's more like you are *listening* to them. As long as you continue to listen, accept and go along with the thoughts, and allow them to act upon you, fear will persist. Trust what you learned earlier in Chapter 14, "Five Effective Tactics. They work; and I can vouch for them personally. As you read my personal experience, see if you can identify how each of the five tactics were part of the solution.

My Personal Experience with Vanquishing Fear

For many years I was afflicted with sudden, almost paralyzing bouts of fear. Being a public speaker and seminar leader, I was in an almost incessant battle with what I called "stage fright." When I was just starting out, I chalked it up to inexperience and thought I'd grow out of it after delivering a number of successful seminars. It never crossed my mind that fear was a malicious assault perpetrated by the adversary. I thought a "case of the butterflies" was just part of the territory of being a newbie. However, as several months and then a few years passed, the fear episodes did not dissipate. In fact, in some cases they got dramatically worse. Once Satan learned how easily I kept falling into his snare, he kept right on using it and even ratcheting it up. (That may apply to you and your fear scenario as well.) When the stakes were high, especially when I had landed a new client with a lot of future potential if the first seminar went well, I'd suffer paroxysms of king-sized, industrial strength anxiety and fear for the weeks, yes weeks, leading up to it. I'd break out in cold sores and experience fitful sleep and sometimes nightmares.

At times I even found myself hoping the client would call up and cancel the gig. But that idiotic thought did nothing to vanquish the fear; it only shifted the pain point. I'd then find myself plagued with fear of poverty and not being able to feed my family. I hadn't yet realized where the fear was coming from. Even though there were clues, I hadn't seen that it didn't matter what the circumstances were—having a seminar to teach or not having a seminar to teach. Either way, the fear would show up suddenly, kind of out of nowhere, and I just endured and continued to suffer the effects of fear.

Over time, one of the things I began to notice was the variation in the intensity of the fear. The greater the possibilities for good that could come from the presentation, the earlier the fear would start, the more frequently it would show up, and the heavier it felt. I also noticed when the bouts of fear would show up, they occurred suddenly without any direct cause. I'd be talking with my wife about what we wanted to do on the weekend, and, wham, out of nowhere I'd get hit with *"Hey, you've got that big seminar coming up with XYZ company in three weeks, and you're totally unprepared.*

You're going to bomb. None of your stuff is good enough for this group. These are seasoned, hard-core corporate warriors who've already heard it all before. They aren't going to buy any of your soft skills stuff. They're going to eat you alive—laugh right in your face."

I found something else to be very instructive. Whether or not I was able to ward off the pre-seminar fears and minimize the suffering SKAM was trying to inflict, the seminars almost invariably went well. The Spirit was there to assist me at the last minute. The moment I opened my mouth and began to speak, the fear evaporated, confidence came, and things went well. Most of the time, the greater the pre-seminar fear, the better the seminar went, and the stronger the confirming feedback. I'd get more positive comments than usual. Driving to the airport to fly home, I'd express my gratitude to the Lord for the opportunity and His help in fulfilling it. I'd also be thinking how unnecessary all the pain and anguish I'd felt in the days or weeks prior had been. Sometimes, I'd feel a loving admonition, "O thou of little faith, wherefore didst thou doubt?" (Matt. 14:31).

Finally, with all the evidence stacked up before me, I made up my mind one day (and, yes, it was just that simple) that I was *finished with it*! On one of those drives back to the airport I just let it all loose and I vented at the top of my lungs a fifty-five-gallon barrel of pent-up rage. It was directed forcefully and personally at the master spook himself and I have not the slightest doubt he heard me and my Heavenly Father heard me. I told Lucifer in no uncertain terms I had finally seen through his nasty little ruse and was sick of it! Never again would I play along with it! I promised him anytime I felt his sneaky, slimy attempt to inject fear into my preparations for a seminar I would take it as a clear sign he was telling me it was going to be a great experience. It would also tell me there must be a lot of good that could come from it, or he wouldn't be messing with my mind. And, with that assurance, I would up my game. Instead of letting fear intimidate me, I would use it to empower me. I'd redouble my preparation efforts. I'd seek more diligently than ever for revelation and guidance about what to include and how to express it.

I have kept that promise. And, it has worked. Rarely do I now get the "pre-seminar fears" anymore and when they start creeping in, I slam the door. I raise my voice and I rebuke the spook, reiterating what I promised above. Invariably, I feel an influx of light and a surge of confidence that's hard to describe.

Fear is a Ploy to Prevent Action

Fear chokes our actions, sometimes to the point of paralysis. We become so bound up in fear we are immobilized on just about any level you care to name—mentally, physically, emotionally, and most of all spiritually. Elder F. Enzio Busche shared a highly instructive experience detailing the origin and impact of fear and the power of love to overcome and dispel it. As a newly ordained general authority, Elder Busche was touring a mission and stayed in the basement of the mission home. In the middle of the night, he was awakened by the mission president, informing him that one of his assistants was upstairs possessed by an evil spirit. The mission president's attempt to cast the evil spirit out had failed, but he was reassured knowing a general authority was in the home. "That was when he came down to wake me up …," Elder Busche related. "I immediately began to pray with a deep, fervent plea for help. I felt so helpless because I had never been in a situation like that."

Elder Busche dressed and went upstairs. "As I went up, I heard noises and unintelligent sounds, and fear began to creep into my heart. I felt that fear come from the ground, from below, trying to sneak into my system. … When I got to the living room, I saw the elder sitting in a chair, shaking all over, making uncontrolled movements, speaking with foam on his lips. His companion and the mission president and his family were all staring at the spectacle with shock and fear." Wrestling with his own fear, and uncertain as to what to do, we can sense the weight of responsibility Elder Busche was feeling coupled with a fervent desire to know the Lord's will and to do it. He recounted what happened next:

> *As I entered the room, it was like a voice said to me, "Brother Busche, you must make a decision now." I knew immediately what decision it was. I had to decide whether to join the fear and amazement and helplessness or to let faith act and let courage come in. I knew, of course, that I wanted to have faith. I wanted to have the power, the priesthood power, and I wanted to know what to do to save the situation.*[8]

At that moment scriptures about perfect love casting out fear came to his mind, particularly Moroni 7:48, which speaks about praying unto the Father with all the energy of heart, *that ye may be filled with the pure love of Christ.* Elder Busche did as he was instructed and prayed with all the energy of his heart that he might be filled with love. He then described the result,

> *After that, it was as if my skull was opened and a warm feeling poured down into my soul—down my head, my neck, my chest. As it was pouring down, it drove out all of the fear. My shivering knees stopped shaking. I stood there, a big smile came to my face—a smile of deep, satisfying joy and confidence.*

Buoyed with "great confidence," he still remained uncertain about what to do next.

> *As I stood there, it was as though someone came and put his arm around me and said, "Let me do this for you. I can take it from here." I was very*

8 Busche, *Yearning for the Living God,* 270.

> *happy with that idea. Then I watched myself do something very strange and surprising. … I went to that young man who was sitting on a chair shaking uncontrollably. I knelt in front of him and put my arms around him, pulling him gently to my chest. I told him, with all the strength of my soul, "I love you, my brother." In the very moment I did that, the evil spirit left. The missionary came to his senses, looked at me and said, "I love you, too." He snapped right out of it and asked what had happened. … It was an exuberant experience of the workings of the spirit of love, which is the Spirit of Christ and by it overcoming all evil.*[9]

As a result of this extraordinary experience, Elder Busche came to understand several priceless truths about fear, the power of the devil, and the power of the love of Christ. He recalled, that not following counsel (in this case the mission rules), a missionary "lost the Spirit and fear entered his soul. The fear allowed the evil spirit to enter." Elder Busche added,

> *The powers of the love of Christ are real. We can control our lives in our families and in our daily routine only when we learn to always be filled with the Spirit of Christ, which is the opposite of the spirit of fear, and which is the spirit of confidence and hope and faith and love. Therefore, in order to be eligible for that spirit, it is so important to keep ourselves away from filth and places of filth.*
>
> *With all the prayers that I was offering, I was still not ready to control my fear until I opened my heart to fill it with love. That was a very holy experience … the Lord gave me the opportunity to learn that our purpose is to fill our souls with love. That has helped me in many ways throughout my life, and I believe that truth contains the essentials for mankind's survival.*[10]

---

9 Ibid., 270-271.

10 Busche, *Yearning for the Living God*, 271-273.

What a trove of spiritual treasures are contained in Elder Busche's experience! Here are a few salient spiritual gems we can ponder and apply:

1) Disobedience (even breaking mission rules) leads to loss of the Spirit, allowing fear to enter and dominate our thoughts and destroy our peace of mind.

2) Allowing fear to dwell in the mind can open the way for evil spirits to enter and take over a person's mortal body.

3) Subject to such direct evil influence, the body will behave abnormally and erratically, indicating the owner is no longer in control.

4) Fear does not come from within us, it is put upon us—literally coming from a lower realm. ("I felt fear come from the ground, from below, trying to sneak into my system.")

5) Praying "with all the energy of my heart," was a key step in overcoming fear and receiving the specific revelation needed to do so.

6) The Spirit of Christ imparts "confidence and hope and faith and love" and is the opposite of the spirit of fear and its fruits—uncertainty, doubt, hopelessness, selfishness and hatred.

7) "Perfect love casteth out fear." This is not imaginary! "The powers of the love of Christ are real" and they oust and defeat the lesser power of the adversary.

8) "Our purpose is to fill our souls with love."

9) Overcoming fear and filling our souls with love is essential for mankind's survival.

In his attempt to defeat you, Lucifer will continually seize opportunities to act upon you. At the top of his list is inflicting and amplifying fear. When you are struck by fear, rather than dwelling on it, you can use your agency and knowledge to turn the tables on the adversary. Keep in mind fear is a hoax perpetrated to deceive you. It's not real at all. Knowing that, you can use the tactics in Chapter 14 on Effective Tactics, which can be applied to fear; and they work.

Facing fears is an integral part of the curriculum Heavenly Father has integrated into this mortal phase of our eternal progression. Throughout your life, SKAM will continue to try to use fear to intimidate you, slow you down, and curtail your righteous works. You can bank on one thing: Every time SKAM tries to block you from proceeding, it is a sign that significant good will come from what you're thinking of doing; and, again, it's not just about you. It's about all the good that others will receive as you overcome your fear. With those thoughts in mind, you can turn to your Heavenly Father and turn up your faith in His love and His providence.

We will devote more attention to asking in faith, nothing doubting in up-coming chapters to add to your effectiveness in vanquishing fear. As you increase your ability to look unto Christ in every thought, your ability to call on your Heavenly Father "in faith, nothing doubting" will grow as the promises of the scriptures and the living prophets come to fruition in your life. You will come to see fear and adversity in an entirely different light. You may even shift from being fearful of fear and being averse to adversity. Just as a pole vaulter views a vaulting pole, overcoming fear can be a means of vaulting you to higher spiritual heights. To remind myself of these higher perspectives and to steel my will to vanquish the fear standing in my way, I use a one-sentence mantra. "Dennis, if it looks like death, it's probably life. Run to it."

CHAPTER 19

Remove From Thee All Doubting

How glorious are the times we live in, especially for those who have received and are hearkening unto the radiant truths of the restored gospel of Jesus Christ. We can sing and we can shout with the armies of heaven, "Hosanna, Hosanna to God and the Lamb!—The visions and blessings of old are returning, and angels are coming to visit the earth. The knowledge and power of God are expanding, the veil over the earth is beginning to burst."[1] These words from this cherished anthem of the Restoration were first sung at the dedication of the Kirtland Temple. During the inaugural days of the first holy House of the Lord dedicated in the dispensation of the fulness of times, the prophetic words of this hymn were literally validated. Angels and the Lord God Himself appeared; and the knowledge and power of God were expanded as priesthood keys were restored by Moses, Elias and Elijah. The validity of those prophetic words still applies. As Elder Neil L. Andersen testified, "Angels have not ceased to minister unto the children of men."[2]

---

1 "The Spirit of God," *Hymns,* no. 2.

2 Neil L. Andersen, "Spiritually Defining Memories," *Ensign,* May 2020, 21. See also Moroni 7:29–30.

I rejoice when I sing "The Spirit of God" and I am especially moved when singing it with a large congregation at a stake or general conference. The unified voices call down a confirming witness of the words we are singing. My heart expands with hope and pounds with joy and resolve as I feel the Spirit bear witness that those words were validated in Kirtland, but not finished. Those blessings and great spiritual experiences are still available to us in our day. Living prophets and apostles, repeatedly remind us that the prophesied "restoration of all things" is on-going. The events that lie ahead of us are to be greater than those that lie behind us.[3] As Primary children, we memorize the ninth Article of Faith: "We believe that [God] will yet reveal many great and important things pertaining to the kingdom of God." The most thrilling part of the hymn is the present progressive tense: "are returning" and "are coming" and "are expanding." The extending of visions, blessings, power and knowledge did not end in Joseph's day any more than they were with the death of the early apostles. Because we worship the unchanging God of miracles, we assuredly know the same privileges are extended to each of us. And it's entirely up to us—each individual—to seek and obtain the blessings Heavenly Father wants to bestow. The degree to which we personally enjoy such glorious blessings rests on the degree of our faith and our willingness to pay the required price. Let us therefore consider our ways—our mindset (faith) and conduct (obedience).

Inspiring Words of the Prophets

The Prophet Joseph Smith invited us to seek for knowledge and spiritual experiences. "It is the first principle of the gospel to know for a certainty the Character of God," he declared, "and to know that we may

3 https://www.thechurchnews.com/leaders-and-ministry/2020-01-01/president-nelson-important-invitation-latter-day-saints-2020-171026.

converse with him as one man converses with another!"[4] Consider also, this glorious statement:

> *God hath not revealed anything to Joseph, but what he will make known unto the Twelve, and even the least saint may know all things as fast as he is able to bear them, for the day must come when no man need say to his neighbor, Know ye the Lord; for all shall know Him (who remain) from the least to the greatest.*[5]

One of the outstanding hallmarks of President Russell M. Nelson's tenure is the clear and repeated invitation he openly extended to the members of the Church to seek for Heavenly Father's choicest blessings through personal revelation:

> *I urge you to stretch beyond your current spiritual ability to receive personal revelation, for the Lord has promised that "if thou shalt (seek) thou shalt receive revelation upon revelation, knowledge upon knowledge, that thou mayest know the mysteries and peaceable things—that which bringeth joy, that which bringeth life eternal."*
>
> *Oh, there is so much more that your Father in Heaven wants you to know. As Elder Neal A. Maxwell taught, "To those who have eyes to see and ears to hear, it is clear that the Father and the Son are giving away the secrets of the universe!"*[6]

Significantly, President Nelson repeated verbatim the same plea again in general conference two years later: "I renew my plea for you to do whatever it takes to increase your spiritual capacity to receive personal revelation."[7] One cannot help but connect these words to the scripture in Section 76 cited

4 Smith, *Teachings of the Prophet Joseph Smith,* 345.
5 Ibid., 149.
6 Nelson, "Revelation for the Church, Revelation for Our Lives," *Ensign,* May 2018, 95.
7 Nelson, "Hear Him," *Ensign,* May 2020, 90.

previously. Notice also the direct connection President Nelson makes to the central theme of this book. He even puts it in the form of a promise: "Doing so will help you know how to move ahead with your life, what to do during times of crisis, *and how to discern and avoid the temptations and the deceptions of the adversary.*"[8]

With such inspiring privileges and promises laid before us, one can almost hear the Prophet Joseph Smith speaking to all of us at this very moment: "Shall we not go on in so great a cause? Go forward and not backward. Courage, brethren (and sisters); and on, on to the victory! Let your hearts rejoice, and be exceedingly glad. Let the earth break forth into singing" (D&C 128:22).

The Challenge Before Us

What is the key principle requisite to enjoying these glorious blessings? Faith in the Lord Jesus Christ. And what is it that actually prevents us from experiencing and enjoying them in greater measure? Lack of faith. Bear in mind what we established earlier. Both faith and lack of faith are states of mind. Each is the polar opposite of the other and both are choices. How do we overcome our lack of faith? What is the mental state we are actually dealing with, the one we have to grapple with and vanquish? The state of mind is *doubt!* What is it that undermines our faith as we pray? Doubt. What weakens the priesthood blessings we give and receive? Doubt. What keeps us from receiving more personal revelation? Doubt. If you doubt my answer, take a look at a fractional list of the scriptures about doubt:

> *And immediately Jesus stretched forth his hand, and caught him, and said unto him, O thou of little faith, wherefore didst thou doubt? (Matt. 14:31)*

---

8 Ibid., 90, emphasis added.

> *For verily I say unto you, That whosoever shall say unto this mountain, Be thou removed, and be thou cast into the sea; and shall not doubt in his heart, but shall believe that those things which he saith shall come to pass; he shall have whatsoever he saith fulfilled (JST Mark 11:25).*

> *Now they never had fought, yet they did not fear death; and they did think more upon the liberty of their fathers than they did upon their lives; yea, they had been taught by their mothers, that if they did not doubt, God would deliver them. And they rehearsed unto me the words of their mothers, saying: We do not doubt our mothers knew it (Alma 56:47–48).*

Doubt that limits our spiritual growth can come at any time and in many forms. We will focus on three forms of doubt in particular, two of which we will explore in this chapter: 1) Doubt about worthiness to receive answers to prayers and personal revelation, and 2) Self-doubt about our abilities in general in setting and achieving lofty goals. In the next chapter we will deal with doubt about the restored gospel of Jesus Christ.

Doubt About Worthiness to Receive

Vanquishing doubt is the key requisite for receiving answers to prayers, obtaining revelation, dreams, visions, visitations, healings—yea, all the gifts of the Spirit. This point is made plainly and powerfully by the prophet Moroni:

> *And behold, I say unto you he changeth not; if so he would cease to be God; and he ceaseth not to be God, and is a God of miracles. And the reason why he ceaseth to do miracles among the children of men is because that they dwindle in unbelief, and depart from the right way, and know not the God in whom they should trust.*

> *Behold, I say unto you that whoso believeth in Christ, doubting nothing, whatsoever he shall ask the Father in the name of Christ it shall be granted him; and this promise is unto all, even unto the ends of the earth (Mormon 9:19–21).*

Put another way, vacillation, uncertainty, double-mindedness, halting between opinions—synonyms and euphemisms for doubt—will negate and block the flow of truth, light and power. Lucifer will try with utmost persistence and guile to sow seeds of doubt in our minds. From that point on, it's up to us. All he can do is plant the seeds. If we water and fertilize those seeds and fail to see them as weeds and pluck them out of our mental garden, they will grow. The harvest is spiritual blight. The first fruit is loss of light. Rejecting light results in withdrawal of the Spirit. A degree of darkness fills the void. We reason less soundly; we lose sensitivity to things spiritual and put ourselves in a more vulnerable position. The Spirit will continue to strive with us, but we become less responsive to it. The influence of Satan becomes stronger, and we become less able to recognize his influence for what it is, making it easier to go along with Satan's meddlings. And the cycle repeats, unless we reverse it by hearkening to the Spirit.

We may not notice it at first, for there is somewhat of a time delay in the consequences of choosing both good and evil. President Henry B. Eyring taught this principle.

> *God makes it attractive to choose the right by letting us feel the effects of our choices. If we choose the right, we will find happiness—in time. If we choose evil, there comes sorrow and regret—in time. Those effects are sure. Yet they are often delayed for a purpose. If the blessings were immediate, choosing the right would not build faith. And since sorrow is also sometimes greatly delayed, it takes faith to feel the need to seek*

forgiveness for sin early rather than after we feel its sorrowful and painful effects.[9]

We Have Power Over Our Doubts

We are capable of abolishing doubt. Because doubt is nothing more than a state of mind, it can be utterly dispatched by choosing to reject and replace it. Habits aren't broken, they're replaced; the same applies to thoughts *before* they become habits. Useless, unproductive thoughts are not permanently engraved in your mind. When doubts enter your mind, shift your focal points. Replace them with something better. Belief is a good start. Focus on what you believe. Revisit what you know and how you came to know or believe it. Often that choice will lead you to recall an experience that had a significant spiritual impact upon you. This is the way we can "cast not away therefore (our) confidence" (Heb. 10:35) but rather renew and revitalize it. What great motivation we gain by considering the very beginning of the Restoration. The promise found in the Epistle of James that propelled Joseph into the grove applies just as directly to us:

> *If any of you lack wisdom, let him ask of God, that giveth to all men (and women) liberally, and upbraideth not; and it shall be given him. But let him ask in faith, nothing wavering. For he that wavereth is like a wave of the sea driven with the wind and tossed. For let not that man think that he shall receive any thing of the Lord. A double minded man is unstable in all his ways (James 1:5–8).*

Right there, in plainest of terms, James sets forth in clarity and simplicity what we must do to obtain wisdom from God. The formula that worked for Joseph will work for us: Ask in a believing, focused, state

9 Eyring, "A Priceless Heritage of Hope," *Ensign,* May 2014, 24–25.

of mind without doubting. It is just that simple and just that hard. We're so accustomed in this generation to turn to a technique or algorithm or an app or an appliance to fix a situation or make it easier to do something. In this case, none of those options will do or be necessary. It just comes down to focusing on dispelling doubt.

Remove From Thee All Doubting

The Prophet Joseph Smith asked the Lord about the Apocrypha and was told, "There are many things contained therein that are true, and it is mostly translated correctly" (D&C 91:1). Certainly this passage found in 2 Esdras is one such inspired message:

> *Remove from thee all doubting; and question nothing at all, when thou asketh anything of the Lord; Saying within thyself: How shall I be able to ask anything of the Lord and receive it, seeing I have so greatly sinned against him? Do not think thus, but turn unto the Lord with all thy heart. And ask of him without doubting. … Wherefore purify thy heart from all the vices of this present world; and thou shalt receive whatsoever good things thou shalt ask, and nothing shall be wanting unto thee of all thy petitions; if thou shalt ask of the Lord without doubting.*
>
> *Wherefore, purify thy heart from doubting, and put on faith, and trust in God, and thou shalt receive all that thou shalt ask.*
>
> *But if thou shouldst chance to ask somewhat and not [immediately] receive it, yet do not therefore doubt, because thou has not presently received the petition of thy soul. … But do not leave off to ask, and then thou shalt receive. Else if thou shalt cease to ask, thou must complain of thyself, and not of God, that he has not given unto thee what thou didst desire.*

> *Consider therefore this doubting, how cruel and pernicious it is. ... For this doubting is the daughter of the devil, and deals very wickedly with the servants of God.*
>
> *Despise it, therefore, and thou shalt rule over it on every occasion. ... Faith cometh from above, from God; and hath great power. But doubting is an earthly spirit, and proceedeth from the devil, and has no strength. Do thou therefore keep the virtue of faith, and depart from doubting in which is no virtue, and thou shalt live unto God.*[10]

We are taught and encouraged to develop faith as a little child. What is the cardinal characteristic of little children? They haven't yet been trained to doubt; they just readily, unquestioningly believe. They don't have to take a doubt management course or go on a doubt loss diet. They simply open their minds and believe.

The Pernicious Ploy of Self-Doubt

The most vexing doubt of all—the one the adversary inflates and exploits more than any other—is doubt about ourselves. It's the one that immediately pops up when we contemplate the promise of James. We read "Giveth to *all* men liberally...." and instantaneously doubts arise to block our belief. We think, "Does that mean *me*? Will God answer *me* just like he did Joseph?" Those thoughts barely start to form in our heads when SKAM comes roaring into the intersection to invalidate the promise: "Hey, settle down there, Dennis. Who do you think you are, entertaining a question like that? Joseph was a foreordained prophet. You're a nobody. You have no stature in the church. Look at all Joseph had going for him that you don't have. He was a poor, undereducated plow boy with no training or schooling. Oops. Ah...forget that. I mean

10 *The Lost Books of the Bible and The Forgotten Books of Eden,* (USA: William Collins & World Publishing Company, Inc., 1976), 2 Hermas 9:1–11, 221–222.

he was *supposed* to go into the grove that day. He couldn't help it. Joseph's boyish faith had nothing to do with this. He was simply *destined* to be the prophet of the restoration. You're just an ordinary member of the church, if that. Get real."

Nothing holds a more vicious grip on our minds than the plague of self-doubt. SKAM wields it with relentless frequency and power. Far more insidiously than any external critic, we are pelted with a seemingly incessant onslaught of self-doubting thoughts from our internal critic—SKAM, the Skeptic Against Me. No one is exempt from this nemesis. Feelings of inadequacy and self-doubt beset all of us from time to time. No matter how accomplished we are, that negative inner voice lurks in our heads, ever ready to eagerly pounce on any good or positive idea we entertain and smear it with dark, greasy doubts. A compelling example is illustrated in the excellent documentary on Fred Rogers, *Won't You Be My Neighbor.* After years of creating incredibly valuable material, Fred Rogers took a hiatus from writing and starring in *Mr. Roger's Neighborhood.* Later, he decided to undertake another project. We might assume, based on the quantity of evidence of how gifted he was and how successful he had been, he would come back to the keyboard with brimming confidence, empowered with rejuvenated energy. But we would be wrong. Here is the personal memo, Rogers typed to himself as he was about to commence on the new project.

> *Am I kidding myself that I'm able to write a script again? Am I really just whistling Dixie? I wonder. If I don't get down to it I'll never really know. Why don't I trust myself? Really that's what it's all about ... that and not wanting to go through the agony of creation. AFTER ALL THESE YEARS IT'S JUST AS BAD AS EVER. I wonder if every creative artist goes through the tortures of the damned trying to create? Oh, well, the hour cometh and now IS when I've got to do it. GET TO*

IT, FRED. GET TO IT! … But don't let anybody ever tell anybody else that it was easy. It wasn't.[11]

What makes this memo so priceless for all of us is to know we are all waging the same battle with the nay-saying skeptic within who tries to stop us from being and doing our best, and maximizing the good we can do in the world. SKAM wants to nip all that good and all those positive possibilities in the bud—preempting all the good and positive effects that could flow from our work. The voice in our head urges us to stay in our lane, settle for less, avoid exertion and, above all, "DO NOT put yourself out there where you are sure to fail and make a fool of yourself, becoming the butt of jokes and other people's disdain." From Fred's memo we derive the invaluable reassurance that we're not the only ones wrestling with inner demons, and that self-doubt is a standard weapon used against all of God's children. Over and above that, Rogers shows us what to do to win the battle. We defy the voice and proceed to do exactly what it tells us not to do or try. Vincent Van Gogh said, "If you hear a voice within you say you cannot paint, then by all means paint and that voice will be silenced."[12]

When you ignore or fight through the doubt and take action, you discover the voice was a liar. Few, if any of the threatened disasters or humiliations occur. The fears and doubts that once seemed so formidable and certain turn out to be anything but formidable and certain. There is nothing real or substantial to them at all. Right from the start of the fears, you were capable of succeeding and you now have the perfect evidence—you called SKAM's bluff and you acted contrary to the doubt and, by moving forward, disproved it.

Three weeks after typing his memo, Rogers added this handwritten addendum: "It wasn't easy, but it was good. The five new scripts about

11 Fred Rogers, https://www.nytimes.com/2018/06/05/movies/mister-rogers-wont-you-be-my-neighbor.html.

12 Vincent Van Gogh, https://www.goodreads.com/author/quotes/34583.Vincent_van_Gogh.

school are nearly complete and I can see how helpful they can be. This I must remember!"[13] When we are being assaulted by the Skeptic Against Me, let us summon the will and energy to turn the tables and do exactly what the intruder is *telling us not* to do. We can all get better at rebuking the enemy and winning the battle by detecting, then disagreeing, then disobeying and defying the voice.

13 Rogers, https://www.nytimes.com/2018/06/05/movies/mister-rogers-wont-you-be-my-neighbor.html.

CHAPTER 20

The Trap of Walking in One's Own Way

Before we leave the subject of combatting doubt, let's explore a significant challenge many wrestle with in the latter days. With so much misinformation and distorted facts, coupled with strident opinions, it becomes increasingly easy to become confused and lose our bearings. Sincere questions of what is true and what is not puts us in a very similar position to the boy Joseph Smith who was caught up in "a war of words and tumult of opinions" (Joseph Smith History 1:10). Exhibiting a degree of common sense beyond his years, Joseph decided the only sure way to know the truth about God was to quit listening to the contending voices and go to the source. So he did as James suggested. He asked God. Why should our quest to know the truth be any different? Are times all that different in terms of finding out what God wants us to do with our lives? The only difference may be in the quantity and venom of the differing opinions, which in our times have greatly escalated.

One thing is certain. Spending hours soaking in the claims and accusations of faceless commentators speaking without authority or divine inspiration are our modern version of the blind leading the blind. Asking their opinion of who God is and who Joseph Smith was is a little bit like asking a barber if you need a haircut. You already know the answer you'll get. Hence, I offer a few thoughts on pride and humility, on hubris and submissiveness—and on trusting in the arm of God rather than the arm of flesh.

Two Incontrovertible Facts

In the movie, *Rudy*, which is based on the experience of Daniel "Rudy" Ruettiger, who grew up idolizing Notre Dame football, we learned that Ruettiger's boyhood dream of one day playing for the Fighting Irish came after a notable trial of his faith. Overcoming major obstacles—dyslexia, lack of tuition money, and being under-sized for collegiate football—he battled his way onto the team, spending most of his time on the practice squad with scant hope of ever playing in a game. One particular scene in the movie remains in my mind. With his chances dimming that he'll ever reach his dream, Rudy goes to the Catholic church on campus to pray and seek God's help. There he encounters Father Cavanaugh and the two get into a conversation:

> *Rudy: "Maybe I haven't prayed enough."*
>
> *Father Cavanaugh: "I'm sure that's not the problem. Praying is something we do in our time. The answers come in God's time."*
>
> *Rudy: "Have I done everything I possibly can? Can you help me?"*
>
> *Father Cavanaugh: "Son, in 35 years of religious studies, I've come up with only two hard incontrovertible facts: there is a God. And I'm not him."*[1]

---

1 *Rudy,* https://www.youtube.com/watch?v=eRFc5RqaTmw.

Be Still and Know that I am God

One of Satan's most subtle snares preys upon the blindness stemming from human pride. The apex of human arrogance is reached when we mortals deign to prescribe what kind of being God should be and how He should conduct His relationship with His children. We don't think of it in terms of actually creating God's job description for Him, but that's exactly what we do. It is also very difficult *not* to align our personal conception of God with the prevailing "wisdom" of the day in which we live, blending it with our own interpretation of what life should be like and the way we want things to be. In effect, we believe there is a God, but forget that we're not Him. Furthermore, based on what we've discussed thus far, we might also suspect that some of our assumptions might be heavily influenced by the adversary. However, God has reserved the right to be God and to think and act according to His infinitely greater wisdom and eternal perspectives. Through the prophet Isaiah, Jehovah said, "For my thoughts are not your thoughts, neither are your ways my ways, saith the LORD. For as the heavens are higher than the earth, so are my ways higher than your ways, and my thoughts than your thoughts" (Isaiah 55:8–9).

The Apostle Paul found it very difficult to convince the Jews in his day that God had the right to institute a higher law. The Law of Moses, having served its purpose, was replaced with higher commandments and a different sacramental way of honoring and remembering the God of Israel. The moment Christ declared from the cross, "It is finished! Into thy hands I commend my spirit," the sacrificing of the firstborn, unblemished male lambs which Israel had offered for centuries went instantly from approved and acceptable to disapproved and unacceptable. A vast majority of Jews were so stuck in their own rigid paradigm of how God should do His work, they utterly failed to recognize Jesus as their God and Promised Messiah. They even cried out for the Savior to be crucified because the Messiah they saw before them—beaten, scourged and bleeding—humbly submitting

His will to that of the Father—did not fit their mental image of what the Messiah was supposed to look like and do. The Messiah they had conjured was supposed to incinerate the wicked, oppressing Romans, return Israel to its former glory and world supremacy, and feed them bread on a daily basis. Moral of the story: Beware of hubris (excessive pride) and imposing *your* paradigm of God onto God.

In the first and final analyses, God's will reigns supreme, not ours. He determines the rules, not us. Obedience to what He commands is the definition of righteousness. Disobedience to what He commands is the definition of sin and wickedness. In the Book of Mormon, Nephi who had grown up knowing the laws of God from his childhood, knew the commandment "Thou shalt not kill." Nevertheless, for a higher purpose and in the wisdom of God, he was "constrained by the Spirit" to kill Laban. At first, Nephi recoiled because this whispering of the Spirit flew in the face of all he had been taught and all he had lived. The Spirit issued the command a second time and then a third before Nephi set aside his preconceptions and yielded to the will of the Lord. God does not always give reasons why, but in this case He did. The Spirit said, "Behold the Lord slayeth the wicked to bring forth his righteous purposes. It is better that one man should perish than that a nation should dwindle and perish in unbelief" (1 Ne. 4:13). Nephi might not have recognized it, but he was being asked the question Heavenly Father has asked of other prophets such as Abraham: "Which is greater? The rules and commandments or the One who sets the rules and issues the commandments?" Nephi had to set aside his conception of right and wrong in order to keep the commandment so that a higher purpose in God's wisdom would be fulfilled. Had Nephi stuck to his preconceptions and not slain Laban, he would have disobeyed a direct commandment from the Lord.

Moral of the story: Beware of hubris and imposing *your* paradigm of God onto God.

Another case in point. If you were to ask a thousand people whether killing one's offspring was right or wrong, it would be stunning if you got one exception. People would emphatically say, "That's definitely wrong." Yet, Father Abraham—the father of many nations, a man revered for his peerless character and righteousness by three great religions, Islam, Judaism, and Christianity—was asked by God to do just that. What a gut-wrenching test it was for Abraham to be commanded to offer up his son Isaac in place of a lamb. Abraham not only had the same cultural and spiritual conflicts as Nephi, he also had two additional elements that made his submissiveness to the Lord the supreme example of faith and obedience to the will of God.

In the Book of Abraham in the Pearl of Great Price, we are first introduced to Abraham at a moment of extreme crisis. He is lying bound on an altar about to be offered by his idolatrous father as a human sacrifice to a false god. Calling upon God with all the energy of his soul, Abraham is delivered and the wicked priest who was about to slay Abraham was slain instead. Fully convinced of the obvious, Abraham wrote, "In the land of the Chaldeans, at the residence of my fathers, I, Abraham, saw that it was needful for me to obtain another place of residence" (Abraham 1:1). The salient point here is also obvious. Would there be anything more repugnant or abhorrent to Abraham who narrowly escaped being sacrificed on an altar himself to now be asked to do that very thing—offer *his* son on an altar to *his* God?

The son Abraham is being asked to sacrifice is not just any son; it is his *promised* heir, the one and only son of his beloved and faithful wife Sarah. This is the son Abraham and Sarah had been promised decades prior by a personal visitation of Jehovah. At the time, Abraham and Sarah were in their prime—hale and attractive. They were faithful, successful missionaries who brought hundreds, if not thousands, to believe in and accept Jehovah as their God. They were known for their hospitality and charity, serving people of all nationalities and cultures. Yet the years passed. Year after year went by. No promised son was conceived in Sarah's womb. Neither Abraham nor Sarah voiced one word of complaint. No murmuring word escaped their tongue. They just believed in God's promise and served on. Eventually, Sarah passed the age of fertility and was no longer physically capable of conceiving and delivering a child. Then, finally and miraculously, the promise was fulfilled. When all boundaries of sensible hope were exceeded, the Lord gave Abraham and Sarah the capacity. Sarah conceived and delivered the promised son and named him Isaac, meaning "laughter" because, when Sarah overheard the words of the angel that she would bear a son, overwhelmed by joy and gratitude, she "laughed within herself" (Gen. 18:12).

Given the weight of all that preceded Isaac's birth and the joy his parents experienced in rearing him into young manhood, how could the test be greater than the one administered to Abraham and Isaac? It certainly broke their hearts as well as every religious paradigm they had ever held. Yet, Abraham and Isaac went ahead and promptly departed to Moriah, where they were committed to fulfilling whatever the Lord required, no matter what. Would your paradigm—your expectations of what a loving God would or should do allow for this? Would your heart allow you to think that it would be *fair* or *right* for God to require such a thing? Abraham offered. He raised his knife. His mind said "thrust" and the synapses in the muscles fired. The knife was headed for Isaac's throat and would have struck, but an angel at that very last instant halted Abraham's descending wrist and intervened. Abraham had answered rightly that same question asked of Nephi: Which is greater? The rules and commandments or the One who sets the rules and gives the commandments?

Moral of the story: Beware of hubris and imposing *your* paradigm of God onto God.

Walking in Your Own Way

When you take it upon yourself, knowingly or unintentionally, to decide what God should do, how He should govern His kingdom, lead His Church, and think you know better than He what the apostles and prophets He has personally selected should do or say, you are in effect designing your own god. You are creating a god unto yourself according to your likes and preferences, your biases and values, which are tainted by the weaknesses and assumptions of other people—the tweets, posts and podcasts in the media where anyone can assert and pontificate without guidance or constraint of the Spirit. The scriptural term for this mindset and practice is "trusting in the arm of flesh," about which we are repeatedly warned.

An explicit warning to all who live in the dispensation of the fulness of times is given in the first section of the Doctrine and Covenants. Just before He bears witness of the calling and role of the Prophet Joseph Smith, the Lord foretells and describes the operating paradigm of many that will prevail in the latter days.

> *The day cometh that they who will not hear the voice of the Lord, neither the voice of his servants, neither give heed to the words of the prophets and apostles, shall be cut off from among the people;*
>
> *For they have strayed from mine ordinances, and have broken mine everlasting covenant;*
>
> *They seek not the Lord to establish his righteousness, but every man walketh in his own way, and after the image of his own god, whose image is in the likeness of the world, and whose substance is that of an idol, which waxeth old and shall perish in Babylon, even Babylon the great, which shall fall (D&C 1:14–16).*

Moral of the story: Beware of hubris and imposing *your* paradigm of God onto God.

When we step back and look at our willingness to trust the opinions of self-appointed critics more readily than the opinion of God, do we not see how vain and arrogant we are? How much wiser we are to heed the counsel, "Be still and know that I am God," and let God be God. Hubris is the grease on the slippery slope of disappointment and loss of light. When we humble ourselves before God and ask for understanding and pray with a sincere heart and real intent to accept His answers and abide by His ways, we have an entirely different experience. We have an abiding sense of peace infused in all we do, even or especially when we face challenges and trials. I have yet to see someone who has succumbed to their doubts and let criticism of the Lord's anointed run rampant, live a calm life of inner peace. And the more they get wrapped up in their carnal security, the more unsettled and contentious they become.

During His mortal ministry the Lord warned his disciples against absorbing the "leaven of the Pharisees" (Luke 12:1). The Pharisees were the most judgmental sect among the Jews of Jesus' day. They were the first to find fault and point out the flaws in the conduct of others. They were so good at it, they were able to find fault after fault in the conduct of their God who modeled what a perfect life looks like before their very eyes. "This man is a sinner," they cried. "Look at him and his disciples eating corn on the Sabbath day with unwashed hands. How profane can they be?" Pharisaic attitudes exist today. Is your vision impaired by your own hypercritical eye that is quick to find sin in the conduct of others while exonerating your own? Has the fermenting leaven of the Pharisees that produces sour dough become the earthly manna you partake of daily?

At the time of Jesus, the leaders of the Jewish nation—the ones who should have been the first to recognize the Messiah and urge others to accept him—were so filled with their conceit they were unable to recognize their God as he lived among them working miracle after miracle. And, what lay at the heart of their error and blindness? They were fanatically and unbendingly committed to *their* interpretation of how God should be God. How much wiser were the group of Nephites spoken of in the Book of Helaman who were persecuted, ridiculed and scoffed at by those who were puffed up in their pride and self-assessment of how wise they were.

> *And in the fifty and first year … there was peace also, save it were the pride which began to enter into the church—not into the church of God, but into the hearts of the people who professed to belong to the church of God.*
>
> *And they were lifted up in pride, even to the persecution of many of their brethren. Now this was a great evil, which did cause the more humble part of the people to suffer great persecutions, and to wade through much affliction.*
>
> *Nevertheless they did fast and pray oft, and did wax stronger and stronger in their humility, and firmer and firmer in the faith of Christ, unto the filling their souls with joy and consolation, yea, even to the purifying and the sanctification of their hearts, which sanctification cometh because of their yielding their hearts unto God (Hel. 3:33–35).*

He that hath an ear, let him hear.

Christ's Disciples Have Known Suffering

The Messianic prophecies of Isaiah and other Old Testament prophets have more than one true fulfillment. They have many and apply to the Messiah's servants as much as to the Messiah himself. Isaiah says the visage of the Messiah would be marred more than any man. It is heart-breaking to envision its literal fulfillment on the body of the Savior after He had been so brutally disfigured through the beatings, scourging, lacerations, and piercings inflicted upon his physical body. Throughout the ages, many of Christ's followers have suffered all manner of violence, pain and indignities for their devotion to Him who suffered beyond anything man can suffer except unto death (Mosiah 3:7). On the night of May 23, 1823, Moroni, the angelic tutor sent to prepare Joseph Smith for his mission wasted no time informing the boy that he, too, would follow in the steps of the Master.

> *He called me by name, and said unto me that he was a messenger sent from the presence of God to me, and that his name was Moroni; that God had a work for me to do; and that my name should be had for good and evil among all nations, kindreds, and tongues, or that it should be both good and evil spoken of among all people (Joseph Smith History 1:33).*

Just as the carpenter's son from Nazareth was the Rock of Salvation for all who would believe on his name[2] and a stone of offense and a stumbling block for others,[3] so also has the farmer's son from Palmyra been the fulcrum of division in the latter days—an inspired seer stone[4] for some and a rock of offense for others.

What About Joseph Smith?

Yes, what about Joseph? Throughout Joseph's life, both good and evil was spoken of him; and both the impugning and extolling of his character and motives continue to this day. If you choose to believe that Joseph was a fraud, then you will come to certain conclusions that are anything but certain. But because you look for evidence to confirm your point of view, you will follow that conclusion up with explanations to "prove" that Joseph was undoubtedly a fraud. You will then try to make a case for how corrupt and evil a man Joseph was. You will cobble together a case that he was

2 John 1:12; Hel. 5:12.
3 Acts 4:11; 2 Ne. 18:14; JST 1 Peter 2:7.
4 2 Ne. 3:6–7, 11; D&C 21:1.

a narcissist and did what he did for adulation and popularity. You will contend that the introduction of plural marriage and his attempts to keep it secret are a clear sign that Joseph was a sex-crazed womanizer and a lying scoundrel. You will argue that he did what he did for the love of wealth and fortune because even from an early age he was nothing more than a gold digger. For good measure, you might also claim that Joseph's whole motive was to gather enough followers who would be so devoted that they would support him financially for the rest of his life, enjoying a life of ease and comfort. And finally, you might contend that the only people who actually stood by Joseph Smith and continued to believe in his divine calling were backwoods hicks who were duped by a cunning charlatan because they were too uneducated, unsophisticated, and mentally deficient to see through the ruse. And then that description will have to be extended to include all of the nitwits who are still following him and his successors today.

If, on the other hand, you choose the position that Joseph Smith was truly called of God and was the man "who did more, save Jesus only, for the salvation of men in this world, than any other man that ever lived in it" (D&C 135:3), you will wind up in a much different place. Such is the case for those who have obtained an initial witness by the Spirit of Joseph's calling, and who have clung to it. Those who have maintained their belief and paid the price to study, fast, obey, and continue on the road of repentance have been guided by the Spirit to understand deeper layers of truth. And, building on the rock of personal revelation upon which Jesus said He would build His Church, they have been blessed with insights and explanation far more satisfactory and fulfilling than ones set forth by the unbelievers. They have found that all that was promised the saints can be given, because they doubted their doubts before they doubted their faith, and the rewards they obtain are beyond description or price.

It all comes down to whom you choose to believe—the spook or the Spirit. If you choose to allow SKAM to have his way with your thoughts, you will become increasingly dark. On the other hand, if you reject the lies and choose to follow the enticings of the Holy Spirit you will become increasingly full of light. For, "he that receiveth light, and continueth in God, receiveth more light; and that light will grow brighter and brighter until the perfect day" (D&C 50:24). Jesus Christ, the Eternal God, taught this doctrine during His mortal ministry:

> *Lay not up for yourselves treasures upon earth, where moth and rust doth corrupt, and where thieves break through and steal:*
>
> *But lay up for yourselves treasures in heaven, where neither moth nor rust doth corrupt, and where thieves do not break through nor steal:*
>
> *For where your treasure is, there will your heart be also.*
>
> *The light of the body is the eye: if therefore thine eye be single, thy whole body shall be full of light.*
>
> *But if thine eye be evil, thy whole body shall be full of darkness. If therefore the light that is in thee be darkness, how great is that darkness (Matt. 6:19–23)!*

The Lord is warning His disciples about where they put their attention. If your focus is on seeking the truth and light of the gospel you will find what you look for and receive the corresponding reward. If your focus is on the things of the flesh and the baubles of the world, you will also find what you look for.

Notice the interesting phrase the Lord uses: "if thine eye be evil." Obviously, He is not talking about the literal orb in the socket below the eyebrow, He is talking about one's point of view, the "eye of the beholder," mentioned earlier in the book. The eye sees what the beholder looks for. If you are looking for something to condemn, you will find it. If you are looking for something virtuous, lovely or of good report or praiseworthy, you will find it. People find what they look for. Notice, however, that one's point of view is a choice, and Jesus is saying to guard it well. For, if you do not exercise good judgment and follow the dictates of the Holy Spirit, you'll certainly be influenced by the adversary. "A man cannot serve two masters" (Matt. 6:24; 3 Ne. 13:24).

As it is with our attitudinal choices, so it is with our point of view regarding Joseph Smith. There is no middle ground. He either was a prophet of God or he was a false prophet and a servant of the devil. Jesus told us how to distinguish between the true prophets and the false. "By their fruits ye shall know them" (Matt. 7:16, 20). I will mention the fruits of the Prophet and of the Church he founded later on. For now, let me reason with you about the stack of claims leveled against him mentioned above.

If Joseph was looking to dupe people for the sake of luxury, fortune and gain: looking for a life of ease and quiet tranquility for himself and those he loved the most—the choices he made could not have been less on the mark. What's more, when those supposed reasons for Joseph to continue perpetrating his hoax backfired and blew up in his face, and the total opposite resulted instead, why in heaven's name would he continue the charade? From the moment he openly shared the good news that the Apostle James was right—that God was willing to give to all men liberally, and he'd even appear to them—he was thrust into a maelstrom of difficulty and incessant persecution that never relented. After over twenty-four years of harassment, trumped up law suits, imprisonment, accusations, betrayals, constant threats—he was murdered by a mob.

Joseph submitted to the law that was supposed to protect him, knowing as he did that he was "going like a lamb to the slaughter." As he and Hyrum left for Carthage, Joseph paused and turned in his saddle to look at Nauvoo, "The City Beautiful," knowing full well he would never see the city, the nearly-built temple, nor his family again. Even in that fateful hour, Joseph exhibited a righteous dignity, born of his absolute assurance that he had seen a vision and he knew it and he knew that God knew it; and he could not nor would not deny it. Quite some faith and backbone for a fraud. The final public statement he uttered was an additional prophecy: "I go like a lamb to the slaughter; but I am calm as a summer's morning; I have a conscience void of offense towards God, and towards all men. I shall die innocent, and it shall yet be said of me—he was murdered in cold blood" (D&C 135:4), which was fulfilled.

Ask yourself, "Would a fraud, a charlatan or a babbler (labels given him by his critics) have endured what he endured and conducted himself as Joseph did? For how long would you, or anyone you know, put up with the fury of hell that Joseph Smith did?" I submit just one of many specific examples of the kind of trying experiences Joseph endured. On March 24, 1832, while staying in the home of John Johnson—because they had no home of their own—Joseph, Emma, and two of their young adopted children were harassed and assaulted in the most egregious fashion. Joseph was dragged from his bedroom in the dead of night. His attackers strangled him until he blacked out, tore off his shirt and pants, beat and scratched him, and jammed a vial of poison against his teeth until it broke. After tarring and feathering him, they left him for dead. Joseph limped back to the Johnson's house and cried out for a blanket. Through the night, his friends scraped off the tar until his flesh was raw.[5] Luke Johnson, son of John, added additional details,

> *[Joseph] was stretched on a board, and tantalized in the most insulting and brutal manner; they tore off the few night clothes that he had on, for the purpose of emasculating him, and had Dr. Dennison there to perform the operation; but when the Dr. saw the Prophet stripped and stretched on the plank, his heart failed him, and he refused to operate.*

---

5 Richard Bushman, *Joseph Smith: Rough Stone Rolling,* (New York: Vintage Books, a division of Random House, Inc., 2005), 178.

> *One of the assailants fell on the naked Joseph, and "scratched my body with his nails like a mad cat," blaspheming, "God damn ye, that's the way the Holy Ghost fall on folks."*[6]

Emma was forced from the house with one of the children in her arms and threatened with murder and rape. The child who was ripped from Joseph's arms wound up on the floor and, due to exposure to the cold that night, died five days later of pneumonia. When Joseph managed to get back inside the Johnson home, Emma and others worked throughout the night to scrape the tar and feathers off his body. Even so, the horror of such an ordeal did not deter the prophet. The next morning, he stood at the pulpit to preach the gospel of Jesus Christ to the assembled audience that included some of the mobbers. "With my flesh all scarfied and defaced, I preached to the congregation as usual, and on the afternoon of the same day baptized three individuals."[7]

This attack was not the last degrading and insolent act inflicted upon Joseph and Emma. Yet despite all this, at no time did Joseph ever waver in his testimony. What possible motivation could a fraud have to maintain his deception in the face of such hardship across two decades? Stalwart to the end, Joseph faced it all, enduring all the bitterness for the sake of the Lord Jesus Christ up to and including June 27, 1844.

"By their fruits you shall know them." In the manner of Joseph's faith and perseverance is a bushel of impressive fruit, as are the fruits of his labors. No other religious organization can compare with the rise and continuous growth of The Church of Jesus Christ of Latter-day Saints. In fact, the question any person who leaves the Church has to answer is "Where do you go to find anything to equal or surpass it? Where do you go and unto whom do you hearken in order to replace the doctrines of the

---

6 Bushman, *Joseph Smith: Rough Stone Rolling,* 179.
7 Ibid., 179.

restored gospel?" The answer the Apostle Peter gave to the same question posed to him by the Lord himself holds validity today. John records, "From that [time] many of his disciples went back and walked no more with him. Then said Jesus unto the twelve, 'Will ye also go away?' Then Simon Peter answered him, 'Lord, to whom shall we go? Thou hast the words of eternal life'" (John 6:66–68).

Getting Back on the Covenant Path

The way back is to humbly look unto Christ in every thought and doubt not. Those who scoff at the straightforward counsel for cultivating the Spirit given by the Lord's prophets are like the children of Israel in Moses' time. After being bitten by poisonous serpents (how appropriate the analogy to the venomous bloggers and podcasters of today), the afflicted were invited to gaze upon the serpent [Christ] raised up upon a cross. Yet some perished because they were unwilling to set aside their pride and simply look at the symbol of Christ atoning for their sins.

> *Behold a type was raised up in the wilderness, that whosoever would look upon it might live. And many did look and live. But few understood the meaning of those things, and this because of the hardness of their hearts. But there were many who were so hardened that they would not look, therefore they perished … because they did not believe that it would heal them (Alma 33:19–20).*

The thought that leads the bitten in our generation astray is a prideful belief that they are above what they derisively refer to as "the Primary answers." "Why don't we ever hear anything new in general conference? It's just the same old oatmeal, regurgitated over and over again." Their pride leads them to look for a more "sophisticated" path than study of the scriptures, daily prayer, and regular temple worship. Yet, if they would be humble enough to heed the counsel of their leaders and *actually do the work,* they would discover the spiritual power that comes from applying the Primary answers and "see that by small means the Lord can bring about great things" (Alma 37:6).

Steps to return to the covenant path:

1) Study (not just superficially read) the scriptures. Every day.
2) Pray with real intent to understand the scriptures and obtain the Spirit and put into practice what the Spirit prompts. Every day.
3) Be willing to heed the promptings advising you to give up certain things. Make sacrifices to perform service you routinely shunned or dismissed in the past.
4) Stop playing with snakes. Continuing to feed yourself the fare that fosters doubts is just another form of the definition of insanity. You don't get lean and fit by eating junk food. It's even sillier to take a nip of arsenic now and then, just to be fair with your intake of heathy food.

These four steps are the essence of going to the Lord for the answers to your doubts. If you truly want to know the truth about God and the people He chooses to represent Him, amid the tumult of opinions on posts and podcasts, you ultimately have to reach the same conclusion as Joseph Smith did. He wasn't willing to stake his salvation on opinions and accusations. He even concluded he couldn't appeal to the Bible (let alone the Internet) for a true definitive answer, for it was spun and wrested in so many different ways. He realized that *only God could tell him the truth.* If you lack wisdom, ask of God! Instead of trying to disprove something, seek to prove it with an open mind and sincere intent. As promised in the Epistle of James, God will give to you liberally without scolding, if you will ask in sincerity and faith—meaning with an explicit promise that if He gives you the answer, you will embrace it and live it. No matter what.

Turn to your Heavenly Father. Replant the seed of faith. Alma declared, "Even if ye can no more than *desire to believe,* let this desire work in you, even until ye believe" (Alma 32:27). Nurture the seed of belief by awakening and arousing your faculties to practice even a small portion of the word. Sister Wendy W. Nelson offers a specific way to "awaken and experiment upon [God's] words":

> *Would you be willing to try an experiment for 30 days? Daily kneel and thank your Heavenly Father for the scriptures. Tell Him the one question you most need to have answered that day. Plead to have the Holy Ghost with you as you read. Then open your scriptures anywhere, and read until you find the answer. Try it for 30 days and see what happens.*[8]

Belief doesn't have to be perfect to be powerful. Keep it simple. Listen to general conference or study the most recent conference issue of the *Liahona*. Select just one admonition with a promise given by the living prophet. I'm talking about an "if you will … , I promise you …" statement. Then do it! Do what you're asked to do. Work at it. Keep it going. Let the consequence follow. It will not be long before you start feeling the positive spiritual effects. You will receive confirmation through the Spirit that the promise was of God and is real. You will see, feel, experience the benefits and blessings occurring in your life, just as promised. In time you will receive a clear witness that the living prophet is in fact God's mouthpiece. With that knowledge you will know that all his predecessors were likewise God's mouthpiece, especially including the Prophet Joseph Smith!

I urge you to cease trying to make God and Joseph Smith fit into your paradigm—your interpretations and assumptions of what God should be

8 Wendy Nelson, "Becoming the Person You Were Born to Be," *Worldwide Devotional for Young Adults,* January 10, 2016.

like and how he should treat, teach and test his other children—including those who may be much further along the path than you. God has no other choice than to work with imperfect beings. We're all He's got to work with. Nevertheless, He has proceeded to unfold, gradually, step by step the most amazing religious organization on the face of the earth—The Church of Jesus Christ of Latter-day Saints. There is nothing that comes close to its scope and its momentum. For instance, take the Lord's charge to His disciples as He ascended from Galilee into heaven two millennia ago. "Go ye therefore, and teach all nations, baptizing them in name of the Father, and of the Son, and of the Holy Ghost" (Matt. 28:19). Where on earth today do you find an organization coming closer to fulfilling that great missionary charge; and getting it done with an army of unpaid teenagers and young adults?"

What other church has a sensible answer to the long-standing question among Christians, "If baptism is required to enter the kingdom of heaven, then what of the babies who died or people throughout the ages who never even heard the name Jesus?" The Church of Jesus Christ of Latter-day Saints not only has a biblically supported answer in the form of vicarious work for the dead, but also a world-wide undertaking of family history research along with over two hundred temples dotting the earth where those ordinances are performed. Consider the worldwide humanitarian efforts. There was a time when the Church members were suffering so much persecution there were hardly sufficient resources to keep the saints alive. But, today as the Church has come of age, it can take care of itself and goes much further than that. Governmental and humanitarian leaders throughout the world marvel at the Church's welfare system. Thousands of people have been helped by saints in yellow t-shirts, who've voluntarily showed up to help them in times of disaster. Tons of food, water, clothing, shoes and other necessities have been delivered to sustain lives caught up in various crises.

Again, I ask where is there an organization to equal it here upon the earth? Step back and look at it from the perspective of the 1840s when the Prophet and his brother Hyrum lay dead in the basement of the Nauvoo house with their mother and sobbing wives and children grieving in shock. The feeble, impoverished Church should have died and vanished in no time. But it didn't. It struggled but it thrived, supported and empowered by the hand of God. Those who have doubts about the Prophet Joseph Smith would do well to heed the wisdom spoken by Gamaliel of the Sanhedrin when, after the death of the Savior, Peter and John were arraigned for healing in the name of Jesus.

> *When they heard that, they were cut to the heart, and took counsel to slay them. Then stood there up one in the council, a Pharisee, named Gamaliel, a doctor of the law, had in reputation among all the people … and said unto them, Ye men of Israel, take heed to yourselves what ye intend to do as touching these men. (Acts 5:33–35).*

The revered Jewish leader then reminded his colleagues in the Sanhedrin of various examples of pretenders and imposters who had their brief moment in the sun and who gathered a small group of followers, and whose movements came quickly unraveled and perished on their own. Then he offers wisdom that remains applicable today: "And now I say unto you, Refrain from these men, and let them alone: for if this counsel or this work be of men, it will come to nought: But if it be of God, ye cannot overthrow it; lest haply ye be found even to fight against God" (Acts 5:38–39).

Moral of the story: Beware of hubris and imposing your paradigm of God onto God; or how He should go about testing His prophets as well as testing us.

CHAPTER 21

Winning the Battle of Discouragement

No one is immune or exempt. Everyone experiences it. Most of us have waged some intermittent, and in some cases prolonged, battles with discouragement. Satan is ever vigilant to inflict discouraging language into our heads to stop us in our tracks and push hope onto the back burner. Elder Gene R. Cook confirmed whose voice it is that promotes discouragement in our heads. "I hope you are not really down on yourself or think you are not worth very much. That is the devil speaking. He is the one who keeps pounding away to make you feel that you are not worth much. That is not the Lord speaking."[1]

In the allegory, *The Pilgrim's Progress,* author John Bunyan used an apt metaphor to describe a portion of the journey the pilgrim named Christian must pass through to arrive at his desired destination, the Celestial City. Along his route, Christian encounters many trials and obstacles to obtain salvation. He must pass through the Slough of Despond and overcome Giant Despair. The Slough of Despond symbolizes a standard part of the

1 Cook, "How to Discourage Discouragement," *New Era,* January 2003.

testing we all experience in our mortal probation. In modern terms, we would call this testing "bouts of discouragement," and all "pilgrims" face it at several points along their journey. It just comes with the territory. All pilgrims grapple with fear, doubt and discouragement. In Bunyan's prose, he explains:

> *[T]herefore is it called the Slough of Despond: for still [soon] as the sinner is awakened about his lost condition, there ariseth in his soul many fears, and doubts, and discouraging apprehensions, which all of them get together, and settle in this place; and this is the reason of the badness of this ground.*[2]

According to Bunyan, it wasn't until Christian got serious about his salvation that fears, doubts, and discouraging apprehensions showed up, and that they *arose in his soul.* How blessed are we who have obtained a testimony of the restored gospel of Jesus Christ! Armed with knowledge of the Plan of Happiness and the rigors of mortality, we are empowered with priceless perspectives. We understand that discouraging apprehensions do not arise out of nowhere: they are injected into our minds by the father of lies and the enemy of our souls.[3] We also come to understand that these apprehensions are an integral part of our coursework and serve an indispensable, invaluable and holy purpose.

From Metaphor to Actuality

Out of the grueling, frigid months of December 1838 to April 1839, when Joseph, Hyrum, and four others languished in the loathsome Liberty Jail, have come three of the most precious sections of our Doctrine and Covenants. They were received as one single flow of divine light, and have been divided into sections 121, 122 and 123. The revelation of reassurance

2 John Bunyan, *The Pilgrim's Progress,* (Hertfordshire: Wordsworth Edition Limited, 199), 14.
3 Moses 4:4; Ether 8:35; 2 Ne. 2:18.

and doctrine came to Joseph on the 110th day of the incarceration that would end seventeen days later on April 6. If you haven't already, consider studying more about the inhumane conditions the prisoners endured, including being served human flesh to eat. Add to that the awareness these brethren had of the dire state of the saints in the region, as well as their families, all of whom had been driven from their homes in the dead of that same winter and whose plight was tenuous and uncertain. Sufficient for our purposes is to know the circumstances were brutal and would be a trial for any person to endure. Note also that the timing of the revelation confirms an important pattern mentioned and illustrated in scripture. Moroni articulated the pattern explicitly: "Faith is things which are hoped for and not seen; wherefore, dispute not because ye see not, for ye receive no witness until after the trial of your faith" (Ether 12:6). The revelatory experience began with Joseph offering a prayer:

> *O God, where art thou? And where is the pavilion that covereth thy hiding place? How long shall thy hand be stayed, and thine eye, yea thy pure eye, behold from the eternal heavens the wrongs of thy people and of thy servants, and thine ear be penetrated with their cries? (D&C 121:1–2).*

Then, in plain and perfect prose coming from the mind of the Lord to the mind of His Prophet, came the words:

> *My son, peace be unto thy soul; thine adversity and thine afflictions shall be but a small moment; And then, if thou endure it well, God shall exalt thee on high; thou shalt triumph over all thy foes (D&C 121:7–8).*

Later in the revelation comes the ultimate explanation:

> *If thou art called to pass through tribulation … if thou art accused with all manner of false accusations; if thine enemies fall upon thee …*

> *and thou be dragged to prison, and thine enemies prowl around thee like wolves for the blood of the lamb … if the heavens gather blackness, and all the elements combine to hedge up the way; and above all, if the very jaws of hell shall gape open the mouth wide after thee, know thou, my son, that all these things shall give thee experience, and shall be for thy good (D&C 122:5–7, emphasis added).*

There in unadorned power and plainness is the reason behind the vicissitudes and tribulation of mortal existence. There is reason and purpose: "All these things shall give [us] experience, and shall be for [our] good." Some things, yea, even the most important things, cannot be learned theoretically or academically. They can only be learned by personal and often painful experience. Were there any other way, we would not have to sip from the bitter cup—the full measure of which our Savior drank without shrinking in Gethsemane and finished on Calvary. This truth was precisely the next utterance that flowed into Joseph's mind: "The Son of Man hath descended below them all. Art thou greater than he?" (D&C 122:8).

Since all of God's children are saved on the same principles and God is no respecter of persons, we can liken these verses unto ourselves. With this last verse, the Lord is telling you and me what we all need to remember. In our hours of trial and heart-wrenching experiences, we all want to hear, just as Joseph did: "Be at peace, my child, I know what you are going through. I understand your pain and your anguish. I know how you feel and will stand by you and sustain you. Hang in there. All this is for a wise purpose in me. Every pang of pain and every heartache will give thee experience and shall be for thy good. And if thou endure it well, thou shalt be exalted on high."[4]

---

4 See D&C 122:7–8.

Joseph Endured It Well

President Wilford Woodruff bore his testimony of the Prophet's strength and valor:

> *When Joseph presented to the Christian world the principles that God had communicated to him, he at once aroused their prejudices; he had to struggle against traditions which they had inherited from their fathers who knew not God nor his ways. … And hence his life was one continual struggle, meeting with opposition on every hand. … He had to wade through deep waters; but he never was discouraged or disheartened notwithstanding he had to contend against foes without and foes within. He never lost sight of the majesty of his calling … and acted in the midst of the people under all circumstances as the man that he was—the prophet of God, the seer and revelator of the last dispensation.*[5]

Particularly meaningful is the phrase, "he had to contend against foes without *and foes within!*" Just as we do, Joseph had to contend with inner foes. Neither Joseph, nor any other prophet, nor even the Lord himself, is exempt from the interference and intrusions of the foe within. All of us are here to pass through trials so we may know good from the evil, by being exposed to evil. Our foes within seek any opportunity to use discouragement to thwart us because it is such a potent weapon for breaking our momentum. As we hold onto our eternal perspectives, we can rally our faith and draw from them and press forward. As endless as our times of discouragement may be or seem, they are but for a short season and will in the end work together for our good, if we walk uprightly.[6]

---

5 Wilford Woodruff, *Journal of Discourses,* 24:52.

6 D&C 90:24 and 100:15.

Discouragement: Lucifer's Last Chance

Satan's strategy to keep us from attaining "all that the Father hath"[7] is not complex. He uses fear and doubt *to prevent us* from starting our "pilgrim's progress;" and he uses discouragement *to stop us* and get us to give up and quit. He's working both ends of the spectrum. We focused on fear and doubt in previous chapters. In this chapter we focus on defeating Satan's ardent efforts to discourage us. Just as Satan's strategy is not complicated neither needs be our response. To defeat discouragement, we go back to the fundamental truth about Satan himself. He's called the "liar from the beginning;"[8] and he's still a liar. He spews lies in our heads about our worth and our hopes of obtaining eternal life. Think about that. Lucifer is telling us that we can't. But he wouldn't tell us that if we couldn't. Putting it more plainly, if Satan says you can't, it actually means you can!

Overcoming Discouragement by Battling the Source

We overcome discouragement by *battling the source, not the symptom.* Satan's cruelest ploy is to turn yourself on yourself. He does this in two ways: to think your *situations* are hopeless and beyond solution and to think *you* are hopeless and beyond salvation. With the testimony of the apostles and prophets, you can resist and reject his lies. His lies are not your thoughts. They are his! You may have to repeat those two short sentences over and over for a while until you feel them deeply. That's a way you can defeat discouragement and its author right at the source. Notice how Elder Jeffrey R. Holland characterized discouragement:

> *I wish to speak today of a problem that is universal and that can, at any given hour, strike anywhere. … I believe it is a form of evil. At least I know it can have damaging effects that block our growth, dampen*

---

7 D&C 84:38.
8 D&C 93:25.

> *our spirit, diminish our hope, and leave us vulnerable to other more conspicuous evils. I address it here this morning because I know of nothing Satan uses quite so cunningly or cleverly in his work. … I speak of doubt—especially self-doubt—of discouragement, and of despair.*

Elder Holland then directly identified the source of discouragement and clearly distinguished Satan's evil purpose in imposing it upon us and the consequences when we succumb to it:

> *Troubles we have all got, but the "germ" of discouragement … is not in the trouble, it is in us. Or to be more precise, I believe it is in Satan, the Prince of Darkness, the Father of Lies. And he would have it be in us. It's frequently a small germ … but it will work and it will grow and it will spread. In fact, it can become almost a habit, a way of living and thinking, and there the greatest damage is done. Then it takes an increasingly severe toll on our spirit, for it erodes the deepest religious commitments we can make—those of faith, and hope, and charity. We turn inward and look downward, and these greatest of Christ-like virtues are damaged or at very least impaired. We become unhappy and soon make others unhappy, and before long Lucifer laughs.*[9]

Identifying SKAM as the actual source of depressive thoughts and feelings gives us the key to defeating them. To begin with, we can adopt a mindset of seeing the higher purpose in the ups and downs of mortality. As we saw in the Diagram,[10] events are neutral until interpreted and assigned a value in our heads. That is where Satan jumps in, endeavoring to churn up dread and despair and, as Elder Holland said, "nothing he uses is more cunning." By divine design, facing disappointment is an important facet of our earthly education. We cannot learn to be effective problem-solvers

9 Jeffrey R. Holland, "For Times of Trouble," *BYU Devotional Address,* March 18, 1980.
10 See Chapter 12.

if we aren't given a few problems to solve. We can actually develop the attitude that facing problems is good news—even an invitation from a loving Heavenly Father for us to grow. SKAM, on the opposite hand, likes to put a negative spin on the word "problem," equating it with bad news. If we ask a friend how another ward member, William, is doing, we might hear, "Not too well," spoken in a somber tone of voice. Reacting to those words, we would likely ask, "Oh, what's the matter?" "Well, William has problems right now." And our natural response might be, "Oh, that's too bad. I'm sorry to hear that." In general, most people have a problem with the word "problem." However, that isn't always the case. If you are visiting with your son's algebra teacher at the beginning of a school year, the conversation might go like this:

Teacher: "I am really excited about having your son in my class. I want you to know I love teaching algebra and I'm committed to having my students become competent and confident in algebra so they can go on to higher things."

You: "That sounds great. How are going to do that?"

Teacher: "We're going to work a lot of problems. We'll work on problems in class, and then I'll give them problems to work on as homework—usually about five problems a week."

You: "Awesome!"

Would it make any sense to say, "Oh I don't think I want my son to solve any problems. I want him to just learn algebra the easy way without having to do that?" Life's problems and challenges are, again, in the eye of the chooser. If we look unto Christ and put our trust in Him, we can cease being shocked when things don't go our way. We can cease to play along when Satan tries to use setbacks as a means of sowing discouragement to stop us from progressing. If we develop the attitude that problems, disappointments and setbacks are an integral part of our probationary state, we take them more in stride. "To the wise," goes the Latin proverb, "to be forewarned is to be forearmed,"[11] which is a point underscored by Elder Holland, "As with any other germ, a little preventive medicine ought to be practiced against those things that make us depressed. Dante said 'When we see the arrow coming, we are less surprised by it.'"[12]

In addition to developing a healthier overall perspective about our personal curriculum here in mortality, we can also apply the counterpunch tactic described in Chapter 14. Elder Larry R. Lawrence shares his experience:

> *Satan effectively uses [discouragement] on the most faithful Saints, when everything else seems to fail. For me, when I begin to feel discouraged, it helps me to recognize who is trying to get me down. This makes me mad enough to cheer up—just to spite the devil.*[13]

Overcome Discouragement by Taking Action

Satan uses discouragement not only to thwart our own progress, he uses it to prevent or reduce the positive impact we can have on other people. If he can discourage us from serving others and doing good works, he wins and everybody else loses. Elder Jacob de Jager is a great example of turning the lemons of discouragement into the lemonade of good works and great spiritual growth.

Due to Elder de Jager's mastery of multiple languages he was an invaluable asset to the Church and presided over the International Mission for a number of years. Growing up under Nazi rule in his native Holland during World War II, he was barred from attending university because he would not sign a "declaration of loyalty" to the Nazi regime. He recounts his experience of dealing with discouragement:

---

11 https://www.phrases.org.uk/meaning/forewarned-is-forearmed.html.

12 Holland, "For Times of Trouble," *Liahona,* January 1982, 6.

13 Larry R. Lawrence, "The War Goes On," *Ensign,* April 2017, 39.

> *My plans to go to a university were stifled. Everything I had been working towards for so long now was truly unattainable. It is an understatement for me to say that this was a great discouragement. But I overcame it and in doing so learned a great lesson by deciding that if you cannot reach one goal then attain another goal. Sure, I had my moments of self-pity; then I decided to look for other options.*[14]

Jacob began to study on his own, nurturing an interest in languages that had no doubt been planted by the Lord in preparation for the mission he would later fill as a general authority. He found a way to study foreign languages by listening to prohibited radio broadcasts from other countries. Later, he served in the Dutch army which at first disappointed him. However, this twist turned out to be advantageous to his future as he learned additional languages while stationed in Asia. As he looked at the broader scope of his life, Elder de Jager could see what he thought were early setbacks and wasted years were actually preparatory steps in Heavenly Father's plan for him. "When I finally became a free man in 1949, I felt like I had spent seven years on hold. But in the same time the Lord had been preparing me in a special way for His later service."[15] In summary of what he had learned about adjusting one's mindset, he wrote:

> *Disappointments can be seen either as a prelude to continued failure in our lives or as occasions for great personal growth and even the beginning of truly outstanding performance. … All human beings experience disappointment. If this hard fact of development were not so, it would be very difficult to explain the joy of personal growth that often follows setbacks.*

---

14 Jacob de Jager, "Overcoming Discouragement," *New Era*, March 1984.

15 de Jager, "Overcoming Discouragement," *New Era*, March 1984.

> *The key, however, is to boldly face disappointments and the pains that accompany them. If you deny them or hide them from view, the chances are great that you will become worn out and fail. If, on the other hand, you meet them in a prayerful attitude asking for inner strength to overcome, the original disappointment will turn into an element of great strength and a firm foundation for further growth. Maybe it is required of all of us to know that through disappointments in life we may also find wisdom and great treasures of knowledge, even hidden treasures.*[16]

Overcome Discouragement by Refusing to Quit

Satan's goal of implanting discouragement is to get us to quit. The way we defeat him is to do the opposite: *We don't quit.* When we feel like quitting, we refuse and press forward. This is the bottom line and essential meaning of "enduring to the end." Elder Jeffrey R. Holland said it with great passion: "Don't give up, boy. Don't you quit. You keep walking. You keep trying. There is help and happiness ahead—a lot of it. ... You keep your chin up. It will be all right in the end. Trust God and believe in good things to come."[17] With an emotion-filled voice of experience, Elder Holland begs us to disregard the disheartening lies of the adversary. The archenemy of our souls sows discouragement by assaulting us with his incessant harangue of "You're not good enough." We've all heard it. You may be hearing it right now. Satan makes it personal. *"You don't have what it takes. Your hopes of eternal life are a delusion. It requires too much. It's too far. It's too high. It's too hard; especially for you. It's way too late. You've already blown it. Your sins are grotesque. You've already passed the point of no return. Give up and stop kidding yourself."*

---

16 de Jager, "Overcoming Discouragement," *New Era*, March 1984.
17 Holland, "An High Priest of Good Things to Come," *Ensign,* November 1999.

According to Heavenly Father's plan for each of us, we will experience our own tailored Abrahamic trials and Gethsemanes, which include a commensurate dose of Satan's venom. For one it may be a birth defect, for another overwhelming financial difficulties. For some it may be poor health, the death of a child or our spouse, or their departure from the Church. Some will have to face abandonment or betrayal. Some will not find a worthy companion despite an ardent desire to marry. Some couples will desire children and their heartfelt requests will not be granted in this life. The trials are varied and the only thing we know for sure is that each is gauged and properly fitted to the individual and are to "give [us] experience" and "all things will work together for [our] good if [we] walk uprightly."

Keenly aware of what is at stake, SKAM tries to rob you of the riches awaiting you for "enduring it well" by filling your mind with reasons to give up and quit. To all of God's children facing the trials of mortality Elder Dieter F. Uchtdorf offered counsel and encouragement:

> *The adversary uses despair to bind hearts and minds in suffocating darkness. Despair drains from us all that is vibrant and joyful and leaves behind the empty remnants of what life was meant to be. Despair kills ambition, advances sickness, pollutes the soul, and deadens the heart. Despair can seem like a staircase that leads only and forever downward. … And to all who suffer—to all who feel discouraged, worried, or lonely—I say with love and deep concern for you, never give in. Never surrender. Never allow despair to overcome your spirit. Embrace and rely upon the Hope of Israel, for the love of the Son of God pierces all darkness, softens all sorrow, and gladdens every heart.*[18]

From the pulpit at Temple Square, we repeatedly hear the clarion call, "Don't quit." How do you obey the counsel; *how* do you *not quit*? You take

18 Uchtdorf, "The Infinite Power of Hope," *Ensign*, November 2008, 22, 24.

it one step at a time. You put one foot in front of the other. Then the other foot in front of that one, and you repeat the rhythm for as long as it takes.

29029

The number 2233 may not mean anything to you. If I asked you to multiply it by the number 13, it might. The product would be 29029, the height of Mount Everest. Jesse Itzler, renowned for breaking all sorts of barriers, is an amazing human being. In January 2018, Itzler challenged an audience of financial planners, among whom was my son Matt, to enter a two-day event he called "Everesting 29029." "Have you got what it takes to climb Mount Everest?" he asked the group and then explained the challenge. The event took place at a ski resort Itzler reserved for a week. The participants hike up a mountain trail adjacent to the main gondola, from the base to the top of the mountain, 2233 feet in vertical distance. When they get to the top, the participants get on the gondola and ride it back down. Then they do it again. They hike to the top and then take the gondola back down to the bottom. Then they do it again, and again. When they have done that thirteen times, they've reached the equivalent of the summit of Mount Everest. Granted it's not the same degree of challenge—no snow, no ice, no yeti or hidden crevasses—and it's not pretending to be. But, if it sounds easy to you, well… it's not.

The participants have thirty-six hours to summit the mountain thirteen times. They start at 6 a.m. on the first day and the competition finishes at 6 p.m. the following day. Participants hike at their own pace; stop whenever they want; sleep if they choose to (and many do not); and eat and drink whatever they like and as much as they want. Of course, there are aid stations along the way, each one manned with medical personnel, including at the top of the mountain.

Matt was smitten with Itzler's energy and accepted the challenge. I have sons and daughters who have all placed high in competitive long-distance running events. My son David, for example, placed in the top ten of a one-hundred-mile race in Arizona, the Javelina Jundred (that's not a typo), and was paced by his sister Rachel, who ran cross-country in high school and college and completed her own 50-miler. This is a trait they must have gotten from their mother. I'm lockstep with Calvin Coolidge who said, "If nominated, I will not run." I bike. The scenery doesn't change fast enough for me when I run.

What I love about Everesting 29029 is how much opportunity it affords the parents and supporters to be involved. In the other long distance running events my children have competed in we'd hardly see them. Some of the time it was only at the start and again at the finish. With Everesting 29029, Susan and I, along with Matt's wife, Katie, were able to ride up on the gondola and get to the top about the time Matt would be arriving, and then ride with him back down on the gondola. We could talk to him and get filled in on how it was going, how he was feeling, and gauge his mental and physical state.

At the time of the event, Matt was forty-one years old and had been an athlete all his life. He worked out regularly and was very fit and strong. He trained extensively for the event, spending hours on the inclined treadmill at the gym. He flew to the site ahead of time and hiked the actual trail several times to know exactly what the course was going to be like and measure his timing. He lives at a low elevation, so for weeks prior, he wore a device that would simulate the oxygen level of the higher elevation of the hike. He did all this so he could be ready to take on the mountain while being a husband, father and owner of his own business.

At 6 a.m. on a sunny August morning, Day 1, Matt commenced. His goal was to complete the first ten ascents before he retired to his tent to sleep on the first day, leaving only three more climbs for the second day. He made Climb 1 in about an hour, hiking with a buddy from Atlanta who was also present at the time Itzler issued the challenge. Good shape. No sweat. (Well, not much, anyway). Same with Climbs 2 and 3. When he started Climb 4 around 11:00 a.m. we could all tell heat was going to soon become a factor. The sun in the high-altitude sky was intense. Climbs 4 and 5 each took over an hour to complete. Riding in the gondola back down the mountain, we could see the challenge starting to take its toll. Both Matt and his friend looked hot, tired, dusty and solemn—the early morning enthusiasm was long gone. They had been hiking non-stop for almost nine hours. Neither spoke much; they just ate and drank as we descended. You could tell doubts were starting to creep in, dragging discouragement along with it. Finally, Matt said, "I don't know. This thing is starting to kick my butt." Now in the late afternoon, the heat seemed tyrannical. Both men began Climb 6, trudging more than hiking as they ascended up the mountain and out of our sight.

Just short of two hours later they reached the top. Both looked exhausted, beat and discouraged. By now Matt had cut a "V" out of the back of one of his hiking shoes to relieve the friction on an area of his ankle that was turning into a blister. Both men spoke about it being "more than they'd bargained for." Discouragement with deep questioning about whether or not to continue was in full bloom. The gondola ride was heavy with downcast spirits.

"Before you start Climb 7, take a good break and let the angle of the sun change," I coached. "Have a good meal. Hydrate as much as you can. Then just commit to do *one more climb*. Forget about everything else. Just commit to summit one more time. That will put you over halfway; and you can then make the decision whether to keep climbing or not."

Climb 7 was the turning point. At the end of it, each made his decision. Matt decided to continue; his buddy decided to end it and go home. Matt said, "The sun will be setting soon and it's getting cooler. I'm going to keep going and do Climb 8." "How's your mindset," I asked. "It's going to be harder climbing alone—nobody to talk to to keep my mind off the pain. My right knee is hurting. That's why I'm limping a little. It's gotten down to *one step at a time.* I'm just telling myself that and concentrating on taking one more step each time I put one down. That's all I know how to do right now."

Climb 8 ended in the dark. Hikers who chose to continue during the night wore headlamps. The temperature had dropped drastically, but the climbing was significantly more difficult on a moonless night. Matt was still clinging to his hope of meeting his original goal of completing Climb 10 before retiring for the night, and set off on Climb 9, which he completed at about 11:45 p.m. "How was it?" we asked. "Hardest one yet… *by far.*" he said in doleful tone. "It's so hard to keep any momentum, because you can't see the terrain well enough to plan your next step until you take it. I'm not doing 10 tonight. It's just not worth it." On the way down in the gondola, shivering due to the cold and exhaustion, our disappointed and totally drained son outlined his plan for the next day. Having come this far, he was more committed than ever and was not about to quit, even though the negative nay-sayer in his head was begging him to do so.

"I have no idea how I'll feel in the morning. I may be so sore and stiff I won't even be able to get dressed. But, for now, I'm going to take a shower, get a massage and get something to eat before I go to sleep. I'm just going to pray I can rally in the morning and get out onto the mountain early. I don't look forward to completing 12 and 13 in the heat of the day."

"What time do you hope to get started?"

"Hopefully, I can wake up around 5 a.m. and be starting Climb 10 about 7:00 a.m."

With that we parted and drove to our hotel twenty-five miles way, and said our prayers, asking the Lord to give Matt the strength he needed to reach this goal.

At 5:00 a.m. my phone buzzed: it was a text from Matt: "I'm up and back on the mountain. Feeling good. Want to get as much climbing in before the heat cranks up." We arrived back to the site about 9 a.m., about the time, we estimated, Matt would be close to completing Climb 11.

When he arrived at the top of Climb 11, we were there to greet him. Right away we could tell our prayers had been answered. He still looked like he'd been through an ordeal, but he had a smile on his face and we could see a bit of the spark we're accustomed to seeing in Matt. "How's was it?" we asked. "Well, it's still tough and my calves are shot. I can't even feel them. The pain receptors in my brain must have given up, I guess. I just keep telling myself, 'Every step is a step closer to the finish.'"

By the time he completed Climb 12, the heat had returned, and it was again draining the energy of the hikers. We could tell Matt's physical tank was ebbing, but we also sensed that his mental strength was not. Hope was shining brightly before him. He knew he had only one last climb ahead of him. This *thought* buoyed his confidence as he visioneered himself crossing the finish line in another hour or so, and he'd have achieved what he set out to do.

At the Top

I wish I could convey the emotion Katie, Susan and I all felt as we witnessed Matt cross the finish line at the top of Climb 13. It was 12:45 p.m., five hours ahead of the deadline. We were cheering and crying without apology or embarrassment. It was a sacred moment and we felt grateful to be part of an unforgettable spiritual experience. Matt walked a few steps past the finish line as his name was announced and a staff member waved a large red flag signifying completion of the challenge. Matt squatted down and leaned forward bowing his head as he put his weight on his hands pressed against the ground. He stayed in that posture for several moments—long enough that the medical person on staff approached him, thinking he might be in physical distress. Then, the son who is not prone to shedding tears, lifted his bowed head, wiped his eyes with the top of his jersey, and stood up to accept the token of victory from a member of the Everesting team—a red baseball cap with the event logo on the front. Priceless.

Perspective

Throughout those two days I had spiritual vibes correlating my experience as an earthly father with a glimpse of what it must be like for our Heavenly Father. More than once I felt the spirit saying, "This is a taste of what the Father feels as he witnesses and supports each one of His children as they struggle to make their climbs back to His presence." I treasure what the Spirit taught me. I could see why Heavenly Father doesn't take away the pain, the blisters, the aching calves, or the exhaustion—and why He allows Satan to cast doubts and discouragement into the mix, making the whole thing even harder. *It's the hard stuff that makes it great!!*

As the climbs for Matt got harder and harder, and his enthusiasm melted into doubt and discouragement, he had to dig down and find strength and courage he didn't know he had. He had to pray more fervently and constantly for Heavenly Father's help and blessing in order to keep taking every one of those "one steps at a time." It's the hard stuff that makes us reach out with the "real intent" and "all the energy of heart" the Book of Mormon describes. With each "one step at a time," Matt was waging and winning a battle over Satan and his mortal body. Ever so gradually his overcoming of physical pain, doubt and discouragement was accomplishing something sacred and sanctifying—the growth of his spirit, the extension of the limits of his faith in himself, and amplification of his gratitude and faith in Jesus Christ who strengthened him. Matt knew in his extremity he wasn't doing it on his own. One of the miracles he received occurred in the early hours of the second day. "I'd only been asleep about three hours when I suddenly woke up. There wasn't a bit of soreness or stiffness in my body. I felt completely replenished and rejuvenated. I was alert, confident and ready to hit it. I know that was an answer to prayer—a gift from my Heavenly Father."

Let Us Not Be Discouraged When We Feel Discouraged

When it seems dark and hopeless or painful and purposeless, let us put our trust in Jesus Christ and call upon the Father in His holy name. May we remember: It's the hard stuff—for Christ and for us—that brings to pass justification and sanctification! May we look unto Christ in every thought and never forget the ultimate climb the Savior had to make in order for our climbs to have any meaning. A clear sign we are exercising our faith is when we can be grateful for the hard stuff. Again, it helps to remember the pattern. The most significant part of life-transforming events, that part we all need to be the most grateful for, is not the easy start. Nor is it the grand and glorious finish. It's the hard stuff in the middle in *between* the easy starts and the glorious finishes that makes the whole thing great. For that reason, we can even be grateful for doubts and discouragement. Without them acting upon his mind, Matt's victory would not have had the inner power it did. Without Climbs 6, 7, 8 and 9, Climb 13 would have had no glory.

Very few will escape moments where it seems like all we can do is endure. It is in those hours when "enduring it well" comes down to taking one more step. And then another. Although it may not seem so at that moment, one step at time is not only sufficient to qualify as "enduring it well," it is also heroic.

SECTION FOUR

Looking Unto Christ in Every Thought

"Oh, there is so much more that your Father in Heaven wants you to know. As Elder Neal A. Maxwell taught, 'To those who have eyes to see and ears to hear, it is clear that the Father and the Son are giving away the secrets of the universe!'"

—President Russell M. Nelson, "Revelation for the Church, Revelation for Our Lives," *Ensign,* May 2018, 95, quoting Elder Neal A. Maxwell, "Meek and Lowly," *BYU Devotional Address,* October 21, 1986.

CHAPTER 22

Believing in a God of Promises

We believe in a God of promises. We believe in gifts of the Spirit. We believe God will yet reveal many great and important things pertaining to the kingdom of God. We believe in the literal gathering of Israel and the restoration of the ten tribes to the lands of their inheritance. We believe the New Jerusalem will be built upon the American continent and we believe Christ will reign personally upon the earth. And we long for the day when all that was promised the saints shall be given. Why? Because God has *promised* these things, and we believe in a God who keeps His promises.

Parley Parker Pratt and Thankful Halsey believed in God's promises. By the fall of 1829, the newly-wedded Pratts had created for themselves an enviably comfortable life and lifestyle for the times in which they lived. Through hard work and diligence, they owned a comfortable home surrounded by farm acreage they had carved out of the Ohio forest about thirty miles west of Cleveland.

> *A small frame house was now our dwelling, a garden and a beautiful meadow were seen in front, flowers in rich profusion were clustering*

about our door and windows; while in the background were seen a thriving young orchard of apple and peach trees, and fields of grain extending in the distance, beyond which the forest still stood up in its own primeval grandeur, as a wall to bound the vision and guard the lovely scene.[1]

Even before he and Thankful were married, Parley had devoted himself to years of diligent study of the Bible. He was thoroughly enthralled with the life and teachings of the Lord Jesus Christ and the establishment and growth of the Church He founded as described in the gospels and The Acts of the Apostles. He grew close to the Spirit and the Holy Ghost tutored him.

At the commencement of 1830, I felt drawn out in an extraordinary manner to search the prophets, and to pray for an understanding of the same. My prayers were soon answered, even beyond my expectations; the prophecies of the holy prophets were opened to my view; I began to understand the things which were coming on the earth—the restoration of Israel, the coming of the Messiah, and the glory that should follow. I was so astonished at the darkness of myself and mankind on these subjects that I could exclaim with the prophet: surely, "darkness covers the earth, and gross darkness the people."[2]

As he and Thankful continued to enjoy their home and the fruits of their labors, Parley felt compelled by the Spirit to share his scriptural knowledge with friends and neighbors in the area and became regarded as a gifted preacher. Through fortuitous events, Parley became reconnected with an older brother, William, whom he had not seen for over five years and assumed was dead.

---

1 Parley P. Pratt, *Autobiography of Parley Parker Pratt,* (Salt Lake City: Deseret Book Company, 1938, reprinted 1976), 31.

2 Pratt, *Autobiography of Parley Parker Pratt,* 33.

> *This was a joyful and unexpected meeting of two brothers. He immediately accompanied me home, and was introduced to my wife and our little farm in the wilderness, where we spent some days together. He admired my wife; but above all my farm. "Brother Parley," said he, "how have you done all this? When we were last together you had no wife, no farm, no house, no orchard, and now you are here with everything smiling around you." I replied that hard work had accomplished it all.*[3]

William was just short of aghast when Parley informed him that he and Thankful were about to leave the self-made paradise they'd worked so hard to create, being perfectly willing to walk away from it all and never see it again. When William asked for an explanation, Parley began sharing with him "the gospel and prophecies as they had been opened" to him. He told William that the Spirit had rested upon him so powerfully he could not rest but needed to share his knowledge with as many as would listen. Still William protested,

> *If I had fifty acres of land, a comfortable house, a fine orchard, a beautiful garden, with meadow land, grain, and above all, such beautiful flowers and … all these things the work of our own hands, I am sure I would stay and enjoy the same while I lived; and the world might go on its own jog. … Besides, how are you to get your living? This is your all; you have toiled for years to obtain it, and why not now continue to enjoy it?*[4]

Parley replied, "Why, sir, I have bank bills enough, on the very best institutions in the world, to sustain myself and family while we live." He assured William the promissory notes he had could never fail and would

3 Ibid., *33–34*.
4 Pratt, *Autobiography of Parley Parker Pratt,* 34.

ever be honored by the institution that issued them. When William asked if he could see the bills, Parley opened a large pocketbook containing the valued promissory notes. On ordinary paper, written in Parley's own hand, were passages from the Bible—promises and prophecies taken from the pages of scripture Parley had studied out, absorbed deeply into his soul, and reverenced as literally true and valid.

> *Parley: Now, William, are these the words of Jesus Christ, or are they not?*
>
> *William: They certainly are; I always believed the New Testament.*
>
> *P: Then you admit they are genuine bills?*
>
> *W: I do.*
>
> *P: Is the signer able to meet his engagements?*
>
> *W: He certainly is.*
>
> *P: Is he willing?*
>
> *W: He is.*
>
> *P: Well, then, I am going to fulfill the conditions to the letter on my part. I feel called upon by the Holy Ghost to forsake my house and home for the gospel's sake; and I will do it, placing both feet firm on these promises with nothing else to rely upon.*[5]

What faith is manifested in these words! Placing his trust in the promptings of the Spirit and in the fidelity of the Lord Jesus Christ, whom he had not as yet heard or seen, Parley Pratt was prepared to give his all. In his mind, no earthly comfort, no worldly wealth, nothing the best of mortal life had to offer equaled, let alone excelled, the wealth the Lord had

---

5 Pratt, *Autobiography of Parley Parker Pratt,* 35.

to offer those who will believe in Him enough to give their all. So Parley and Thankful Pratt believed the promises of the Lord and they acted upon them with full purpose of heart.

Think again on what basis they made such a total sacrifice and leap of faith. They had in their possession fewer canonical books of scripture than we have—only one of the standard works. They had not heard with their own ears the solemn testimonies of *living* apostles and prophets as we have, which we too often take so casually as ho-hum ordinary statements. They had not been supplied with inspired manuals to study with their families to pray over and ponder. There were no bookstores, websites or smartphones for them to obtain scriptural commentaries, biographies and other books laden with doctrinal guidance. And, they could not have even begun to conceive of having in reasonable proximity to their home a house of the Lord where they could receive personal revelation about the scriptures and even greater ordinances than baptism.

The Pratts treasured and made the most of what they had; and they studied diligently and prayed about the words of ancient prophets, apostles, and inspired evangelists. And they *believed in them.* Parley and Thankful Pratt did not take those holy words and testimonies as beautiful literary prose or heart-warming stories. They took them *literally.* Before the two brothers parted, William made a significant statement we all could ponder. "Well," said he, "try it, if you will; but, for my part, although I always believed the Bible, I would not dare believe it literally, and really stand upon its promises, with no other prop."[6]

Human Testimony and Human Testimony Only

Before Parley Parker Pratt was called to be an apostle in the initial Quorum of the Twelve, before he was baptized by water and the Spirit,

6 Pratt, *Autobiography of Parley Parker Pratt,* 35.

before he had spoken with angels or seen the face of the Lord, he believed the testimony of those witnesses God set before him. He received promptings and whisperings of the Spirit that "wrought upon him" as he continued to pray and study and teach and live the gospel to the best of his imperfect ability. By doing all these things, he proved for himself, just as the Prophet Joseph Smith had done, that God is no respecter of persons, and He gives to all men liberally if they ask and act in faith without doubting.

Just three years after departing his homestead in Ohio, Elder Pratt received spiritual confirmations far beyond his expectations. While others doubted and even betrayed the prophet, Parley's believing heart soaked up every word that fell from Joseph's lips as though from the Lord Himself. In the summer of 1833, Elder Pratt was called to teach a branch of the School of the Prophets, called the School of Zion located in Independence, Missouri. His efforts so pleased the Lord, he was commended in a revelation now found in the Doctrine and Covenants: "I, the Lord, am well pleased that there should be a school in Zion, and also with my servant Parley P. Pratt, for he abideth in me" (D&C 97:3). Parley's study, faith and obedience to the Spirit—ever willing to set aside the cares of the world—resulted in further privileges and promises of the Lord: "And I will bless him with a multiplicity of blessings, in expounding all scriptures and mysteries to the edification of the school, and of the church in Zion" (D&C 97:5).
A significant part of the curriculum of "scriptures and mysteries" Parley expounded was what we now call The Lectures on Faith. Upon specific direction from the Prophet Joseph Smith, Elder Pratt memorized and delivered the lectures verbatim to the sixty people who attended. The powerful conclusion of Lecture Two reads as follows:

> *Let us here observe, that after any portion of the human family are made acquainted with the important fact that there is a God, who*

> *has created and does uphold all things, the extent of their knowledge respecting his character and glory will depend upon their diligence and faithfulness in seeking after him, until, like Enoch, the brother of Jared, and Moses, they shall obtain faith in God, and power with him to behold him face to face.*
>
> *We have now clearly set forth how it is, and how it was, that God became an object of faith for rational beings; and also, upon what foundation the testimony was based which excited the inquiry and diligent search of the ancient saints to seek after and obtain a knowledge of the glory of God; and we have seen that it was human testimony, and human testimony only, that excited this inquiry, in the first instance, in their minds. It was the credence they gave to the testimony of their fathers, this testimony having aroused their minds to inquire after the knowledge of God; the inquiry frequently terminated, indeed always terminated when rightly pursued, in the most glorious discoveries and eternal certainty.*[7]

Today we are blessed with the fruits of the labors and sacrifices and teachings of the early members of The Church of Jesus Christ of Latter-day Saints such as Thankful and Parley Pratt. We are blessed with resources galore to assist us in our studies and receive constant counsel from the living president and prophet of the church along with fourteen other prophets, seers and revelators. May we never take any of these gifts of the Spirit for granted. Let us hearken to the words of the Apostle Paul:

> *Wherefore seeing we also are compassed about with so great a cloud of witnesses, let us lay aside every weight, and the sin which doth so easily beset us, and let us run with patience the race that is set before us,*

7 Smith, *Lectures on Faith,* Lecture Second, 55-56, emphasis added.

Looking unto Jesus the author and finisher of our faith; who for the joy that was set before him endured the cross, despising the shame, and is set down at the right hand of the throne of God (Heb. 12:1–2).

And What Glorious Promises We Have!

How comforting and inspiring are the words of Moroni regarding the universal, all-inclusive nature of God's promises to His children—men, women, old, young, early starters, and late bloomers—all are included. The adversary tries to make us think otherwise—that some way or another, we are disqualified, excluded, and left out. If such a thought has become part of how you view yourself, please replace that false notion with these reassuring words of the Apostle Peter: "Of a truth I perceive that God is no respecter of persons: But in every nation he that feareth him, and worketh righteousness, is accepted with him" (Acts 10:34–35). And, as you do so, savor again this sublime confirming testimony from the prophet Moroni:

And behold, I say unto you he changeth not; if so he would cease to be God; and he ceaseth not to be God, and is a God of miracles.

And the reason why he ceaseth to do miracles among the children of men is because that they dwindle in unbelief, and depart from the right way, and know not the God in whom they should trust.

Behold, I say unto you that whoso believeth in Christ, doubting nothing, whatsoever he shall ask the Father in the name of Christ it shall be granted him; and this promise is unto all, even unto the ends of the earth (Mormon 9:19–21).

Let us lay aside every weight of doubt and hesitation. As literal spirit sons and daughters of the Most High, let us treasure in our hearts each word of promise He declares and seek our Father's guidance and strength in obtaining them. Specifically, let us study three glorious promises found in the Doctrine and Covenants, and let us *believe* them and take them *literally*!

D&C 42: 61

> *If thou shalt ask, thou shalt receive revelation upon revelation, knowledge upon knowledge, that thou mayest know the mysteries and peaceable things—that which bringeth joy, that which bringeth life eternal.*

D&C 76: 5–10

> *For thus saith the Lord—I, the Lord, am merciful and gracious unto those who fear me, and delight to honor those who serve me in righteousness and in truth unto the end.*
>
> *Great shall be their reward and eternal shall be their glory.*
>
> *And to them will I reveal all mysteries, yea, all the hidden mysteries of my kingdom from days of old, and for ages to come, will I make known unto them the good pleasure of my will concerning all things pertaining to my kingdom.*
>
> *Yea, even the wonders of eternity shall they know, and things to come will I show them, even the things of many generations.*
>
> *And their wisdom shall be great, and their understanding reach to heaven; and before them the wisdom of the wise shall perish, and the understanding of the prudent shall come to naught.*
>
> *For by my Spirit will I enlighten them, and by my power will I make known unto them the secrets of my will—yea, even those things which eye has not seen, nor ear heard, nor yet entered into the heart of man.*

D&C 84: 33–40

For whoso is faithful unto the obtaining these two priesthoods of which I have spoken, and the magnifying their calling, are sanctified by the Spirit unto the renewing of their bodies.

They become the sons of Moses and of Aaron and the seed of Abraham, and the church and kingdom, and the elect of God.

And also all they who receive this priesthood receive me, saith the Lord;

For he that receiveth my servants receiveth me;

And he that receiveth me receiveth my Father;

And he that receiveth my Father receiveth my Father's kingdom; therefore all that my Father hath shall be given unto him.

Worthy of contemplation are the words that follow this great promise extended to women and men who worthily enter into the temple and keep their covenants. So firm and sure are these "promissory notes" that the Father binds himself *with an oath* to honor them!

And this is according to the oath and covenant which belongeth to the priesthood. Therefore, all those who receive the priesthood, receive this oath and covenant of my Father, which he cannot break, neither can it be moved (D&C 84:39–40).

These magnificent promises declared in this "revelation on priesthood"[8] pertain to Heavenly Father's daughters just as much as to His sons. As he addressed the sisters of the Church in a session of general conference, President Russell M. Nelson, declared this truth:

8 See heading of D&C 84.

How I yearn for you to understand that the restoration of the priesthood is just as relevant to you as a woman as it is to any man. Because the Melchizedek Priesthood has been restored, both covenant-keeping women and men have access to "all the spiritual blessings of the church" or, we might say, to all the spiritual treasures the Lord has for His children.

Every woman and every man who makes covenants with God and keeps those covenants, and who participates worthily in priesthood ordinances, has direct access to the power of God. Those who are endowed in the house of the Lord receive a gift of God's priesthood power by virtue of their covenant, along with a gift of knowledge to know how to draw upon that power.

The heavens are just as open to women who are endowed with God's power flowing from their priesthood covenants as they are to men who bear the priesthood. I pray that truth will register upon each of your hearts because I believe it will change your life.[9]

Transforming lives is the primary purpose of God's covenants and supernal promises to us, His children! Extending blessings and joys beyond description or measure, He invites us to set aside the transient baubles of mortality and seek in dedicated earnestness the everlasting joys of Eternal Life. For each of us who will do so, He will do more than change our life, *He will change us*—our very nature and character—even to the degree we shall be like Him.

Let Us Accept His Invitation and Choose His Ways

In the writings of Jeremiah, we find a prophecy and a promise delivered by Jehovah to His people when they were held captive in Babylon.

9 Nelson, "Spiritual Treasures," *Ensign,* November 2019, 77.

Knowing that prophecies of the ancient prophets have more than one true fulfillment, we can learn much from Jeremiah's words as we liken them unto our day and ourselves. The Lord has urged us to "go ye out of Babylon" (D&C 133:7). Babylon represents a society centered on worldliness and an economy based on deception and greed. It doesn't take much of a stretch to make the connection to the times in which we live. Jeremiah prophesied of the Lord's relationship and the promise He makes to His people when they come out of Babylon. Hear, then, the Lord's promise to you and me:

> *Then shall ye call upon me, and ye shall go and pray unto me, and I will hearken unto you. And ye shall seek me, and find me when ye shall search for me with all your heart (Jeremiah 29:12–13).*

May we all go forward with the same earnest faith, commitment and courage as Thankful and Parley Pratt, demonstrating with all our hearts, as they did, that we believe in a God of promises.

CHAPTER 23

Obtaining Strength Beyond Your Own

Of the stunning promises the Lord our God has pronounced, none is more plain and precious than this one:

> *Verily, thus saith the Lord: It shall come to pass that every soul who forsaketh his sins and cometh unto me, and calleth on my name, and obeyeth my voice, and keepeth my commandments, shall see my face and know that I am (D&C 93:1).*

This striking verse is unique in how clearly the requirements for obtaining the promise are spelled out. Holding fast to the same faith and hope as Parley and Thankful Pratt, let us study this glorious promise line by line:

"Verily, thus saith the Lord:"

The Lord Jesus Christ is known as "The Word"[1] and "The Truth."[2] In the first section of the Doctrine and Covenants, He declares how sure His pronouncements are: "And though the heavens and the earth pass away,

1 John 1:1–2.
2 John 14:6.

my word shall not pass away, but shall all be fulfilled" (v. 38). Knowing the Lord's word is sure, we prepare our minds for the first word: "verily."

We are mistaken if we suppose "verily" to be a trite word of beginning. He who is the God of truth and cannot lie, is not saying this casually. This is a wake-up call—an earnest invitation—to devote our attention and embrace what is to follow. We might consider it to be a shortened version of a prelude question posed to prophets on the verge of receiving a vision—"Believest thou all the words I *shall speak*?"[3] We do well to focus and open our hearts to receive the pearl He is about to offer.

"It shall come to pass that every soul . . ."

How energizing is the word *every*. It undergirds and strengthens our faith that what is to be said applies to *us*! With this one word, the Lord reaffirms He is no respecter of persons. Whoever obeys the law upon which a given blessing is predicated will surely receive the associated blessing, for it is irrevocably decreed. This single word connects powerfully to "who giveth to *all* men liberally" and the Prophet Joseph Smith's grand declaration, "God hath not revealed anything to Joseph, but what He will make known unto the twelve, and *even the least* saint may know all things as fast as he is able to bear them."[4]

". . . who forsaketh his sins and cometh unto me,"

Forsaking sins and coming unto the Lord is a blessed, spirit-empowered invitation, which can be summed up in one word: repentance. Repentance is the pathway to healing and sweet forgiveness for those who look unto Christ in their thoughts. Neil L. Andersen said, "The Lord's desire that we come unto Him and be wrapped in His arms is often an invitation to repent. 'Behold, he sendeth an invitation unto all men, for the arms of

3 Ether 3:11; 1 Ne. 11:4–5.

4 Smith, *Teachings of the Prophet Joseph Smith,* 149, emphasis added.

mercy are extended towards them, and he saith: Repent, and I will receive you'" (3 Ne.9:14).[5] Satan has succeeded in his sinister goal of distorting the true character of God as a loving parent, convincing the general population instead that Heavenly Father is an angry old man, quick to condemn and slow to forgive. Embedding that falsehood, he then equates repentance to punishment, urging us to avoid it by cloaking it in a shroud of fear and dread. In truth, repentance is the soothing balm to heal our wounds, relieve our burdens, and bring us into the embrace of our loving Heavenly Father.

The essence of repentance is to do exactly what the Lord requests in His promise. We give up all that separates us from Him in our thoughts and actions and come unto him with a humble heart, submitting our will to His. The coupling of "forsaking our sins" and "coming unto Him" is significant. For the only way we completely forsake our sins is by coming unto Him—to learn what to forsake and gain the power to do it. In our fallen state with the additional weight of the sins we commit, we are unable to free ourselves of the burden we now carry or heal the wounds we incur in this mortal state. Hence the poignancy of the Lord's solicitous invitation, "Come unto me, all ye that labor and are heavy laden, and I will give you rest. Take my yoke (as opposed to the yoke of bondage) upon you, and learn of me; for I am meek and lowly in heart (as opposed to proud, mean-spirited and hypercritical); and ye shall find rest unto your souls; for my yoke is easy, and my burden is light" (JST Matt. 11:28–30).

As Moroni made his final entry on the plates, he reiterated God's invitation and assured us that we do not have to do it on our own willpower. "Yea, come unto Christ," he pleads, "and be perfected in him, and deny yourselves of all ungodliness; and if ye shall deny yourselves of all ungodliness and love God with all your might, mind and strength, then is his grace sufficient for you, that by his grace ye may be perfect in Christ

5 Andersen, "Repent . . . That I May Receive You," *Ensign,* November 2009, 40.

(Moroni 10:32). Our mortal strength is not, nor ever will be, sufficient. As we do our best to forsake the world and our sins, Christ's grace will enable and strengthen us every step along the way. Empowered by His grace, we will incorporate more truth and light into our souls and eventually be perfected in Christ.

Sacrificing Our Sins

In the Book of Alma, the remarkable saga of the mission of the four sons of Mosiah to the Lamanite people includes the account of the conversion of a Lamanite king (Alma 20). Actually, he was a king of kings. One of his vassal kings, Lamoni, was taught by Ammon and had received the Holy Ghost. As Lamoni's father, also a king, hears this news, he is outraged and threatens to slay Lamoni. Ammon steps in and the king turns on Ammon to slay him instead. Ammon disarms the enraged father, who then begs for Ammon's mercy. "If thou wilt spare me I will grant unto thee whatsoever thou wilt ask, even to half of the kingdom" (Alma 20:23). Later, this king of kings allows Ammon's brother, Aaron, to teach him the gospel. After a lengthy doctrinal discussion, the king is so impressed and touched by the Spirit, a mighty desire wells up inside him. This desire is so great, the king is willing to go beyond the price he was willing to pay to save his mortal life—half his kingdom. He is prepared to give up *everything*—everything that stands in his way from receiving the eternal joy Aaron had described. "Behold, said he, I will give up *all that I possess*, yea, I will forsake my kingdom, that I may receive this great joy" (Alma 22:15, emphasis added). No doubt thrilled with how deeply the teachings had been received, Aaron gave instruction: the king must repent of all his sins—make a profound commitment to forsake and never return to his sins, bow down before God and call on His name in faith, believing that God will grant his request. The king immediately complies. Without hesitation, he does what Aaron asked him to do. He doesn't just bow, he prostates himself on the ground and cries mightily, saying "…if thou art God, wilt thou make thyself known unto me, and I will give away all my sins to know thee, and that I may be raised from the dead, and be saved at the last day" (Alma 22:17–18). This king must have been a man who faithfully honored his commitments—a man whose word was his bond. For, upon this one earnest pronouncement, he was overwhelmed by the power of the Holy Ghost and, like his vassal son, Lamoni, was also born again.

For most of us—actually for all of us—truly forsaking all our sins is a journey, not an instantaneous event. That includes the Lamanite king as well. For the rest of his mortal days, he must faithfully maintain his commitment, never returning to his past ways. Forsaking our sins is more than a verbal renouncement, it requires a complete revision of our purpose, priorities and pastimes—a new way of thinking and being. All idols and idle pursuits must be put away, so we may worship the only true God and Him only. None of us fallen mortals can accomplish that on our own. Even a sincere, in-depth confession of one's sins and transgressions is made only with the assistance and strength of the Spirit.

The great news in all of this is how eager the Father and the Son are to help us, and how pleased they are when we ask for their help. Due to agency, they cannot respond until we ask. Christ is the source of our power to forsake our sins. With and through His grace, He provides strength beyond our own every step of the way. What makes repentance a journey we cannot make alone, stems from the stiff resistance we get from the adversary, who constantly works to appease the pangs of an uneasy conscience by smothering it with rationalizations, self-justifications, and excuse-making. In his book *The Divine Gift of Forgiveness,* Elder Neil L. Andersen, writes about the "twin bullies of pride and fear:"

> *[Fear and pride] are twin bullies because they work together in hopes of preventing us from making the important decisions that will bring*

us to Jesus Christ. Fear and pride immediately attempt to counter our positive thoughts of faith and prayer and our determination to become the person God wants us to be. False pride and erroneous fear are connected because of our mortal insecurities, which Satan constantly tries to use against us.[6]

Knowing the transforming power of the Atonement of Jesus Christ, the adversary will do all in his power to prevent, or at least delay, God's children from forsaking their sins and coming unto Christ.

The Faith to Forgive

One might not view withholding forgiveness as a sin, but it is. It's a sin against ourselves and it's a sin against Christ—the One who suffered the unspeakable anguish required of divine justice so He could forgive our sins. One of the steps we must take in forsaking our sins and coming unto Christ is to forgive and leave the administration of justice up to Him. Those who come to realize the healing power of forgiveness know firsthand why we are commanded to forgive. All who forgive without reservation experience the healing power of the Atonement of Jesus Christ. Consider this account shared by one who works as a mentor in an Addiction Recovery Program:

It would've been better if I'd never been born!" lamented Jim as he sat looking at the desk with tears in his eyes. Where do feelings of such anguish and despondency come from? Since a young teen, Jim had struggled with addictive behavior and overwhelming feelings of hopelessness, shame and failure.

Fortunately, Jim was willing to be brutally honest with himself. Finally admitting he could not do it on his own, he sought relief from the

6 Neil L. Andersen, *The Divine Gift of Forgiveness,* (Salt Lake City: Deseret Book Company, 2019), 122.

constant anguish he felt by entering an addiction recovery program. That is how I first met Jim and began working with him. Through the many appointments during the first year I met with him, he never once smiled or laughed at any situation or made jovial comment. As I share his history you will see why.

When Jim was fifteen months old, his father made the decision to leave his mother and three other siblings. Tremendous hardship was placed upon his mother. She worked two and three jobs in an effort to survive financially. Once in a while, his father would show up and stay with the family for a few hours. Then he'd fade out of their lives for a number of months. Holidays, birthdays and other special events were acknowledged sporadically and unpredictably by the man he knew as his "biological father." Year by year feelings of hostility and anger grew as he recognized the void in his life due to the absence of a father figure.

At a fairly young age he was introduced to pornography. At first he viewed it out of curiosity, but he soon found the sexual images helped to numb the painful feelings smoldering within his heart. Jim unintentionally found himself deeply entrenched in an addiction to the distorted sexual images that numbed his pain. His need for more lurid forms of pornography continued to escalate.

There were periods of time when he would "white knuckle" his addiction and remain clean for a few weeks but never for a sustained period. He always relapsed back into the demoralizing world of pornography.

Eventually, mustering all the courage he could find within his soul, he humbly approached his bishop and pled for help in resolving his addiction. Jim came away from the interview with hope and a desire to fully recover through the blessings of the Atonement of Jesus Christ.

Jim was referred to an addiction recovery program based on the church's 12-Step program done on a one-to-one basis rather than in a group.

Each step required considerable commitment, time and accountability on Jim's part, as he processed and applied each of the principles taught. The concept of a loving Heavenly Father seemed to resonate in his soul as never before. The seed of transformation began to grow as he nourished it with heartfelt prayer, scripture study and humility. In due course, Jim was made aware of the miracles available through the Atonement of Jesus Christ—particularly both the redeeming power and the enabling power of Jesus Christ that could heal his heart and change his life.

Having grown up in the church and having served a mission, Jim thought he understood the teachings of the Savior regarding forgiveness. As his faith in Jesus Christ grew, he was able to better understand principles of truth in a profound and meaningful way, including the principle of forgiveness, giving him a new perspective.

During one particular appointment, Jim was asked to make a list of individuals he had offended in his life and from whom he needed to seek forgiveness. He also created an additional list of individuals whom he needed to forgive. Interestingly his father's name did not appear on that significant list. A pointed question was asked to the solemn-faced young man, "Where is your father's name?" Immediately, Jim's face turned red and there was definite anger in his voice as he blurted out "You expect me to forgive him? After all that he has done to me and my family?" Then he asserted "I could never do that!"

In the following weeks there were numerous discussions focused on the teachings of a loving Heavenly Father and Savior regarding forgiveness, love and basing one's life on truth. In particular, attention was drawn to Doctrine and Covenants 64:9–10: "Wherefore, I say unto you, that ye ought to forgive one another; for he that forgiveth not his brother his trespasses standeth condemned before the Lord; for there remain in him the greater sin. I, the Lord, will forgive whom I will forgive, but of you it is required to forgive all men."

After considerable deliberation, Jim recognized if he didn't bring himself to forgive his father the heavy burden of pain would continue to fuel his addiction. But how could he accomplish such a daunting task? Deep-seated feelings of anger and animosity had festered in his soul for nearly twenty years.

Jim was advised to write a letter of forgiveness to his father which seemed to be a simple task. At the next appointment he read the proposed letter. It started out kindly but then deteriorated to "if you hadn't done … I wouldn't have felt … " sentences. Jim was asked to rewrite his letter and simply, unconditionally forgive his father in a brief, succinct statement. A week later he returned with a new one-page letter which was an improvement but still lacked one key element. He needed to feel the genuine love and peace that accompanies unconditional forgiveness. Additionally, Jim was asked to pray for the well-being of his father and the betterment of his life, and to ask his father for forgiveness if he had offended him in any way over the many years of their strained relationship. Jim shook his head but agreed to pursue the suggestions.

During the month of December there was a four-week recess with no contact with his mentors. At the first appointment of the year, in walked a grinning version of the Jim his mentors had seen a month ago. A major transformation had taken place. When asked how he was doing, a smiling Jim stood up and walked to the white board. In large letters he printed "Good!" Then he paused for a moment and boldly printed "Good" two more times. Energetically he elaborated, stating he was "Good" with his mother, siblings and friends; and he was "Good" with his dad!

Jim went on to explain he had met with his father and simply said, "Dad, I forgive you for any offenses of the past; and if I have offended you in any way, I ask you to forgive me." Surprised, his father stood there in a state of shock. Peace and love flowing from unconditional forgiveness permeated Jim's soul as he departed. Amazingly, after years of anguish, in a matter of a few moments, his entire burden of pain was lifted from his soul. It was lifted by our loving Savior Jesus Christ who paid the full and ultimate price so the miracles of healing and transformation could be granted to those who put their trust in Him and do what He requires for the power of His Atonement to flow to them. And along with the burden of pain that was lifted so was the grip of his addiction to pornography. That too was healed. When asked about where his battle with pornography stood, his two word response was priceless. "It's gone!" he said.

Addiction free, Jim is now a positive, happy young man leading his ward in gospel studies and a leader in significant stake activities. He deeply feels the unlimited possibilities of his true divine potential as a son of a loving Father in Heaven and Savior. Like all of Father's children, Jim is meant to experience happiness in his journey through mortality.[7]

Forsaking our sins is a soul-expanding, guilt-obliterating and joy-producing journey. Once we start the trek and make some progress, and look back to where we were, we often want to use words like "amazing" and "astounding." Satan wants us to believe the exact opposite. He will tell

7 Personal correspondence from Daniel B. Madsen, MD, used with permission.

us we're getting nowhere. He will continue to hammer at our self-worth and try to belittle our efforts. As you make progress, your heart will swell with gratitude for Jesus Christ who embraces and empowers you as you continue to repent, forsake your sins and come unto Him.

Forsaking One Sin at a Time

Another aspect of the analogy of a journey holds true. As we move forward, we gain priceless perspectives. We discover things we could not have seen at earlier stages of the trek. It's not until reaching certain new vantage points that we are able to see ourselves more clearly—where we are and what the next leg of the journey must be. It's like the Savior's metaphor of beams and motes. We can't even see the motes we need to remove until we've removed a beam or two that have been obscuring our view. Don't let SKAM jump in and tell you that finding more motes is bad news. As you grow closer to Christ and feel His suggestions of what next to throw out of your handcart, it's usually more exhilarating than daunting. Even when you're asked to leave behind a once-cherished pastime, it doesn't take long to recognize what a meaningless waste it actually was and how much more you are deriving from putting your focus on higher things.

Elder D. Todd Christofferson related a friend's experience of forsaking overlooked sins and the gift of repentance:

> *I fell into a dream in which I was given a vivid, panoramic view of my life. I was shown my sins, poor choices, the times … I had treated people with impatience, plus the omissions of good things I should have said or done. … [A review of] my life was shown to me in just a few minutes, but it seemed much longer. I awoke, startled, and … instantly dropped to my knees beside the bed and began to pray, to plead for forgiveness, pouring out the feelings of my heart like I had never done previously.*

Prior to the dream, I didn't know that I [had] such great need to repent. My faults and weaknesses suddenly became so plainly clear to me that the gap between the person I was and the holiness and goodness of God seemed [like] millions of miles. … While on my knees I also felt God's love and mercy that was so palpable, despite my feeling so unworthy … I can say I haven't been the same since that day. … My heart changed. … What followed is that I developed more empathy toward others, with a greater capacity to love, coupled with a sense of urgency to preach the gospel. … I could relate to the messages of faith, hope, and the gift of repentance found in the Book of Mormon [as] never before.[8]

To be sure, this beautiful experience offers us much spiritual insight and incentive to press forward with steadfastness in Christ, ever praying for the necessary revelation we need to forsake our sins and come unto Christ.

Christ: The Author and Finisher of Our Repentance

How great the gift the Father has given mankind in sending His Son! "For God so loved the world, that he gave his Only Begotten Son, that whosoever believeth in him should not perish, but have everlasting life" (John 3:16). Next to the Son, and eternal life itself, stands the gift of repentance and the miracle of forgiveness, both of which are made possible through the Atonement of Jesus Christ, and without which all mankind would be forever lost (1 Ne. 10:6; Mosiah 16:4). Once we make sinful choices in this fallen state, there is nothing any of us can do to redeem ourselves or overcome our fallen state. Thus, even the *possibility* of repentance is a gift of immense value, granted to us by the Savior.

As illustrated in the experience of Elder Christofferson's friend, Christ is willing to bestow two additional gifts to assist us. First, although we strive

8 D. Todd Christofferson, "The Living Bread Which Came Down from Heaven," *Ensign,* November 2017, 37–38.

to do our best, still one glaring fact remains: we cannot repent of things we don't see as being errors. Sincere disciples are not intentionally trying to cover their sins as do the wicked, they are simply unaware of omissions and commissions committed through lack of awareness. "Prior to this dream, I didn't know that I had such great need to repent." What a blessing it is for the Lord to awaken us to our spiritual possibilities. He stands ready to lovingly guide us to recognize where we can improve and what we need to forsake. A greater awareness of "what lack I yet" is a gracious gift only He can bestow.

The second gracious gift he offers to help us forsake our sins is the gift of humility. In our fallen state, it is impossible for us to comprehend how holy and glorious our Father and His Son truly are. The disparity between Their holiness and our current state of progression makes the Grand Canyon seem like a ditch. Even that comparison is insufficient. Yet, when we are ready, this reality, rather than discouraging us, ignites in us a great impetus to repent and seek the attributes of Christ, as in the case of Elder Christofferson's friend.

Bringing Gifts to the Lord

Elder Christofferson offered us a lustrous insight about the law of sacrifice and how we may strengthen our relationship with the Lord:

> *In ancient times when people wanted to worship the Lord and seek His blessings, they often brought a gift. For example, when they went to the temple, they brought a sacrifice to place on the altar. After His Atonement and Resurrection, the Savior said He would no longer accept burnt offerings of animals. The gift or sacrifice He will accept now is "a broken heart and a contrite spirit." As you seek the blessing of conversion, you can offer the Lord the gift of your broken, or repentant, heart and your contrite, or obedient, spirit. In reality, it is the gift of yourself—what you are and what you are becoming.*

> *Is there something in you or in your life that is impure or unworthy? When you get rid of it, that is a gift to the Savior. Is there a good habit or quality that is lacking in your life? When you adopt it and make it part of your character, you are giving a gift to the Lord. Sometimes this is hard to do, but would your gifts of repentance and obedience be worthy gifts if they cost you nothing? Don't be afraid of the effort required. And remember, you don't have to do it alone. Jesus Christ will help you make of yourself a worthy gift. His grace will make you clean, even holy.*[9]

Besides making repentance and forgiveness possible, Jesus Christ continually extends the inspiration, mercy, and power we need to offer Him our broken heart and contrite spirit—the ultimate sign of complete repentance. What greater gift can we give Him than to humbly accept the gift of His atoning sacrifice with full purpose of heart, ensuring that His suffering for us was not in vain?

9 Christofferson, "When Thou Art Converted," *Ensign*, May 2004, 12.

CHAPTER 24

Prayer: Sign of Faith and Portal to Power

Elder Jeffrey R. Holland helps us grasp the role of prayer in obtaining the Lord's promise of seeing His face: "It is significant that one of the ultimate evidences God has of our belief in Deity is that we are seen and heard praying … It is the key to the miraculous manifestations of heaven and the personal companionship of the Holy Comforter(s)."[1] May those words ring from the mountain tops and continually resonate in our souls.

"And Calleth on My Name"

Wherever we may be on the path of truth, prayer is the essential portal of communication connecting us with our Father in Heaven. Need we look any further than to the Savior and the example He set of constant prayer to His Father? "And when he had sent the multitude away, he went up into a mountain apart to pray: and when the evening was come, he was there alone" (Matt. 14:23). "And in the morning, rising up a great while before day, he went out, and departed into a solitary place, and there prayed"

---

1 Jeffrey R. Holland, *Christ and the New Covenant,* (Salt Lake City: Deseret Book Company, 2003), 280.

(Mark 1:35). "And it came to pass in those days, that he went out into a mountain to pray, and continued all night in prayer to God. And when it was day, he called his disciples and of them he chose twelve, whom also he named apostles" (Luke 6:12–13). Can we pattern our lives after the life of the Savior without recognizing the frequency of prayer in the Savior's mortal life and the extent to which he applied Himself?

When we desire to commune with God in a way that brings significant blessings and power into our lives, we must hearken to the priceless instruction on prayer given by President Russell M. Nelson:

> *We need to pray from our hearts. Polite recitations of past and upcoming activities, punctuated with some requests for blessings, cannot constitute the kind of communing with God that brings enduring power. Are you willing to pray to know how to pray for more power? The Lord will teach you.*[2]

I cannot think of a conference message that had a greater impact on me than this one. What dimensions of prayer and revelation opened up! And I testify of the truthfulness of these words to those who will accept the invitation to pray to know how to pray for more power. In particular, I bear testimony of the truth of the five words in the last sentence: "The Lord will teach you." What greater promise could we receive from a living prophet? It echoes very similar words of the Prophet Joseph Smith, "The best way to obtain truth and wisdom is not to ask it from books, but to go to God in prayer, and obtain divine teaching."[3] When one prophet affirms the words of another, such words merit our fullest attention.

After delivering the soul-provoking question—"are you willing to pray to know how to pray for more power?"—President Nelson gives us indications of how the Lord will teach us. He counsels us to:

---

2 Nelson, "The Price of Priesthood Power," *Ensign,* May 2016, 68.

3 Smith, *Teachings of the Prophet Joseph Smith,* 191.

(1) Pray from your heart;

(2) Study *earnestly* (his emphasis, not mine) the doctrine of Christ;

(3) Worship in the temple regularly.[4]

Lest this third point be overlooked as mere repetition of "things we already know," I suggest really pondering and praying about the additional counsel President Nelson gave immediately following this statement: "The Lord will teach you."

> *The Lord loves to do His own teaching in His holy house. Imagine how pleased He would be if you asked Him to teach you about priesthood keys, authority, and power as you experience the ordinances of the Melchizedek Priesthood in the holy temple. Imagine the increase in priesthood power that could be yours.*[5]

As a further clue, note that President Nelson's reference note takes us to D&C 84:19–20 which is not talking about the keys of administration, but rather "the *key of the mysteries of the kingdom, even the key of the knowledge of God.*"

Following the leadership and guidance of the living prophets, we are beckoned to seek higher levels of prayer, leading us to elevate our communication with the Father in the name of Jesus Christ. If we are taking to heart what they teach, we are not just checking in with our "want list." We are praying for greater knowledge—for answers to doctrinal questions—for personal revelation. We are praying to know the will of the Lord for us and we are praying for *power.*

President Henry B. Eyring invited us to follow the example of the Prophet Joseph Smith using the *prayer of faith* to grow in spiritual power and obtain continuous revelation:

---

4 Nelson, "The Price of Priesthood Power," *Ensign,* May 2016, 68.
5 Nelson, "The Price of Priesthood Power," *Ensign,* May 2016, 68.

> *Joseph Smith is an example of how to grow in … spiritual power. He showed us that the prayer of faith is the key to revelation from God. He prayed in faith, believing that God the Father would answer his prayer. He prayed in faith, believing that only through Jesus Christ could he be freed from the guilt he felt for his sins. And he prayed in faith, believing that he needed to find the true Church of Jesus Christ to gain that forgiveness. Throughout his prophetic ministry, Joseph Smith used prayers of faith to obtain continuous revelation. As we face today's challenges and those yet to come, we too will need to practice the same pattern.*[6]

Consider with care, "*He prayed in faith, believing God the Father would answer his prayer.*"

Believing God Answers *Your* Prayers

We must believe God not only answers prayers, we must believe that God answers *our* prayers. Why is this so difficult? As discussed in an earlier chapter, Lucifer throws every personal doubt he can conjure up to undermine our faith. The Prophet Joseph Smith taught us how to deflect those doubts. We must hold and retain in our minds "a *correct* idea of his character, perfections and attributes."[7] The central characteristic of God is love (1 John 4:8). It is His utmost perfection, His primary attribute. He does not just show love or feel love for us. He *is* love. The God who loved us first (1 John 4:19), is the God who answers prayers. He cannot be otherwise. To be otherwise would be completely contrary to his very character—who He is and why He lives the kind of life and performs the kind of work He does.

No promise in the scriptures is declared more often than this: "Ask, and it shall be given you; seek, and ye shall find; knock, and it shall be opened

6 Eyring, "Prayers of Faith," *Ensign,* May 2020, 28.
7 Smith, *Lectures on Faith,* Lecture Third, 4.

unto you."[8] In heart-touching logic, the Lord reasons with us, endeavoring to dispel our doubts about Heavenly Father responding to us with love and generosity:

> *For* every one *that asketh receiveth; and he that seeketh findeth; and to him that knocketh it shall be opened.*
>
> *Or what man is there of you, whom if his son ask bread, will he give him a stone?*
>
> *Or if he ask a fish, will he give him a serpent?*
>
> *If ye then, being evil, know how to give good gifts unto your children, how much more shall your Father which is in heaven give good things to them that ask him? (Matt. 7:8–11).*

It is as though Christ is saying, "Before you go to call on the Father in my name, be still and think about the attributes of Him to whom you are praying. Envision Him as a loving parent. Dispel any doubts Satan may be casting into your mind by reminding yourself who He is and your relationship to Him—you are His *child* and He has no other motive than to bless you."

Knowing Satan will try to undermine the faith and prayers of those who seek a witness of the truthfulness of the Book of Mormon, notice what Moroni writes at the culmination of the whole book. Just before engraving the sterling promise —"And when ye shall receive these things…"—on the last plate, Moroni does something intentional. He asks us to "remember how merciful the Lord hath been unto the children of men, from the creation of Adam even down until the time that ye shall receive these things, and ponder it in your hearts" (Moro. 10:3). And what's the "it" he wants us to ponder? The "it" is not the book itself. It's "*how merciful the Lord has been*" from the creation up to the moment the asker is about

8 Matt 7:7; Luke 11:9; 3 Ne. 14:7, 27:29; D&C 4:7, 6:5, 11:5, 12:5, 14:5, 49:26, 88:63.

ask! And he invites the asker to *ponder* that thought—setting the stage for asking to receive a witness from God.

Reminders to remember God's goodness abound in the teachings of the apostles and church leaders. Elder Dale G. Renlund made this point,

> *Throughout time, even and especially during difficult times, prophets have encouraged us to remember the greatness of God and to consider what He has done for us as individuals, as families, and as a people. … The consistency of pleas from prophets to reflect on the goodness of God is striking. Our Heavenly Father wants us to recall His and His Beloved Son's goodness, not for Their own gratification but for the influence such remembrance has on us. By considering Their kindness, our perspective and understanding are enlarged. By reflecting on Their compassion, we become more humble, prayerful, and steadfast.*[9]

In the footnotes associated with this statement, Elder Renlund cited nineteen scriptural references to support this vital point!

God Answers Sincere Prayers

The loving, merciful, gracious character of God is such that he cannot answer some prayers and ignore others. Our God answers all sincere prayers, as Elder Gene R. Cook testified:

> *Sometimes some of us go on our own strength because we have not obtained the confidence that, if we'll humble ourselves before God, and ask, that He will answer. I believe that with all my heart; I know that to be a fact. I believe there was never a humble prayer ever offered, once, by member or non-member, whomever he may be, ever once since the days of Adam, that was not answered. There was never a sincere, humble request made that He didn't respond to.*[10]

---

9 Renlund, "Consider the Goodness and Greatness of God," *Ensign,* May 2020, 41, emphasis added.
10 Cook, "Receiving Answers to Prayers," Audio CD.

Elder Cook pinpointed a critical requisite for receiving answers to prayers: humility and sincerity. Nothing regarding worthiness or righteousness or extensive knowledge of the scriptures or position in the Church is mentioned. Above all of those virtuous assets, God requires a contrite state of mind.

> *And whoso knocketh, to him will he open; and the wise, and the learned, and they that are rich, who are puffed up because of their learning, and their wisdom, and their riches—yea, they are they whom he despiseth; and save they shall cast these things away, and consider themselves fools before God, and come down in the depths of humility, he will not open unto them (2 Ne 9:42).*

Dallas and Emily Called Upon God

Dallas grew up in a less-active family and was baptized by his grandfather at age eight. Through the intervening years Dallas' testimony was nurtured by devoted priesthood leaders. Although he had some rough spots in high school, he qualified to serve a mission. During his mission, he began to correspond with a returned missionary, Emily, who became his future wife.

> *I knew without a doubt I would marry her. I knew it because I had a troubled past. I had made a lot of mistakes in high school, had done drugs and was involved in things that took me away from the spirit of the Lord. But I knew she was strong and that between the two of us we could have an eternal family.*

And that is what happened. Within a few months of Dallas' return from his mission, he married Emily in the temple. Life was great!

However, thirteen years and four kids into the marriage, things began to change. Dallas began hanging out with old "friends" from high school; and he and Emily slacked off doing the "gospel basics." "We kind of got complacent," Dallas said, "and were just going through the motions."

Emily started taking classes, working towards a degree in psychology, and she began to pick up on the change in Dallas. In her studies on addictive behavior, she became convinced Dallas was showing signs of addiction. To what extent she did not know until later. When she approached Dallas with her suspicions, he denied everything. So she sought counsel from her bishop, who was already aware of some of the problems they were facing. The bishop counseled Emily to increase her prayers and her fasting and emphasized that she attend the temple at least weekly. This was a real stretch for Emily as she had not attended the temple for many months. But she humbly complied and made temple attendance a regular part of her weekly activities.

At first the prayers, fasting and temple attendance did not seem to make a difference. In fact, things seemed to be getting worse despite Emily's diligence. Dallas left home and continued his downward spiral.

> *I knew Dallas was unhealthy. I knew that his problems were fixable, however. But the addictions had so much control on him there was nothing more I could do. It was very hard for me, and all I could do was say, "Okay, Heavenly Father, I'm fully putting my trust and confidence in you." That was the first time I ever remember having to give my will over to my Heavenly Father. It was very hard. It was very uncomfortable because I wanted to know how this was going to end up.*

Temple worship was the key to getting answers to her prayers. It was in the temple that Emily received the strong impression she needed to divorce Dallas. She didn't want to take this step, but she knew this was what Heavenly Father was telling her to do. She immediately obeyed. The news hit Dallas hard and he took a nosedive. He describes being at a point where he had lost hope. Things were bleak and he knew he was losing everything valuable in his life.

Emily continued to pray and receive Heavenly Father's promptings of specific things she should do. She obeyed each one.

> *I continued to go to the temple once or twice a week, even as Dallas completely went into a spiral. I reached out to my family and close friends and we had a fast. Heavenly Father guided me one hundred percent in every single thing I did. It was in that fast that Dallas' heart began to soften but he still wasn't all there. He just was very combative. Basically, he was just fighting himself because he figured I wasn't going to forgive him for the things he had done, so what's the point?*
>
> *I think the defining moment came on a Saturday. Our son, Matthew, had a football game and I could tell just by talking to Dallas on the phone that he was high and not really there. I told him he could not come to the house to pick up Matthew. He insisted and I refused. When I got off the phone, I sent the kids to a family member's home. Matthew was the only one home with me when Dallas came and was pounding on the door. He was irate. I knew I needed to get proof on my side, so I called the police. I had changed the locks, but Dallas was still pounding when the police arrived. He eventually calmed down and left.*
>
> *At the game, I noticed I had all my family and friends surrounding me and I looked down at Dallas on the far end all by himself. I realized this was the life he had chosen. He had chosen the recreational drugs and alcohol and all these other addictions over what I have—my family and friends.*

That night, Emily received a distinct impression to hold one more fast for Dallas. Again, she obeyed. She invited some close friends and family members to fast with her for what she felt was a "last ditch effort." She later recalled, "I knew Heavenly Father had the ability to humble Alma the younger and bring people in the scriptures to their knees, and I was trying to have the faith that that could happen to Dallas."

In the meantime, Dallas, under the heavy influence of the adversary, had grown despondent and had decided life wasn't worth living. Planting suicidal thoughts in Dallas' head, Satan was on the verge of winning his battle over this son of God. But, even in these darkest hours, there is the voice of light and hope—a pleading voice to not give up—it's never too late. Dallas said,

> *We are taught that when you are doing wrong, the Holy Ghost leaves you. I think that is not always true. It may be tougher to feel him, but at no point does he ever leave us. We become distant from him, at least I felt that in my own life. But when I was at my worst that is when I felt him the most. At that point, I had lost everything. I had nothing else to lose. I had lost my wife; I had lost my eternal family; I was about to lose my business; so in my eyes it wasn't worth being on this earth. So, I tried to end it.*

This was precisely at the time Emily and all those supporting her and Dallas were beginning their fast for him.

> *All alone in my office in the middle of my overdose, I knew precisely when Emily knelt in prayer to start her fast for me. I could feel her faith bringing the strength I needed. And I sank to me knees and prayed one of the most fervent prayers I have ever had in my life. 'Please, Heavenly Father, if you pull me out of this, I will never touch any of it again in my life.' That was it. I never broke the Word of Wisdom ever again.*

During the next weeks Dallas was able to detoxify himself, "white knuckling" it at his brother's house. He then went through the 12-step addiction recovery program, individual counseling sessions, and regular drug testing. He passed every one of them; and he and Emily got back together and remarried. She still attended the temple regularly by herself as Dallas went through the repentance process with his priesthood leaders. Reflecting back on the times when he was on the verge of losing everything—his wife, his children, his membership in the Church, and his life—he maintained his promise to the Lord.

> *I had made some pretty stupid decisions throughout that period of my life, so I had to face a disciplinary council and was disfellowshipped for a year. It was a year of suffering, but I came to realize what is truly important in life. You don't always realize what you have until you don't have it anymore—you know, giving my children father's blessing before school, giving my wife a blessing when she was sick. I had lost that portion of my life.*

The night he was disfellowshipped Dallas had made a promise to the stake president that he would keep all the conditions required by the council, and the stake president made a promise in return: if Dallas was true to his word, he'd be reinstated in the Church in one year. Exactly one year later, at 10:30 p.m. Dallas was able to meet with his bishop. At 11:00 p.m. he met with the stake president and, before the clock struck midnight, he received his temple recommend. It was a joyous moment.

> *That was probably the first time in ten years, maybe twelve, that I was truly worthy to actually hold a temple recommend and I was truly able to feel the Atonement in my life and see it work in my wife's life. After all the stuff I put her through, the Atonement was just as much for healing for her as it was for forgiveness for me.*[11]

Key Lessons

Dallas and Emily's experience is inspiring and what is even more inspiring is that their story is not uncommon. When the full account of

11 Personal correspondence from Dallas and Emily Neville, used with permission.

this dispensation is manifest, we will see how in so many ways, and so many times, and in numbers beyond counting, Heavenly Father and His Son Jesus Christ have answered prayers and bestowed grace upon those who "call upon His name" in humility and faith.

Here are key lessons to be derived from Dallas and Emily's experience and others like theirs:

1. Emily prayed constantly—in her home, in the temple, in her heart.
2. She was obedient and followed the counsel of her priesthood leaders.
3. She humbled herself and God answered her, time and time again.
4. She obeyed God's promptings without questioning, even when it was hard.
5. She exercised faith especially in the dark moments and never gave up hope.
6. She believed the promises in the scriptures and applied them to herself and her situation.
7. Like Alma in the Book of Mormon and others in extreme agony because of his sins, Dallas cried out to the Lord for deliverance.
8. Dallas faithfully did the work necessary to fulfill the conditions set for repentance by his priesthood leaders.
9. He persevered, even when suffering, and kept his covenant with the Lord and with his stake president.
10. Dallas was given the power to forsake his sins and not return to them through the grace of Jesus Christ and the power of His Atonement.

CHAPTER 25

The Mindset of Prayer

Heavenly Father not only answers all sincere and humble prayers, *He always answers "Yes"* or He bestows something better. As we ponder upon the character of God and His goodness and love, it is hard to arrive at any other conclusion. You have likely already experienced this truth yourself. As you look back over the course of your life, you can identify times when you at first felt disappointed when something you asked for did not come to be. Then, down the road later on, you are able to see the Lord's loving hand in your life. In the stead of what you once so ardently wanted, He has bestowed upon you something significantly better, especially for your eternal growth and happiness, and you have probably gone to your knees in gratitude for the greater blessing, acknowledging His superior wisdom. Again, I say, He always answers yes, or He gives something better. He has to. It is His very nature to deal with His children in a loving and provident manner. He cannot do otherwise.

When we fully accept this principle, we find it imparts an irreplaceable level of confidence in our prayers and in our trials. We no longer have to pine or sulk or doubt God's love for us. We can simply be still and know that He is God. We can then press forward, knowing in time His generosity and wisdom will be manifest. We will see His hand in what has transpired and how it has worked for our good because we walked uprightly.

"Sister Deaton, I Have Two Baby Boys that Need Adoption."

Three years into our marriage, when I was in dental school, Susan and I were fasting and praying to become parents. We were living the commandments and each of us held positions in our ward requiring a substantial commitment of time. We loved our ward, our callings, and our schooling; all was well except we were not yet parents. Eventually, we sought medical advice. The doctors we consulted told us we had a low likelihood of ever having children of our own. This was deeply sobering news to us, but we remained hopeful. Knowing infertility was a trial for at least two of our ancestral mothers in the House of Israel, Sarah and Rachel, we prayed constantly and fasted frequently with only one blessing in mind. We wanted to have a naturally born child. We were not adamantly opposed to adoption. We were well aware adoption is also a divinely guided process to get spirits into the arms of the parents Heavenly Father has selected. Still, we hoped and prayed on.

With graduation a little over a year away, we decided to make one final effort to prevail with the Lord and, if that did not succeed, we would seek to qualify for adoption. Fasting again we felt inspired to make a covenant with Heavenly Father: "Dear Heavenly Father, if you will send us one child, bone of our bone and flesh of our flesh, we will continue to serve thee with all our hearts. And we covenant with thee to take as many additional children as you choose to send us. We will never interfere with the conception process in any way; we will just leave it all in your hands and receive all the children you want to give us."

A couple of months passed with no results. Susan was the Young Women's president in our ward. One night after Mutual, Susan was approached by the bishop just as she was about to head home with a carload of Mutual girls to drop off at their homes on the way. Having no idea about our situation and prayers, Bishop Wilden's conversation was brief and to the point. "Sister Deaton, you know a lot of the women in the ward, including the younger couples. I have two baby boys who need to be placed for adoption. Do you know anyone who might be interested in adopting?"

There may have been burnt tire marks left behind in the church parking lot. Our car may have not gotten to a complete stop before Susan hurried the girls out the door in front of their homes. I wouldn't doubt there were skid marks in front of our mobile home as the car screeched to a halt. What I do know for sure is there was one very excited wife telling her very surprised husband about her conversation with the bishop. "Dennis, there's not just one; there are two! We've fasted and prayed—this has got to be the answer to our prayers! What do you think?!" My first reaction was, "Wow, maybe this *is* it. Maybe this is how it's all going to unfold. This *could be* the answer to our prayers. Let's pray about it tonight and see what the Lord has to say." We prayed well into the night but felt no answer one way or the other. We turned out the lights and fell asleep. Somewhere in the night I awoke which was unusual for me. I lay in bed for a while and with sleep not returning, I knelt and prayed about the matter of adopting those babies. It didn't take long. Very distinctly I received the impression these little boys were not to be ours, and we needed to be patient a little longer—nothing more concrete than that—just the impression to be patient and wait. In the morning I shared the impression with Susan. I could tell immediately how disappointed she was and it pained me to see her fallen countenance. She did not protest. She just asked in a subdued tone, "Are you sure?" Inexperienced as I was in the principle of personal revelation, my answer was a soft, "pretty sure." My dear wife is a covenant keeper. When she makes a covenant that's it, no waffling. She had made a covenant in the temple to sustain her husband and she was not about to break it. With no elaboration, she called the bishop and said, "Bishop, I don't know of anyone who is ready to adopt those babies."

In less than three months we were overjoyed with the news we were expecting! Those who have been in our situation understand the immense joy we felt. The following April, our firstborn child, a darling little girl with lots of dark black hair arrived, whole and healthy. We named her April Joy. In due course, she was followed by eight siblings, six brothers and two sisters. The first eight were all born with the same dark hair and brown eyes. The ninth was born with lots of hair too, but it was light blonde. I said to Susan, "Well that may be it; we've run out of toner."

Like many of you, my first experience with calling on God for a specific revelation was an eye-opener and a faith-builder. Over the years, this experience has been added upon manifold, just as the Prophet Joseph Smith said it would be,

> *A person may profit by noticing the first intimation of the spirit of revelation; for instance, when you feel pure intelligence flowing into you. It may give you sudden strokes of ideas, so that by noticing it, you may find it fulfilled the same day or soon; i.e., those things that were presented into your minds by the Spirit of God, will come to pass. And, thus by learning the Spirit of God and understanding it, you may grow into the principle of revelation, until you become perfect in Christ Jesus.*[1]

Believe and Envision

Believe He is there. Envision your prayers being heard. Return to your open-to-any-possibility childhood mentality when you used visioneering to project yourself into all sorts of exciting adventures. I vividly remember reenacting movie scenes with my friends in our backyards. We'd run them

---

1 Smith, *Teachings of the Prophet Joseph Smith,* 151.

over and over, taking turns playing the roles of the screen heroes of our day. If you can relate, such adolescent mental activities should have been precursors for more mature and spiritually significant application later in life. I fear, however, many of us have set aside that faculty and let it go dormant, labeling it childish and something we needed to grow out of.

Believe and envision when you pray. This practice is simple and yet profound and powerful. We make it hard (or Lucifer tells us it's hard and we believe him). With childlike simplicity and openness when you pray, believe Heavenly Father is right there, present with you, accepting your gratitude, listening to your concerns, receiving your petitions, answering your questions, responding to your pleas. Envision Him as your loving Heavenly Father—the epitome of kindness, mercy and love—seated before you on the mercy seat, attentive to your words and willing to do whatever will be in your best interest. President Gordon B. Hinckley said, "The marvelous thing about prayer is that it is personal, it's individual, it's something that no one else gets into, in terms of your speaking with your Father in the name of the Lord Jesus Christ... He stands ready to help. Don't ever forget it."[2]

Approach Him in Deep Reverence

I cherish Moroni's description of a time the Lord appeared to him: "And then shall ye know that I have seen Jesus, and that he hath talked with me face to face, and that he told me in plain humility, even as a man telleth another in mine own language, concerning these things" (Ether 12:39). Can one read these words and not be deeply touched with the thought that it's the Lord speaking in plain humility? It brings a lump to the throat and tears to the eyes, yet I offer a caution here and a recommendation.

The caution: Knowing that the God we worship will speak with us as one person speaks with another, I suggest we always bear in mind, who

2 Gordon B. Hinckley, *Teachings of Gordon B. Hinckley*, (Salt Lake City: Deseret Book Company, 1997), 468.

that "other person" actually is. He is the Lord Omnipotent, the Eternal Father, the creator of Heaven and Earth. Becoming too casual in our prayers weakens them. We are not in a casual, off-the-cuff chat with our buddy. The scriptures use the word "fear" as the appropriate attitude for approaching Deity. Not fear in the sense of being afraid or frightened of God, the higher definition of the term "fear" conveys the sense of utmost respect and reverence, even awe.

The recommendation: Pause before you begin to pray. Employ visioneering. Picture the majesty of who you are about to address, and it will produce a reverent mindset, shifting you into an attitude of respect and humility that makes an enormous difference in the level of communication you have with the Lord.

Listen with the Expectation of an Answer

Envision a two-way communication, where He listens when you speak and you listen when He speaks. This is a major key we so often overlook. "The trouble with most of our prayers," says President Hinckley, "is that we give them as if we were picking up the telephone and ordering groceries—we place our order and hang up." [3]

Believe in immediate answers. Yes, of course, there are many instances when the Lord's answer will take time and will unfold on His timetable. But we often pray as though *all* of our prayers are answered that way. It seems as though SKAM has convinced us that prayer is like interaction through snail-mail. We put in our request, and it takes a week or so before we get an answer back. If we will listen—really tune our spiritual ears to the wavelength of the Spirit—we will come to know for a certainty that immediate answers are not a rarity; they are the norm. In fact, there will be times when we haven't even completed our sentence, that the Lord will

3 Hinckley, *Teachings of Gordon B. Hinckley,* 469.

give us His answer. Such experiences will become more common as we *believe* He is listening and we listen like we believe it! Really take time to listen. Prayers take on a whole new dimension when we spend more time thanking, praising and listening than asking.

Listen with Real Intent

The best way for me, by far, to show Heavenly Father I'm listening and serious about receiving His guidance and revelations is to have a pen and pad by the place where I kneel. Being poised to write, coupled with an attitude of acting on what will be given, accentuates my listening. At times there will be a silent pause when no impressions come. Occasionally the pauses are lengthy. Yet, when I stay focused and just listen patiently, it is seldom I don't begin to receive an impression. Then, almost always, as I jot down the first thought, another thought follows it. And I write. Then another follows and I write. I write until the inspiration pauses and I wait a little longer. Sometimes, I get the sense the conversation is complete; and I close. Other times, applying a suggestion given by Elder Richard G. Scott,[4] I ask "Is there more?" Often there is, and more will come; and I record it.

Not long after being set apart as president of the church, President Nelson and his wife Wendy came to Arizona to speak to a huge audience, most of them youth. Tears came to my eyes when Sister Nelson shared some rather surprisingly intimate details of what it's like to be the wife of God's living prophet. She mentioned she knows when to leave the room when revelation is flowing to her husband. She mentioned how exuberant he is when he has his "yellow pad" filled with messages he has captured as the Lord directs His Church. She also mentioned how earnestly President Nelson is in immediately getting to work on what he receives—which brings us to the next indispensable point.

4 Scott, "To Acquire Spiritual Guidance," *Ensign,* November 2009, 8.
5 See D&C Section 101, particularly verses 6 & 7.

Act Immediately

Act immediately on the answers. This point cannot be overstated. Treating the Lord's counsel lightly and being slow to respond closes the window of revelation and divine guidance. Early saints in Jackson County learned this lesson the hard way.[5] The children of Israel spent forty years tramping through the desert because of their lack of faith and tepid response to the Lord's invitation to them to enter the promised land in the strength of Jehovah. In Ecclesiastes we read, "When thou vowest a vow unto God, defer not to pay it; for he hath no pleasure in fools: pay that which thou hast vowed. Better is it that thou shouldest not vow, than that thou shouldest vow and not pay" (Ecclesiastes 5:4–5). I pray these suggestions will be useful to you and bless your life as much as they have mine.

CHAPTER 26

Obedience

"And Obeyeth My Voice and Keepeth My Commandments"

God whispers before He speaks, and when He speaks it is with a mild, gentle voice which entices and invites. Never does He exert the slightest degree of compulsion upon the agency of His children. Soft-spoken President Howard W. Hunter modeled what he taught:

> *God's chief way of acting is by persuasion and patience and long-suffering, not by coercion and stark confrontation. He acts by gentle solicitation and by sweet enticement. He always acts with unfailing respect for the freedom and independence that we possess. He wants to help us and pleads for the chance to assist us, but he will not do so in violation of our agency.*[1]

Frequently, throughout his mortal ministry the Lord uttered the phrase: "He that hath ears to hear, let him hear," suggesting that His disciples need to attune their listening and make effort to open their ears so they can hear the Lord's voice. We have become so accustomed to the strident voices of hucksters and barkers on the commercial midway who raise their voices

---

1 Howard W. Hunter, "The Golden Threads of Choice," *Conference Report,* October 7, 1989.

to demand our listening, we become insensitive to the whisperings of the Spirit and overlook them. "Sometimes the Lord waits hopefully on His children to act on their own," said President Ezra Taft Benson, "and when they do not, they lose the greater prize, and the Lord will either drop the entire matter and let them suffer the consequences or else He will have to spell it out in greater detail. Usually, I fear, the more He has to spell it out, the smaller is our reward."[2]

The greater spiritual rewards come to those who are earnestly listening and quick to obey. These traits are highly pleasing to the Lord. Notice the primary quality by which Ammaron recognized the spiritual potential of the ten-year-old Mormon in selecting him to undertake the monumental stewardship of curating the thousand-year collection of sacred records of the Nephite nation. "Ammaron said unto me: I perceive that thou art a sober child, and art quick to observe"[3] (Morm. 1:2) The antithesis also holds true. Those who are slow to obey pay a penalty. Due to greed, speculation and slothfulness, the saints who had gathered to Independence Missouri to build up Zion and the New Jerusalem, hearkened to the avaricious voice of the adversary and ignored the voice of the Spirit. In Section 101 of the Doctrine and Covenants, the Lord explained why He "suffered the affliction to come upon them" (D&C 101:2):

> *Behold, I say unto you, there were jarrings, and contentions, and envyings, and strifes, and lustful and covetous desires among them; therefore by these things they polluted their inheritances.*
>
> *They were slow to hearken unto the voice of the Lord their God; therefore, the Lord their God is slow to hearken unto their prayers, to answer them in the day of their trouble.*

---

2 Ezra Taft Benson, *Teachings of Ezra Taft Benson,* (Salt Lake City: Bookcraft, 1988), 530.

3 According to Merriam-Webster dictionary "To watch carefully" is the fourth definition of the word *observe.* The first definition is the best suited to Ammaron's intent: "To conform one's action or practice."

In the day of their peace they esteemed lightly my counsel; but, in the day of their trouble, of necessity they feel after me (D&C 101:6–8).

Put plainly, if you seek the Lord's favor, be quick to obey.

Alma Acted Promptly

A sterling example of being "quick to obey" is the prophet Alma in the Book of Mormon. Having been bitterly rejected by the people of Ammonihah, including being spat upon as he was being reviled, Alma headed for home. He had been away for quite some time. He had labored diligently, putting in long hours preaching and praying for the people. He had a rightful claim to a bit of time to recoup his strength and enjoy a few days of peace and rest. He may have been thinking very similar thoughts as he made his way homeward. As he journeyed, weighed down with sorrow and "anguish of soul because of the wickedness of the people who were in the city of Ammonihah," Alma was intercepted by an angel (Alma 8:14). He was commended in glowing terms and then commanded to return to the city of Ammonihah, the city of spitters and revilers, to declare another message. Without a moment's hesitation or "You mean, *right now*?" Alma "*returned speedily* to the land of Ammonihah" (Alma 8:18).

Three Modern Examples

Brother Ed J. Pinegar, an author and beloved educator, shared an eye-opening experience.

A number of years ago I recall being in attendance at a regional conference of several BYU stakes in which Elder Boyd K. Packer of the Quorum of the Twelve was presiding. Because the meeting was taking place in the cavernous Marriott Center and the audience was occupying only a fraction of the seats, Elder Packer requested that all those seated higher up in the auditorium move down closer to the stage. Only a few

> *of the attending students responded. Most did not move. The meeting continued, nevertheless, and good counsel was given by him and a number of other attending General Authorities and their wives.*
>
> *During a subsequent meeting with the leaders of the stakes, Elder Packer shared enlightening detail concerning what had transpired. He told the leaders that the message which was intended to be delivered that day had been withheld because of the disobedience of so many in the congregation, and another message was given instead.*
>
> *Thus, absent a broken heart and a contrite spirit on the part of so many there, the attendees had relinquished a grand opportunity to hear the exact words of counsel and receive the blessing that the Lord intended for them to have that day. The words of Alma echo strongly: "And they that will harden their hearts, to them is given the lesser portion of the word" (Alma 12:11). This experience was discussed widely throughout these stakes afterward, and many learned valuable lessons from it.*[4]

Second Example

A second example of being quick to obey is Sister Susan Bednar, wife of Elder David A. Bednar, as told in his words,

> *Before attending her sacrament meetings, Sister Bednar frequently prays for the spiritual eyes to see those who have a need. Often as she observes the brothers and sisters and children in the congregation, she will feel a spiritual nudge to visit with or make a phone call to a particular person. And when Sister Bednar receives such an impression, she promptly responds and obeys. It often is the case that as soon as the "amen" is spoken in the benediction, she will talk with a teenager or*

4 Ed J. Pinegar, *Teachings and Commentary on the Old Testament,* (Salt Lake City: Covenant Communications, Inc., 2005), 275.

> *hug a sister or, upon returning home, immediately pick up the phone and make a call. As long as I have known Sister Bednar, people have marveled at her capacity to discern and respond to their needs. Often they will ask her, "How did you know?" The spiritual gift of being quick to observe has enabled her to see and to act promptly and has been a great blessing in the lives of many people.*[5]

Sister Bednar's example calls to mind the words of Alma, "By small and simple things are great things brought to pass and small means in many instances doth confound the wise" (Alma 37:6); and they also confound the wiles of the adversary who would have us delay our immediate actions.

Third Example

The third example is closer to home and to my heart. While serving as bishop, I grew particularly close to the Kinneard family. Sister Rosalyn Kinneard served as the president of the Relief Society and was admired throughout the ward for her loving ways and selfless service. She was a widow still raising a family—her husband, Doug, had died in a tragic plane crash a few years prior. One of her sons, Curtis, an adult with special needs, was still living at home along with a younger sister. In many ways Curtis functions as a man in his twenties. In other ways he functions as a ten-year-old child. At the beginning of a priesthood meeting, as was often the case, the back of the meeting room was filled with bearers of both priesthoods, the Aaronic and Melchizedek. Only a few brethren, sparsely populated the front rows. As the meeting room was fairly large for the size of the group, the counselor in the bishopric conducting the meeting invited the brethren to please come forward and fill in the empty seats. A few, perhaps less than ten percent, of the brethren in the back responded. Tears filled my eyes and ran down my cheeks as I witnessed humility and immediate obedience personified. Curtis

---

5 David A. Bednar, *Increase in Learning,* (Salt Lake City: Deseret Book Company, 2011), 55.

Kinneard had gotten up out of his seat on the third row. He walked politely up to the very front row, moved over to the middle chair and took his seat. Resonating in my head were the words of the Lord, "Verily I say unto you, Whosoever will not receive the kingdom of God as a little child, shall in no wise enter therein" (JST Luke 18:17). Those words, coupled with Curtis' example, called me to repentance. For, if I had not been sitting up front as the presiding officer, I would have been sitting on the third or fourth row. I am one-hundred-percent sure I would have remained there when the leader had asked the brethren to move forward. I would have said to myself, for SKAM has trained me well, "Oh, Dennis, you don't need to move. You're already one of the ones sitting towards the front. You're perfectly fine where you are. This doesn't apply to you; you're an exception. This applies to others." If I were more alert to opportunities to not justify my obedience and just look for ways to obey and do so more readily and willingly, I could have followed Curtis and said, "This applies to me; I'm not an exception. I'm not as far up to the front as I could be. I'll obey and move up closer."

Being quick to obey is a far bigger deal than most of us realize. This attitude and its corresponding actions represent our submitting of our will to the will of the Father—a central feature of the ministry of the Savior. "My meat is to do the will of him that sent me," he said (John 4:34), and "I came down from heaven, not to do mine own will, but the will of him that sent me" (John 6:38). May we follow Him and do likewise.

By *Every* Word that Proceedeth from the Mouth of God

Immediately following His supernal promise that *all the Father hath* will be given to those who magnify their callings and receive Him and those He sends, comes a caution: "I now give unto you a commandment *to beware* concerning yourselves, to give *diligent heed* to the words of eternal life. For you shall live *by every word* that proceedeth forth from the mouth of God" (D&C 84:43–44, emphasis added).

The Lord stresses how vital it is to give heed—yea, *diligent heed*—to the words of eternal life. Half-hearted effort is insufficient. Lucifer would have us think otherwise. He's constantly conning us into believing we can obtain the blessings of God at a discounted price. Discounting proves to be an effective commercial marketing tactic, but it flatly doesn't work in spiritual matters. "What we obtain too cheaply we esteem too lightly," wrote the inspired Thomas Paine: "It is dearness only that gives everything its value. Heaven knows how to put a proper price upon its goods."[6] This truth aligns with teachings of the Prophet Joseph Smith.

> *The question is frequently asked, 'Can we not be saved without going through with all those ordinances?' I would answer, 'No, not the fulness of salvation.' Jesus said, There are many mansions in my Father's house, and I will go and prepare a place for you. House here named should have been translated kingdom; and any person who is exalted to the highest mansion has to abide a celestial law, and the whole law too.*[7]

Once Satan gets us to view ourselves as an exception to counsel, he further strokes our pride by enticing us to believe we are superior to others. This "exceptional" thinking is not a slippery slope, it's an open elevator shaft to disappointment. Salvation is not obtained through a cafeteria plan where we can pick and choose which commandments apply to us and which ones don't. Only those who humble themselves and follow the example of the Savior, allowing their will to be swallowed up in the will of the Father, become joint heirs with Christ inheriting all the Father hath. True disciples are not selective when it comes to keeping the commandments of God. They strive to live by *every word* that proceedeth forth from the mouth of God.

---

6 Thomas Paine, *The American Crisis,* No. 1, 1776.
7 Smith, *Teachings of the Prophet Joseph Smith,* 331.

Unless I miss my guess, SKAM just hit some readers with the old rant, "You'll never make it—it's too hard—there are way too many commandments for you to keep." As a pill for the headache caused by this standard pitch, let us turn to Elder Jeffrey R. Holland.

> *Around the Church I hear many who struggle with this issue: "I am just not good enough." "I fall so far short." "I will never measure up." I hear this from teenagers. I hear it from missionaries. I hear it from new converts. I hear it from lifelong members. … For some [Satan] has turned the ideals and inspiration of the gospel into self-loathing and misery-making. …*
>
> *What I now say in no way denies or diminishes any commandment God has ever given us. I believe in His perfection, and I know we are His spiritual sons and daughters with divine potential to become as He is. I also know that, as children of God, we should not demean or vilify ourselves, as if beating up on ourselves is somehow going to make us the person God wants us to become. No! With a willingness to repent and a desire for increased righteousness always in our hearts, I would hope we could pursue personal improvement in a way that doesn't include getting ulcers or … feeling depressed or demolishing our self-esteem. That is not what the Lord wants for Primary children or anyone else who honestly sings, "I'm trying to be like Jesus."*[8]

Sister Michelle D. Craig, of the Young Women General Presidency, gave wise counsel about avoiding this satanic attempt to derail us:

> *We should welcome feelings of divine discontent that call us to a higher way, while recognizing and avoiding Satan's counterfeit—paralyzing discouragement. This is a precious space into which Satan is all too*

8 Holland, "Be Ye Therefore Perfect—Eventually," *Ensign,* November 2017, 40.

eager to jump. We can choose to walk the higher path that leads to seek for God and His peace and grace, or we can listen to Satan, who bombards us with messages that we will never be enough."[9]

I pray these assurances will calm our troubled souls and stifle the voice of hopelessness and discouragement Satan constantly foments to get us to give up and quit. I also pray He will not lead any of us to taking our foot off the pedal and coasting. Between those two extremes there is a healthy, "happy median." Elder Neal A. Maxwell applied the term "divine discontent" to that healthy spiritual state of mind the Savior wants us to embrace. He taught, "It is left to each of us to balance contentment regarding what God has allotted to us in life with some divine discontent resulting from what we are in comparison to what we have the power to become. Discipleship creates this balance on the straight and narrow path."[10]

Heavenly Father will help each of us find the balance appropriate for each chapter of our life as it unfolds. Satan will endeavor to contradict that truth, telling us everything has to be done perfectly and at this moment right now or all is lost. Marjorie Hinckley gave wise counsel on setting priorities at different times in our lives:

> *Think about your particular assignment at this time in your life. It may be to get an education, it may be to rear children, it may be to be a grandparent, it may be to care for and relieve the suffering of someone you love, it may be to do a job in the most excellent way possible, it may be to support someone who has a difficult assignment of their own. Our assignments are varied and they change from time to time.*[11]

The Lord is our Good Shepherd caring for each of us on our journey. As we draw near to Him and listen to the still small voice, He tutors us in a

9 Michelle D. Craig, "Divine Discontent," Ensign, November 2018, 53.
10 Maxwell, "Becoming a Disciple," *Ensign,* June 1996, 18.
11 Marjorie Pay Hinckley, *Small and Simple Things*, (Salt Lake City: Deseret Book Company, 2003), 44.

personal loving way. Through the inspiration of the Holy Ghost, He gives each of us our personal agenda and task list, customized to our individual needs, capacity, callings, situations and desires of our hearts.[12] It is these personalized commandments given through the Spirit that most fit the phrasing, "obeyeth my voice and keepeth my commandments." As we do the spiritual work to hear Him and act upon the promptings we receive, we grow closer and closer to our Lord and "wax stronger and stronger in our humility, and firmer and firmer in the faith of Christ unto the filling (our) souls with joy and consolation" (Hel. 3:35), and obtaining the promise given in D&C 93:1.

And that's the key. It's precisely the reason why "calleth on my name" precedes "obeyeth my voice, and keepeth my commandments" in the divine staircase of instructions on how we come to know our Savior. Each of us must continually seek and obey the personal revelation we receive from the Lord at any given moment as the Author and Finisher of our faith.

12 See Chapter 8, *Ground Rules of the Battle*.

CHAPTER 27

Accessing Power Through Faith in Jesus Christ

The marvelous culmination of the Lord's requirements set forth in D&C 93:1 is expressed in nine glorious words of promise, "*shall see my face and know that I am!*" What a sublime thought! Were it not bolstered with such credible testimony, the idea of any mortal soul being permitted to enter God's presence while in the flesh—see His face and converse with Him—would be beyond belief. Yet, such is the truth.

Who has not been touched while reading Moroni's testimony that he had "seen Jesus and that he hath talked with me face to face . . . in plain humility . . . in mine own language?" (Ether 12:39). Then, assuring us that he was not somehow singularly favored, he invites us to seek for the same experience. "And now, I would commend you to seek this Jesus of whom the prophets and apostles have written" (Ether 12:41). Throughout his ministry, the Prophet Joseph Smith encouraged the saints to seek diligently to know the Lord as he did. "I am going to enquire after God; *for I want you all to know him* . . . It is the first principle of the Gospel to know for a certainty the Character of God, and to know that we may converse with him as one man converses with another."[1]

Would it shock you to know that Heavenly Father is highly disappointed when we *don't* take this opportunity seriously, even to the point He is angry when His people refuse to pursue these invitations given through his servants? Consider what the Lord revealed in September 1832:

> *And this greater priesthood administereth the gospel and holdeth the key of the mysteries of the kingdom, even the key of the knowledge of God.... For without this no man can see the face of God, even the Father, and live. Now this Moses plainly taught to the children of Israel in the wilderness, and sought diligently to sanctify his people that they might behold the face of God; But they hardened their hearts and could not endure his presence; therefore, the Lord in his wrath, for his anger was kindled against them, swore that they should not enter into his rest while in the wilderness, which rest is the fulness of his glory. Therefore, he took Moses out of their midst, and the Holy Priesthood also (D&C 84:19-26).*

We Live Below Our Privileges

While in the First Presidency, Elder Dieter F. Uchtdorf delivered an enlightening message in the priesthood session of April 2011 General Conference:

> *The fact that our Heavenly Father would entrust this power and responsibility to man is evidence of His great love for us and a foreshadowing of our potential as sons of God in the hereafter. Nevertheless, too often our actions suggest that we live far beneath this potential. When asked about the priesthood, many of us can*

1 Smith, *Teachings of the Prophet Joseph Smith*, 345, emphasis added.

> *recite a correct definition, but in our daily lives, there may be little evidence that our understanding goes beyond the level of a rehearsed script. Brethren, we are faced with a choice. We can be satisfied with a diminished experience as priesthood bearers and settle for experiences far below our privileges. Or we can partake of an abundant feast of spiritual opportunity and universal priesthood blessings.*[2]

One has to wonder what is holding us back from rising up and anxiously engaging ourselves in obtaining a greater measure of the blessings available in this the dispensation of the fulness of times. Are we like the Nephites of old who have been so prospered and pampered financially we have been lulled away into carnal security saying, "All is well in Zion; yea, Zion prospereth, all is well," allowing the devil to cheat our souls and lead us away carefully down to hell?" (2 Ne. 28:21). Has Lucifer succeeded in seducing us with the deceitfulness of riches? (Matt. 13:22; Mark 4:19) Such are questions one must ask and answer for oneself.

As an additional piece of testimony to provoke introspection, consider this experience shared by Elder F. Enzio Busche:

> *At a Christmas social once, I was sitting next to a woman from a recently opened country in Eastern Europe who was in the West for the first time. … [S]he was a convert of a little over a year. I asked her how she liked America, and she was very enthusiastic and positive and had many good things to say. … Suddenly, she stopped and said, "I wish I could invite all the members of my Salt Lake ward to come to my home branch." I asked her about her branch.*

> *She told me about the poor circumstances they were all living in and about how difficult it was for the members to get to their Sunday meetings and the many sacrifices that they joyfully made. She said*

2 Uchtdorf, "Your Potential, Your Privilege," *Ensign,* May 2011, 58.

> *the most inspiring time for the members in her branch was testimony meeting. … They all looked forward to hearing their fellow members report about the Lord's working in their lives. They, of course, would not part until everyone had given a testimony because they were all anxious to share the many miracles happening around them. They could not say enough about the love and most gracious care of the Lord. Then she said, "Once in a while, we have holy angels visit and comfort and strengthen us." She added with a smile, "Can you imagine? I have found people in Salt Lake City who have never seen an angel." She laughed as if that were the strangest thing she had ever heard.*[3]

If we were to ask the Prophet Joseph Smith what one thing holds us back the most in our quest to obtain the blessings and promised privileges pertaining to both this life and the next, his answer might well be this:

> *Because faith is wanting, the fruits are. No man since the world was had faith without having something along with it. The ancients quenched the violence of fire, escaped the edge of the sword, women received their dead, etc. By faith the worlds were made. A man who has none of the gifts has no faith; and he deceives himself, if he supposes he has. Faith has been wanting, not only among the heathen, but in professed Christendom also, so that tongues, healings, prophecy, and prophets and apostles, and all the gifts and blessings have been wanting.*[4]

In the eleventh chapter of the epistle to the Hebrews we read: "Without faith (in Jesus Christ) it is impossible to please him: for he that cometh to God must believe that he is, and that he is a rewarder of them that diligently seek him" (Heb. 11:6). The Apostle Paul goes on to list a stunning pantheon of the faithful souls who experienced miracles and

---

3 Busche, *Yearning for the Living God,* 233–234.
4 Smith, *Teachings of the Prophet Joseph Smith,* 270.

attained great spiritual heights *by faith.* Similarly, Moroni makes an equally impressive list of spiritual attainments and miracles manifest among the descendants of Lehi which were also obtained *by faith* (Ether 12:10-19). Little wonder faith in the Lord Jesus Christ ranks as the first principle of the gospel. To grasp the power and effects of faith, the Prophet Joseph Smith stated, "Faith is not only the principle of action, but of power also, in all intelligent beings, whether in heaven or on earth."[5] Elder Bruce R. McConkie wrote, "Faith applies in all spheres. All intelligent beings—be they gods, angels, spirits, or men—all operate by its power."[6]

Faith, the Foremost State of Mind

States of mind are not permanent features or set characteristics indelibly etched into your spirit. They are creations of your intelligence of spirit. This creator within can learn to create better creations. Indeed, if you and I are to progress to the full extent of our spiritual birthright and potential, we must. We must create better, more powerful *states of mind.* We must develop unshakeable faith in the Lord Jesus Christ. Elder Orson Pratt, Apostle of the Lord and eloquent theologian, wrote: "Faith is not an abstract principle, separate and distinct from the mind, but it is a certain condition or state of the mind itself."[7] In this one sentence, Elder Pratt has set forth more pure truth on the subject of faith than found in many volumes written on the subject. It merits our careful consideration and absorption.

Orson Pratt was not only one of the original twelve apostles in the dispensation of the fulness of times, he was also a noted mathematician and scientist. Having a mind with a scientific bent and being a man not given to hyperbole, when he refers to "an abstract principle" he is not using the term

---

5 Smith, *Lectures on Faith,* Lecture First, 13–17.

6 Bruce R. McConkie, *A New Witness for the Articles of Faith,* (Salt Lake City: Deseret Book Company, 1985), 164.

7 Pratt, *The True Faith,* 1.

loosely. And we derive powerful insights about faith by not rushing past his statement. "Abstract" is the opposite of "concrete or physical." When he says faith is *not* an abstract principle, he is trying to lead us away from false notions about faith which prevailed in his day and still exist in ours. For many, faith is a lukewarm, passive mental posture—mere acceptance or acquiescence to an idea. The phrase, "You'll just have to take it on faith" becomes the slogan and excuse for being mentally and spiritually lazy. Rather than searching and pondering, seeking for enlightenment and understanding through study, prayer and fasting; it means you simply accept or surrender. That conception of faith is the polar antithesis of the truth. True faith is a firm, powerful, energetic state of mind—one that activates effort, hard work, sacrifice and repentance.

Elder Pratt wanted to put us on a firmer foundation. As a scientist, he put faith in the same category as the laws of physics and the fundamental forces of nature, such as gravity, magnetism, electrical and atomic energy. Rightly so. Faith is most certainly a genuine power. Though you cannot see gravity, you can nevertheless feel it. In fact, you can feel both the presence and the absence of gravity. The reality of gravity can be validated by its effects, despite not being able to see it, smell it, or grasp and hold onto it or weigh it on a scale.

With this understanding, we proceed to absolutely priceless insights. According to Elder Pratt, there is one marked difference between faith and the physical forms of energy just mentioned. Magnetism and atomic energy are physical forces and phenomena, separate and apart from the mind. They exist in the domain of the outside physical universe. They are the external working energies and forces manifest as the awe-inspiring phenomena of the physical universe. Faith is *not* one of those. Faith is unique: it is not abstract, but neither is it a physical force. Faith does not exist "separate and apart from the mind," rather, "it is a certain condition or state of the mind itself." Elder Pratt is saying a state of mind can become so powerful it can influence and alter, yea, manage and control, the physical energies and forces of the universe. Faith isn't one of the physical principles, it's the one that governs them! And it's a state of mind!

Faith Is a Choice!

Here is the next blockbuster truth: If faith is a state of mind, then faith is *also a choice*! So are doubt, disbelief and fear, as we have discussed in previous chapters. Because faith is a state of mind, it falls in the purview of the agency of each intelligence. Like all other traits and capabilities of the intelligence, it must be cultivated by choice. It cannot be forced or imposed. It must be sought and developed. Elder L. Whitney Clayton, of the Presidency of the Seventy, wrote:

> *Belief and testimony and faith are not passive principles. They do not just happen to us. Belief is something we choose—we hope for it, we work for it, and we sacrifice for it. We will not accidentally come to believe in the Savior and His gospel any more than we will accidentally pray or pay tithing. We actively choose to believe, just like we choose to keep other commandments.*[8]

President Henry B. Eyring said: "Every child in each generation chooses faith or disbelief. Faith is not an inheritance; it is a choice."[9] Elder Neil L. Andersen also taught:

> *Faith in the Lord Jesus Christ is not something ethereal, floating loosely in the air. Faith does not fall upon us by chance or stay with us by birthright. It is, as the scriptures say, "substance …, the evidence of things not seen." Faith emits a spiritual light, and that light is*

8 L. Whitney Clayton, "Choose to Believe," *Ensign,* May 2015, 38.
9 Eyring, "Helping Students Inquire of the Lord," February 2013, https://www.churchofjesuschrist.org/media/video/2013-02-1340-133-helping-students-inquire-of-the-lord?lang=eng.

> *discernible. Faith in Jesus Christ is a gift from heaven that comes as we choose to believe and as we seek it and hold on to it. Your faith is either growing stronger or becoming weaker. Faith is a principle of power, important not only in this life but also in our progression beyond the veil. By the grace of Christ, we will one day be saved through faith on His name. The future of your faith is not by chance, but by choice.*[10]

Elder L. Whitney Clayton added further instruction:

> *Alma's call for us to desire to believe and to "give place" in our hearts for the Savior's words reminds us that belief and faith require our personal choice and action. We must "awake and arouse (our) faculties." We ask before it is given unto us; we seek before we find; we knock before it is opened unto us. We are then given this promise: "For every one that asketh, receiveth; and he that seeketh, findeth; and to him that knocketh, it shall be opened. … The decision to believe is the most important choice we ever make. It shapes all our other decisions."*[11]

Having complete respect for our agency, Heavenly Father's plan allows you and me complete freedom of choice even in these matters of enormous eternal consequence. He will beckon, invite and inspire us to come unto Him and choose to walk the path that leads to eternal joy and happiness. But, under no circumstances will God infringe upon the agency of His children.

And You Don't Have To

You don't have to do any of this. You are not constrained or compelled to take upon yourself any of the characteristics of godliness. You don't have to pray or repent or seek salvation. You are called and you are supported by the Father, the Son and the Holy Ghost, but you don't have to accept

---

10 Andersen, "Faith Is Not by Chance, but by Choice," *Ensign,* November 2015, 65.
11 Clayton, "Choose to Believe," *Ensign,* May 2015, 37.

their invitation or partake of any of it. You don't have to progress one inch further than you are right now. And you will still be loved and blessed beyond measure, as we all are. You can stay just as you are for as long as you choose. You always have been, are now, and ever will be the chooser, choosing your own destiny. You can choose to go part way and stop if you choose. You can even choose to turn around and go back; and some do. You can retrogress as in the case of Esau and David. You can even fall as in the case of Lucifer, Cain and Judas. Just know this. You are progressing, retrogressing or parked in neutral according to the states of mind you choose to cultivate.

Know this as well: Exaltation in the kingdom of heaven is a personal quest. We are not saved as a Church. We are not saved as a family. We are not even saved as a couple. Only I can repent of my sins. No one else can do it for me. What Joseph Smith believed and what he saw enlightens my mind, gives me hope and shows me the way. I will ever be grateful to the Prophet Joseph Smith for introducing me to the eternal verities that lead me to Christ. I will ever be grateful for the clear explanations of the Atonement of my Savor set forth in the Book of Mormon, which Joseph translated. But the truth is: I must act upon the truths of the restored gospel, and do so with all my heart or, for me as an individual it all goes for naught. Joseph himself said: "Reading the experiences of others, or the revelation given to them, (including his) can never give us a comprehensive view of our condition and true relation to God. Knowledge of these things can only be obtained by experience through ordinances of God set forth for that purpose."[12] Great is the consequence of our choices. Even the cumulative effect of so-called small everyday choices have marked impact upon the present and the future. No choice ranks higher than the choice to believe in God the Eternal Father, His Son Jesus Christ, and in the Holy Ghost.

---

12 Smith, *Teachings of the Prophet Joseph Smith,* 324, emphasis added.

Disbelief is Also a Choice

The antithesis of faith is disbelief and it, like faith, is also a choice. As the Holy Spirit is continually enticing us to put off the natural man and become saintly through the Atonement of Christ the Lord, there is an opposing voice continually whispering in our ears to choose disbelief and become carnal, sensual, and devilish. As hard as it may be for us to imagine, sons and daughters of Adam and Eve rejected the eyewitness testimony of their parents, who had walked and talked with God in the Garden of Eden and chose to disbelieve.

> *And Adam and Eve blessed the name of God, and they made all things known unto their sons and their daughters. And Satan came among them, saying: I am also a son of God; and he commanded them, saying: Believe it not; and they believed it not, and they loved Satan more than God. And men began from that time forth to be carnal, sensual, and devilish (Moses 5:12–13).*

As it was with the children of Adam and Eve, so it was in the family of Lehi and Sariah. In the face of major spiritual evidence—Spirit-empowered teachings, testimonies and warnings of a prophet father, a prophet brother and an angel, confirmed by miracle after miracle of deliverance—some of Lehi and Ishmael's children chose to disbelieve. Further on in the Book of Mormon, a congregation of adults hearkened to the angel-authored discourse of King Benjamin and experienced a mighty change of heart and were born of the Spirit. Undoubtedly, they taught their children with love and diligence the truths that transformed their lives. Yet, notwithstanding, many of their children chose disbelief.

> *Now it came to pass that there were many of the rising generation that could not understand the words of King Benjamin, being little children at the time he spake unto his people; and they did not believe*

> *the tradition of their fathers. They did not believe what had been said concerning the resurrection of the dead, neither did they believe concerning the coming of Christ (Mosiah 26:1–2).*

The Price of Disbelief

Those who choose to disbelieve pay a price. Notice the consequences in the cases mentioned above. Adam and Eve's children "began from that time forth to be carnal, sensual and devilish" (Moses 5:13). Laman and Lemuel became "hard in (their) hearts" and "blind in (their) minds" (1 Ne. 7:8), and so insensitive to things spiritual that even though they had seen an angel, and heard God's voice, they were past feeling and could not feel God's words (1 Ne 17:45). And, of the disbelieving children of King Benjamin's people it was said, "because of their unbelief they could not understand the word of God and their hearts were hardened…" and they "remained so ever after, even in their carnal and sinful state; for they would not call upon the Lord their God" (Mosiah 26:3–4).

In our dispensation, the Lord chastised members of the Church in similar terms for the same reason, "And your minds in times past have been darkened because of unbelief, and because you have treated lightly the things you have received—which vanity and unbelief have brought the whole church under condemnation" (D&C 84:54–55). The correlation between disbelief and the loss of light is significant. When our minds become darkened, we suffer spiritually debilitating consequences. Loss of light means loss of spiritual power. Temptations have a stronger impact and the traps and snares of the adversary gain a greater hold and tighter grip upon us. It becomes easier for Satan to take hold of the steering wheel, shoving our will to the side, as our ability to resist him and his power weakens. Lucifer can literally take hold as we lose control of our will. Those who choose disbelief, succumbing to Satan's influence and surrendering their wills to the adversary become servants first, then children, of the devil. This is the exact opposite of those who choose belief, yielding to the enticings of the Holy Spirit and surrendering their hearts, knowingly and willingly, unto God. They too begin as servants—servants of the Lord; and, by faith and obedience they become spiritually begotten sons and daughters of Christ. Oh, how significant are the daily choices we make. One seemingly small decision after another inches us ever closer to one pole or the other. Each intelligence ultimately obtains the end result of his or her choices. The rule of thumb for the choosing is given in the Doctrine and Covenants:

> *And that which doth not edify is not of God, and is darkness. That which is of God is light; and he that receiveth light, and continueth in God, receiveth more light; and that light groweth brighter and brighter until the perfect day (D&C 50:23–24).*

Almost beyond our ability to comprehend are the end results that stem from choosing light over darkness, day by day, one small righteous choice adding upon another, drawing ever closer to our Lord and Savior Jesus Christ. The more we can hold in our minds the images of those who have built upon their belief until they have perfected it, and passed from belief to faith to knowledge, the more we can do as they have done and receive as they have received.

Daughter, Be of Good Comfort, Thy Faith Hath Made Thee Whole

One of the most instructive and inspiring of our Lord's miracles recorded in the New Testament is the healing of the woman "having an issue of blood" (Mark 5:25; Luke 8:43). What makes this miracle so remarkable is that it appears to have occurred without the conscious intention of the Savior. The healing occurred due to faith exerted by the woman, solely on her initiative and state of mind. The setting is so essential to this salient point, we will revisit it.

Jesus has been approached by Jairus, one of the rulers of the synagogue in Capernaum, Jesus' "own city" (Matt 9:1; Mark 2:1). Jairus' daughter lay on the brink of death and this good man threw himself at the feet of the Master and prayed He would come and heal her. Without hesitation Jesus responds and goes with him with intention of proceeding directly with some degree of haste to the home of Jairus. By now Jesus' reputation as a healer and teacher has billowed, and he is followed by crowds wherever he goes on a parallel with rock stars of today. "And much people followed him, and thronged him" (Mark 5:22–24).

Picture now an entourage making its way through narrow and crowded streets. Jesus, led by Jairus and accompanied by his disciples, is making His way through an amassed swarm of admirers, curious citizens and, one cannot doubt, a number of people burdened with various afflictions, desirous of a healing miracle as well. One among them is "a certain woman, which had an issue of blood twelve years" (Mark 5:25). Over those years, she had done her diligent best to find a remedy on her own, exhausting her financial means to no avail. Still, she suffered on. Quite possibly, the unnamed certain woman was similar to the aged Simeon, who "came by the Spirit into the temple," when Mary and Joseph brought Jesus to be presented. Perhaps, she too was in the crowd having been prompted in her prayers to find Jesus and draw near enough to touch him. She "came in the press behind Him, and touched the border of his garment" (Mark 5:27; Luke 8:44). Three seemingly insignificant details beg mentioning. First, she came up behind him, not in his field of vision. Jesus would have had no awareness of her physical approach. Second, she did not touch his person, only the *border*, the uttermost fringe, of his garment. Even if she had made physical contact with his body, he scarcely would have detected it given the press of the crowd, the reaching and pawing, along with the clamoring voices of people calling out to be heard and gain the Lord's attention. Third, Mark writes, "For she said," not shouted, not called out, simply "she said" and it's hard not to picture it being only an unvocalized inner thought. Indeed, Matthew records, "For she said *within herself,* If I may but touch his garment, I shall be whole" (Matt 9:21). One could even think it might have been that very thought that distilled upon her mind as she prayed at home—the Spirit urging her to find Jesus and come unto Him that day and helping her focus her faith sufficient to be healed. Repeating in her mind "If I may touch but his clothes, I shall be whole" (Mark 5:28), she put her faith into action. She reached out and managed to touch the hem of his outer garment. "And immediately her issue of blood stanched" (JST Luke 8:44)! "Straightway the fountain of her blood was dried up; and she felt in her body that she was healed of that plague" (Mark 5:29). She felt it! She knew it! At long last, after all those years, she was healed!

Wait. It gets better. "And Jesus, immediately knowing in himself that virtue had gone out of him, turned him about in the press, and said, Who touched my clothes?" At this statement, Peter and His disciples are stunned and mystified. Here is Jesus, surrounded by a mob, pushed, jostled and pressed upon from every angle as in an adoring mosh pit, and he's asking, "who touched me?" The disciples are thinking, "What? Who touched you? They all touched you. Everybody did. Everybody's laying their hands on you. You're being mauled!" "And Jesus said, Somebody hath touched me: for *I perceive that virtue is gone out of me*" (Luke 8:46, emphasis added). Now we arrive at the crux of this miracle and the glorious good news it holds out for all of us. The word translated "virtue" by the King James translators is "dunamis," from the root word "dunami," meaning force or *power,* the same root of the word *dynamo* in English. At the moment the woman touched the border of Christ's garment, there was an *actual transfer of power* from the body of the Lord to the body of the woman! He *felt* it! She *felt* it—"she *felt* in her body that she was healed of that plague." He that hath ears, let him hear and ponder.

"And when the woman found that she was not hid, she came trembling, and falling down before him, she declared unto him before all the people for what cause she had touched him and how she was healed immediately" (Luke 8:47). Fearing she had done something inappropriate, possibly even spiritually illegal, she trembles before the Lord. As we think about this moment of suspense, awaiting the Lord's response, we do well to also admit the singular and unusual nature of this healing miracle. No oil or water or even spit and mud was applied as Jesus did at other times. There was no laying on of hands, nor any pronounced words of blessing from the lips of the Lord. It's almost as though she obtained her miracle without the Lord's permission, intention or will. It was certainly without his initial awareness. As we contemplate this moment, we cannot help but feel how much love and joy and righteous pride the Lord must have felt for this certain woman at this moment. One can almost visualize tears coming to his eyes, maybe even a lump in his holy throat, as he smiles lovingly upon her, as he puts her mind at ease with the words, I would guess every one of us wants to hear Him say to us, "Daughter, be of good comfort, thy faith hath made thee whole" (Matt. 9:22). "Go in peace, and be whole of thy plague" (Mark 5:34). Not many passages of scripture give us more hope, incentive and *direction* in our quest to come unto the Lord Jesus Christ and be healed than this one. It conveys such monumental meaning and instruction about faith preceding and precipitating miracles.

Too often we let Satan undermine our faith by believing him when he tells us it's not up to us. It's up to the whim and wishes of the Lord. "If you don't catch him on a good day, he may not grant your prayers" is the erroneous "logic" Satan dispenses. SKAM is trying to obscure the fact that it's up to us as much, or maybe more, than it's up to the Lord! As repeatedly stated in scripture, the Lord works with men "according to their faith" (2 Ne. 26:13), meaning we are the primary factor in this equation. We hold the key to the transfer of power in our behalf. The Lord is ever ready and certainly has more than an ample storehouse of power to bestow any and every blessing. Whether or not we receive, and the degree to which we receive, His blessings are "predicated on the laws irrevocably decreed in the heavens before the foundation of this world." Such are the teachings of the Book of Mormon:

> *And it came to pass that I, Nephi, beheld the pointers which were in the ball, that they did work according to the faith and diligence and heed which we did give unto them (1 Ne.16:28).*
>
> *And that he manifesteth himself unto all those who believe in him… working mighty miracles, signs, and wonders, among the children of men according to their faith (2 Ne. 26:13).*
>
> *For behold, I am God; and I am a God of miracles; and I will show unto the world that I am the same yesterday, today, and forever; and I work not among the children of men save it be according to their faith (2 Ne. 27:23).*

Elder Gene R. Cook testified,

> *I bear witness we live far below our possibilities in working with the Lord. I bear witness we're too quick to turn to our own strength, and not rely on Him—maybe for fear that it won't work, maybe for fear of our own inadequacies. But I bear testimony that we can all learn how to do it better, and have much greater results from the heavens; and I bear that testimony in the name of Jesus Christ. Amen.*[13]

Life is a Creation

Life is a creation and we're the ones who get to create it. By now you know that I am not saying we created our intelligence. You know I am not

---

13 Cook, *Receiving Answers to Prayers.*

saying we created our own spirit. You know I am not saying we created the earth or the heavens or the plan of happiness. I am saying we are responsible for who we are, and what we accomplish with the infinite opportunity and generosity our Heavenly Father is offering and providing through His great plan of happiness. My intent is to unite two significant ideas to rivet your focus on how much authority, power, and opportunity you possess to create and lead a life filled with spiritual experiences and growth made possible by the power of Jesus Christ, Our Lord and Our Savior.

Idea One: Elaine Cannon said,

> *Accountability is the natural product of agency and is the basis of the plan of life. We are responsible for our own actions and accountable to God for what we choose to do with our lives. Life is God's gift to us, and what we do with it is our gift to him.*[14]

Idea Two: Brigham Young said,

> *With regard to our property, as I have told you many times, the property which we inherit from our Heavenly Father is our time, and the power to choose in the disposition of the same. This is the real capital that is bequeathed unto us by our Heavenly Father; all the rest is what he may be pleased to add unto us.*[15]

Combine those two ideas with points emphasized in this book and what do we come up with? You and I are in charge of what we think, what we feel, say, and do, and what results we get and how far we go in life. We are in charge of whether we believe in the gospel of Jesus Christ or not. We are in charge of how much faith we exercise or how much doubt we carry. We are in charge of whether we pray or not, how intently or casually we

---

14 Elaine Cannon, "Agency and Accountability," *Conference Report,* October 1983.
15 Young, *Journal of Discourses,* 18:354.

pray, how often we pray, how reverently we approach the throne of mercy and grace. We are responsible for our moods, our demeanor, our emotions, our disposition, our "personality." We are in charge of how hard we strive to cultivate the virtues exemplified perfectly in the life of our Savior—our empathy and compassion or lack thereof. We are responsible for how much effort we put into controlling our temper, cultivating meekness, developing patience, granting our forgiveness.

Now connect these realities with a major message in this book. Lucifer will do anything and everything in his power to confuse us about these truths. He will dissuade us from believing them and acting upon them. He will lie to us about true doctrines and the scriptures. He will spin and twist their meaning, purpose and intent. He will stir up contradictions to mislead us and delay or thwart our progress up the covenant path. He will persuade us that we have little control, and bear virtually no responsibility, for our conduct or character. He will demean us and discourage us and cast doubts a plenty into our minds to convince us none of this concerted effort is necessary or possible.

Yet, if we will latch onto the truth and embrace it and nurture our faith and relationship with the Father and the Son, the truth will prevail. We will go forward, deflecting the voice of the adversary, hearkening to the voice of the Father and the Son, step by step, until we obtain every promise in its fullest measure and bask in the realms of light where nothing is withheld.

CHAPTER 28

The Promised Rewards

Perhaps the most subtle and seldom recognized fear imposed by Lucifer is the fear of doctrine. He spreads a number of false ideas to prevent us from undertaking a diligent, consistent study of the greater truths of the restored gospel. To some, he sells us on the idea that it's simply not necessary. Elder Richard G. Scott warned of this deception. "Be wise and don't let good things crowd out those that are essential. What are the essential ones? *They are related to doctrine*," he said. Then he directly points out the fallacy, "While some may not understand or agree, I testify that it is not sufficient to be baptized and then live an acceptable life avoiding major transgressions. … Whether you intend to or not, when you live as though the Savior *and His teachings* are only one of many other important priorities in your life, you are clearly on the road to disappointment and likely on the path to tragedy."[1] To others, the adversary tries to frighten and intimidate us, insinuating that it's dangerous to delve too deeply. "You might discover something that will shake your testimony. It's better to play it safe and just stick to the milk of the gospel; you might choke on the meat."[2]

---

1 Scott, "Jesus Christ, Our Redeemer," *Ensign,* May 1997, 58, emphasis added.

2 See 1 Cor. 3:2.

We can't stay put, content with a cursory knowledge of the truths of the gospel and the doctrine of Christ. Nor can we expect our upward trek from one truth to a higher, along the rod of iron, to not have a share of trials of our faith. Significantly, in describing his vision of the tree his father Lehi saw, Nephi twice uses the words "press forward" (1 Ne. 8:24, 30). Do not those words strongly suggest that the quest for knowledge leading to the tree whose fruit "was desirable above all other fruit" (1 Ne. 8:12–15) requires effort and struggle? And does it not imply that we need to be undertaking that effort?

The need for the saints to open their minds and strive harder weighed heavily on the mind of the prophet Joseph Smith.

> *I have tried for a number of years to get the minds of the Saints prepared to receive the things of God; but we frequently see some of them, after suffering all they have for the work of God, will fly to pieces like glass as soon as anything comes that is contrary to their traditions: they cannot stand the fire at all. How many will be able to abide a celestial law, and go through and receive their exaltation, I am unable to say, as many are called, but few are chosen.*[3]

We need not harbor fears, sown by Satan, of learning too much or that by prayerfully searching the scriptures we run the risk of "going off the deep end." The journey up the path to eternal life will require us to learn and expand our understanding of many things we think we have "down pat." We do well to heed the counsel of Elder Jeffrey R. Holland to not cast away our confidence when we encounter a new insight or two along the path. "Beware the temptation to retreat from a good thing," he warned. "If it was right when you prayed about it and trusted it and lived for it, it is right now."[4] If you have felt the witness of the Spirit from time to time in your

3 Smith, *Teachings of the Prophet Joseph Smith*, 331.

life, testifying that the "seed is good" and the testimonies of the apostles and prophets are true, then hold to that witness. Refuse to doubt it, no matter what "mists of darkness" Satan may brew up. If you will not cast away your confidence in God and His plan, gospel questions and seeming scriptural contradictions will actually become the fulcrum to greater insight, sacred personal revelation, and a stronger witness of the truthfulness of the restored gospel of Jesus Christ and the mission of the Prophet Joseph Smith.

It is imperative we see the vital role trials of faith play in our quest for eternal life and embrace them. Obtaining the greatest of all the gifts Heavenly Father has for His children, is *of necessity* an upward ascending climb. It's the cardinal hallmark of our journey, for it demands our utmost efforts and continuous stretching of our faith. Without the testing there would be no growth or glory. And it is precisely *in* the gloomy valleys of temptation and on the withering mountains of trial that we must look unto Christ. Yea, we must look to Him in every thought. Christ has the answers to every one of our questions. Christ has the explanation for every one of the seeming contradictions he knew we would face. For, it is in those moments that we must turn to Him and Him alone for the answers. And he will give to any and all of us liberally, without scolding, if we ask Him in faith.

Christ alone has the power each of us needs to live the truths we will be taught as we ascend the path. He is our Savior! He is the author and the finisher of our faith (Heb. 12:2). Anyone who tries to go it alone with an "I'll figure it out on my own" attitude will, putting it bluntly, miserably fail. As part of his final entry on the plates he forged and engraved, Nephi plainly declares:

> *And now, my beloved brethren, after ye have gotten into this strait and narrow path, I would ask if all is done? Behold, I say unto you, Nay;*

---

4 Holland, "Cast Not Away Therefore Your Confidence," *BYU Devotional Address,* March 2, 1999.

for ye have not come thus far save it were by the word of Christ with unshaken faith in him, relying wholly upon the merits of him who is mighty to save.

Wherefore, ye must press forward with a steadfastness in Christ, having a perfect brightness of hope, and a love of God and of all men. Wherefore, if ye shall press forward, feasting upon the word of Christ, and endure to the end, behold, thus saith the Father: Ye shall have eternal life.

And now, behold, my beloved brethren, this is the way; and there is none other way nor name given under heaven whereby man can be saved in the kingdom of God. And now, behold, this is the doctrine of Christ, and the only and true doctrine of the Father, and of the Son, and of the Holy Ghost, which is one God, without end. Amen (2 Ne. 31:19–21).

For the remainder of Nephi's personal record—2 Nephi chapters 32 and 33—he is solemnly testifying that "Men must pray and gain knowledge for themselves from the Holy Ghost" (2 Ne. 32, chapter heading). When questions arise, and they surely will, the answers will come, for every member of the Godhead wants you to keep probing and learning more truth. Most importantly, the answers will come from the source you can trust, the one and only source you can really count on, the same Holy Spirit that first bore witness to you to begin with.

Maintain and exercise faith, be patient and diligently hang onto the iron rod—knowing the Holy Ghost has already told you what you know thus far is true. Then look to the Lord and appeal in earnest prayer for the Holy Ghost to teach you and open the door to a greater understanding of the truth. Rather than wading through the weed patch of half-truths and uninspired posts and tweets on the internet, the Holy Ghost will surely guide you to inspired answers. He has to; that is precisely His role in the Godhead! The specific mission of the Holy Ghost is to testify of the Father and the Son and to lead all of God's children to all truth (John 16:13). The Holy Ghost is not annoyed by your seeking honest answers to sincere questions. Many times, He will be the one to plant a question, so you will be motivated to study and pray with more diligence and specificity.

For these and other reasons, Satan wants to discourage and intimidate latter-day saints when they hear the word "doctrine." He desperately wants us to shy away from doctrine. He wants to make studying doctrine and receiving revelation seem hard and difficult, as though it's beyond our capability, attainable only by the scholarly elite. All this is done to prevent us from delving more deeply into the scriptures, while the apostles and prophets are encouraging, even begging, us to do so. Hear the Prophet Joseph Smith's plea given near the end of his life, "I advise all to go on to perfection, and search deeper and deeper into the mysteries of Godliness."[5] Perhaps it's the word "mystery" that throws us. SKAM immediately tries to direct our thoughts to things like murder mysteries by Agatha Christie and horror novels by Stephen King. These thoughts trigger feelings of foreboding, danger and consorting with evil—things we know instinctively to avoid. The Bible Dictionary, however, gives us the correct scriptural intent of the term: "Mystery. Denotes in the New Testament a spiritual truth that was once hidden but now is revealed, and that, without special revelation, would have remained unknown.... The modern meaning of something incomprehensible forms no part of the significance of the word as it occurs in the New Testament" (Bible Dictionary, 736).

Why does Lucifer want us to avoid study of doctrine? Because it changes us! As emphasized in an earlier chapter, studying and understanding true doctrine changes us for the better, not just in a general way but in the

5 Smith, *Teachings of the Prophet Joseph Smith*, 364.

precise spiritual way God wants us to change. President Boyd K. Packer, a gifted teacher, uttered many memorable statements. The one I hear quoted most often by other church leaders is this: "True doctrine, understood, changes attitudes and behavior. The study of the doctrines of the gospel will improve behavior quicker than a study of behavior will improve behavior."[6] *Study* of the doctrine implies and requires more than regular and routine *reading* of the scriptures, as uplifting and comforting as that may be. Again, the Prophet Joseph Smith emphasized, "Reading the experiences of others, or the revelation given to them, can never give us a comprehensive view of our condition and true relation to God. Knowledge of these things can only be obtained by experience through ordinances of God set forth for that purpose."[7]

To obtain "all that the Father hath" requires us to exert our minds—to search and strive for greater understanding, going deeper than the surface layer. Diligent study of the doctrine of the restored gospel leads to genuine transformation because it requires the guidance and close companionship of the Holy Ghost. As we work to obtain revelation, the Holy Ghost reveals more and more truth and light. Simultaneously, we are not only gaining greater knowledge, we are obtaining more of the Savior's power to live and apply the truths we are learning. This ennobling and sanctifying process begins modestly, and it gains momentum as we continue to pursue it. Line upon line, we grow stronger as the light within us grows "brighter and brighter until the perfect day" (D&C 50:24), meaning we approach perfection as we strive to obtain a perfect knowledge. We are not just transformed by knowledge but also *through the process of obtaining the knowledge.*

The scriptures provide the map. Studying, pondering, and applying the doctrine is the actual journey—the journey that leads to eternal life. If

6 Packer, "Do Not Fear," *Ensign*, May 2004, 79.
7 Smith, *Teachings of the Prophet Joseph Smith*, 324.

SKAM is trying to discourage and dissuade you from deeper study of the scriptures, then that's your clue that it's precisely what you should do. The Prophet Joseph Smith taught, "It is impossible for a man to be saved in ignorance" (D&C 131:6).

What We Search For

Consider two more rules of the mind: 1) The mind does not solve *general* problems; 2) The mind does not achieve *vague or indefinite* goals. Applying these laws to our quest for eternal life, it makes sense that Heavenly Father would give us specific milestones to strive for and attain along the path. At one time in my life, like many I suppose, I would have phrased my spiritual goal in broad general terms, such as "to return to my Heavenly Father and dwell eternally in His presence." This is a worthy expression. Yet, expressed as it is, it's too broad. Greater spiritual progress and experiences occur when we have defined focal points and, as part of the restoration, the Prophet Joseph Smith provided them.

At a conference of the Twelve, the Prophet gave commentary on several important doctrines. What he taught in this discourse amounts to a road map—a step by step progression, if you will—that provides specific milestones which serve as focal points and a way to gauge our progress to the tree whose fruit is "most desirable above all things" (1 Ne. 11:21–23). The date was June 27, 1839, exactly five years to the day prior to his martyrdom. After giving instruction on the first principles, Joseph focused on the doctrines of resurrection and election, and cited the words of the Apostle Peter:

> *Wherefore the rather, brethren, give diligence to make your calling and election sure: for if ye do these things, ye shall never fall: For so an entrance shall be ministered unto you abundantly into the everlasting kingdom of our Lord and Savior Jesus Christ (2 Pet. 1:10–11).*

As Peter did, the Prophet exhorted those present to "make [their] calling and election sure,"[8] and also linked it with the words of Paul about being "sealed with the Holy Spirit of Promise…that we may be sealed up unto the day of redemption" (Eph. 1:13–14). Joseph is equating these specific doctrinal terms to the broad goal of "attaining the celestial kingdom," giving it more definition. Consider then "making ones calling and election sure" and "sealed with the Holy Spirit of Promise" as the destination on the map of our mortal journey. The next words from the Prophet Joseph Smith are even more explicit and inspiring:

> *This principle ought (in its proper place) to be taught, for God hath not revealed anything to Joseph, but what He will make known unto the Twelve, and even the least Saint may know all things as fast as he is able to bear them, for the day must come when no man need say to his neighbor, Know ye the Lord; for all shall know Him (who remain) from the least to the greatest. How is this to be done? It is to be done by this sealing power, and the other Comforter spoken of, which will be manifest by revelation.*[9]

Two Comforters

The Prophet Joseph Smith focuses our attention and clarifies our priorities by framing the journey of all journeys as the obtaining of two Comforters.

> *There are two Comforters spoken of. One is the Holy Ghost, the same as given on the day of Pentecost, and that all Saints receive after faith, repentance, and baptism. This first Comforter or Holy Ghost has no other effect than pure intelligence.*[10]

8 Smith, *Teachings of the Prophet Joseph Smith,* 149.
9 Ibid., 149.
10 Ibid., 149.

Receive the Holy Ghost

To grasp the precious pearls Joseph presented, we must be clear on what it means to *receive the Holy Ghost*—the first Comforter. In General Conference October 2010, Elder David A. Bednar described what it means to actually receive the Holy Ghost.

> *My message focuses on the importance of striving in our daily lives to actually receive the Holy Ghost. … The ordinance of confirming a new member of the Church and bestowing the gift of the Holy Ghost is both simple and profound. … By the authority of the holy priesthood and in the name of the Savior, the individual is confirmed a member of The Church of Jesus Christ of Latter-day Saints, and this important phrase is uttered: "Receive the Holy Ghost."*

Note carefully Elder Bednar's explanation of what the phrase "receive the Holy Ghost" means and what it doesn't mean:

> *The simplicity of this ordinance may cause us to overlook its significance. These four words—"Receive the Holy Ghost"—are not a passive pronouncement; rather, they constitute a priesthood injunction—an authoritative admonition to act and not simply to be acted upon. The Holy Ghost does not become operative in our lives merely because hands are placed upon our heads and those four important words are spoken. As we receive this ordinance, each of us accepts a sacred and ongoing responsibility to desire, to seek, to work, and to so live that we indeed "receive the Holy Ghost" and its attendant spiritual gifts.*[11]

For clarification and emphasis, let us note the following distinction in terms:

11 Bednar, "Receive the Holy Ghost," *Ensign*, November 2010, 95.

- The Holy Ghost is the third member of the Godhead, a personage of Spirit (D&C 130:22).
- The Gift of the Holy Ghost is the *right* to receive the Holy Ghost based on keeping the covenant of baptism.
- Receiving the Holy Ghost is the baptism of fire and the Holy Ghost; being born again; sanctification (3 Ne. 27:20; Moro. 6:4).

Thus, there is a difference between receiving *the gift* of the Holy Ghost and actually *receiving* the Holy Ghost. The gift bestowed at confirmation is the *right* to receive the Holy Ghost based on fulfilling the requisites to receive the Holy Ghost, as taught by Elder Bruce R. McConkie:

> *The saints in this day go through the ordinance of the laying on of hands which gives them the gift, which by definition is* the right to receive the companionship of the Spirit. *If and when they are worthy, they are then immersed in the Spirit, as it were,* thus actually enjoying the gift.[12]

We qualify to receive the Holy Ghost by using our agency to exercise and act upon a mighty desire to receive the first Comforter. We do our part by earnestly seeking, repenting, studying, serving and comforting others, striving to live according to the covenant we made at baptism. Due to *the gift* of the Holy Ghost received at confirmation, the Holy Ghost continually works with us—teaching, testifying, and bestowing truth, light and grace upon us, gradually sanctifying us—thus helping us every step of the way to qualify for His full and constant companionship.

Receiving the Holy Ghost should be our foremost priority—uppermost in our minds and in our prayers. The Book of Mormon provides a classic

12 Bruce R. McConkie, *Doctrinal New Testament Commentary*, (Salt Lake City: Bookcraft, 1976), Vol. 1, 857, emphasis added.

confirmation of this truth. You will recall after Christ's resurrection and forty-day ministry to His flock in the Old World, the Lord visited His other sheep in the Americas. In third Nephi we read:

> *[A]nd behold, he stretched forth his hand unto the multitude, and cried unto them, saying: Blessed are ye if ye shall give heed unto the words of these twelve whom I have chosen from among you to minister unto you, and to be your servants; and unto them I have given power that they may baptize you with water; and after that ye are baptized with water, behold, I will baptize you with fire and with the Holy Ghost; therefore blessed are ye if ye shall believe in me and be baptized, after that ye have seen me and know that I am (3 Ne. 12:1).*

At the end of that marvelous day of divine teachings and spiritual experiences, the group returned to their homes. Understandably, they shared the news that Jesus was going to appear the next day and it was "noised abroad." Keep in mind that the people gathering were good people. They were not perfect, but they were righteous enough to be spared during the cataclysmic destructions that literally sundered the rocks around them. These were people who had not cast out and persecuted the prophets sent unto them. They were "spared because [they] were more righteous than they" who had rejected the prophets (3 Ne. 9:13).

Throughout the night and into the early hours of the morning a multitude gathered. The body was so numerous they were divided into twelve groups, each tutored by one of the twelve ordained disciples in all the doctrine Jesus had taught the previous day. Note what occurred before Jesus appears on the second day; it's symbolic of what we must also do. After receiving the teachings by the twelve was completed, the congregations "knelt again and prayed to the Father in the name of Jesus" (3 Ne 19:5–8). *And what did they pray for?* The record states, "And they did pray for that which they most desired; and they desired that *the Holy Ghost should be given unto them."* Keep in mind that these people praying to receive the Holy Ghost were not being introduced to the gospel and the testimony of the Spirit for the very first time. They were not unacquainted with the Holy Ghost. They had felt the influence and power occasionally and intermittently. They had heard and heeded the prophets to a degree that they were not obliterated in the destruction. Yet, most of them had not lived valiantly enough to receive the Holy Ghost in the fullest sense of the term.

Receiving the Holy Ghost is synonymous with such scriptural terms as "the baptism of fire and the Holy Ghost, born of the Spirit, birth of the Spirit, conversion, born again, and spiritually begotten (Alma 7:14; John 3:1–13; Mosiah 27:24–29). These terms are more literal than poetic or figurative. In the June 27 discourse cited next, the Prophet explains how literal the new birth can be:

> *The first comforter or Holy Ghost … is more powerful in expanding the mind, enlightening the understanding, and storing the intellect with present knowledge of a man who is of the literal seed of Abraham, than one that is a Gentile, though it may not have half as much visible effect upon the body; for as the Holy Ghost falls upon one of the literal seed of Abraham, it is calm and serene; and his whole soul and body are only exercised by the pure spirit of intelligence; while the effect of the Holy Ghost upon a Gentile, is to purge out the old blood, and make him actually of the seed of Abraham. That man that has none of the blood of Abraham (naturally) must have a new creation by the Holy Ghost. In such a case, there may be more of a powerful effect upon the body, and visible to the eye, than upon an Israelite, while the Israelite at first might be far before the Gentile in pure intelligence.*[13]

---

13 Smith, *Teachings of the Prophet Joseph Smith,* 149–150.

Clearly, receiving the Holy Ghost is a transformative experience. People so cleansed and purified lose every desire for sin and are animated by an unquenchable loving desire to serve God by serving all of God's children. Note how Mormon describes the sons of Mosiah after their conversion: "Now they were desirous that salvation should be declared to every creature, for they could not bear that any human soul should perish; yea, even the very thoughts that any soul should endure endless torment did cause them to quake and tremble" (Mosiah 28:3).

Elder Parley P. Pratt described the effects of receiving the gift of the Holy Ghost thus:

> *The gift of the Holy Ghost adapts itself to all these organs or attributes. It quickens all the intellectual faculties, increases, enlarges, expands, and purifies all the natural passions and affections, and adapts them, by the gift of wisdom, to their lawful use. It inspires, develops, cultivates, and matures all the fine-toned sympathies, joys, tastes, kindred feelings, and affections of our nature. It inspires virtue, kindness, goodness, tenderness, gentleness, and charity. It develops beauty of person, form, and features. It tends to health, vigor, animation, and social feeling. It invigorates all the faculties of the physical and intellectual man. … In short, it is, as it were, marrow to the bone, joy to the heart, light to the eyes, music to the ears, and life to the whole being.*[14]

Thus, we may correctly add to our list of synonymous terms for being born again and the baptism of fire and the Holy Ghost the term "quickened in the inner man" (Moses 6:65).

Lorenzo Snow's Account

Consider President Lorenzo Snow's account of his baptism of water and of the spirit:

14 Parley P. Pratt, *Key to the Science of Theology,* (Salt Lake City: Deseret Book Company, 1978), 61.

I was baptized by Elder John Boynton, then one of the Twelve Apostles, June, 1836, in Kirtland, Ohio. Previous to accepting the ordinance of baptism, in my investigations of the principles taught by the Latter-day Saints, which I proved, by comparison, to be the same as those mentioned in the New Testament taught by Christ and His Apostles, I was thoroughly convinced that obedience to those principles would impart miraculous powers, manifestations and revelations. With sanguine expectation of this result, I received baptism and the ordinance of laying on of hands by one who professed to have divine authority; and, having thus yielded obedience to these ordinances, I was in constant expectation of the fulfillment of the promise of the reception of the Holy Ghost.

The manifestation did not immediately follow my baptism, as I had expected, but, although the time was deferred, when I did receive it, its realization was more perfect, tangible and miraculous than even my strongest hopes had led me to anticipate.

Some two or three weeks after I was baptized, one day while engaged in my studies, I began to reflect upon the fact that I had not obtained a knowledge of the truth of the work—that I had not realized the fulfillment of the promise "he that doeth my will shall know of the doctrine," and I began to feel very uneasy. I laid aside my books, left the house, and wandered around through the fields under the oppressive influence of a gloomy, disconsolate spirit, while an indescribable cloud of darkness seemed to envelop me. I had been accustomed, at the close of the day, to retire for secret prayer, to a grove a short distance from my lodgings, but at this time I felt no inclination to do so. The spirit of prayer had departed, and the heavens seemed like brass over my head. At length, realizing that the usual time had come for secret prayer, I concluded I would not forego my evening service, and, as a matter of formality, knelt as I was in the habit of doing, and in my accustomed retired place, but not feeling as I was wont to feel.

I had no sooner opened my lips in an effort to pray, than I heard a sound, just above my head, like the rustling of silken robes, and immediately the Spirit of God descended upon me, completely enveloping my whole person, filling me, from the crown of my head to the soles of my feet, and O, the joy and happiness I felt! No language can describe the almost instantaneous transition from a dense cloud of mental and spiritual darkness into a refulgence of light and knowledge, as it was at that time imparted to my understanding. I then received a perfect knowledge that God lives, that Jesus Christ is the Son of God, and of the restoration of the holy Priesthood, and the fullness of the Gospel.

It was a complete baptism—a tangible immersion in the heavenly principle or element, the Holy Ghost; and even more real and physical in its effects upon every part of my system than the immersion by water; dispelling forever, so long as reason and memory last, all possibility of doubt or fear in relation to the fact handed down to us historically, that the "Babe of Bethlehem" is truly the Son of God; also the fact that he is now being revealed to the children of men, and communicating knowledge, the same as in the Apostolic times. I was perfectly satisfied, as well I might be, for my expectations were more than realized, I think I may safely say in an infinite degree.

I cannot tell how long I remained in the full flow of the blissful enjoyment and divine enlightenment, but it was several minutes before the celestial element which filled and surrounded me began gradually to withdraw. On arising from my kneeling posture, with my heart swelling with gratitude to God, beyond the power of expression, I felt—I knew that He had conferred on me what only an omnipotent

> *being can confer—that which is of greater value than all the wealth and honors worlds can bestow.*[15]

When, where and in what manner this infinitely precious gift is bestowed rests upon the Lord. He who does all things in wisdom and in love for the good of each of His children will determine the bestowal, for it is only through Him and His infinite Atonement that such glorious gifts can be realized. Our role is to accept responsibility and exercise greater faith to do everything in our power to prepare and fulfill our side of the equation. Until we receive the Holy Ghost no other priority, spiritual or temporal, exceeds this one.

Suggestions from an Apostle of the Lord

Elder Bednar offered specific suggestions for cultivating a rich relationship with the Holy Ghost:

> *What should we do to make this authorized admonition to seek the companionship of the third member of the Godhead an ongoing reality? Let me suggest that we need to (1) sincerely desire to receive the Holy Ghost, (2) appropriately invite the Holy Ghost into our lives, and (3) faithfully obey God's commandments.*[16]

Speaking specifically of faithfully obeying, Elder Bednar puts what we know, do and are about in the church into a sharper perspective. He points out: "Everything the Savior's gospel teaches us to do and become is intended to bless us with the companionship of the Holy Ghost."

Then he expanded on his statement:

> *Praying, studying, gathering, worshipping, serving, and obeying are not isolated and independent items on a lengthy gospel checklist of things to*

---

15 Eliza R. Snow, *Biography and Family Record of Lorenzo Snow,* (Salt Lake City: Deseret News Company, 1884, 7–9.
16 Bednar, "Receive the Holy Ghost," *Ensign,* November 2010, 95.

> *do. Rather, each of these righteous practices is an important element in an overarching spiritual quest to fulfill the mandate to receive the Holy Ghost. The commandments from God we obey and the inspired counsel from Church leaders we follow principally focus upon obtaining the companionship of the Spirit. Fundamentally, all gospel teachings and activities are centered on coming unto Christ by receiving the Holy Ghost in our lives.*[17]

Now in possession of a clear understanding of what it means to receive the Holy Ghost, the first Comforter, we can appreciate and rejoice in Joseph's description of the Second Comforter, the culminating component of our spiritual journey.

The Second Comforter

> *The other Comforter spoken of is a subject of great interest, and perhaps understood by few of this generation. After a person has faith in Christ, repents of his sins, and is baptized for the remission of his sins* and receives the Holy Ghost, *(by the laying on of hands), which is the first Comforter, then let him continue to humble himself before God, hungering and thirsting after righteousness, and living by every word of God, and the Lord will soon say unto him, Son, thou shalt be exalted. When the Lord has thoroughly proved him, and finds that the man is determined to serve Him at all hazards, then the man will find his calling and his election made sure, then it will be his privilege to receive the other Comforter, which the Lord hath promised the Saints, as is recorded in the testimony of St. John (John 14:12–27).*
>
> *Now what is this other Comforter? It is no more nor less than the Lord Jesus Christ Himself; and this is the sum and substance of the*

17 Ibid., 95.

> *whole matter; that when any man obtains this last Comforter, he will have the personage of Jesus Christ to attend him, or appear unto him from time to time, and even He will manifest the Father unto him, and they will take up their abode with him, and the visions of the heavens will be opened unto him, and the Lord will teach him face to face, and he may have a perfect knowledge of the mysteries of the Kingdom of God; and this is the state and place the ancient Saints arrived at when they had such glorious visions—Isaiah, Ezekiel, John upon the Isle of Patmos, St. Paul in the three heavens, and all the Saints who held communion with the general assembly and Church of the Firstborn.*[18]

A Remarkable Complementary Relationship

As you ponder and pray about the doctrine of the two Comforters expounded by the Prophet Joseph Smith, you will come to recognize *a grand complementary relationship* between the June 27 discourse and the promises we have studied set forth in the Doctrine and Covenants. How do we best magnify our callings, receive His servants, and receive Christ so He can introduce us to the Father, as stipulated in D&C 84? By undertaking the works required to receive the first Comforter, the Holy Ghost. How do we cultivate companionship of the Holy Ghost? By forsaking our sins, coming unto Christ, calling on His name and obeying His voice, as specified in D&C 93:1. Now note how clearly this is explained by Nephi, he who delights in plainness:

> *Do ye not remember that I said unto you that after ye had received the Holy Ghost* [First Comforter] *ye could speak with the tongue of angels? And now, how could ye speak with the tongue of angels save it were by the Holy Ghost?*

18 Smith, *Teachings of the Prophet Joseph Smith,* 150–151.

> *Angels speak by the power of the Holy Ghost; wherefore, they speak the words of Christ. Wherefore, I said unto you, feast upon the words of Christ* [The scriptures and words of Christ's messengers]*; for behold, the words of Christ will tell you all things what ye should do* [Promptings and whisperings of the Spirit to receive the Holy Ghost].
>
> *For behold, again I say unto you that if ye will enter in by the way, and receive the Holy Ghost,* [First Comforter] *it will show unto you all things what ye should do* [In order to receive the Second Comforter].
>
> *Behold, this is the doctrine of Christ, and there will be no more doctrine given until after he shall manifest himself unto you in the flesh* [Second Comforter]. *And when he shall manifest himself unto you in the flesh, the things which he shall say unto you shall ye observe to do (2 Ne. 32:2–3, 5–6).*

Equally significant and notable is the verse immediately following these plain and precious teachings: "And now I, Nephi, cannot say more; the Spirit stoppeth mine utterance, and I am left to mourn because of the unbelief, and the wickedness, and the ignorance, and the stiffneckedness of men; for they will not search knowledge, nor understand great knowledge, when it is given unto them in plainness, even as plain as word can be" (2 Ne. 32:7). He that hath an ear, let him hear.

The Power of the Doctrine of Christ

When rightly understood, is not the true doctrine of Christ life transforming? Does it not awaken and inspire us to reach higher and strive harder? Will it not improve behavior quicker than a study of behavior will improve behavior? Yes, it will! It will when we will take it to heart, act on it, and seek after more. It will when we call upon Christ in faith and rebuke the fiery darts the adversary inflicts upon us. It will when we learn to intercept the steady stream of doubts Satan sows, and we turn our thoughts to Christ. It will when we choose to let belief supplant unbelief and choose to put our trust in Christ and the power of His Atonement.

May we all accept our loving Savior's invitation to "look unto me in every thought; doubt not, fear not. Behold the wounds which pierced my side, and also the prints of the nails in my hands and feet; be faithful, keep my commandments, and ye shall inherit the kingdom of heaven. Amen" (D&C 6:36–37)!

Acknowledgements

Pertaining to the Book Itself

Many people have spent many hours plying their gifts and skills in the publication of this book, each of them making a unique and valuable contribution. Specifically, I express thanks to Mike Higgins and Tori Spencer who waded through the first bulky manuscript and provided valuable suggestions to pare it down; Dr. Michael L. Wright who offered timely encouragement and moral support in the early stages; President R. Dean Arnson, who was particularly generous with his time, willingly reading the entire manuscript and providing invaluable suggestions, and for the sustaining priesthood blessing; Dr. Daniel B. Madsen for his insights and the inspiration for Chapter 1; Cecily Condie who did the research and polling that finalized the title; Mary B. Johnston whose professional content editing produced major improvements; Michelle Mulford whose final proofing was amazingly thorough; Christine Deaton for the photography; artist Danny Hahlbohm whose painting *Speak to the Storm* seemed to be created especially for this cover; Christine Van Wagenen and Roxanne Thayne and the team at Rooftop Publishing who so effectively coordinated all the components involved in producing such an exceptional presentation of the written message; my brother Gary and his wife Teresa, and my sister JaLee Harris and her husband Mark, who provided support throughout the process; and, a special note of appreciation to my granddaughter Sabrina Stewart who gave up valuable vacation beach time to advise and polish Section Four and, last but not least, Talmage Thayne who labored patiently making corrections so the audio book might also accomplish the ends the Lord desires.

Pertaining to the Professional Development of the Author

It feels both awkward and shallow to attempt to express sufficient appreciation to individuals to whom no amount of thanks, written or verbal, could be nearly enough. Highest on the list, second only to my devoted eternal companion, Susan, is Reece A. Bawden, my loyal and able business partner—co-founder of the human development training company first known as Mind Masters Institute, then TimeMax, and now Quma Learning Systems. In the prime of our lives, for two amazingly exciting decades, we worked shoulder to shoulder to validate the principles of Mind Management and Visioneering—that against daunting odds, one can actually create a sensory-rich, emotion-laden vision of what you want to do and who you want to be and, with generous help of the Lord, accomplish it. Linked in that endeavor, each adding his or her considerable strength at timely moments along the way, I express sincere appreciation to Dan Hartman, Brent Bawden, Clyde Bawden, DeAnn Kettenring, Steve Hardison, Steve Chandler, Ken Cook, Evan Nielsen, Steve Bodhaine, Larry Capps, Chelcie Dunlap, Patricia Cox, and Scott Sandberg.

Pertaining to the Personal and Spiritual Development of the Author

With deepest gratitude and affection I acknowledge and honor nine choice spirit sons and daughters of the Perfect Father: April, Jared, Matthew, Jacob, Timothy, Rachel, Christian, Emily, and David. They are stars each, rising in their own galaxy, and further advanced than I, who agreed to be children of an imperfect mortal father, granting me opportunities to learn lessons I sorely needed to learn, often at their expense. I could not be more privileged to be a witness, up close and personal, of their individual greatness and unique talents, let alone to have the honor to call each one a beloved son or daughter.

And now comes the impossible. How does one express even a miniscule fraction of the immense gratitude one feels and owes one's eternal companion? I have been blessed beyond measure and what I deserve to have married Susan Spencer of Price Utah in the Salt Lake Temple. She is beautiful, brilliant and multi-talented; and, above all, devoted to the Lord Jesus Christ. How do you thank someone who has made the environment you've lived in for over five decades a paradise through her elevated talents in so many arts and aspects of her profession—sewing, quilting, tatting, stained glass art, home decorating, gardening, landscaping? How do you thank someone whose life's work could have been in any number of other highly respected professions requiring above average intelligence and drive, but who willingly and happily chose to be "a mother of a large family of children," and was pregnant for 81 months of her life and delivered all nine of our beloved children naturally, and then loved and served them with all her heart? How do you thank someone who never once winced or whined when business or church callings, or preparations for the same, took precedence. How do you thank someone who for over fifty years has continually sacrificed her own interests in favor of yours? No words however skillfully crafted could do justice. All I can say is that I have through these years felt like the most blessed man on earth; and living worthy enough to continue our courtship through the eternities has been by far my greatest hope and motivation.

BIBLIOGRAPHY

Allen, Richard J. *Teachings and Commentary on the Old Testament.* Salt Lake City: Covenant Communications, Inc., 2005.

Anderson, Neil L. "Faith Is Not by Chance, but by Choice." *Ensign,* November 2015.

________, "Repent. . . That I May Receive You," Ensign, November 2009.

________, *The Divine Gift of Forgiveness.* Salt Lake City: Deseret Book Company, 2019.

Ballard, M. Russell. "Pure Testimony." *Ensign,* November 2004.

Beck, Julie B. "Remembering, Repenting and Changing." *Ensign*, May 2007.

Bednar, David A. "And Nothing Shall Offend Them." *Ensign,* November 2006.

________, *Increase in Learning.* Salt Lake City: Deseret Book Company, 2011.

________, "Receive the Holy Ghost." *Ensign,* November 2010.

________, "We Believe in Being Chaste." *Ensign,* May 2013.

Begley, Sharon. *Train Your Mind, Change your Brain.* New York: Ballantine Books, 2007.

Benson, Ezra Taft. *The Teachings of Ezra Taft Benson.* Salt Lake City: Bookcraft, 1988.

________, "Think on Christ." *Ensign,* April 1984.

Bridge of Spies. Directed by Steven Spielberg. Filmed in 2015. Distributed by Touchstone Pictures.

Busche, F. Enzio. *Yearning for the Living God.* Salt Lake City: Deseret Book Company, 2004.

Bunyan John. *The Pilgrim's Progress.* Hertfordshire: Wordsworth Edition Limited, 1996.

Bushman, Richard Lyman. *Joseph Smith: Rough Stone Rolling.* New York: Vintage Books, a division of Random House, Inc., 2005.

Cannon, Elaine. "Agency and Accountability." *Conference Report,* October 1983.

Chandler, Steve. *Crazy Good.* Anna Maria, FL: Maurice Bassett, 2015.

Christofferson, D. Todd. "The Living Bread Which Came Down from Heaven." *Ensign,* November 2017.

________, "When Thou Art Converted." *Ensign, May 2004.*

Clayton, L. Whitney. "Choose to Believe." *Ensign,* May 2015.

Cook, Gene R. "How to Discourage Discouragement." *New Era,* January 2003.

________, *Receiving Answers to Prayers,* Audio CD, Salt Lake City: Deseret Book Company, 1991.

Craig, Michelle. "Divine Discontent." *Ensign,* November 2017.

Crick, Sir Francis. *The Astonishing Hypothesis: The Scientific Search for the Soul,* New York: Touchstone, 1994.

Deaton, Dennis R. *The Book on Mind Management,* Mesa: Quma Learning Systems, 1994, 2003.

de Jager, Jacob. "Overcoming Discouragement." *New Era,* March 1984.

Dew, Sheri. "God Wants a Powerful People." Deseret Book Audio Library, Salt Lake City: Deseret Book Company, 2004.

Dickinson, Emily. *The Complete Poems of Emily Dickinson.* Edited by Thomas H. Johnson. Boston, New York, London: Little, Brown and Company, 1960.

Editors of Encyclopedia Brittanica. *Encyclopedida Brittanica.* February 12, 2016.

Eyring, Henry B. "A Child of God." BYU Devotional, October 21, 1997.

________, "A Priceless Heritage of Hope." *Ensign,* May 2014.

________, "Helping Students Inquire of the Lord," February, 2013. *https://www.churchofjesuschrist.org/media/video.*

________, "Holiness and the Plan of Happiness." *Ensign,* November 2019.

________, "Prayers of Faith." *Ensign,* May 2020.

Frankl, Viktor E. *Man's Search for Meaning.* New York: Simon & Schuster, 1984.

Gates, Bill. "One-on-One with Bill Gates." Article by Scott Eason, cnbc.com. August 29, 2007.

Goodreads. *https://www.goodreads.com/quotes.*

Hamilton, Alexander. *"Alexander Hamilton Quotes." Quotes.net.* STANDS4 LLC, 2020. Web. 27 Oct. 2020, <.https://www/quotes.net/53508.

Hinckley, Gordon B. In *Teachings of the Presidents of the Church: Gordon B. Hinckley.* Salt Lake City: The Church of Latter-day Saints, 08862.

________, *Teachings of Gordon B. Hinckley.* Salt Lake City: Deseret Book Company, 1997.

________, "You Are a Child of God." *Ensign,* May 2003.

Hinckley, Marjorie Pay. *Small and Simple Things.* Salt Lake City: Deseret Book Company, 2003.

Holland, Jeffrey R. "An High Priest of Good Things to Come." *Ensign,* November 1999.

________, "Be Ye Therefore Perfect—Eventually." *Ensign,* November 2017.

________, "Cast Not Away Therefore Your Confidence." *BYU Devotional Address,* March 2, 1999.

________, *Christ and the New Covenant.* Salt Lake City: Deseret Book Company, 1997.

________, "For Times of Trouble." *BYU Devotional Address,* March 18, 1980.

________, "For Times of Trouble." *Liahona,* January 1982.

Hunter, Howard W. "The Golden Threads of Choice." *Conference Report,* October 7, 1989.

Hyde, Orson. Given in Tabernacle, Great Salt Lake City, February 12, 1860. In *Journal of Discourses, Volume 7.* Liverpool: Amasa Lyman, London: Latter-day Saints Book Depot, 1860.

Hymns of the Church of Jesus Christ of Latter-day Saints. Salt Lake City: The Church of Jesus Christ of Latter-day Saints, 1985 (revised in 2002).

Kelly, Walt. "Pogo" Comic Strip syndicated by Fantagraphics, New York: Simon & Schuster, October 4, 1948 – July 20, 1975.

Kimball, Spencer W. *Faith Precedes the Miracle.* Salt Lake City: Deseret Book Company, 1973.

________, *The Miracle of Forgiveness.* Salt Lake City: Bookcraft, 1969.

Latin proverb. https://www.phrases.org.uk/meaning/forewarned-is-forearmed.html.

Lawrence, Larry R. "The War Goes On." *Ensign,* April 2017.

Lewis, C. S. *Mere Christianity.* New York: HarperCollins Publishers, 1952.

Madsen, Daniel B. Personal interaction used with permission.

Mandela, Nelson. *Long Walk to Freedom.* Boston, New York, London: Little, Brown and Company, 1994, 1995.

Maxwell, Neal A. "According to the Desires of [Our] Hearts." *Ensign,* November 1996.

________, "Becoming a Disciple." *Ensign,* June 1996.

________, "But For a Small Moment." *BYU Devotional Address,* September 1, 1974

________, "Grounded, Rooted, Established, and Settled." *BYU Devotional Address,* September 15, 1981.

________, "Meek and Lowly." *BYU Devotional Address,* October 21, 1986.

________, "Swallowed Up in the Will of the Father." *Ensign,* November 1995.

McConkie, Bruce R. *A New Witness for the Articles of Faith.* Salt Lake City: Deseret Book Company, 1985.

________, *Doctrinal New Testament Commentary, Volume 1.* Salt Lake City: Bookcraft, 1976.

________, *Mormon Doctrine,* 2nd Edition, Salt Lake City: Bookcraft, 1966.

________, "Our Relationship with the Lord." *BYU Devotional Address.* March 2, 1982.

________, *The Mortal Messiah, Book 1.* Salt Lake City: Deseret Book Company, 1979.

McKay, David O. *Gospel Ideals.* Salt Lake City: The Improvement Era, 1953.

________, *Secrets of a Happy Life.* Salt Lake City: Bookcraft, 1967.

Nelson, Russell M. "Hear Him." *Ensign,* May 2020.

________, "President Nelson Extends Important Invitation to All Latter-day Saints in 2020." *The Church News, January 1, 2020.*

________, "Revelation for the Church, Revelation for Our Lives." *Ensign,* May 2018.

________, "Spiritual Treasures." *Ensign,* November 2019.

________, "The Price of Priesthood Power." *Ensign,* May 2016.

________, "We Can Do Better and Be Better." *Ensign,* May 2019.

Nelson, Wendy. "Becoming the Person You Were Born to Be." Worldwide Devotional for Young Adults, January 10, 2016.

Netflix, *The Social Dilemma.* Documentary edited by David Coons

Neville, Dallas. Personal story used with permission.

Neville, Emily. Personal story used with permission.

Nibley, Hugh. *Enoch the Prophet, The Collected Works of High Nibley: Volume 2.* Salt Lake City: Deseret Book Company, 1986.

Oaks, Dallin H. "Truth and the Plan." *Ensign,* November 2018.

Paar, Jack. *I Kid You Not.* New York: Pocket Books, Inc., 1959, 1960.

Packer, Boyd K. "Do Not Fear." *Ensign,* May 2004.

________, "The Brilliant Morning of Forgiveness." *Ensign,* November 1995.

Paine, Thomas. *The American Crisis,* No. 1, 1776.

Parkin, Bonnie D. "Personal Ministry: Sacred and Precious." BYU Devotional Address, February 13, 2007.

Phinney, Davis. Permission granted by Davis Phinney Foundation for Parkinson's. September 30, 2020.
Pinegar, Ed J. *Teachings and Commentary on the Old Testament.* Salt Lake City: Covenant Communications, Inc., 2005.
Pratt, Orson. *The True Faith*. Liverpool, England: 1856.
Pratt, Parley P. *Autobiography of Parley Parker Pratt.* Salt Lake City: Deseret Book Company, 1938, reprinted 1976.
________, *Key to the Science of Theology.* Salt Lake City: Deseret Book Company, 1978.
Price, April. "100% Awesome Podcast", aprilpricecoaching.com.
Purdy, Amy. TED talks. *Ted.com/talks/amy-purdy-living-beyond-limits.*
Renlund, Dale G. "Choose You This Day." *Ensign,* November 2018.
________, "Consider the Goodness and Greatness of God." *Ensign,* May 2020.
Rogers, Fred. "Won't You Be My Neighbor." *New York Times.com.* June 5, 2018, https://www.nytimes.com/2018/06/05/movies/mister-rogers-wont-you-be-my-neighbor.html.
Rossell, Dina. Permission granted to use excerpt from talk given in sacrament meeting, 2020.
Rudy and Priest scene from movie "Rudy". https://www.youtube.com/watch?v=eRFc5RqaTmw.
Russell, Lana. Permission granted to use excerpts from talk given in sacrament meeting, 2019.
Rutledge, Thom. *Life Without Ed.* New York: McGraw-Hill. 2004.
Schaefer, Jenni. *Life Without Ed.* New York: McGraw-Hill. 2004.
Schwarzenegger, Arnold. *https://www.muscleandfitness.com/features/active-lifestyle/arnold-schwarzeneggers-muscle-building-mental-strategy.*
Schwartz, Jeffrey M., M.D. *The Mind and the Brain.* New York: HarperCollins Publishers, 2002.
Schweitzer, Albert. Quotes at www.goodreads.com.
Scott, Richard G. "Jesus Christ, Our Redeemer." *Ensign,* May 1997.
________, "To Acquire Spiritual Guidance." *Ensign,* November 2009.
Smith, George Albert. In "Think on Christ." *Ensign,* April 1984.
Smith, Joseph, Jr. *History of the Church of Jesus Christ of Latter-day Saints, Volume 3.* Edited by B. H. Roberts. 2d ed. rev 7 vols. Salt Lake City: Deseret Book Company, 1970.
________, *History of the Church of Jesus Christ of Latter-day Saints, Volume 4.* Edited by B. H. Roberts. 2d ed. rev 7 vols. Salt Lake City: Deseret Book Company, 1970.
________, comp. *Lectures on Faith.* Salt Lake City: Deseret Book Company, 1985.
________, *Teachings of the Prophet Joseph Smith,* Selected by Joseph Fielding Smith. Salt Lake City: Deseret Book Company, 1976.
Smith, Joseph F. Delivered in the Assembly Hall, Salt Lake City, February 17, 1884. In *Journal of Discourses, Volume 25.* Liverpool: John Henry Smith, London: Latter-day Saint Book Depot, 1884
________, In *Teachings of the Presidents of the Church: Joseph F. Smith.* Salt Lake City: The Church of Latter-day Saints, 35744.
Smith, Joseph Fielding. *Answers to Gospel Questions, Volume 3.* Salt Lake City: Deseret Book Company, 1960.

Snow, Eliza R. *Biography and Family Record of Lorenzo Snow.* Salt Lake City: Deseret News Company, 1884.

________, In *Hymns of the Church of Jesus Christ of Latter-day Saints.* Salt Lake City: The Church of Jesus Christ of Latter-day Saints, 1985.

Snow, Lorenzo. Delivered in Tabernacle, Great Salt Lake City, October 11, 1857. In *Journal of Discourses, Volume 5.* Liverpool: Asa Calkin, London: Latter-day Saints Book Depot, 1858.

________, Delivered in Tabernacle, Great Salt Lake City, January 14, 1872. In *Journal of Discourses, Volume 14.* Liverpool: Albert Carrington, London: Latter-day Saints Book Depot, 1872.

________, *The Teachings of Lorenzo Snow.* Salt Lake City: Bookcraft, 1996.

The Lost Books of the Bible and The Forgotten Books of Eden. USA: William Collins & World Publishing Company, Inc. 1976.

Tanner, N. Eldon. *Conference Report,* October 1966.

The Social Dilemma. Netflix Documentary edited by David Coons

Uchtdorf, Dieter F. "The Infinite Power of Hope." *Ensign,* November 2008.

________, "The Love of God." *Ensign,* November 2009.

________, "The Merciful Shall Obtain Mercy." *Ensign,* May 2012.

________, "Your Potential, Your Privilege." *Ensign,* May 2011.

Van Gogh, Vincent. https://www.goodreads.com/author/quotes/34583.Vincent_van_Gogh.

Whitney, Orson F. *Life of Heber C. Kimball.* Salt Lake City: The Kimball Family, Juvenile Instructor Office, 1888.

________, *Through Memory's Halls: The Life Story of Orson F. Whitney, as Told by Himself.* Independence, MO: Zion's Printing and Publishing, 1930.

Widtsoe, John A. *Conference Report.* April 1950.

Wikipedia. *"Know Thyself."* //https:www.en.wikipedia.org.

Williamson, Marianne. *A Return to Love.* New York: HarperCollins Publishers, 1992.

Wilcox, Ella Wheeler. *World Voices.* New York: Hearst's International Library Company, 1916.

Wirthlin, Joseph B. "The Unspeakable Gift." *Ensign,* May 2003.

Woodruff, Wilford. delivered in Nephi, January 27, 1883. In *Journal of Discourses, Volume 24.* Liverpool: John Henry Smith, London: Latter-day Saints Book Depot, 1884.

Young, Brigham. Delivered in Tabernacle, Great Salt Lake City, April 9, 1852. In *Journal of Discourses, Volume 1.* London: F.D. and S.W. Richards, 1854.

________, delivered in Tabernacle, Great Salt Lake City, February 17, 1856. In *Journal of Discourses, Volume 3.* Liverpool: Orson Pratt, London: Latter-day Saints Book Depot, 1856.

________, delivered in Tabernacle, Great Salt Lake City, November 28, 1857. In *Journal of Discourses, Volume 6.* Liverpool: ASA Calkin, London: Latter-day Saints Book Depot. 1859.

________, remarks made in Bowery, Great Salt Lake City, July 28, 1861. In *Journal of Discourses, Volume 9.* Liverpool: George Q. Cannon, London: Latter-day Saints Book Depot, 1862.

_______, delivered in the Semi-Annual Conference, held in the Temple, St. George, April 6, 1877.

In *Journal of Discourses, Volume 18.* Liverpool: Joseph F. Smith, London: Latter-day Saints Book Depot, 1877.

Ziglar, Zig. *See You at the Top*. Greta, LA: Pelican Publishing Company, 1975, 1977, 2000, 2003, 2005, 2010.

INDEX

DENNIS R DEATON is co-founder of Quma Learning Systems and a nationally known corporate educator and motivational speaker. He received his BA from the University of Utah and his DMD degree, cum laude, from Washington University in St. Louis.

He is also co-founder of Grand Key Education which provides online mindset and emotional regulation training for teens. He has authored Money: *An Owner's Manual; The Book On Mind Management; and Ownership Spirit: The One Grand Key That Changes Everything Else.*

Dennis has taught numerous Adult Education courses for the Church Education System, and was a regular speaker at BYU Campus Education Week for 22 years. He and his wife Susan are the parents of nine children; and he currently serves as a stake patriarch and temple worker.

Lovingly dedicated to my wife, Sally, my son, Alex, and my daughter, Stephanie

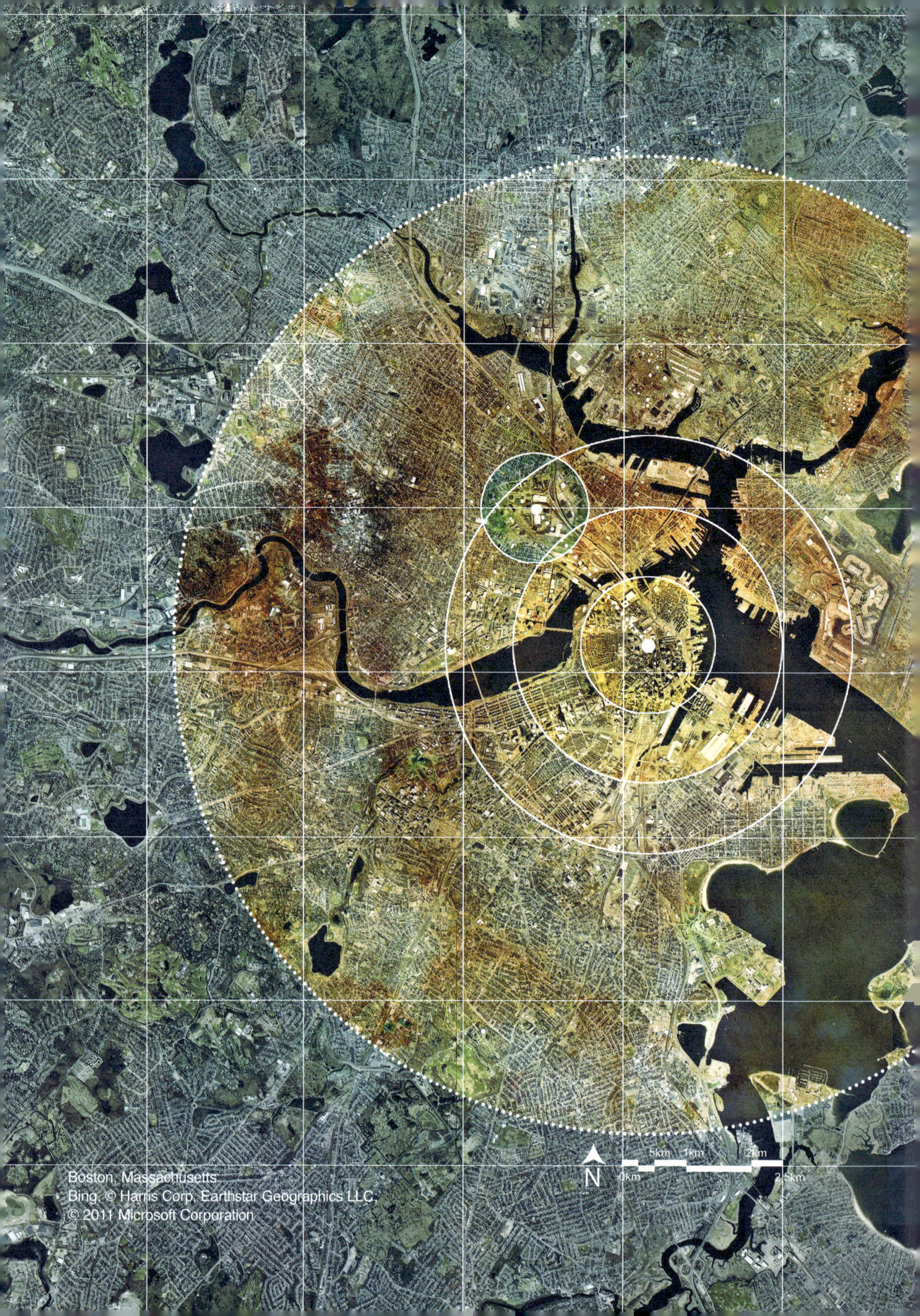

N
.5km
1km
2km
0km
2.5km
Boston, Massachusetts
Bing, © Harris Corp, Earthstar Geographics LLC,
© 2011 Microsoft Corporation

Transforming the Mid-Polis

Conversations on the Mid-Polis Condition

Introduction
Bruce Lindsey, Stephen White & Paul Lukez

Contributors
Interboro Partners, LTL Architects,
MIT Senseable City Lab, MONOLAB,
Paul Lukez Architecture, Dagmar Richter,
URBANUS, June Williamson, WSP Architects,
Ken Yeang, Zhejiang University

Artists & Photographers
Benjamin Edwards, Sarah McKenzie,
Julie Mehretu, Peter Vanderwarker

With Students' Contributions
Washington University In St. Louis &
Roger Williams University

Editor
Paul Lukez

OSCAR RIERA OJEDA
PUBLISHERS

Table of Contents

Opening Notes

0.0

Istanbul, Türkiye
Bing, © Harris Corp,
Earthstar Geographics LLC;
© 2011 Microsoft Corporation

Mid-Polis World Key Map

0.1

CITIES IN ALPHABETICAL ORDER:

1 Amsterdam, The Netherlands
2 Barcelona, Spain
3 Berlin, Germany
4 Boston/Somerville, Massachusetts, USA
5 Columbia, Maryland, USA
6 Columbus, Ohio, USA
7 Copenhagen, Denmark
8 Denver, Colorado, USA
9 Dubai, United Arab Emirates
10 Düsseldorf, Germany
11 Guatemala City, Guatemala
12 Hangzhou, Zhejiang, China
13 Istanbul, Türkiye
14 Jerusalem

15 Johannesburg, South Africa
16 Lagos, Nigeria
17 Los Angeles, California, USA
18 Melbourne, Australia
19 Mumbai, India
20 Nanhai, Guangzhou, China
21 Nanjing, Jiangsu, China
22 New York, New York, USA
23 Paris, France
24 Rio de Janeiro, Brazil
25 Rome, Italy
26 Rotterdam, The Netherlands
27 San Diego, California, USA
28 São Paulo, Brazil
29 Shanghai, China
30 Singapore, Republic of Singapore
31 Suzhou, Jiangsu, China
32 Valparaíso, Chile
33 Washington, D.C., USA
34 Zürich, Switzerland

The City is a Tree **0.2**

Christopher Alexander's seminal essay "A City is Not a Tree," published in 1965, outlined a powerful idea wherein cities gain their vitality from dynamic and overlapping relationships. Drawing from his earlier background in mathematics, Alexander's "tree" was contrasted with a "semi-lattice structure," both coming from set theory. He also made a distinction between "natural" cities – those that had grown spontaneously (semi-lattice) – and "artificial" cities – those that had been designed and planned (tree). While powerful in its analogy, Alexander's essay misses the possibility that all cities are always simultaneously spontaneous and planned, natural and artificial. It would be hard to call the city wall of Nanjing spontaneous, yet its persistently changing effect on the city continues to define it today.

The mid-polis, being in the middle, can be understood as a part of the city that, at this moment, has been planned and is in need of spontaneity. It could also be described as a section of the city that is artificial and in need of nature. Here I use "natural" in reference to both the environment and spontaneity. Landscape architects use the term "eco-tone," which refers to the overlap of distinct ecologies. Eco-tones are areas of greater diversity, greater vitality, and greater resiliency – in short, a place where things change. This is the potential for the mid-polis to be natural. The question is: "Can the natural and the spontaneous be planned and designed?"

This question underlies the research, projects, and essays in this book. The very structure of the book suggests an important methodology through the diverse partnerships, multiple scales, geographic differences, and at times mutually exclusive points of view that are required to approach a necessary richness of understanding. As Jane Jacobs has said, "There is no use wishing it were a simpler problem." This book also suggests that, while it is true that cities are unique, they also share patterns, climates, morphologies, and uses that are similar

by **Bruce Lindsey**

Former Dean & Current E. Desmond Lee Professor, Sam Fox School of Design & Visual Arts, Washington University in St. Louis

and can be models for other cities. In other words, cities can learn from each other. This is especially true for the mid-polis, since it is predominantly new and persistently changing.

The urban design program at Washington University in St. Louis was founded in 1962 by faculty members Fumihiko Maki and Roger Montgomery. The program, from its inception, included faculty and students from around the world. We are proud that this has continued through the work of visiting faculty members and architect Paul Lukez, through our partnership with Roger Williams University, and through the cooperation of students from both universities. In the next 40 years the mid-polis will be the city. Our efforts will be to make it a tree designed to generate life in all of its nature and spontaneity.

Foreword **0.3**

Transforming the Mid-Polis is an important work in the early 21st century, when new forms of environment, culture, and architecture are emerging in many locations around the world, beyond the city as it has been traditionally considered. Paul Lukez contributed enormous drive to this work and developed insights through collaboration and comparison, bringing people and issues into public view. Here they gather leading figures and firms active in contemporary world architecture, urbanism and the arts alongside faculty and students from several American universities, all within a framework of theory, precedents, analyses, strategies, designs, and artistic responses for evaluating the mid-polis condition they define.

One of the strengths of a book like this is its presence within a conception that environmental potentials and solutions are beyond the ability of one mind, group, or location to provide solutions for, and varied responses to, place(s) and culture(s). This book's central message is: We need to live in awareness of and with each other, and we need to work together to test and compare current and previous efforts, in order to create decent, compelling environments ourselves, and to continue to do so into the future.

Elements of *Transforming the Mid-Polis* recall concerns of earlier thinkers. Patrick Geddes' *Cities in Evolution* and Ian McHarg's *Design With Nature* come to mind as works that sought to consider human and environmental health as a basis for sustainable form, and they were based on an evolutionary/transformational sensibility. What distinguishes *Transforming the Mid-Polis* from similar works is Lukez's identification of a scale of attention that can be successfully addressed through design in many comparative situations and with varied typologies. This extremely important contribution offers great promise for the quality of the constructed environment, and is spatial rather than diagrammatic.

by **Stephen White**

*Dean, Cummings School of Architecture,
Roger Williams University*

The authors' focus on transformation and transformational strategies is appropriate in our contemporary situation, and it probably could have been appropriate as well in the pre- and post-World War II eras when cultures and settlements were often cleared to make way for the singular heroic visions of imperial and modern urbanism, in the guise of "urban renewal." Many relevant concepts and strategies put forward by leading figures are present in *Transforming the Mid-Polis*. To name only a few:

• June Williamson and Ellen Dunham-Jones' theory of incremental metropolitanism;
• Nashid Nabian and Carlo Ratti's awareness that the mid-polis, "once vague, is morphing into a complex network of connections"; and
• Ken Yeang's identification of architectural strategies that advance green design.

Transforming the Mid-Polis provides a frame of reference and a methodology that are large and inclusive in scope without being reductive, offering appropriate strategies for developing variations of fitness to place and culture. Many can find a place worth living in the examples in this book, and many can contribute well to the work. What an extraordinary perspective to share with others, especially leading world figures, as well as faculty and students who need to emerge as future leaders.

Current Somerville rail corridor from Boston, photo by Peter Vanderwarker

Introduction

0.4

The Mid-Polis, A Global Phenomenon

Postwar urban scholars such as Leon Krier,[1] Colin Rowe,[2] and Kevin Lynch[3] focused their research on the center of the traditional city form – one that had grown and developed compactly while retaining a coherent, legible urban structure. This generation of writers and scholars aimed to understand a city's underlying order as a way to apply learned urban planning lessons to contemporary cities needing repair from the destructive effects of war, urban renewal, or poorly developed growth patterns.

As urban planners better understood the characteristics and typologies of the urbanism advanced by Krier, Rowe, Lynch et al., those new standards were gradually integrated into practice from the 1970s onward. Special attention was paid to the roles of streets, blocks, and public space played in creating pedestrian-friendly cities. The scarred, neglected urban cores of Baltimore, Berlin, and other major metropoleis were slowly stitched into a new kind of urban fabric inspired by traditional city planning principles while accommodating the needs and required amenities of contemporary urban life.

The attention dedicated – in both academic halls and the field – to the city and its urban core has benefited urbanists and city dwellers alike. Yet the problems emerging from metropolitan growth were not as clearly understood, nor were their solutions. The late 1980s and early 1990s saw the emergence of the New Urbanism movement, which sought to apply traditional city planning principles to suburbs and other urban growth areas. Andres Duany,[4] Elizabeth Plater-Zyberk,[5] Peter Calthorpe,[6] and others demonstrated, through their writings and design work, how pedestrian-oriented development patterns could reconstitute urbanism, even as a pocket within a larger metropolis. In re-thinking the metropolis, Rem Koolhaas,[7] Winy Maas,[8] and others accepted and embraced the forces of urban modernity – even its radical scale shifts and crassness – recognizing the overpowering momentum of larger economic, social and political dynamics.

by **Paul Lukez**

Paul Lukez Architecture

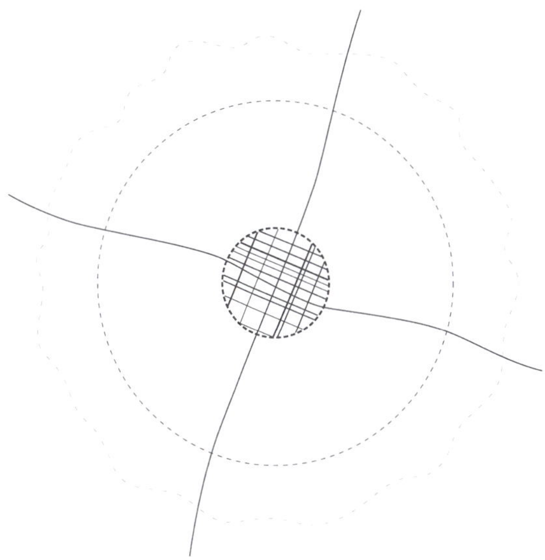

The traditional city Mid-Polis

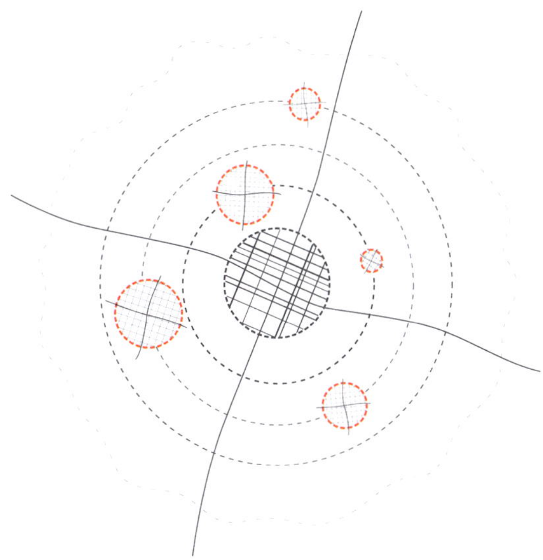

The concentric metropolis development

In the "double oughts" (2000-2009), a wave of research and writing focused on the suburbs, a long-time underexplored area of urban design and study. Built on the work of Peter Rowe,[9] writers such as Anne Vernez-Moudon,[10] Ellen Dunham-Jones,[11] June Williamson,[12] Miles L. Berger,[13] Paul Lukez,[14] and Margaret E. Farrar[15] examined theories about suburban structure and typologies. Chiefly they sought to define remedies for retrofitting and repairing suburbs into more sustainable environments.

Understanding the third condition: The Mid-Polis

While the last 60 years of research and design work have yielded valuable lessons for the city's center (the first condition) and its suburbs (the second condition), more abstruse are those large swaths of urbanity located between a metropolis's urban core and its ever-expanding suburban fringe. This is understandable, since this third urban condition is but a relatively recent phenomenon. With time, postwar suburban developments have mutated into new, sometimes unpredictable metropolitan patterns. Maturing suburbs in the inner-ring of 1950s and 1960s development have been neglected or abandoned in many cities such as Cleveland and Detroit. Later iterations of suburban development have contributed to the perpetually growing girth of the contemporary metropolis. Their growth patterns have varied according to time, location, and the whims of the developers. Consequently, they are harder to classify typologically.

Metropolitan form has also mutated into a variety of forms and types, based on historic, economic and political contexts. (See the next chapter for descriptions of the different metropolitan typologies.) Where the metropolis was once considered a natural outgrowth of a city extending its tentacles into the landscape, the current size and complexity of metropolitan form has yielded highly varied shapes and forms, even as neighboring metropoleis mutate as part of a new regional mega-polis, e.g., Manhattan with the New Jersey municipalities across the Hudson. In developing countries, cities

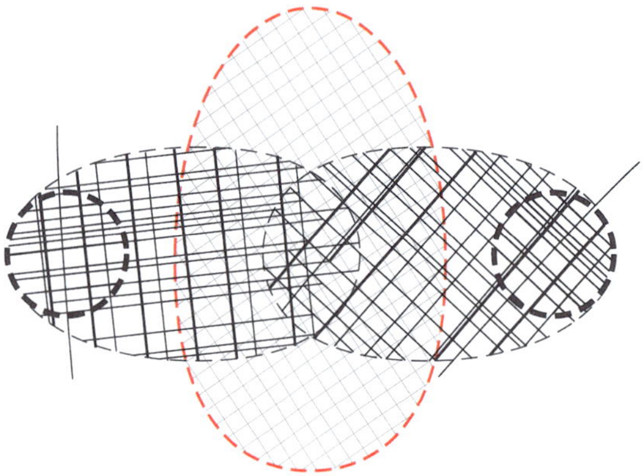

Blurring

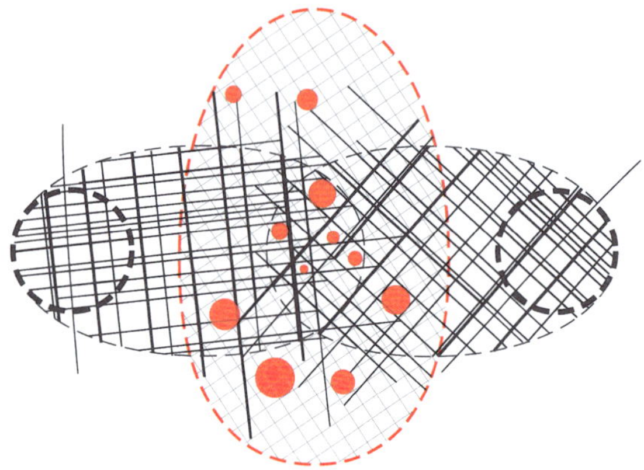

New Mid-Polis

are leapfrogging suburbs. High-speed rail lines are turning neighboring cities into suburbs by virtue of their temporal proximity. (For instance, Hangzhou is but a 30-minute train ride from Shanghai, some 120 miles away.)

What, then, is the mid-polis, this third form of metropolitan urbanity that is neither urban nor suburban? Its simplest definition is locational, i.e., those urban conditions between a city's core and the metropolis's outer edge. While this definition defines locus, it tells us less about the content of those urban conditions found within this metropolitan envelope. Therein lie both the challenge and the potential to understand these areas. They constitute a large portion of our metropoleis, but their content, structure and tissue are difficult to define in simple terms, perhaps because they take so many forms and types and are still evolving.

Despite its indefinite categorization, the mid-polis merits further study and exploration. To begin, we may consider some of its characteristics:

• The mid-polis contains most of our living and working spaces. U.S. Census 2020 data indicate that 80% of the U.S. population live in urban areas, a 9% increase from 68.5% in 2000.[16] Furthermore, the Pew Research Center reported that, in 2018, more than half of the total U.S. population (183.4 million people) lived in the 52 largest metropolitan areas, and its 50 largest metro areas now hold about half of the U.S. population.[17] Nonetheless, the mid-polis is least well served by integrated networks of infrastructure or public amenities.

• The mid-polis often comprises areas that were once on the edge of a city or metropolitan district. Like the rings of a giant redwood tree, the aggregate growth of the metropolis is registered temporally. What was once the edge of the city or metropolis is now "mid" – in the middle – of the metropolis.

• What is "mid" can sometimes be subsumed into a city's "core" or become an urban "node" in its own right.

• Since many mid-polis areas were based on suburban development patterns, it is not surprising that, like so many suburbs, they lack a strong identity, one with distinctive qualities differentiating one development from another. Hence a carpet of urbanity lacking diversity sprawls across many metropolitan areas.

• As a region within the metropolis, the mid-polis comprises many places connected more through chance adjacencies than by systematic intent.

Sometimes these places have boundaries defined by infrastructure, landscape features, or pronounced changes in urban tissue. Other abutting developments may merge into each other as part of a sprawling metropolitan terrain.

• The mid-polis also contains “leftover” urbanism, where underutilized industrial and infrastructural areas leave scars within and between metropolitan neighborhoods and districts.

• As the girth of the metropolis increases, the mid-polis spatially disconnects from the metropolis's urban core or rural edge.

• Where sprawling development patterns govern, the mid-polis may lack a series of integrated nodes for wayfinding, logical circulation systems, or distinctive landmarks.

• Given the ad-hoc development patterns of the mid-polis, its urban structure is neither coherently defined nor legible (e.g., New Jersey). For instance, the vast swath of urban development patterns of all kinds found in the southern part of Bergen County, N.J., located among Manhattan, Newark, and Paterson, N.J., represents highly idiosyncratic defined urban morphologies, resulting from historical circumstances and chance.

• The mid-polis represents the full spectrum of places: urban, suburban, ex-urban, and rural.

The mid-polis is evolving into new urban forms. While some mid-polis conditions have been referred to as “inner suburbs” or “maturing suburbs” over the last 3,000 years of urban development, we are still laying the foundations of a new form of urbanism, one that is metropolitan in scale. This new and evolving metropolitan configuration has not yet revealed its true form, structure or identity, as it is still responding to rapidly changing societal needs and technological innovations. Yet we are at a stage in its development at which changes can be made that would influence its future evolution so that, taken as a whole, the means and methods by which we inhabit the earth's fragile surface can be ameliorated to better serve nature and humanity.

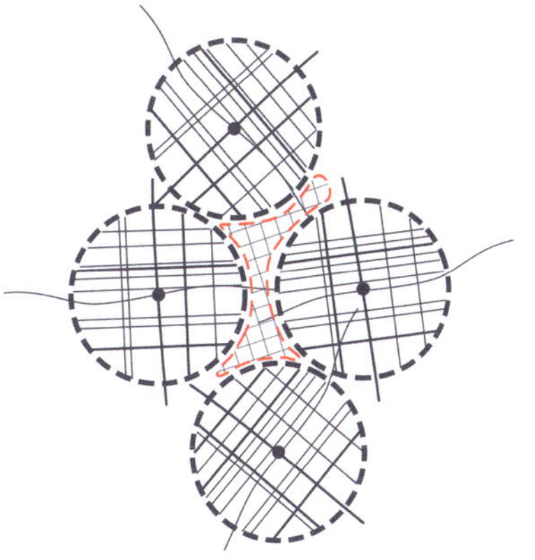

The Mid-Polis connected amorphously

Why investigate the mid-polis, and why is it important?

The mid-polis deserves further study for many reasons. As the size of metropolitan cores in developed countries shrinks in population, the metropolitan boundary's landmass often increases as populations shift outward. The mid-polis's area and population thus increases. More importantly, the mid-polis represents those places where so many city-dwellers live, work and play. Yet it lacks the distinctive qualities – character, landmarks, connectivity to other places – that support and enrich its residents' daily lives. The mid-polis condition has not always fulfilled its potential as an exemplary urban form, given its strategic location within its urban environs. This is especially true in cities that underwent rapid suburban development from the 1950s into the 1970s and now find their inner-belt suburbs compromised, decayed and neglected. The mid-polis terrain of the postwar era has often been scarred by less thoughtfully considered infrastructural projects, e.g., highways and rails. These regions (inner suburbs) have often been bisected, sliced and diced into smaller fragments. Sometimes this has hastened urban decay along the highways and rail lines that divvy up the mid-polis terrain into a fragmentary urban terrain.

Emerging Mid-Polis - Somerville, MA, USA, photo by Peter Vanderwarker

As energy costs continue to rise, the viability of suburban and exurban development in the distant orbit of the metropolitan core will decline. Thus developers, companies and institutions will seek locations closer to established neighborhoods and infrastructure systems within the mid-polis. For example, Washington, D.C., is experiencing a large movement of capital and corporate investment into Tyson Corner and other former suburban outposts, establishing them as mid-polis nodes within the larger D.C. metropolis.

As demand and development pressures increase in these underdeveloped mid-polis sites, planning and design tools must be tailored to address the issues associated with transforming the mid-polis. First, we must understand the full scope of mid-polis morphology, structure, infrastructure, land use, building types, and physical characteristics, as well as the numerous forces that contribute to its current identity and character. Building a repository of mid-polis case studies can help discern patterns and trends found in metropoleis worldwide.

From this understanding, planning, design and development strategies can be conceived to address the mid-polis general conditions as well as more idiosyncratic local conditions. These studies may facilitate the development of more comprehensive, coherent guidelines and tools for transforming the mid-polis, so it strengthens communities within the metropolis and, by extension, the metropolis itself.

Structure of the Book

This publication represents the collaborative efforts of many contributors across the globe. The book's concept arose from a joint urban design studio conducted between Southeast University in Nanjing, China, and Washington University in St. Louis, Missouri, USA, in the spring of 2010. Dean Dong Wei of SEU and Dean Bruce Lindsey of WUSTL generously supported the studio and research exchange between their respective universities. Prof. Bao Li of SEU sparked the interest of Southeast University Press in an initial commitment to publish a book on the mid-polis. In addition, Dean Steven White of Roger Williams University in Bristol, Rhode Island, USA, orchestrated additional research support from his students in the spring of 2011, further advancing the content research included in the final book.

As an international collaboration, planners, architects, writers, artists, and students were encouraged to contribute their commentaries, designs, and visions as they related to the mid-polis topic. These in turn were filtered through a series of thematic filters, with their respective chapters. A description of each chapter follows:

Part 1.0: Theoretical Underpinnings
What is the Mid-Polis?
What are the theoretical implications generated by viewing this urban condition through the lens of the mid-polis typologies?

These are some of the questions pondered in the first selection of essays by defining the mid-polis and its many types and classifications. Strategies for transforming the mid-polis are illustrated through typological diagrams.

Prof. June Williamson, co-author of *Retrofitting Suburbia*,[18] focuses on the origins of the mid-polis in North America's suburban terrain. Prof. Carlo Ratti and Nashid Nabian characterize the mid-polis through the advanced application of analytical digital tools developed in Prof. Ratti's Senseable City Lab at MIT.

Dr. Ken Yeang, FAIA (Hon), DMPN (Malaysia), PhD (Cantab), AADipl (UK), APAM, FSIA, RIBA, ARAIA (Hon), FRIAS (Hon), of Malaysia explores strategies for converting our metropoleis and their mid-polis sites into sustainable nodes.

Part 2.0: Mid-Polis Analysis
This chapter starts to build a repository of case studies that identify mid-polis characteristics. Six richly illustrated case studies from metropoleis worldwide are documented and analyzed by urban design students from Washington University in St. Louis. Each case study reveals development patterns over time and their roles in generating the contemporary mid-polis.

Part 3.0: Mid-Polis Transformations
The above mid-polis site analyses form the foundational proposals for transforming a mid-polis site through architectural and planning strategies. Complementing these proposals are six projects featuring diverse mid-polis opportunities from around the world, all generated by graduate students of architecture and urban design at Roger Williams University and Washington University in St. Louis.

Before - morphology suburban strip base map

After - morphology suburban strip iteration

Eco Auto-Tek - Brickbottom, Somerville, image by Paul Lukez Architecture

Part 4.0: In-Depth Mid-Polis Projections – Somerville - Boston, MA

Students from Washington University studied a mid-polis site in Somerville, Massachusetts, in the United States. The students conducted an in-depth investigation of a Metro Boston mid-polis, the Inner Belt of Somerville.

Part 5.0: Prominent Designers' Responses

Here, student projects are followed by redevelopment proposals from academics and architectural professionals who have researched the mid-polis or designed projects in this realm. Projects from the United States, France, Holland, Denmark, Switzerland, and China are represented here. The work of Interboro Partners, LTL Architects,

Prof. Dagmar Richter, WSP, MONOLAB, URBANUS, Prof. Xu Lei, Prof. Wang Ka, and Paul Lukez Architecture illustrate new mid-polis transformation strategies.

Part 6.0: Visionaries' & Artists' Reponses

While most of this book investigates the mid-polis with academic and professional planning/design tools in mind, the artists represented in this section offer a liberating perspective on the mid-polis.

The mid-polis liminal space is richly layered and interwoven in Julie Mehretu's paintings of Berlin, where the boundaries between solid and immaterial dissolve, giving visual form to the complexity of urban life in flux. In works like Berlin Platze, traces of past and present architecture overlap, revealing the city's enduring scars in the mid-polis – visible and invisible markers of transformation.

Sarah McKenzie depicts Denver and its accelerated pace of construction as her subject. Her paintings highlight the latent, if not fulfilled, potential of the city's fast-paced, unplanned production.

Ben Edwards' colorful cityscape images amplify the ephemeral elements of the contemporary mid-polis in places such as Washington, D.C. Liberated from the metropolis's more permanent structure, signs, symbols, lights, and surface dominate in Edwards' renderings.

Part 7.0: Conclusion

This chapter explores the following questions: How can we better understand the mid-polis in its current condition?

How can the mid-polis be transformed over time?

Will its fate be left to chance and historical circumstances? Or can it be regenerated into a higher form of urbanity, one that can support convivial communities while sustaining economies and ecologies?

If so, what actions and strategies will be required to realize this goal?

Notes

[1] Krier, Leon. *The Architecture of Community.* Washington, D.C.: Island Press, 2011.

[2] Rowe, Colin, and Prof. Fred Koetter. *Collage City.* Cambridge, Mass.: The MIT Press, 1984.

[3] Lynch, Kevin. *The Image of the City.* Cambridge, Mass.: MIT Press, 1958.

[4] Duany, Andres, Elizabeth Plater-Zyberk, and Jeff Speck. *Suburban Nation: The Rise of Sprawl and the Decline of the American Dream.* 10th Anniversary Edition. New York: North Point Press, 2010.

[5] *Ibid.*

[6] Calthorpe, Peter. *The Next American Metropolis: Ecology, Community, and the American Dream.* Third edition. Princeton, N.J.: Princeton Architectural Press, 1995.

[7] Koolhaas, Rem. *Delirious New York: A Retroactive Manifesto for Manhattan.* New York: The Monacelli Press, 1997.

[8] Maas, Winy. *Visionary Cities: 12 Reasons for Claiming the Future of our Cities.* Rotterdam: nai010 publishers, 2010.

[9] Rowe, Peter. *Making a Middle Landscape.* Cambridge, Mass.: The MIT Press, 1992.

[10] Vernez-Moudon, Anne. *Monitoring Land Supply with Geographic Information Systems: Theory, Practice, and Parcel-Based Approaches.* New York: Wiley, 2000.

[11] Dunham-Jones, Ellen, and June Williamson. *Retrofitting Suburbia: Urban Design Solutions for Redesigning Suburbs.* Updated Edition. New York: Wiley, 2011.

[12] *Ibid.*

[13] Berger, Miles L. *They Built Chicago: Entrepreneurs Who Shaped a Great Citys Architecture.* Los Angeles: Bonus Books, 1992.

[14] Lukez, Paul. *Suburban Transformations.* Princeton, N.J.: Princeton Architectural Press, 2007.

[15] Farrar, Margaret E. *Building the Body Politic: Power and Urban Space in Washington, D.C.* Champaign, Ill.: University of Illinois Press, 2008.

[16] U.S. Census Bureau Newsroom. *Growth in Urban Population Outpaces Rest of Nation, Census Bureau Reports.* United States Census Bureau, U.S. Department of Commerce, March 26, 2012.

[17] Florida, Richard. *The Fading Differentiation Between City and Suburb*, Urban Land Magazine, urbanland.uli.org, January 1, 2013.

[18] Dunham-Jones, *op.cit.*

Theoretical Underpinnings

1.0

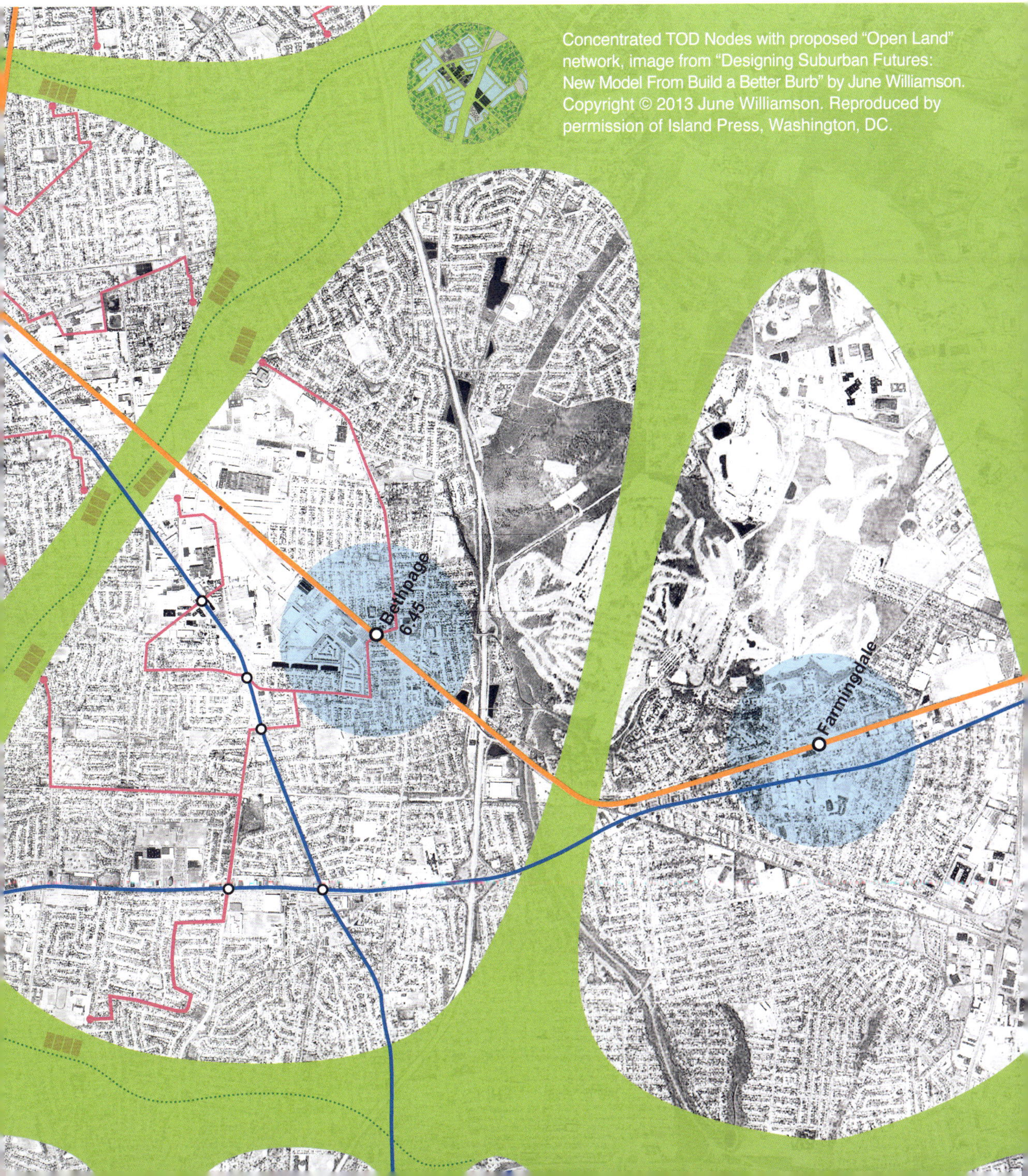

Concentrated TOD Nodes with proposed "Open Land" network, image from "Designing Suburban Futures: New Model From Build a Better Burb" by June Williamson. Copyright © 2013 June Williamson. Reproduced by permission of Island Press, Washington, DC.

Classification of Mid-Polis

1.1

Fundamentally, the mid-polis is easy to define. It represents those places which are between a metropolis's center and its outer edge. However, the appearances and conditions of a city and its mid-poleis come in many shapes, sizes, and configurations. In addition, many factors can influence the characteristics of a mid-polis, including its content, topography, and location. Other drivers include demographic, economic, cultural, and historical forces. This chapter seeks to typologically classify some of the many mid-polis conditions. By no means exhaustive, this is a first step in better understanding the common and differentiating features of the mid-polis found around the world.

Mid-Polis typologies:

by **Paul Lukez**

Paul Lukez Architecture

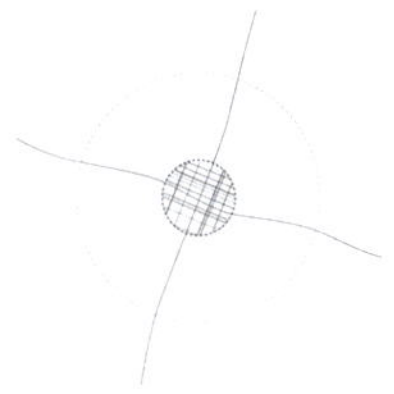

1. The Traditional City Mid-Polis

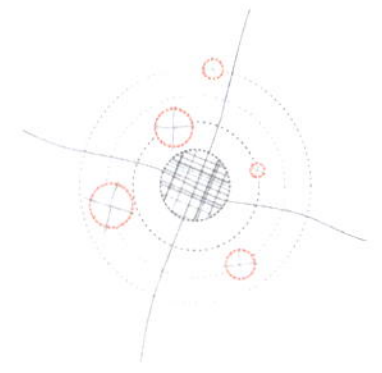

2. The Concentric Metropolis

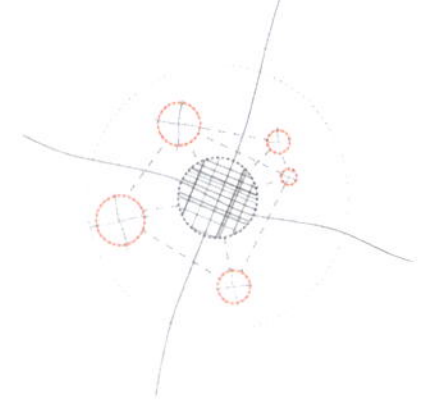

3. The Metropolis as a Collection of Smaller Mid-Poleis

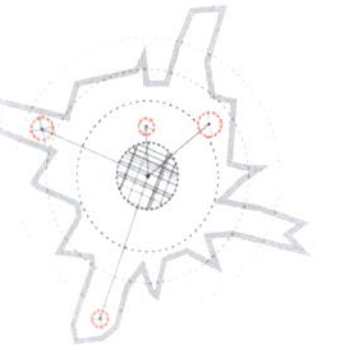

4. The Metropolis as a Collection of Interconnected Mid-Poleis

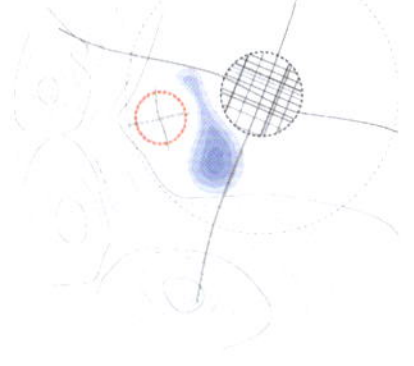

5. The Metropolis with Strong Topographic and Natural Features: Water and Mountains

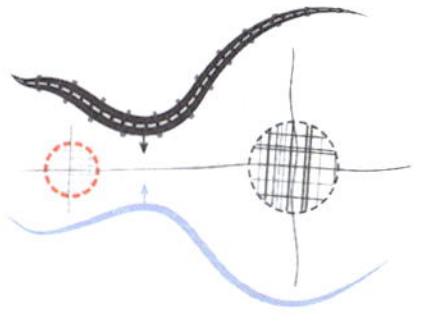

6. The Elongated Mid-Polis

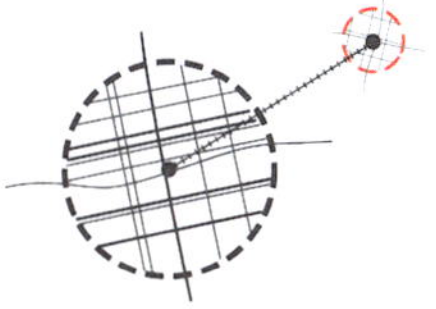

7. The Mid-Polis as a Satellite

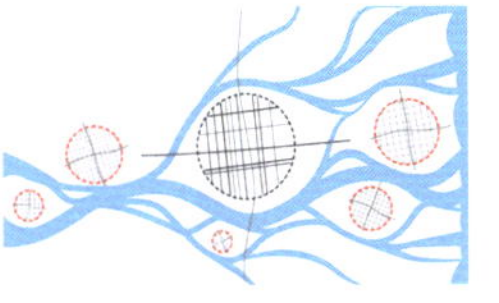

8. The Mid-Polis in the Delta

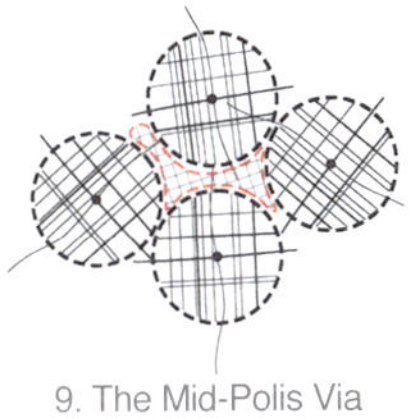

9. The Mid-Polis Via Amorphous Leftover Space

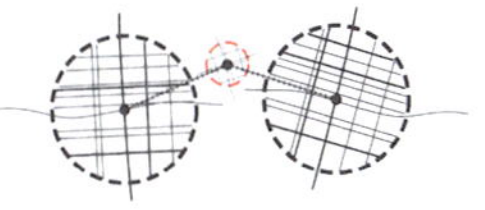

10. The Mid-Polis Between Two Metropoleis

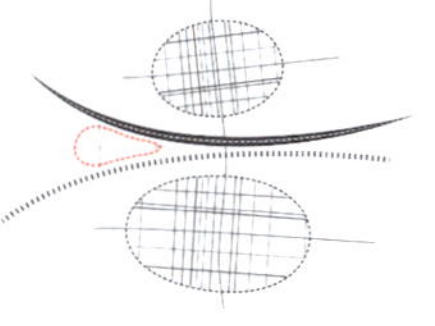

11. The Mid-Polis Bounded by Infrastructure

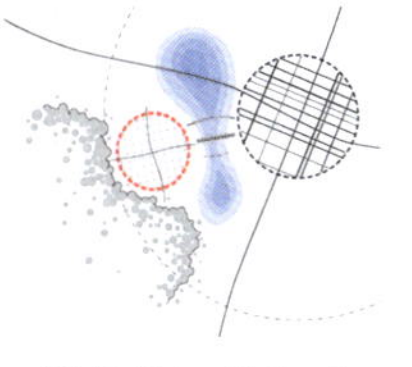

12. Bridging Natural Mid-Polis Features

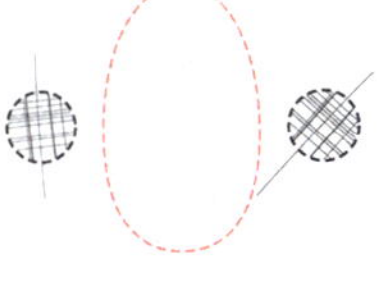

13. The Metropolis with Strong Natural Mid-Polis Features: Farms and Forests

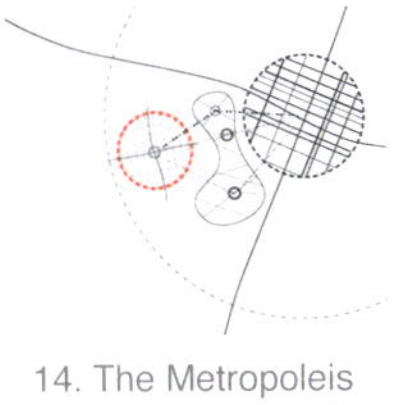

14. The Metropoleis Comprising Multiple Mid-Polis Morphologies

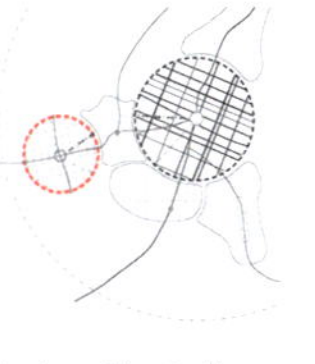

15. Fusing Dissimilar Morphologies

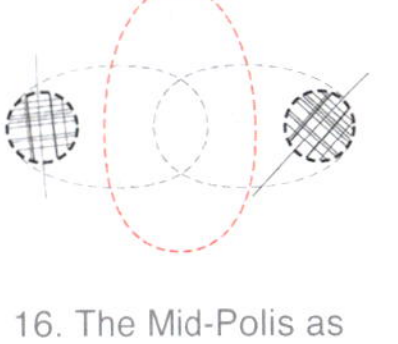

16. The Mid-Polis as Open Space: Carved Out of the Metropolis

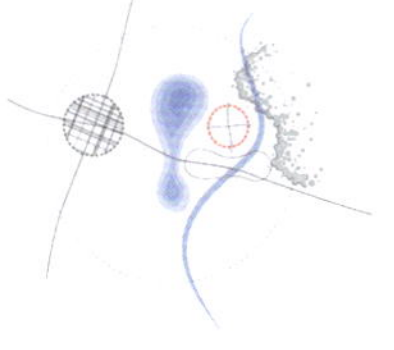

17. Connecting Open Space to Adjacent Mid-Polis Neighborhoods

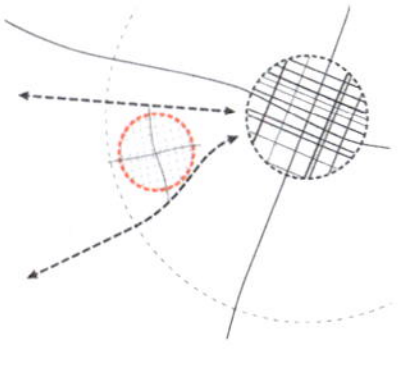

18. The Mid-Polis Squeezed by Infrastructure

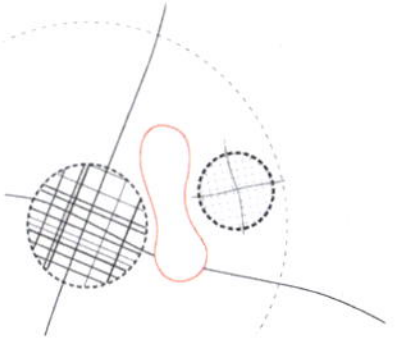

19. The Mid-Polis Through Modern Conflict

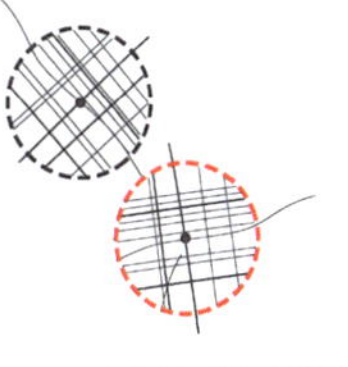

20. Dueling Mid-Poleis Within Larger Metropolitan Areas

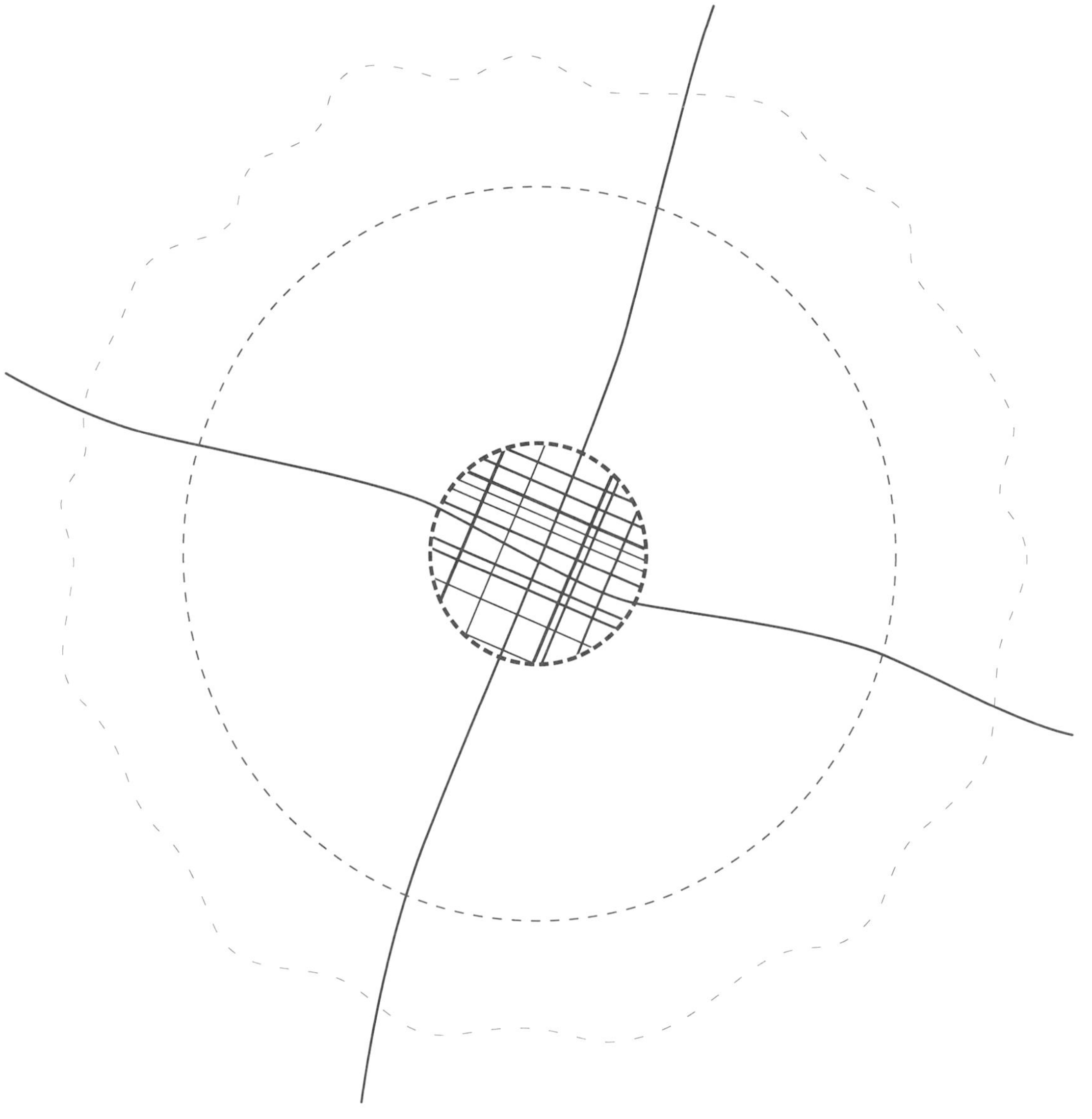

1. The Traditional City Mid-Polis

Indianapolis, Columbus (OH), Milan

As the city's core capacity is met, gradual and even sudden growth spreads outward. This is evident in cities without topographic or infrastructural constraints on this growth. For example, Indianapolis, Indiana, and Milan, Italy, are located in largely flat terrains, such that they have expanded outwardly, unencumbered by topographic constraints.

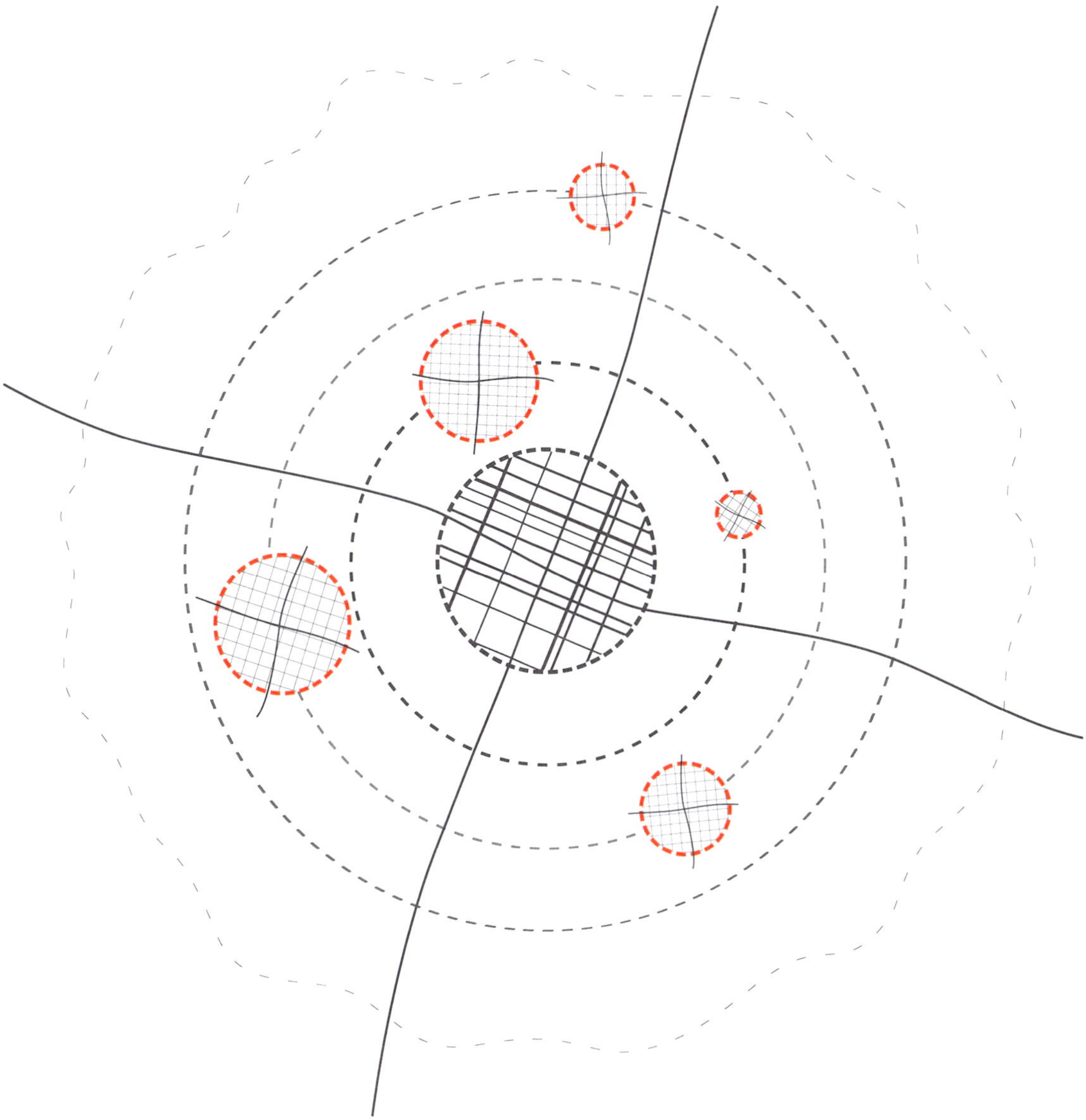

2. The Concentric Metropolis

Beijing, Nanjing, Moscow, Cologne, Vienna

Mid-poleis can grow concentrically in easily discernable patterns, like rings in a tree. These are found more commonly in historic walled European and Asian cities. Cologne, Germany, and Nanjing, China, for instance, exhibit this growth form with traces of their ancient walls and fortifications.

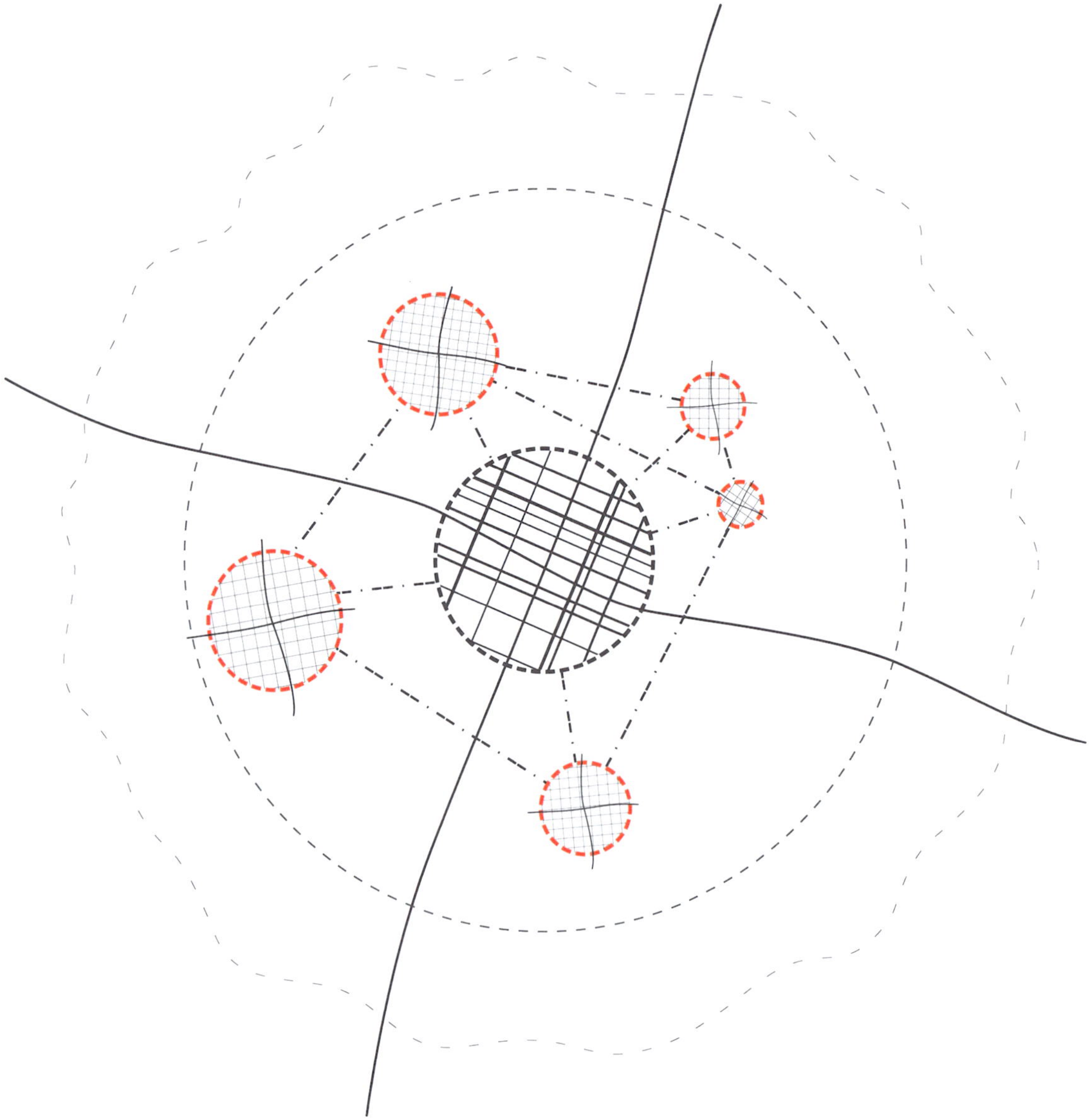

3. The Metropolis as a Collection of Smaller Mid-Poleis

Boston, London, Shanghai

Depending on their geographical and historical circumstances, mid-poleis are sometimes a collection of smaller poleis. For instance, greater Boston incorporates smaller well-established communities such as Dorchester, Cambridge, Somerville, Newton, Salem, and Lexington. Each of these smaller communities was established concurrently along with Boston proper. As they grew over time, they merged into a larger metropolitan area anchored by Boston and its harbor.

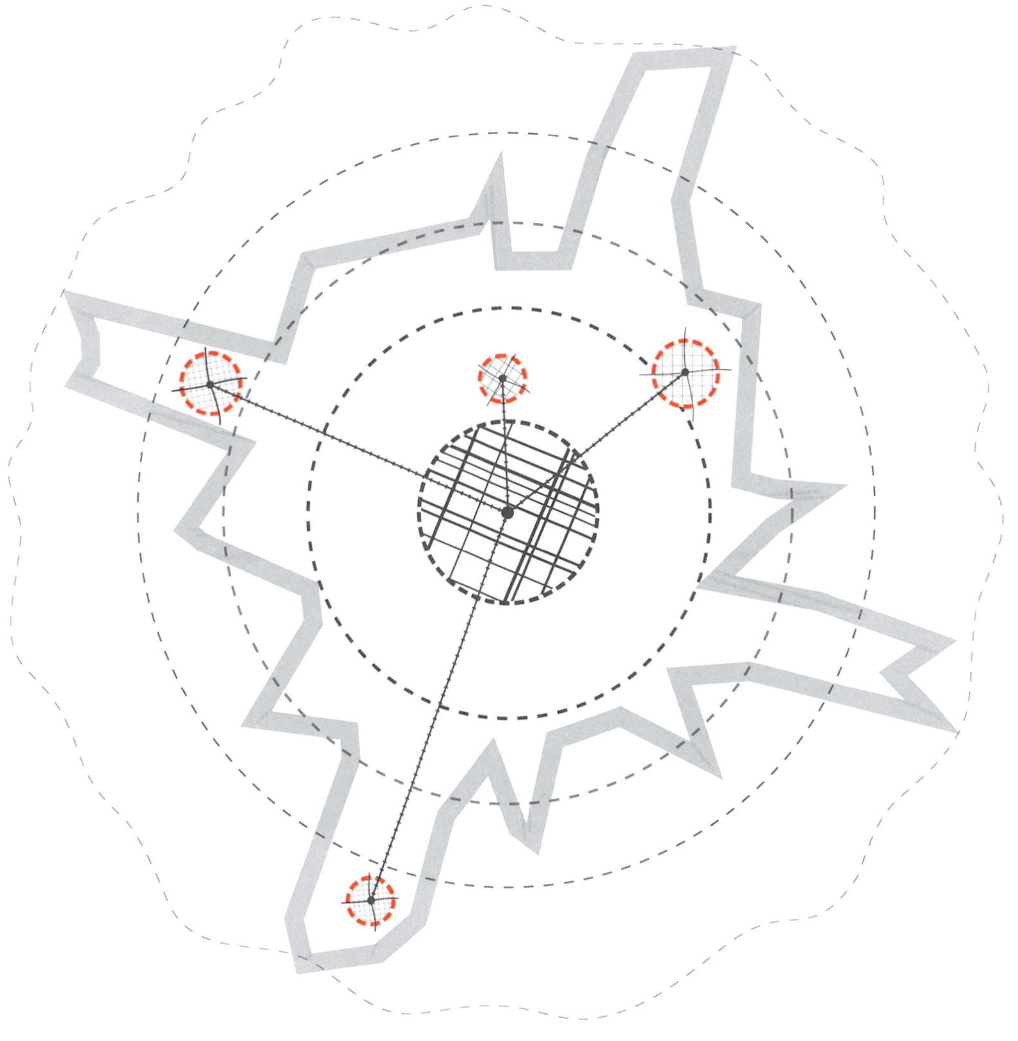

4. The Metropolis as a Collection of Interconnected Mid-Poleis

Paris, Tokyo, Los Angeles

Sometimes these smaller poleis are strongly interlinked by networks of roads, rail lines and infrastructures built over time. These networks can grow in a spoke-and-hub pattern, as seen in Paris, or a net-like system of infrastructure (subway, rail, highways) can interconnect the mid-poleis, as in Tokyo. Los Angeles, with its vast web of highways, exemplifies a collection of intertwined mid-poleis.

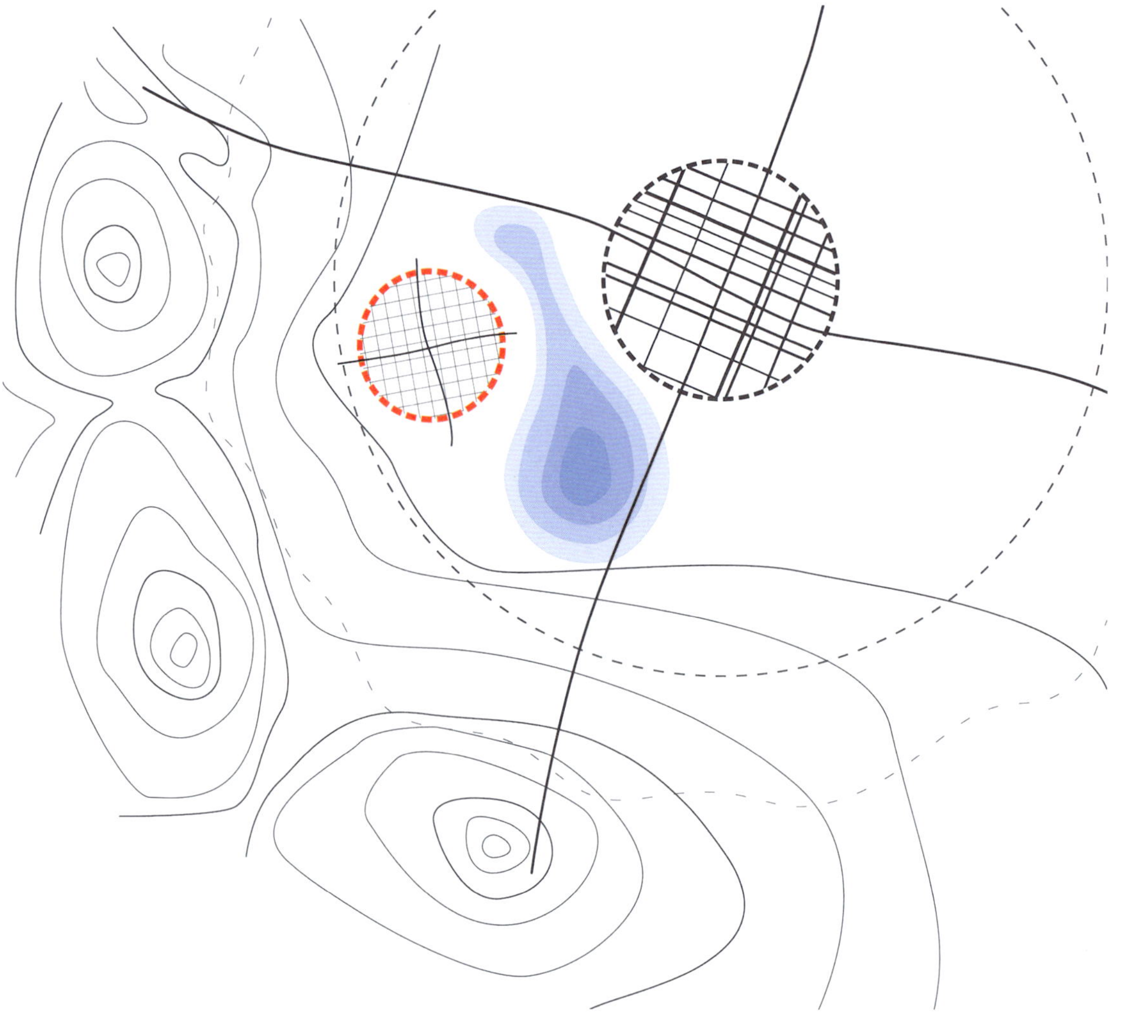

5. The Metropolis with Strong Topographic and Natural Features: Water and Mountains

Vancouver, Hangzhou, Rio de Janeiro, Singapore, San Francisco

Where prominent natural features or topography limit metropolitan growth, the metropolis often comes up against the challenges of strong topographic features as part of its evolution. Mountains, lakes, rivers, harbors, and wetlands can force development to adapt to these limitations, often turning them into positive attributes that can nurture their growth. Conversely, steep hills and mountains can constrain metropolitan growth, limited only to the degree to which buildings and supporting infrastructural systems can overcome these limitations. For instance, the steep topography found in places like San Francisco, Rio de Janeiro, and Hong Kong have forced developers and builders to be inventive in adapting building typologies (rowhouses or towers) to a city's topography while increasing site density. The result is not only visually dramatic, but also helpful in optimizing land use for creative development purposes.

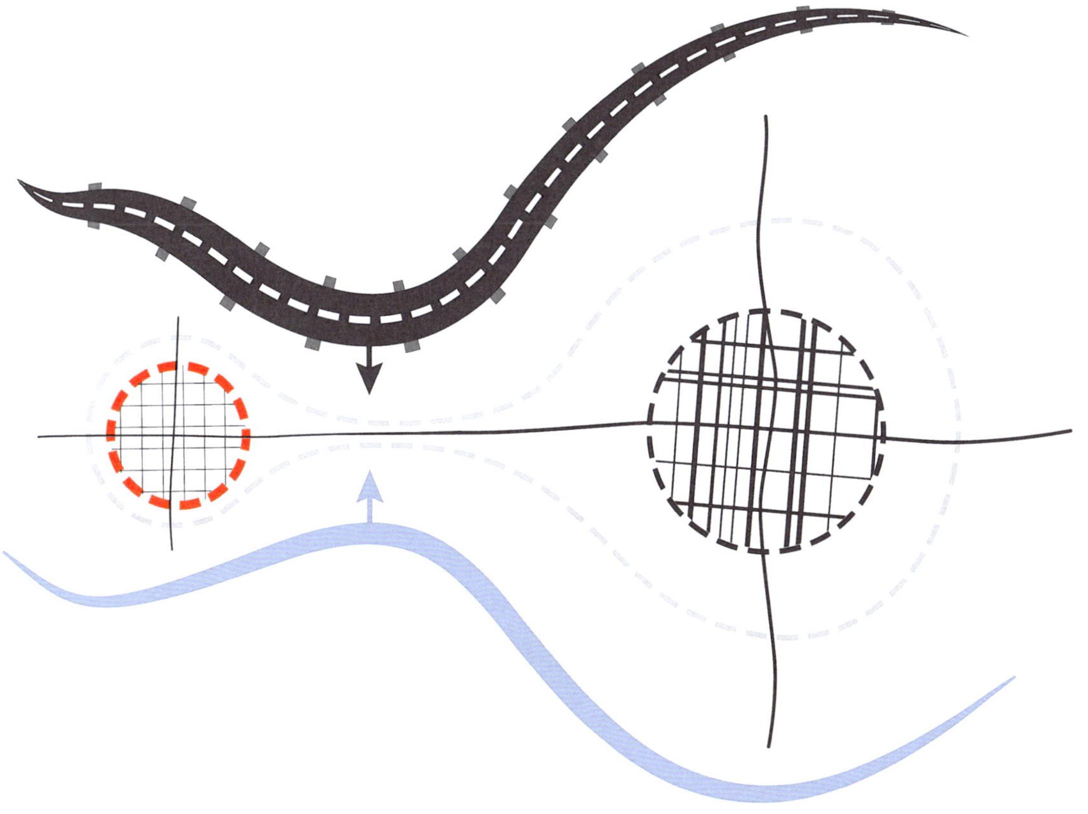

6. The Elongated Mid-Polis

Cairo, Düsseldorf

Natural and man-made constraints can shape the metropolis. For instance, cities dependent on rivers grow over time along their banks, taking on an elongated metropolitan profile, e.g., Cairo and Düsseldorf. The land along the riverbanks may not always be wide enough to accommodate growth patterns. The available terrain may be further pinched by natural landforms, such as mountains and gullies, or large infrastructure systems running parallel to the river.

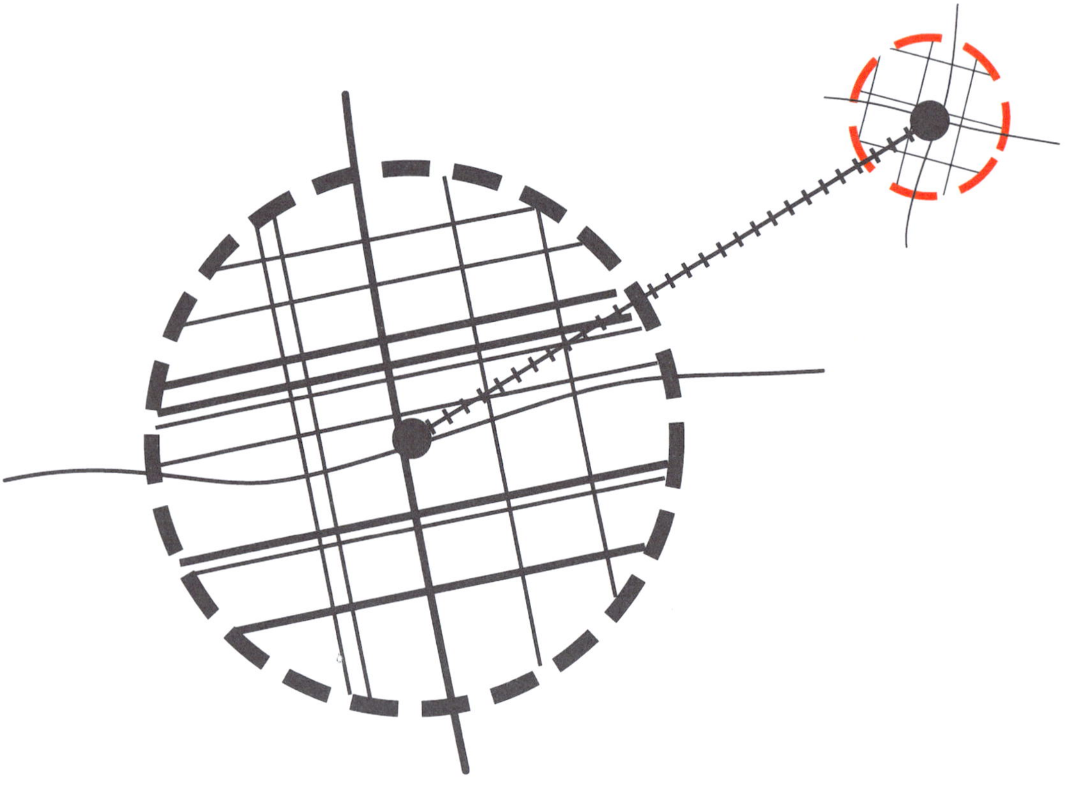

7. The Mid-Polis as a Satellite

Potsdam, Suzhou, Versailles

The mid-polis is not always embedded in a continuous carpet of urbanity that comprises the classic metropolitan form. Instead, the mid-polis can be a separate entity, yet within the outer orbit of the metropolis proper. Forces causing this may include limits on land development, such as protecting and preserving farmland.

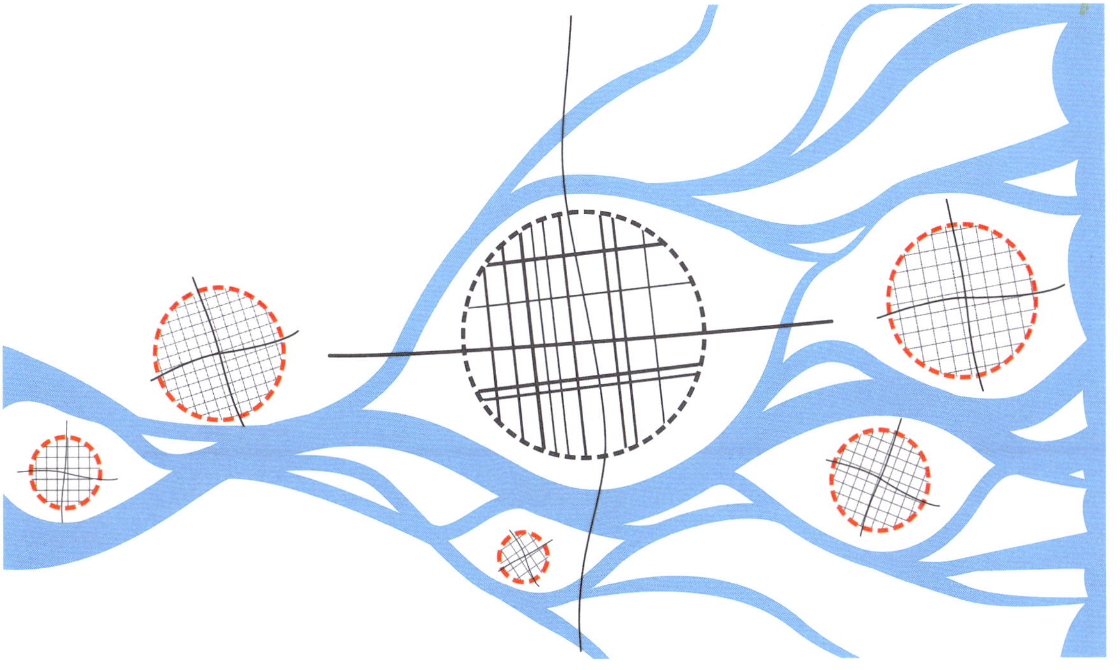

8. The Mid-Polis in the Delta

Guangzhou, New Orleans, Alexandria in Egypt

Nowhere is the force of water felt more than in cities built by the delta of a major river. They often owe their existence to the river but also are vulnerable to natural disasters associated with local climate and ecology. Alluvial land requires city builders to position their structures strategically, finding a balance between exposure to trade and protection from natural disasters. New Orleans, Alexandria in Egypt, and the Pearl River Delta (anchored by Guangzhou) are three examples of delta-shaped metropolitan areas. These cities illustrate different urban development patterns in the river delta, but in all cases, the form of the city is determined first and foremost by the shape, dimensions, physical characteristics, and ecology of the river.

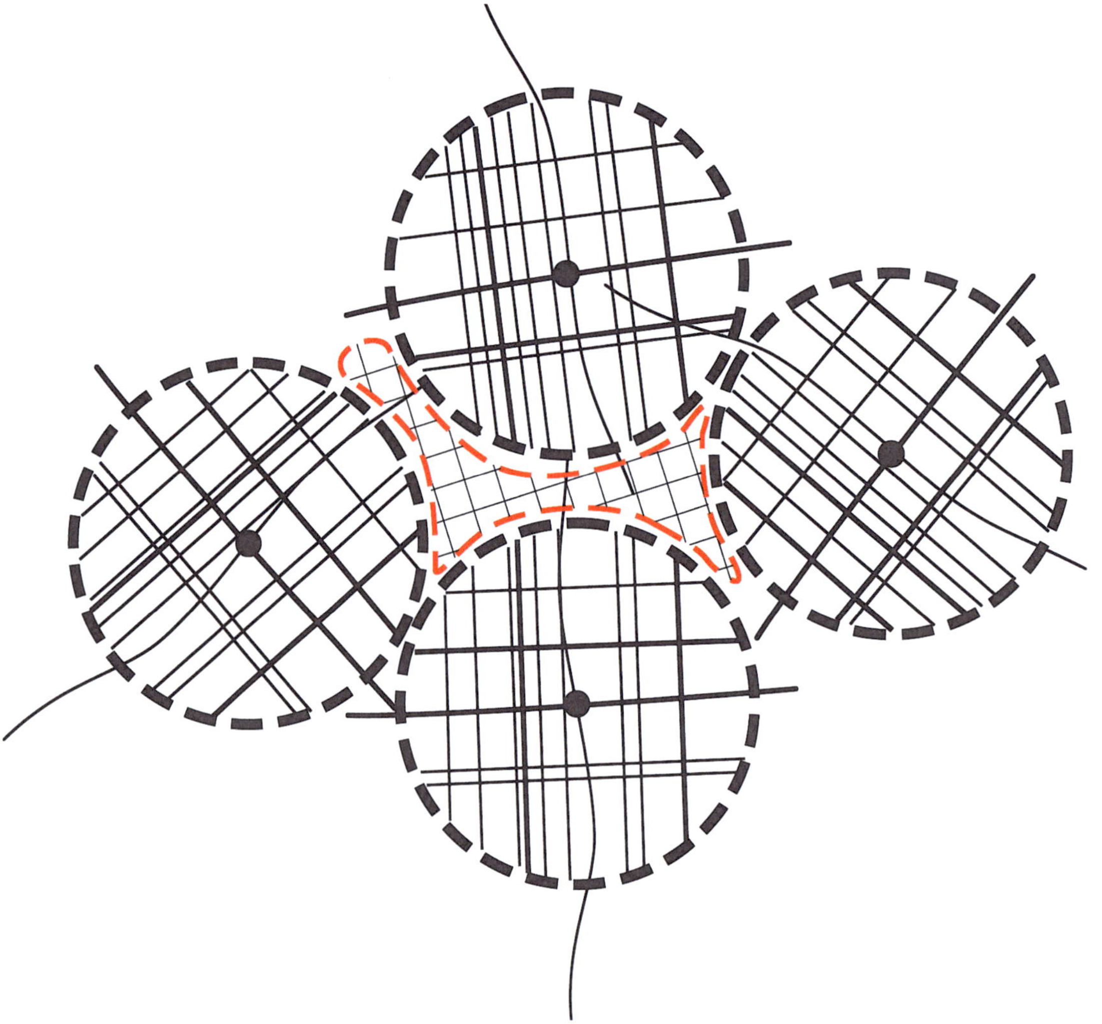

9. The Mid-Polis Via Amorphous Leftover Space

Detroit, Ruhr Valley, Manchester in the UK

Where the metropolis comprises distinctive neighborhoods and villages, amorphously shaped zones and districts may occupy the space between the neighborhoods. These in-between spaces can encompass landscape features such as parks and valleys, or they can be infrastructure corridors. For instance, highways and rail lines often run through the flatter terrains that valleys, floodplains or wetlands offer. These areas often attract industry, as their land is cheaper and infrastructure-accessible. As cities mature and industries fail, large swatches of land between neighborhoods can be vacated, leaving a void in the metropolitan fabric. This is evident in such industrial cities as Detroit, Michigan, and Manchester, UK.

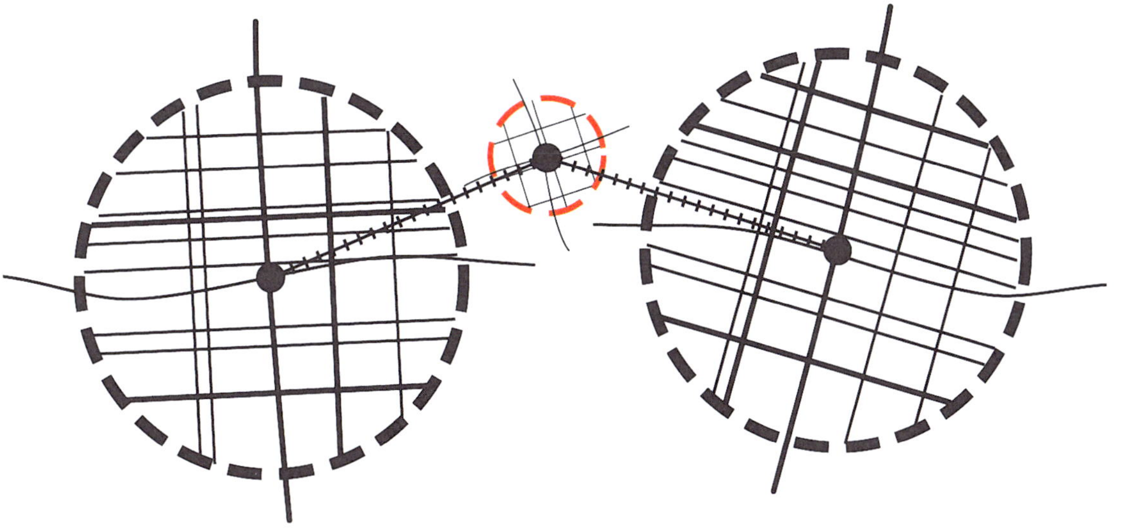

10. The Mid-Polis Between Two Metropoleis

Tokyo-Yokohama, Baltimore-Washington

As cities evolve into larger metropolitan areas, their domains can infringe upon the outer reaches of a neighboring metropolis. Eventually these metropolitan areas merge into a larger mega-polis. Examples include Tokyo-Yokohama and Baltimore-Washington, where urban development is unrelenting. Before two metropolitan areas are fused, though, towns and villages between them may also be expanding, becoming established municipalities in their own right. Columbia, Maryland, is such a case.

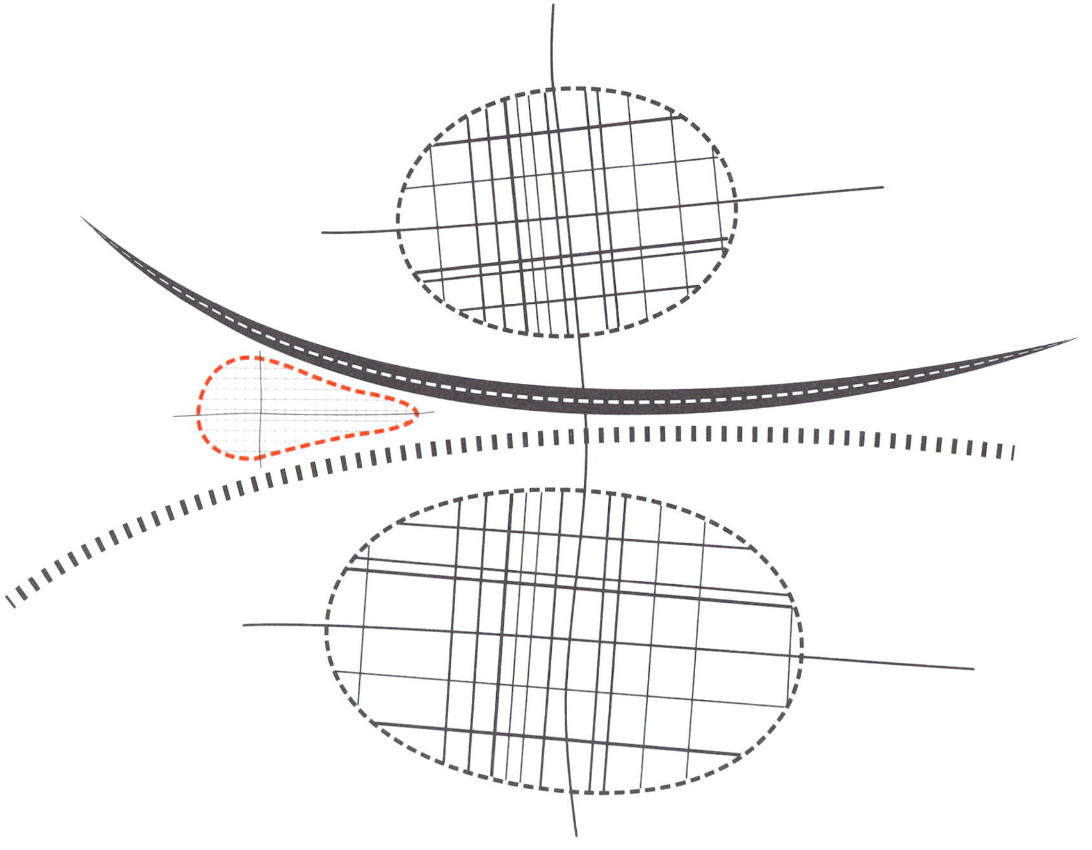

11. The Mid-Polis Bounded by Infrastructure

Paris, Washington, D.C., Seoul

As a metropolis grows in breadth and density, infrastructure systems supporting connections between a city's core and its outer boundaries must expand commensurately. As a result, quaintly scaled streets have expanded into avenues and even highways. These systems can cut through mid-polis conditions, e.g., La Défense, a major business node west of Paris's Arc de Triomphe. Or they can encircle or bound mid-poleis. For example, Reston, Virginia, outside of Washington, D.C., was built up over time, such that its boundaries were defined by highways linking Dulles Airport to the city.

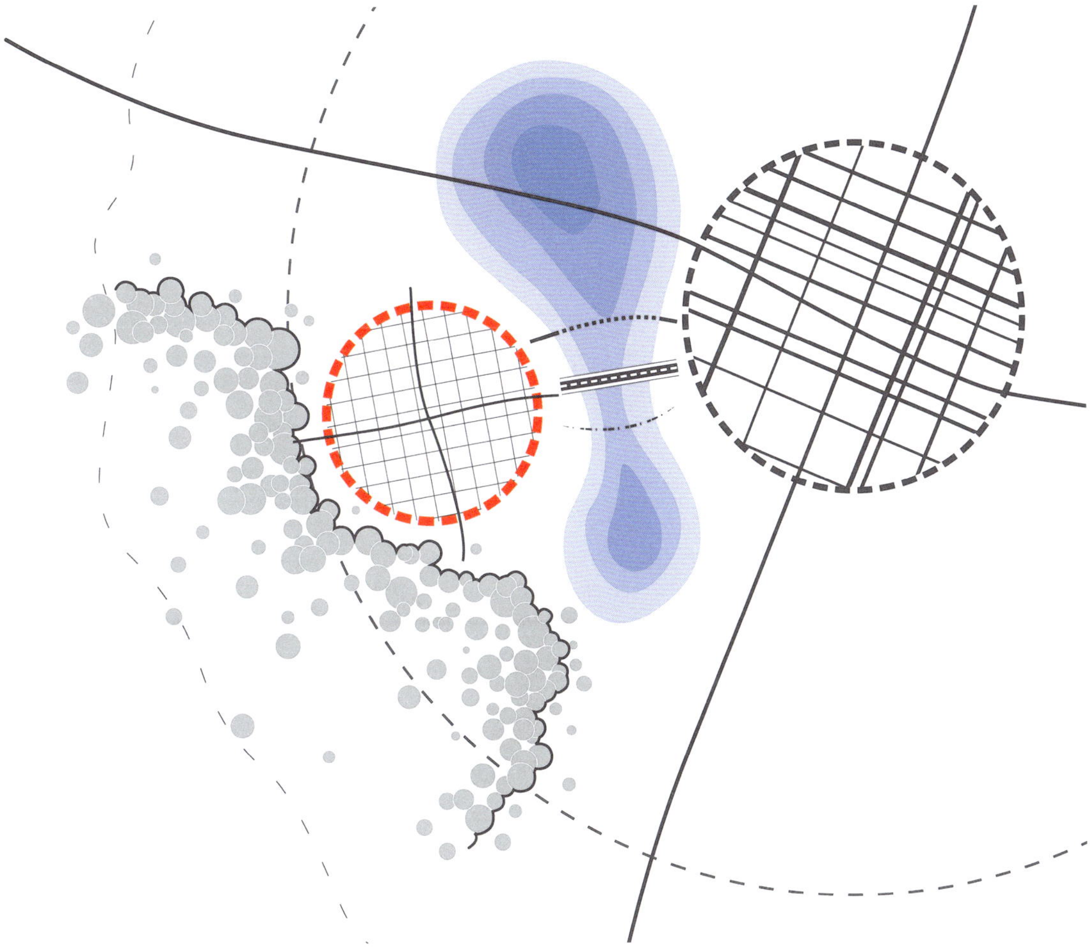

12. Bridging Natural Mid-Polis Features

New York, Rotterdam, Venice, Sydney

Where prominently scaled natural features limit urban development, major infrastructure elements can be used to link areas separated within the larger metropolis. For instance, New York is a collection of five interconnected boroughs, with Manhattan as its economic and cultural core. The extensive system of bridges, rail lines, subways, tunnels, ferries, and even cable cars (the Roosevelt Island Tramway) link the metropolis's distinctive neighborhoods despite their spatial displacement from one another. Similarly, other cities with strong water features, such as Venice, Amsterdam, and Sydney, generate a metropolitan fabric where infrastructure, natural features, and urbanized areas are interwoven to create a unique identity.

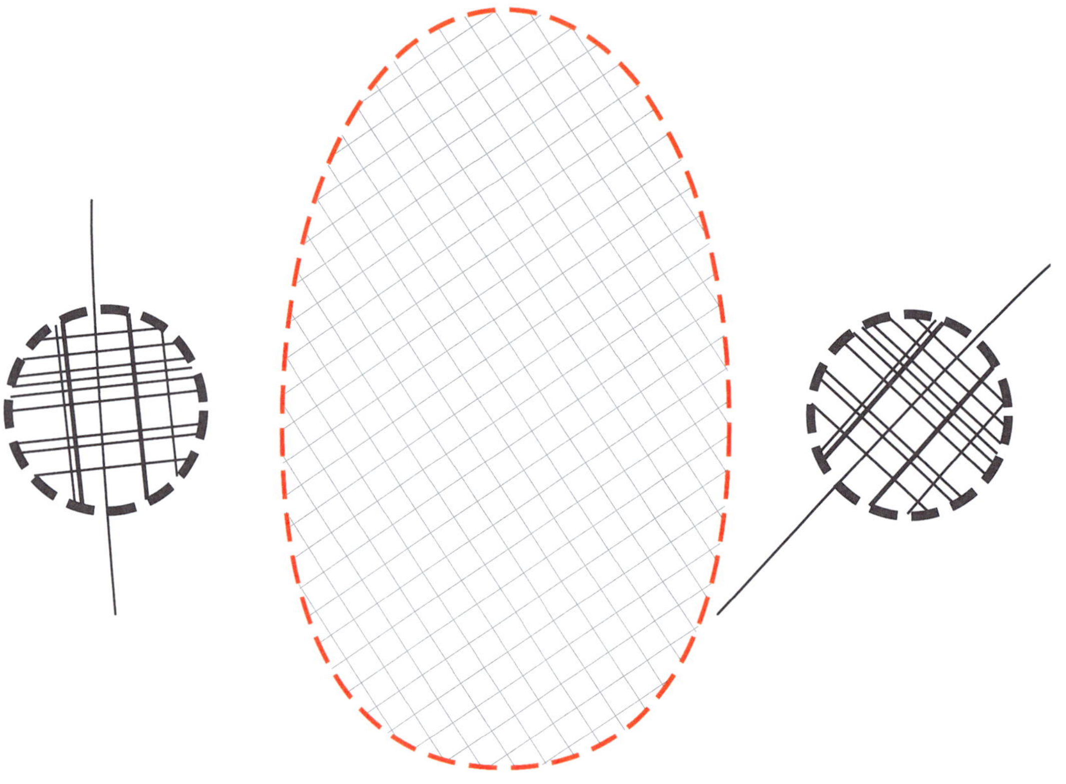

13. The Metropolis with Strong Natural Mid-Polis Features: Farms and Forests

Randstad, Portland (OR), Ottawa

Natural boundaries such as mountains, forests, and lakes need not limit urban growth. Instead, they can be protected from development through the boundaries defined by people and governments. For instance, the Dutch mega-polis known as the Randstad – comprising Amsterdam, Rotterdam, The Hague, Utrecht, and other towns – collectively forms an urban development ring around a largely rural center. The Randstad's interior farmlands are protected by zoning restrictions and conservation laws. Consequently, urban development is coordinated along the perimeter of these protected landscapes. Similarly, Portland, Oregon, and Ottawa, Ontario, Canada, limit their outward growth by defining strict zoning limits on land development outside their city perimeters. The desired result is to create denser metropolitan areas, surrounded by natural environments.

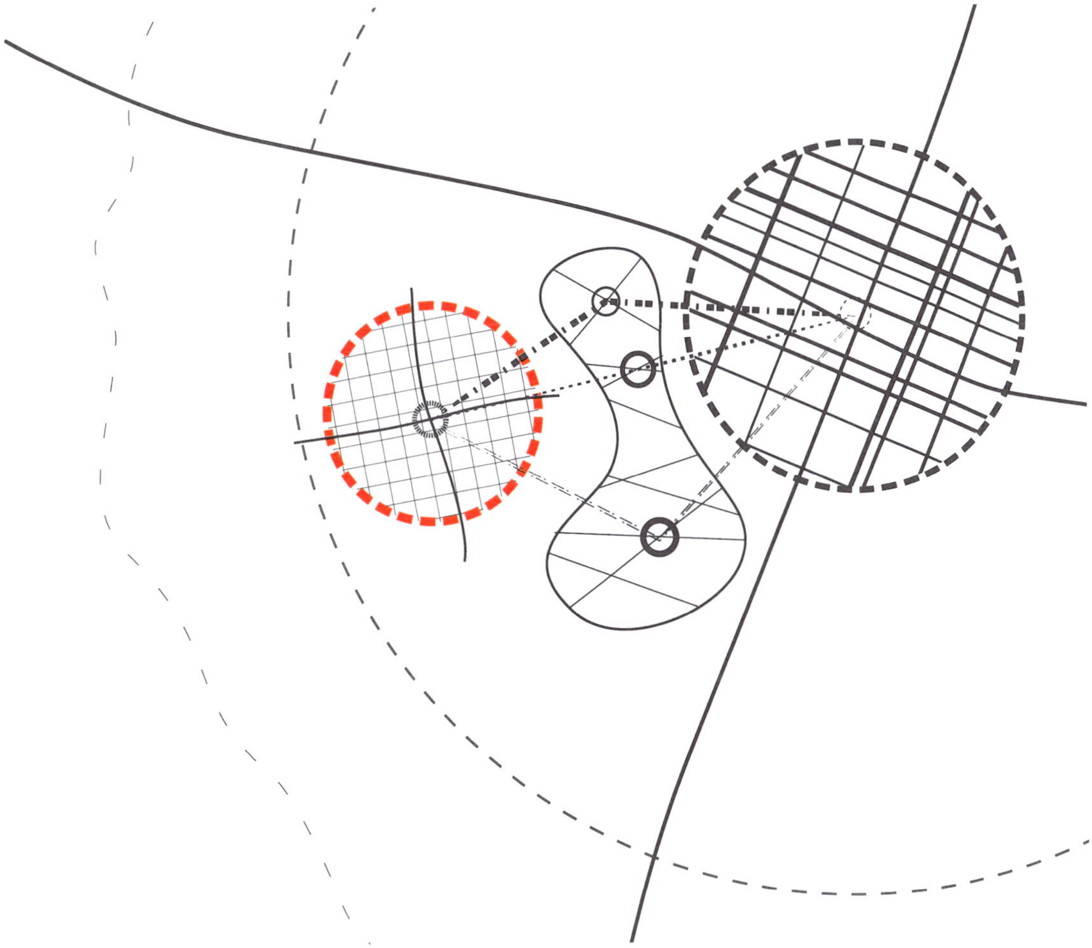

14. The Metropoleis Comprising Multiple Mid-Polis Morphologies

Madrid, Cologne, Athens

Some cities, such as Madrid and Athens, are made up of distinctive neighborhoods, each with its own pattern of streets and blocks. Their outlines are also discernable in a map or figure-ground plan. Yet their compact adjacencies create a compact metropolitan fabric. This urban pattern often results from development tendencies that occurred over distinct and separate waves of development.

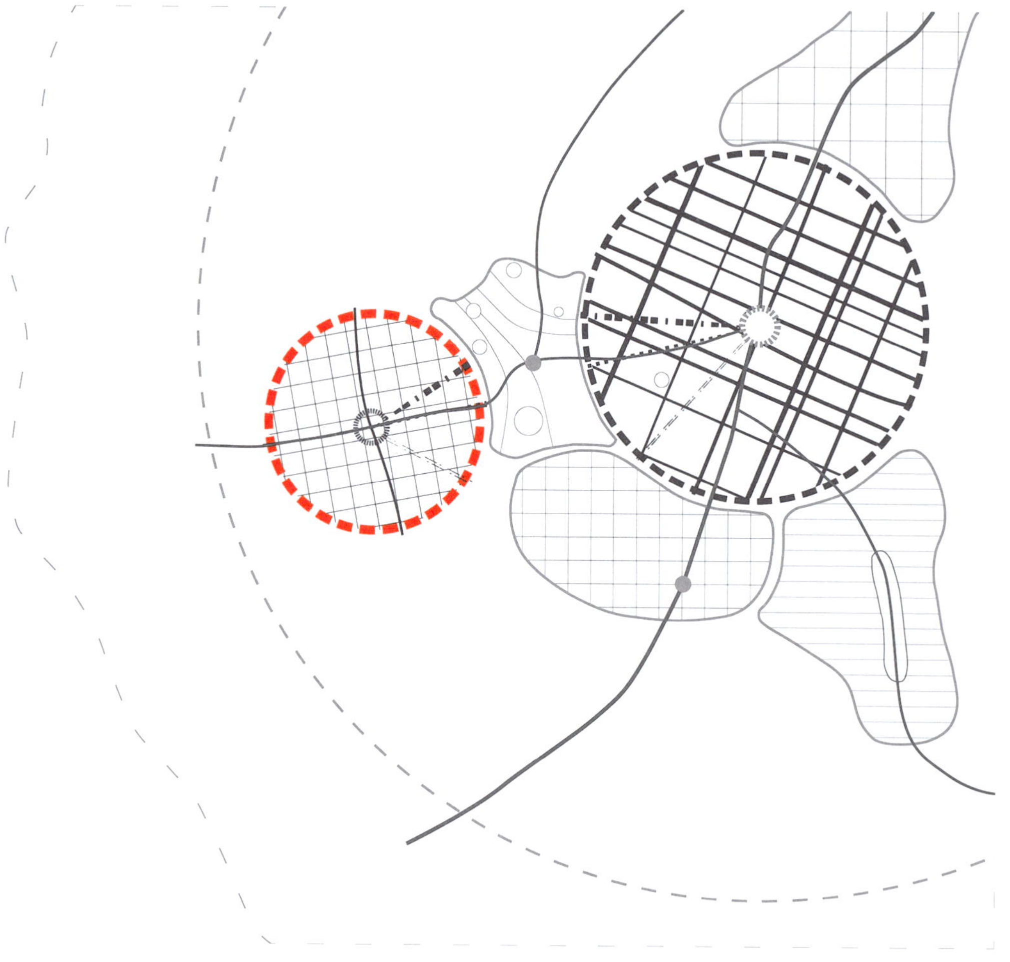

15. Fusing Dissimilar Morphologies

Vienna, Chicago

For metropoleis with distinctive neighborhood street patterns and spatial structures to function as a coherent whole, adequately scaled street and infrastructure systems must be overlaid and incorporated into this type of urban patchwork quilt. Avenues, parks, subways, and other linkage systems need to interconnect the neighborhoods to create an integrated network of nodes. The districts outside Vienna's Ringstrasse achieve this goal. Major roads, parks, tramlines, and subways cut through districts, connecting them one to the other, to the city's historic core, and to points beyond. Similarly, Chicago's broad avenues – some registered to the underlying street grid, others radiating from the city's core – help to fuse the city's many neighborhoods into a larger metropolis.

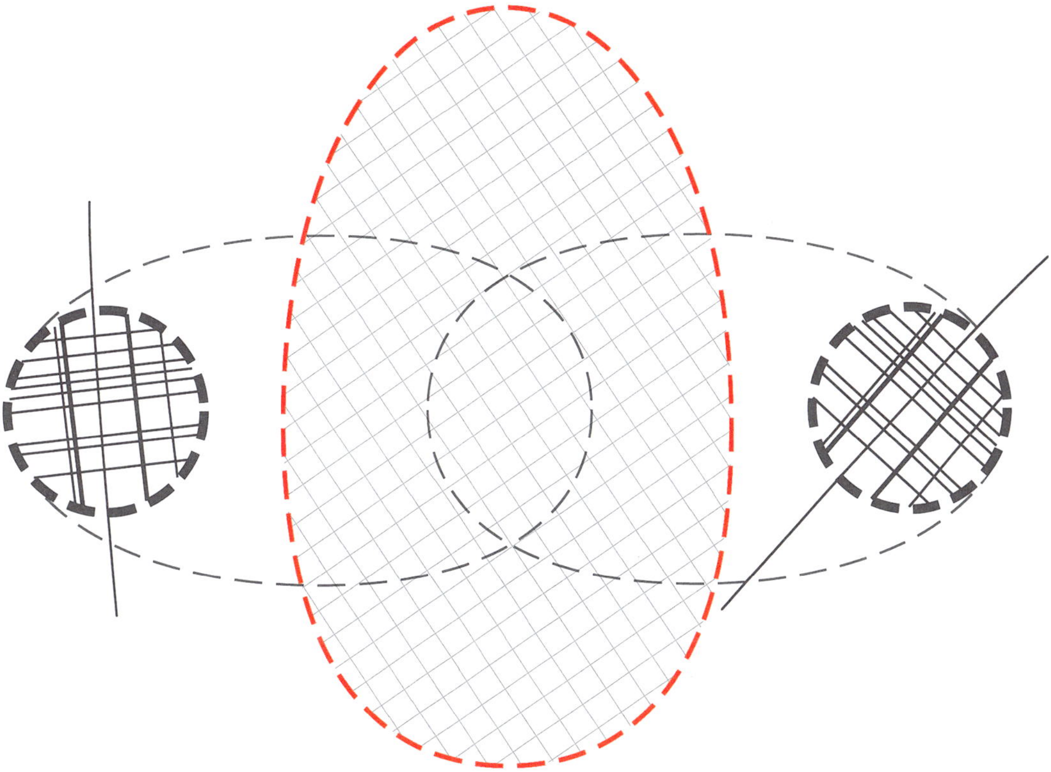

16. The Mid-Polis as Open Space: Carved Out of the Metropolis
Berlin, New York, London

A metropolis does not consist of built areas alone. Open spaces and parks are a welcome relief from overly dense development patterns. The parks can be small and interspersed regularly throughout the metropolis, or a city may benefit from parks large enough to constitute a mid-polis, e.g., New York's Central Park and London's Hyde Park. The Tiergarten in Berlin and the Vondelpark in Amsterdam are of a scale that impacts the organization of not only the neighborhoods that abut them, but also the metropolis itself. In each of these cities, the properties and neighborhoods adjacent to these large parks benefit from their proximity to nature. Quality of life is enhanced for residents, while the edge of the park helps to define the local spatial experience and the larger organization of the city and its neighborhoods. For instance, New York's Fifth Avenue clarifies the identity and interaction of Central Park, on one side, and the Upper East Side neighborhood. This edge also contributes to the overall organization of Manhattan.

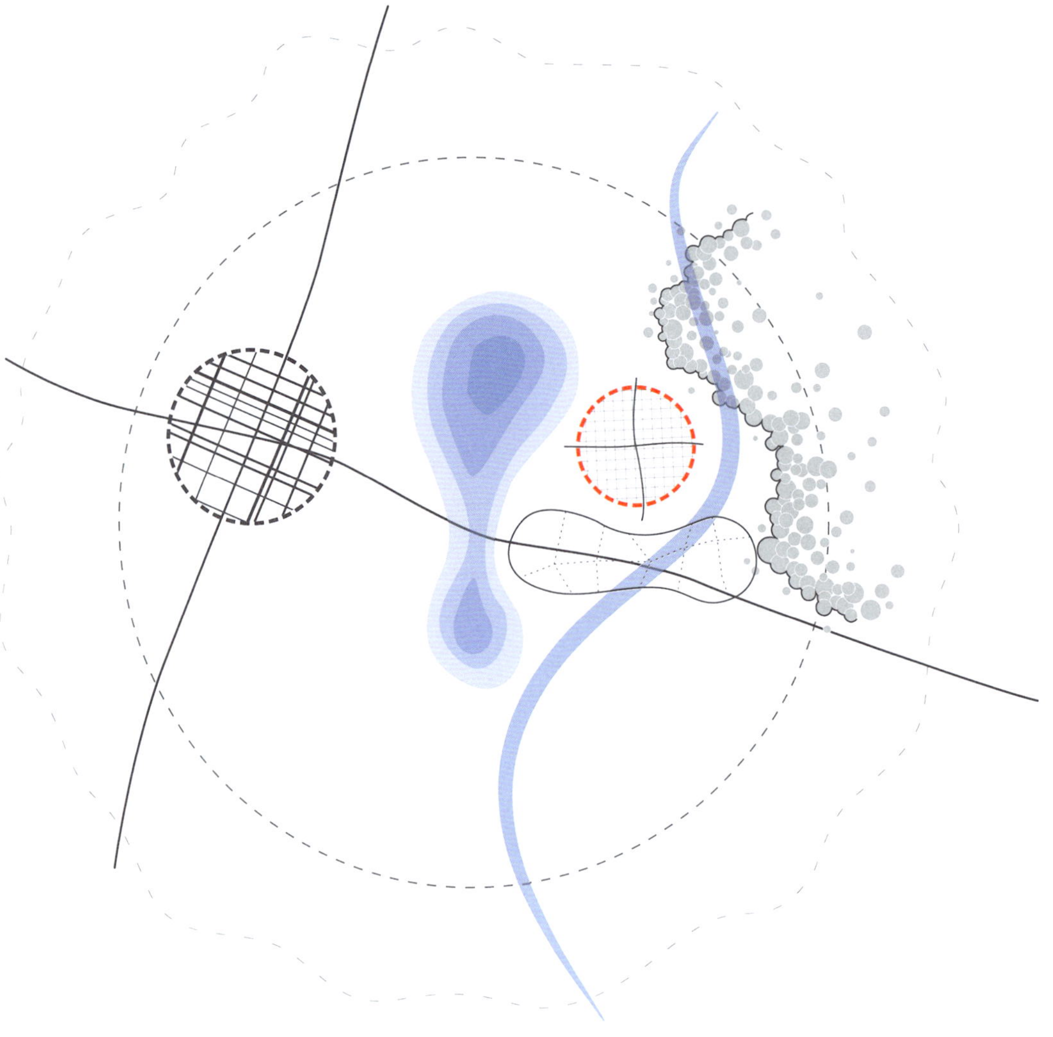

17. Connecting Open Space to Adjacent Mid-Polis Neighborhoods

Copenhagen, Singapore

A mid-polis as an open space can be designed in two ways: (1) It can be an autonomous, discrete area with its own spatial structure intended to be entirely separated from the surrounding city, e.g., Tokyo's Imperial Palace, a vast landscape in the heart of Tokyo's center that is inaccessible to the public. (2) It can be publicly connected to the surrounding network of streets and neighborhoods, e.g., New York's Central Park, where a cleverly concealed major thoroughfare cuts laterally through the greenspace, connecting the city's East and West sides. In addition, cities such as Copenhagen and Singapore have extensive linear green networks, open water, and natural preserves that are linked with the surrounding urban fabric. Over time, such mid-polis communities are known for how nature is integrated into the fabric of the neighborhood.

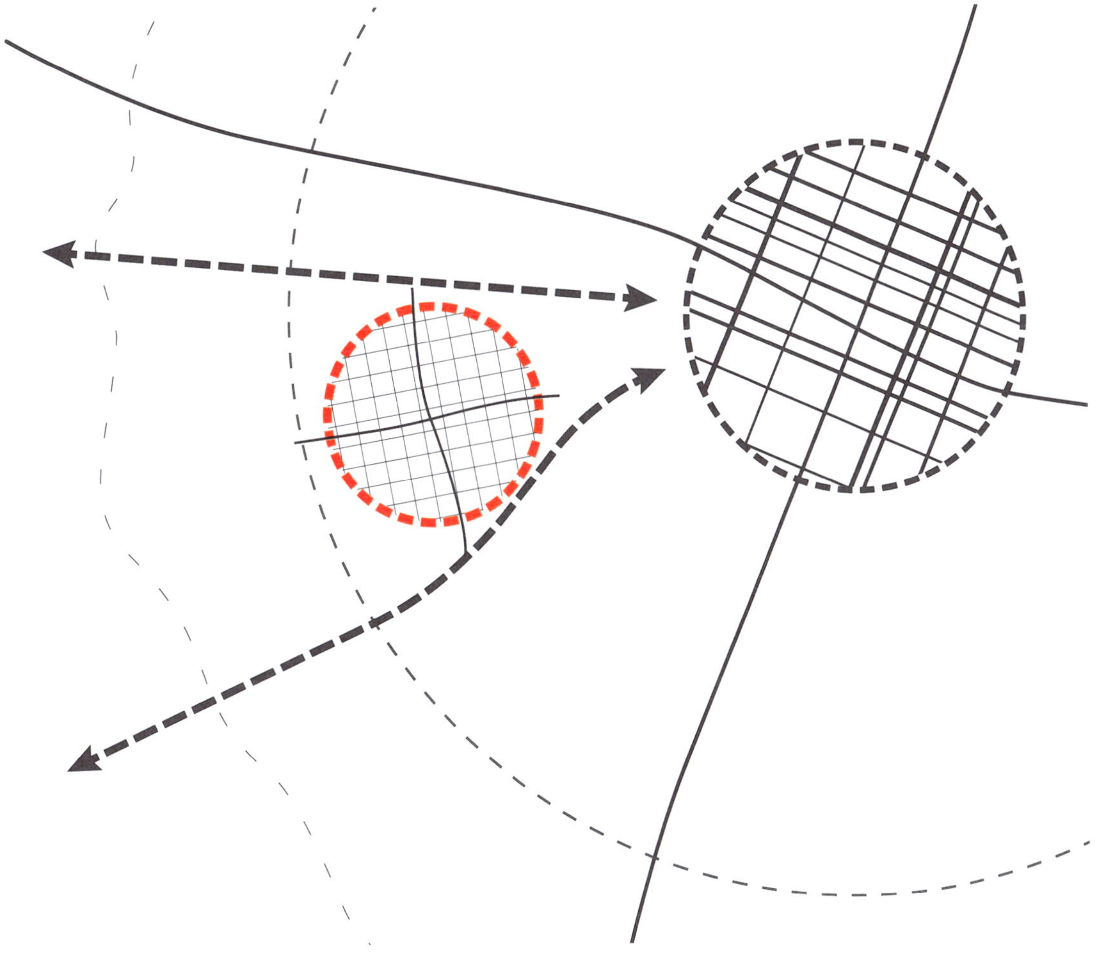

18. The Mid-Polis Squeezed by Infrastructure

Brooklyn, New York; Southwark, London; Kowloon, Hong Kong

As the metropolis's size and population increases, the demands on the capacity of the infrastructural systems must grow commensurately. When the girth of the metropolis broadens, new layers of infrastructure are overlaid onto the metropolis. The closer you get to the city center or important nodes within the metropolis, the greater the density of these systems tends to become. Consequently, some neighborhoods within the metropolis can be squeezed, sliced, or even separated from the grain of the larger metropolis. Examples of this condition are in Brooklyn, New York; Southwark, London; and Kowloon, north of Hong Kong Island.

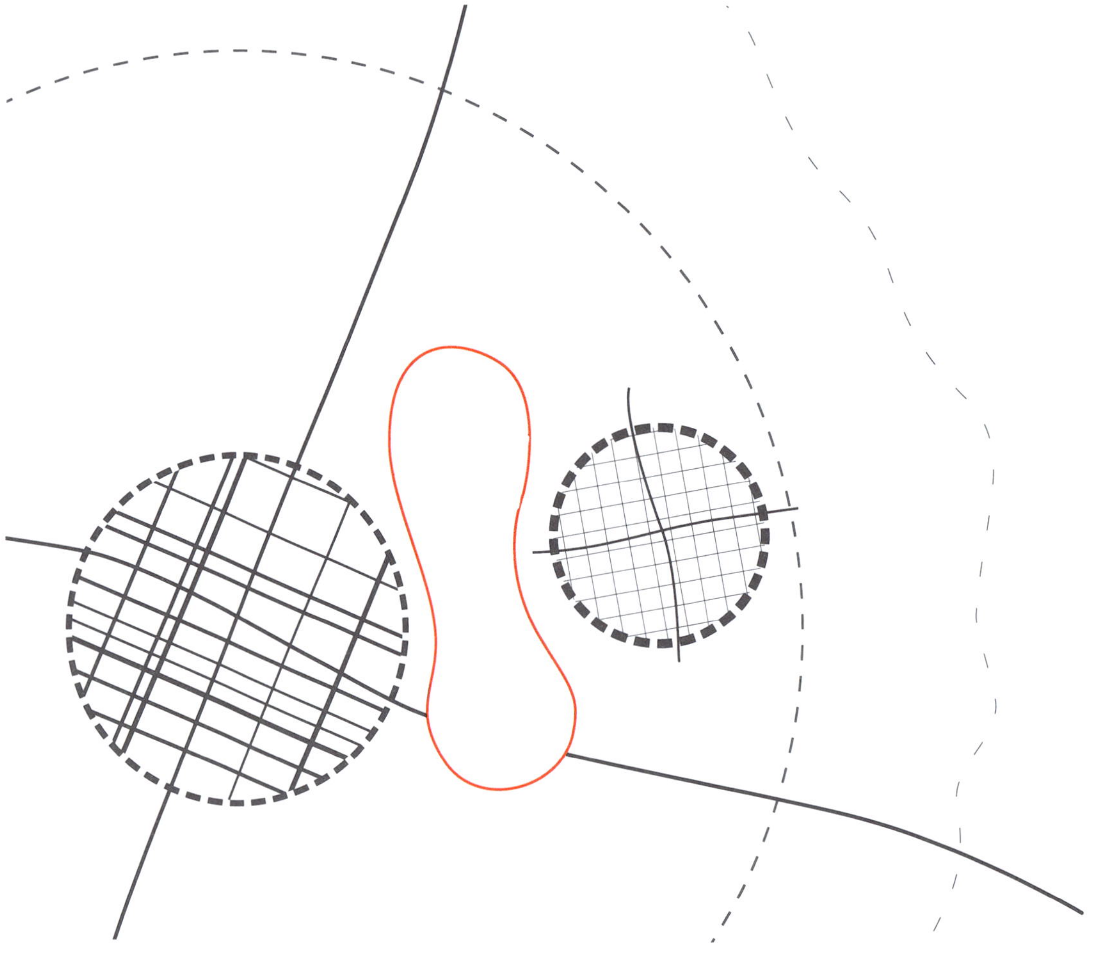

19. The Mid-Polis Through Modern Conflict

Berlin, Jerusalem, Johannesburg

In particular locations worldwide, modern warfare and imposed separation brought on by politics, religion and race can generate buffer areas between two opposing factions. For decades after World War II, Berlin split into capitalist and communist sectors on either side of the no-man's land abutting the Berlin Wall until the wall fell in 1989. Similarly, Jerusalem was separated into religious sectors: the Muslim Quarter, the Christian Quarter, the Jewish Quarter, and the Armenian Quarter. Johannesburg was also known for separating the cities into apartheid-driven divisions. Finally, Belfast, during the "Troubles," was zoned into Catholic and Protestant regions. Today, most of these urban buffer areas are dissolved, creating mid-polis regions with conditions ripe to be redeveloped through infill and re-inhabitation.

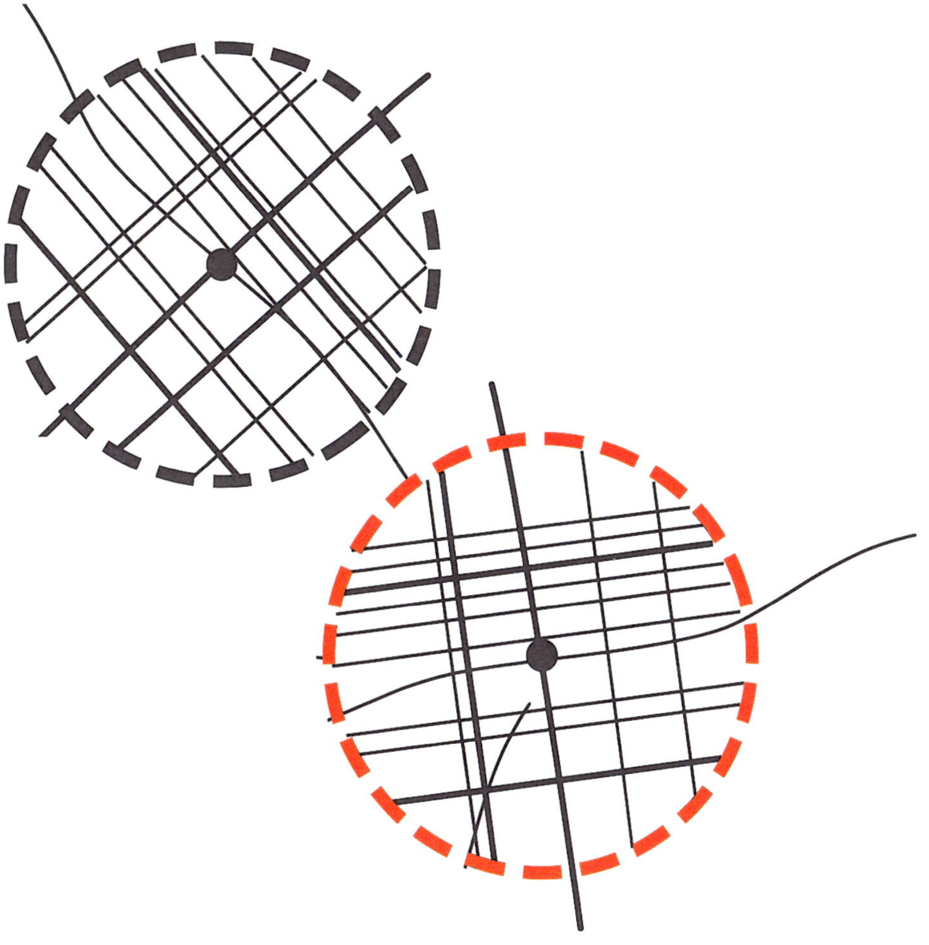

20. Dueling Mid-Poleis Within Larger Metropolitan Areas
Shanghai, New York, London

As cities grow and mature, the needs of residents and markets result in expansion outside the original central business, commercial and cultural districts. Often these expansions leapfrog natural or topographic boundaries or inhabit and re-energize existing neighborhoods through economic and physical transformation. For instance, Shanghai is divided between the historic urban center of Puxi and its contemporary counterpart, Pudong, on the opposite sides of the Huangpu River. Where each urban node has office space, hotels, retail and cultural amenities, the urban experience is very different from that in the other node. These nodes both compete and complement each other's functions and markets. Thus, they can simultaneously thrive because of the overwhelming market demands within the larger metropolitan region. Similarly, the resurgence of Manhattan's wealth, livability index, and housing market has propelled Brooklyn's redevelopment. Squeezed out of pricey Manhattan real estate, many residents have crossed the East River to many of Brooklyn's amenity-rich neighborhoods, e.g., Clinton Hill, Greenpoint, Williamsburg. Ironically, many of these districts in Brooklyn have become unaffordable, since their popularity as desirable neighborhoods increased.

Strategies for Transforming the Mid-Polis

1.2

Developing the Underutilized Mid-Polis

Some mid-poleis are fully integrated as part of a metropolis, comprising a network of adjacent neighborhoods and districts. They may possess a strong sense of identity, harnessing the urban landscape efficiently and effectively, while more underutilized districts may lack a strong sense of identity. Consequently, less integrated mid-poleis do not optimize land-use and other valuable urban resources and amenities, such as open space and fresh air. Overcoming the challenges presented by underutilized typologies will require a design and planning strategy that transforms the urban landscape, its typologies, and underlying ecologies. Maximizing urban utility, while strengthening the district's identity, is worthwhile and important to elevating the overall health of a metropolis. Neglect, on the other hand, can yield tumor-like voids in the metropolitan body.

Types of Mid-Polis Challenges

Lack of Identity

Where the mid-polis is part of a sprawling urban carpet, the identity of communities within this zone may be undifferentiated. They may include a mix of unremarkable streets, buildings, materials, and spaces. Such locations will lack a sense of place, failing to create a region that fosters strong connections between people and place.

Civic identity arises in part out of the way in which unique and idiosyncratic elements (buildings, materials, spaces, institutions) come together to support a community and its needs. In addition, variation in the types of spaces, their configurations, and their locations can contribute to a community's identity. Whether or not a community has a sense of identity can be determined by asking these kinds of questions:

Can you determine the extents of a community, defined not only by its legal boundaries, but also by its spatial, social, demographic, and economic characteristics?

by **Paul Lukez**

Paul Lukez Architecture

Highways transformation

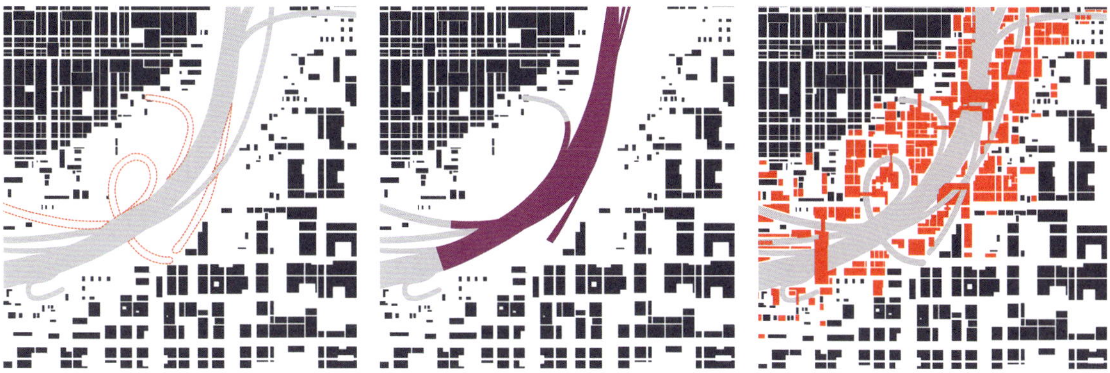

Erasure

Modification

Iteration

Is there a coherent and legible order to a community's physical and spatial organization?
Is the community image-able – that is, are there physical characteristics that make the community memorable?

Does a community have qualities that make it distinct from its neighboring community?

<u>Weak Part-to-Whole and Whole-to-Part Connections</u>

The relationship between the mid-polis and its surrounding environment in the metropolis is critical. This highlights the "part to whole" and "whole to part" relationship between the mid-polis and the metropolis. If the identity of the mid-polis is strong and unique, it can still be identifiable as part of a larger metropolitan area. The mid-polis's identity is shaped in part by the collection of communities that constitute its larger domain. Is the metropolis made up of communities that are different but clearly related, like siblings in a family? Or does the metropolis comprise a very diverse array of communities, each unrelated to the other in type, character or appearance? In either case, the mid-polis must contribute to the identity of the metropolis in a way that creates positive urban experiences while allowing its identity to evolve.

<u>Natural and Man-Made Obstacles</u>

Sometimes large swaths of a metropolis act as considerable obstacles within the metropolis, limiting connections among adjacent communities. These obstacles come in man-made as well as natural forms. For instance, oversized infrastructure systems can separate and divide communities. Similarly, abandoned industrial complexes and commercial complexes can inhibit the connectivity among neighborhoods within a community or metropolis. Prominent natural features such as mountains, hills, lakes, and rivers can also impede the connectivity among districts. Instead of becoming a point of interest around which complimentary uses cluster, they divide and separate districts by virtue of their scale.

Underutilized highway territory, photo by Peter Vanderwarker

Curtailed Land-Use Due to Adjacent Infrastructure and Facilities

Some metropolitan areas have underutilized sections within their domains, such that the highest and best uses of these sections are not being realized. This condition may result from many different circumstances. Most commonly, land alongside highways underperforms, either because noise levels make it less desirable, or because overly generous easements are set aside for future growth. Similarly, land parcels next to various industrial facilities are not optimized. Urban development patterns can also affect land-use trends, in such a way that land situated among adjacent larger-scale development patterns presents challenges. This is because either the geometry of the respective street patterns is not well designed and coordinated, or the boundary of each development does not fit its neighboring one. As a patchwork quilt of evolving urban development patterns, the metropolis can provide planners and developers with land parcels that await higher, better development uses.

Fighting the Forces of Entropy Through Renewal

To survive and mature over time, the mid-polis requires refurbishment and renewal. The lifecycle needs of buildings and supporting urban infrastructure demand this, as the forces of entropy and decay take hold. The opportunity to use lifecycle repairs – not only to revive existing built environments, but also to integrate new sustainable technologies and systems – is opportune. Furthermore, the landscape can be restored where it has been damaged and integrated into the metropolis where it is absent. If the mid-polis condition can be transformed to accommodate this growth, it becomes a catalyst – an ideal terrain for renewal in the existing metropolis.

Types of Transformation

Of course, the built environment can be transformed in many ways. The following three categories – (1) Transformation by Type, (2) Transformation by

Scale / Infrastructure, and (3) Transformation by Urban Landscape – are not intended to be exhaustive, but are a small sampling of how urban transformations might be considered.

Transformation Strategies by Type:
The urban environment comprises buildings (public and private, old and new), infrastructure (roads, highways, rail, etc.), and landscape (built or natural). Facilities in the mid-polis can be transformed, building by building. Finding new uses for old structures can help repair, energize, cohere, and beautify a mid-polis. Upgrading a building's appearance and systems improves a building's performance and, by extension, the community. New buildings can also be added as needed; buildings as infills can fix the gaps in the mid-polis's urban fabric. A balance of public and private use should be added as required to support the needs of the community.

Transformation Strategies by Scale / Infrastructure:
Infrastructure elements, such as highways and rail lines, often separate communities and districts within the mid-polis. "Taming" infrastructure, by either submerging highways or mitigating their environmental impacts in other ways, can contribute to mid-polis repair. Large multi-lane boulevards can be tamed by adding tree-lined dividers and pedestrian/bike paths where possible. Designated bus lanes speed up service as a cheaper, more flexible system than subways.

Transformation Strategies by Urban Landscape:
Landscape is the lungs of the city, providing fresh air to its inhabitants. Yet so often landscape features are considered an urban luxury, or they are poorly designed and/or disconnected from one another, thus reducing their benefit. Urban landscapes should not be regarded merely as formally designed parks. Instead, they can be integrated into a larger network of softscape features. Transforming the landscape, resuscitating it, or re-establishing its presence in the mid-polis can have positive effects on the adjacent buildings and infrastructure elements, especially if these development strategies are integrated.

Transformation by Scale: Top-Down vs. Bottom-Up

The scale of transformational development strategies depends in part on whether or not the proposed changes are driven by a top-down, bottom-up, or hybrid approach.

Top-Down Development Strategies
Top-down strategies are often generated by governments, institutions, or large-scale private developers. They have the power, financial resources, and decision-making tools to exercise their will within the metropolis. As the urban community becomes more complex in its physical, social, economic and political structure, these tools are not only useful but sometimes necessary to make large-scale development changes.

Examples of government-driven transformations include the ambitious infrastructure projects of Robert Moses in New York City; Oscar Niemeyer in Brasilia, Brazil; or Georges-Eugène Haussmann in Paris. In Las Vegas, the enormous casino projects by such developers as Wynn Casinos represent city-making driven by private enterprise. Similarly, China is witnessing the development of enormous housing and multi-use projects by both private developers and government agencies.

Bottom-Up Development Strategies
Bottom-up development strategies rely on more organic processes. Often market-driven, bottom-up processes respond to local needs and available resources. This scale of development is smaller and is phased incrementally. The resources invested match those available to residents, shopkeepers, small businesses, and community organizations. As the need for development arises and resources for it are made available, these resources are released with little coordination or regard for what neighbors are doing.

When (re)developing the mid-polis, questions arise: What kind of infrastructure is available to support bottom-up development patterns? Can the results of such patterns help to promote positive solutions to the challenges facing the mid-polis? Examples of bottom-up development abound. In their rawest form, the favelas of Rio de Janeiro, Brazil, and Lagos, Nigeria, represent residents building their shelters with very limited available resources.

A Hybrid Approach

Ideally, the mid-polis can be transformed through a hybrid approach, a thoughtful blend of top-down and bottom-up strategies. Where the scope of development requires large-scale or mid-scale interventions, public or private, the appropriate institutions can build the necessary transformative developments, be they building-based, infrastructure-based, or landscape-based. If well-designed, these larger-scale developments can spur future smaller-scale ones by capturing latent market forces or serving as an economic catalyst.

Numerous strategies of this kind have been tried in the US and Europe over the last 40 years. Some of the most successful ones, e.g., the Promenade Plante in Paris, have transformed old train tracks into a multifaceted pedestrian and bicycle path system, which in turn spurred the redevelopment of the 12th Arrondissement, a one-time downtrodden, overlooked part of Paris. Similarly, American cities such as Baltimore have used publicly financed projects such as stadiums and harbor improvements to regenerate the inner harbor just south of Baltimore's downtown area and urban heart into a vibrant commercial, cultural and residential extension of the historic American city.

Transformation by Process

The following discussion will present a more conceptual framework for thinking about the transformation of the mid-polis, which can support the more pragmatic options already presented. A more global definition of transformation implies change, change brought to the qualitative properties of an object or system. In urban design, transformation can take many forms. It assumes, though, a pre-existing condition: a city, its neighborhoods and districts, its infrastructure, its buildings and parks. For discussion purposes, mid-polis transformations could require three stages: erasure, generative modification, and iteration.

Erasure

Erasure is optional but often used in urban transformations in which something needs repair, replacement or relocation. Erasure takes something away from its original or last position. It presents an opportunity to set the stage for new transformations. Material elements that are taken away can range in type, material, or scale. The resources expended to remove something from its original location must be validated by what is left in its absence, or by what is added to a prepared site. For instance, if a roof on a building fails, the old roof is removed (erased) at a cost. This cost is justified by the added value in improved performance and security that a new weatherproof roof provides its users.

In urban design, the decision to erase is both practical and value-laden. If part of a city simply fails to meet a community's needs, city elders must reconfigure, redesign and/or rebuild those parts that do not work. This process is easier for infrastructure systems; for example, an overburdened water-sewer system can be erased and replaced with a new one. However, this choice becomes more complicated when considering where people live, work and recreate in a city. To erase a home, shop or park is a value-driven decision, based on the values of a community and its residents. Besides the direct value of a city's buildings, infrastructure and parks provided to its citizenry, these urban components also contribute to the city's history and culture.

In deciding when and what to erase in a city, erasure helps to define a city's useful history, i.e., which elements will contribute now and in the future to a place's evolving history. Western cities, especially those rooted in Roman culture, are replete with examples of ancient foundations and walls reused to support new structures and functions in newly configured spaces. Similarly, abandoned industrial complexes have progressively been redeveloped for new uses, e.g., housing, offices, etc. These older structures are retained in full or in part. They contribute to a history that is not encapsulated and preserved as an artifact by inviting the layering of new additions.

Mid-polis condition - Columbus, Ohio, USA
Bing, © Harris Corp, Earthstar Geographics LLC, © 2011 Microsoft Corporation

Low density industrial landscape, Somerville, Massachusetts, photo by Peter Vanderwarker

Modification

Modification of an urban site can involve a number of operations, including adding or altering the location of elements such that the intervention is a catalyst for future development. These new interventions can generate new construction patterns, which in turn influence, or even determine, the order of new development patterns. Modifications come in the form of addition or reconfiguration.

Modification Through Addition

Modification through addition can include adding to existing structures, infrastructures, or landscapes. It can operate at multiple scales from small to large. The simplest example of this is moving furniture (systems) within an existing space. The addition of a temporary structure brought onto a site to support special events can also represent a form of spatial modification through addition.

Modification Through Reconfiguration

Modification through reconfiguration includes existing elements and spaces, such that the material mass of a place does not change. Instead, the arrangement of elements relative to each other and their context is altered and deployed in a new order. The wear and tear of everyday use also pushes the entropy of the building's material and structural properties. Similarly, the forces of nature change a city's natural landscape, parks and spaces.

Iteration

Iteration implies repetition of a set of actions or processes that are related to one another or are derivative. Iteration, as a design and development process, builds on the themes formed during the generative modification phase of a place's transformation. That is, the urban and building typologies and their inherent patterns (e.g., repetitive street grid, common parcels sizes, open space typologies) can generate rich urban textures.

In urban design, iterative transformations are often carried out thematically. These iterative themes can depend upon how the original land was surveyed, parceled and inhabited by generations. Subsequently, each place develops a culture unique to its landscape, people, society, and evolving history. The way iterative transformations take place over time will be informed by both the themes established early in a city's history and how these themes can be used to accommodate the changing needs of an evolving culture, history, and unforeseen circumstances.

For instance, Indiana's counties were parceled using the surveyor's grid. This geometry worked well and was laid out neatly for most of this very flat state. However, its southern part is hillier, especially where the sinuous Ohio River borders Kentucky. In these regions the surveyor's grid is less effective: here it must morph, bend, and curve to accommodate the rolling landscape and winding river.

In the north of the state, roads run straight to the horizon. In the south, they curve and bend as needed. These road patterns also affect the geometries of the towns in their respective regions: Indianapolis is a gridded utopia, while just 60 miles south, Bloomington's gridded street plan is violated by subtle shifts in street geometry to negotiate the hillier terrain. Consequently, subsequent transformations to each city's plan are thematically related to urban dimensions and geometries established at the city's genesis. Today, Indiana University's expansive campus mixes straight and curving geometries.

An urban development pattern is established through the parceling of land and the subsequent road network development among those parcels. The iterations enabled these cities and towns to use these road and land division structures to meet the needs of a growing populace. The same land-parceling patterns were employed statewide to subdivide counties into land tracts, then into parcels, and ultimately into buildable lots for commercial or residential construction. Roads were laid within these newly occupied districts, defining new blocks that were then subdivided into smaller lots and occupied by new houses and businesses. The iterative process continues until the land is fully occupied, at which point what has already been built must be erased in part or completely for further development to occur.

Economic and social forces determine how useful iterative building and development cycles are to their community in the long term. The suburban model of building tract homes across the landscape is one kind of generative modification that has been iterated across the US. However, its

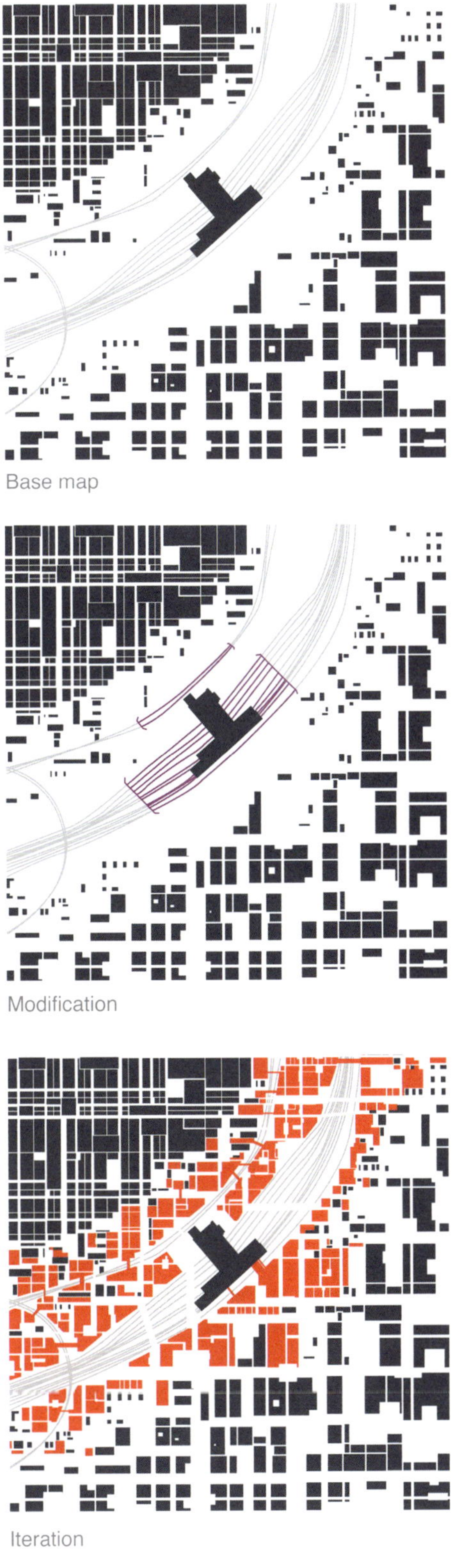

Base map

Modification

Iteration

Train tracks transformation

useful life as a development model may come to an end as the limits of resources such as energy, land and finance require more efficient models.

Thus, the mid-polis is an urban terrain that can be found to be in a state of flux. Can existing generative modifications repair their illnesses? Or must new forms of development be introduced and iterated to meet present and future urban needs? By definition, the iterative process stops when: (1) the design problem or challenge is met and achieved; (2) land and resources required to sustain the iterative process are exhausted or satiated; and (3) the generative modification model has failed to meet its performance standards and requires replacement or reconceptualization.

To determine how to transform the mid-polis, we must determine its current stage of development and the kinds of interventions that stage of development require: erasure, generative modification, and/or iteration. This will allow for a strategic deployment of design and material resources.

Applying Transformational Processes to Mid-Polis Typologies

The following diagrams are intended to illustrate how the three transformational processes – erasure, generative modification, iteration – are applied to a variety of mid-polis conditions. The larger goal is to repair the mid-polis or enhance its ability to contribute to the larger metropolis as a vibrant district. In the cases illustrated below, this larger goal is achieved by: (1) improving the connections between districts severed by natural obstacles or poor development patterns; (2) creating a new, more coherent reading of spaces being transformed or redeveloped; and (3) maximizing the development potential by using both built and natural typologies within each district.

<u>Body of Water</u>
Rivers and other large bodies of water can limit continuities among districts and regions within the greater metropolis. Plus, through years of industrialization and transportation shifts, waterway corridors have seen a wide range of uses and transformations. In the 21st century, land adjacent to various waterways can find appropriate uses for modern business, living and industry, and be used to enhance the waterfront as a contributing element within the metropolis.

<u>Natural Topography</u>
Steep terrain or other natural features can serve as obstacles in the development of a metropolis. New building typologies and supporting infrastructure elements can be introduced to use land formerly thought to be uninhabitable, in a manner symbiotic with the landscape, as seen in Italy's medieval hill towns and Chile's mountain cities. Natural topography can also help to create stronger connections to neighboring districts.

<u>Natural Forests</u>
Forests and parks nourish the city, its inhabitants, and its underlying ecology. Yet, how to make these forests and parks accessible to urban residents while assuring their sustenance is an important issue. Promoting forested natural landscape developments in bustling urban areas is critical in sustaining quality of life and good health. The Bois de Boulogne in Paris, Central Park in New York, and Vondelpark in Amsterdam are a few examples of forests and parks inextricably linked to the daily life of urbanites.

<u>Farmland</u>
As a precious commodity, farmland is threatened by runaway metropolitan development. Farms that survive urban development are frequently found on the fringes of the metropolis. However, urban farms need not be limited to the urban edge, but can be interwoven into the fabric of a metropolitan tapestry. Urban farms provide local produce for residents, and offer a welcome visual reprieve from dense urban development patterns. The air is re-oxygenated, and the presence of landscape can be physically and emotionally uplifting for urban residents. Portland, Oregon, and The Randstad in Holland are excellent case studies for integrating urban farming into larger metropolitan areas.

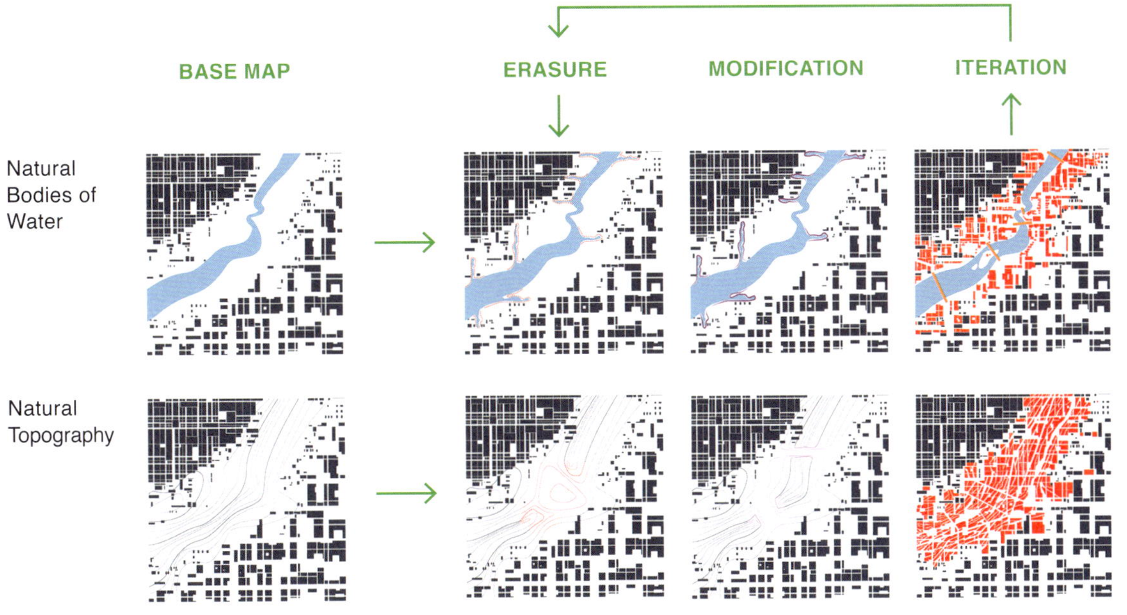
BASE MAP
ERASURE
MODIFICATION
ITERATION
Natural Bodies of Water
Natural Topography

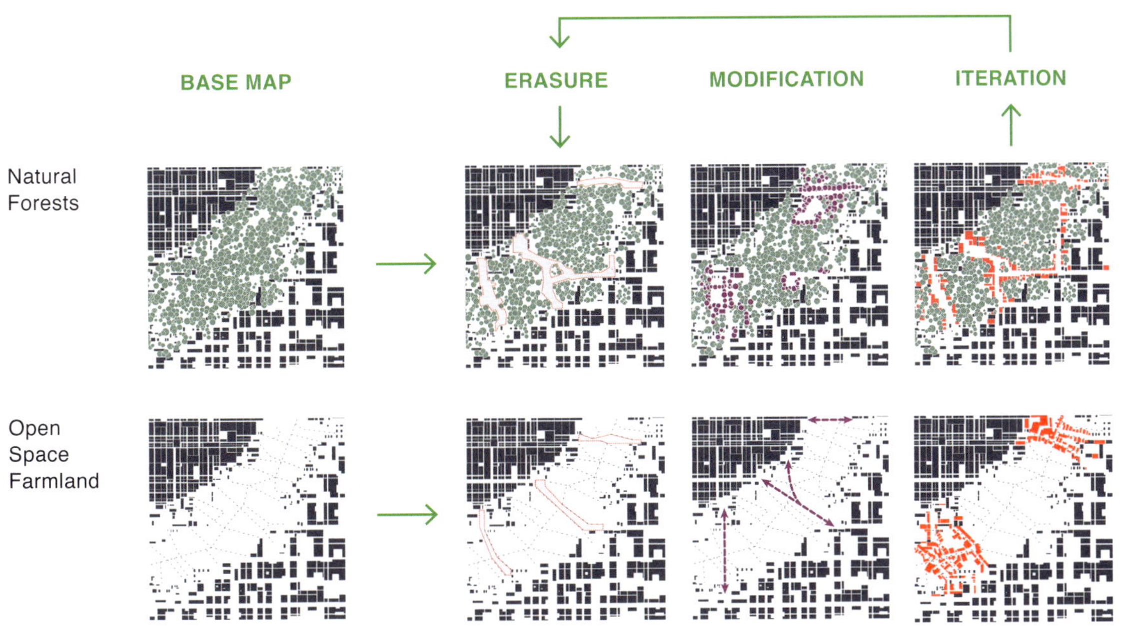
BASE MAP
ERASURE
MODIFICATION
ITERATION
Natural Forests
Open Space Farmland

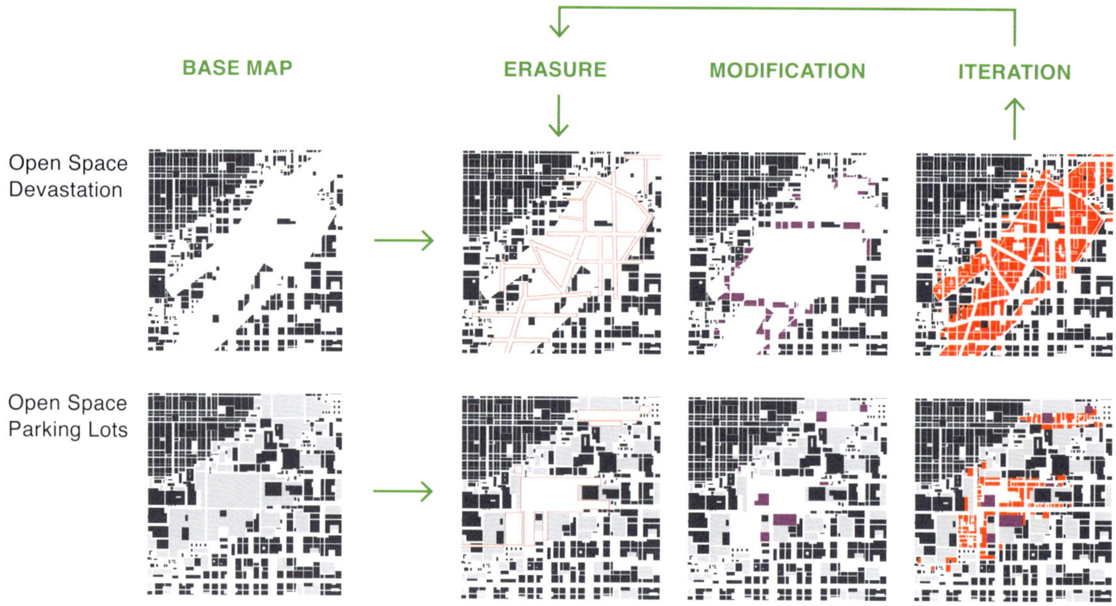

Devastated Open Space

The scars of war, political division, urban renewal, or mass exodus can leave their scars within a modern metropolis. These damaged terrains can be stitched back together, using existing or new forms of infrastructure and road networks as a means of creating a framework for new development. Belfast, Berlin, Tokyo, Detroit, Johannesburg, New Orleans, and other cities affected by economic or natural disasters must define appropriate strategies for repairing the wide expanses of physical and political devastation.

Parking Lots

The transformation of vibrant urban inner cities into a collection of massive parking-lot rings has plagued many American metropoleis such as Houston, Texas, and Cleveland, Ohio. Similarly, the “strip” has become an armature for large-scale parking lots servicing commercial development. Integrating new and better parking design practices into urban planning will allow reduction of large expanses of asphalt found in suburbia. As the true value of land escalates, new typologies that combine buildings, landscapes and parking will emerge and help reduce hardscapes in the mid-polis.

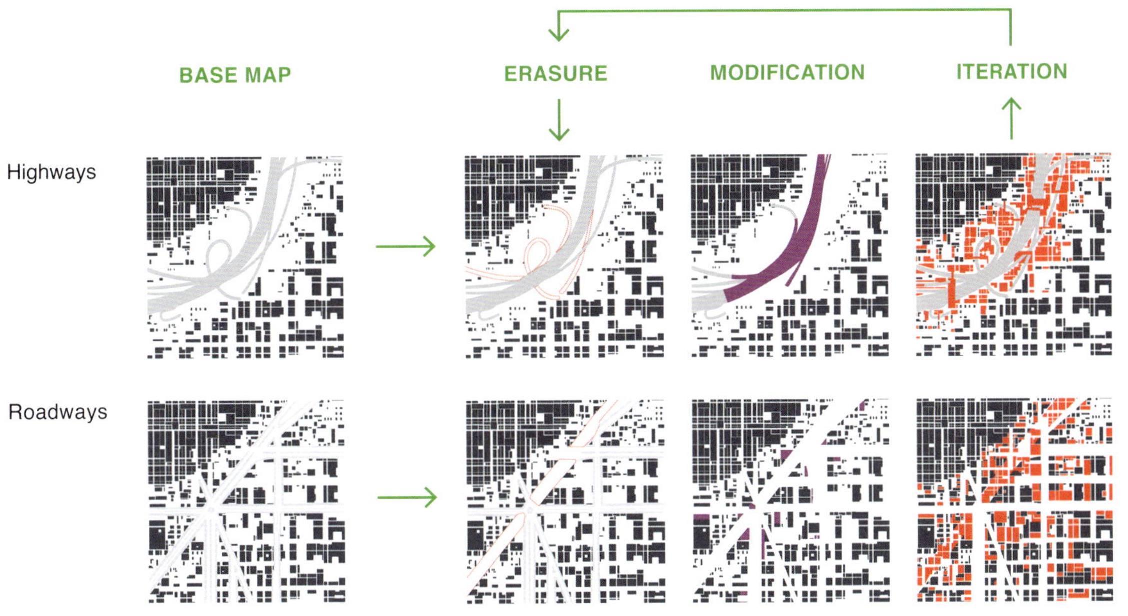

Highways

The land along the highway is often underutilized, particularly across the United States and Canada. This land can be filled in with appropriate uses or landscapes that treat the infrastructure as something valuable and usable. A better understanding and usage of space around highways can also enhance the opportunities to re-connect neighborhoods divided by such infrastructure.

Roadways

Some road networks expand to accommodate higher traffic counts. Streets become broad boulevards that separate adjacent neighborhoods. Taming the scale of the boulevard can be achieved in many ways, e.g., island medians, trees, trams, walkways, and busways. The boulevards' spatial quality can also be defined more prominently by strengthening their edge. Vancouver, Paris, and Boston are cities with broad but well-defined boulevards, which accommodate traffic while creating comfortably scaled pedestrian experiences.

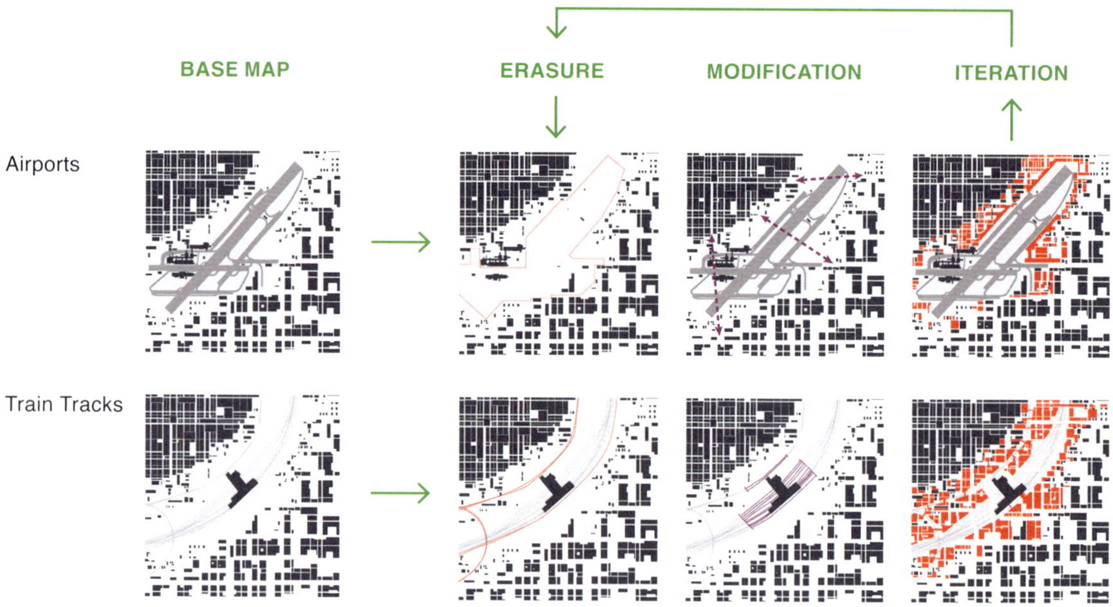

<u>Airports</u>

Since many larger airports are on a metropolis's outskirts, their effectiveness can be leveraged by linking them to a city's multimodal transportation network and assigning them multiple uses: business, retail, conference, hospitality, and even museums. Amsterdam's Schipol Airport and Frankfurt's International Airport each exemplify an airport evolving into a thriving Aeropolis. Schipol is linked to points near and far by car, subway, bus, and high-speed railways. In addition, many ex-urban airports are enveloped by open fields and encroach urban development. These include Dulles Airport in Dulles, Virginia.

<u>Train Tracks / Stations</u>

Rail lines typically slice through the urban fabric without sensitivity to residents in adjacent neighborhoods. Their technical requirements make them less malleable than streets supporting bus lines. Furthermore, their size, geometry and noise levels impact what can be built around the station and its tracks. Building alongside the tracks with appropriate uses, or covering over certain parts of the tracks, allows train lines to co-exist with the districts and neighborhoods of the metropolis. Cities such as Paris, Stuttgart, Chicago, Hong Kong, and New York have created higher-value districts by either transforming their rail lines and adjacent neighborhoods, covering their tracks, or integrating their tracks with neighboring districts and the more industrial uses of those districts.

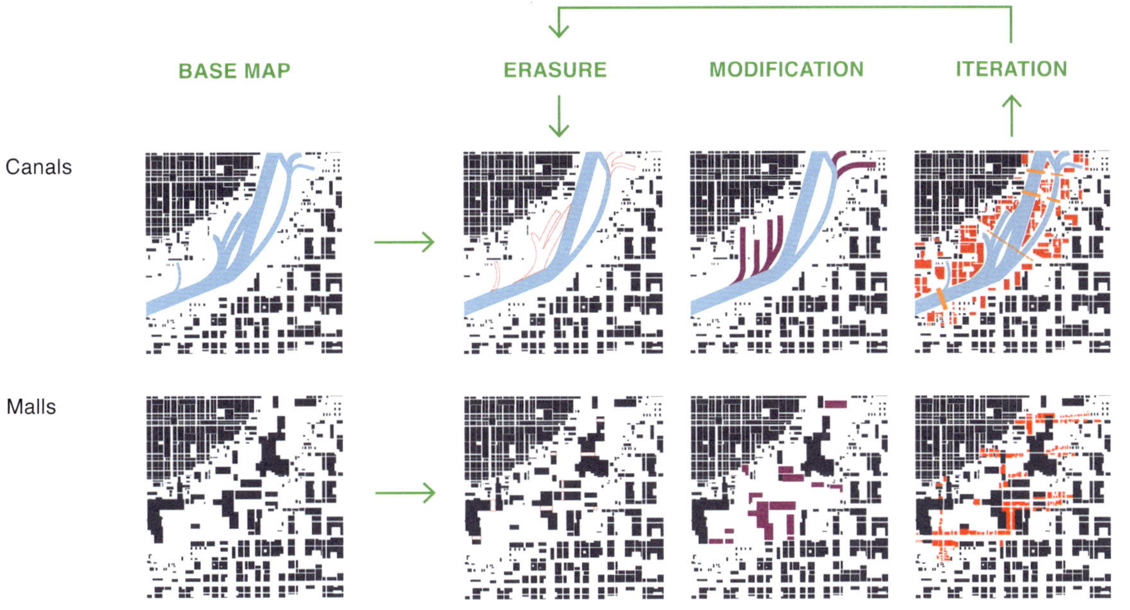

Canals and Harbors

Canals and harbors can present major challenges if revamped into higher, more impactful developments within a metropolis. Their location, their considerable scale, and the size of the machinery and equipment servicing the harbors can limit redevelopment strategies. Thus, canals and harbors require customized strategies scaled to meet the challenge, so they can build on the unique qualities of their districts. Hamburg's Haffenstadt is a massively successful example of the transformation of Hamburg's inner harbor into a new multi-use district. Similarly, Baltimore's Inner Harbor and Melbourne's Docklands are examples of districts that transformed harbor areas into vibrant communities with unique qualities of place that link them to their past.

Malls

Malls have wreaked havoc on traditional city planning principles. Their scale is intimidating, while the resultant streetscape is sacrificed for vehicular convenience. Consequently, malls have created an urban hodgepodge in the metropolis. However, they can be transformed and reintegrated into new dense centers highlighting community-oriented programs; such is the case of the conversion of the Villa Italia Mall in Belmar, Colorado. This mall conversion now includes a range of uses (housing, office, retail, and other amenities) and is integrated into a pedestrian-friendly district. Similarly, Assembly Square in Somerville, Massachusetts, converted a site occupied by a small mall, a Home Depot, and fields of parking. Today it is a vibrant community with strong connections to the adjacent water and parkways along the Mystic River. Also noteworthy is the once successful (then dying) mall on the West Side of Los Angeles. UCLA has since purchased it and converted it into a research park promoting advanced sciences and technology research companies. In all cases, the importance of scale and human centric design is key to each project's success.

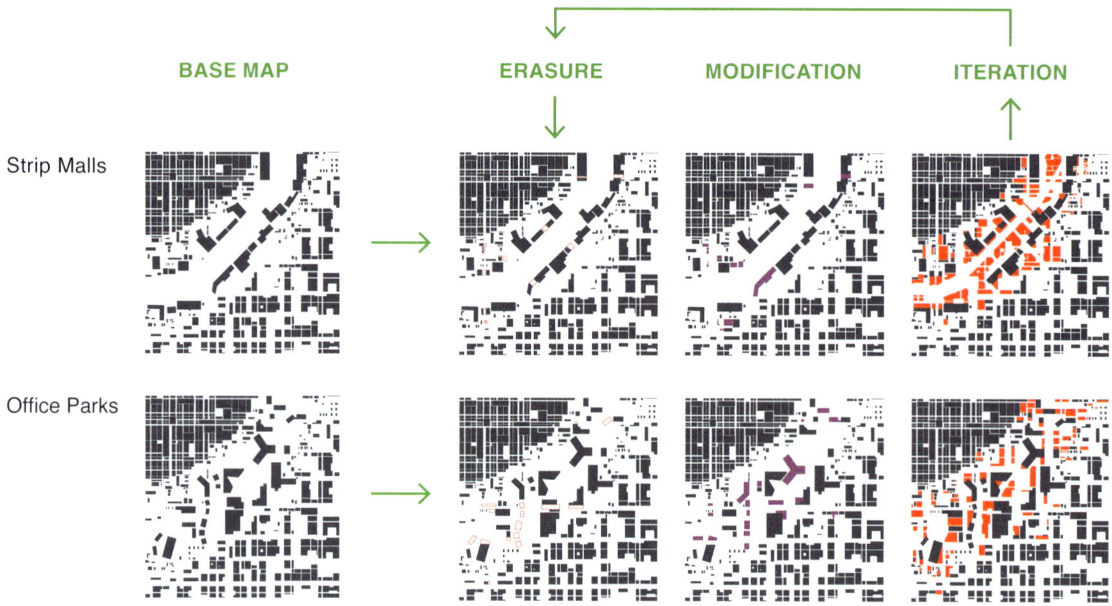

Strip Malls
Less imposing than regional malls, but equally destructive to the metropolitan fabric, the traditional strip mall typically runs parallel to thoroughfares. Each strip mall requires its own parking lot and entrance, thus limiting pedestrian access. Because of their small scale, new buildings and other various uses can occupy oversized parking lots. Over time, a new kind of streetscape can emerge, balancing pedestrian and vehicular needs.

Office Parks
The design of office parks is driven by zoning calculations tied to parking square foot ratios. Consequently, developers try to maximize the size of the buildings and parking area with little regard for the shape of the spaces created. New strategies for reinhabiting office complexes through erasure and modification can create a new kind of urban fabric. Fringe regions in Atlanta and Washington, D.C., are witnessing the transformation of once-suburban office parks into a new kind of urban satellite metropolitanism.

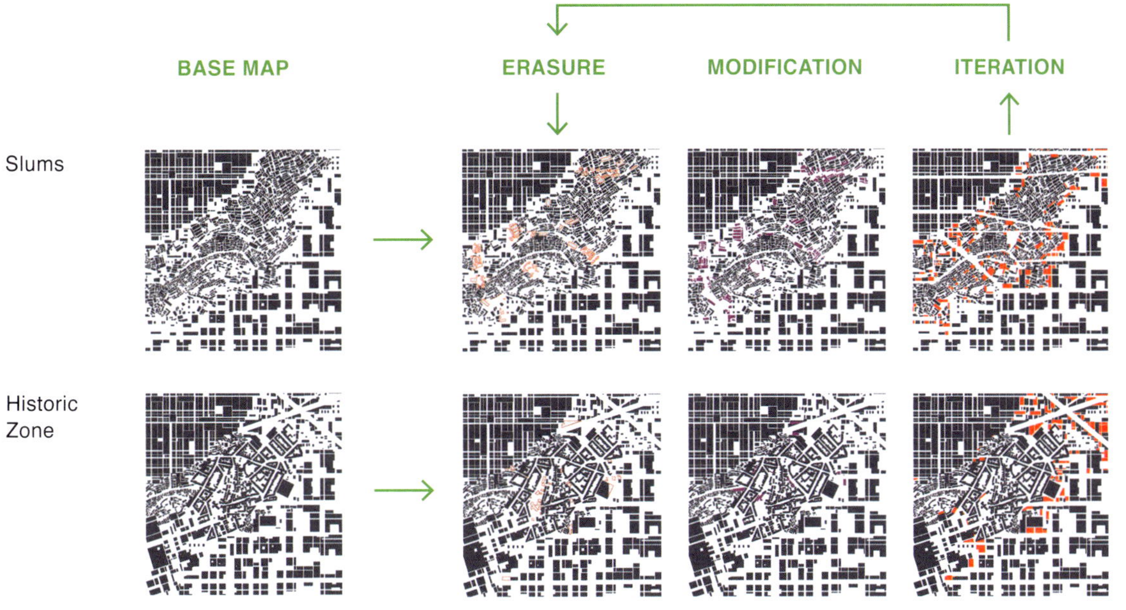

<u>Slums</u>
Slums, the impoverished districts of urban centers large and small, have diverse names: shantytowns, ghettos, banlieues, favelas, even "dumps" or "ratholes." Using found materials, slum housing developments can evolve into full-fledged communities. The challenge is to find ways to integrate services, infrastructure, and public space within these maturing urban regions and neighborhoods. The process of layering infrastructure and services in slums is emerging in Lagos, Nigeria; Mumbai, India; and Rio de Janeiro, Brazil.

<u>Historic Zone</u>
Historic districts should be preserved whenever possible. Their design limits street traffic. Historically significant buildings and delicate development patterns can limit new construction. Yet, new infrastructure systems such as subways, surface buses, and strong pedestrian corridors can help to integrate these historic enclaves within the contemporary districts around them. Such conditions can be seen in Barcelona, Munich, Boston, and Shanghai.

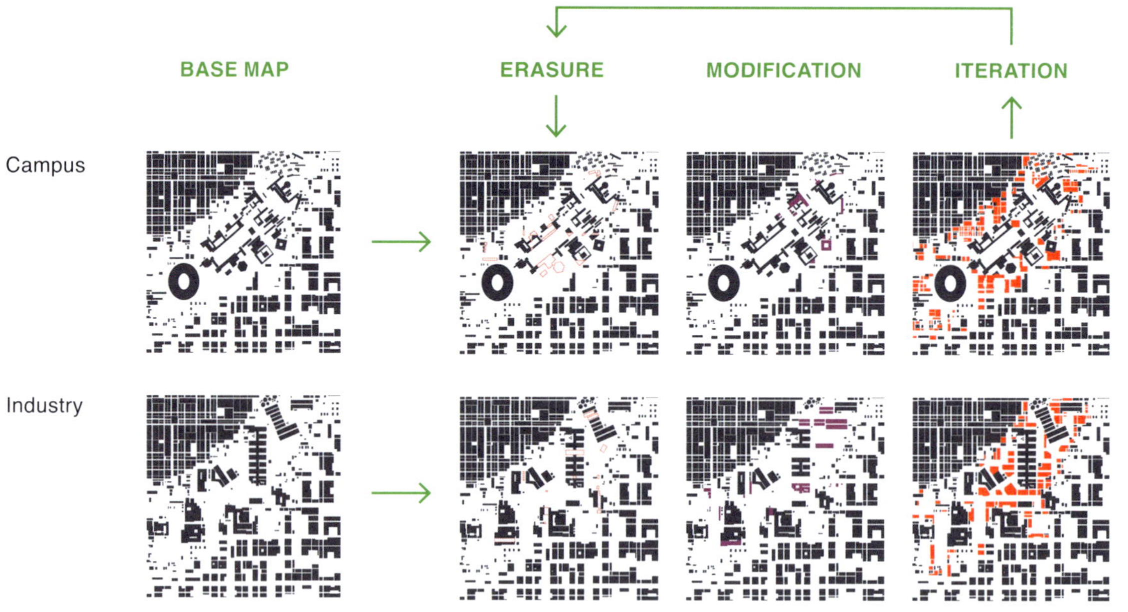

Campus

The relationship between "town" and "gown" has always triggered sensitive conversations, as cities try to balance the needs of a university and the town that supports its services and uses. The campus and its boundaries in a town can be blurred or distinctively and autonomously delineated. Either way, the campus design mindset is useful in re-thinking strategies for transforming the mid-polis. There are so many different campus-town precedents to consider as transferable and replicable models for transforming the mid-polis.

Industry

Finally, an assortment of large-scale, often carbon-intensive manufacturing centers has become a set of opportunities for converting industrial artifacts into revived programs. One of the most impressive conversions is the 798 Art Zone, a mid-polis in Northeast Beijing. Once a busy industrial complex, the Art Zone is now packed with studios and galleries featuring contemporary artworks by some of China's up-and-coming artists. Public space, sprinkled with teahouses and restaurants, creates a unique and culturally engaging spectacle, recalling the past in its preservation of industrial fragments while harnessing youthful creative energy.

Across the globe, in Pittsburgh, Pennsylvania, a dramatic conversion of a large steel mill (Mill 19) today houses robotic and high-tech companies while preserving the complex's unique industrial-era architecture. The most dramatic industrial conversion may be found in the Landschaftspark in Duisburg-Nord in Germany, where a remarkable park is interwoven into the remnants of the once-abandoned industrial facility.

Conclusion

The section above serves as a guide to how to transform underperforming mid-poleis. First and foremost, the underlying defects and challenges presented by a deficient mid-polis need to be compiled, evaluated, and understood. Commonly defined urban analysis tools can be harnessed to determine foundational pathologies. Once defined, a range of transformational strategies can be deployed, including transformation by urban type, building type, infrastructure, and decision-making processes, whether top-down or bottom-up. This book also offers a more specific set of transformational tactics, including operations of erasure, and modification.

Each of these process-oriented tactics can be applied to a range of urban and building typologies found in a specific site, due for transformation. Through an iterative engagement with the site, the desired transformations can be generated over time to fit the evolving needs of a community and mid-polis.

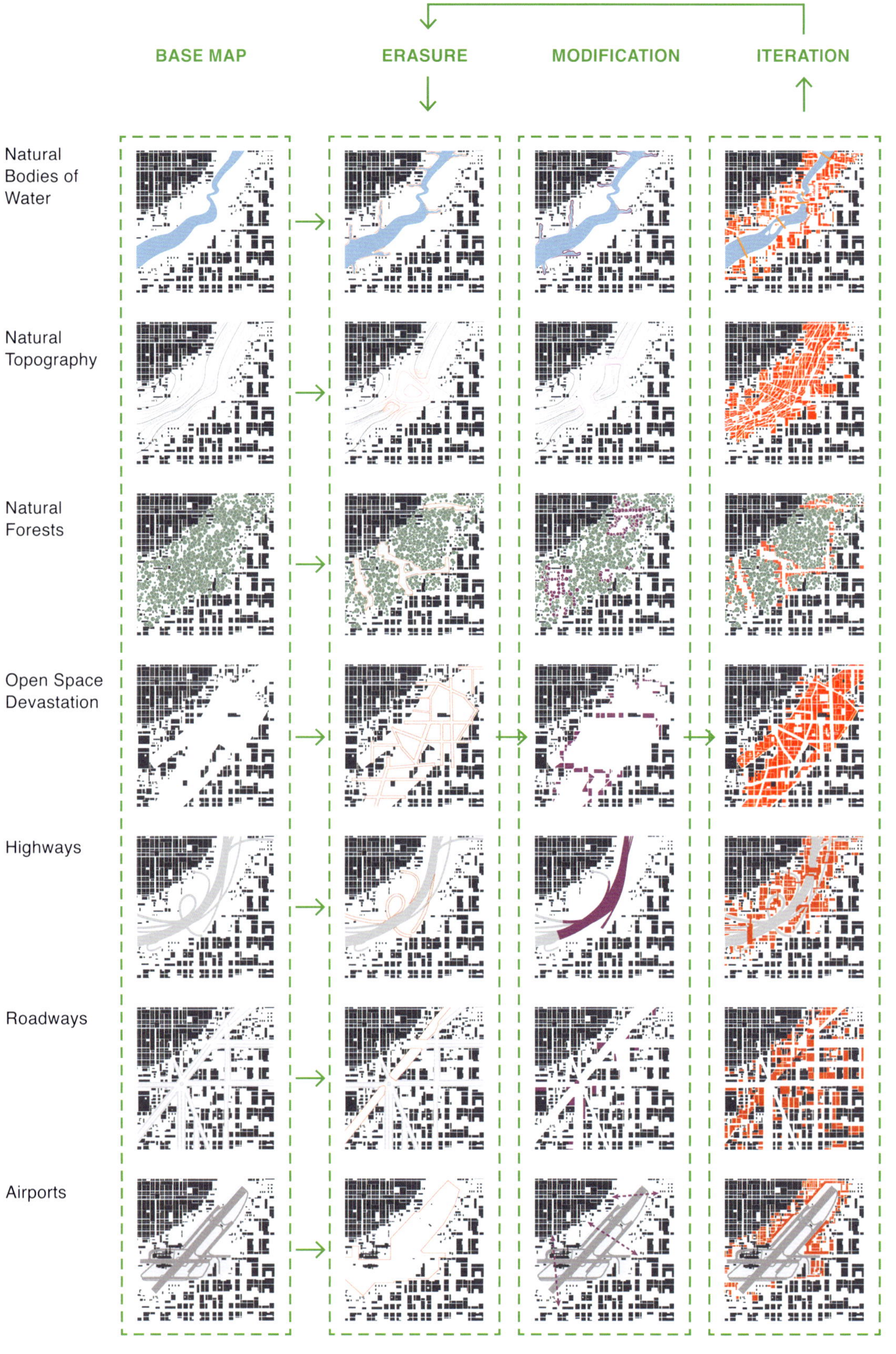
BASE MAP
ERASURE
MODIFICATION
ITERATION
Natural Bodies of Water
Natural Topography
Natural Forests
Open Space Devastation
Highways
Roadways
Airports

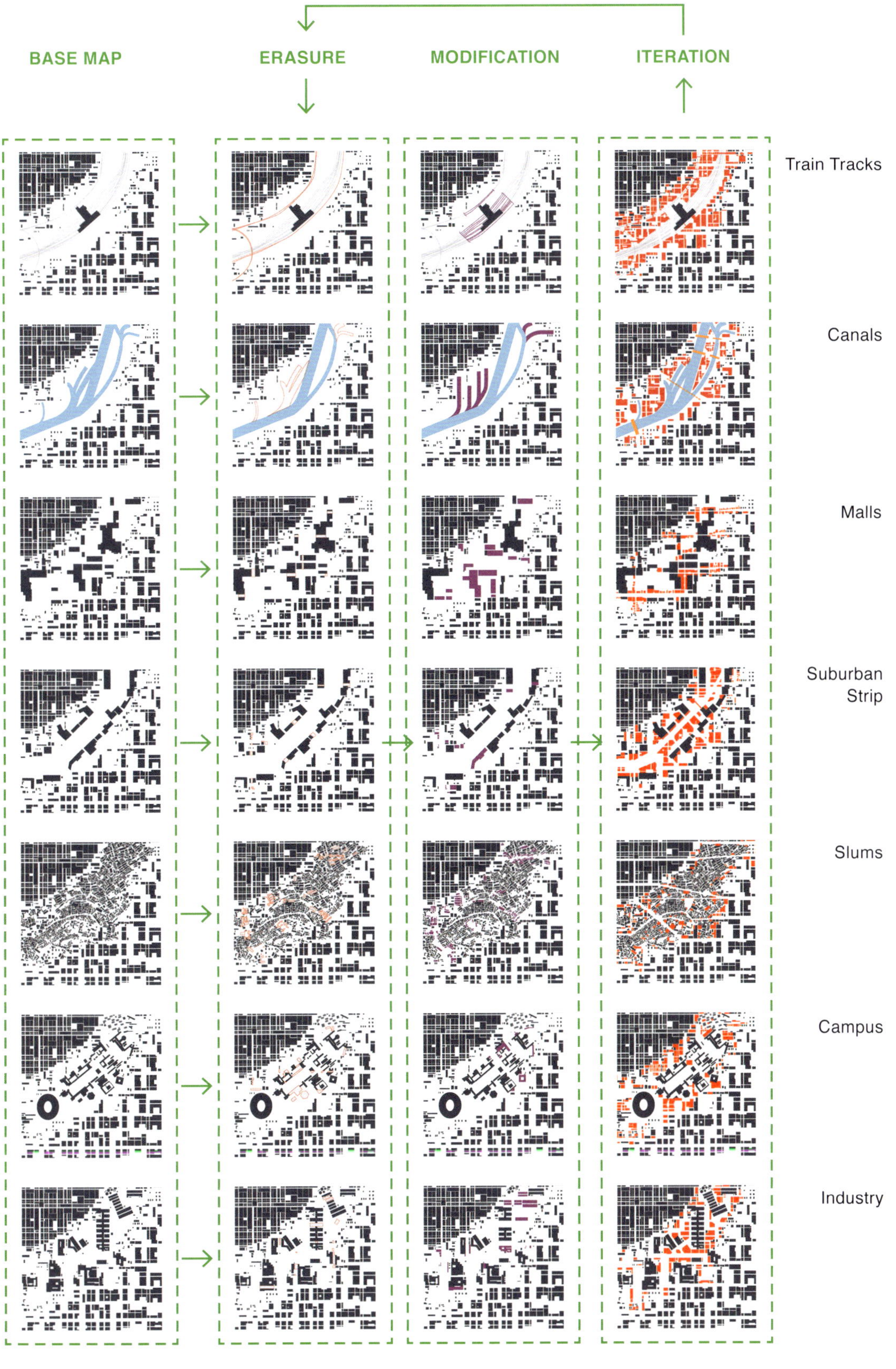
BASE MAP
ERASURE
MODIFICATION
ITERATION
Train Tracks
Canals
Malls
Suburban Strip
Slums
Campus
Industry

The Transforming Territory of North American Suburbs

1.3

The dominant North American "territory" is suburban. The United States is over 80% urbanized, with about a third of its population living in center cities, and over half in suburban municipalities. But what is happening now in terms of urban form and development is a reciprocal process between center cities and their suburbs. Cities are the proliferation of standardized suburban development types such as big-box chain stores, though often built in non-prototypical (i.e., vertical) configurations to adapt to urban morphologies of smaller blocks and higher densities. At the same time, we are experiencing the densification and diversification of nodes and corridors in suburbs, the subject of my research into retrofitting suburbia.

Various dynamics drive suburban retrofitting, and they have only intensified in the wake of the 2008 economic meltdown:

• Combating the contribution of GHG emissions to climate change requires reducing the high ecological footprints of suburban dwellers, which are three times on average those of urbanites, due to frequent driving patterns and energy-inefficient detached dwellings.

• Demographic change in suburbs is leading to a smaller percentage of households with children, primarily due to longer life spans and the aging of the baby-boom generation. Change is also due to the growth of immigrant gateway suburbs, as well as a pronounced rise in suburban poverty. US suburbs are much more diverse than generally assumed.

• The aging of the physical fabric of the "first-suburbs" (the communities built out from the 1940s to the 1960s), especially of cheaply built commercial properties, has produced an overabundance of "underperforming asphalt" in our dramatically over-retailed suburban landscapes.

So, what to do? Ellen Dunham-Jones and I coined the term "incremental metropolitanism" to refer to a polycentric vision that could be advanced by the retrofitting of appropriate sites, both by densifying

by **June Willamson**

Bernard and Anne Spitzer School of Architecture, The City College of New York

and diversifying nodes along transit-served corridors and by de-densifying other failed sites for ecological repair.

We identify three main strategies or approaches for retrofitting, alone or in some combination: (1) re-inhabitation, (2) redevelopment, and (3) re-greening. Regulatory, financing, and other barriers to applying these strategies exist, but they are being systematically addressed in creative ways, especially by committed new urbanists.

Re-inhabitation

The re-inhabitation strategy applies various forms of adaptive reuse or reprogramming of older retail sites, such as strip malls and big-box stores, which can be permanent or temporary. Re-inhabitation often entails a shift from private to public use, such as a branch library or government offices, but it also can engage the entrepreneurial energy of new immigrants and others who open small, community-oriented service businesses. This strategy is now used short-term by leasing vacant storefronts to arts groups or other nonprofits in order to "keep the lights on," such as the ArtSpace initiative at Crestwood Court Mall in St. Louis, Missouri.

Re-development

Retrofitting by redevelopment, or the scrapping and rebuilding of a site, usually results in transition from a single-use, car-dependent configuration to one that is mixed in use, transit-served (or servable) and, often, higher-density. Much of my research concerns urban design solutions for mixed-use redevelopment of large suburban "campus tissue," a morphology of large parcels with multiple buildings, all for a single use, such as shopping malls, garden apartments, and office parks. Redevelopment can introduce a new morphology of urban blocks and streets – an "instant urbanism." The somewhat radical proposition is that the new morphology, once established, can spur an incremental transformation that unfolds over time in a way that the campus tissue could not. It can also support transition to post-carbon modes of transit, such as biking and walking.

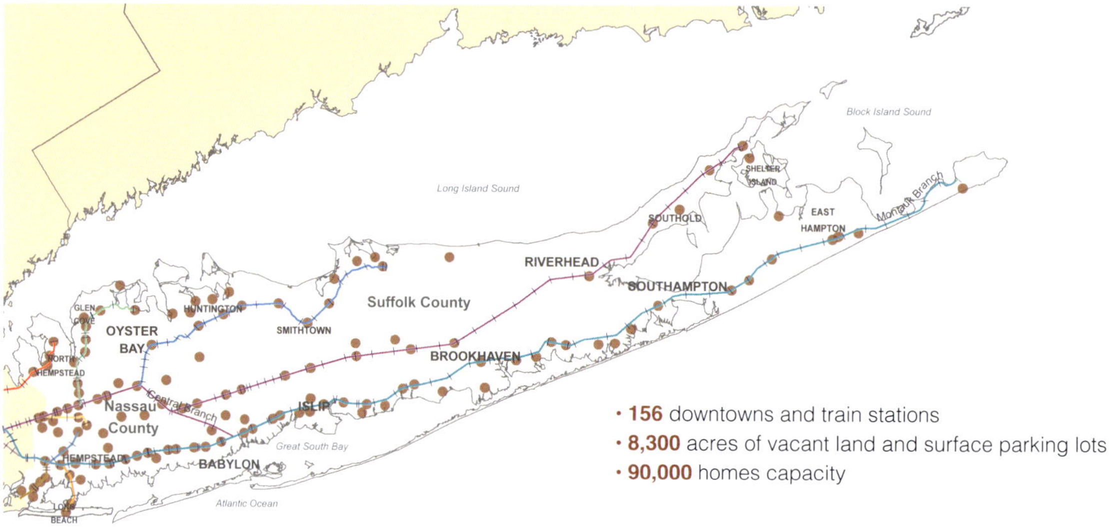

Long Island rail network emanating eastward from New York City © 2010, June Williamson

Re-greening

Re-greening can range from the introduction of small civic spaces, parks and green roofs to large-scale ecological repair of watersheds and wildlife corridors damaged by decades of suburban development in sprawl patterns. The de-densification of poorly located commercially developed sites – a land-banking of sorts – is an important aspect of retrofitting, to be considered alongside the densification of nodes and corridors. The Red Fields to Green Fields initiative, supported by the City Parks Alliance and others, is an example of dramatically scaling this idea up to the level of the Federal Treasury Department, to address something like $3 trillion in commercial real estate loans that will come due in the next five years and threaten the solvency of many regional banks. The idea is to employ land use, or "territory," in the mid-polis to prevent direct taxpayer bailouts. Another form of re-greening is the suburban farming movement, which promotes the conversion of suburban lawns to vegetable gardens and chicken coops. This type of change can also have significant legal hurdles, in the form of Homeowners Association CC&Rs (covenants, codes and restrictions) and restrictive R-1 zoning regulations.

The potential for incremental metropolitanism was demonstrated in the eastern suburbs of New York City, on Long Island, home to almost 3 million suburbanites. I had the honor to organize the 2010 "Build a Better Burb" open-ideas competition for the nonprofit Long Island Index, an organization that commissions "indicator studies" to track the performance of the region according to several metrics: economy, health, education, environment, governance, and communities. The Index commissioned a study of the amount of vacant land and surface parking lots within a half-mile of 156 downtowns and commuter rail stations. They found 8,300 acres, roughly equivalent to the land area of Manhattan south of 50th Street.

The competition (buildabetterburb.org; website now defunct) asked designers to consider bold new uses and forms for this land that might address the many challenges the region is facing as it matures from a booming suburbanization economy. The projects of two dozen finalists illustrated a range of fascinating ideas, suggesting new directions for the next generation of suburban retrofits: using under-capacity commuter and school buses for local freight transport, moving office parks to downtowns and converting the land to intensive organic farms, intensifying the construction of accessory dwelling units, reintroducing the shop-house typology, sequestering carbon in highway verges and just about everywhere else, chopping up malls and putting housing on top, expanding biking, and figuring out clever bottom-up ways to pay for it all.

REINHABITATION Lake Grove Village, Oregon

REDEVELOPMENT Wyandanch Rising, New York

REGREENING Meriden Green, Connecticut

These sequences of aerial photographs document suburban retrofits of three sites. (Top) Lake Grove Village, the reinhabitation of a strip shopping center near Portland, Oregon, illustrates the urban design tactic of subtracting narrow passages to break up the building mass, add access to the rear, and provide shared area for "third place" sociability. (Center) Wyandanch Rising, in the Town of Babylon on Long Island, New York, is gradually infilling depaved commuter parking lots and industrial brownfield sites adjacent to a newly rebuilt train station with deeply affordable new housing and community amenity spaces. (Bottom) Before regreening, the urban renewal-era Meriden Hub mall sat squat in a parking lot. The mall was demolished, the brook daylit, and the land regraded into a stormwater park, a sophisticated piece of green infrastructure, called Meriden Green, surrounded with new and relocated subsidized housing. Source: Diagram by June Williamson, 2024.

Deciphering the Ambiguity 1.4

Toward a More Efficient Mobility Within the Mid-Polis

Our contemporary metropolitan areas are perpetually transforming into more complex organisms. As a result, the ambiguous landscape between the city's traditional core and its suburbs is becoming a domain that accommodates a network of distribution and exchange of capital, human, and material resources between the inner urban condition and its outer fringes. The mid-polis, once the vague terrain accommodating singular vehicular links and portals of transmission between the urban core and the low-density residential suburbs, is morphing into a complex network of connections that expand the reach of the core, offering a multiplicity of routes for transferring resources from the core to the fringes, and vice versa. Under such circumstances, with the multiplication of choices, concerns about optimizing the circulation of resources are raised:

• What is the most efficient way of getting from point A to point B – one being in the city's core, the other in its suburbs – once more than one route becomes available to take?

• Which route offers the path of minimum resistance in terms of traffic?

• Which route is the most ecologically responsible one when it comes to leaving a carbon footprint while distributing material resources within the ever-expanding urban terrain?

• With the intensification of the mid-polis condition, what are the new points in space that gain centrality?

• Are we witnessing the emergence of a new series of points of interest within the mid-polis, new urban centers, so to speak?

• Or is the mid-polis's role in the urban condition limited to a transition zone, a connection for the transference of capital, material and human resources between the urban core and the suburban fringes?

In discerning the dynamics of the contemporary metropolitan area, conventional tools fall short in deciphering the complexity of its logics of operation.

by **Nashid Nabian and Carlo Ratti**

MIT Senseable City Lab

We need new tools for understanding the urban condition and its multifaceted dynamics. A true understanding would not only allow for well-informed decisions at the level of those who manage the city within the top-down, hierarchical structure that institutions provide, but could also be shared by the residents to create a feedback loop, offering new possibilities for optimizing spatial practices in a bottom-up approach: what is sensed and deciphered about the city would be fed back to its residents to provide them with real-time information, based on which they could make well-informed decisions.

The questions to be answered here are:

• What can be sensed about the urban condition?

• What are the different mechanisms for delivering this information back to those who inhabit the city?

These questions fall under the more general research field of urban informatics. We deduce conclusions about various matters, including the cities we inhabit, based on recognizing certain patterns of information, by looking at data generated as a by-product of their internal or external operations. Occasionally, the recognized patterns reveal unexpected aspects of the phenomena we try to decode. In reality, the contemporary city is the cradle of information about the various spatial-temporal dynamics it contains, and recognizing patterns in such information would reveal aspects of urban life that are invisible at first glance, or even unexpected.

• How can we sense a city?

• How can we collect information about it?

• How can we experience the space of urbanity through revealing patterns that are not initially visible, but recognized by investigating the collected information?

• Finally, how can such temporal processes – that is, the recognized patterns – become available to inhabitants?

Figure 1
Concept diagram for *viral* sensing

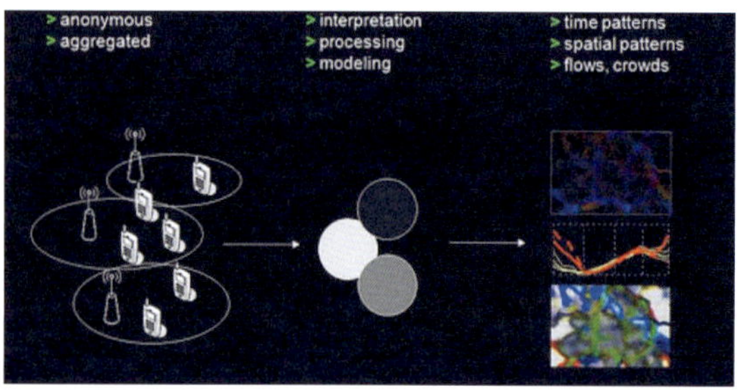

Figure 2
Diagram of workflow for *viral* sensing project that taps into used data from cellular networks, such as the *Current City* project

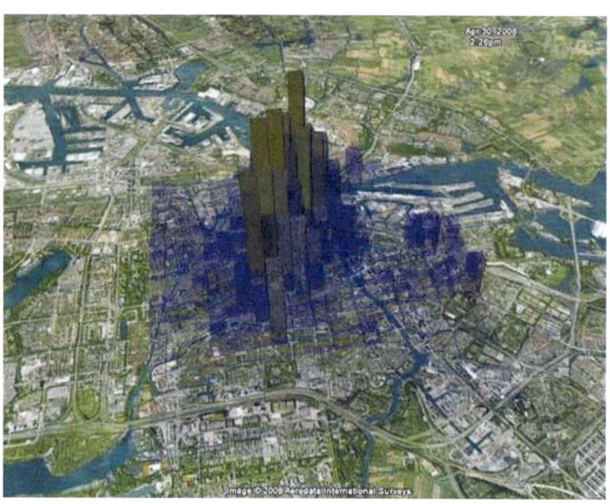

Figure 3
Current Amsterdam project: A vision of Amsterdam during the national festivity of Queen´s Day 2008. The analysis of mobile phone traffic reveals people´s presence and movement

To this end, we would like to propose three different, yet categorically connected, urban sensing practices that would provide both citizens and urban practitioners with a new understanding of how metropolitan areas perform, particularly in terms of the efficient use of mobility networks and infrastructures for the distribution of material and human resources. These approaches utilize research development projects at MIT Senseable City Lab, a research initiative at Massachusetts Institute of Technology Department of Urban Planning that focuses on situated technologies and their application to architecture and urban practices.

One approach is to leverage existing systems that have been developed for other reasons but can function as a source of information about how our cities operate. A great example is the cellphone network, and how usage analysis can provide hints about the distribution of a cellphone-using crowd within the city. Called *crowdspotting*, this practice can yield useful information about land use and the temporal patterns in which inhabitants use their city.[1] In the context of urban informatics, we define this as *viral* sensing, since the computational algorithms of such sensing practices install themselves on the digital networks that already augment cities, much as a virus settles in an already operational environment within another organism in order to support its internal bio-processes. The premise of such sensing practices is that the contemporary subject involuntarily leaves digital traces on various networks that are juxtaposed over urban areas every time a credit card is used, a text message or email is sent, an outgoing search-engine query is submitted, a phone call is made, a social profile is updated, a photo is uploaded or tagged on a network, or a purchase is made on a major online store's web-site. Concurrently, an entry with the time and location of any of these actions is added to a dataset on a central server, administered and maintained by the organizational entity providing the platform for these and hundreds of other day-to-day operations. Once the datasets are spatially and temporally attached to entities and phenomena

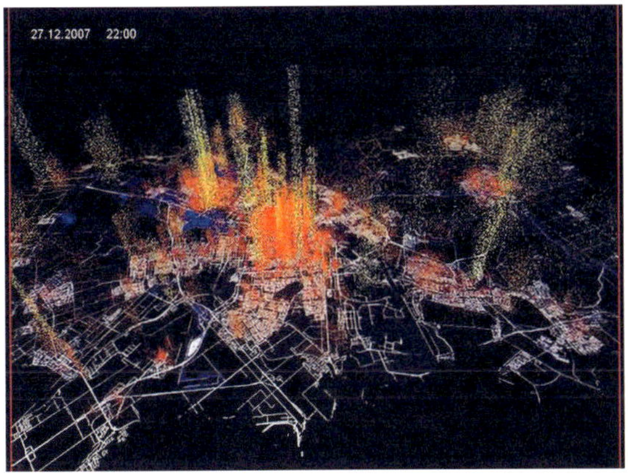

Figure 4
Current Amsterdam project: text messaging activity at 22:00 hours (10 pm) four days before New Year's Eve 2007 in Amsterdam

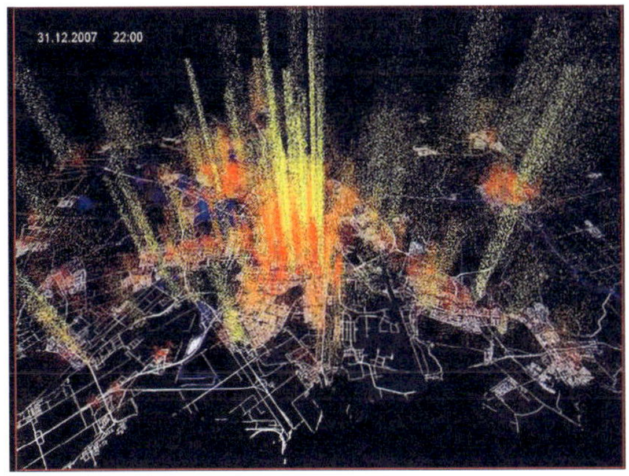

Figure 5
Current Amsterdam project: text messaging activity at 22:00 hours (10 pm) on New Year's Eve 2007 in Amsterdam

in the physical terrain, the urban landscapes that accommodate these traces are transformed into info-scapes. An info-scape, in this sense, is a digital terrain both temporally and spatially associated with the physical terrain. (Fig. 1)

An example of implemented *viral* sensing projects is The **Current City** project (Current Amsterdam and Real-time Rome)[2]. The **Current City** project looks at how positions and activities of mobile phones can be used to "sense" people's presence. When aggregated at the highest possible level, mobile location data do not impinge upon the privacy of individuals, but can return important information about the concentration and relative weights of human activities in the urban environment, as well as flows and patterns of city use. Visualizations and analyses of such data can be obtained in as close to real-time as possible. Such visualizations allow us to answer various questions regarding the dynamics of a city:

- How many people are in a given area?

- Where is traffic piling up?

- What percentage of people have left the critical area?

- What is the current demand for public transportation?

- How many people will look at that billboard?

- What is the pattern of inflow and outflow of people from the city?

- What's the hottest spot in town right now?

- Finally, does the mid-polis activity equal or even supersede the urban core?

(Fig. 2-8)

Another example of executed network projects is **Borderline**, which developed a novel, fine-grained approach to regional delineation, based on analysis of networks of billions of individual human transactions in the United Kingdom. Given a geographical area and some measure of the strength of links among its inhabitants, **Borderline** shows how to partition the area into smaller, non-overlapping regions while minimizing the disruption to each person's links. In **Borderline** we tested our method on the largest non-Internet human network, inferred from a large telecommunications database in Great Britain. Our partitioning algorithm yields geographically cohesive regions that correspond remarkably well with administrative regions, while unveiling unexpected spatial structures that had previously only been hypothesized in the literature. We also quantify the effects of partitioning, showing, for instance, that

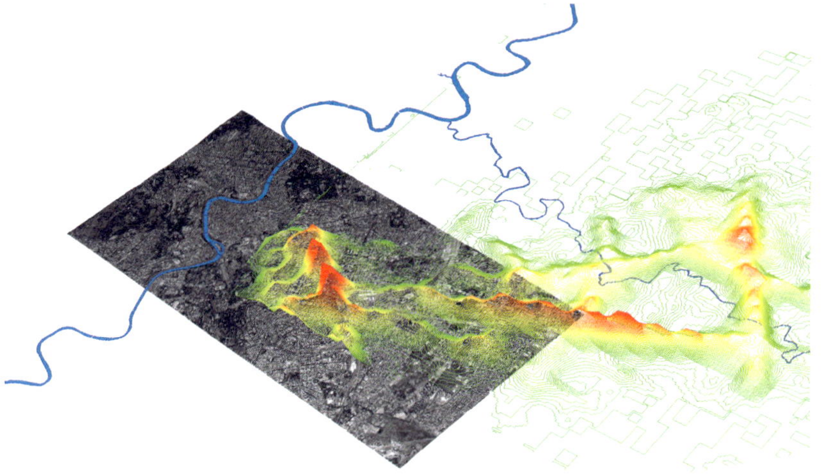

Figure 6
Real-Time Rome project: Aggregate picture of data transferred through the Telecom Italia cellphone network

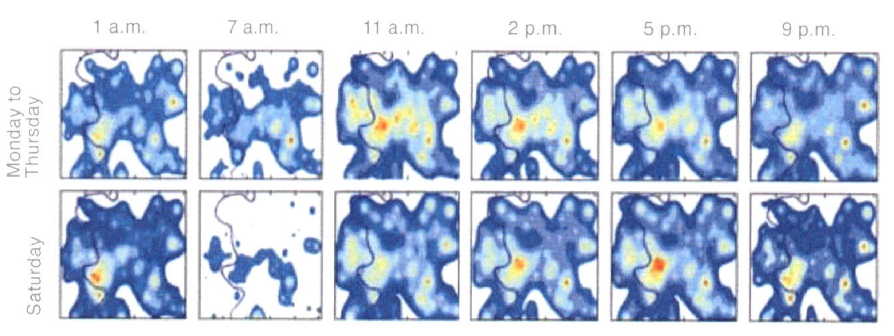

Figure 7
Real-Time Rome project: Aggregate picture of cellphone-use signatures used to draw land-use maps from mobile usage patterns that resemble the actual land-use map of Rome

Figure 8
Real-Time Rome project: Illustration mapping the mean velocity and dominant direction of mobile phone users on the Telecom Italia Network

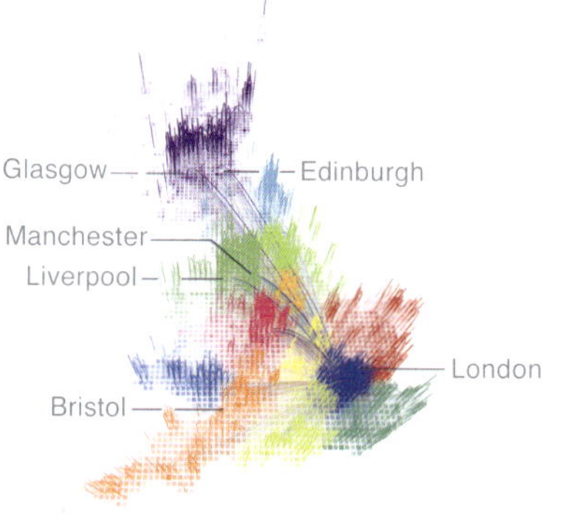

Figure 9
Borderline project: The geography of talk in Great Britain

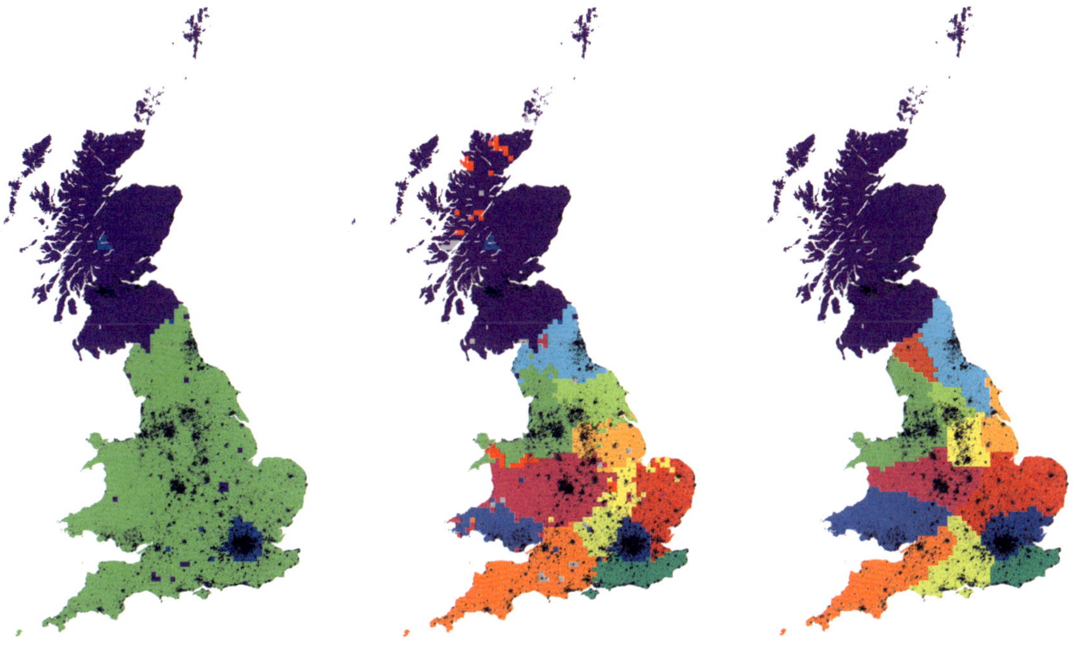

Figure 10
Borderline project: The core regions of Britain, obtained by combining the output from several modularity optimization methods

the effects of a possible secession of Wales from Great Britain would be twice as disruptive for the human network as a secession of Scotland from the United Kingdom would. (Fig. 9 and 10)

The second approach is to use customized sensor networks, comprising centrally managed sensing agents embedded within the fabric of the city, to decode various urban flows. To this effect, the sensors operate as smart dust saturating the space of urbanity, extracting large amounts of data about the processes contained within the built environment and constructed spaces, and channeling these data to a central control and command mechanism. From there, these data are aggregated, managed, and used as the basis for how the monitored space of the city should be regulated and actuated. In urban-sensing mechanisms that operate based on networks with central control and command structure, with algorithms that allow for the context-sensitive interpretation of the information transmitted to the database, we arrive at spatial scenarios in which entire geographic regions are digitally augmented by the ubiquity of these sensor/transmitter devices. In the extreme version of this scenario, one can envision a world in which any object is capable of sensing its context and reporting it back to a central data-management facility, where its identity, its real-time location, and its contextual state are cross-referenced, stored, and managed computationally. (Fig. 11)

An example of implemented sensor network projects is the **Trash Track** project.[3] The project consists of digitally enhanced tags that were attached to objects and could report their location to an Internet backbone infrastructure via the cellular network. **Trash Track** made use of these location-reporting tags to track urban disposal and study the efficiency of the urban waste-removal chain. The platform allowed designers and planners to analyze the acquired data and make well-informed high-level decisions about how the given constructed landscape is managed.

Therefore, a multiplicity of questions about the dynamics of the urban removal chain could be addressed empirically: Is our removal chain efficient? Is hazardous waste managed properly? Or are there loopholes in our system that need to be taken care of? Is the recycled waste really recycled, or does it end up in dumps? The **Trash Track** system can have a great impact on the nature of the perceptual relationship a city or region develops with its waste-disposal habits. (Fig. 12-14)

Finally, in the third approach we consider more grassroots, bottom-up systems for sensing the dynamics of cities based on decoding the voluntary traces that Internet users leave behind. This presents a contrast to *viral* sensing, where the involuntary digital footprints of contemporary urbanites are the basis for making sense of city dynamics, and sensor networks employ a top-down architecture linked to a central database. User-generated content sharing platforms allow everybody to report his or her experience to others in real-time, and in a multi-modal, high resolution format. This leads to the possibility of thinking of each urbanite as a human sensor, an agent for sensing and reporting on his or her individual experience through tapping into data generated by user-contributed content on these platforms. Hence, we arrive at the third possibility of urban sensing: *crowdsourcing.*[4]
(Fig. 15)

An example of implemented *crowdsourcing* projects is **Los Ojos del Mundo/The World's Eyes.**[5] The project focuses on revealing the dynamic of civic landscapes, as viewed and collaboratively reported by their inhabitants. For example, the attractiveness and popularity of places and events are revealed by visualizing the density of user-generated data in particular, the photographs tagged with information about their location and time uploaded by online photo-sharing sites. Then, user-generated electronic trails based on the sequences of photographs are used to reveal the presence and movement of visitors in a city. Such data visualizations that geo-localize the content generated by the user's experience of a given urbanity reveal how occupants interpret their cities, e.g., which locations are considered more or less important, and what the eyes of the people there capture. (Fig. 16 and 17)

To understand the mid-polis, and to arrive at a more efficient connection between the city's core and fringes, we need to situate it within the larger context of the polis itself, discerning how today's cities are inhabited and experienced by contemporary urbanites. Deciphering the ambiguities of the urban condition lets us transform matters of concern about the efficient management of our cities and responsible citizenship into matters of fact – for example, how to maintain a symbiotic relationship between the city and its ecological context when it comes to decisions about regulating the traffic of people and goods, material, and capital. Perhaps the best way to approach the emerging condition of the mid-polis is to examine how new tools offered by digital and telecommunications technologies arrive at a real-time urbanism, a perpetual feedback loop between urban dynamics and citizens with access to a holistic view of how their cities perform in real-time, and how individual decisions can affect the city's performance on a larger scale.

Figure 11
Concept diagram for sensor networks

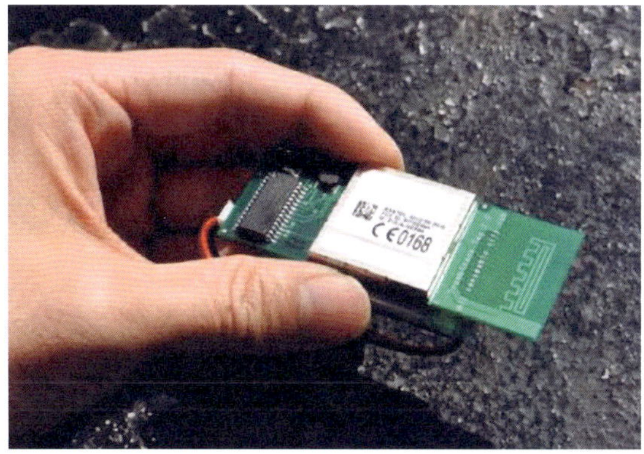

Figure 12
Trash Track project: Custom designed electronic tag

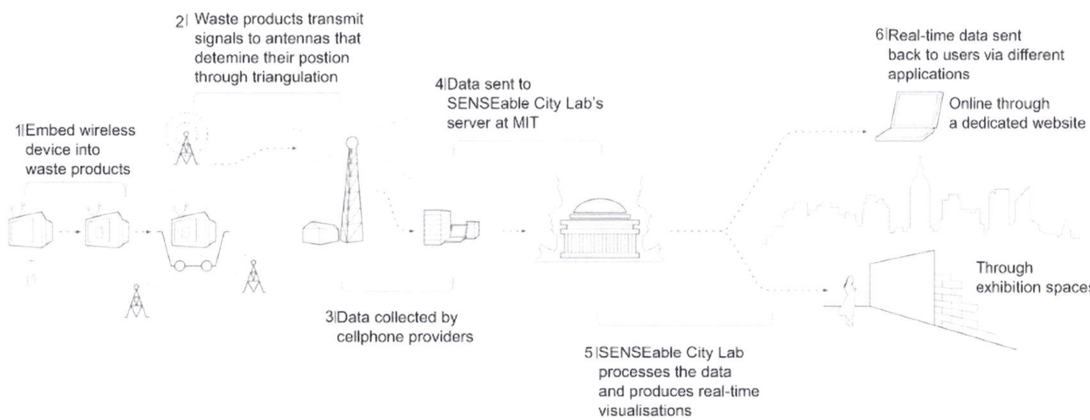

Figure 13
Trash Track project: Diagram illustrating how the trash tag periodically measures its location and reports those data to the server via the cellular network

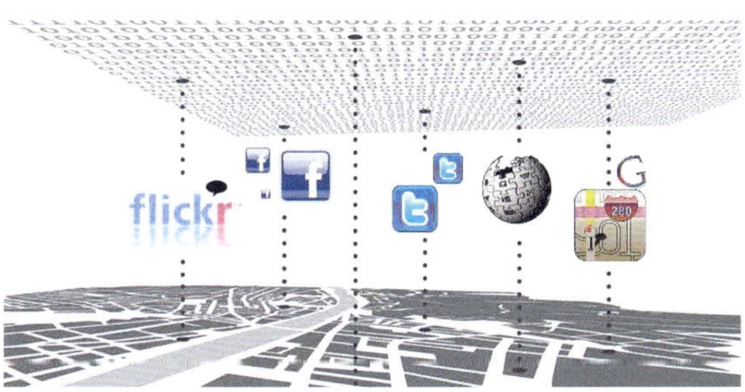

Figure 15
Concept diagram for *crowdsourcing*

Figure 14
Trash Track project: Sample visualization tracking a tagged aluminum can as it travels through the city's garbage collection network. (Right)

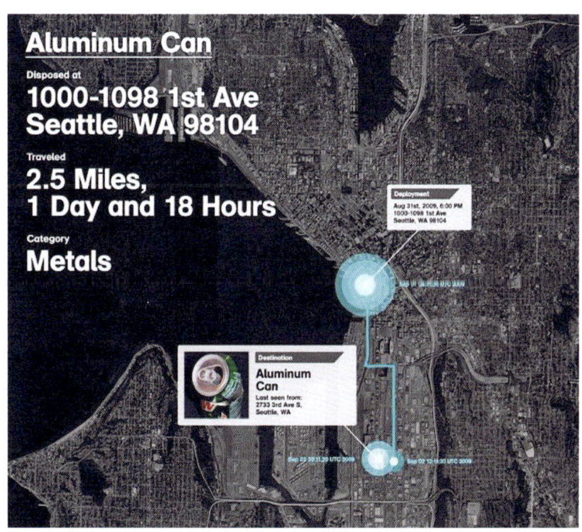

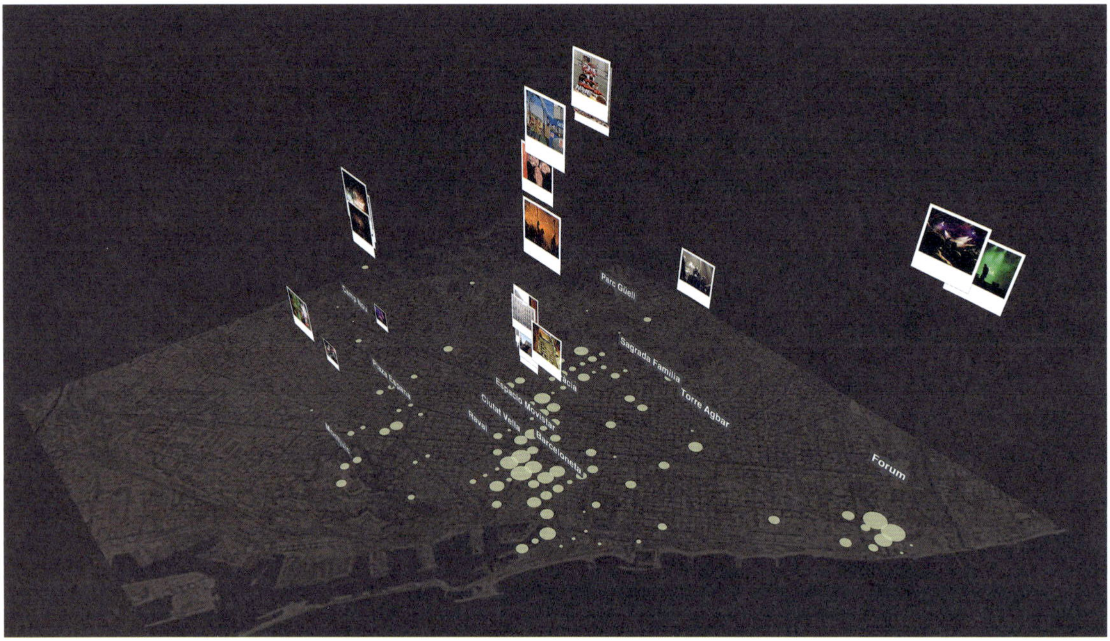

Figure 16
Los Ojos del Mundo/The World's Eyes project: An animation of the photos geo-tagged to different neighborhoods of Barcelona with descriptive tags that relate to "partying" in the summer of 2007, shows that Barcelona's Old Town (Ciutat Vella) is where one goes to have fun. Image by MIT Senseable City Lab: The World's Eyes (2007)

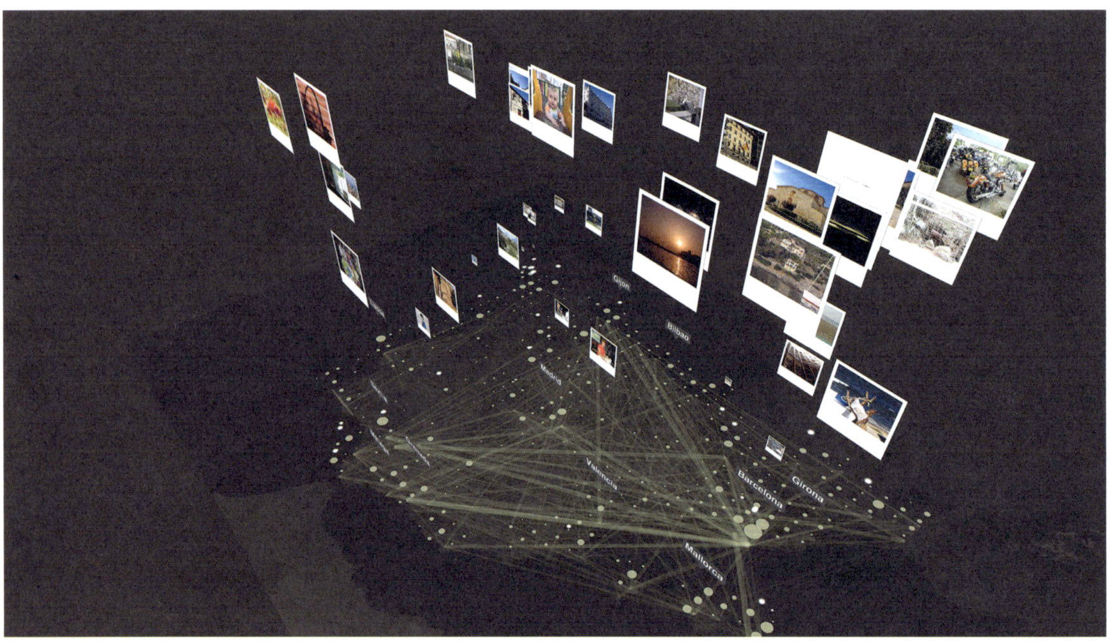

Figure 17
Los Ojos del Mundo/The World's Eyes project: Another visualization in the same set looks at how Spain is photographed by tourists over the course of one year. The photos overlap in certain locations and expose places that attract the photographer's gaze. In other locations the absence of images is eye-catching, revealing the more introverted parts of Spain. Image by MIT Senseable City Lab: The World's Eyes (2007)

Notes

[1] Calabrese, Francesco, Francisco C. Pereira, Giusy Di Lorenzo, L. Liu, and Carlo Ratti. *"The Geography of Taste: Analyzing Cell-phone Mobility and Social Events."* In Proceedings of the 8th International Conference on Pervasive Computing, 2010.

[2] Project credits are as follows: Current City Organization: Euro Beinat: Co-Founder, Director I Filippo Dal Fiore: Co-Founder, Director I Bartosz Hawelka: Chief Data Specialist I Richard Duivenvoorde-Webmapping: Senior Consultant I Paolo Santoro: Server and Data model Specialist I Karolina Stanislawska: Web Client Specialist I Joao Oliveirinha: Web 2.0 Consultant I Natalia Oprowska: Graphics Consultant I Pavlas Kazakopoulos: Chief Science Officer MIT Senseable City Lab/ Aaron Koblin: Visualizations, Aaronkoblin.com I Francesco Calabrese I Assaf Biderman I Carlo Ratti I Andrea Vaccari I John Steenbruggen-Rijkswaterstaat I With the financial support of: the Dutch Ministry of Transport, Public Works and Water Management (Rijkswaterstaat): WnT (Wegen naar de Toekomst) and WINN (Water Innovatie Bron) Politic Amsterdaml In collaboration with: KPN Mobile.

[3] Project credits, MIT Senseable City Lab: Carlo Ratti: Director I Assaf Bidennan: Assoc. Director I Dietmar Offenhuber: Team Leader I Eugenio Morello: Team Leader I Musstanser Tinauli: Team Leader I Kristian Kloeck!: Team Leader I Lewis Girod: Engineering I Jennifer Dunnam / E Roon Kang I Kevin Nattinger I Avid Boustani I David Lee Programming I Alan Anderson I Clio Andris I Carnaven Chiu I Chris Chung I Lorenzo Davolli I Kathryn Dineen I Natalia Duque Ciceri I Samantha Earl I Sarabjit Kaur I Sarah Neilson I Giovanni de Niederhausem I Jill Passano I Elizabeth Ramaccia I Renato Rinaldi I Francisca Rojas I Luis Sirota I Malima Wolf I Annin Linke: Video.

[4] Pereira, Francisco C., Andrea Vaccari, Fabien Giardin, Carnaven Chiu, and Carlo Ratti. *"Crowdsensing in the Web: Analyzing the Citizens' Experience in the Urban Space."* Senseable City Lab, MIT, USA, n.d.

[5] Project credits, MIT Senseable City Lab: Carlo Ratti: Lab director I AssafBidermann: Associate Director I Fabien Girardin: Project Leader I David Lu: Visual Designer I Andrea Vaccari: Data mining. Universitat Pompeu Fabra: Ernesto Arroyo: Interaction designer.

Strategies for Designing our Green-Built Environment 1.5

We are all only too aware of the numerous pressing global social issues that need to be addressed. These include addressing abject poverty; providing clean water, adequate food and enclosures, and proper sanitation; and so forth. But ultimately if we do not have a clean environment such as clean air, clean water and clean land, all of those other pressing global social issues become even more difficult and costly to resolve. Thus saving our environment has to be the most vital issue that humankind must address today, feeding into our fears that this millennium may be our last.

For the designer, the compelling question is: How do we design for a sustainable future? Globally, businesses and industries face similar concerns about seeking to understand the environmental consequences of their functions and processes, to envision what these might be if sustainable, and to take action to realize this vision with comprehensive, ecologically benign strategies, with new business models and new production systems, materials, and processes. More than these, our human society must change to a sustainable way of life. We need to change how we live, behave, work, create, eat, learn, move about.

We would be mistaken to regard green design as simply about eco-engineering. These engineering systems are indeed an important part of green design (see "gray ecoinfrastructure" below), giving us an acceptable level of comfort that is sustainable, while such technologies continue to rapidly develop and advance toward greener, cleaner engineering solutions for our built environment. However, it must be clear that eco-engineering is not the only consideration in green design.

Nor is green design just about rating systems (LEED, BREEAM, carbon profiling, etc.). These are certainly useful checklists and guidelines but are not comprehensive. They are useful as partial tick-lists of reminders of some of the key items to consider in green design or for comparing buildings and masterplans using a common standard. They have also been useful in proselytizing green design to a wider audience. However, by not being

by **Ken Yeang**

(Dr.), FAIA (Hon), DMPN (Malaysia), PhD (Cantab), AADipl (UK), APAM, FSIA, RIBA, ARAIA (Hon), FRIAS (Hon)

T.R. Hamzah & Yeang Sdn Bhd

Completed Fusionopolis Complex - Northwest of Downtown Singapore

comprehensive and ecologically holistic (an aspect crucial in ecodesign), many designers who achieved the highest LEED rating (such as platinum) would ask: What's next? Where do we go from here?

Clearly, green design has entered the mainstream of architecture. Ask any architect today about green design, and you will find the same pitch about the use of renewable energy systems (photovoltaics, wind generators, etc.), compliance to accreditation systems, carbon profiling, planning as new urbanism, etc. We need to question whether this is all there is to green design. The contention here is: achieving effective green design is much more than the above, and green design is not as easy as it has been contended. It is complex. While it is still incomplete, a number of design strategies can be adopted in combination to arrive as close as we can to the goal of achieving a state of stasis between our built environment and the natural environment.

Fusionopolis green roof,
© 2009 T.R. Hamzah & Yeang Sdn. Bhd.

I. Four Strands of Ecoinfrastructures

The first design strategy is to view green design in terms of weaving four strands of ecoinfrastructures, color-coded here as follows:

• the "gray" (the engineering infrastructure being the eco-sustainable cleantech engineering systems and utilities);

• the "blue" (water management and the closing of the water cycle by design with sustainable drainage);

• the "green" (the green ecoinfrastructure, or nature's own utilities which must be linked); and

• the "red" (our human-built systems, spaces, hardscapes, society, legislative and regulatory systems).

Green design is the seamless and benign blending of all of these four sets of ecoinfrastructures into a system. This concept provides a platform for green design. Like the factors in DNA (by Crick and Watson), which reduces a complex concept into four simple sets of instructions, these four sets of ecoinfrastructures and their integration provide the integrative bases for green design and planning the blending of all four sets of infrastructures into a system.

Fusionopolis green roof,
© 2009 T.R. Hamzah & Yeang Sdn. Bhd.

Green Ecoinfrastructure

Green ecoinfrastructure is vital to every design and master plan. It parallels the usual gray urban infrastructure of roads, drainage systems, and utilities. This green ecoinfrastructure is nature's utilities. It is the interconnected network of natural areas and other open green spaces within the biome that conserves natural ecosystem values and clean air and water. It also enables the area to flourish as a natural habitat for a wide range of wildlife besides delivering a wide array of benefits to humans and the natural world alike, such as providing habitats linked across the landscape that permit fauna (such as birds and animals) to move freely. This ecoinfrastructure is nature's functioning infrastructure (equivalent to our human-made engineering infrastructures, designated here as gray, blue, and red ecoinfrastructures), and, in addition to providing cleaner water and enhancing water supplies, it can also result in some, if not all, of the following outcomes: cleaner air; a reduction in heat-island effect in urban areas; a moderation in the effects of climate change; increased energy efficiency; and the protection of source water.

Incorporating an ecoinfrastructure is thus vital to any ecomasterplanning endeavor. Without it, no matter how clever or advanced the eco-engineering systems are, the design or master plan remains simply a work of engineering, and can in no way be called an ecological master plan nor, in the case of larger developments, an ecocity.

These linear flora and fauna corridors connect existing green spaces and larger green areas within their locality and to the landscape of the hinterland, and can create new larger habitats in their own right, perhaps in the form of newly linked existing woodland belts or wetlands, or existing landscape features (such as overgrown railway lines, hedges and waterways). Any new green infrastructure must also clearly complement and enhance the natural functions of what is already there in the landscape.

In the master-planning process, the designer identifies existing green corridors, routes and green areas, and possible new routes and linkages for creating new connections in the landscape. At this point additional green functional landscape elements or zones can also be integrated, such as linking to existing waterways that also provide such ecological services as drainage to attenuate flooding.

This ecoinfrastructure takes precedence over the engineering ecoinfrastructure in the master plan. By creating, improving and rehabilitating ecological connectivity of the immediate environment, the ecoinfrastructure turns human intervention in the landscape from a negative into a positive. Its environmental benefits and values are as a green armature and framework for natural systems and functions that are ecologically fundamental to the viability of the locality's plant and animal species and their habitats, such as healthy soils, water and air. It reverses the fragmentation of natural habitats (as a consequence of urban sprawl and transportation routes, etc.) and encourages increases in biodiversity to restore functioning ecosystems while providing the fabric for sustainable living, and safeguarding and enhancing natural features.

This endeavor by design to connect the landscape must extend to the built form both horizontally and vertically. An obvious demonstration of horizontal connectivity is the provision of ecological corridors and links in regional and local planning that are crucial for making urban patterns more biologically viable. Connectivity over impervious surfaces and roads can be achieved by using ecological bridges, undercrofts and ramps. Besides improved horizontal connectivity and ecological nexus, vertical connectivity with buildings is also necessary, since most buildings are not single-story but multistory. Design must extend the ecological corridors vertically upward, with the ecoinfrastructure traversing a building from the foundations and landscape at the ground to create habitats on the walls, terraces and rooftops.

Gray Ecoinfrastructure

Gray infrastructure is the usual urban engineering infrastructure, such as roads, drains, sewerage, water reticulation, telecommunications, and energy and electric power distribution systems. We need not be prescriptive of any specific engineering system, but must require these systems to be clean technologies of low-embodied energy and carbon-neutrality as much as possible while integrating with the green infrastructure, rather than vice-versa.

Blue Ecoinfrastructure

Parallel to the ecological infrastructure is the water infrastructure (the blue ecoinfrastructure), where the water cycle should be managed to close the loop. This, however, is not always possible in locations with low rainfall. Rainfall must be harvested, and water must be recycled. The surface water from rain must be retained within the site and returned to the land for recharging of groundwater and aquifers by means of filtration beds, pervious roadways and built surfaces, retention ponds, and bioswales. Water used within the built environment (both gray and black water) must be reused sustainably as much as possible.

Site planning must consider the site's natural drainage patterns and provide surface-water management such that rainfall remains within the locality and is not drained away into water bodies, which is then lost. Combined with the green ecoinfrastructure, stormwater management enables the natural processes to infiltrate, evaporate and transpire, or capture and use stormwater on or near the site where it falls, while potentially generating other environmental benefits.

Waterways should not be culverted or deculverted as engineered waterways, but should be replaced with the introduction of wetlands and buffer strips of ecologically functional meadows and woodland habitats. Sealed surfaces can reduce soil moisture and leave low-lying areas susceptible to flooding from excessive run-off. Wetland greenways must be designed as sustainable drainage systems to provide ecological services. Green buffers can be used together with linear green spaces to maximize their habitat potential.

Ecodesign must create sustainable urban drainage systems that can function as wetland habitats. This not only alleviates flooding, but also creates buffer strips for habitat creation. While the widths of the buffer may be constrained by existing land uses, their integration through linear green spaces can allow for wider corridors. Surface-water management maximizes habitat potential. Intermittent waterway tributaries can be linked up using swales.

Red (or Human) Ecoinfrastructure

This human ecoinfrastructure is our human community, its built enclosures (buildings, houses, etc.), hardscapes, and regulatory systems (laws, regulations, legislation, ethics, etc.). This is the social and human dimension that is often missing in the work of many green designers. It is evidently clear that our present profligate lifestyles, our economies and industries, our mobility, our diet and food production, etc., must be changed to be sustainable.

II. Seamless & Benign Biointegration

The second design strategy is to regard green design as the seamless, benign environmental biointegration of the synthetic and the artificial (the human-made) with the natural environment. It is the failure to successfully biointegrate that is the root cause of all of our environmental problems. In effect, if we are able to biointegrate all of our businesses, industrial processes and functions, all of our built systems, and essentially all we do or make in our built environment (which by definition includes our buildings, facilities, infrastructure, products, refrigerators, toys, etc.) with the natural environment in a seamless and benign way, there will in principle be no environmental problems whatsoever. Successfully achieving this is, of course, easier said than done, but herein lies our challenge.

We can draw an analogy here between ecodesign and prosthetic design in surgery. A medical prosthetic must integrate with its organic host, the human body. Failure to integrate successfully results in dislocation in one or in both. By analogy, this is what ecodesign should achieve: a total physical, systemic and temporal integration of our human-made built environment and our activities with our organic host being the natural environment within in a benign, positive way. Ecodesign thus successfully biointegrates our artificial systems both mechanically and organically with its host system, the ecosystems in the biosphere.

Our design for biointegration can be regarded in three aspects: physically, systemically, and temporally.

Singapore R&D Mid-Polis
Legend
1 Signature High Rise Luxury Condominium
2 Luxury Villa Cluster
3 Exclusive Office Tower
4 Sports Center
5 School
6 Restaurants
7 Hotel
8 Landscape Area
9 Open Green Space
10 Ecological Corridor
11 Water Retention Pond
12 Main Entrance with Security
13 Security
14 CMO's Villa
15 Director's House
16 Elevated Water Tank

Urban Fringe Data Center
Kuala Lumpur, Malaysia

Physical and systemic integration requires a discernment of the ecology of the locality. Any activity arising from our design or our businesses/ industries must physically integrate benignly with the ecosystems. To achieve this, we must first understand the locality's ecosystem before imposing any human activity or built system upon it. Every site has an ecology with a limiting capacity to withstand stresses imposed upon it, which, if stressed beyond this capacity, becomes irrevocably damaged. Consequences can range from minimal localized impact (such as the clearing of a small land area for access) to the total devastation of the entire land area (the clearing of all trees and vegetation, leveling the topography, diversion of existing waterways, etc.).

We need to ascertain the locality's ecosystem structure, energy flow, species diversity and other ecological properties and processes. Then we must identify which parts of the site (if any) can permit different types of structures and activities, and which parts are particularly sensitive. Finally, we must consider the likely impacts of the intended construction and use over time.

This is, of course, a major undertaking. It must be done diurnally over the year, and in some instances over several years. To reduce this lengthy effort, landscape architects developed the "sieve-mapping" technique for landscapes. We must be aware that this method is an abbreviated approach that generally treats the site's ecosystem statically and may ignore the dynamic forces taking place between the layers and within an ecosystem. Between each of these layers are complex interactions.

Another major design issue is the systemic integration of our built forms and its operational systems and internal processes with the ecosystems in nature. This integration is crucial because, if our built systems and processes do not integrate with the natural systems in nature, they will remain disparate, artificial items and potentially pollutive and destructive to the ecology of the locality. Their eventual integration after their manufacture and use can happen only through biodegradation. Often, this requires a long-term natural process of decomposition.

Temporal integration involves the conservation of both renewable and nonrenewable resources to ensure that these are sustainable for future generations. This includes designing for low-energy built systems that are less dependent or non-dependent on the use of non-renewable energy resources.

III. Ecomimesis

The third design strategy is to regard green design as "ecomimesis," or the imitation of the attributes and properties of ecosystems – that is, their processes, structure, features, and functions. This is one of the fundamental premises for ecodesign. Our built environment must imitate ecosystems in all respects, e.g., recycling, using energy from the sun through photosynthesis, and developing systems that head toward increasing energy efficiency, achieve a holistic balance of biotic and abiotic constituents, etc.

Nature without humans exists in stasis. Can our businesses and our built environment imitate nature's processes, structure, and functions, particularly its ecosystems? For instance, ecosystems have no waste. Everything is recycled inwardly. Thus, by imitating this, our built environment will produce no waste. All emissions and products are continuously reused, recycled within, and eventually reintegrated with the natural environment, in tandem with efficient uses of energy and material resources.

Ecosystems in a biosphere are definable units containing both biotic and abiotic constituents acting together as a whole. From this concept, our businesses/industries and built environment should be designed analogously to the ecosystem's physical content, composition and processes. For instance, besides regarding our architecture as simply art objects or engineering-serviced enclosures, we should regard it as artifacts that need to be operationally and eventually integrated with nature.

Data Center interior - Kuala Lumpur, Malaysia

As is self-evident, the material composition of our built environment is almost entirely inorganic, whereas ecosystems contain a complement of both biotic and abiotic constituents, or of inorganic and organic components, which need to be reversed.

Our myriad of construction, manufacturing and other activities are, in effect, making the biosphere more and more inorganic, artificial, and increasingly biologically simplified. To continue without balancing the biotic content means simply to add to the biosphere's artificiality, thereby making it increasingly more and more inorganic and synthetic. This results in the biological simplification of the biosphere and the reduction of its complexity and diversity. We must reverse this trend and balance our built environment with greater integral levels of biomass, ameliorating biodiversity and ecological connectivity in the builtforms.

Ecodesign also requires the designer to use green materials and assemblies of materials, and components that facilitate reuse, recycling and reintegration for temporal integration with the ecological systems. We need to be ecomimetic in our use of materials in the built environment. In ecosystems, all living organisms feed on continual flows of matter and energy from their environment to stay alive, and all living organisms continually produce outputs. Here, an ecosystem generates no waste, one specie's waste being another specie's food. Thus matter cycles continually through the web of life. It is this closing of the loop in reuse and recycling that our human-made environment must imitate.

IV. Ecodesign as Restoring Impaired Environments

Fourth, ecodesign can be regarded as not only the creation of new artificial "living" urban ecosystems or rehabilitating existing built environments and cities but also the restoration of existing impaired and devastated ecosystems regionally within the wider landscape of our designed system. Ecodesign must look beyond the limitations of the project site, and at the larger context of the locality. Where needed, we should improve the ecological linkages between our designed systems and business processes and the surrounding landscape and hardscapes, not just horizontally, but also vertically.

Fusionopolis exterior details

The Constructed Ecosystem: A conceptual design strategy of a building as a human-made ecosystem featuring vertical landscaping, biodiversity enhancement, renewable energy use, water harvesting and other sustainable design strategies by T.R. Hamzah & Yeang

Achieving these linkages ensures a wider level of species connectivity, interaction, and mobility, as well as a greater sharing of resources across boundaries. Such real improvements in ecological nexus enhance biodiversity and further increase habitat resilience and species survival. Providing new ecological corridors and linkages in regional planning is crucial to making urban patterns more biologically viable. Crucially, we need to apply these concepts to retrofit our existing cities and urban developments.

We must biointegrate the existing inorganic aspects of our built environment and its processes with the landscape so that they mutually become ecosystemic. We must create "human-made ecosystems" compatible with the ecosystems in nature. By doing so, we enhance human-made ecosystems' abilities to sustain life in the biosphere.

V. Ecodesign as a Self-Monitoring System

The fifth strategy for ecodesign is to regard our designed system as a series of interdependent environmental interactions whose constant global and local monitoring (e.g., through GPS and biosensors) is necessary to ensure global environmental stasis, enabling an anticipatory approach to, and the immediate repair and restoration of, environmental devastations by humans, natural disasters, and the inadvertent negative impacts of our human-built environment, activities and industries. These sets of environmental interactions must be monitored for appropriate corrective action to be immediately taken to maintain global ecological stability.

The above are strategies that can be adopted singularly or in combination. Green design must go beyond conventional rating systems such as LEED or BREEAM. While these are indeed useful indexes for providing a common basis for comparing the greenness of building designs, they are not totally effective design tools. They are not comprehensive enough in approaching the issues of environmental design at the local, regional and global levels.

Ecological design is still very much in its infancy. The completely green building or green ecocity does not yet exist. We need to do more theoretical work, technical research and invention, environmental studies and design interpretations before we can have a truly green built environment. We all need to continue this great pursuit.

Mid-Polis Analysis 2.0

Aerial map of Amsterdam with Zuidas, image by Matthew Kleinmann

Historical Transfer and the Edge as Metaphor

2.1

Istanbul, Türkiye, is one of the largest cities in the world, containing a population of over 15 million with an annual growth rate of 1.2%. Today, the area within the Istanbul province covers approximately 5,461 km^2 with a history that spans the periods of the Roman Empire, the Byzantine Empire, the Latin Empire, the Ottoman Empire, and what is now the modern Republic of Türkiye. Located on both the European and Asian continents, its long history as the capital of the western world during antiquity and the subsequent empires that followed, contributes to its unique identity. While the district of Fatih, which contains the Old City, has been densely populated for quite some time, the regions that have sprung up around it are the result of relatively recent immigration and utilitarian support for the city center that has produced specific mid-polis development patterns around the core. One area of interest lies within the Zeytinburnu and Ataköy districts of Istanbul along the edges of the Old City near the Yedikule Fortress to the east and working-class suburbs to the west.

Various infrastructural elements interweave through the area, including the ancient city wall of Theodosius II, the suburban railway lines that feed into the city center, and an assortment of major highways. The convergence of these elements, along with the topographical, environmental and historical factors of the site, provide a multi-layered and unique area of interest. They have been fundamental in shaping the physical fabric of the site as it exists today. The space in-between the urban and suburban fabrics is a result of the convergence of particular infrastructural, environmental and social elements that have transformed over time to create what is described in this study as the mid-polis condition. It has enormous potential to accommodate various typical unique urban programming needs within the existing city fabric between the center and edge.

by **Yusheen Yang**
Washington University in St. Louis

MID-POLIS: ISTANBUL, TÜRKIYE

Site aerial

Area identified as the mid-polis condition

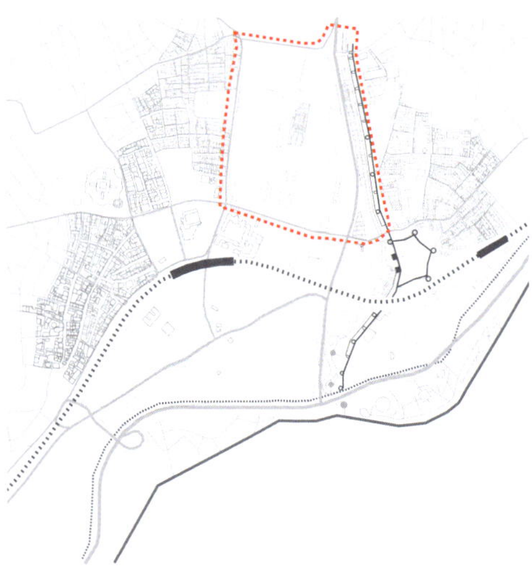

Area of interest

Zone and degrees of open space

Topography

Agricultural land

Double walls of the city

Mosques

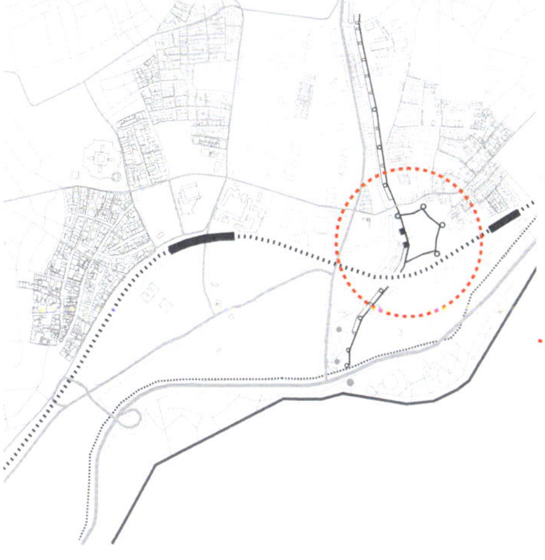

Area of interest

Site constraints vs. public spaces

Roman Colony Origins **2.2**

Barcelona, with over 2,000 years of history, has a long urban tradition that has nurtured a dense and compact urban form through a process of growth rather than remodeling. Its history is an episodic account of change and expansion, which has given the city its current physical form of varying urban conditions. As a result, what was once the center of this ancient Roman colony is today a mid-polis between the modern city center to the north and the expansive urban waterfront to the south. In time, the old Roman streets have become a welcome transition between both regions, creating a rich fabric of dense organic urban life between the planned modern center and waterfront. Within Barcelona's contemporary fabric emerges a new mid-polis condition, as the articulation of a historic urban space positioned between two major nodes.

In the district of Ciutat Vella, within Barcelona's ancient Roman village are the remains of its original city. Remnants of the original city wall, urban grid, and public monuments are subtly woven into the functions of daily modern life. The urban space is shaped by internalized monumentality, informal open space, topography, and urban fabric. It works as a collection of historic artifacts and characteristics of the Ciutat Vella. The significance of these historic artifacts can be found in the intricacy of their adjacencies and interactions with time: how the old interfaces with the new within the adjacent nodes of city center and waterfront edge. Altogether, this is an intriguing study of urban evolution, where the original city center has been superseded by the modern center and in turn has become a rich mid-polis condition.

MID-POLIS: BARCELONA, SPAIN

by **Adria Longenderfer**
Washington University in St. Louis

Barcelona, Spain
1900 - 2010

Barcelona, Spain
500 BC

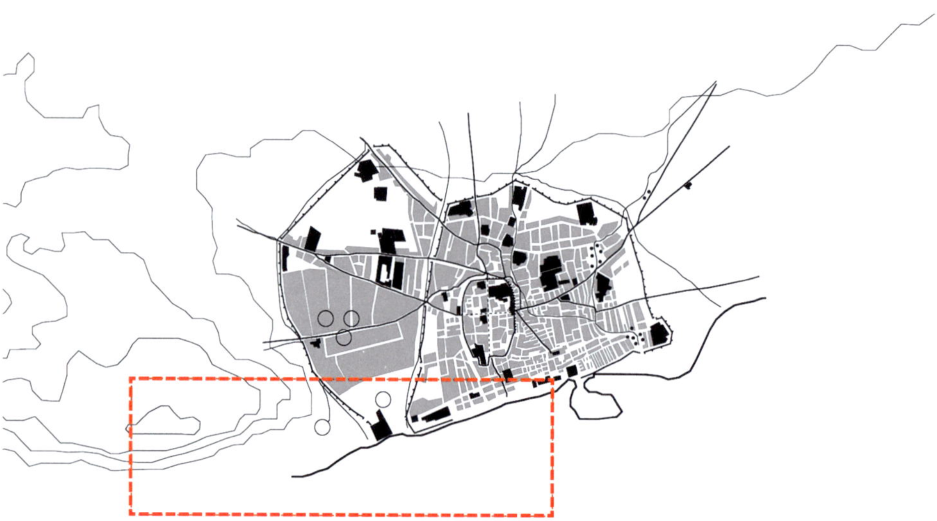

Barcelona, Spain
1350 - 1700

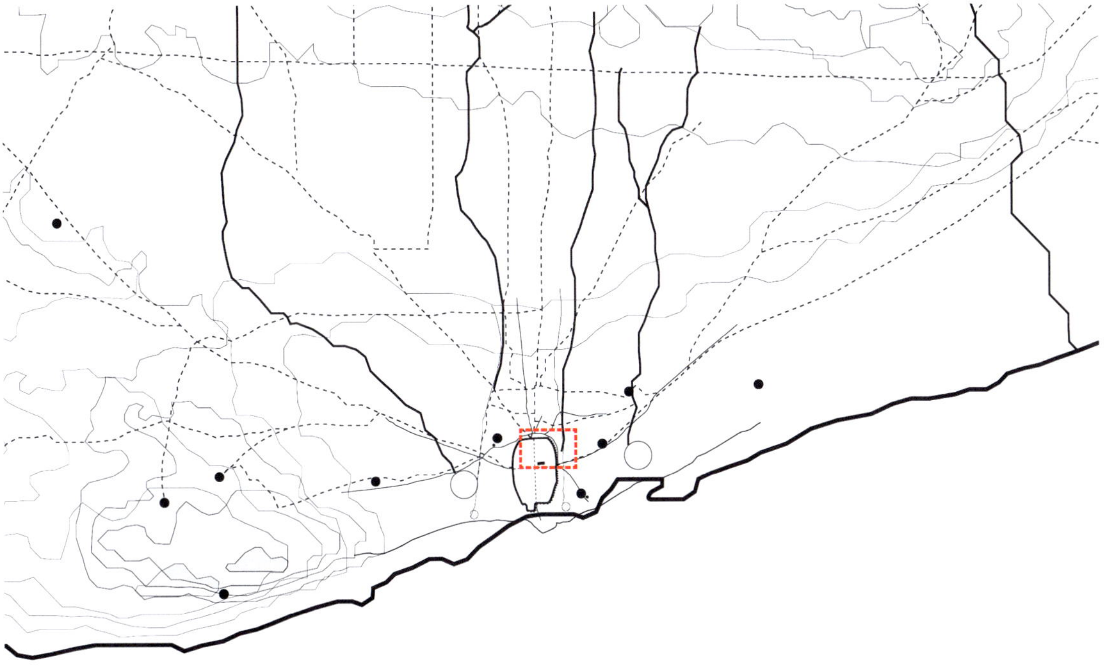

Barcelona, Spain
500 BC - 800 AD

Barcelona, Spain
1700 - 1850

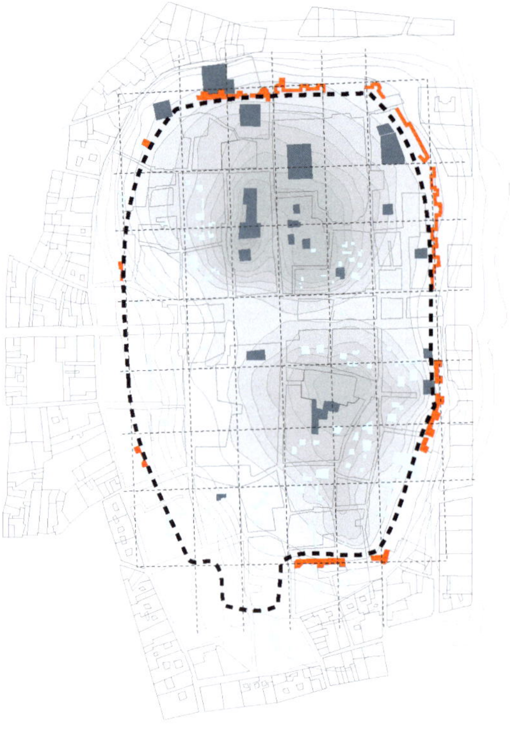

Private open space composite

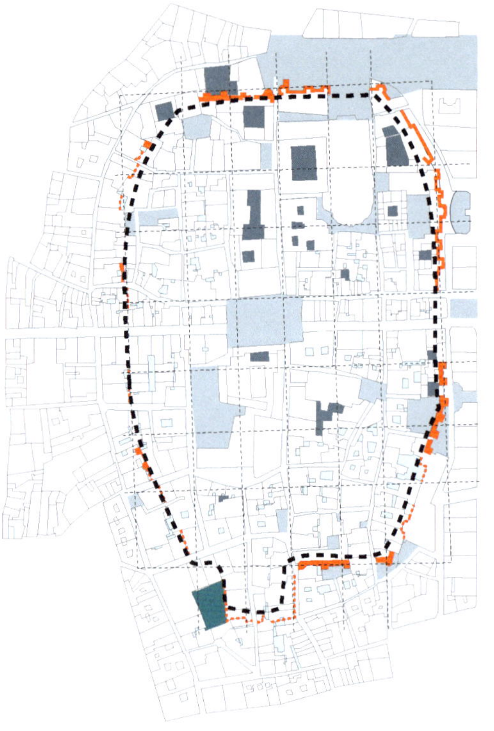

Public open space composite

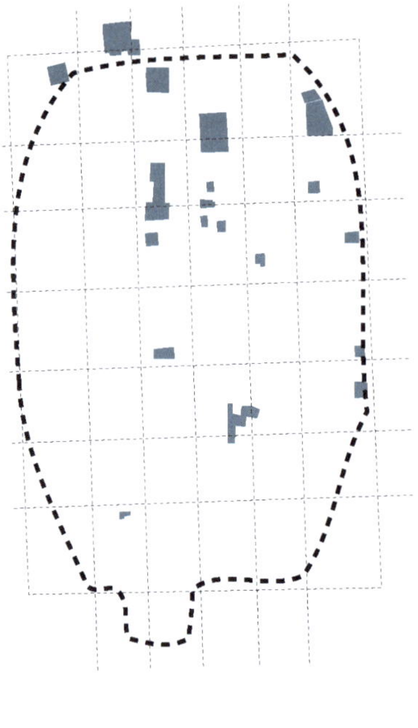

Public space, internal monuments

Traces of history

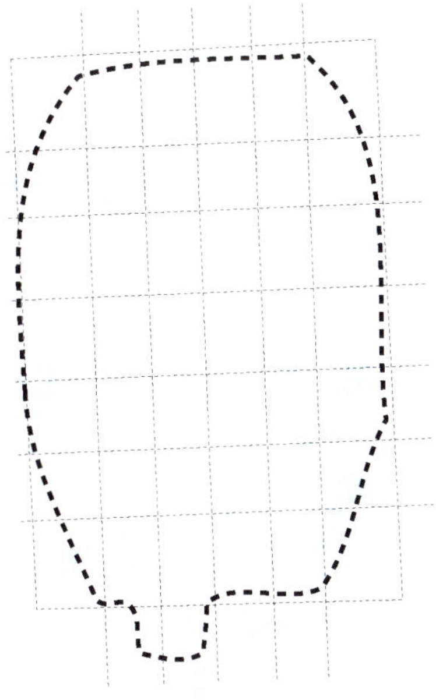

Open space and private space

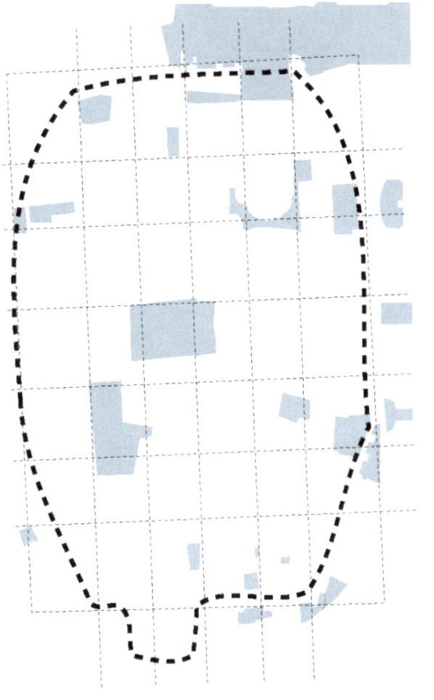

Private open unbounded exposed

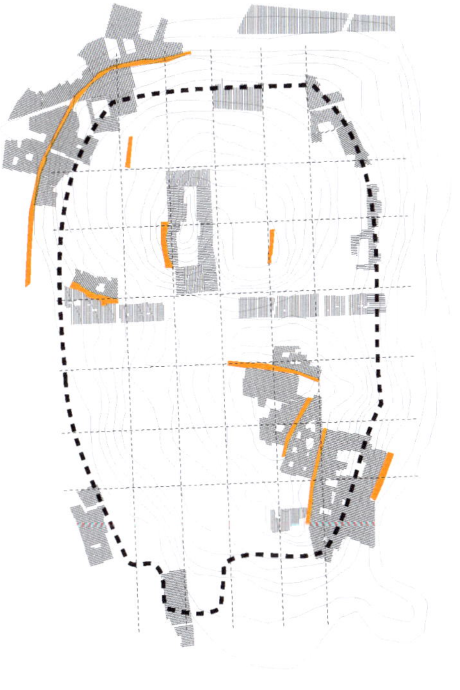

Block, grain and topographical relationship

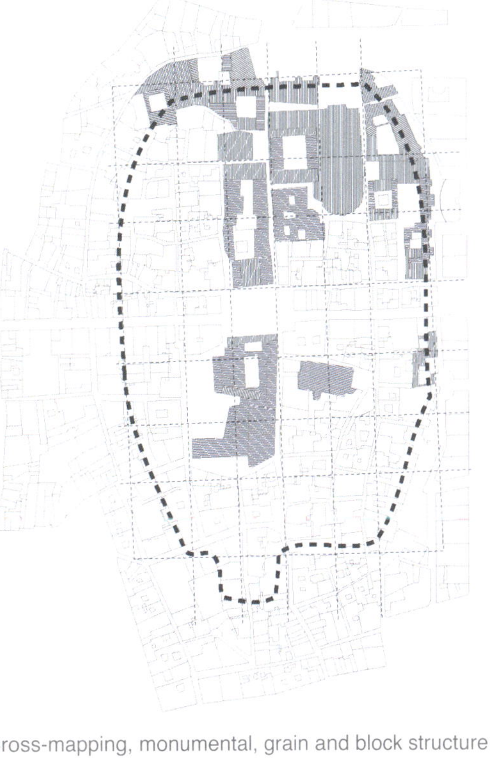

Cross-mapping, monumental, grain and block structure

Epicenter of Cultural Crossroads **2.3**

Jerusalem is a place of extensive history and cultural conflict. Having existed under various empires and religious systems across four millennia, the city has been constantly rebuilt and shaped by countless cultural forces, both native and foreign. As a result, it has yielded a unique modern condition that is still at the center of much controversy: the division between Israel and Palestine within the city since 1948. To this day, the city and its environs are highly coveted by both sides.

In addition, since the United Nations-mandated "no-man's land" buffer between the Israeli and Palestinian portions was lifted in 1967, this once-unusable land just outside the old city's western wall has been a new center of modern contention and gradual contemporary infill. At the same time, it provides room for a mid-polis condition where both Palestinian and Israeli development can begin to blur just outside the city center.

Jerusalem's "no-man's land" buffer was established by the United Nations in 1948 and enforced until 1967. This area is situated between the ancient walled city center to the east, held by the Palestinians, and the urban environs to the west, held by the Israelis. The city has expanded in a northeastern direction, primarily due to topographic conditions. The result is an urban area composed of complex layers shaped through various historical conditions in the 20th century, including the United Nations' "no-man's land" condition during the political conflicts between Israel and Jordan.

Today, the region has become a unique growing mid-polis condition due to the city's 20th-century history of modern conflict.

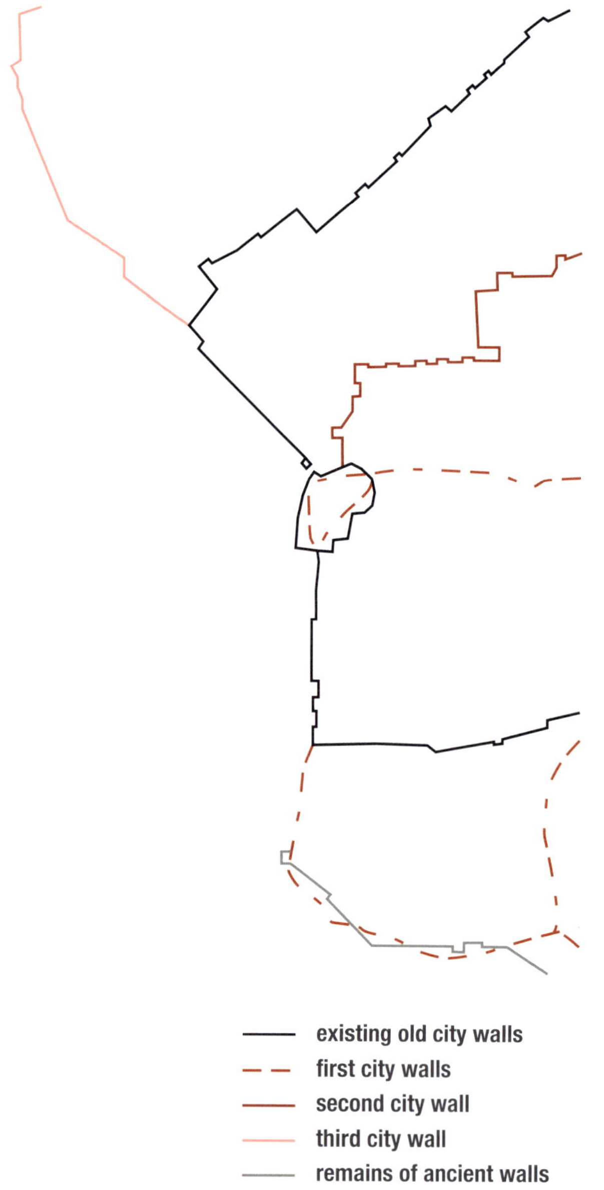

by **Matthew Kuebler**

Washington University in St. Louis

MID-POLIS: JERUSALEM

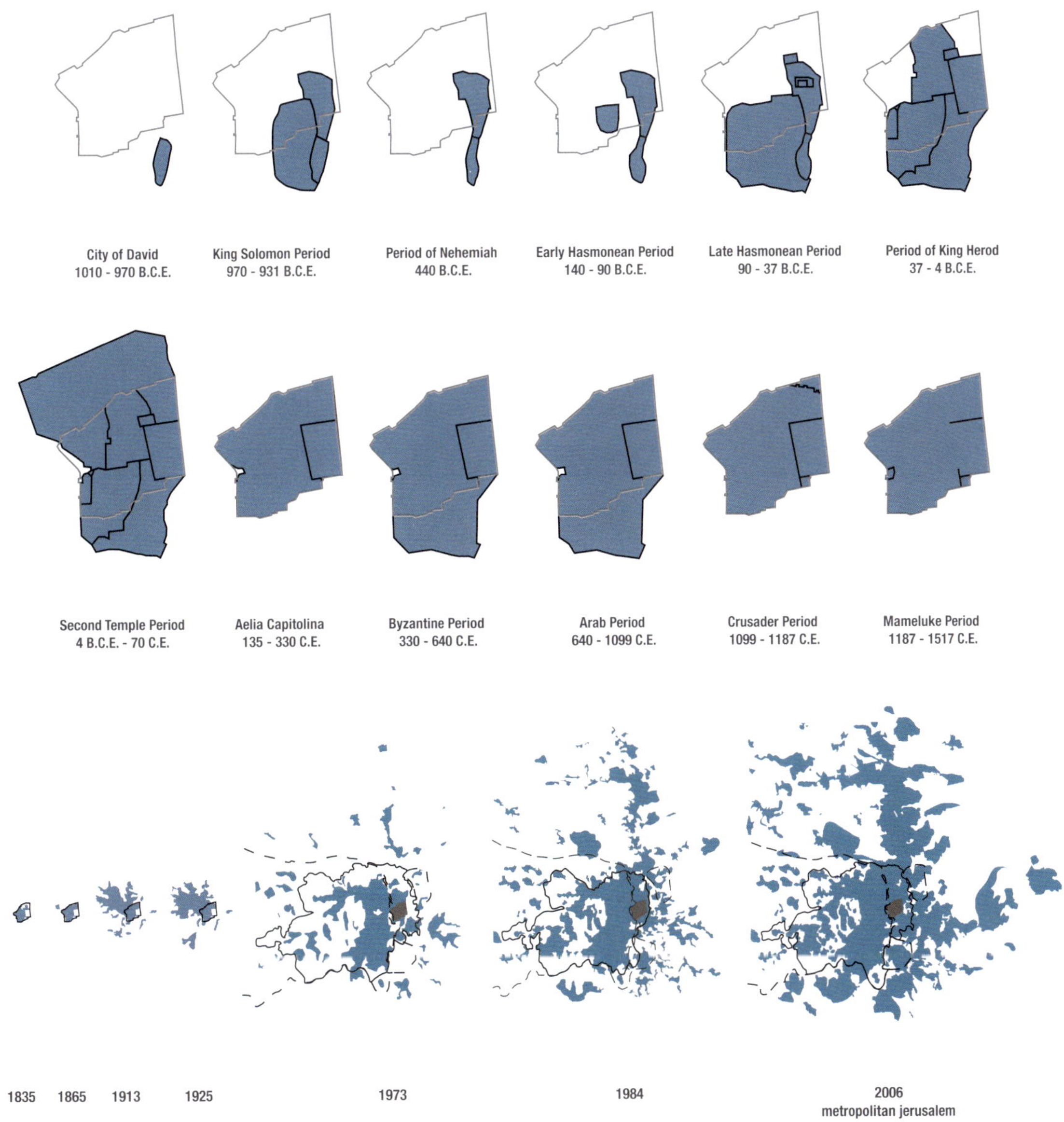

Growth and expansion of Jerusalem. Historical evolution of the urban form and city walls.

1947-1967 Geopolitical boundaries

Israeli Jerusalem (west city)
Jordanian Jerusalem (east city)
U.N.-mandated "no man´s land"

Topographic relationship

Gates & Districts

Gates of the old city
1. Jeffa Gate
2. New Gate
3. Damascus Gate
4. Herods´ Gate
5. Lions´ Gate
6. Dung Gate
7. Zion Gate

Old city districts
A. Christian Quarter
B. Muslim Quarter
C. Armenian Quarter
D. Jewish Quarter
E. Temple Mount

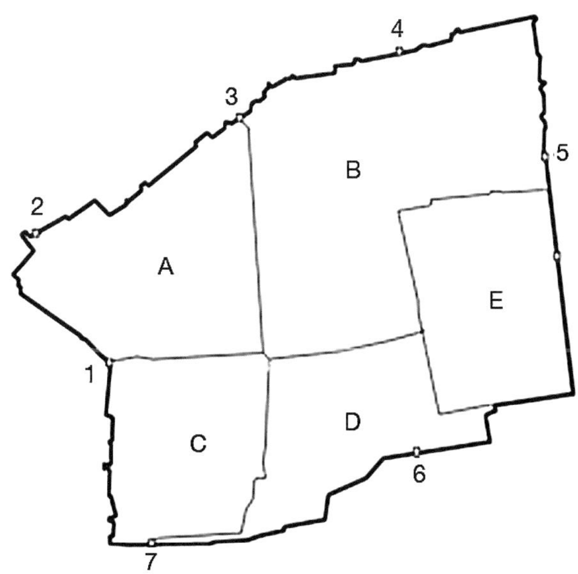

1865

1912

2006

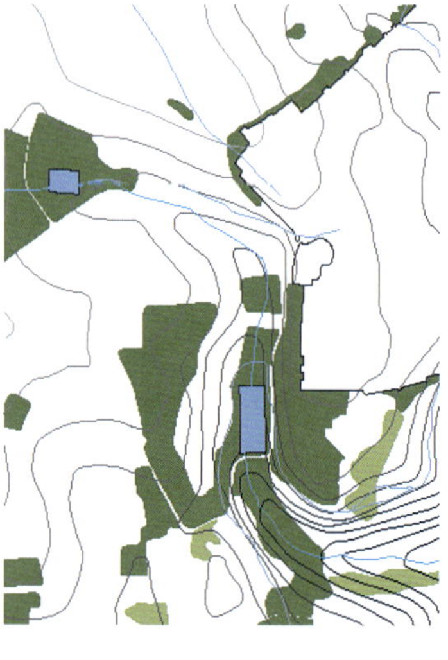

Natural systems

Filled landscape

Urban composition

Investigative site conditions

- buildings
- roadways
- public realm beyond old city
- carved public realm
- public gardens
- private gardens

Scaling the Edge 2.4

Valparaíso, Chile, is nestled between two extraordinary geographic features: the city's picturesque bay, and the steep cliffs of the mountainous countryside. The historic city developed as a seaport due to its naturally protected north-facing harbor, contained by cliffs rising 150 meters within one kilometer inland. Before the building of the Panama Canal, Valparaíso was a key stop along the journey between the Atlantic and Pacific oceans. The multi-national immigrants that have settled in the city over centuries are reflected in the existing diversity of building typologies and construction. The city's growth spurts, combined with its unique geographic constraints, provide insight into how unplanned urban spaces developed around the region. The spontaneous expansion of the periphery, in contrast to the planned, measured and adjusted central grid of the city center, resulted in pockets of unused land. In time, modern redevelopment initiated a shift toward reuse of this initially overlooked and inaccessible land, resulting in distinct building clusters scattered across the terrain.

Much of the modern, large-scale infrastructure in Valparaíso has capitalized on land previously thought to be unusable. Funicular systems that developed in response to the demand for access to the central town from the hilly outskirts have changed this dynamic of the city. In addition, public transport continues to have a weighted importance with the growing line of trolley buses in the center and a newer series of tunnels allowing port traffic to circumnavigate the congestion of the historical central district. This has allowed Valparaíso's traditional public spaces in the city and surrounding nodes to expand into space originally used exclusively for automobile traffic.

Finally, the historic port city has strengthened its rail ties with Chile's capital of Santiago while redirecting more seaport traffic to the newer modern port systems in San Antonio to the south. As a result, more of the city's original flat-port terrain can be used for new housing, hotels, and local commercial initiatives between downtown and the city's mountainous edges.

by **Christian Clerc**

Washington University in St. Louis

MID-POLIS: VALPARAÍSO, CHILE

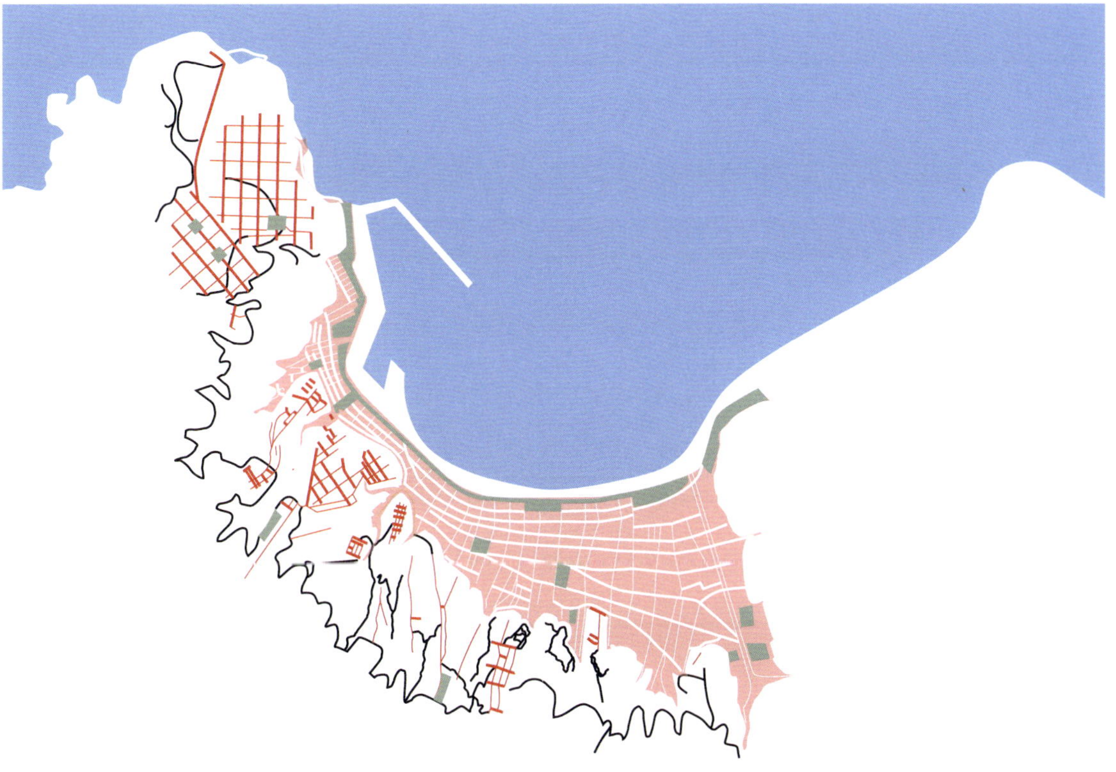

City grids

Valparaíso urban aerial map © 2011 Microsoft Corporation © 2010 DigitalGlobe

Enlarged aerial site map © 2011 Microsoft Corporation © 2010 DigitalGlobe

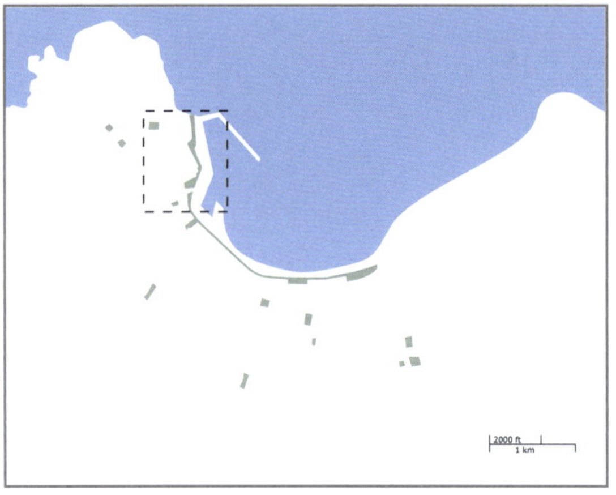

Public space

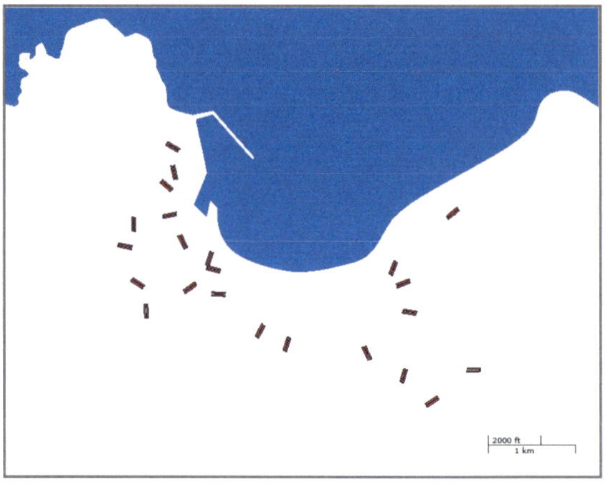

Funiculars

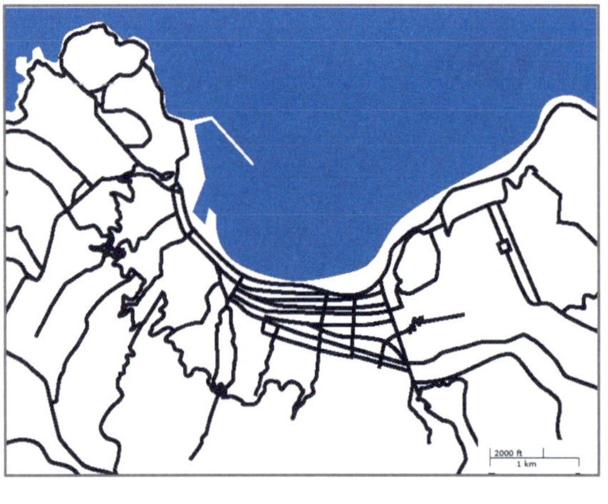

Major roads

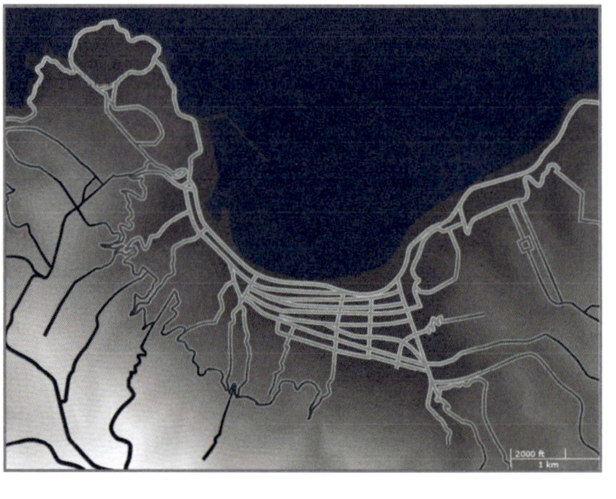

Roads and topography

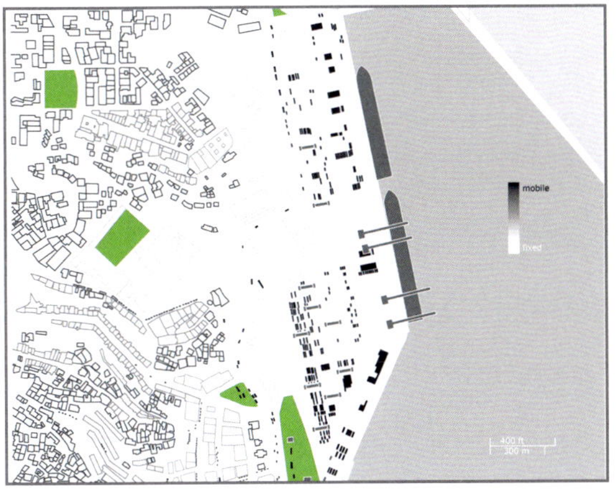

Transitory objects

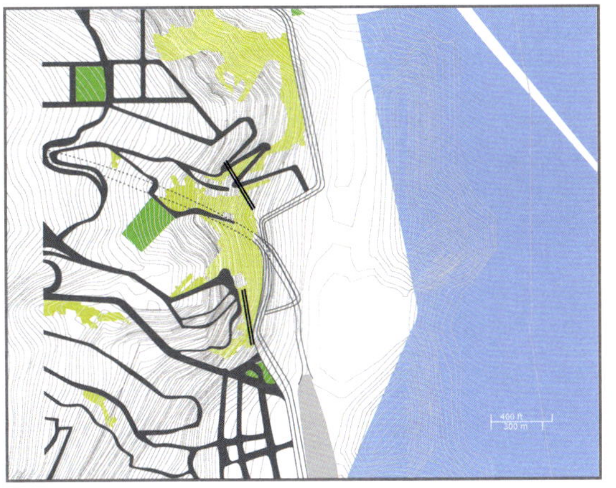

Overlaid space and systems
(transportation, open space, topography)

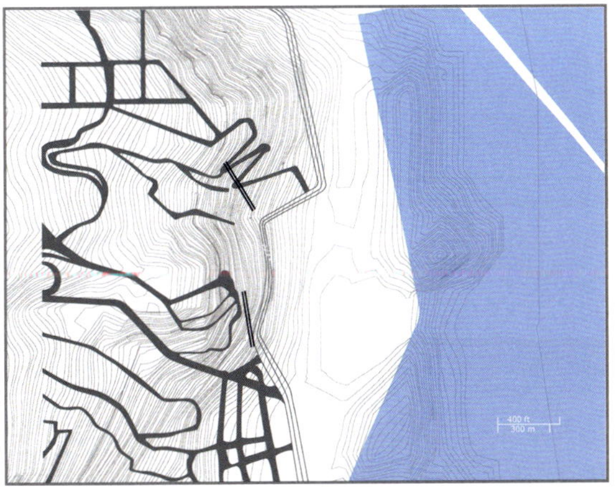

Transportation (highways, roads and funiculars)

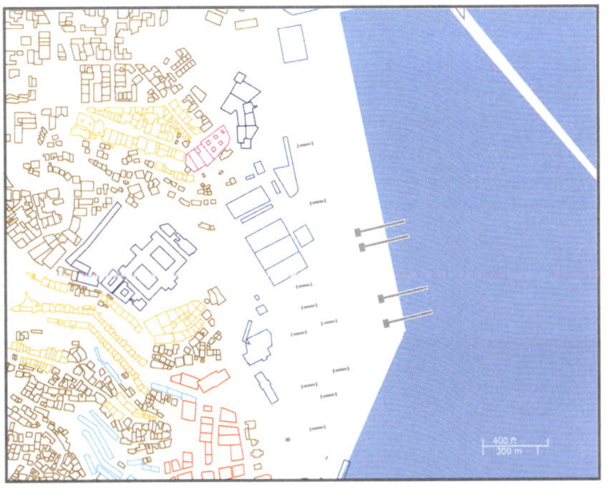

Building clusters

A Political and Social Struggle 2.5

Johannesburg is a city with a short but tumultuous history. Founded in 1886 when massive gold and diamond reserves were found nearby, the city was a boomtown at the turn of the 20th century. However, the city was shaped by racial segregation and discrimination from the start and is still trying to eliminate decades of community division across the metro area. Since the removal of South Africa's apartheid law, a new process of access and diversity has begun to coalesce in the once-divided city. However, the urban division is still apparent. Johannesburg's segregated history has created a city of extraordinary contrasts. Probably the greatest example of this division lies to the north and east: the wealthy business district of Sandton and the large, impoverished black township of Alexandra. In-between is the small prospective mid-polis of Wynberg, a potential middle ground between both communities a few miles from the city core.

For most of its history, during and after apartheid, Wynberg has worked as a utilitarian industrial park buffer between Sandton and Alexandra. On both sides of the otherwise generic industrial node is the full spectrum of urban life in South Africa. To the east, you have the Alexandra township, anchored by two massive hostels designed by the apartheid government to curtail family growth within the black population. To the west, you have the office towers and mansions of Sandton. However, in the 1990s, once Sandton was merged with Alexandra after apartheid as part of the city's new unified eastern district, the region began to blur decades of development based on class and race lines.

As a result, Wynberg is a new critical mid-polis opportunity between both communities – downtown Johannesburg, the financial hub of South Africa which accounts for 16% of the country's gross domestic product, and the suburban fringe. As time progresses and the pressure to redevelop inner-city land for stronger urban uses grows, low-rise industry will continue to move to the fringe and will allow new housing development opportunities to develop

by **Sarah Hill (Burnett)**

Washington University in St. Louis

MID-POLIS: JOHANNESBURG, SOUTH AFRICA

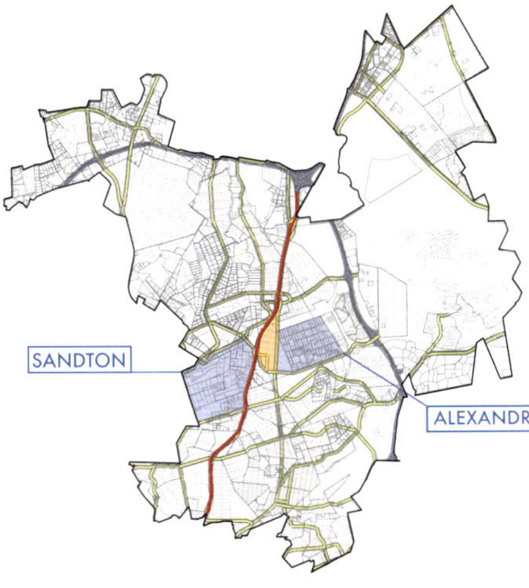

Region E (blue and yellow)

• 14% population of greater Johannesburg
average age range of population: 17-35
• 87% Black African population

in these inner-city communities. Wynberg in time can become a strong middle-class community of local industry, commerce, and residential space that starts to blur the lines between Sandton's and Alexandra's complicated apartheid history.

sandton

population: 222,415
area: 144 km²
density: 1,500 (people/km²)

midpolis
(Wynberg)

3 km
a world apart

alexandra

population: 394,000 ~ 1 million +
area: 8 km²
density: 45,000 to 81,000 (people/km²)

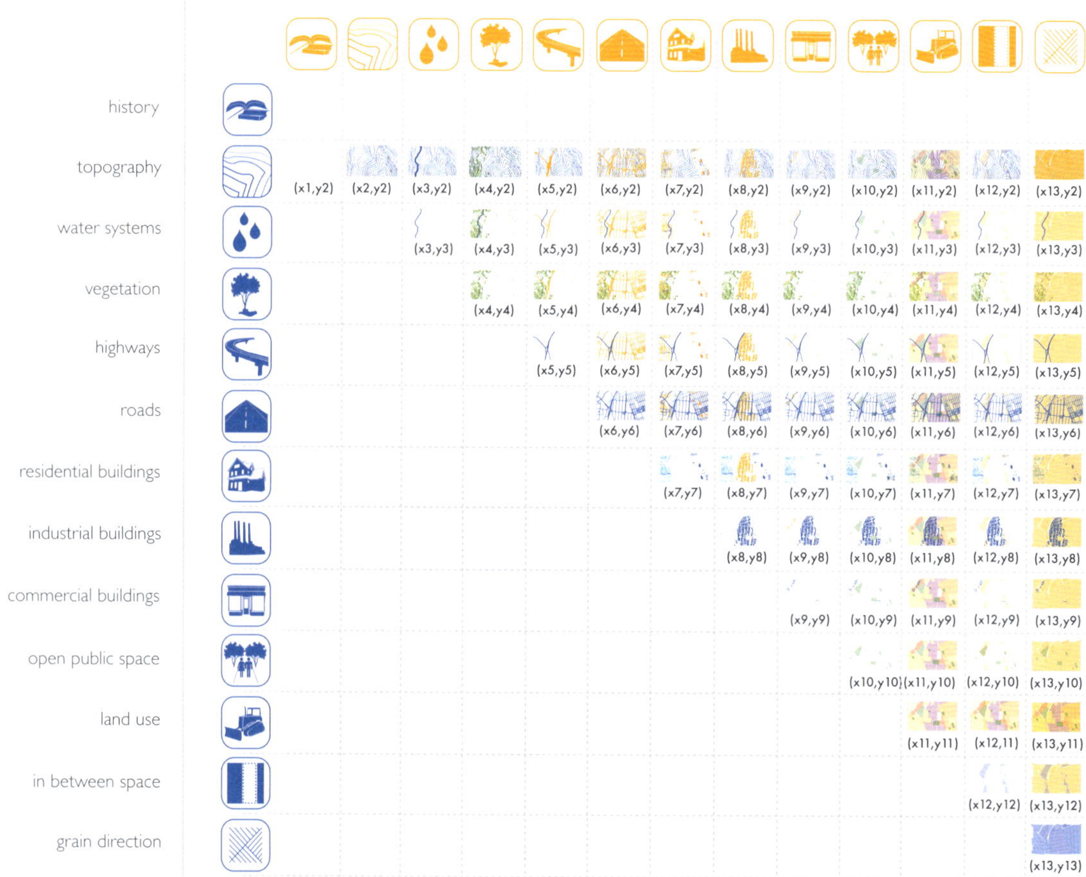

Cross-mapping matrix

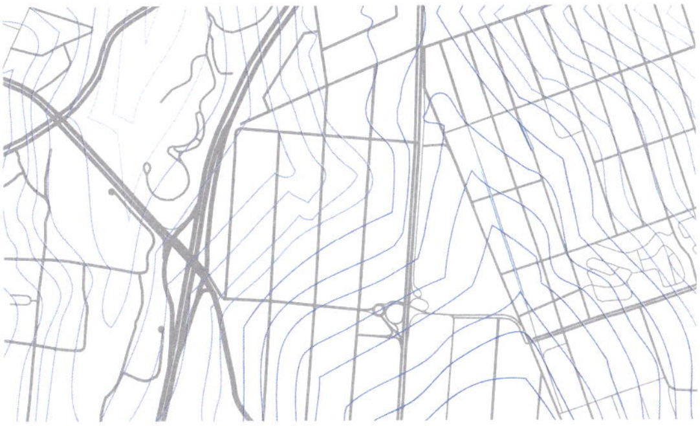

Topography and natural systems

Industrial corridor

Low density
High density

Residential discrepancy

Vegetation

Wynberg, in-between space of Sandton (on the left) and Alexandra (on the right), South Africa

Berlage's Zuidas

2.6

From 1585 to 1672, Amsterdam saw an unprecedented period of growth in the midst of a golden age of international trade. Some four hundred years later, plans were set in motion to expand the city's borders and allow for an integrated system of motorways, canals and public transit across a much broader urban region.

In the 21st century, the city saw another period of urban growth due to its robust international finance market. This boom instigated another wave of growth and the re-start of the city's plan for the Zuidas region in Amsterdam, straddling the city's southern boundary. Once a region originally laid out and designed by the famous Dutch architect and planner, Hendrik Berlage, the site quickly evolved into a vibrant business hub for Amsterdam, strategically located in-between the city's historic center and its outer fringes.

Today, Amsterdam continues to strengthen urban links to the much larger Dutch Randstad, a megalopolis encompassing Amsterdam, Rotterdam, The Hague, and Utrecht. The city and the circularly shaped Randstad continue to densify while balancing nature and urbanity. The Zuidas is at a critical location, interconnecting Amsterdam's metropolis with the megapolis that is the Randstad. Berlage's elegant plan, developed in pre-World War II, still carries the organizational master-planning features that extend into the Zuidas. One of the major master-planning features carried over from Berlage's plan is the district's intersecting layers of transportation, green space, housing and commercial uses.

Berlage did not foresee the arterial highway and high-speed rail lines that feed southern Amsterdam. Their scale is reduced by splitting up large infrastructural elements into spaghetti-like strands, interwoven with greenery, waterways and bike paths. The impact of the modern-day mid-polis infrastructure is tamed and made more humanly scaled, while feeding the utilitarian demands of modern-day financial centers.

MID-POLIS: AMSTERDAM, THE NETHERLANDS

by **Matthew Kleinmann**

Washington University in St. Louis

Aerial map of Amsterdam with Zuidas

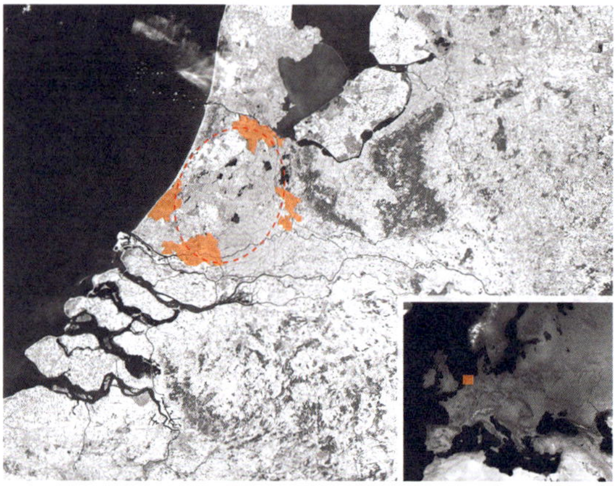

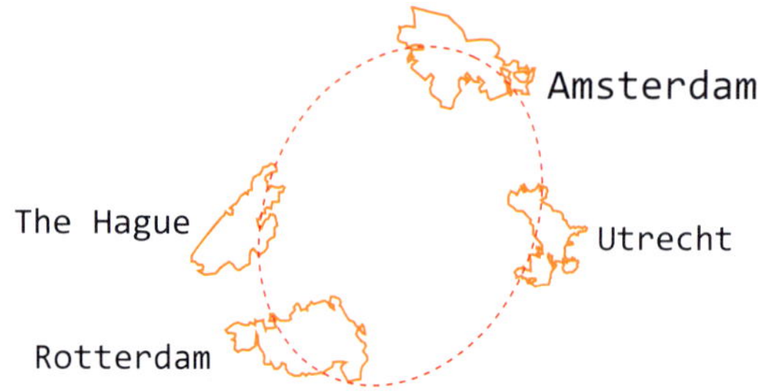

Aerial Map of Holland's Randstad - highlighted

Holland contains four major cities: Amsterdam and Utrecht in the Noordvleugel (North Wing) and The Hague and Rotterdam in the Zuidvleugel (South Wing). These four nodes link with other cities to form the Randstad (rim city). The Randstad has seen many proposals over the years to link the region through high-speed rail and international motorways.

Amsterdam is the capital of and the largest city in the Netherlands. Including the Randstad cities, Amsterdam is the sixth-largest greater metropolitan area in Europe.

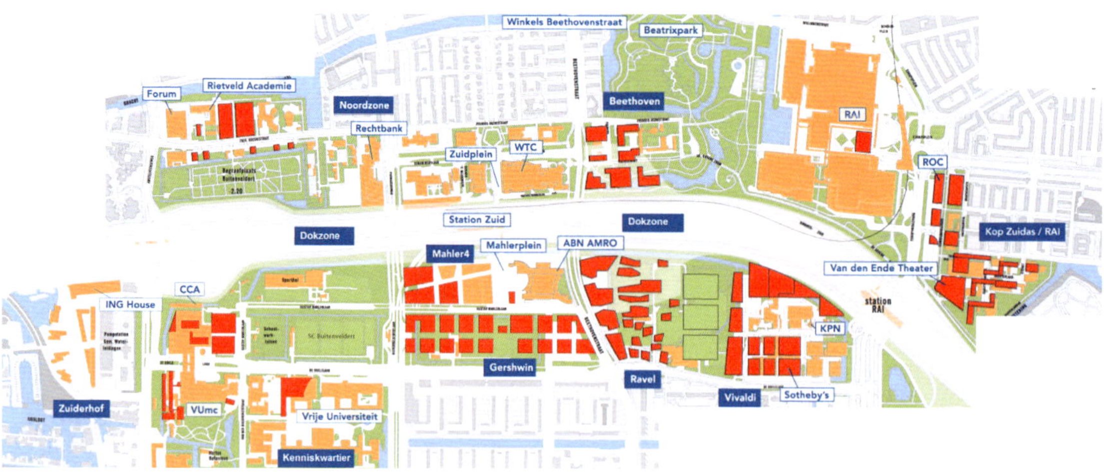

Zuidas Business District - neighborhoods' current plan

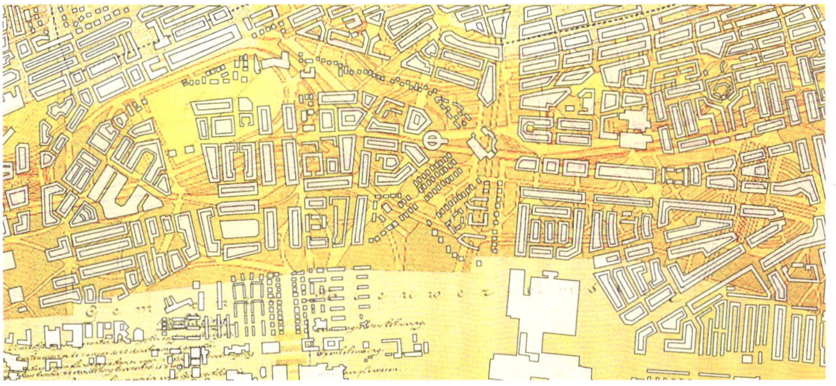

Berlage's plan for Amsterdam 1904

Berlage's initial plan for the southern expansion in 1904 included winding streets and a strong connection to the existing urban fabric. The city council rejected his plan due to its high cost and inefficiency.

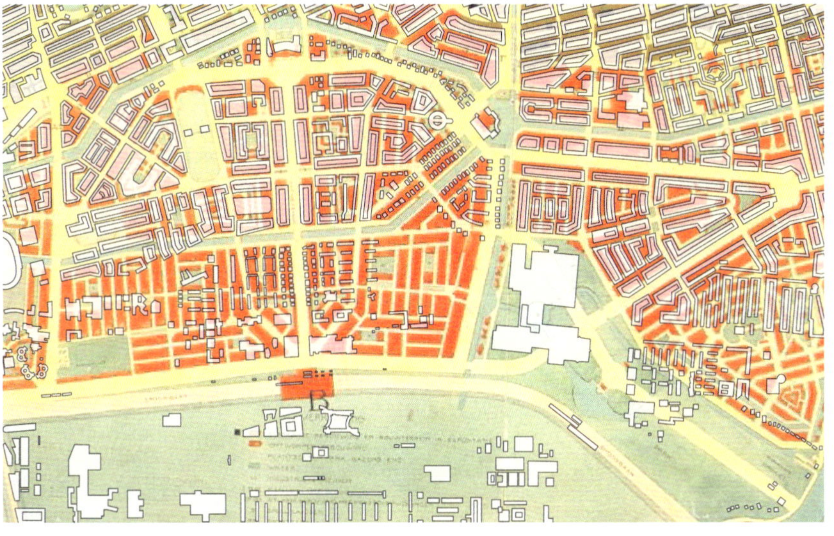

Berlage's plan for Amsterdam 1914

In 1914 Berlage introduced a new plan, this time with straight streets and broad intersections. The plan was a success, with construction approved in 1917, following the style of the Amsterdam School.

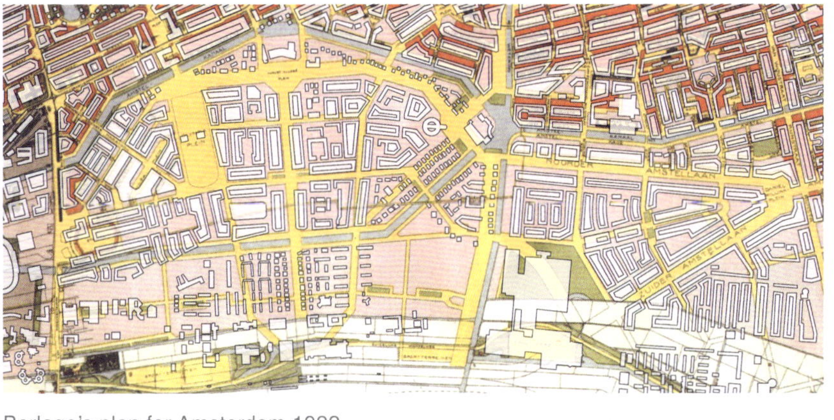

Berlage's plan for Amsterdam 1922

A major feature of the plan was The Apollo area, which included the 1928 Olympic stadium. However, not all of Berlage's scheme was built according to plan, as evidenced by its southern edge.

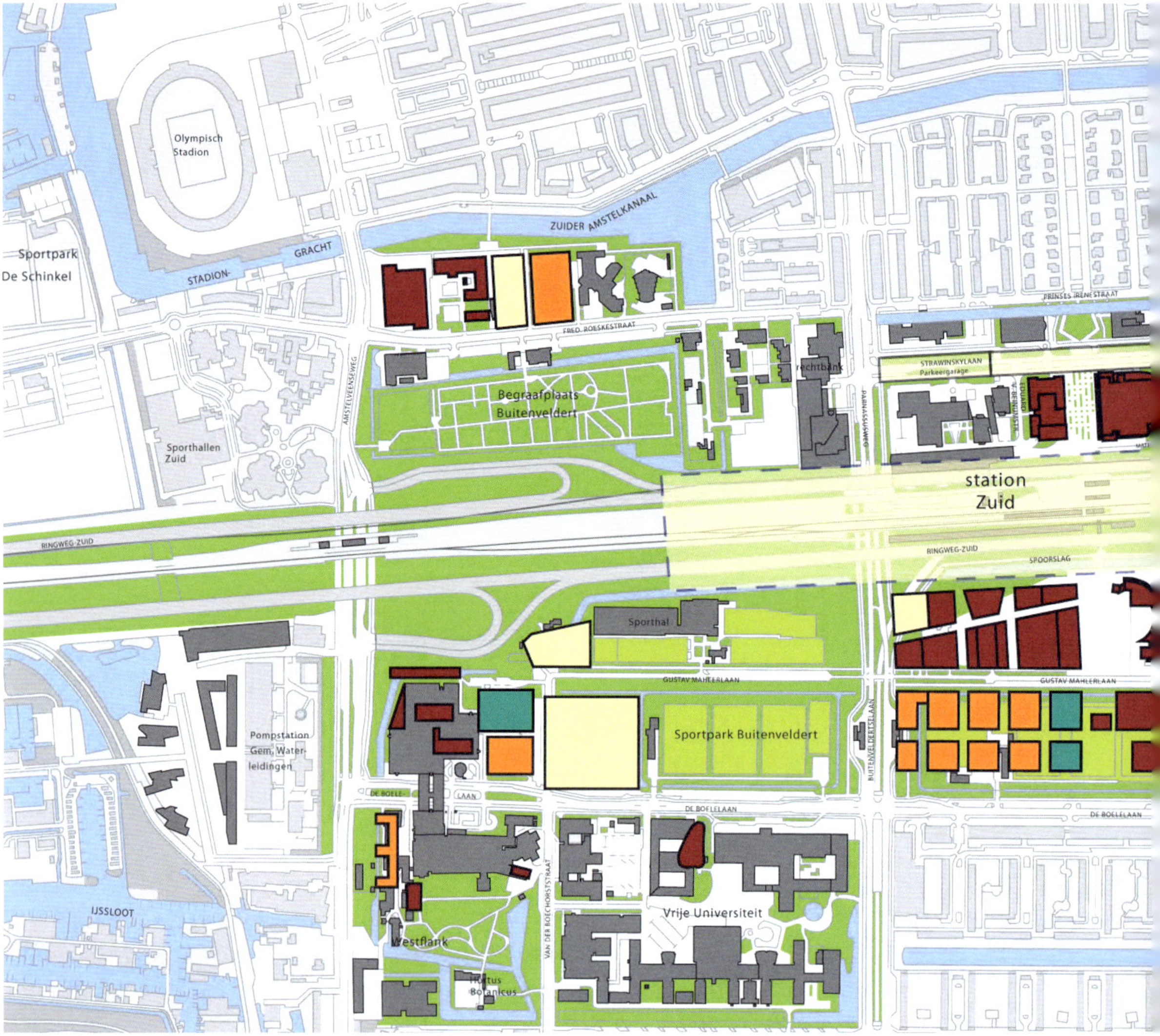

Zuidas Business District - mixed-use programming

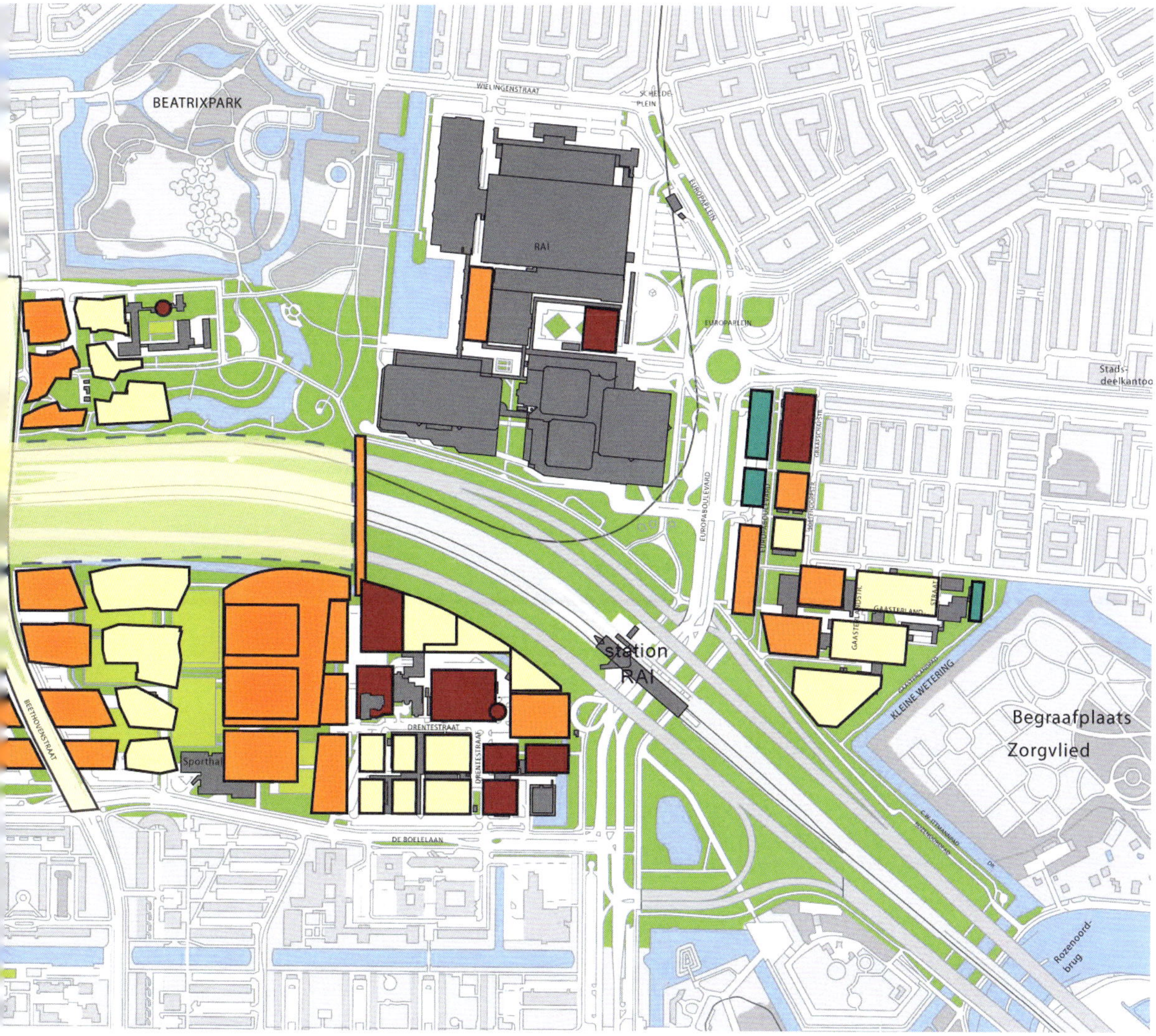
BEATRIXPARK
WIELINGENSTRAAT
RAI
EUROPAPLEIN
EUROPABOULEVARD
Stads-
deelkantoo
station
RAI
DRENTESTRAAT
DE BOELELAAN
BEETHOVENSTRAAT
Sporthal
GAASTERLAND
KLEINE WETERING
Begraafplaats
Zorgvlied
Rozenoord-
brug

Addressing the bridge and river

Utilizing the space underneath

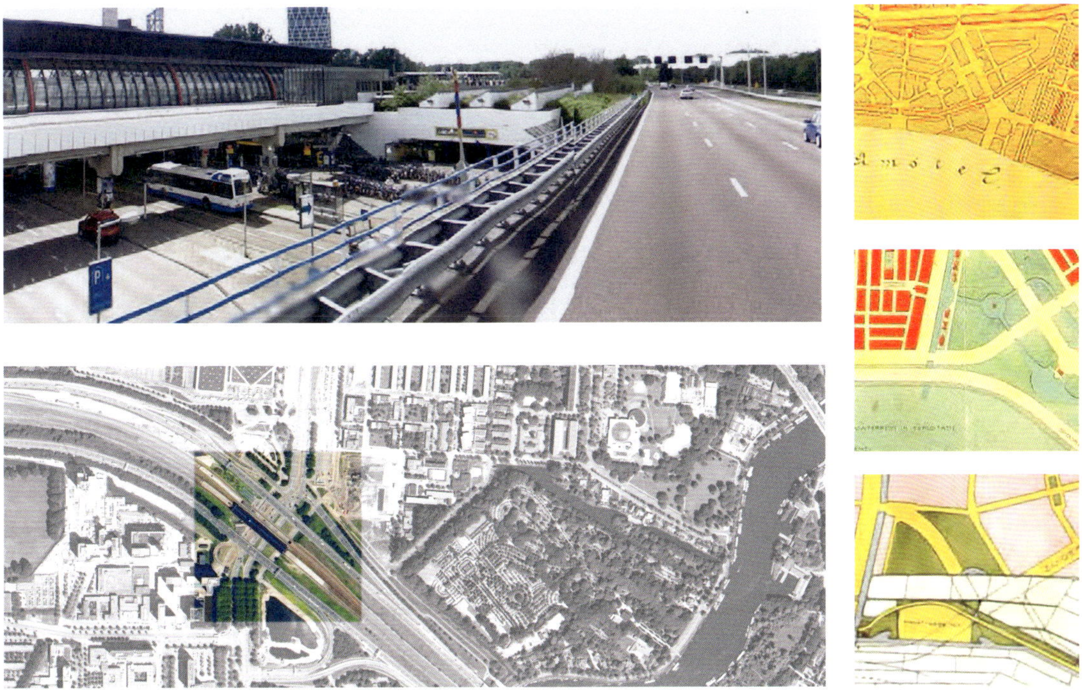

Layering of landscapes as infrastructure

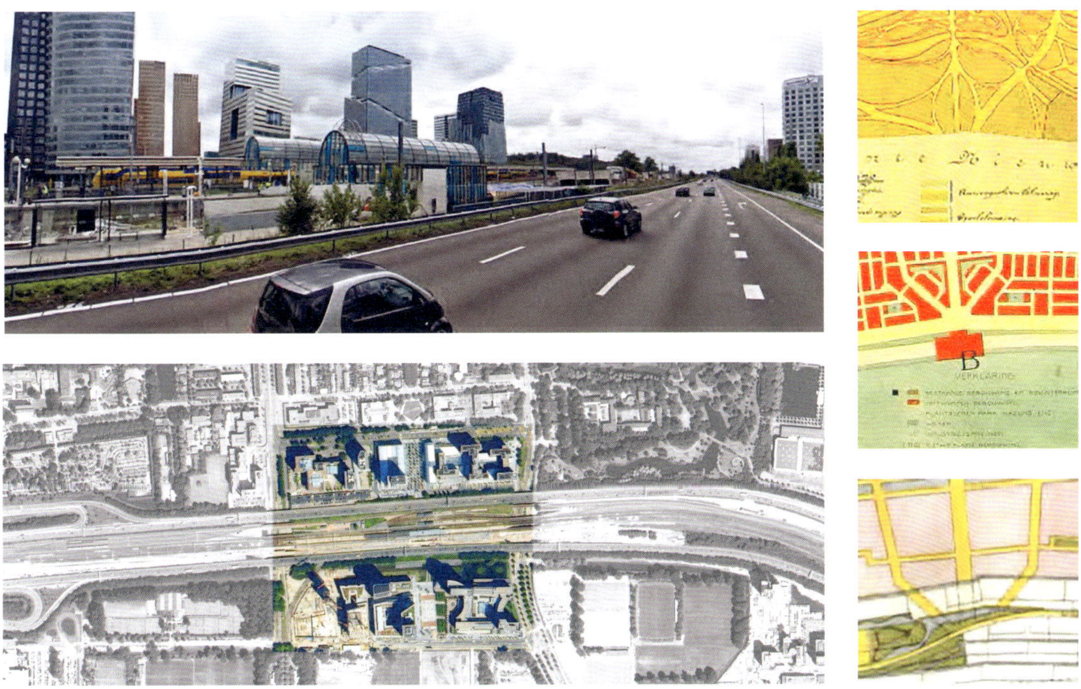

Connecting the old with the new

Mid-Polis Transformations

3.0

Perspective rendering of Boston-Somerville Mid-Polis transformation, image by Adria Longenderfer & Rebecca Sommer (Castellon)

3.1
Fringe Edge to the Inner City
by Bryan Apito & Tom Sherman

Mid-Polis: Düsseldorf, Germany + Rio de Janeiro, Brazil

3.2
Inner Belt / Brickbottom
by Matthew Kleinmann & Matthew Kuebler

Mid-Polis: Boston-Somerville, Massachusetts, USA

3.3
Mall to Mid-Polis Transformations
by Brian Boisvert & Evan Krasik

Mid-Polis: Columbia, Maryland, USA + San Diego, California, USA

3.4
Somerville Brickbottom Stadium
by Adria Longenderfer & Rebecca Sommer (Castellon)

Mid-Polis: Boston-Somerville, Massachusetts, USA

3.5
Global Mid-Polis
by Chris Nelson & Katie Fitzpatrick (Kanakos)

Mid-Polis: Melbourne, Australia + Guatemala City, Guatemala

Fringe Edge to the Inner City

3.1

Düsseldorf
by Bryan Apito

Along the Rhine River between Düsseldorf's city center and its main airport lies the historic town of Kaiserswerth. In-between Kaiserswerth and Düsseldorf is a large expanse of farmland gradually being filled in by low-density sprawl. The farmland is critical to the area's development and is served by a four-mile levee system along Rhine. The goal of this project was to build up the levee region into a dense new waterfront mid-polis of urban life. This academic study proposes reducing urban sprawl while preserving the surrounding farmland.

The infrastructure and residential zones in the new mid-polis run along the river. Particular attention was paid to the area around the A44 highway and the iconic airport bridge that bisects the levee region. This area would become the location for a new Sustainable Agriculture and Ecological Studies College for the existing Heinrich Heine University Düsseldorf. Long glass greenhouses, oriented southward, pierce through the building's shell and peer dramatically over the flat landscape. The school's program is planned and integrated with the area directly near the bridge. A learning platform serves as a school on the water and a place to learn about river ecology. A student-run organic market is lofted below the bridge and opens toward the grassy floodplain below. A tractor barn allows the students and farmers to learn from each other year-round. The barn is lifted on pilotis beneath the bridge. A ferry landing was added to the north side of the bridge, enabling students and visitors to travel to the site without using an automobile.

By adding environmentally friendly transportation routes to Kaiserswerth, the city and suburbs are better connected. Areas of the farmland are sectioned off for public use, so those who live in the city can ferry or bicycle north to Kaiserswerth and tend to a small field or garden. The homes along the river all have direct access to the water and can use the river as a new method of transportation to and from this new waterfront mid-polis.

by **Bryan Apito & Tom Sherman**
Roger Williams University

MID-POLIS: DÜSSELDORF, GERMANY + RIO DE JANEIRO, BRAZIL

Riverfront center entry

Greenhouse facilities

Center with adjacent preserved farmland

Riverfront walk

Central greenhouse stack

Riverfront with boat dock

Front façade

Waterfront edge with preserved farmland

Rio de Janeiro
by Tom Sherman

Rio de Janeiro's poor neighborhoods have swollen in recent decades due to droves of rural migrants moving to the city for work. Today, numerous fringe hillsides and industrial regions around Rio house these new migrants, including a large expanse extending northward and inland from downtown called Zona Norte.

In the heart of this region between the city center and Rio's inland towns, a mid-polis condition can arise as a new community node revolving around sport and other inexpensive gatherings that repair the strained social conditions of the area. The project site lies within the communities of Jacarezinho and Marimba in Zona Norte near an infrastructural nexus of overlapping highways, rail lines and canals that have framed the general growth of each community. Consequently, the proximate land value of this region has dropped, allowing low-rise dense migrant housing to flourish. However, although these regions are poverty-stricken and detached from other parts of the city, they have developed a dense urban integrity that provides easy pedestrian access to numerous urban local settings that can be repaired with nominal funding.

For this project, the region's overused playing field and canal system between the dense Jacarezinho community and the more dispersed Marimba region were selected as the site of a new enhanced mixed-use complex. The new facility was designed to bridge the canal gap by building new modern housing in both Jacarezinho and Marimba while allowing the canal to flow through the site within a new set of urban plazas and residences overlooking the waterway.

Existing conditions

Intervention

Canal corridor bridge

Ground level passage

Central plaza adjacent to stadium

Stadium entry

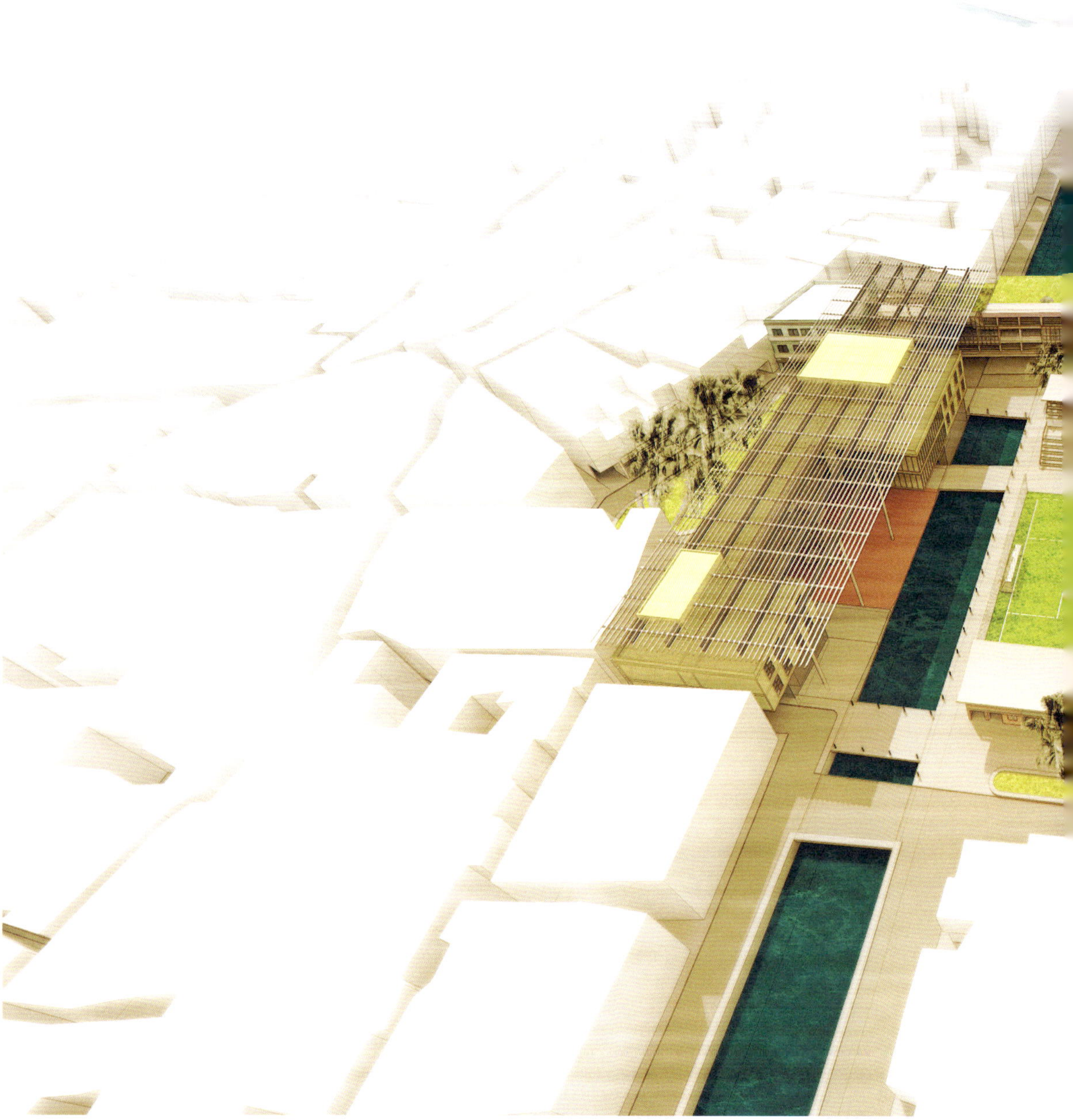

Local stadium infill along canal

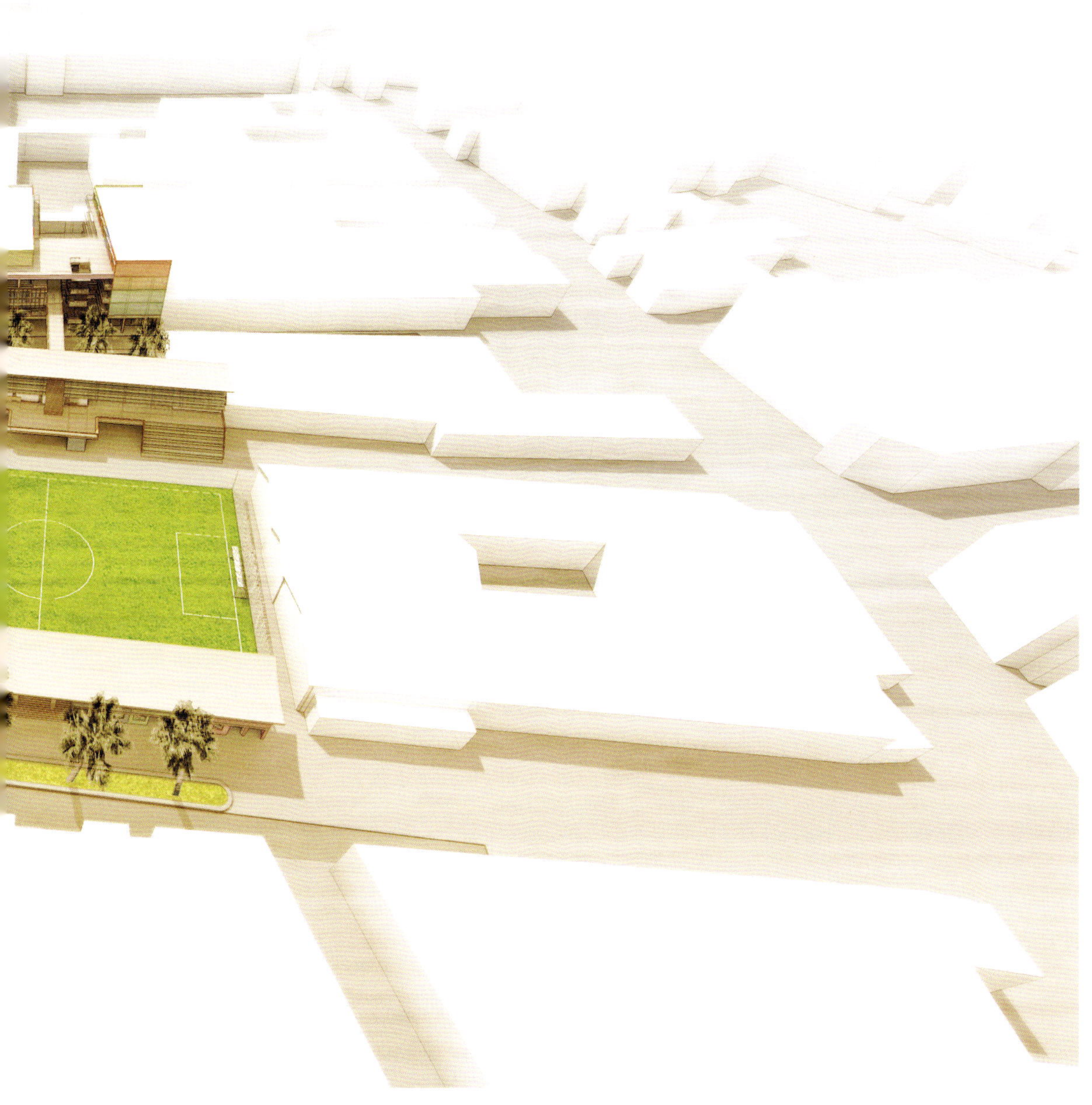

Inner Belt / Brickbottom 3.2

by Matthew Kleinmann

Meant to serve as an American hub for high-speed rail manufacturing, this proposal calls for the creation of a new railway assembly facility. The proposed site plan relies on the distribution method of New England manufacturing to move raw material efficiently through the region. Various rail links converge toward Somerville's Inner Belt. By partnering with Amtrak, the owners of the nearby railway on the southern edge of the site, the new rail car factory benefits from accessible, direct delivery and shipment of all parts to and from their assembly stages via rail. Future connections are made through the buildings, allowing for penetration through the rail berm, offering significant opportunities for the future growth of this facility.

The availability of housing on the site is minimal and generally of low density. By adding new landscape – infrastructure typologies which encourage pedestrian thoroughfare – the landscape is integrated as part of this industrial backdrop. The orientation of the new rail lines helps to generate a new urban block structure, which creates a balanced mix of open and closed spaces. Many of the open spaces generate attractive courtyard spaces. An underground parking structure helps to support denser developments above grade. Many lessons are learned from the Amsterdam Zuidas case study. In the Zuidas district, its eastern edge mixes highway and rail-oriented transportation with an interwoven fabric of landscape typologies, thereby minimizing the impact of larger scale infrastructure in a new development area.

by **Matthew Kleinmann & Matthew Kuebler**

Washington University in St. Louis

MID-POLIS: BOSTON-SOMERVILLE, MASSACHUSETTS, USA

New manufacturing hub with community path corridor and rail edge looking south

General plan

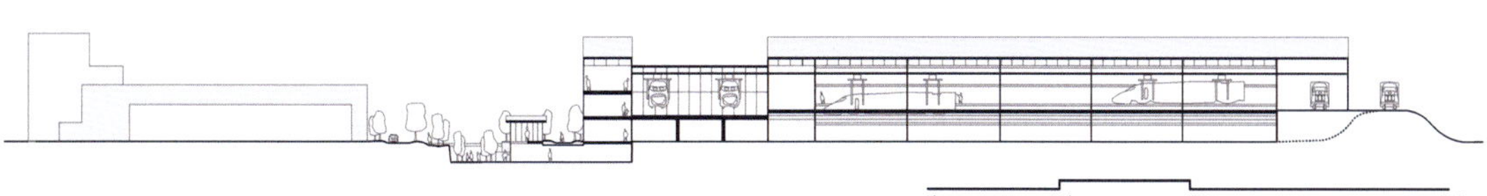

Section

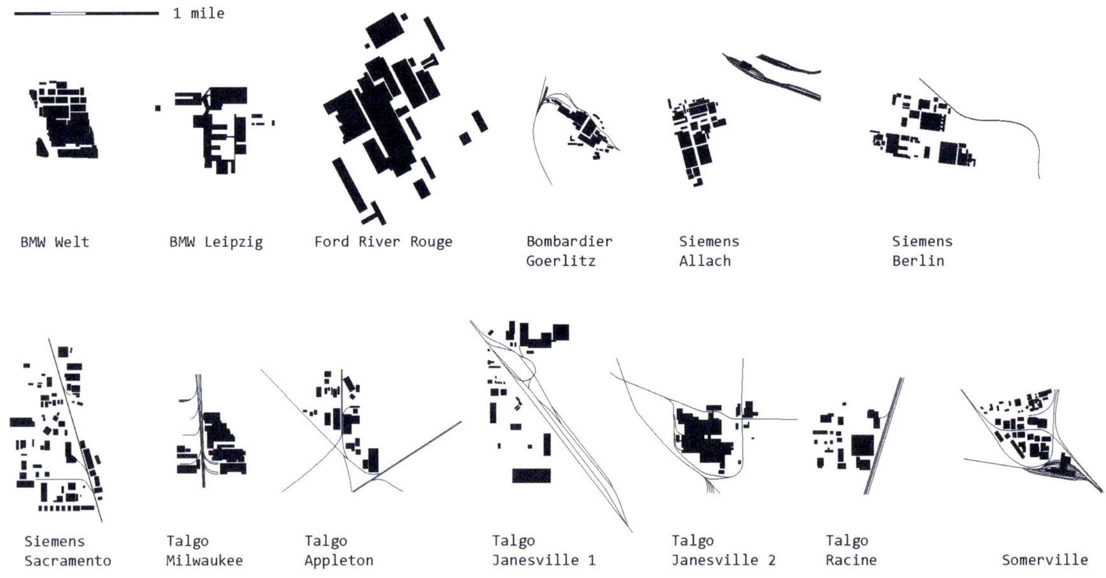

International case studies

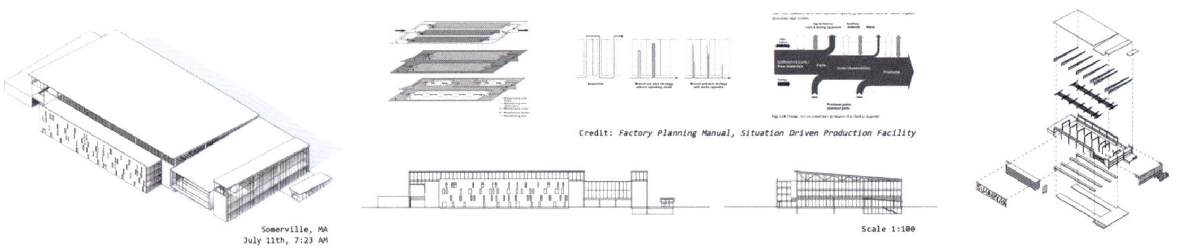

Factory building components

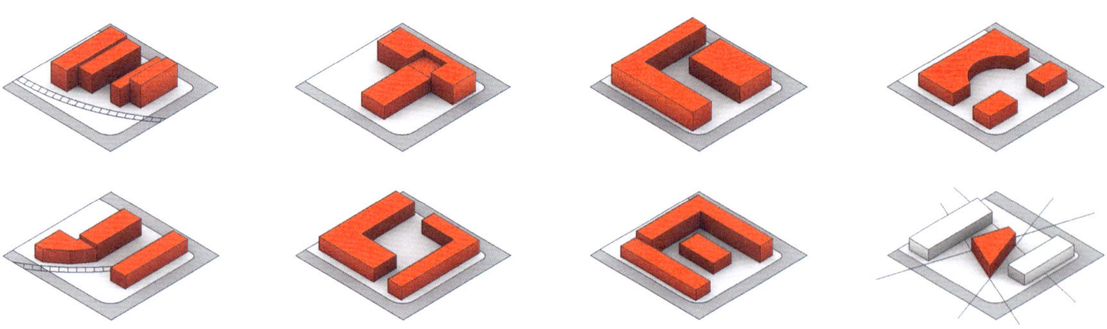

Building infill configurations

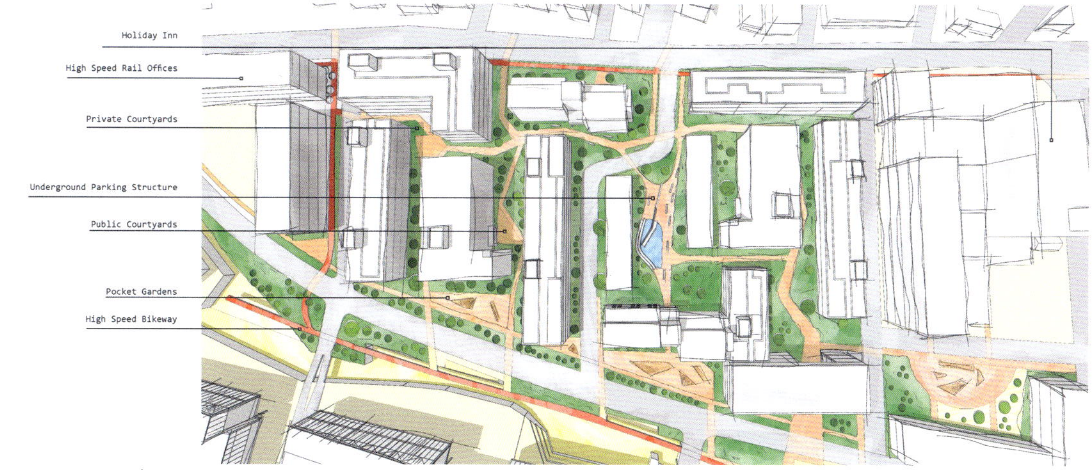

Washington Street Corridor - West

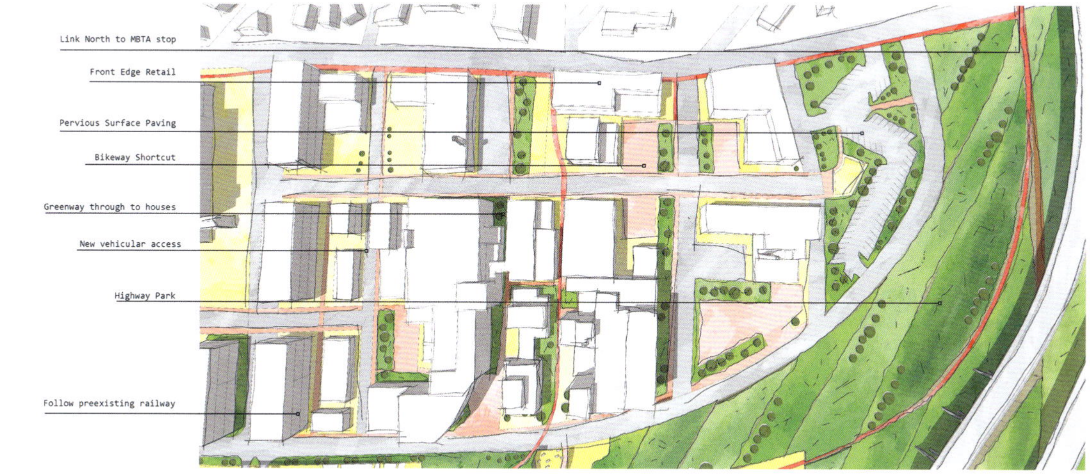

Washington Street Corridor - East

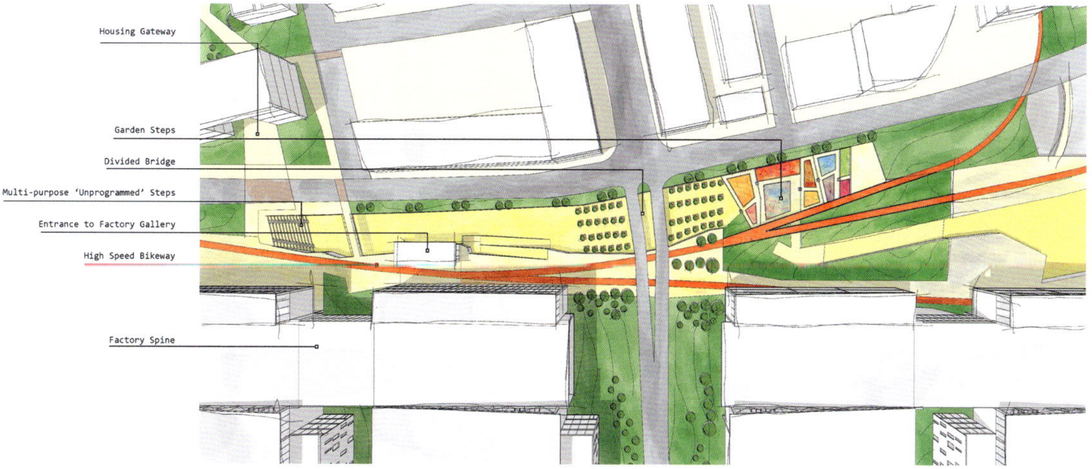

Greenway plaza between Washington Street Corridor and Inner Belt Factory

Greenway corridor

Old and new tied together by open space

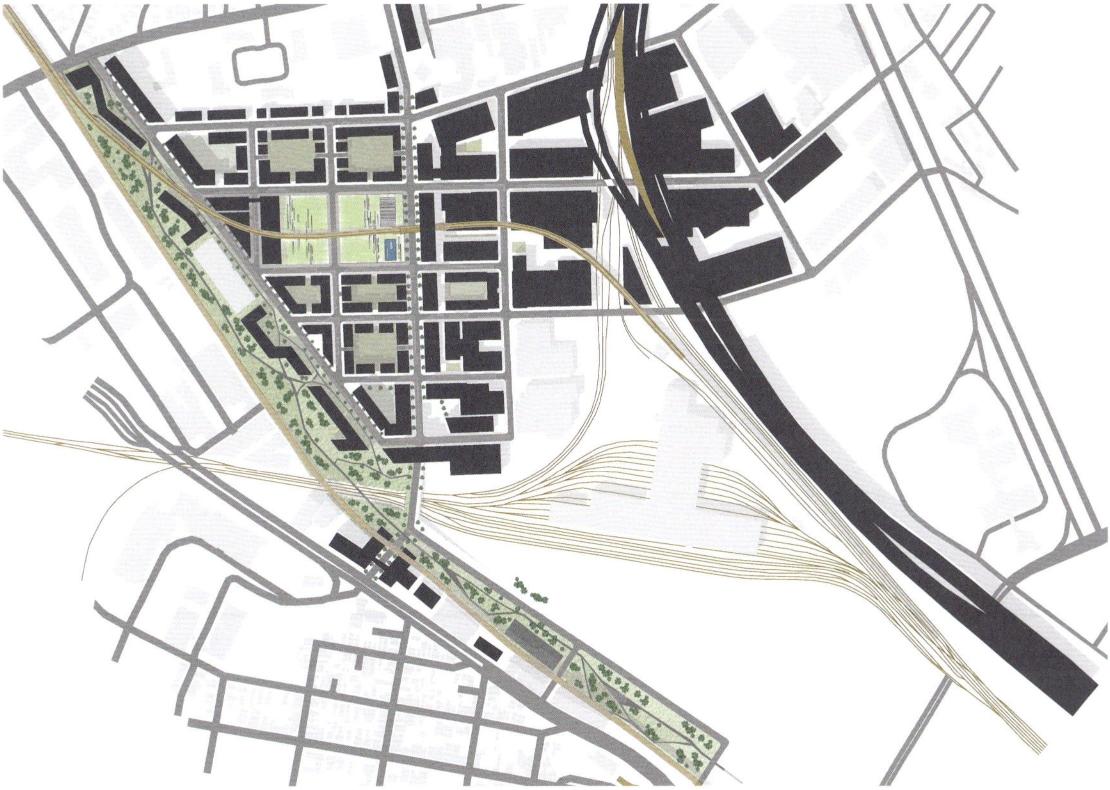

Inner Belt master plan

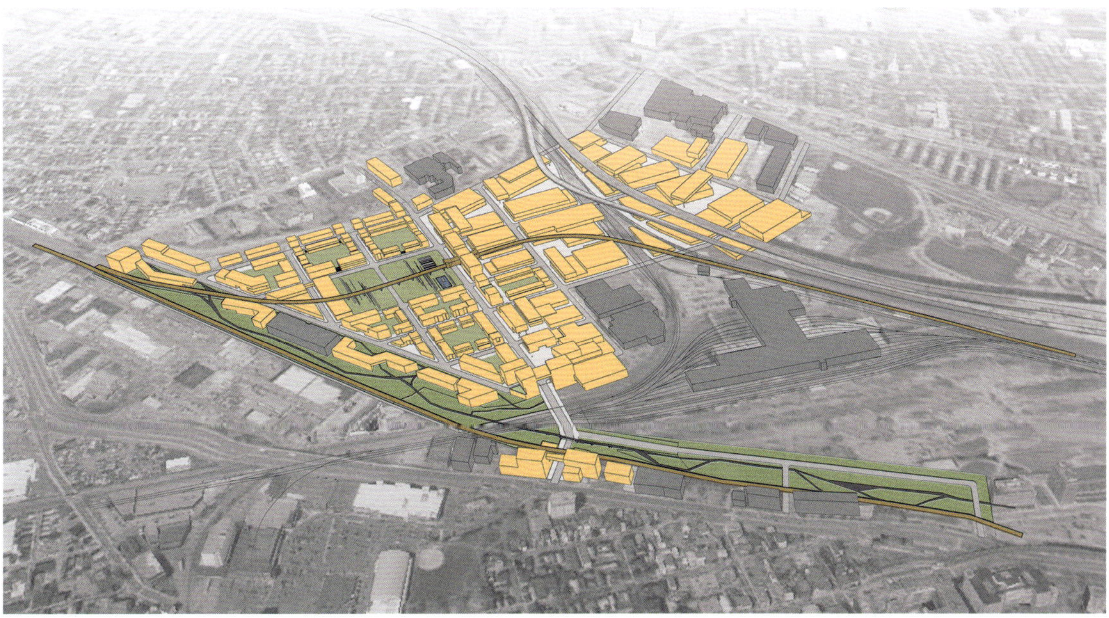

Continuous infill underneath existing rail lines and Interstate 93

by Matthew Kuebler

Since the site consists of a large industrial park with limited access, the primary concern was to provide connections to the adjacent areas. This goal was further complicated by the site's confinement by infrastructural elements on the east, south and west, which presented themselves as barriers. While the current condition lacked organization, density and flow, the site still presented itself with an array of opportunities for improvement. Understanding the history of this part of Somerville was essential to creating a positive transformation and design approach. The presence of industry and infrastructure was not to be removed, merely transformed and consolidated. This act would create more developable land, allowing for the diversification of land uses within the site. Accentuated by the introduction of an urban greenway, an extended mass transit line, and new urban typologies, the site would be transformed into a more inviting, diversified landscape.

The design approach was largely governed by establishing three primary components. The first involved the consolidation of the existing industry into a denser core. The industry was shifted to the west, harnessing land under and adjacent to the elevated freeway, which would otherwise be considered unusable. While this opened up the western edge condition, the second component transformed the eastern edge condition into an urban greenway, establishing a green spine that bridges over the transit rail lines and provides access into Cambridge toward the Charles River and Boston's larger green network. The final component of the design was the creation of a commercial/urban spine at the center of the site. This was used to negotiate and blur the division between the newly created residential blocks and the consolidated industrial core. The result was a design approach that opened the site to adjacent neighborhoods, established more flow and structure in the urban landscape, and minimized the divide between otherwise segregated land uses.

Green spine + open space

Consolidation of industry underneath Interstate 93

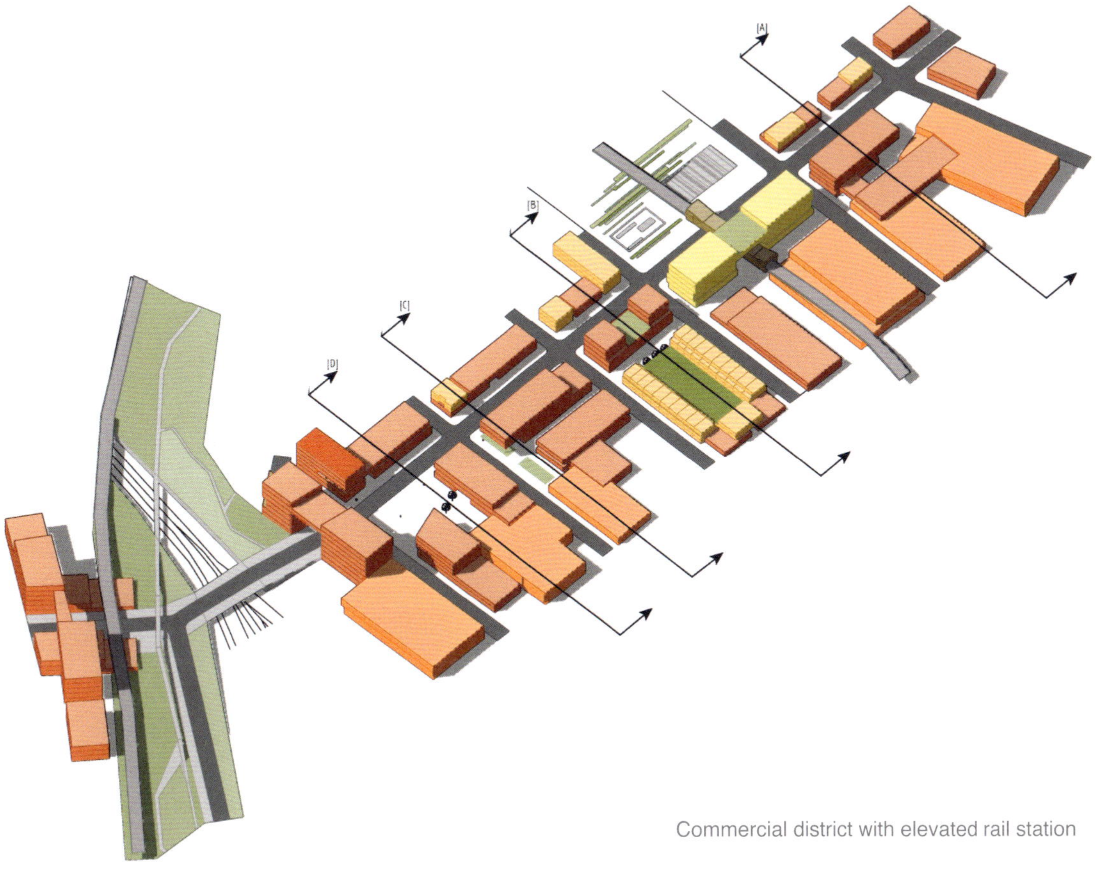

Commercial district with elevated rail station

Elevated rail station details

PROJECT OPTIONS

BUILDING

Courtyard form

Street responsive form

Warehouse form

Responsive form

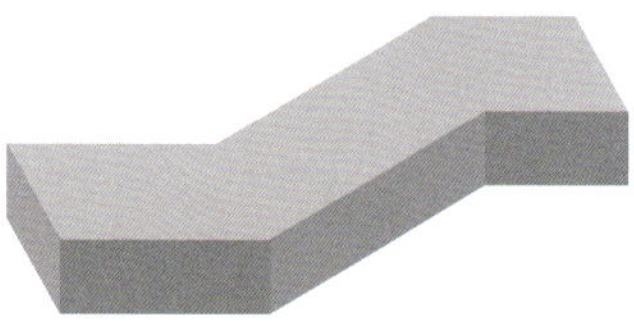

Carved form

SPATIAL

Public square

Expanded sidewalk

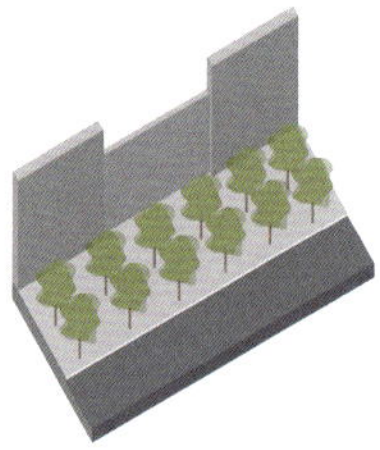

Pathway

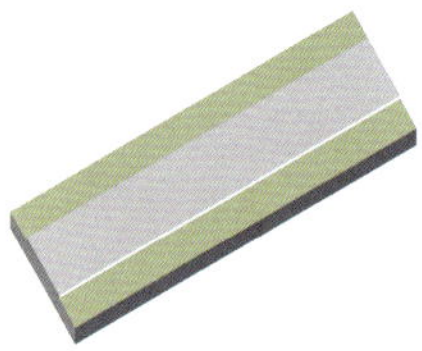

Service space

Semi-private public space

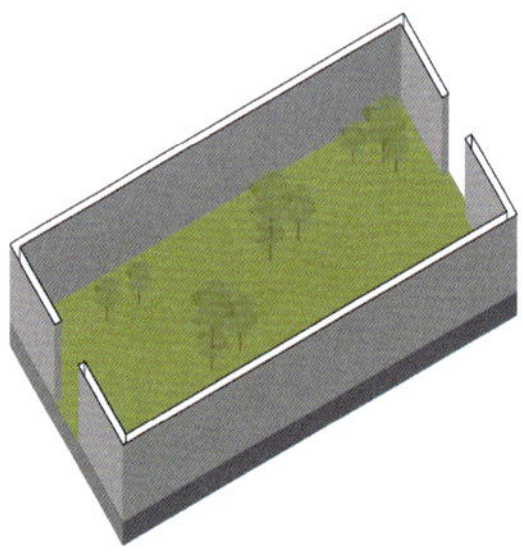

Linear park (greenway)

INFRASTRUCTURE

Road

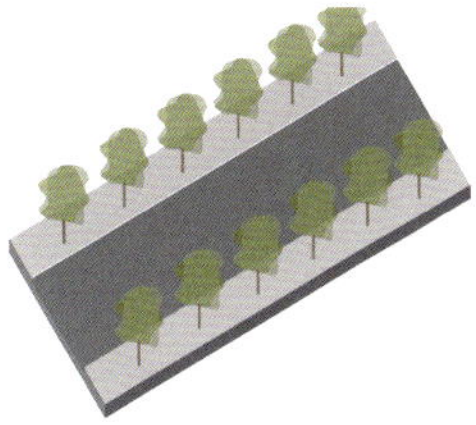

Boulevard

Rail at grade

Rail bridged by landscape

Elevate rail

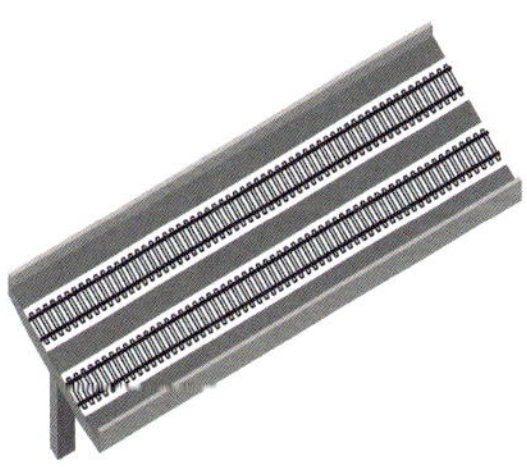

Elevated highway

LANDSCAPE

Recreational

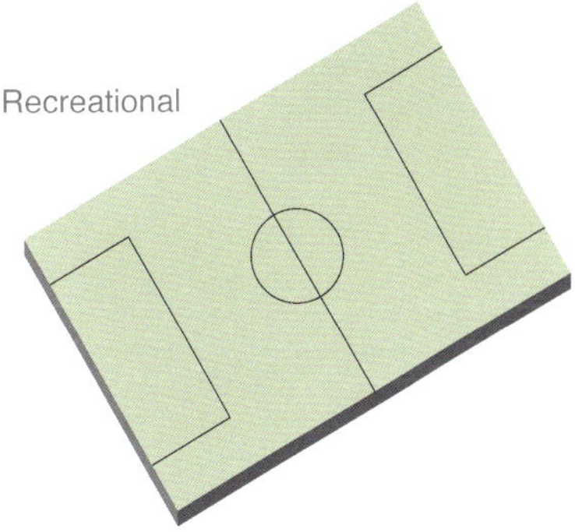

Fluid

Spatial definition

Topographical

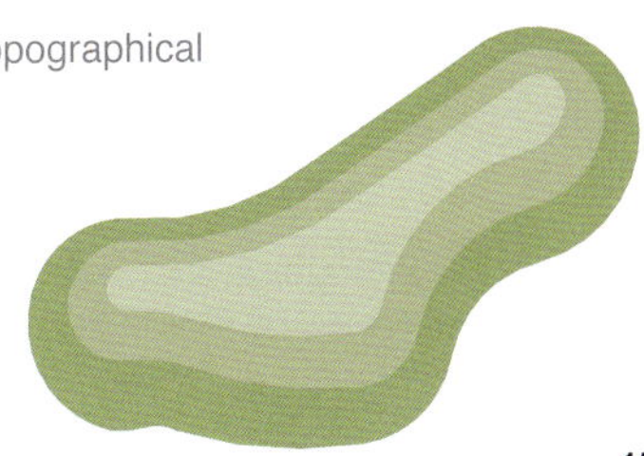

Mall to Mid-Polis Transformations

3.3

A peripheral mall located in proximity to an active transit corridor presents mid-polis conditions that can offer opportunities for transformation, while elevating the quality of the larger metropolis.

Some of these conditions will have a rail corridor running directly through the region, as seen in San Diego, California. While other malls have become the regional transit centers for local communities such as Columbia, Maryland, this city of 100,000 is located in-between Baltimore and Washington, D.C. Both in San Diego and Columbia, the shopping center becomes a major node of transit and retail that can continue to evolve over time into a strong mixed-use community.

In San Diego, the metro area has a large-scale suburban mall and a surrounding shopping district to the north and west, called Grossmont Center in La Mesa. It has a tram service running through the district. The mid-polis already functions as a connected urban node. It can continue to capitalize on this new linkage by redeveloping additional suburban-oriented strip malls alongside the central mall into a denser set of neighborhoods and districts. In time, the mall will continue to evolve into a locale where residents and visitors alike can embrace public transit over more conventional auto-centric patterns of transportation.

Finally, in Columbia, Maryland, the town's large mall functions as the region's central hub and transit node. In addition, the mall property and the shopping facility can be gradually carved up into smaller blocks and open spaces.

Waterfront amenities and varied programming for the mall and its adjacent developments are already evolving into a richer array of uses and amenities. This further anchors Columbia as an attractive mid-polis – poised between two larger cities in the Washington-Baltimore metropolis.

by **Brian Boisvert & Evan Krasik**
Roger Williams University

MID-POLIS: COLUMBIA, MARYLAND, USA + SAN DIEGO, CALIFORNIA, USA

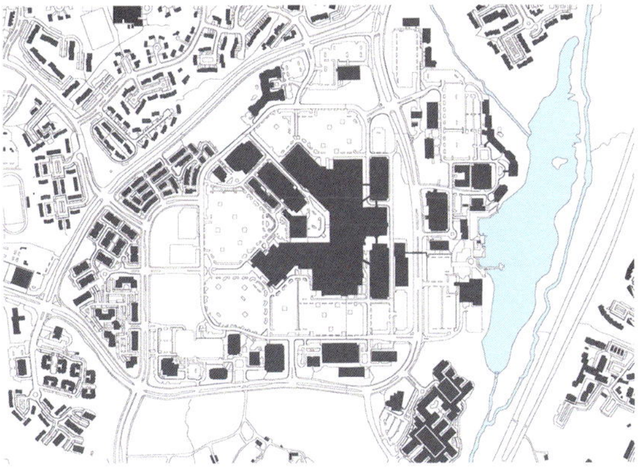

Existing

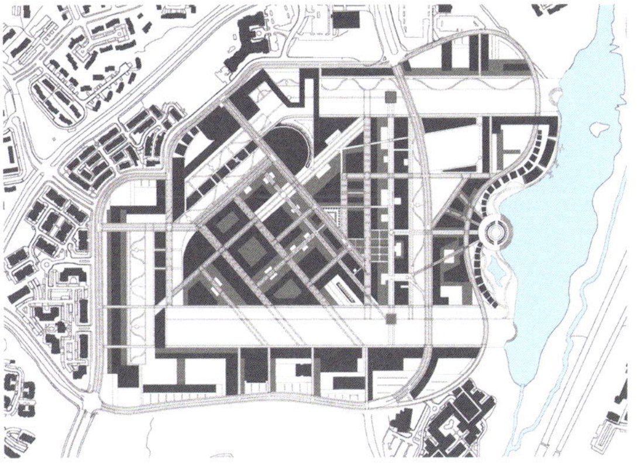

Transformation

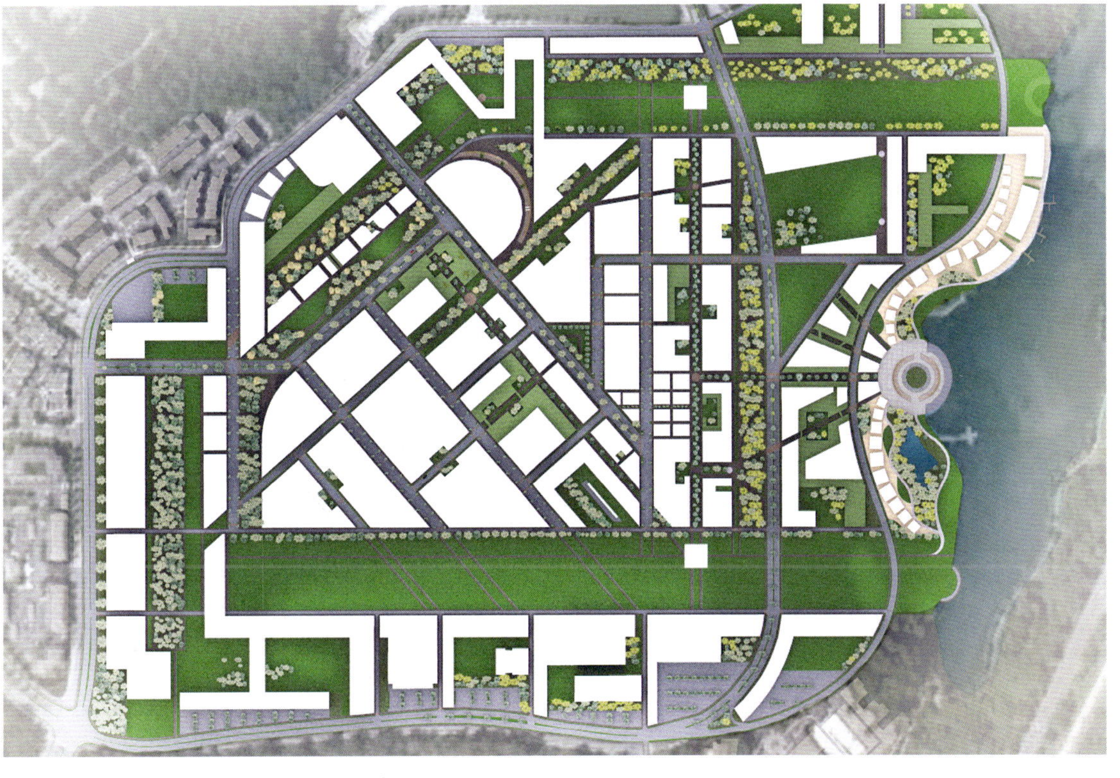

Columbia transformation: open space web

Columbia - Open space web

Columbia - Waterfront plaza

San Diego - Current mall conditions

San Diego - New development adjacent to the existing mall

San Diego - Nighttime activity

Somerville Brickbottom Stadium

3.4

Loosely defined as a gap in the urban fabric that is Boston, Cambridge and Somerville, the Brickbottom district in Somerville, Massachusetts, represents a mid-polis condition that has a multi-layered history. This precedent represents a rich example of industrial forces shaping the environment. One focused on production of cars and industrial components, fabricated in an array of smaller-scale workshops.

Directly adjacent to the Inner Belt (partly located in Somerville and Medford), this district is gritty and rough around the edges. It is a district saved in part by pioneering artists willing to transform industrial concrete-framed buildings into hip and cool studios, lofts and galleries. They were not bothered by the elevated highways and train tracks. Today, this area has been further inhabited by speculative life-science labs and office buildings.

Given the disordinate programs, oversized scale, and amenity-poor qualities that make up the Brickbottom mid-polis, this district begs for a stronger, more cohesive urban intervention. To that end, two sets of initiatives are proposed: one builds on the artists' brand, the other on introducing sports and entertainment.

Fostering a dialogue between preservation and innovation, this proposal seeks to transform the Brickbottom District through urban collage and introducing and layering a range of different building types and open spaces, very much inspired by the architectural language of the current district, and by using the existing rail lines that run through the center of the site as a green spine fed by trams that will connect people and places. A new community of thinking, creating, manufacturing, and living will emerge.

A cornerstone of the proposed Brickbottom district will be the Somerville Center for the Arts. The center's community arts programs will be dedicated to bringing artists to schools, non-profit service agencies and community organizations working with

by **Adria Longenderfer**
& Rebecca Sommer (Castellon)

Washington University in St. Louis

MID-POLIS: BOSTON-SOMERVILLE, MASSACHUSETTS, USA

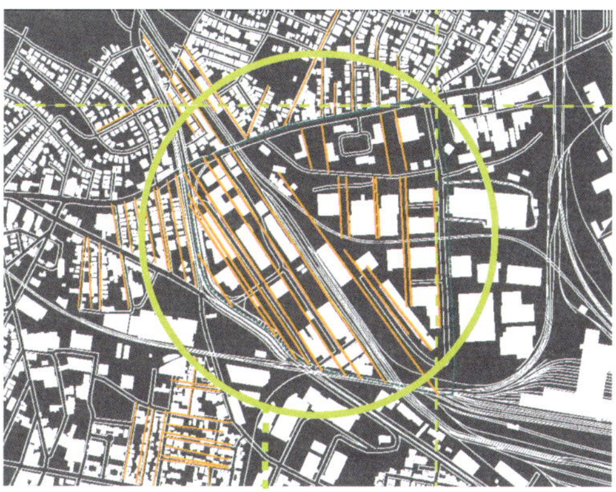

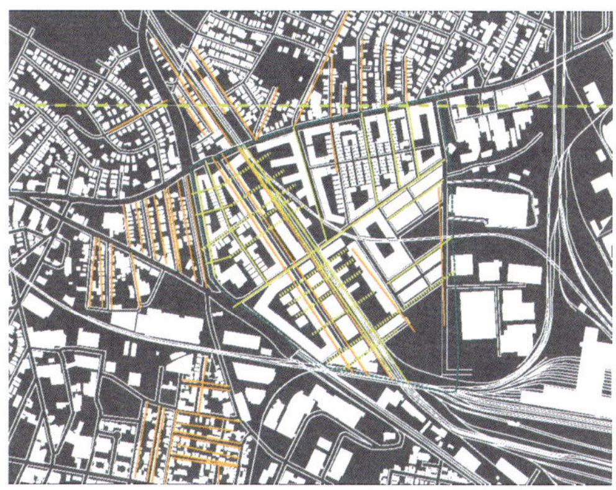

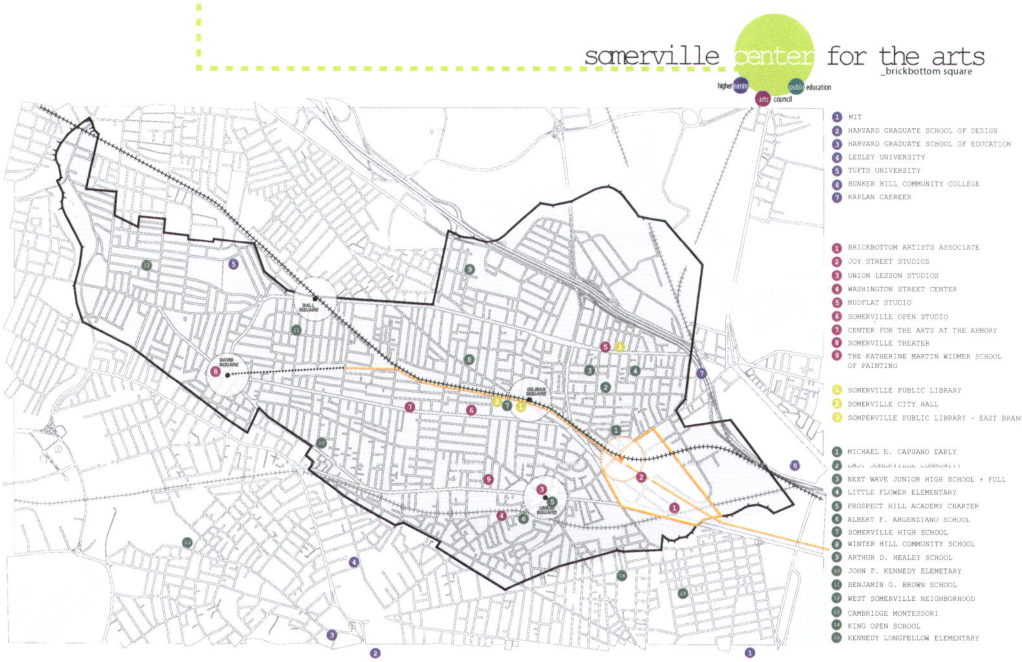

Somerville arts & culture map

Somerville Center for the Arts

Site plan

Public (Art) space

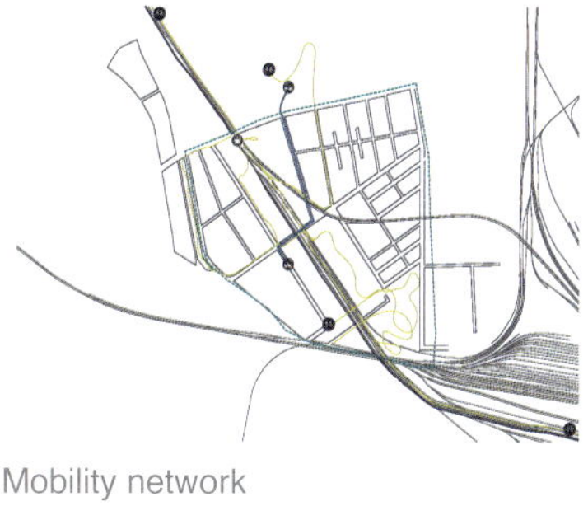

Mobility network

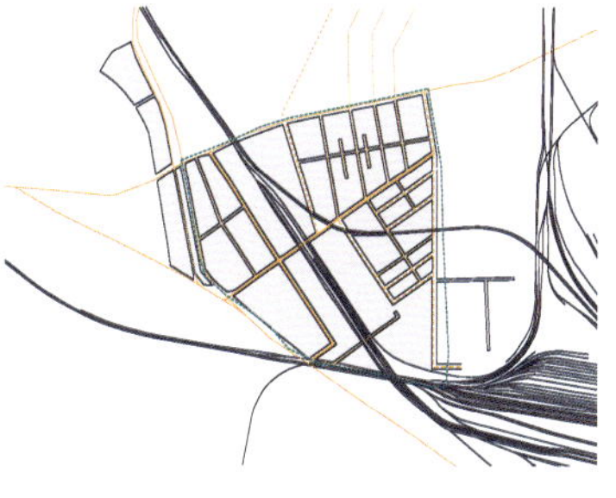

Street network

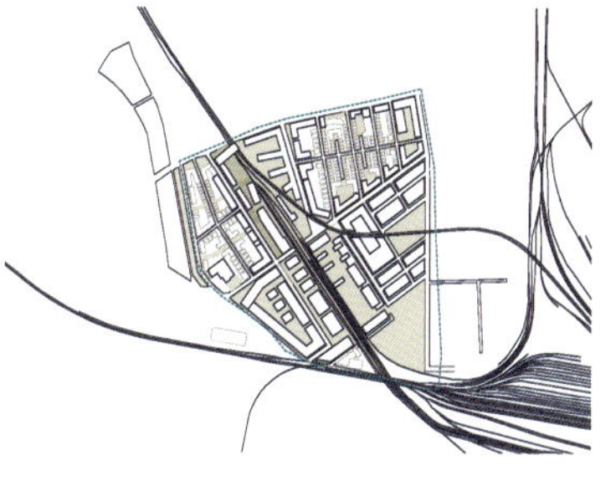

Public spaces

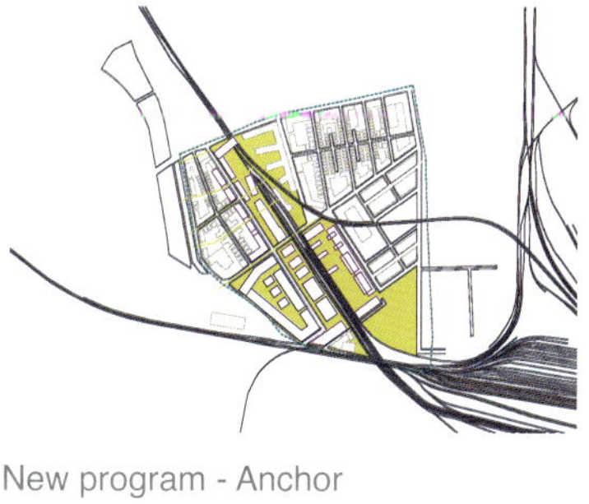

New program - Anchor

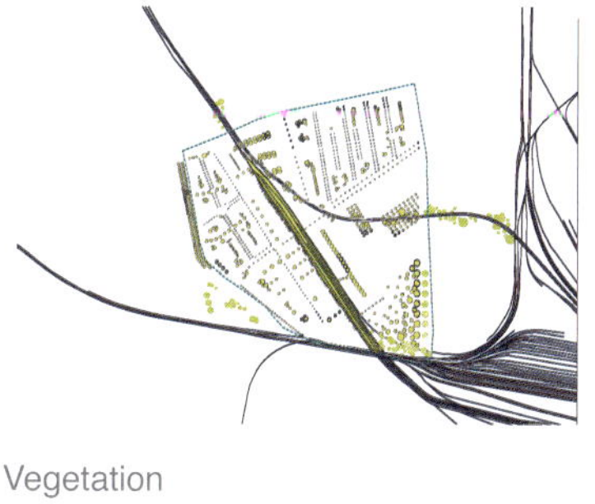

Vegetation

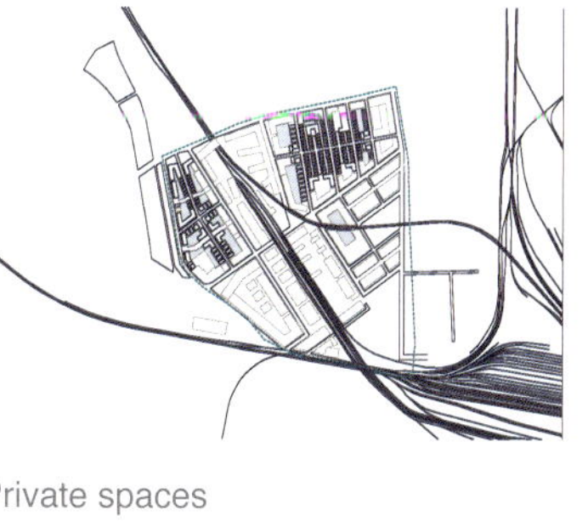

Private spaces

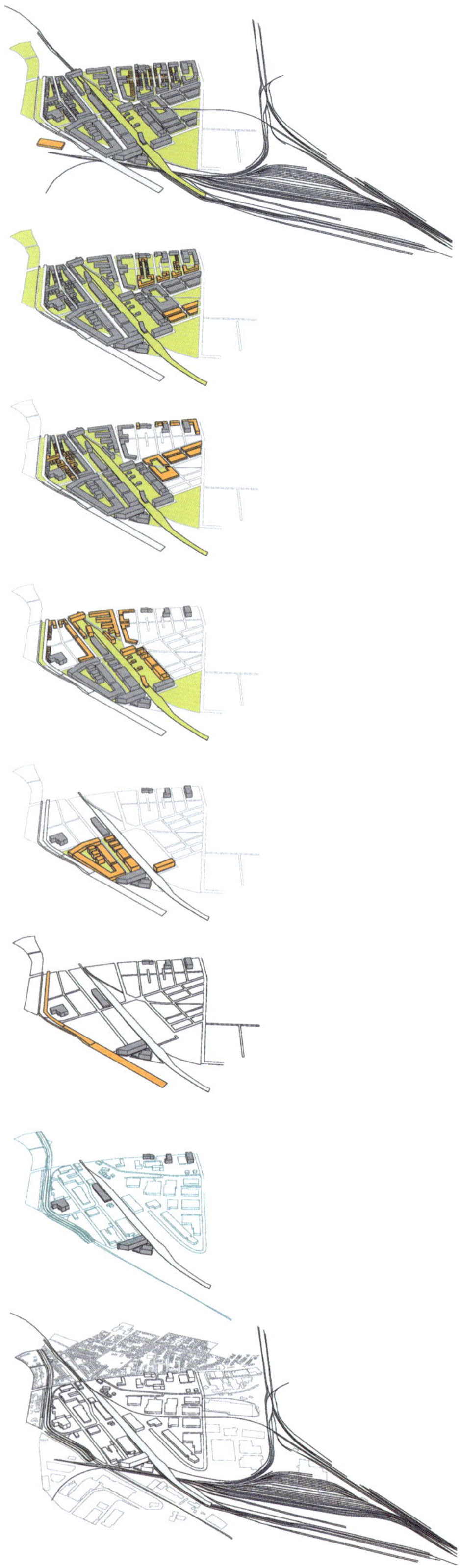

Brickbottom transformation

both children and adults. Ultimately, the mission of the Somerville Center for the Arts at the Brickbottom district will be to promote the arts; to encourage and support artists and their development; to assist arts organizations; and to facilitate communication and cooperation among artists, arts organizations, and other designers in the community.

The Inner Belt and Brickbottom neighborhoods have been at the center of speculation concerning a new potential urban sports hub in Metro Boston. The impending conversion of the McGrath Highway into a boulevard running from Boston to points north will allow Somerville's local urban fabric to extend eastward to the city's recently realized Green Line rail extension. This expansion area is wide enough to accommodate large-scale structures, such as a stadium for American major-league soccer, lacrosse, and regional music/festival events. Thanks to transit, bike and pedestrian access, this district offers attractive development and business opportunities for developers and small business owners alike.

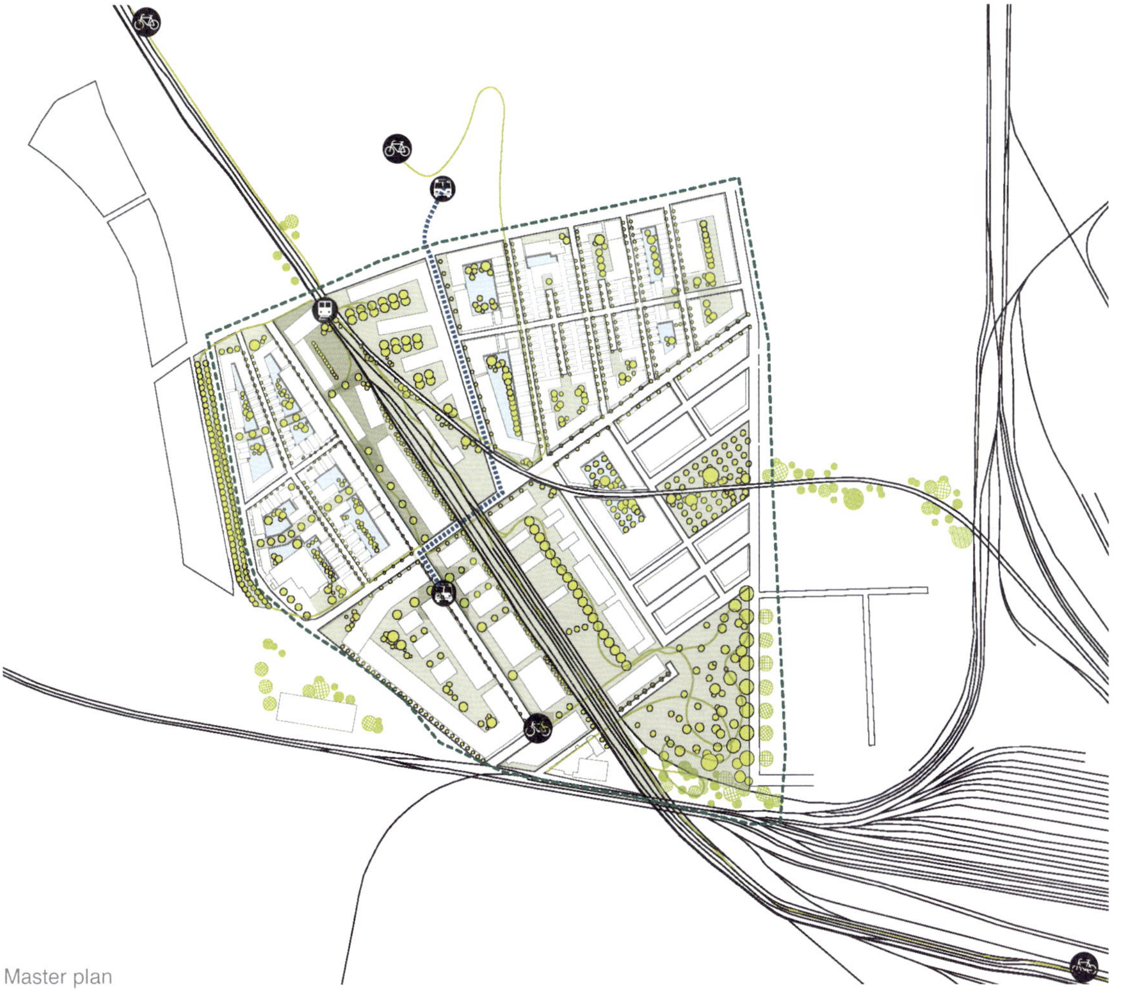

Master plan

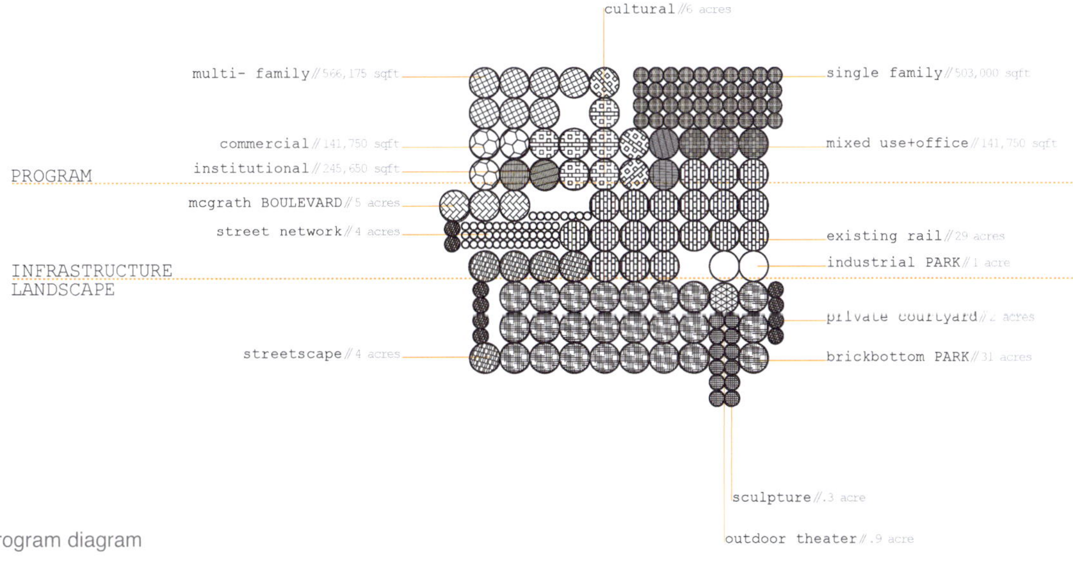

Program diagram

Arena infill alongside preserved Brickbottom artist community

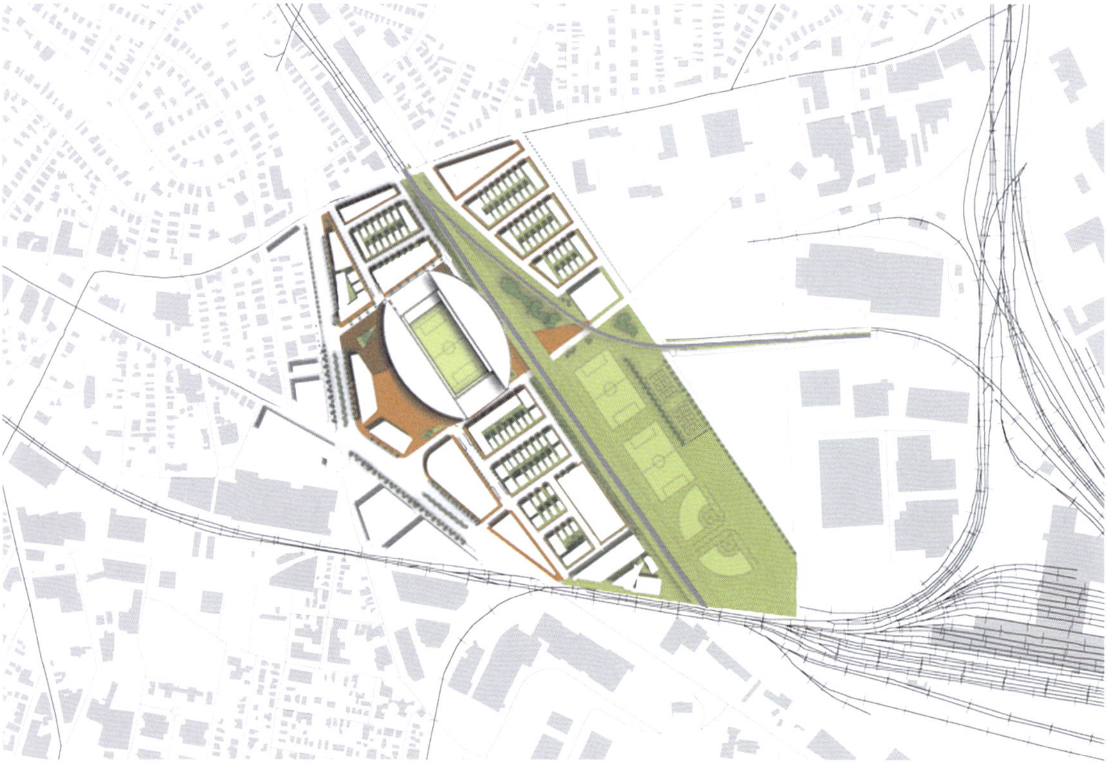

Arena in context

Stadium timeline

A small 25,000-seat stadium fits neatly into this area, bounded in part by the new McGrath Highway and the new Green Line Extension. Much like Boston's famous Fenway Park, which is surrounded by businesses and hospitality amenities, this new soccer stadium anchors a new district that is populated by a range of uses, including much-needed housing.

Thus, the once fragmentary and disjointed Brickbottom area can evolve into a region that supports the arts and sports while offering new housing opportunities and amenities. It is an area that can build on its industrial and arts-oriented past while introducing new uses.

Global Mid-Polis 3.5

Across varied urban communities in both industrialized nations and developing third-world countries, numerous mid-polis conditions can be harnessed for a series of different interventions. Two examples within this spectrum are the industrialized metropolis of Melbourne in Australia and the fledgling national capital of Guatemala City within Central America. Both are vital urban infill conditions in their respective metro areas.

The first example entails the reuse of Melbourne's old industrial harbor for dense urban expansion between downtown to the east and the suburbs to the west. Various rail lines snake through the property, while the city's tram network, the largest system of its kind, can easily expand into the site from downtown and foster decades of new urban growth on land with existing infrastructure, utilities, rail links, and nearby waterfront access.

In contrast, Guatemala City can use the loosely defined open space in a fringe favela to develop a new community center focused on neighborhood development and female empowerment in the growing capital city. Such a facility within walking distance of a large urban swath of the city will serve as a local leadership center within the sprawling region. The new center will house a number of day-to-day operations, such as a school, a medical clinic, and a job placement center, while working as a gathering space for special events. This new complex will not only transform the fringe neighborhood into a new urban node but will also serve as a strong mixed-use community of public open space and amenities for a large urban population in need of services.

Both mid-polis conditions – the industrialized harbor of Melbourne and the favelas of Guatemala City – will become strong productive centers in their own right at different scales of intervention and change.

by **Chris Nelson & Katie Fitzpatrick (Kanakos)**

Roger Williams University

MID-POLIS: MELBOURNE, AUSTRALIA + GUATEMALA CITY, GUATEMALA

Reused Melbourne yards

Melbourne mid-polis - Plaza space

Melbourne mid-polis - Pedestrian corridors

Melbourne mid-polis - Pedestrian bridge

Melbourne mid-polis - Local field

Melbourne mid-polis - Community layers

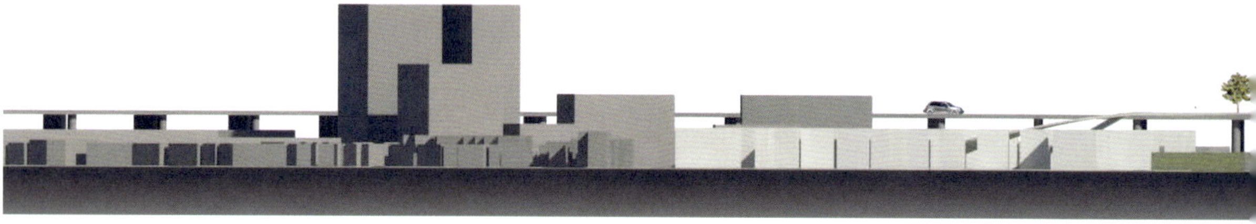

Melbourne mid-polis - Community layers section

Guatemala City - Women's Center master plan

Guatemala mid-polis -Existing conditions

Guatemala mid-polis - Intervention

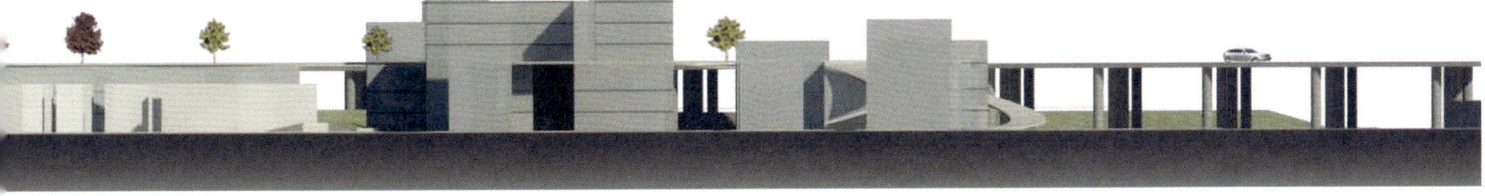

In-Depth Mid-Polis Projections

4.0

Somerville's Brickbottom District, looking toward Boston, photo by Peter Vanderwarker

4.1

Analysis of a Mid-Polis Condition

by Christian Clerc, Sarah Hill (Burnett), Matthew Kleinmann, Matthew Kuebler, Adria Longenderfer, Rebecca Sommer (Castellon), Yusheen Yang

Mid-Polis: Boston-Somerville, Massachusetts, USA

Photographs by Peter Vanderwarker

Analysis of a Mid-Polis Condition

4.1

Boston, Massachusetts, is a prominent business, technology and academic hub in the United States. It is located at the northern terminus of the Boston-Washington, D.C., (or Bos-Wash) corridor – a megalopolis of considerable scale.

Boston's 19th-century history was fueled and dominated by the Industrial Revolution. Conveniently serviced by a harbor feeding Atlantic routes and international markets, Boston's metropolitan area, factories, workshops, and warehouses needed to network new rail lines onto what was a city founded in the 16th and 17th century. After all, greater Boston comprises multiple communities and neighborhoods – Cambridge, Lexington, Brookline, Dorchester, etc. – each of which was its own village and township in the 1600s. Over time, the metropolis infilled the gaps among the villages with more development, so as to blanket the larger greater Boston terrain with contiguous urban growth.

To that end, greater Boston's metropolitan area integrated new rail lines that connected communities as part of a spoke-and-wheel rail network. Consequently, some of the nodes along the spokes become important rail junctions as rail lines crisscrossed the rugged New England landscape, built upon rocky ledges, waterways, wetlands, pastures, and woodlands. Somerville is one such community in which multiple rail lines crisscross through tight and constrained spaces.

Due to its strategic location and layered infrastructure, Somerville thrived as an industrial center, especially in the early 1900s. Factories and workshops were serviced by laborers living in worker-housing typologies. The triple-decker was the most famous workforce typology to offer spacious, affordable housing for workers and their families. By the early 20th century, Somerville evolved into one of the nation's most densely populated towns. Its 4 square miles, housed by over 80,000 people, speak of the efficiency of Somerville's housing and urban typologies.

MID-POLIS: BOSTON-SOMERVILLE, MASSACHUSETTS, USA

by **Christian Clerc, Sarah Hill (Burnett), Matthew Kleinmann, Matthew Kuebler, Adria Longenderfer, Rebecca Sommer (Castellon), Yusheen Yang**

Washington University in St. Louis
Photographs by Peter Vanderwarker

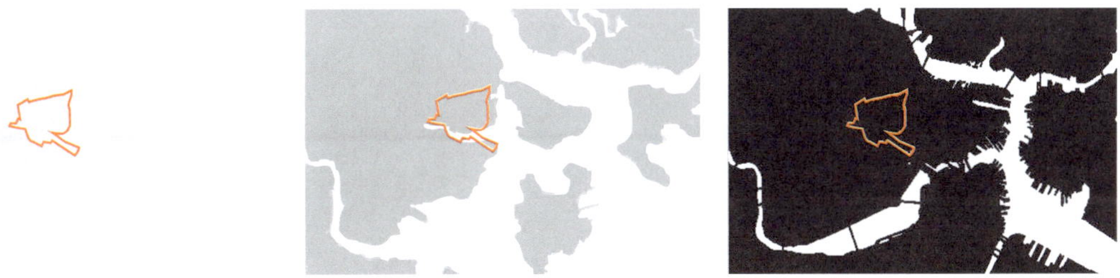

Land expansion 1630-2004

Existing Boston subway map

Site overview

Yet Somerville's future was significantly impacted by post-World War II trends in evolving urban form. The rise of highway systems funneling people from suburbs to city centers was consequential for inner-belt cities such as Somerville. Larger grain infrastructure systems, such as (elevated) highways, found their way into Somerville as well, McGrath Highway being the most prominent. Luckily, civic-minded activists put a halt to several major highway arteries that had been planned to rip through parts of Cambridge, Boston's South End and Roxbury, and parts of Somerville. Reducing the scope of infrastructure systems that fed Somerville's industries meant that the ease with which goods and services could be exchanged was reduced, as was the financial viability of local industries. Consequently, parts of the Somerville's inner-belt area and Brickbottom district declined economically and physically. Warehousing and other low-end land uses began to dominate the area. Neighboring urban nodes such as Union Square suffered as well, as economic activity fell back.

Building placement

Eventually, the 1970s and 1980s started to see the emergence of urban pioneers, particularly artists beginning to inhabit and convert underutilized factories and warehouses into artist studios and workshops. In time, the surrounding urban fabric in Somerville's Brickbottom and Inner Belt districts became more desirable for working and living. People in the suburbs sought a less auto-oriented suburban sprawl lifestyle. Also, local real estate values in Somerville escalated as neighboring Cambridge deregulated its rent-control laws.

Public open spaces

Renters in Cambridge sought more affordable housing in Somerville and other communities. However, these former blue-collar family neighborhoods also started to change due to the forces of gentrification. Simple triple-deckers and two-family homes in Somerville were rehabilitated into fancy condos. Even commercial strips and small retail outlets were eventually forced out of their neighborhoods. As a result, Somerville has been transformed, now strongly associated with an increasingly attractive set of Boston neighborhoods. The flipside of this is that many of the original owners and residents of Somerville have been displaced. Today, Somerville continues to struggle with its success, as it takes pride in its ability to create attractive public spaces and parks while improving its schools, infrastructure, and public services. Yet its success also impacts housing costs beyond what is affordable, certainly for long-time residents and renters.

This in turn has put market pressure on property owners to redevelop underutilized parcels in Somerville for new housing and job opportunities. Southeast Somerville in particular has experienced sustained development pressure, given its raw mix of industrial buildings, scrappy infrastructure, and neglected housing stock. Consequently, there are ongoing plans to transform the elevated McGrath Highway into an elegant tree-lined urban boulevard. In addition, the site has integrated into a new transit station that supports the Green Line Extension, which has improved access to neighboring cities such as Cambridge, Boston, and Brookline. Now Boston's tram line (also referred to as the Green Line) extends from Lechmere Square in Cambridge to Tufts University in Medford – which is on the fringe of Boston's inner beltway. This extension completely changes Somerville's urban dynamics, offering considerable access (within walking distance) to public transportation for 95% of Somervillians. In addition, the Brickbottom site has become a source of ongoing speculation for a new major-league soccer arena. With easy access to two public transit lines, several bus stops, and a central location, Somerville's Brickbottom area presents a unique opportunity for a new arena with a capacity of some 25,000 fans.

Neighborhood context

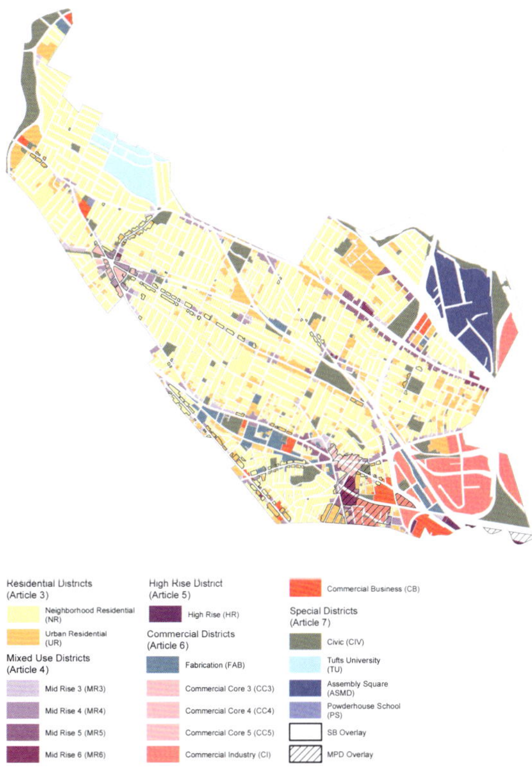

Zoning

Somerville's Brickbottom District, looking toward Boston

Current Somerville rail corridor from Boston

Low-density landscape

Vehicular repository

Zone of Transformation:
Summary Overview of Somerville's Context

Located north of Boston in Middlesex County, Somerville is the most densely populated municipality in the metro area. The city is bounded to the north by the Mystic River and the communities of Medford, Malden, and Everett; to the west by the Alewife Brook and Arlington; and to the east and south by the cities of Boston and Cambridge. Today, Somerville is a changing mix of blue-collar families, young professionals, empty-nesters, college students, and recent immigrants. One-third of Somerville's residents are foreign-born, and more than 50 languages are spoken in Somerville's schools. With a large immigrant population, the city celebrates its diversity through numerous ceremonies, cultural traditions, and holidays. Somerville has historically been a city of renters; while the rest of the nation has homeownership rates around 60-65%, Somerville's homeownership rate is roughly 44%. This is due in part to Somerville's ideal location near greater Boston's major academic institutions. Tufts, Harvard, and MIT are all within walking distance of the city's numerous residential communities, thus many undergraduate and graduate students make Somerville their home.

Since 2000, single-family homes have increased in price by 90%, and condominium prices have increased by 46%, making Somerville unaffordable to many residents. It is known for its large number of squares, which help mark neighborhood boundaries while featuring bustling businesses and entertainment centers. Among the most active today are Davis Square, Union Square, Ball Square, Teele Square, and Magoun Square. Each offers a mix of ethnic restaurants, bars, shops, and small businesses. The Massachusetts Bay Transportation Authority (MBTA) runs the fifth largest public transit system in the country, which serves approximately 1.1 million passengers every day. In metro Boston, about 15% of the population commutes to work using public transit, compared to 25% in Somerville. A range of areas around Boston offers approximate ten-minute walking distances to metro stops. Most of Somerville is now serviced by the MBTA's newly expanded public transit network.

According to 2023 Census Reporter data, 6% of Somerville's residents and workers walk to work, and the city has consistently been ranked among the top 10 walkable cities in the nation, due in part to its ranking as the nation's most family-friendly city, according to a 2023 Coastal Neighborhoods report. Somerville also ranks as the seventh most eco-friendly city for transit in the nation, Realtor.com reported in 2025. The two major multi-use city paths for pedestrians and bicyclists are the Mystic River Path and Davis Square's Community Path, which connects to the Minuteman Bikeway.

The key industries in Somerville are health services, retail, and creative design, which are heavily integrated through both suppliers and customers with regional hubs in Boston and Cambridge. Somerville's local economic base is heavily influenced by three factors: its dense residential population, the nature of its commercial and industrial building stock, and its proximity to Boston. The high residential population supports numerous commercial clusters across the city's small-and medium-sized squares.

Honing In on the Site:
Inner Belt – Brickbottom District

The site is in a low-lying region, historically referred to as Milldam Marsh. Once a wetland connected with the Charles River, the marsh was filled in to allow for various infrastructure networks and eventually development. The site has remained a low-density region among the urban communities of Somerville, Cambridge, and Boston throughout its history. The project site lies mostly within Somerville; however, several parts of the site extend into Cambridge and Boston. This is due to site boundaries that were largely driven by the physical landscape. Today, various road and rail networks running from Boston to the suburbs dissect the site into several large fragments. Although there appears to be a coherent urban grain in the bordering communities, the site itself is a hodgepodge of building types, including large utilitarian industrial structures, big-box outlets, retailers, and artist lofts. Most of the unbuilt open space on the site consists of parking

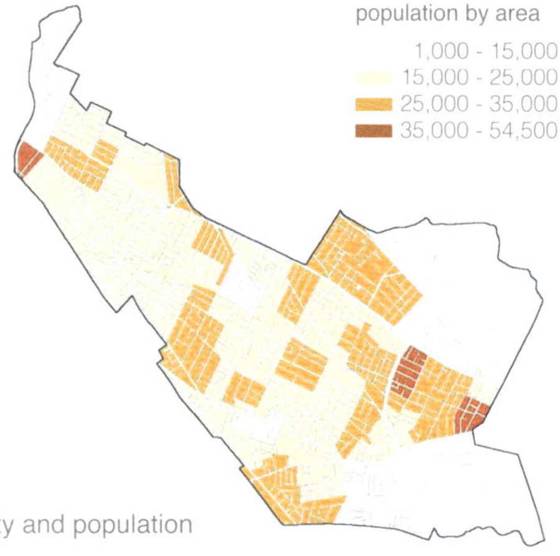

Density and population

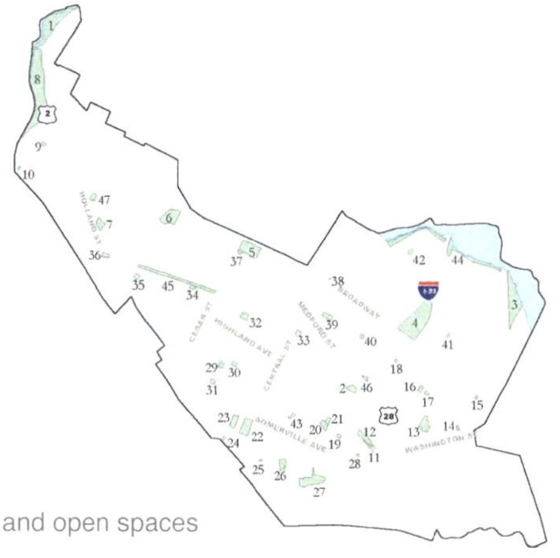

Parks and open spaces

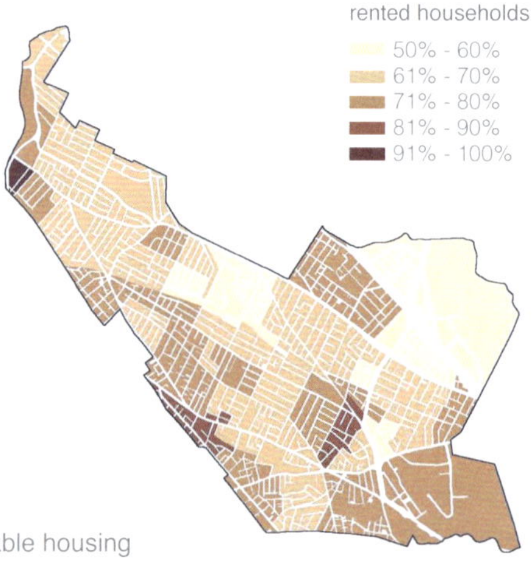

Affordable housing

Tree infrastructure

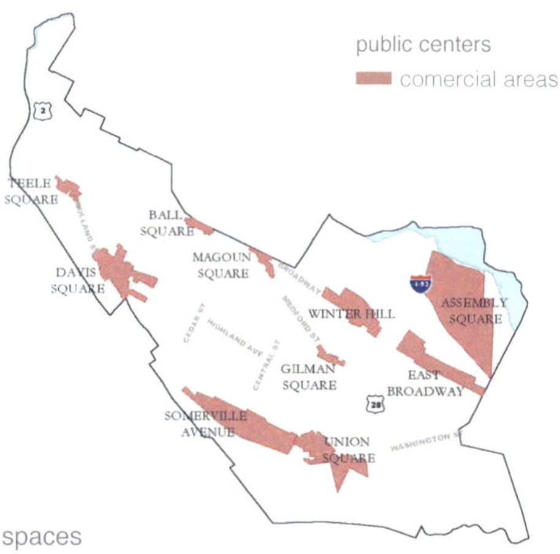

Public spaces

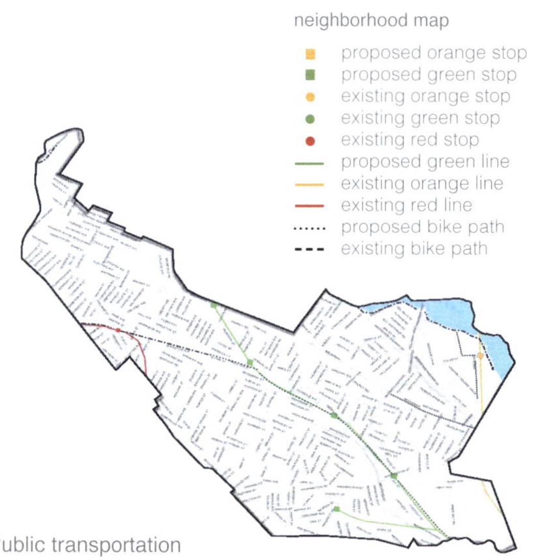

Public transportation

Suburban corridor

Car dealership along McGrath

Hardscape conditions

Elevated McGrath Highway

Conditions under highway

Roadway functional classification

Industrial sectors

lots. Very few public parks or open spaces are found throughout this area, though a series of recreational fields exists to the northeast and south of the site. The site is bordered by several historically significant hilltops, including Prospect Hill, Cobble Hill, and Bunker Hill. Dense residential neighborhoods border the site along its north, west and south boundaries, which include an elementary school and a high school, small retail shops, restaurants, and various community facilities. In addition, the site's fringe is within walking distance of two existing MBTA rail stops – Lechmere along the Green Line to the South, and Sullivan Square along the Orange Line to the North. The Northeast portion of the site is served by a new MBTA Green Line Extension stop at Washington Street.

The overlay of building footprints, community services, and population highlights the relationship among strategic locations for community services and the distribution and concentration of people around the site. These community services, including police and fire stations, educational facilities, libraries, and healthcare facilities, serve as a form of community structure.

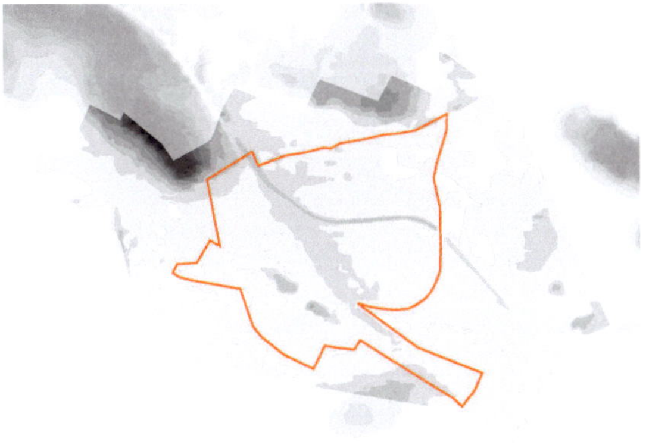

Site topography

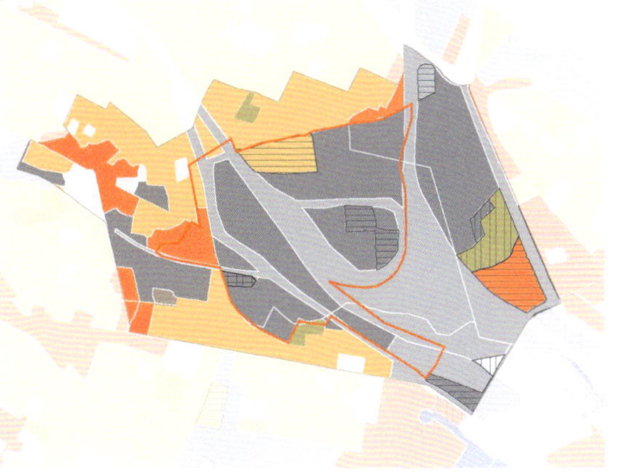

Land use evaluation

Building use

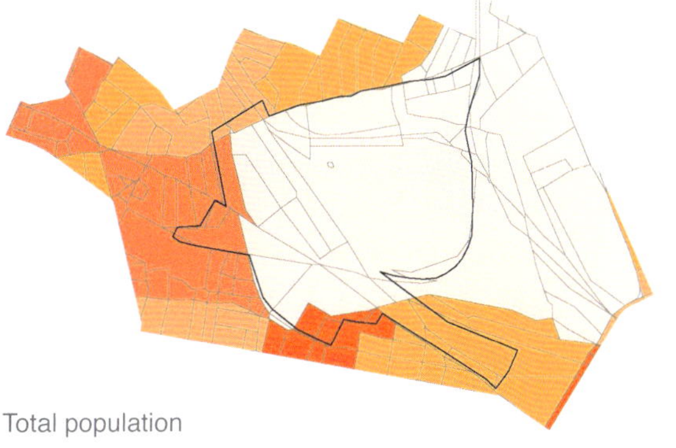

Total population

Community services

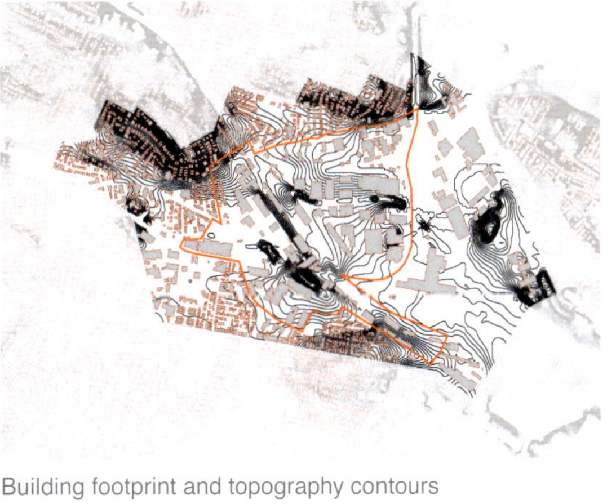

Building footprint and topography contours

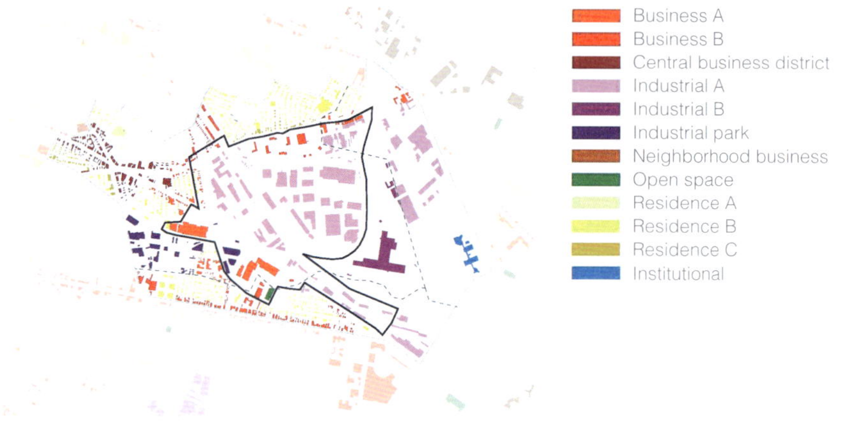

Building footprint and municipal zoning

Forgotten landscapes

The overlay of building footprints and topography reveals the relationship between building typology and site slope. The steeper and higher areas have smaller buildings with a high density of clustering. The low-lying, flat, and flood-prone areas have larger buildings with substantial spacing between them. The development succession is apparent when one evaluates the relationship between street grids and topography. The hill in the lower left-hand corner within Cambridge has a distinctive radial pattern emanating from the subtle topography shift. The manipulation of the terrain by highway and railway ramps is translated clearly by a huge buildup and removal of linear tracts of land. With these conditions, the site can accommodate a series of large facilities.

Conclusion

Somerville's evolution reflects some of the broader narrative of Boston's metropolitan development – in this case, led by industrial development and challenged by post-war infrastructural shifts. Today, Somerville has continued to transform and redefine itself through various cycles of economic and social developments. It consistently stands at the intersection of opportunity and uncertainty like many other mid-polis. Somerville tries to balance growth with its original heritage while embracing innovation and technological advancements. In addition, it continues trying to find a more coherent and thoughtful integration with its adjacent urban fabric and townships.

Prominent Designers' Responses

5.0

5.1
The Critical Path
by Interboro Partners
Mid-Polis: Columbus, Ohio, USA

5.2
Park Tower
by LTL Architects
Mid-Polis: Los Angeles, California, USA

5.3
Harbor Transformation
by DR_D Lab
Mid-Polis: Copenhagen, Denmark

5.4
The Core Area of Automobile City
by WSP
Mid-Polis: Shanghai, China

5.5
Jinshu Commercial Center
by WSP
Mid-Polis: Suzhou, Jiangsu, China

5.6
Shared Green Space
by MONOLAB
Mid-Polis: Rotterdam, The Netherlands

5.7
Urban Tulou by URBANUS
Mid-Polis: Nanhai, Guangdong, China

5.8
Yuhang Courtyard Maze
by Paul Lukez Architecture & Zhejiang University
Mid-Polis: Hangzhou, Zhejiang, China

5.9
Eco Auto-Tek
by Paul Lukez Architecture
Mid-Polis: Somerville, Massachusetts

Rendering of Urban *Tulou*, image by URBANUS

The Critical Path

5.1

Typically, public transportation aims to deliver suburbanites to and from the traditional downtown and to transport people around a traditional, dense, mixed-use downtown. This is because, for many years, movements in and out of the city center were typically the most important.

The rail (Fig. 1) and road (Fig. 2) systems in most American cities are hub-and-spoke, because those are the most efficient configurations for delivering people in and out of a central location.

This movement from periphery to center is certainly still made, but it is no longer as important as it once was. As many urbanists have noted, the monocentric city that characterized the early 20th century (Fig. 3) is being overwritten by a new, polycentric, post-modern city (Fig. 4). In this new city – which illustrates Michael Dear's conceptualization of the fragmented landscape of post-modernism (Fig. 6), in contrast with Ernest Burgess's celebrated Concentric Rings diagram (Fig. 5) – growth happens in residential, commercial and industrial nodes sprinkled around the urbanized region. Here, where the movement from periphery to traditional center is not necessarily more important than the movement between any two given nodes, an ideal public transportation system would look less like a hub-and-spoke web and more like a network (Fig. 7).

While there are a lot of good ideas about how to get people from periphery to center, as well as around the center, there are fewer ideas about how to get people around the nodes between what Mark Robbins has called "the downtown and the small town." Columbus, Ohio, for example, has many transportation plans on the table. The Northern Corridor (Fig. 8) will link the downtown to Ohio State University (OSU) and Polaris Mall on the city's urban fringe, creating a strong, rail-based corridor. The streetcar network (Fig. 9) will make both downtown and the OSU campus more walkable and less autoreliant. The express-bus service running along the city's radial highways connects outer-ring suburbs

MID-POLIS: COLUMBUS, OHIO, USA

by **Interboro Partners**

Tobias Armborst,
Daniel D'Oca & Georgeen Theodore

to the center. These initiatives are critical, but they are informed by a more traditional understanding of the city and are inspired by the more traditional goal of public transportation.

Let us consider where most people in Columbus live (Fig. 10), where most of the region's major employers are, and where most job and population growth is projected to occur (Fig. 11). From that, we can see that these initiatives might have trouble rising to the challenge posed by the new, poly-centric city, and are likely to have a compromised impact.

The Critical Path is a scheme to bring public transportation to this "area between downtown and the small town." Its laboratory is an average three-mile commercial corridor at the edge of Columbus, Ohio. In this typical Midwestern city the automobile is used for close to 90 percent of trips to and from the home, office, and mall. This four-lane road, bracketed by beltway exits, typifies the Midwestern condition: a patchwork of

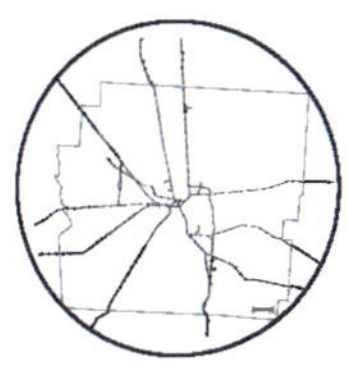

Figure 1
Railway network

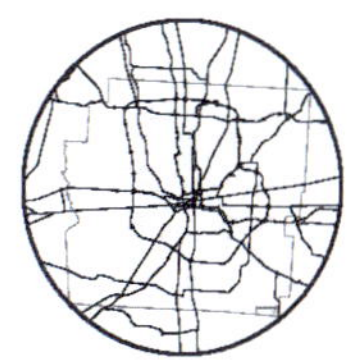

Figure 2
Road network

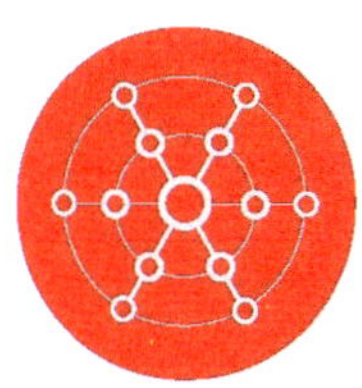

Figure 3
The monocentric city

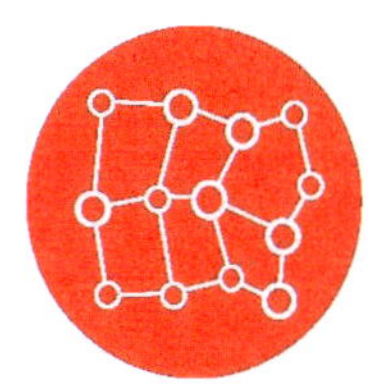

Figure 4
The polycentric city

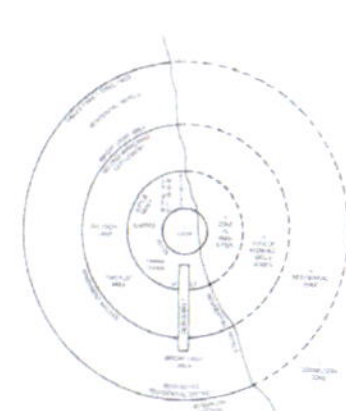

Figure 5
Concentric rings (Burgess)

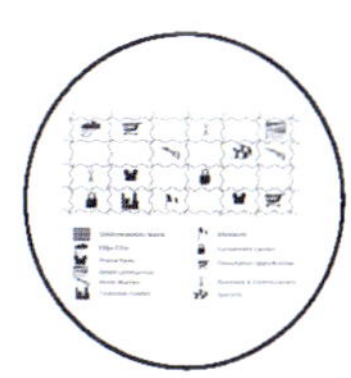

Figure 6
Fragments (Dear and Flusty)

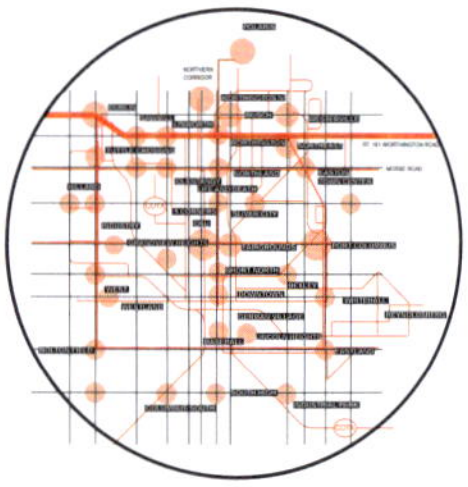

Figure 7
Idealized network system with cross-suburban connectors

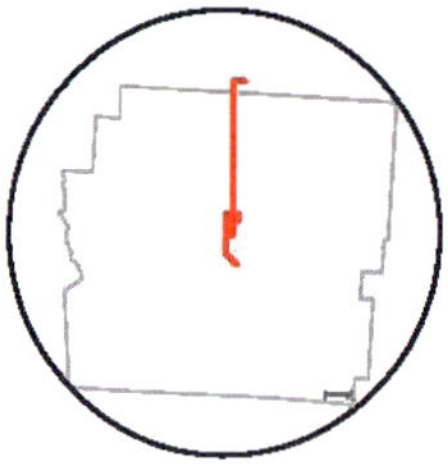

Figure 8
North Corridor project

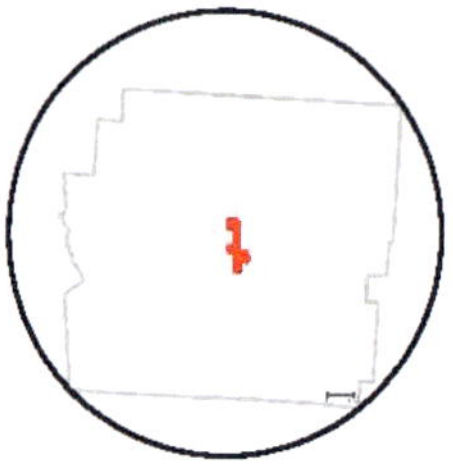

Figure 9
Streetcar system

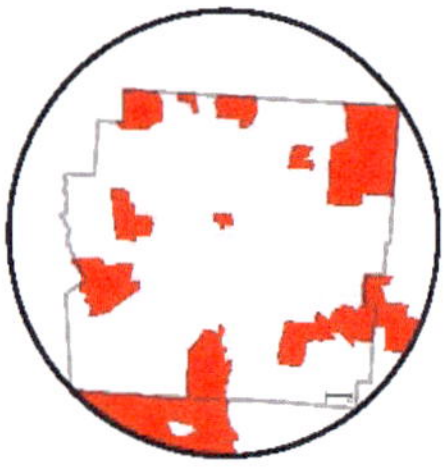

Figure 10
Areas with highest population

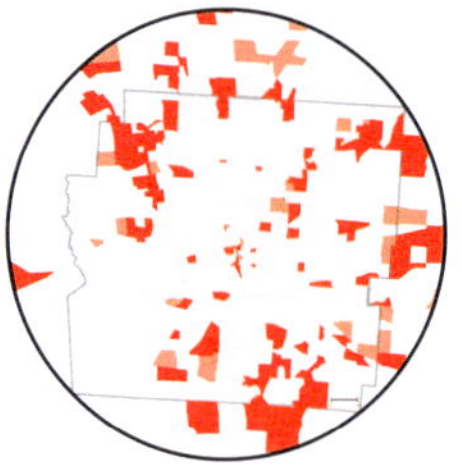

Areas of greatest expected:
Population growth
Employment growth

Figure 11
Areas of greatest expected

light industry, regional retail, modest office buildings, and postwar single-family subdivisions.

To meet this challenge, the proposal outlines a three-part strategy. First, densify nodes and promote mixed-use development so more people live and work within walking distance of centers. Second, expand transit access for the "last mile" by creating connections – such as pedestrian easements – that make nodes truly walkable. Finally, rethink the right-of-way as a multi-functional urban corridor: a hybrid of Parkway, Main Street, and Strip. This includes a central "Fast Lane" for rapid transit and high-occupancy vehicles. Flanking this lane are "Plain Lanes" for regular traffic, with an "Avatarmac" zone encouraging public-facing uses and a "Swale" for landscape and community features. Together, these strategies aim to make transit viable in a polycentric, postmodern city while transforming corridors into new civic spaces. (Fig.12-17)

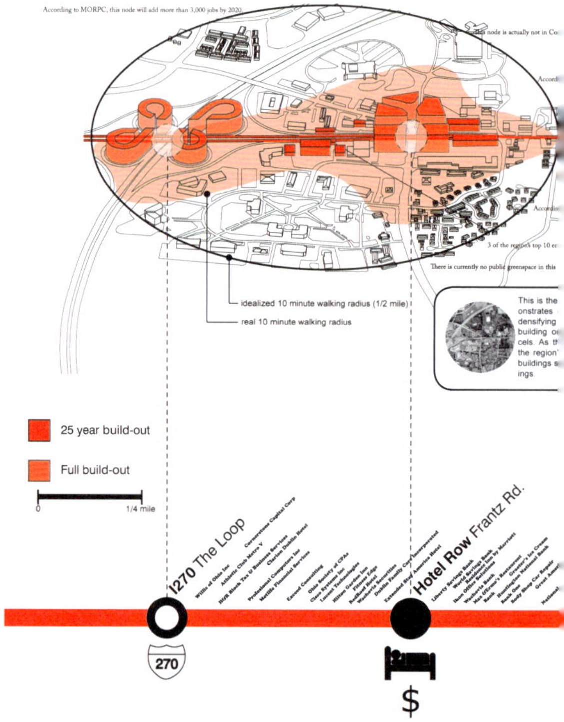

Figure 13
Linworth node withing Columbus Northern Corridor

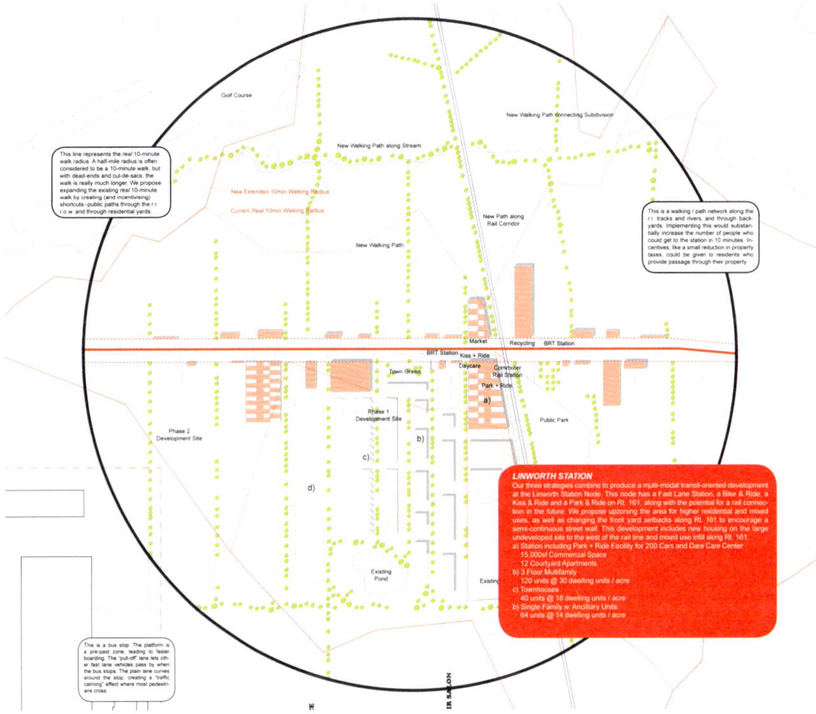

Figure 12
Linworth Center

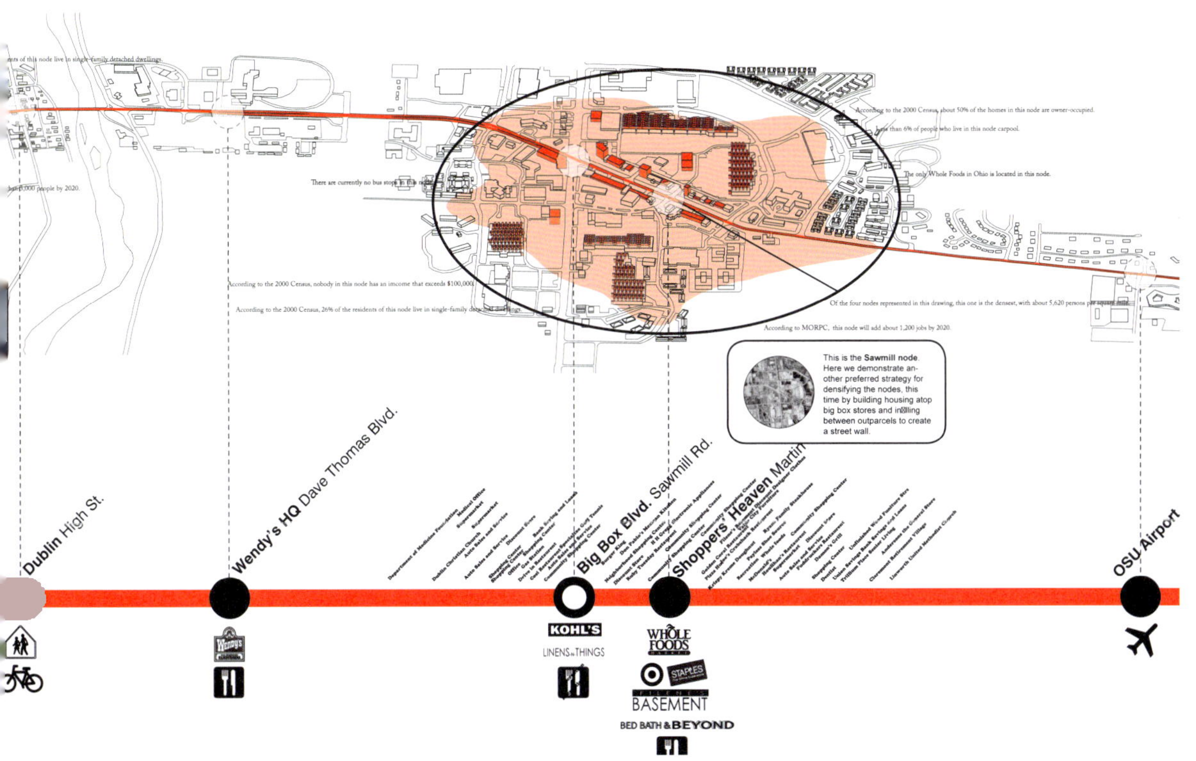

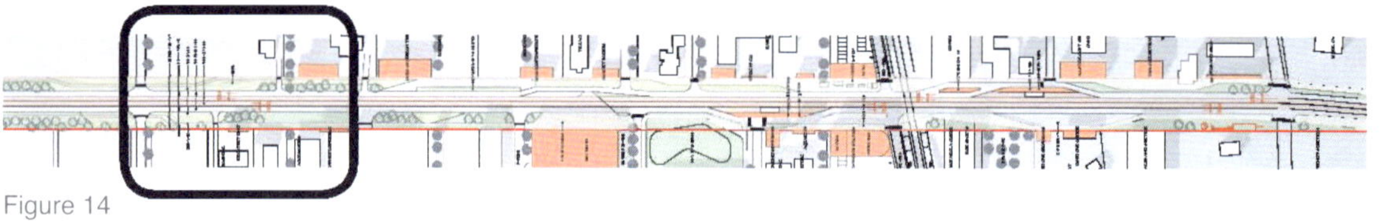

Figure 14
Linworth median

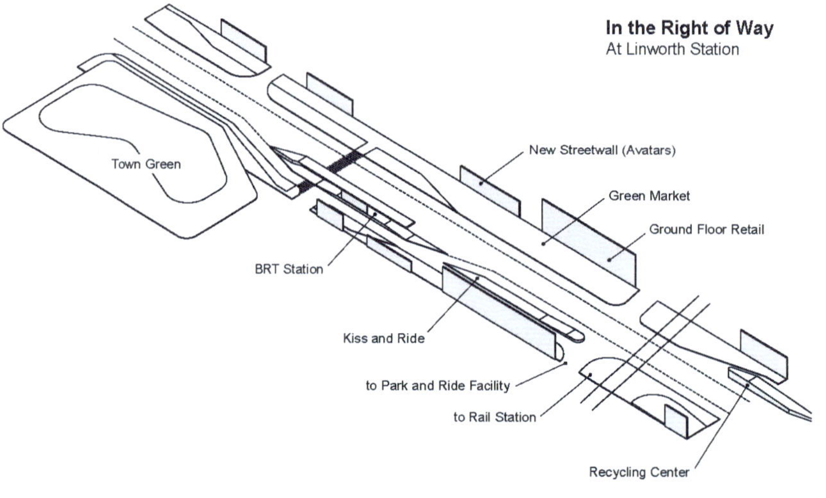

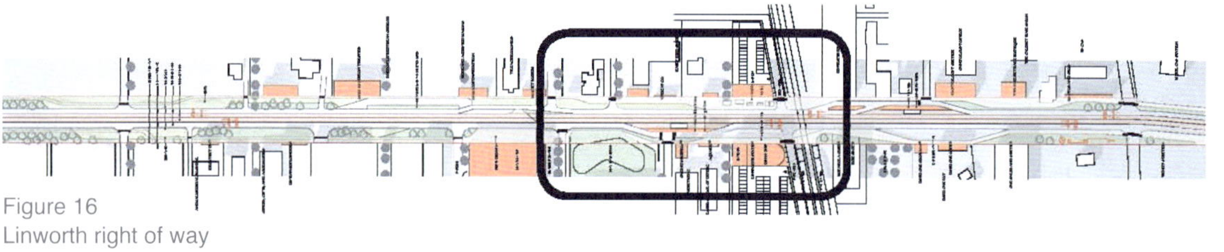

Figure 16
Linworth right of way

Figure 15
Linworth bus corridor

Figure 17
Linworth pedestrian corridor

Park Tower

5.2

The potential future of an electric-vehicle world is explored in this project as a catalyst for rethinking the relationship between cars and programs within the zones around cities that are defined by suburban desires but are pushed toward greater density than suburban models can accommodate.

Harnessing the promised future of clean, quiet electric cars as a catalyst, Park Tower in Los Angeles enables occupants to drive up the skyscraper without leaving noxious fumes or creating excessive engine noise. Suburban desires are thus coupled with an urban building type and footprint. The time-consuming suburban commute is transformed into a seductive urban ascent, complete with panoramic views and urban garden stops.

The ubiquitous nature of automobiles has created a series of complex proportional relationships between the size and type of architectural programs and required parking sizes and numbers. While the dependency of program type and parking is statistically coupled and legislated into building and zoning codes, the potential reciprocal spatial relationship between parking and architectural programs has been left under-exploited. What if the interdependence of spatial function and parking space becomes the catalyst for architectural invention?

Instead of sequestering parking to subterranean levels, what if automobile parking is intertwined into every level of a building, changing in density and frequency to match the required parking allocations of divergent programs of a complex, multi-use Park Tower? While employing a commonplace mix of programs – retail space on the ground level, hotel and office space in the middle, residential on the upper levels – the Tower combines in the manner of a double helix a new intertwining of a continuous drive-through parking garage and a sandwich of occupiable architectural space (Fig. 1). The sectional matings of each program's function and parking are maximized, using the specific ratio of parking-to-program type to establish the rules of exchange.

by **LTL Architects**

MID-POLIS: LOS ANGELES, CALIFORNIA, USA

Paul Lewis,
Mark Tsurumaki & David Lewis

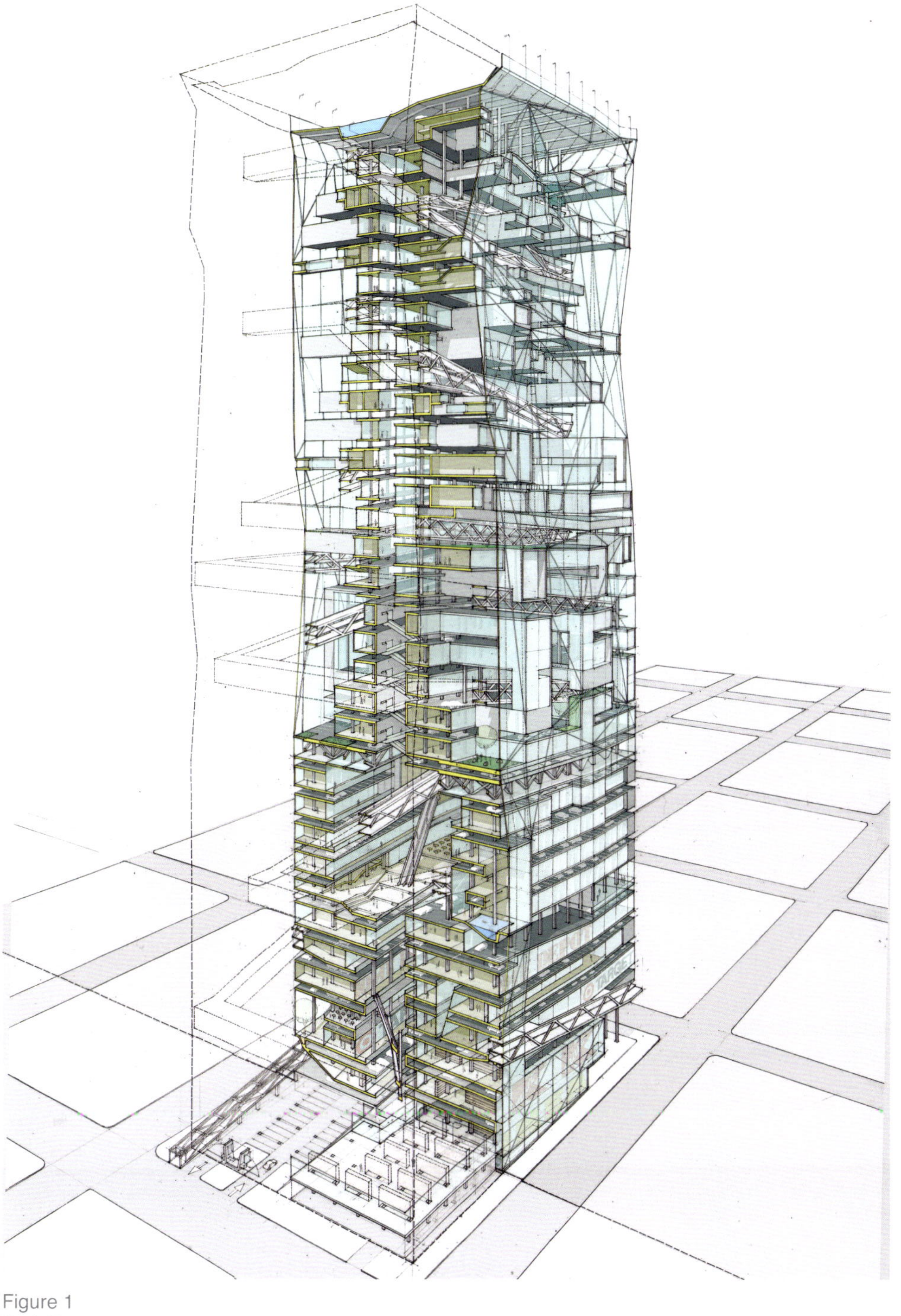

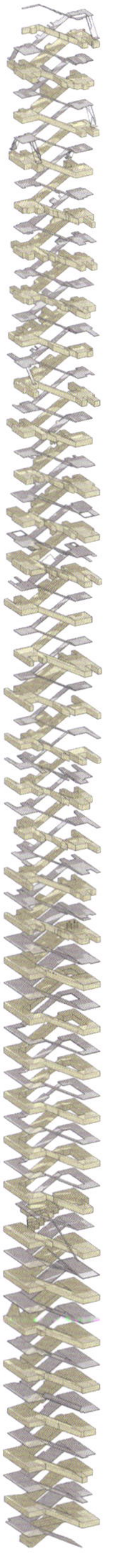

Figure 1
Park Tower section

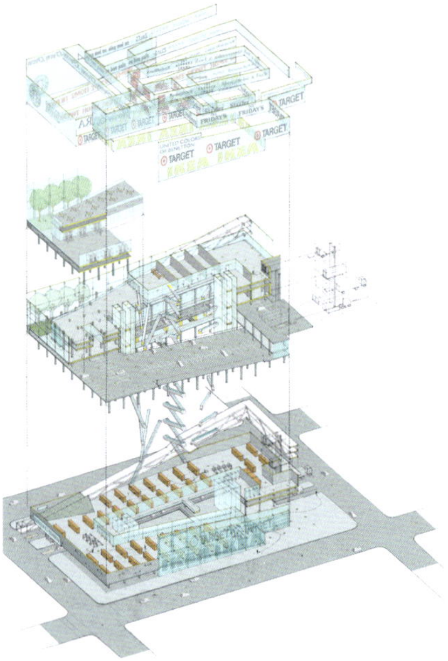

Figure 2
Retail axonometric

To facilitate rapid ascent and descent, an additional speed-lane wraps up through the tower (Fig. 1), enabling the penthouse owner to drive home in the manner of a trip to the top of Hollywood Hills, or the outdoor enthusiast to experience the rooftop SUV testing ground.

Retail (Fig. 2 and 3):
The retail section cross-wires a strip mall with an urban shopping district. Due to the double helix, every parking space has proximity to the stores. A series of escalators rotates through the central atrium, allowing shoppers to seamlessly move between levels. Exterior courtyards introduce green space into the retail spiral, producing complex interactions between the interior and exterior façades of stores.

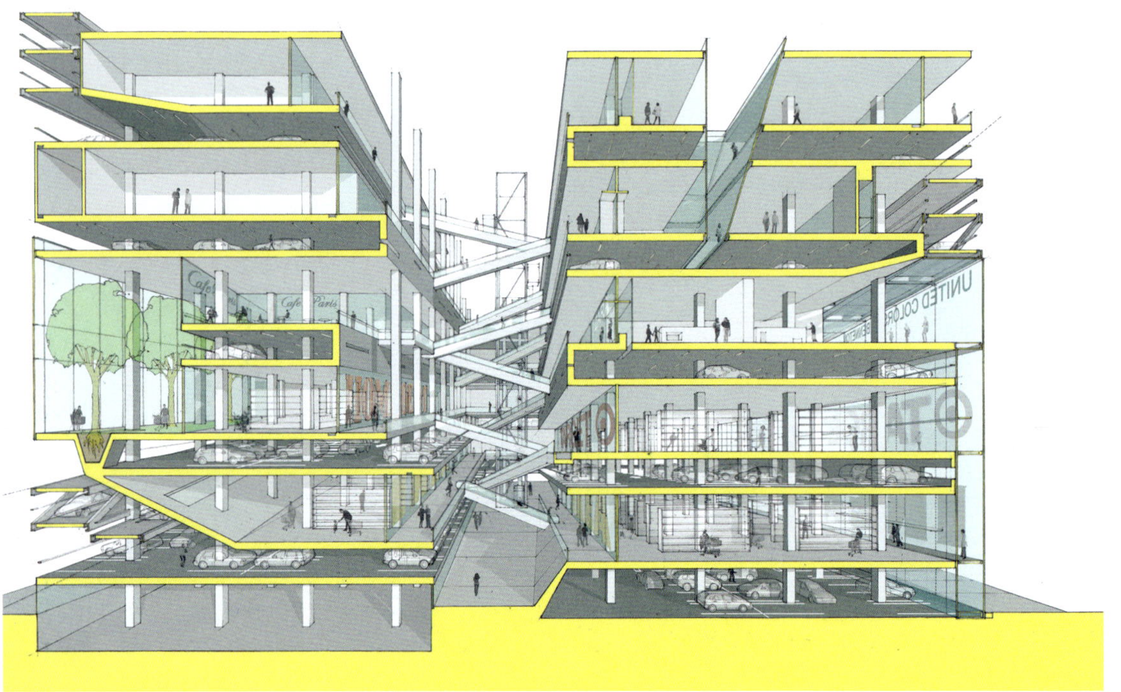

Figure 3
Retail section

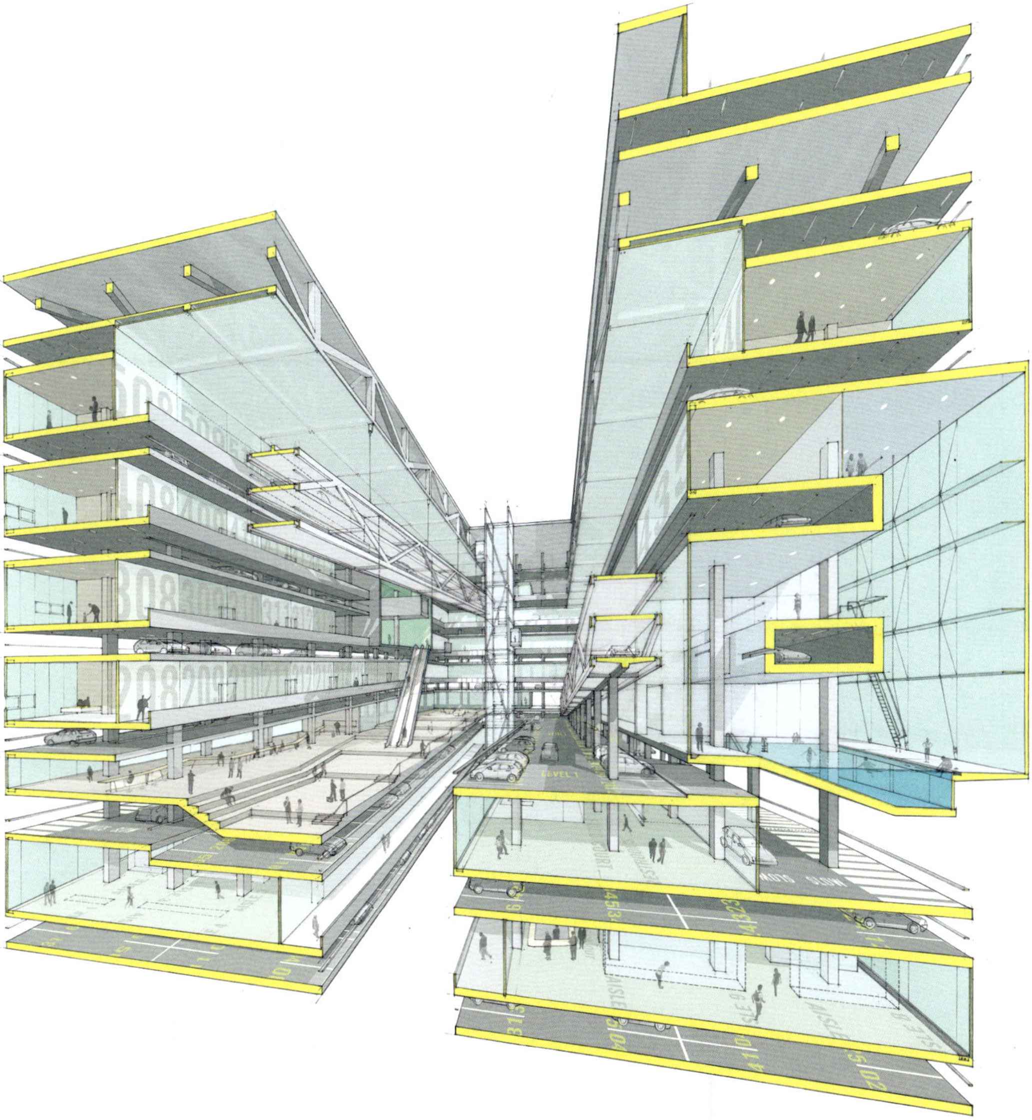

Figure 4
Hotel section

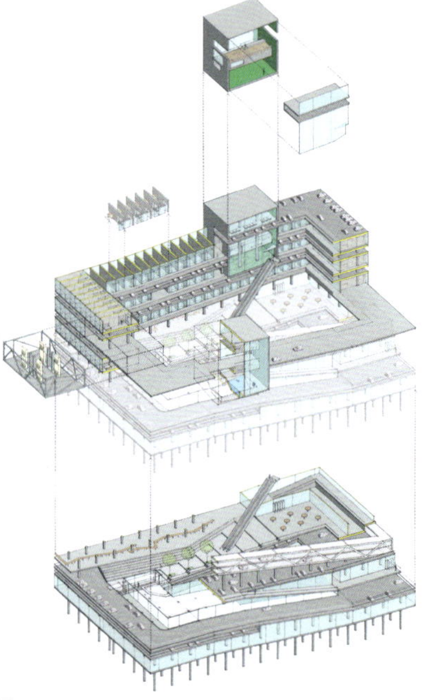

Figure 5
Hotel axonometric

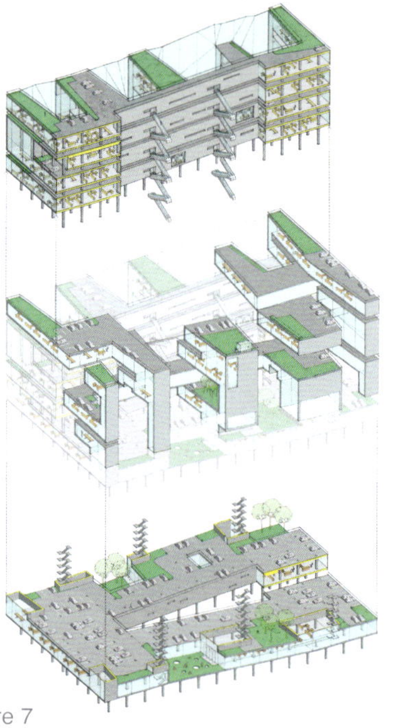

Figure 7
Office axonometric

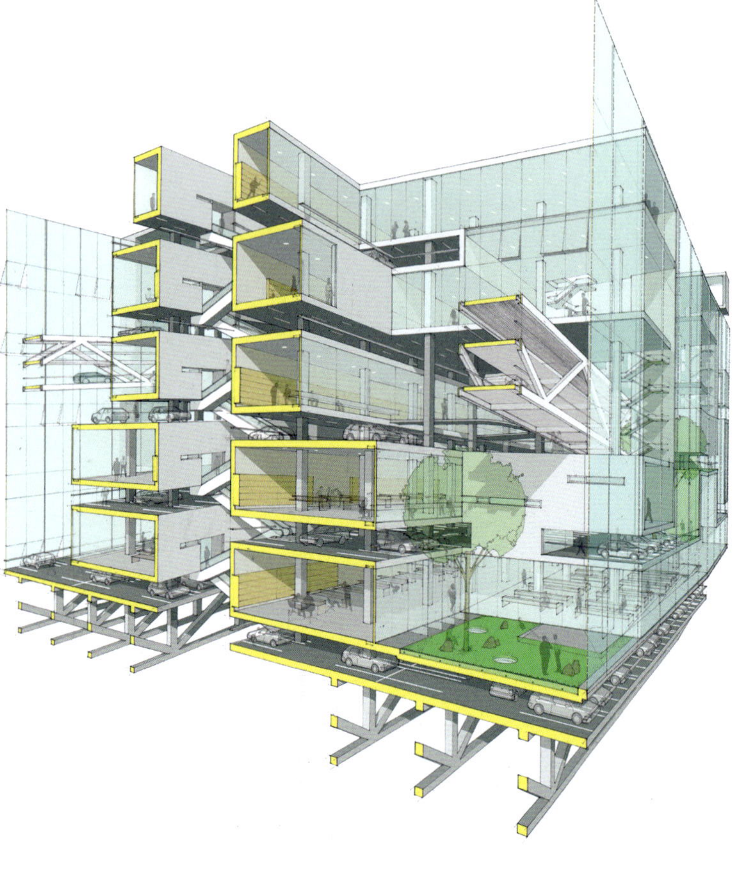

Figure 6
Office section

Hotel (Fig. 4 and 5):
Park Tower's hotel is situated between the retail and office districts, placing business travelers in the center of their two most common activities: shopping and work. This hotel combines the qualities of a grand Piranesian Portman lobby space with a prosaic motel. Alternating spirals of rooms and parking surfaces circle a social atrium, which is animated by two internal express ramps and the requisite glass elevators. Here one has the convenience of parking below one's room (like a motel) while enjoying the spatial amenities of an urban hotel.

Office (Fig. 6 and 7):
The office district is characterized by an increased articulation, with greater amounts of exterior space relative to occupiable interior square footage. The result is a high-rise office park where all unnecessary parking spaces are converted to green space. While the overall form of this section is fairly regular, individual offices within can be configured in unconventional ways, accommodating changing needs of tenants.

Residential (Fig. 8 and 9):
The residential section consists of housing units cantilevered out from a minimal car-ramp surface. Because of the reduced demand for parking in residential areas, most parking needs can be accommodated by the driveway extending as the roof of each apartment. One enters the apartment through the driveway and front lawn, moving down into the house itself. Ubiquitous suburban features of a lawn and driveway are combined into a new form of a high-density vertical neighborhood. A lattice-like membrane of photovoltaic cells provides a buffer zone mitigating weather extremes. The express ramps terminate at an SUV testing ground at the roof, complete with panoramic views. The roof landscape collects rainwater for use within the building.

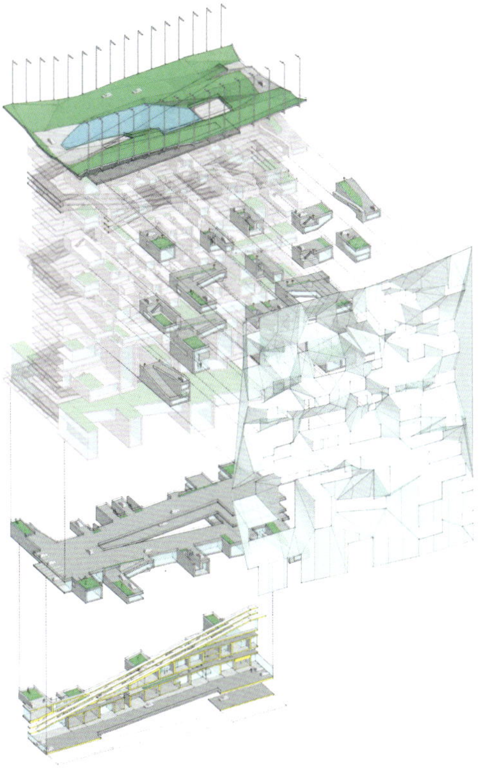

Figure 8
Residential axonometric

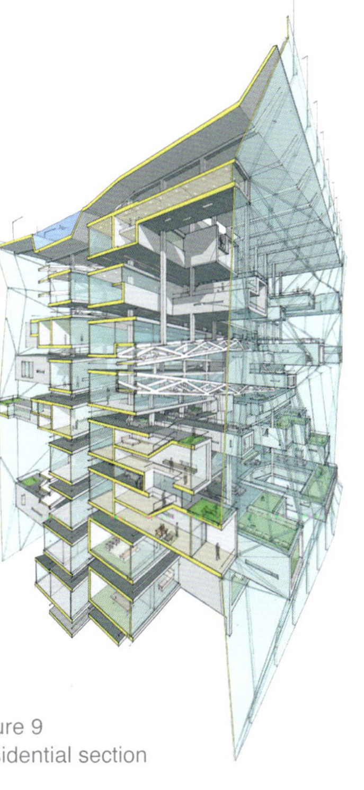

Figure 9
Residential section

Harbor Transformation 5.3

The contemporary metropolitan city comprises a tapestry of development that collapses into an ongoing dynamic ebb and flow. As our cities grew and technology evolved, the infrastructure that had supported the city's performance had to move. Today, enormous landmasses and valuable locations are being freed up between the traditional city center and by-now-established suburbia, because outmoded, cumbersome, traffic-inducing infrastructures must move elsewhere. This opens up exceedingly large spaces in-between that the public has not recognized as city-identifying elements. Nevertheless, this in-between often defines and elaborates the main character of things.

Today, a new generation of large-scale collapsing infrastructures creates opportunities for new cities-within-cities. As we re-examine harbors, ring-roads, inner-city freeways, train lines, and especially airports, these former infrastructural figures on the city map take on a new meaning with an old figure. Through centuries of maps, the public at large recognized many metropoleis as an image. The shape and curves of the Thames in London; the Seine River's peculiar move through Paris; the piazzas, canals and bridges in Venice, Rome and Marrakech; and the shape and layout of the famous parks, castles and public squares of Tokyo and Beijing each gave every city an easily readable identity.

The image of the map had deeply embedded in it a narrative trail that inspired dreams, wide-ranging cultural connections, and memories. The palazzos and their stories of love and hatred; the castles and their power and defeat; the markets and their specialty and gossip; and the harbors with their conquests, military history, and markets attached all gave the map a narrative grounding that was deeply embedded in the citizens' identity. Though the cities had developed through very particular, highly functional needs, their resulting image had stories and memories attached that created rich interwoven atmospheres.

MID-POLIS: COPENHAGEN, DENMARK

by **DR_D Lab**

Dagmar Richter

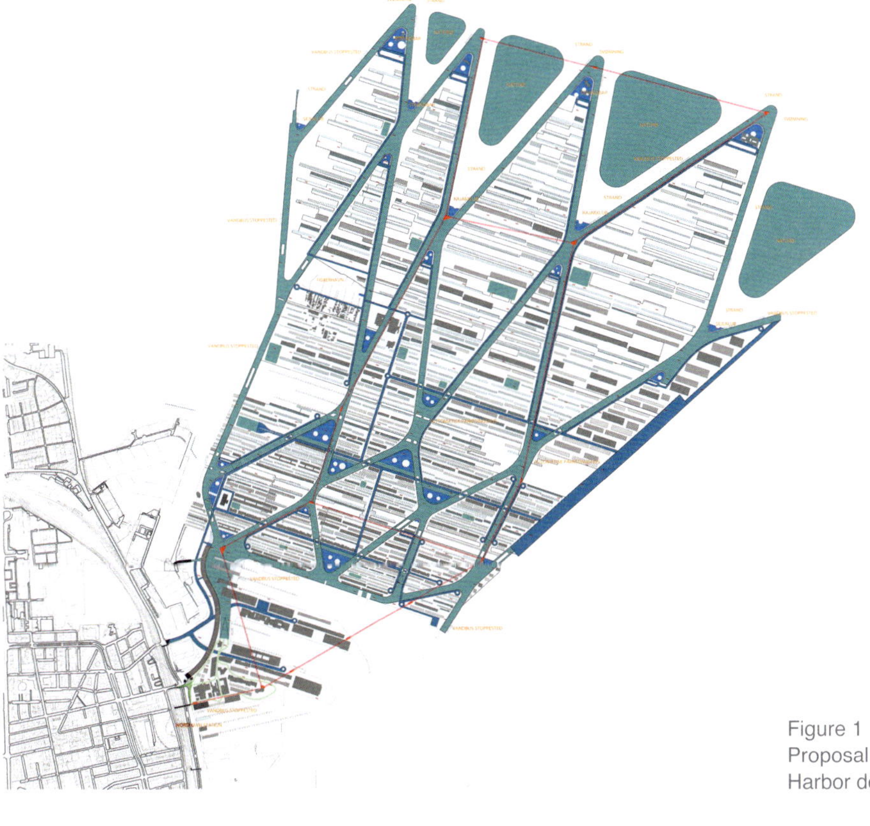

Figure 1
Proposal for Copenhagen Harbor development

Figure 5
Kartoffelrækkerne, the potato rows,
photo by Cris Benton

In the 20th century, the performance reason for a majority of these map figures – e.g., the harbor, the location of the market and square belonging to it, the city walls and their control points – had slowly disappeared. However, the map image of the city remained, as it was telling a story. When development expanded outward and onward, suburbia did not provide a strong visual identity at first; this is directly related to spatial use through history. Moreover, at the time of suburban development, many memories were produced, not through rituals in physical public space, but within such new media as photography, film, TV, and computer screens. Suburban users did not care that much that there was "no there there" as long as they felt at home with the Addams Family or the Simpsons and were orbiting a city center that gave them a clearly defined identity.

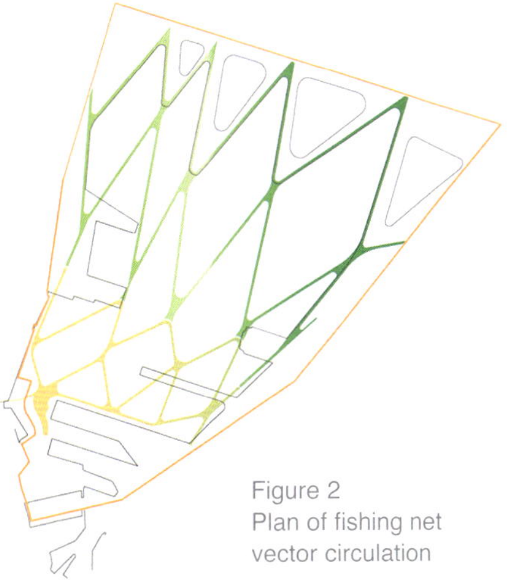

Figure 2
Plan of fishing net vector circulation

Instead of relying solely on the old city centers' figure-ground as the singular physical marker for suburbia's identification, this project aims to identify a distributed network of small identities that take the form of cities-within-cities. The image of this city-within-a-city was to be produced by a map figure that reflected a kind of one-liner for easy recognizability. This map figure was chosen not for performative reasons, but purely for its image and associative quality, as Kevin Lynch expressed it: "Every citizen has had long associations with some part of his city, and his image is soaked in memories and meanings."[1]

Figure 3
Possible barcode of building stripes after 40 years

In the traditional city, the image had an embedded meaning through memory. A new city or city part that has been built up through rapid development does not have a lot of memories attached to its image. Therefore, the following competition proposal for a former container harbor area proposes constructing a map image that provokes open-ended harbor associations for a new city in-between the old center. This new city would be built around a medieval harbor and its northern periphery, which has been developed around sailing clubs and recreational harbors. The developed plan and urban design propose a fast-track narrative through association

Figure 4
Plan of fishing net park network

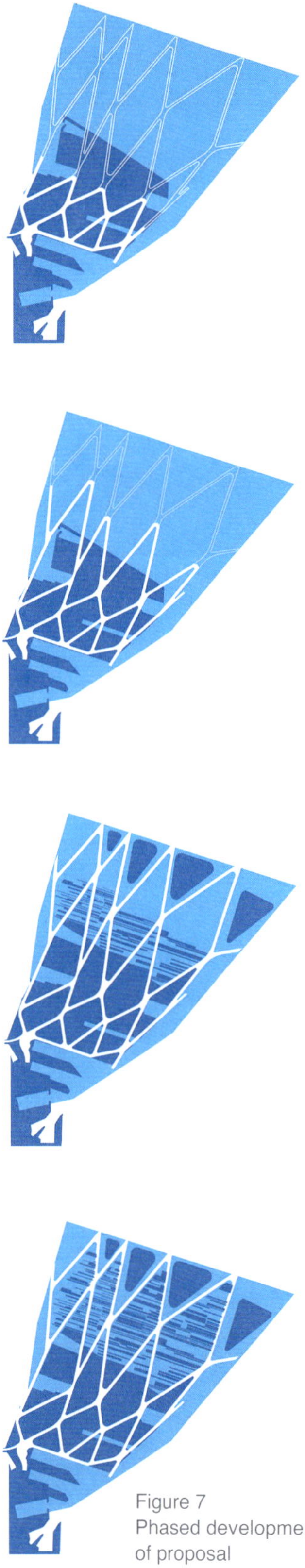

Figure 7
Phased development of proposal

for an area with no memory attached to its place, shaped by the performative requirements for a container harbor with few human users. The plan was designed to regain new meaning by evoking narrative associations instead of particular functions. Instead of reacting to traces that were showing the former harbor functions, the design tried to create an image easily understood and identified: a fishing net (Fig. 2).

The fishing net image created a natural structure that twisted and meandered across the entire site. This structure offered a network of vectors of circulation that accommodated effortless biking, cross-country skiing, and walking, with a cable car using minimal footings. The car traffic was organized through a filtering distribution system using some of the area under the net for computerized parking. The building structure was then overlaid with a strict East-West-oriented fabric of building rows that varied in height, thickness, program and rhythm, depending on current planning and construction needs within a 40-year time span of planning and history (Fig. 3).

The image of the striped structure was directly borrowed from the layout and structure of a famous inner city's former workers' quarter. It striped a large area in the East-West direction with one-stripe housing, a one-stripe garden, and a one-stripe street so the families could grow their own food in the south-oriented garden. The "potato-rows" then became an image that demonstrated the city's commitment through history to sustainability, good orientation, and intimate relationships to landscape and production. This produced a well-structured, socially responsible neighborhood that could accommodate many changes through time (Fig. 5). The project's stripes were to accommodate spaces for work, production, and living in equal measures. As time proceeded, the highly adaptable "fishing net" was to be built always several steps ahead of future development. The always "already there" public network would offer established plant growth and a rich tapestry of already established activities and rituals to support the next phase of construction (Fig. 4).

Figure 6
Proposal for Phase One

The net shape easily establishes the future area of development by subdividing the city into smaller neighborhoods. The stripes' location and shape for the next phase was to be established five years ahead of this phase. To produce established patterns of use and spatial appropriation, the future sites were to be rented out for allotment gardens five years prior to construction. As a result, house sites were tended to early on and, at building time, provided established plant life. The proposed plan was trying to adapt around an unknown dynamic, amid the known direction of the stripes, fishing net and location of public buildings. The rhythm of future stripes was decided a few years before planning time; building height and resulting volumes were to be adapted to the needs of the construction time (Fig. 1 and 6-8).

Note:
[1] Lynch, Kevin. *The Image of the City.* Cambridge, Mass.: MIT Press, 1958.

Figure 8
Perspective of proposal for Copenhagen Harbor development

The Core Area of Automobile City

5.4

The International Automobile City is located in the Jiading District of Shanghai. As one of six industrial bases of Shanghai, it has great development potential for automobile manufacturing, research, trade, and related services. As one of three city areas of Jiading New City, it serves as a city center.

The Core Area is located in southwest International Automobile City near Anting Old Town, Anting New Town, Kunshan Huaqiao, Huangdu, and other surrounding metropoleis. As this area demands a variety of uses, this project serves multiple functions: a public recreation center for International Automobile City, commercial center, automobile exhibition center, automobile trading area, research and administration training center, park, golf course, and residential community. The Core Area is not only a localized center, but also the regional public activity center. It is designed as a newly patterned town with traditional town spirit that enriches urban life, making it modern and livable. The project's sustainability, humanity, and functions are all derived from and influenced by the city's structure.

By incorporating the subway into the planning of the core area, a linear city layout emerges, mingling buildings with green areas. At the heart of the design, emphasis is placed on integrating industry with urban functions. Many regional service centers were developed to create efficient, fair, and citizen-friendly service systems. The group development model is also applied in the plan: by increasing road density, decreasing each plot area, and optimizing openings, plot use is more efficient. As a result, the mixed-use zone mainly consists of medium-height buildings and medium density. The public and private area ratio is balanced by increasing public areas to create neighborly communities. Linking the Core Area to external infrastructures is important in this project, so subway stations are coordinated to create open boundaries, and traffic

by **WSP**

*Wu Gang, Zhang Ying,
Chen Ling & Knud Rossen*

MID-POLIS: SHANGHAI, CHINA

International Automobile City - Jiading District northwest of the City Center

River corridor

High-density corridor

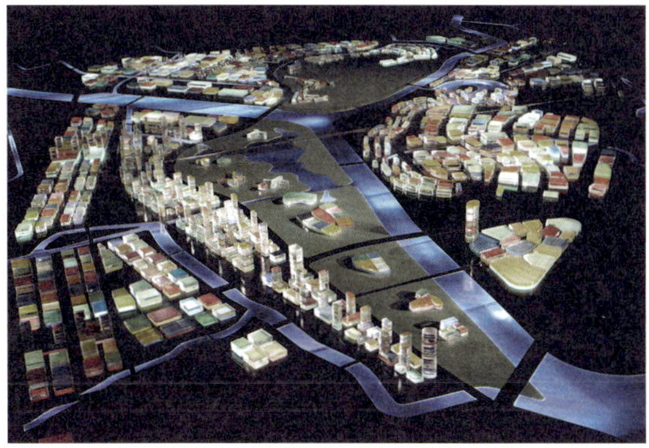

Open space

systems of other districts and cities are plugged into the Core Area to heighten connectivity of the city's plots. Likewise, by linking interior functions and the exterior environment, multiple city functions interact and are integrated with each other.

The riverside greenbelt is introduced to the Core Area, forming a landscaped park that runs from east to west. As a result, the entire region is separated into north and south zones surrounded by water features and parks, consequently improving land value. A riverside landscape linking both zones makes the riverside more interesting, interactive, and diverse in conjunction with riverside recreation and commercial facilities, which provide space dedicated to visitor entertainment. The building heights are controlled so as to complement the rhythm of the city's horizon.

Jinshu Commercial Center **5.5**

The project is situated within Suzhou Industrial Park. Drawing on Suzhou's rich urban fabric and enduring traditions, the designer seeks to create a contemporary commercial destination that resonates with the city's traditional heritage.

Our initial design idea came from the analysis of the existing neighborhood-style building typology, integrating courtyards, atria, and passageways. These spatial elements define the urban blocks, foster communal gathering spaces, and generate a distinctive spatial morphology that reflects Suzhou's traditional residential and commercial culture and character.

In terms of design methods, the team adopted a strategy of breaking down the whole into smaller parts, introducing multiple axes, and incorporating shifts and turns in the building masses. Since the site is nearly square, three concentric, progressively smaller squares form the typological framework of the complex. Following this framework, commercial units are arranged to create fluid street-like spaces, each unit engaging with the pedestrian realm. The existing T-shaped road at the center defines a square central plaza, complemented by an array of landscape lighting and strategically heightened building volumes along the edges. This makes the central plaza the focal point of the entire commercial district.

The proposal studies four distinct program types – shops, restaurants and bars, clubs and entertainment venues, a kindergarten – approaching them from a typological perspective. The basic building module is set at 9.00 by 7.20 meters (roughly equivalent to 29.5 ft by 23.6 ft), establishing a clear construction logic while allowing flexibility for diverse, evolving uses over time.

A double-skin façade system gives the development a cohesive and recognizable identity. The outer layer consists of sun-shading metal mesh. It partly screens the air-conditioning units and expresses an introverted, enclosed character. In contrast, the façades facing the interior courtyards create a livelier, more open atmosphere. This

by **WSP**

Wu Gang, Zhang Ying
Chen Ling & Knud Rossen

MID-POLIS: SUZHOU, JIANGSU, CHINA

Roofscape

juxtaposition between the inner and outer façades embodies a balanced dialectical relationship in traditional culture between openness and reserve, like Suzhou's traditional urban blocks.

Courtyards serve as not only extensions of interior activities but also emotionally resonant spatial backdrops. Depending on how future users plan to open up or close off the courtyard, and to choose materials and ways to define their boundaries, a courtyard could transform into a public plaza or become a fully enclosed service yard, accommodating evolving user needs over time.

Arrangement

Courtyard view

Base configuration

Courtyard nighttime view

Shared Green Space **5.6**

Rotterdam lags behind on two issues compared to other cities. First, it has little functional green public space. Second, it neglects the potential uses for citizens and tourists of its 94-km waterfront possibilities along the Maas River. The Rotterdam-based design practice of Monolab has taken the initiative to confront these issues through its Green River project.

Green River consists of two elements:

1. A Monolab upgrade of the Westersingel, the green axis running parallel with the Coolsingel main boulevard, would connect tiny fragments of green plots, make the city center healthier and more human, and improve its absorption of rainwater. Green River also connects two dedicated public buildings on both sides: in the North, the renewed Central Station: in the South, the 'Rotterdam Green Building,' a cultural hotspot designed by Monolab.

2. In the urban window of this building, a site originates where the city is connected to the river. The Euromast Park is linked to a new, permanent beach on the Maas River.

According to Jan Willem van Kuilenburg, principal of Monolab Architects: "...through Green River we have united city and river again. Rotterdam has a dramatic lack of usable green space within its downtown district. The few city parks, like the Zuiderpark and Kralingse Bos, are too remote. The city center only has the hidden Euromast Park and the Westersingel green axis. In our proposal we made a quantum leap by introducing a green shared space for pedestrians, cyclists and vehicles. The new green and deliberately vulnerable surface has a larger buffer capacity for rainwater, and certain existing buildings along the axis will have green façades and roofs".

"We also planned the multifunctional and embedded 'Green Rotterdam Building' on the Westerkade quay, connecting Green River with the Maas River through a permanent beach. This initiative

MID-POLIS: ROTTERDAM, THE NETHERLANDS

by **MONOLAB**

Jan Willem van Kuilenburg

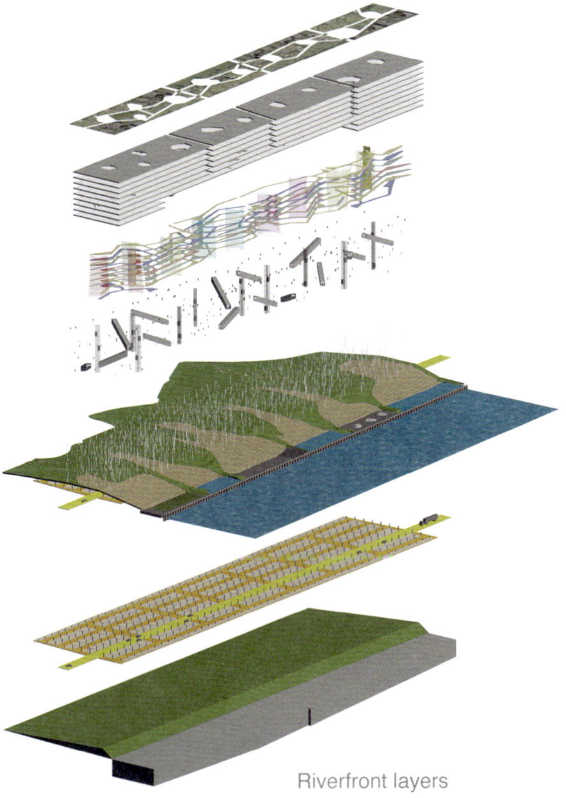

Riverfront layers

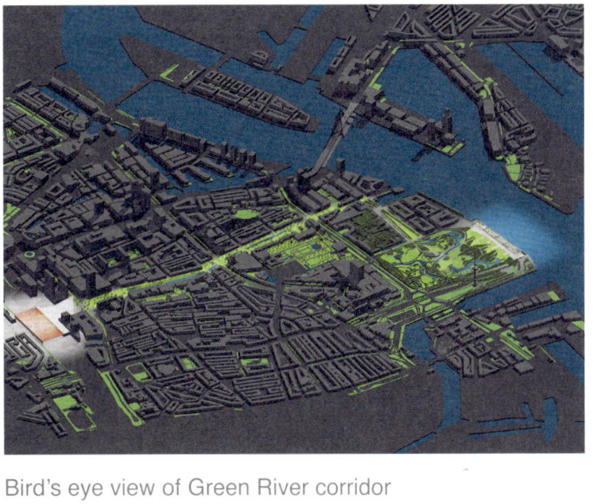

Bird's eye view of Green River corridor

Riverfront structure

Riverfront complex

Riverside complex underside

Riverside beach

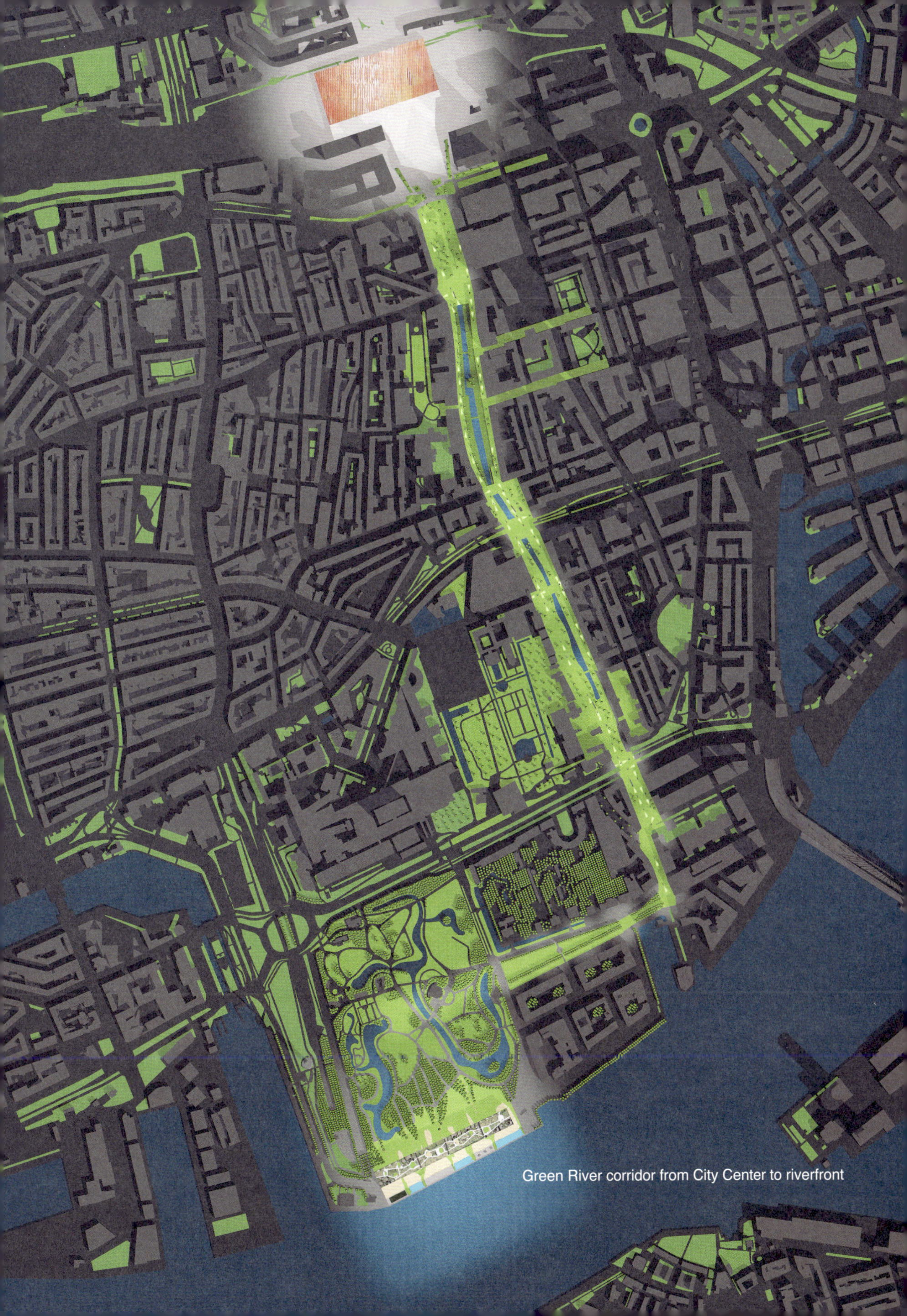

Green River corridor from City Center to riverfront

contributes to the transformation of Rotterdam, the city that lost its westward moving world harbor – the city that never really was connected with its Maas River except for purely logistical reasons but boasts a 94-km waterfront within its Ring. Many cities have already realized [the potential of] their waterfronts [and made the most of it]."

"It is about time for Rotterdam to take action. Green River is our proposal [to achieve that directive as a contribution to its] citizens and tourists. The tourist industry is the largest in the world and will double in the next twenty years. I expect that Rotterdam will regret it if it misses out on this huge opportunity. The city cannot simply attract tourism through [episodic] 'hit and run' events all the time. The city also has a responsibility to realize a structural quality within its public space. We make this first move by linking the inner city to the river through this project that serves both its citizens and the larger market..."

Sustainable transport network

Green spine

Green intervention through the city

Urban Tulou

5.7

Tulou is a type of dwelling unique to the Hakka people. It is a communal residence between the city and the countryside, integrating living, storage, shopping, religion, and public entertainment into one single building entity.

Traditional units in *tulou* are evenly laid out along their perimeter, like modern slab-style dormitory buildings, but with greater opportunities for social interaction. By introducing a "new *tulou*" to modern cities and by carefully experimenting with its form and economy, one can transcend the conventional modular dwelling into urban design. Our experiments explored ways to stitch the *tulou* within the existing urban fabric, which includes green areas, overpasses, expressways, and residual land left over by urbanization. The cost of residual sites is low due to incentives provided by the government; this is an important factor for the development of affordable housing. The proximity of each *tulou* building to the others helps to insulate the users from the chaos and noise of the outside environment, while creating an intimate, comfortable environment inside.

Integrating the living culture of traditional Hakka *tulou* buildings with affordable housing is not only an academic issue but also implies a more important yet realistic social phenomenon. The living conditions of impoverished people are now gaining more public attention.

The research of *tulou* dwelling is characterized by comprehensive analyses ranging from theoretical hypothesis to practical experimentation. The study examined the size, space patterns, and functions of *tulou*. The new programs also inject new urban elements into the traditional style, while balancing the tension between these two paradigms. As a consequence of such comprehensive research, the *tulou* project has accumulated layers of experience in various aspects. The project provided a platform for an in-depth discussion on feasibilities and possibilities of contextualizing the variable metamorphoses of traditional dwelling modules with an urban reality. It also introduced a series of publications and forums on future hypothetical designs for a "new *tulou* project." The logic and design process of the *tulou* program set up a solid foundation and excellent precedent for translating research-based feasibility studies into design realization.

by **URBANUS**

Liu Xiaodu & Meng Yan

MID-POLIS: NANHAI, GUANGDONG, CHINA

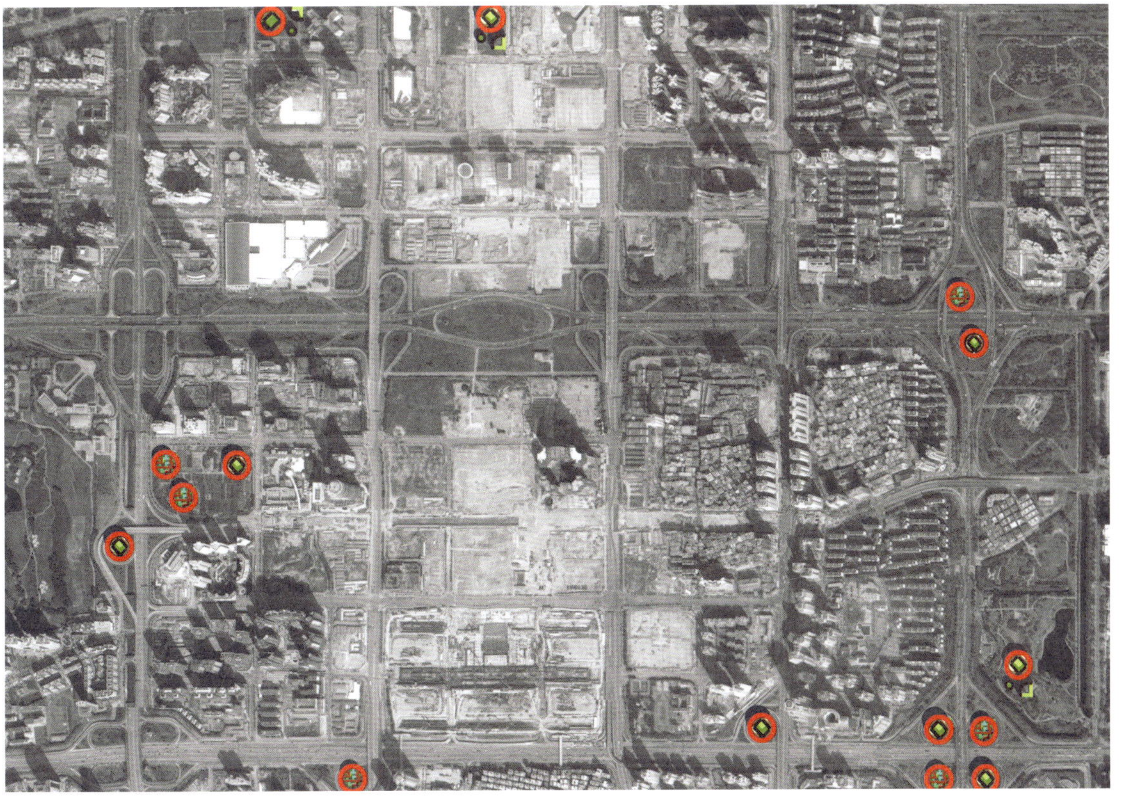

Tulou city collage, image by URBANUS

Fujian *Tulou*, photographer - Huang Zhanpeng

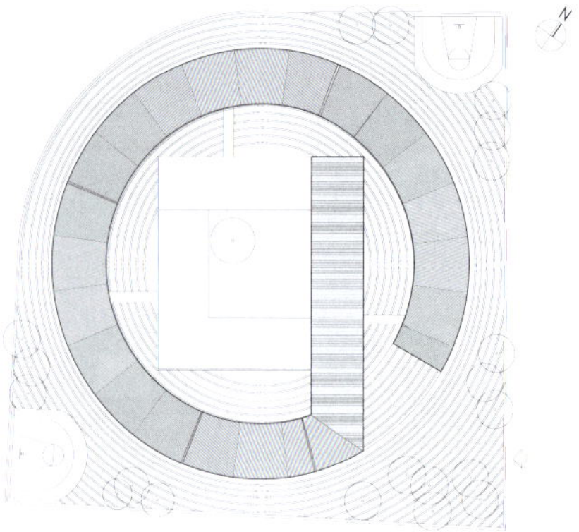

Tulou plan

Massing

Configurations

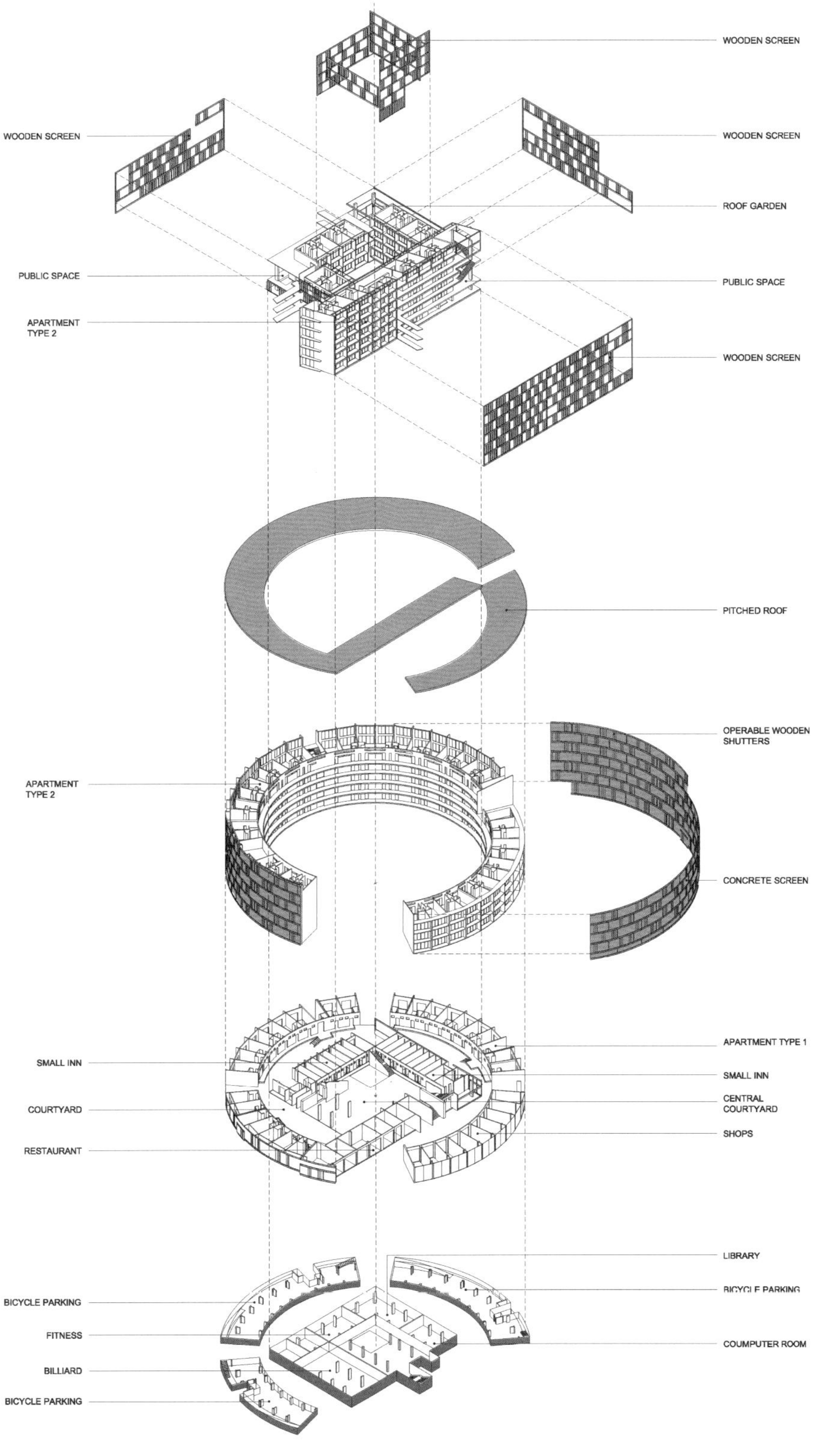

Tulou affordable housing components

Public space of *Tulou*, photo by URBANUS

Exterior view of *Tulou,* photographer - Yang Chaoying

Bird's-eye view of *Tulou*, photographer -Yang Chaoying

Exterior view of *Tulou*, photographer - Yang Chaoying

Courtyard view of *Tulou*, photographer - Yang Chaoying

Yuhang Courtyard Maze

5.8

Hangzhou is a massive city of five million citizens to the south and east of Shanghai within the Yangtze River Delta megalopolis. The metro area population has surged in the last few years due to waves of rural migrants coming to the city for work and the completion of the Shanghai-Hangzhou high-speed rail line. As a result, the city's inner-city districts are under tremendous pressure to expand.

Today, the Yuhang District of Hangzhou abuts the city center on the northeastern boundaries of the city proper. The entire region has begun to see an onslaught of new redevelopment demands. These call for larger, denser communities around the metro area for commercial, educational and residential applications. One such region is located 15 kilometers outside of Hangzhou's city center. Currently the region is flourishing, thanks in part to a new subway line linking the city center with the district's urban landmarks, including its expanding universities, educational and research facilities. This location, close to the city but not in Hangzhou's ex-urban periphery, makes it an attractive region for development.

Leveraging the research capacities of the universities, Hangzhou decided to build a series of new research-oriented districts within the city's existing inner-city fabric. Our firm was asked to help facilitate the development of one of these districts within a limited design competition in collaboration with Prof. Xu Lei and Prof. Wang Ka of Zhejiang University. Our proposal called for the transformation of local courtyard typologies as a building block into a new kind of urban fabric, interweaving urbanity and landscape. The landscape is organized around waterways that are intertwined with the landscape and supporting road and public transit network. Together, all of these elements provide residents, researchers, and visitors direct and immediate contact with nature and urbanity.

While the typology of the courtyard block structure is clear, the courtyards vary widely in

MID-POLIS: HANGZHOU, ZHEJIANG, CHINA

by **Paul Lukez Architecture & Zhejiang University**

Paul Lukez, Xu Lei & Wang Ka

geometry, orientation, and the organization of paths, trees and landscapes. Similarly, the perception of public spaces changes, depending on the way each space is approached. Slight shifts in the paths within the courtyard create unexpected chance encounters with nature and visitors.

This proposal demonstrates strategies for inhabiting the mid-polis region (between city center and ex-urban regions) such that a sense of sophisticated urbanity can co-exist with nature. This environment can help elevate the creativity of researchers and administrators alike, while nature permeates our senses and sense of well-being.

Preliminary massing studies (top)
Research and technology headquarters (bottom)

Yuhang - canal fabric

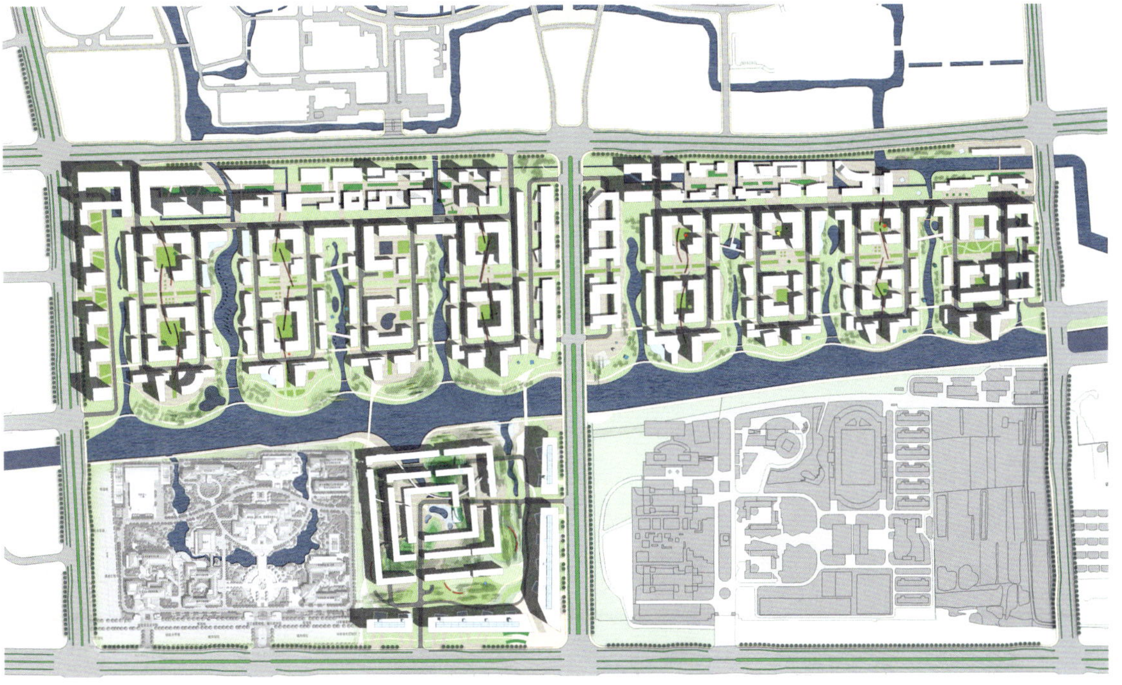

Site plan

Yuhang courtyard waterscape

Eco Auto-Tek

5.9

Creating a New Community – Technology for the Future

The Brickbottom's condition has evolved through the iterative transformations of infrastructure. Railroads bisected and traversed the site. The surveyor's grid has been built, erased, and rebuilt over time. The elevated McGrath Highway cuts through the site. Despite its strategic location, the site is territorially isolated, limited by difficult access and visual barriers. Consequently, the Brickbottom district generates only a fraction of its potential economic value.

This proposal seeks to create a new economic engine by integrating traces of the site's rich automotive history, as well as building on the academic / research capacity of local institutions such as MIT, Harvard, and Tufts University. As the centerpiece of this proposal, we propose the development of a new armature, a research factory. It will house startup incubator businesses (sometimes funded by large automobile manufacturers) related to the development of advanced automotive technologies and systems. The research factory will anchor the development of a new community. It will include artist housing, shops and amenities, a system of parks and open spaces, and easy access to the T and the proposed Somerville community bike path. In addition, this proposal embraces infrastructure by creating new pedestrian and vehicular connections to adjacent neighborhoods, as well as points remote via public transportation.

Site History and Programming Opportunities
The Brickbottom district has been, and continues to be, the home of automotive / mobility-related industries. The Somerville Board of Trade noted in 1900 that Kiley Wagons had an excellent reputation for perfect workmanship, durability, and superior finish. Kiley also built all kinds of bodies for automobiles. More recently, Herb Chambers has expanded his Mercedes facilities in the neighborhood. High-quality fabricators of bicycle components operate in the district as well.

by **Paul Lukez Architecture**

Paul Lukez

MID-POLIS: SOMERVILLE, MASSACHUSETTS

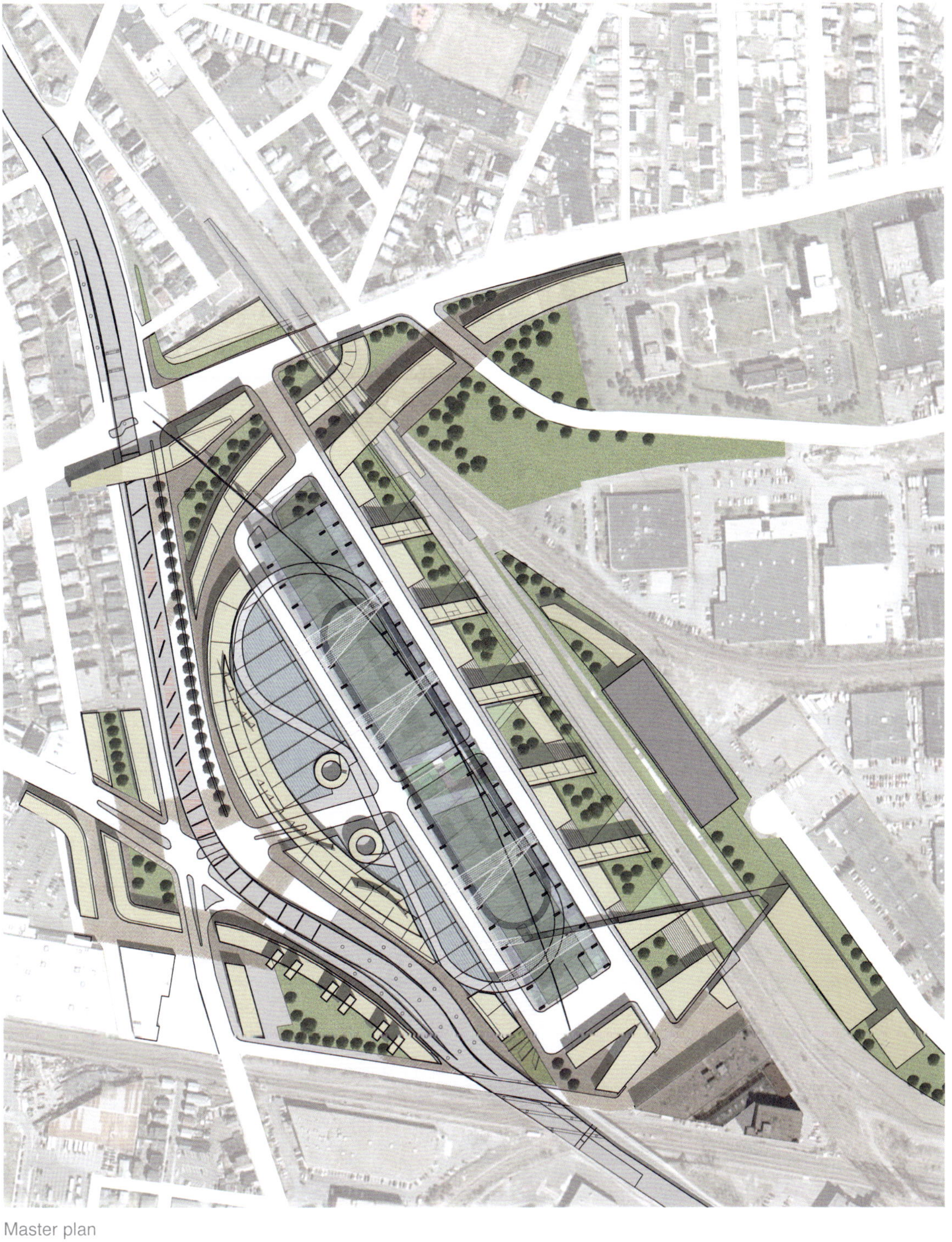

Master plan

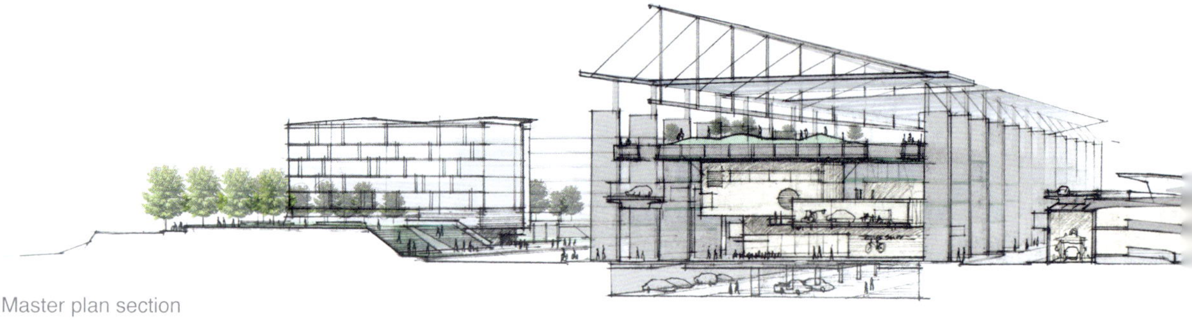

Master plan section

The Need

Public and business-sector awareness of the need to develop sustainable, advanced modes of mobility is increasing. Major automobile manufacturers such as GM and Toyota are actively searching for places to further develop new energy-efficient vehicles and their technologies. These manufacturers are also funding significant research programs in design and energy optimization at local research universities, such as MIT's Car of the Future Program, as part of the institute's Smart City Project initiative. These programs could spur new startup firms associated with this growing industry sector. Brickbottom is ideally situated to meet this need, given its centralized location, access to transportation infrastructure, and intellectual capital from Boston's research community.

Program Elements

<u>The Automotive Research Facility</u>

A large physical and spatial framework occupies the center of the site, providing startups with flexible space for automotive and alternative vehicle research. This framework occupies a long central volume, where a luminescent canopy provides a visual landmark within and beyond the site. Its upper terraces, protected in part by photovoltaic panels, provide a lush landscape and welcome reprieve from the urban streetscape at grade.

<u>The Showrooms / Workshops</u>

Glistening showrooms run the full length of McGrath Highway, which has been reconfigured into a landscaped boulevard. Visitors learn about new technologies and prototypes; attached workshops allow technicians to service and modify their inventions.

<u>The Tracks</u>

A raised track, some 30 feet above grade, enables visitors and researchers to test-drive new vehicles and prototypes. Inspired by the Fiat Factory in Turin, this new track weaves along the workshop's roofscapes and through the research factory, offering drivers dramatic views of the surrounding cityscape and glimpses of the industry's inner workings. A separate bike track soars overhead, providing expansive views of Boston, Cambridge and Somerville.

<u>Public Transportation – The T</u>

Currently, the site is accessible from the Orange Line subway less than half a mile away. A new Green Line T station is perched over the site's Washington Street Bridge, creating a new direct gateway to the community along an east-west axis.

<u>Housing</u>

The Brickbottom artists community's strength and character is extended along the length of the bike path. Its form and geometry mediate the site's complex morphology, creating a series of interconnected courtyards.

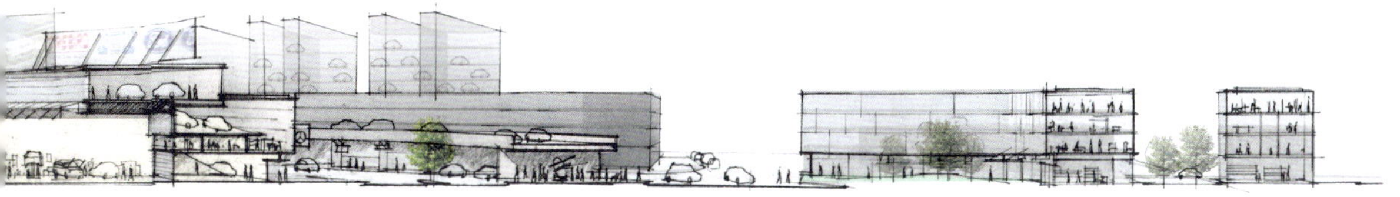

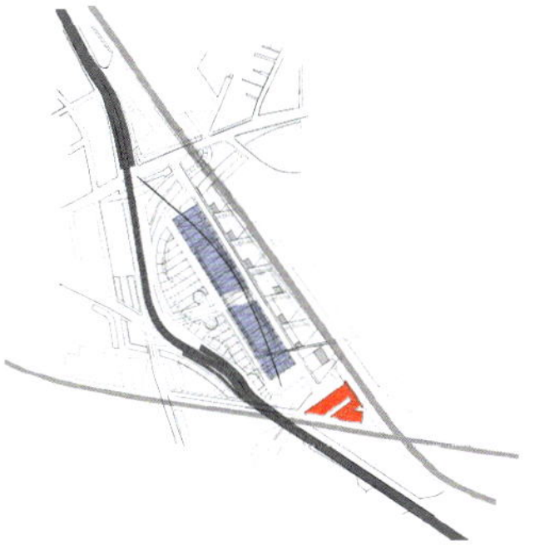

Automotive research facility

Housing

Showrooms / workshops

Parks and public spaces

The tracks

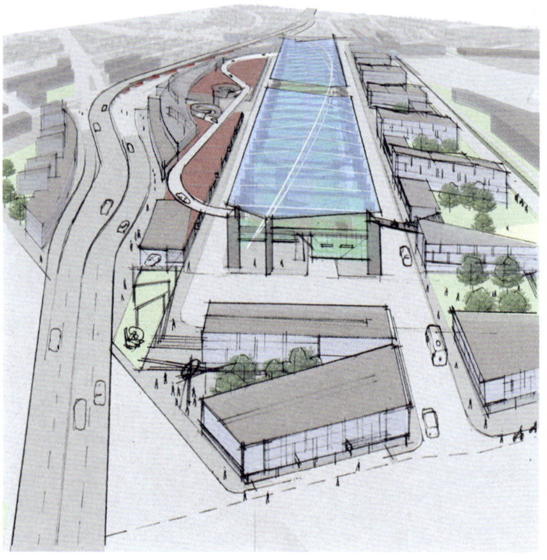

Aerial view from the south

View across transit station

View from McGrath Highway

Office and Retail Spaces

New office buildings, whose fluid forms are inspired in part by the McGrath Highway's geometry, provide support services for the research factory. These buildings help shape public spaces, repair the tattered urban fabric, and define important urban moments of thresholds and gateways. Upper floors hold offices; lower floors house shops and amenities. Additional shops along a tree-lined boulevard provide for the everyday needs of residents and workers.

McGrath Re-inhabited

Through the reconfiguration of the northbound lane of McGrath Highway into a boulevard, the space under the highway can be converted into new uses (retail, galleries and clubs). Concurrently, new pedestrian connections could traverse the once great divide of McGrath Highway.

Parks and Public Spaces

A network of public spaces occupies multiple levels and terraces in this new community. The presence of landscape permeates the once-barren ground, offering occupants and visitors views of lush vegetation.

Phasing

Phasing begins with the identification of the Brickbottom artists community as the anchor for any new development, then proceeds in several steps. First, the reconfiguration of McGrath Highway streamlines traffic flow and improves the site's connectivity. Then the construction of the landmark central open frame houses the new automotive research factory. State-of-the-art dealerships, followed by mechanical service centers, connect research operations to sales and service opportunities. The elevated test track and accompanying bike track create a unique user experience.

Residential capacity is expanded with a string of housing complexes, and the community path is integrated into the site with small-scale commercial development. The site's increased activity draws potential investors and commercial

Bird's-eye view of the master plan

development into the surrounding community, further tying Brickbottom to adjacent districts.

The final stage of development creates numerous open plazas and green passageways. Gardens line the community path as a permeable edge for pedestrian access into the site.

Visionaries' & Artists' Responses

6.0

Ether Study (What), 2007. Inkjet on paper, 22.5" x 30" by Benjamin Edawrds

6.1
Julie Mehretu
Text by Paul Lukez

Mid-Polis: Berlin, Germany

6.2
Sarah McKenzie
Text by Paul Lukez

Mid-Polis: Denver, Colorado, USA

6.3
Benjamin Edwards
Text by Paul Lukez

Mid-Polis: Washington D.C., USA

Julie Mehretu

6.1

Berlin's violent and divisive 20th-century history overshadowed centuries of comparably gradual historical development. The unprecedented layering of trends and historical undercurrents – imperialism, defeat, buildup, annihilation, breakup, Cold War, reunification, and healing – have transformed Berlin into a contemporary urban environment unlike that of any other modern city. This multitude of shifts transformed the German capital into a patchwork of 19th- and early 20th-century urbanism, where past bombardments and divisions are still apparent across the terrain of open space, often born out of historical circumstance.

This unique urban condition has created a loose mesh of mid-polis conditions in the last several decades. Some are inhabited by healing urban infill; others are regions that withstood years of unrest. Decades after World Wars I & II and the Cold War, Berlin is gradually filling in the gaps in its urban terrain, through both contemporary and retroactive processes. Ranging from the construction of Norman Foster's glass dome of the Reichstag to the contemporary towers of Potsdamer Platz, Berlin has rebounded by generating new urban zones among once-blighted historic structures and centers.

In contrast, other regions have been deliberately demolished, reconstructed, destroyed, and restoratively replicated. For instance, the Palace of the Republic is one such landmark that demonstrates this iterative form of urbanism. After the war-damaged Berlin City Palace was demolished in 1950–51, the Palace of the Republic was constructed on its site between 1973 and 1976. It was later closed in 1990 and subsequently demolished from 2006 to 2008. The Humboldt Forum now occupies the site, incorporating rebuilt baroque façades and the reconstructed dome of the historic City Palace. This process of building on traces of past building sites, erasing and rebuilding new structures – sometimes in reference to historic precedents, other times ignoring such influences – provides a complex reading of Berlin's urban reality.

Text by **Paul Lukez**

MID-POLIS: BERLIN, GERMANY

Black City, 2007
Ink and acrylic on canvas, 120 x 192 inches (304.8 x 487.7 cm), François Pinault Collection, Photography Credit: Tim Thayer, Courtesy of the artist and Marian Goodman Gallery, New York © Julie Mehretu

Detail of Black City, 2007
Ink and acrylic on canvas, 120 x 192 inches (304.8 x 487.7 cm), François Pinault Collection, Photography Credit: Tim Thayer, Courtesy of the artist and Marian Goodman Gallery, New York © Julie Mehretu

Berliner Plätze, 2009
Ink and acrylic on canvas, 120 x 168 inches (304.8 x 426.7 cm), Commissioned by Deutsche Bank AG in consultation with the Solomon R. Guggenheim Foundation for the Deutsche Guggenheim, Photography credit: Matthias Schormann, Courtesy of the artist, carlierlgebauer, Berlin and Marian Goodman Gallery, New York © Julie Mehretu

Detail of Berliner Plätze, 2009
Ink and acrylic on canvas, 120 x 168 inches (304.8 x 426.7 cm), Commissioned by Deutsche Bank AG in consultation with the Solomon R. Guggenheim Foundation for the Deutsche Guggenheim, Photography credit: Matthias Schormann, Courtesy of the artist, carlier|gebauer, Berlin and Marian Goodman Gallery, New York © Julie Mehretu

Sarah McKenzie

6.2

Denver is a relatively young city, founded in 1858. Its growth was spurred by the discovery of gold. The Gold Rush intensified in its early years, so much so that four villages combined to become Denver proper. This is itself a kind of early mid-polis transformation.

In the 1870s, Denver leveraged its ideal location at the foothills of the Rockies and its adjacency to the great plains of the Midwest to become a major rail hub. Traces of Denver's extensive rail infrastructure are still evident in today's city maps, and its landmarks (e.g., Union Station) recall the city's origins as a place of thriving mercantile trade. As Denver grew during the early 1900s, city planners were influenced by the City Beautiful movement, such that major streets, e.g., Sherman Street, are terminated by major monuments, such as the golden-domed Colorado State Capitol.

This view of urban planning changed radically during post-World War II. Like the rest of the country, cities were subject to the radical overlay of highways feeding and cutting through American cities. These highway networks helped to feed growing suburban tracts outside of cities. Because of Denver's largely flat terrain, its suburbs were ideal for tract housing development, as depicted in Sarah McKenzie's paintings. An ever-expanding zone of suburban development emerged out of the prairies east of the city, all built one wood stud at a time. The wood-frame technology was simple and adaptable, making it easy for developers to meet the demand for housing and community.

In the 1980s, the city's growth patterns and demand for more housing and communities came up against geographic limits. In particular, the conflicting demands for improved infrastructure (air and road) required a radical solution. Stapleton International Airport, originally built in 1929, was in dire need of repair and ultimately replacement. Located 10 miles east of Denver, it had been encroached upon by suburban

Text by **Paul Lukez**

MID-POLIS: DENVER, COLORADO, USA

Black Box, 2010. Oil and acrylic on canvas, 60 x 60 inches

Aerial 62, 2002. Oil on canvas, 48 x 48 inches
Right page: Aerial 69, 2002. Oil on canvas, 72 x 48 inches

developments on its perimeter. The need for a new airport was significant, and resulted in the proposal for the new, massive Denver International Airport. It is situated on a vast grassland some 20 miles northeast of downtown Denver. Occupying the largest land area of any airport in the U.S., it is the nation's third largest airport measured by passenger volume.

When Stapleton International Airport was demolished, its land was turned into an ambitiously scaled multi-use development, under the direction of a master plan developed by Forest City Enterprises. The plan for this new mid-polis is called Central Park. Inhabited by over 30,000 people, it is still growing as its master plan is built out. The master plan borrows from some principles of New Urbanism, emphasizing open spaces and pedestrian access. Interestingly, remnants of the original airport are being reused, such as the control tower and some hangars.

This project and its history demonstrate how the development and subsequent transformation of mid-polis conditions can happen in an accelerated fashion, especially when large infrastructure systems serve as catalysts for changing the metropolitan status quo.

Aerial 52, 2002. Oil on canvas, 24 x 72 inches

Benjamin Edwards

6.3

Washington, D.C., is a fascinating city to study vis-à-vis the mid-polis paradigm. This book has focused on the metropolitan space amid the less-populated outer boundaries and the denser urban core. This historic capital city offers an intriguing counterpoint, where the center is more vacuous and the periphery is denser. The center is reserved for federal monuments, museums, and important government buildings, and is complemented by correspondingly coordinated open spaces. The National Mall provides the armature for this mix of scales and uses.

The original kernels of today's Washington, D.C., plan can be found in Pierre Charles L'Enfant's 1791 master plan, selected by George Washington himself. It has since been modified and amended over the past 230 years, most notably in 1814, when the city was burned down by British forces during the War of 1812, and in 1902, when the McMillan Plan, named for Senate Park Commission Chairman James McMillan, updated L'Enfant's plan to correct, or strengthen, urban plan features and connections among landmarks. The McMillan Plan also enhanced the mix of gridded streets and blocks sliced by strong diagonal avenues, creating public spaces and nodes at intersecting geometries. Some of Benjamin Edwards' paintings capture the mix of grid and diagonals in a gravity-liberated rendition of urban space.

Perhaps more impactful to the metropolitan region over the past centuries were the demographic shifts, especially during the Civil War, when southern slaves sought refuge in Washington. More recently, the development of two systems of mobility – subway and highway – radically redefined the city and its future development. The Washington Metro began construction in 1976, feeding inner- and outer-belt neighborhoods outside the city center. This much-praised subway system helped to bolster town centers along the Metro's route. More established inner-belt communities, such as Georgetown, Arlington, and Alexandria, were absorbed into the city's transportation network, while farther places, such as Tysons Corner Center,

Text by **Paul Lukez**

MID-POLIS: WASHINGTON D.C., USA

Landscape, 1995-1996. Acrylic on canvas, 74" x 110"

Ether Study (What), 2007. Inkjet on paper, 22.5" x 30"

were fed a steady stream of workers, shoppers and visitors alike, creating a denser urban node in an underutilized mid-polis. Fortuitously, mid-polis nodes, including Tysons Corner Center, are also served by the Metro and the Capital Beltway (I-495), integrating and concentrating economic and social activities in the metropolis.

Washington, D.C., is therefore fertile ground for mining mid-polis case-studies, given both its rich national history and its more recent contemporary developments. It is a city that will continue to evolve in potentially productive ways, making the most of a well-developed infrastructural system.

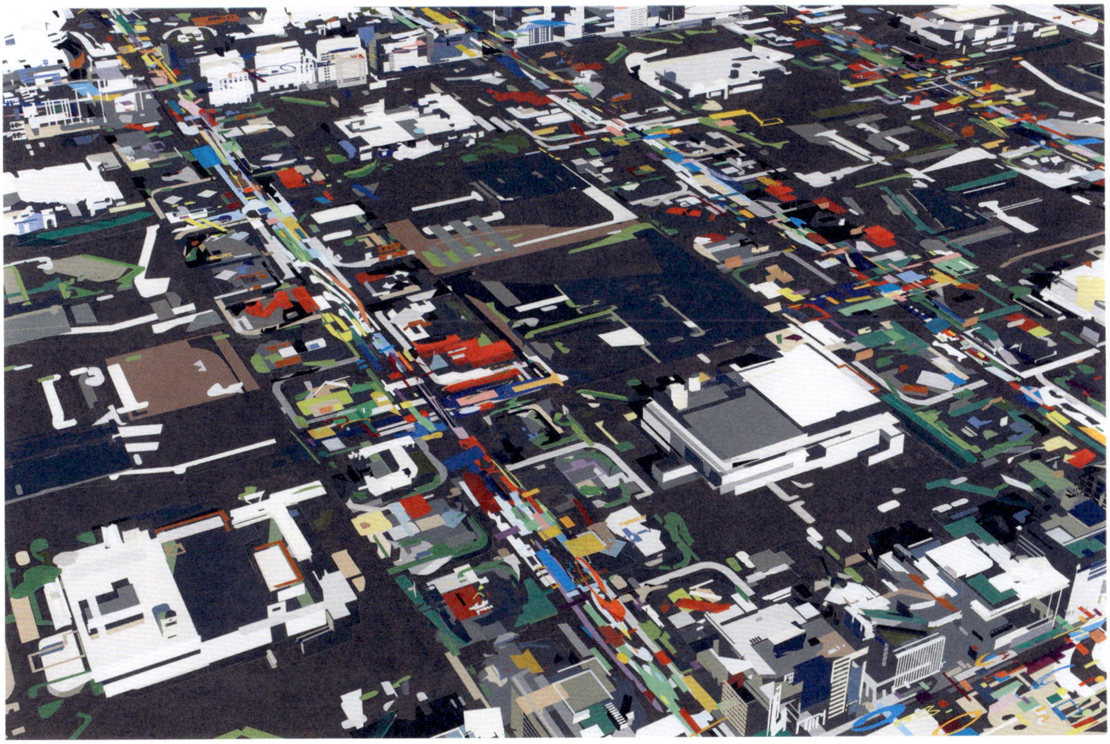

Freedom Through Order, 2008. Acrylic on canvas, 54" x 84"

Worship, 2008. Acrylic on canvas, 54" x 84"

Conclusion 7.0

“Burlington Re-Visited” a mid-polis “Traces” drawing by Paul Lukez & Patrick Zhang

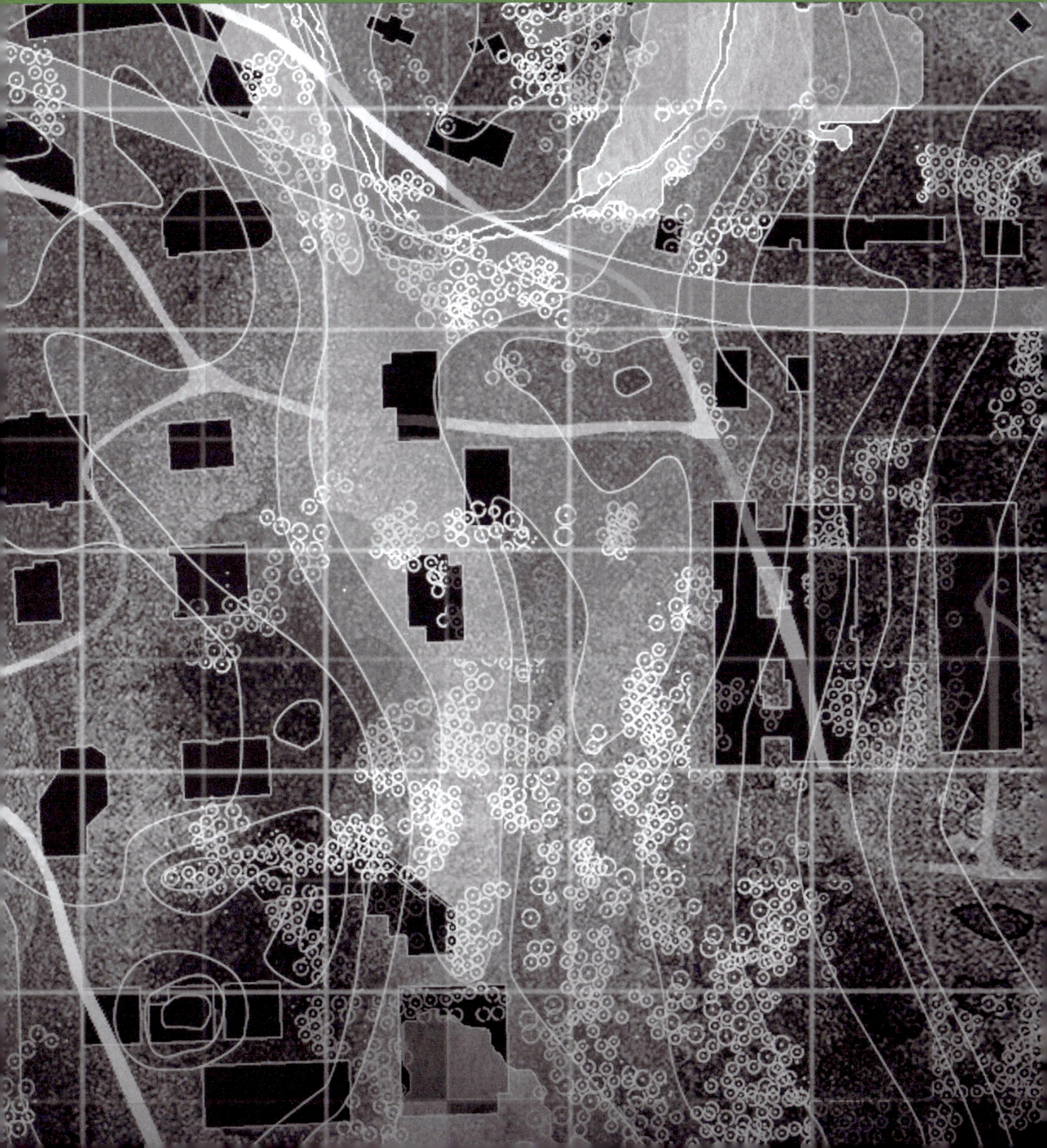

Conclusion

7.1

Mid-Polis as the New City

This book is merely the beginning of an investigation into a new and evolving urban condition driven by larger worldwide demographic and economic shifts. Urban demographers predict that, by 2050, over 70% of the world's population will reside in urbanized areas, an increase from 50% of today's population.[1] This means some 2 billion people will be urbanized within the next twenty-plus years, which is the equivalent of constructing a new city for a population of 1 million every week in that time frame.[2]

However, people around the world are not urbanized in the same way. Yes, some are housed in sparkling new cities in China, built specifically to house people and commerce. The shotgun marriage between those two components can be uneasy, unnatural, and often at loggerheads and cross-purposes with one another. Instant cities, urban utopias, and fast-track workers' towns rarely foster the rich interplay among culture, people and economy that is found in more mature cities. The Brazilian capital of Brasilia, the Nigerian capital of Abuja, and the many ghost-towns of China illustrate the challenges and flaws of this strategy.

In other cases, rapid urbanization occurs more organically where urban migrants flock to existing metropoleis. South and Central America are replete with examples: Lima, Peru; Quito, Ecuador; Tegucigalpa, Honduras; and Mexico City, to name a few. These migrants densify parts of existing cities to overflowing capacities, or they settle in underutilized or neglected urban voids, thereby creating pockets of newer development. The favelas of Rio de Janeiro, Brazil, are but one example of these phenomena. These newly inhabited second- and third-tier urban voids constitute the beginnings of new neighborhoods. Sometimes they are independent of adjacent neighborhoods; other times they are parasitically interwoven with abutting or contiguous neighborhoods and districts.

All of these trends are indicative of larger societal forces at play, ones that 19th- and 20th-century by Paul Lukez

concepts of urbanism could not address. Instead, fresh solutions are required to confront the problems these trends present, e.g.: Where will all these people go? How will they be housed and schooled? Where will they work? What kinds of economies will sustain them? What kinds of infrastructure systems will need to be overlaid onto areas already occupying part of the larger metropolis? And how will these systems be tied into existing, overtaxed infrastructures?

Many important mid-polis transformation issues are tied to sustainability. What resources will the ever-expanding mid-polis require? How will its inhabitants access these resources? Will they be sustainable over time? This, of course, Is tied to not only exhausting valuable energy resources, but also our ecosystem's ability to provide food, water and fresh air over the long term. For this purpose, can we create a network of new high-intensity vertical farms within the evolving mid-polis as a self-sustaining cluster or node?

The European medieval city could be a fruitful model to investigate, where small-to-mid-sized metropoleis bounded by city walls or natural terrain often had their own farms and water sources within town limits. This allowed their individual citizenries to survive droughts, floods, and other hostile climatic incidents. Portland, Oregon, also offers valuable lessons in creating boundaries around urban centers. District zoning defines what urban uses are allowed within the city's boundary and outside its more rural outer boundary.

More recently, the concept of the *15-minute city* has emerged as a powerful urban design concept. Prof. Carlos Moreno's concept organizes the city into overlapping zones of mixed uses readily accessible by public transit, bikeways and pedestrian paths. Residents are able to gain access to all the products and services that are required in daily life within 15 minutes, whether by public transit, bike or foot. This model recognizes the impact that technology has had on our lifestyle, regarding the ability to work remotely and buy locally. This reduces the need for large, centralized facilities and systems in the city, enabling a more malleable urban model supporting spaces and lifestyles scaled for people.[3]

Paris, Singapore, Utrecht, and many cities around the world are applying this concept. This model can be retroactively applied to mid-polis conditions. The 15-minute city is also compatible with the Transit Oriented Development (TOD) concept endorsed by the New Urbanists.[4] Similarly, pedestrian pocket developments and principles of campus planning, whether applied to housing or corporate-focused developments, may all be applied to the mid-polis condition.[5] Taken together, the metropolitan domain can be made more efficient and habitable as newly constituted and transformed mid-polis conditions become important nodes linked to a polycentric metropolis.

Such conditions can really take transformative root as they begin to cover large swaths of a country's land mass (e.g., the Pearl River Delta Metropolitan Region in China, the Bos-Wash Corridor from Boston to Washington, D.C., Ruhrgebiet in Germany, Lagos in Nigeria, Caracas in Venezuela). A more human life and ecologically integrated societal framework need a reprieve from the increasing density, congestion and pollution of never-ending urbanity. (Imagine what New York City would be like without Central Park.) Connections to nature, recreation, and places to congregate are critical to sustaining the quality of private and civic health. What networks of public space can be interjected into the metropolis? Can the pockets of mid-polis development serve as the beginning of a system of public spaces, some of which contain nature or community gardens?

These questions, important as they may be, are ultimately a subset of a larger one: What is the new form of urbanity for the 21st century? After all, in the decades and centuries to come, the mid-polis condition will increasingly frame the human experience. Consequently, we must develop urban models that can evolve symbiotically so existing urban landscapes and natural ecologies can co-exist in a way that supports and enriches the well-being of cities and the lives of their citizens.

This book is intended to highlight and raise awareness of these issues, as new solutions are sought for more site-specific problems. It is a resource that both frames the larger issues and lays the groundwork for more extensive research and applied practice. In the end, we hope this book will challenge planners, urban designers, developers, government officials, leaders, and citizens alike to arrive at solutions that will ultimately provide more efficient, sustainable, lively forms of urbanity, ones that can be both capable of handling increasingly complex sets of design parameters and resilient to economic, social, political and ecological disruptions. Only then can the mid-polis fulfill its potential as a generative, catalytic building block for 21st-century urbanity.

Notes

[1] *U.N.: World Population Increasingly Urban*, The Associated Press, CBSNews.com, February 26, 2008.

[2] McKenzie, Fiona. *Welcome to the Future: Drivers and Trends that will Shape Australia*, discussion paper for the Australian Futures Project, a multi-sector, non-profit, and non-partisan initiative hosted by La Trobe University, Melbourne, Victoria, Australia, August 2013.

[3] Carlos Moreno, *The 15-minute City: A Solution to Saving Our Time & Our Planet*, Hoboken, N.J.: John Wiley & Sons, 2024.

[4] Calthorpe, Peter. *The Next American Metropolis: Ecology, Community, and the American Dream.* Third edition. Princeton, N.J.: Princeton Architectural Press, 1995.

[5] Gregory T. Havens. *Pedestrian Pockets – A New Suburban Paradigm?* Cambridge, Mass.: Massachusetts Institute of Technology, Department of Urban Studies and Planning, 1992.

“Burlington Re-Visited” a mid-polis “Traces” drawing by Paul Lukez & Patrick Zhang

Acknowledgments **7.2**

This book originated out of a design studio I was asked to teach by Professor Bruce Lindsey, who was then Dean of the Sam Fox School of Design and Visual Arts at Washington University in St. Louis (WUSTL). As a visiting professor of architecture, I proposed developing a joint studio with Prof. Boa Li and Vice-Dean Dong Wei of the Department of Architecture of Southeast University (SEU) in Nanjing, China, with the intent of exploring the *Transformation of the Mid-Polis.* Dean Lindsey endorsed this proposal.

Consequently, first and foremost, I owe special thanks to Dean Bruce Lindsey for his generous support of the Nanjing Studio. Also, I will always appreciate Prof. Bao Li and Vice-Dean Dong Wei, who so graciously hosted the joint WUSTL - SEU studio. Their contributions to the joint studio were very valuable.

I also want to extend my thanks to Dean Stephen White, AIA, of Roger Williams University (RWU) in Bristol, Rhode Island. His long-standing support of this book project helped to sustain its intellectual development and momentum, and ultimately to fund a studio and exhibit at RWU focused on the mid-polis. I will always value his friendship.

Kudos also to members of that first joint studio (WUSTL and SEU), whose enthusiasm helped propel this project forward. WUSTL's graduate students come to the studio from a wide range of backgrounds, helping to feed the design and exploration process. Sarah Hill (Burnett), Rebecca Sommer (Castellon), Christian Clerc, Matt Kleinmann, Matthew Kuebler, Adria Longenderfer, and Yusheen Yang must all be recognized for their exemplary work in the studio. Boa Li's students were equally creative in their design proposals. They include Chen Yu, Hao Ji, Li Xiaoxi, Meng Cheng, Shi Xiaoxia, Song Kai, Wang Xin, Wu Huanyu, Yin Xi, and Yu Xiaoge.

In addition to the students mentioned above, I want to show my appreciation to all the graduate students from Roger Williams University, including Bryan Apito, Brian Boisvert, Katie Fitzpatrick (Kanakos), Evan Krasik, Chris Nelson, and Tom Sherman. Their imaginative interpretations of the various transformations of the mid-poleis brought fresh perspectives to the book.

by Paul Lukez

Of those affiliated with my office who contributed to the book in one way or another, I am grateful to Nicholas Caruso, AICP, Assoc. AIA; to Jing Cai, for her organizational and graphic design skills; and to Matt Uminski, a talented graphic designer, for elegantly shaping the book's presentation during the early phases of its compilation and design. Bryan Apito's diagrams intricately illustrate the many types of mid-polis conditions explored in the book, particularly Jue Zhan's persistence in communicating with Chinese contributors.

And, most emphatically, I wish to thank I-Ting Lee (aka Tina Lee) and Safia Dziri, both of whom work with Paul Lukez Architecture (PLA) as highly valued colleagues. Their contributions to the book's editing, graphics, and organizational tasks helped bring this project to completion, despite the many challenges a multinational endeavor of this scale requires. I am forever grateful to Tina and Safia.

Not to be forgotten is Todd Larson, who has worked with me as an editor and colleague on all things related to writing. Todd is uniquely talented and capable, and brings an editorial filter and voice to projects that require a subtler reading of architectural issues and history. His talent and good nature are powerful qualities that serve architects and writers invaluable benefits.

I appreciate the enthusiastic support provided by Oscar Riera Ojeda, founder of Oscar Riera Ojeda Publishers, and his team, including Carrie Tang, Florencia Damilano and Juan Pablo Sarrabayrouse. Oscar Riera Ojeda has an outstanding reputation for creating artfully produced books whose content and graphic design elevate the reader's experience. It is an honor to be part of their catalog.

Finally, I wish to dedicate this book to my family, my wife Sally, my son Alex, and my daughter Stephanie. Their patience and support came in large doses, sustaining my spirit. I will always be grateful to them for their enduring love.

Paul Lukez FAIA
Lexington, Massachusetts, USA
August 30, 2025

Biographies 7.3

Contributors

Interboro Partners — New York City, USA
Tobias Armborst, Daniel D'Oca, Georgeen Theodore

Interboro Partners is an architecture, urban design and planning practice focused on public projects for the public good. The firm was established over twenty years ago by Tobias Armborst, Daniel D'Oca, and Georgeen Theodore, FAIA. The partners work today among a team of twelve in Brooklyn, NY. Interboro began its practice by winning a series of international design competitions in which they focused on places that faced challenges (dead malls, shrinking cities, inner-ring suburbs), and by building a series of groundbreaking temporary public space projects for the LMCC, MoMA PS1, and the Venice Biennale. Today, Interboro works for, and with, cities and communities that face disinvestment, crime, and climate injustice, such as Detroit, St. Louis, and the South Bronx.

Bruce Lindsey — St. Louis, Missouri, USA
Former Dean of Architecture,
& Current E. Desmond Lee Professor,
Sam Fox School of Design & Visual Arts,
Washington University in St. Louis

Bruce Lindsey has made significant contributions to introductory, sustainable, and community design education. Prior to becoming Dean of Architecture at Washington University in St. Louis, he was head of Auburn University's School of Architecture from 2000 to 2006. He also taught at Carnegie Mellon University, where he was associate head of the School of Architecture from 1994 to 2001. Lindsey holds bachelor's and master's degrees in art from the University of Utah and a master's degree in architecture from Yale University.

LTL Architects — New York City, USA
Paul Lewis, Marc Tsurumaki, David Lewis

Founded in 1997 by Paul Lewis, Marc Tsurumaki, and David Lewis, LTL Architects (Lewis.Tsurumaki.Lewis) is an architecture partnership that explores the opportunistic overlaps among form, program, and materiality. With over 27 years of practice in projects ranging from ground-up buildings to dynamic interiors and speculative research, LTL Architects has refocused its practice on the role of embodied carbon and the architectural potentials of plant- and earth-based materials and reuse. The firm's principals are on the faculty at Princeton University, Columbia University, and Parsons School of Design.

MIT Senseable City Lab — Cambridge, Massachusetts, USA

Carlo Ratti — Cambridge, Massachusetts, USA, and Milan, Italy
Professor/ Massachusetts Institute of Technology, Politecnico di Milano
Director/ MIT Senseable City Lab
Founder/ CRA-Carlo Ratti Associati
Curator/ Venice Architecture Biennale 2025

An architect and engineer by training, Carlo Ratti runs the design and innovation studio CRA-Carlo Ratti Associati and teaches at the Massachusetts Institute of Technology, where he directs the MIT Senseable City Lab. He is also a professor at the Politecnico di Milano. He graduated from the Politecnico di Torino and the École Nationale des Ponts et Chaussées in Paris and later earned his M.Phil. and Ph.D. at the University of Cambridge, U.K. His work has been exhibited worldwide at venues such as the Venice Biennale, the Design Museum in Barcelona, the Science Museum in London, and The Museum of Modern Art in New York. He is the curator of Venice Architecture Biennale 2025.

Nashid Nabian — Tehran, Iran
Tehran Urban Innovation Center, Former post-doctoral fellow at MIT Senseable City Lab

Dr. Nabian earned her Doctor of Design degree from the Harvard Graduate School of Design. She is a co-founder of (Shift) Process Practice, an award-winning architecture studio based in Tehran. She is also the director and co-founder of Tehran Urban Innovation Center (TUIC), a design-by-research,

research-by-design initiative, dedicated to developing ideas for smart urban solutions in contemporary Iranian cities. In the 2010s, Nashid Nabian was a postdoctoral fellow at the Massachusetts Institute of Technology (MIT) Senseable City Lab.

MONOLAB — Rotterdam, The Netherlands
Jan Willem Van Kuilenburg

Jan Willem Van Kuilenburg is the Principal of MONOLAB, a studio for advanced research and design in urbanism and architecture founded in 1999. The office adheres to the theory that simplicity (mono) is linked to experiment (lab) in design processes fueled by our accelerating culture. Mr. Van Kuilenburg also teaches at MA+U, the Fontys Academy of Architecture and Urbanism in Tilburg.

Paul Lukez Architecture — Somerville, Massachusetts, USA
Paul Lukez

Paul Lukez is a graduate of the Massachusetts Institute of Technology (MIT) with over thirty years of professional experience in architectural and urban design. He is the author of *Suburban Transformations* (Princeton Architectural Press, 2007) and multiple articles on urban transformation. He has twenty years of teaching experience as a professor and visiting professor at MIT, Washington University at St. Louis, Tsinghua University, and Roger Williams University, among others. His firm (Paul Lukez Architecture) has received over 60 design awards. He was named a Fellow of the American Institute of Architects in 2011.

Dagmar Richter — New York City, USA
DR_D Lab, Pratt Institute

Dagmar Richter is a Professor at the Pratt Institute's Undergraduate Architecture Department. Her design studio, DR_D, is known for design research and experimental projects. Two monographs, *XYZ* from Princeton Architectural Press and *Armed Surfaces* from Black Dog Publishing, are documenting her work from 1986 to 2004. She was Chair at Cornell University and taught at Cooper Union, the Rhode Island School of Design, Harvard GSD, Columbia University, Art Academy in Stuttgart and Berlin, and UCLA.

URBANUS — Shenzhen + Beijing + LXD, China
Liu Xiaodu, Meng Yan, Wang Hui

Founded in 1999, URBANUS is a think-tank providing strategies for urbanism and architecture. URBANUS is committed to the modernist belief that architecture is a pivotal force for a better life, hence architects should push the boundary of their traditional role and be a progressive force in society. Since 2019, the three founding partners, guided by a shared framework of URBANUS principles, have led design studios independently as principal architects. Currently, Meng Yan directs URBANUS Shenzhen studio, Wang Hui oversees URBANUS Beijing office and Liu Xiaodu heads a cross-disciplinary design atelier. Urban *Tulou* was completed in 2008, led by Liu Xiaodu and Meng Yan.

Stephen White — Bristol, Rhode Island, USA
Dean, Cummings School of Architecture, Roger Williams University

Stephen White, AIA has been Roger Williams University's Dean of the School of Architecture since 1997, where he also co-founded both the Center for Macro Projects and Diplomacy and the Community Partnerships Center, focusing on transforming local and global environments. White authored *Building In the Garden: The Architecture of Joseph Allen Stein in India and California* with support from the Ford Foundation. He has worked in New Delhi, Amsterdam, London, San Francisco, and St. Louis.

June Williamson — New York City, USA
Bernard and Anne Spitzer School of Architecture, The City College of New York

June Williamson is Professor and former Chairperson of the Architecture Department at the City College of New York. She is co-author, with Ellen

Dunham-Jones, of *Retrofitting Suburbia: Urban Design Solutions for Redesigning Suburbs*, winner of the 2009 PROSE Award for Architecture and Urban Planning, and *Case Studies in Retrofitting Suburbia: Urban Design Strategies for Urgent Challenges*, winner of the 2021 Great Places Award for Books. She is the author of *Designing Suburban Futures*, which documents Build a Better Burb, a 2010 ideas design competition for the next generation of suburban downtowns that she created for the nonprofit Long Island Index, a project of the Rauch Foundation.

WSP Architects — Beijing, China + Munich, Germany
Wu Gang, Zhang Ying, Chen Ling, Knud Rossen

WSP Architects is an international innovation-oriented design firm. All four principal architects and landscape designers – Wu Gang, Zhang Ying, Chen Ling, Knud Rossen – have worked on a range of public facilities, large-scale industry centers, enterprise headquarters, social housing projects, commercial centers, recreational facilities, theme parks, and landscaped environments in various cities and towns in China, Europe, and Africa.

Ken Yeang — Kuala Lumpur, Malaysia
FAIA (Hon), DMPN (Malaysia), PhD (Cantab), AADipl (UK), APAM, FSIA, RIBA, ARAIA (Hon), FRIAS (Hon), T.R. Hamzah & Yeang Sdn Bhd

Dr. Ken Yeang is an architect, planner, ecologist and author best known for his ecology-based architecture and master plans. He is Principal of Hamzah & Yeang (Malaysia) and former Chairman and Director of Design of Llewelyn Davies Yeang (U.K.). He studied at Cheltenham College (Gloucestershire), completed his architectural education at the Architectural Association School in London, and received a doctorate at Wolfson College, Cambridge University (U.K.).

Zhejiang University — Hangzhou, China

Wang Ka
Associate Professor of School of Civil Engineering and Architecture, Zhejiang University
Deputy Director of the Institute of Architectural Design and Theory, Zhejiang University

Dr. Wang Ka, Associate Professor at Zhejiang University, specializes in urban design, green buildings, and architectural pedagogy. He has published extensively, spearheaded award-winning projects, and completed numerous acclaimed urban and architectural designs.

Xu Lei
Former Professor of School of Civil Engineering and Architecture, Zhejiang University
Former Director of the Institute of Architectural Design and Theory, Zhejiang University

Dr. Xu Lei is a former Professor at the School of Civil Engineering and Architecture, Zhejiang University, and served as Director of the university's Architectural Design and Research Institute. For many years, he has taught undergraduate and graduate students while conducting research on green building design, as well as urban design theories and methods.

Artists & Photographers

Benjamin Edwards — Washington, D.C., USA

Benjamin Edwards was born in Iowa City, Iowa, in 1970 and was raised in the San Francisco Bay Area. He received a Bachelor of Arts degree in art from the University of California, Los Angeles, in 1992, and a Master of Fine Arts in painting from the Rhode Island School of Design in 1997. In his artwork he portrays the balance and the laws that regulate the dystopia of the city of the future. He exhibited in the USA, Europe, and Asia. His works are in prestigious museum collections such as the Carnegie Museum of Art in Pittsburgh, PA, and the Museum of Modern Art in New York City, N.Y. He lives and works in Washington, D.C.

Sarah McKenzie — Boulder, Colorado, USA

Sarah McKenzie (sarahmckenzie.com) is a visual artist based in Boulder, Colorado. Her paintings document our built landscape, exploring changes in our architecture (what we build) for evidence of societal, economic, and cultural shifts (why we build). Her most recent work explores the dynamics of institutional space, as manifested in American museums and prisons. Sarah has exhibited her paintings nationally, including shows with the Walker Art Center, the Carnegie Museum of Art, the Yale School of Architecture, the New Mexico Museum of Art, the Aspen Art Museum, and the Museum of Contemporary Art Denver, among other venues. Her paintings have been featured in *Art Forum, The New York Times, The Denver Post, Dwell* magazine, *and New American Paintings.* She received a Joan Mitchell Painters and Sculptors Grant in 2012, the Alexander Rutsch Award for Painting in 2019, and the Marion International Fellowship for the Visual and Performing Arts in 2021. In addition to her studio practice, Sarah teaches visual art classes inside the Colorado Department of Corrections (CDOC) through a non-profit she cofounded in 2024, Impact Arts (impactartsco.org). She also develops and curates exhibition opportunities for artists impacted by the criminal-legal system.

Julie Mehretu — New York City, USA

Julie Mehretu was born in Addis Ababa, Ethiopia, in 1970 and lives and works in New York City. Mehretu is a recipient of many awards, including the Officer of the Ordre des Arts et des Lettres by the French Ministry of Culture in 2025, the MacArthur Fellowship in 2005, and the U.S. Department of State Medal of Arts Award in 2015. Her work has been exhibited extensively in museums and biennials such as the Carnegie International (2004–05), Sydney Biennial (2006), Solomon R. Guggenheim Museum, New York (2010), dOCUMENTA (13) (2012), Sharjah Biennial (2015), Museu de Arte Contemporânea de Serralves, Porto, Portugal (2017), Kettle's Yard, University of Cambridge, U.K. (2019), and the 58th International Art Exhibition, La Biennale di Venezia, Italy (2019). Recent notable exhibits include Kunstammlung NRW Düsseldorf, Germany (2025), Palazzo Grassi-Pinault Collection, Venice, Italy (2024) and the Museum of Contemporary Art, Sydney, Australia (2025).

Peter Vanderwarker — Boston, Massachusetts, USA

Peter Vanderwarker is a freelance photographer and author whose work interprets both the natural and man-made environments. His prints are in the collections of the Museum of Fine Arts, Boston, and the Addison Gallery of American Art at Phillips Academy, Andover, Mass. He is represented by Gallery NAGA, Boston. Peter has a degree in Architecture from the University of California Berkeley, and was a Loeb Fellow at Harvard University. He has received grants from the National Endowment for the Arts and the Graham Foundation for his work. He was a frequent collaborator with the late Robert Campbell, architecture critic of *The Boston Globe*; together they authored *Cityscapes of Boston: An American City Through Time* (Boston: Houghton Mifflin Company, 1992).

Former Students

Bryan Apito — Master of Architecture, Roger Williams University

Brian Boisvert — Master of Architecture, Roger Williams University

Christian Clerc — Master of Architecture + Master of Urban Design, Washington University in St. Louis

Katie Fitzpatrick (Kanakos) — Master of Architecture, Roger Williams University

Sarah Hill (Burnett) — Master of Urban Design, Washington University in St. Louis

Matthew Kleinmann — Master of Architecture + Master of Urban Design, Washington University in St. Louis

Matthew Kuebler — Master of Urban Design, Washington University in St. Louis

Evan Krasik — Master of Architecture, Roger Williams University

Adria Longenderfer — Master of Architecture + Master of Urban Design, Washington University in St. Louis

Chris Nelson — Master of Architecture, Roger Williams University

Tom Sherman — Master of Architecture, Roger Williams University

Rebecca Sommer (Castellon) — Master of Architecture + Master of Urban Design, Washington University in St. Louis

Yusheen Yang — Master of Urban Design, Washington University in St. Louis

Bibliography 7.4

Books

Adhya, Anirban, and Philip D. Plowright. ***Urban Design Made by Humans: A Handbook of Design Ideas.*** New York: Routledge, 2023.

Alexander, Christopher W., Sara Ishikawa, and Murray Silverstein. ***A Pattern Language: Towns, Buildings, Construction.*** Oxford, U.K.: Oxford University Press,1977.

Allen, Stan. ***Points + Lines: Diagrams and Projects for the City***. New York: Princeton Architectural Press, 1999.

American Planning Association. ***Planning and Urban Design Standards.*** Hoboken, N.J.: John Wiley & Sons, Inc., 2006.

Arets, Wiel. ***Stills.*** Rotterdam: 010 Publishers, 2010.

Ascher, Kate. ***The Works: Anatomy of a City***. New York: The Penguin Press HC, 2005.

Ballesteros, Mario. ***Verb Crisis.*** Barcelona: Actar, 2008.

Barnett, Jonathan. ***Planning for a New Century: The Regional Agenda.*** Washington, D.C.:Island Press, 2000.

Barnett, Jonathan. ***Redesigning Cities.*** Washington, D.C.: American Planning Association, 2008.

Beatley, Timothy. ***Green Urbanism: Learning from European Cities.*** Washington, D.C.: Island Press, 2000.

Benfield, Kaid. ***Solving Sprawl: Models of Smart Growth in Communities Across America.*** Washington, D.C.: Island Press, 2001.

Bentley, Ian. ***Urban Transformations: Power, People and Urban Design.*** New York: Routledge, 1999.

Berger, Alan. ***Drosscape: Wasting Land in Urban America.*** New York: Princeton Architectural Press, 2007.

Berger, Miles L. ***They Built Chicago: Entrepreneurs Who Shaped a Great City's Architecture.*** Los Angeles: Bonus Books, 1992.

Berke, Philip R., David R. Godschalk, and Edward J. Kaiser, with Daniel A. Rodriquez. ***Urban Land Use Planning.*** Fifth Edition. Champaign, Ill.: University of Illinois Press, 2023.

Bertaud, Alain.***Order without Design: How Markets Shape Cities.*** Cambridge, Mass.: The MIT Press, 2018.

Belanger, Pierre. Landscape as Infrastructure Landscape Journal, 28, no. 1 (2009), pp. 79-95. Bohl, Charles C. ***Place Making: Developing Town Centers, Main Streets, and Urban Villages.*** Washington, D.C.: Urban Land Institute, 2002.

Bokov, Anya, ed. ***Edge as Center, Envisioning the Post-Industrial Landscape - Somerville, MA.*** Somerville, Mass.: Mayors Office of Strategic, Planning and Community Development, 2007.

Bosselmann, Peter. ***Urban Transformation: Understanding City Design and Form.*** Washington, D.C.: Island Press, 2008.Botchwey, Nisha, Andrew L. Dannenberg, and Howard Frumkin (eds.). Making Healthy Places. Second Edition. Washington, D.C.: Island Press, 2022.

Brook, Daniel. ***A History of Future Cities.*** New York: W.W. Norton & Co., Inc., 2014.

Bruns-Berentelg, Jurgen. Interviewed by Yoco Fukuda Noennig, ***Toward a New Balance for the Inner City of the 21st Century, Architecture and Urbanism, No. 459***, December 2008.Burdett, Ricky. The Endless City. London: Phaidon Press, 2008.

Cache, Bernard and Sanford Kwinter. ***Phylogenesis Foas Ark: Foreign Office Architects.*** Barcelona: Actar, 2004.

Calabrese, Francesco, Francisco C. Pereira, Giusy Di Lorenzo, L. Liu, and Carlo Ratti. ***"The Geography of Taste: Analyzing Cell-phone Mobility and Social Events."*** In Proceedings of the 8th International Conference on Pervasive Computing, 2010.

Calthorpe, Peter. ***The Next American Metropolis: Ecology, Community, and the American Dream.*** Princeton, N.J.: Princeton Architectural Press, 1997.

Calthorpe, Peter. ***The Regional City.*** Washington, D.C.: The Island Press, 2001.

Calthorpe, Peter. ***Urbanism in the Age of Climate Change.*** Washington, D.C.: The Island Press, 2010.

Calvino, Italo. ***Invisible Cities.*** Rome: Giulio Einaudi, 1972.

Campbell, Robert, and Peter Vanderwarker. ***Cityscapes of Boston: An American City Through Time.*** Boston: Houghton Mifflin Company, 1992.

Castells, Manuel. ***The Informational City.*** London: Basil Blackwell, 1989.

Corvoro, Robort. ***The Transit Metropolis: A Global Inquiry.*** Washington, D.C.: Island Press, 1998.

Chase, John, ***Margaret Crawford, and John Kaliski. Everyday Urbanism.*** New York: The Monacelli Press, 1999.

Chiarella, Donald. ***The History of Urban Planning and Cities.*** Morrisville, N.C.: Lulu Press, Inc., 2005.

Christensen, Julia. ***Big Box Reuse.*** Cambridge, Mass.: The MIT Press, 2008.

Colenbrander, Bernard, Michelle Provoost, and Rem Koolhaas. ***Dutchtown: A City Center Design*** by OMA/ Rem Koolhaas. Rotterdam: NAi Publishers, 2000.

Couch, Chris. ***Urban Planning: An Introduction.*** London: Bloomsbury Academic, 2016.

Cronon, William. ***Uncommon Ground: Rethinking the Human Place in Nature.*** New York: W. W. Norton, 1996.

Cowan, Rob. ***Essential Urban Design: A Handbook for Architects, Designers and Planners.*** London: RIBA Publishing, 2021.

Cullingworth, Barry, and Roger W. Caves. ***Planning in the USA: Policies, Issues, and Processes.*** Milton Park, Abingdon-on-Thames, Oxfordshire, U.K.: Routledge, Taylor & Francis Group, 2013.

Cushing, Debra Flanders, and Evonne Miller. ***Creating Great Places: Evidence-based Urban Design for Health and Wellbeing.*** New York and Milton Park, Abingdon-on-Thames, Oxfordshire, U.K.: Routledge, 2020.

Davidson, Cynthia. ***Eisenman/Krier: Two Ideologies.*** New York: Monacelli Press, 2005.

Dear, Michael, and Allen J. Scott (eds.). ***Urbanization and Urban Planning in Capitalist Society.*** New York: Routledge Library Editions, 2018.

Diamond, Jason. ***The Sprawl: Reconsidering the Weird American Suburbs.*** Minneapolis: Coffee House Press, 2020.

Dover, Victor, and John Massengale. ***Street Design: The Secret to Great Cities and Towns.*** Hoboken, N.J.: John Wiley & Sons, Inc., 2014.

Duany, Andres, Elizabeth Plater-Zyberk, and Jeff Speck. ***Suburban Nation: The Rise of Sprawl and the Decline of the American Dream.*** San Francisco: North Point Press, 2000.

Dunham-Jones, Ellen, and June Williamson. ***Retrofitting Suburbia: Urban Design Solutions for Redesigning Suburbs,*** Updated Edition. New York: Wiley, 2011.

Etingoff, Kimberly (ed.). ***Sustainable Cities: Urban Planning Challenges and Policy.*** Palm Bay, Fla.: Apple Academic Press, 2017.

Farr, Douglas. ***Sustainable Urbanism: Urban Design With Nature.*** Hoboken, N.J. John Wiley & Sons, Inc. 2007.

Farrar, Margaret E. ***Building the Body Politic: Power and Urban Space in Washington, D.C.*** Champaign, Ill.: University of Illinois Press, 2008.

Fotsch, Paul Mason. ***Watching the Traffic Go By: Transportation and Isolation in Urban America.*** Austin: University of Texas Press, 2007.

Franck, Karen A., and Quentin Stevens. ***Loose Space: Possibility and Diversity in Urban Life.*** New York: Routledge, 2006.

Friedman, Avi. ***Fundamentals of Sustainable Urban Design.*** Cham, Switzerland: Springer, 2021.

Fulton, Bill. ***Place and Prosperity: How Cities Help Us to Connect and Innovate.*** Washington, D.C.: Island Press, 2022.

Garreau, Joel. ***Edge City: Life on the New Frontier.*** New York: Random House, 1991.

Garvin, Alexander. ***The American City: What Works, What Doesn't.*** New York: McGraw-Hill, 2013.

Garvin, Alexander. ***What Makes a Great City.*** Washington, D.C.: Island Press, 2016.

Gehl, Jan. ***Cities For People.*** Washington, D.C.: Island Press, 2010.

Gehl, Jan. ***Life Between Buildings: Using Public Space.*** New York: Van Nostrand Reinhold, 1987.

Glaeser, Edward. ***Triumph of the City: How Our Greatest Invention Makes Us Richer, Smarter, Greener, Healthier, and Happier.*** New York: Penguin Press, 2011.

Goodman, William I., and Eric C. Freund. ***Principles and Practice of Urban Planning.*** Chicago: Institute for Training in Municipal Administration, 1968.

Graham, Wade. ***Dream Cities: Seven Urban Ideas that Shape the World.*** New York: HarperCollins, 2016.

Guberman, Marc, Jacob Reidel, and Frida Rosenberg, ed. ***Perspecta 40 Monster.*** The Yale Architectural Journal. Cambridge, Mass.: MIT Press, 2008.

Hack, Gary, Eugénie L. Birch, Paul H. Sedway, and Mitchell J. Silver (eds.). ***Local Planning: Contemporary Principles and Practice.*** East Windsor, N.J.: ICMA Press, 2009.

Hall, Peter. ***Cities of Tomorrow: An Intellectual History of Urban Planning and Design in the Twentieth Century.*** Hoboken, N.J.: Wiley-Blackwell, 2002.

Hall, Peter. ***Urban and Regional Planning.*** Fourth Edition. London and New York: Routledge, 2005.

Harvey, David. ***Rebel Cities: From the Right to the City to the Urban Revolution.*** London: Verso, 2012.

Havens, Gregory T. ***Pedestrian Pockets – A New Suburban Paradigm?*** Cambridge, Mass.: Massachusetts Institute of Technology, Department of Urban Studies and Planning, 1992.

Hayden, Dolores. ***A Field Guide to Sprawl.*** New York:W.W. Norton & Co., 2004.

Hayden, Dolores. ***The Power of Place: Urban Landscapes as Public History.*** Cambridge, Mass.: The MIT Press, 1997.

Inman, Robert P. (ed.) ***Making Cities Work: Prospects and Policies for Urban America.*** Princeton, N.J.: Princeton University Press, 2009.

Jacobs, Allan B. ***Great Streets.*** Cambridge, Mass.: MIT Press, 1995.

Jacobs, Jane. ***The Death and Life of Great American Cities.*** New York: Random House, 1961.

Jacobs, Jane. ***The Economy of Cities.*** New York: Random House, 1969.

Jackson, Kenneth. ***Crabgrass Frontier: The Suburbanization of the United States.*** Oxford: Oxford University Press, 1985.

Kaspirisin, Ron. ***Urban Design: The Composition of Complexity.*** Second Edition. New York and Milton Park, Abingdon-on-Thames, Oxfordshire, U.K.: Routledge, 2020.

Kelbaugh, Douglas. ***Repairing the American Metropolis: Common Place Revisited.*** Seattle: University of Washington Press, 2002.

Kidokoro, Tetsuo. ***Sustainable City Regions: Space, Place and Governance.*** New York: Springer, 2008.

Koolhaas, Rem et al. SMLXL. New York: Monacelli Press, 1997.

Koolhaas, Rem. ***Delirious New York: A Retroactive Manifesto for Manhattan.*** New York: The Monacelli Press, 1997.

Koolhaas, Rem. ***Mutations.*** New York: Actar, 2001.

Krieger, Alex. ***City on a Hill: Urban Idealism in America from the Puritans to the Present.*** Cambridge, Mass.: Belknap Press at Harvard University Press, 2019.

Krieger, Alex, and William S. Saunders. ***Urban Design.*** Minneapolis: University of Minnesota Press, 2009.

Krier, Leon. ***The Architecture of Community.*** Washington D.C.: Island Press, 2009.

Kukla, Quill R. ***City Living: How Urban Dwellers and Urban Spaces Make One Another.*** New York:Oxford University Press, 2021.

Kunstler, James Howard. ***The Geography of Nowhere: The Rise and Decline of America's Man-Made Landscape.*** New York: Free Press, 1993.

Larco, Nico, and Kaarin Knudson. ***The Sustainable Urban Design Handbook.*** New York: Routledge, 2024.

LeGates, Richard T., Frederick Stout, and Roger W. Caves, eds. ***The City Reader.*** 7th Edition. Milton Park, Abingdon-on-Thames, Oxfordshire, England, U.K.: Routledge, 2020.

Levy, John M., Sonia A. Hirt, and Casey J. Dawkins. ***Contemporary Urban Planning.*** 12th Edition. New York: Routledge, 2024.

Lukez, Paul. ***Suburban Transformations.*** New York: Princeton Architectural Press, 2007.

Lynch, Kevin. ***Good City Form.*** Cambridge, Mass.: The MIT Press, 1984.

Lynch, Kevin. ***The Image of the City.*** Cambridge, Mass.: The MIT Press, 1960.

Maas, Winy. ***Visionary Cities: 12 Reasons for Claiming the Future of our Cities.*** Rotterdam: nai010 Publishers, 2010.

Maas, Winy, and Jacob van Rijs. ***FARMAX: Excursions on Density.*** Rotterdam: 010 Publishers, 2006.

MacDonald, John, Charles Branas, and Robert Stokes. ***Changing Places: The Science and Art of New Urban Planning.*** Princeton, N.J.: Princeton University Press, 2019.

Marohn, Charles R., Jr. ***Strong Towns: A Bottom-up Revolution to Rebuild American Prosperity.*** Hoboken, N.J.: John Wiley & Sons, Inc., 2020.

Mars, Roman, and Kurt Kohlstedt. ***The 99% Invisible City: A Field Guide to the Hidden World of Everyday Design.*** New York: Dey Street Books, 2020.

Mathias, Ruth. ***Smart Growth And Climate Change: Regional Development, Infrastructure and Adaptation.*** Cheltenham, U.K.: Edward Elgar Publishing, 2006.

McHarg, Ian L. ***Design with Nature.*** Hoboken, N.J.: John Wiley & Sons, Inc., 1995.

McKenzie, Fiona. ***Welcome to the Future: Drivers and Trends that will Shape Australia.*** Discussion paper for the Australian Futures Project, a multi-sector, non-profit, and non-partisan initiative hosted by La Trobe University, Melbourne, Victoria, Australia, August 2013.

Mitchell, William. ***Reinventing the Automobile.*** Cambridge, Mass.: The MIT Press, 2010.

Mitchell, William. ***Smart City 2020***. Metropolis Magazine, April 2006.

Montgomery, Charles. ***Happy City: Transforming Our Lives Through Urban Design.*** New York: Farrar,Straus and Giroux, 2013.

Montgomery, John. ***Making a city: Urbanity, vitality, and urban design.*** Journal of Urban Design, Vol. 3, No. 1, 1998.

Montoya, Kid. ***The Sustainable Urban Planning Handbook: A Thorough Guide to Urban Design for Architecture, Planning and Development, Ecology and Environmental Engineering for Sustainable Living.*** Kid Montoya, 2024.

Moreno, Carlos. ***The 15-minute City: A Solution to Saving Our Time & Our Planet.*** Hoboken, N.J.: John Wiley & Sons, 2024.

Moskowitz, P.E. ***How to Kill a City: Gentrification, Inequality, and the Fight for the Neighborhood.*** New York: Bold Type Books, an imprint of Hachette Book Group, 2017.

Mostafavi, Mohsen and Gareth Doherty. ***Ecological Urbanism.*** Baden, Switzerland: Lars Muller, 2010.

Mumford, Lewis. ***The City in History: Its Origins, its Transformations, and its Prospects.*** New York: Harcourt, Brace and World, 1961.

Murphy, Connor. ***City Planning: How Citizens can Take Control.*** Tucson, Ariz.: Wheatmark, 2021.

MVRDV. ***Mvrdv: Km3: Excursions on Capacity.*** Barcelona: Actar, 2006.

Newman, Oscar. ***Defensible Space.*** New York: Macmillan, 1973.

Olmsted, Frederick Law. ***Civilizing American Cities: Writings on City Landscapes.*** New York: Grand Central Publishing, 1997.

Park, Robert, Ernest W. Burgess, and Roderick D. McKenzie. *The City.* Chicago: University of Chicago Press, 1925.

Parker, Simon. *Urban Theory and the Urban Experience: Encountering the City.* New York: Routledge, 2004.

Pereira, Francisco C., Andrea Vaccari, Fabien Giardin, Carnaven Chiu, and Carlo Ratti. *"Crowdsensing in the Web: Analyzing the Citizens' Experience in the Urban Space."* Senseable City Lab, MIT, USA, n.d.

Rein, Richard K. *American Urbanist: How William H. Whyte's Unconventional Wisdom Reshaped Public Life.* Washington, D.C.: Island Press, 2022.

Rojas, James, and John Kamp. Dream, Play, *Build: Hands-on Community Engagement for Enduring Spaces and Places.* Washington, D.C.: Island Press, 2022.

Romero, Simon. *Destination Sao Paulo, Metropolis Magazine*, October 2000.

Rossi, A. *The Architecture of the City - Oppositions Books.* Cambridge, Mass.: The MIT Press, 1984.

Rouse, David, and Rocky Piro. *The Comprehensive Plan: Sustainable, Resilient, and Equitable Communities for the 21st Century.* Milton Park, Abingdon-on-Thames, Oxfordshire, U.K.: Routledge, 2021.

Rowe, Collin and Fred Koetter. *Collage City.* Cambridge, Mass.: The MIT Press, 1984.

Rowe, Peter G. *Making a Middle Landscape.* Cambridge, Mass.: The MIT Press, 1992.

Ruby, Ilka. *The Challenge of Suburbia.* Hoboken, N.J.: John Wiley & Sons, Inc., 2004.

Rusk, David. *Cities without Suburbs.* 3rd Edition. Washington, D.C.: The Woodrow Wilson Center Press, 2003.

Rybcynski, Witold. *Makeshift Metropolis: Ideas About Cities.* New York: Scribner, 2010.

Sadik-Khan, Janette, and Seth Solomano, *Street Fight: Handbook for an Urban Revolution.* New York: Viking Press, 2016.

Safdie, Moshe. *The City After the Automobile: An Architect's Vision.* New York: Basic Books, 1997.

Saffron, Inga. *Sprawl Brawl*, Metropolis Magazine, September 2007.

Samuels, Robert. *Timeless Cities: A Blueprint for Livable and Sustainable Urban Ecology.* 2021.

Sassen, Saskia. *The Global City: New York, London, Tokyo.* Princeton: Princeton University Press, 2004.

Saunders, William S. (ed.). *Urban Planning Today: A Harvard Design Magazine Reader.* Introduction by Alexander Garvin. Minneapolis: University of Minnesota Press, 2006.

Schwarz, Terry, ed. *Pop-Up City.* Kent, Ohio: Kent State University – Cleveland Urban Design Collaborative, 2009. Soderstrom, Mary. Green City: People, Nature, and Urban Life. Montreal: Vehicule Press, 2006.

Sennett, Richard. *Building and Dwelling; Ethics for the City.* New York: Farrar, Straus and Giroux, 2018.

Sorkin, M. *Michael Sorkin Studio: Wiggle.* New York: Springer, 1998.

Speck, Jeff. *Walkable City: How Downtown Can Save America, One Step at a Time.* New York: Farrar, Straus and Giroux, 2012.

Speck, Jeff. *Walkable City Rules: 101 Steps to Making Better Places.* Washington, D.C.: Island Press, 2018.

Steiner, Frederick R., and Kent Butler (eds.). *Planning and Urban Design Standards.* Hoboken, N.J.: John Wiley & Sons, Inc., 2006.

Taylor, Nigel. *Urban Planning Theory Since 1945.* Thousand Oaks, Calif.: SAGE Publications, 1998.

Thompson, Nato, et al. *Experimental Geography: Radical Approaches to Landscape, Cartography, and Urbanism.* New York: Melville House, 2009.

Torrens, Nicholas (ed.). *Contemporary Urban Planning.* New York: Clanrye International, 2018.

Urban Design Associates. *The Urban Design Handbook: Techniques and Working Methods. New York and London: W.W.* Norton & Company, 2003.

U.S. Census Bureau Newsroom. *Growth in Urban Population Outpaces Rest of Nation, Census Bureau Reports.* United States Census Bureau, U.S. Department of Commerce, March 26, 2012.

Van der Ryn, Sim, and Stuart Cowan. *Ecological Design.* Washington, D.C.: Island Press, 1996.

Vance, James E. *The Continuing City: Urban Morphology in Western Civilization.* Baltimore: The Johns Hopkins University Press, 1990.

Venturi, Robert, Steven Izenour, and Denise Scott Brown. *Learning from Las Vegas.* Cambridge, Mass.: The MIT Press, 1977.

Vernez-Moudon, Anne. ***Monitoring Land Supply with Geographic Information Systems: Theory, Practice, and Parcel-Based Approaches.*** New York: Wiley, 2000.

Waldheim, Charles. ***The Landscape Urbanism Reader.*** New York: Princeton Architectural Press, 2006. Weber, Rachel, and Randall Crane (eds.). The Oxford Handbook of Urban Planning. Oxford and New York: Oxford University Press, 2011.

Whyte, William H. ***City: Rediscovering the Center.*** Philadelphia: University of Pennsylvania Press, 2009.

Whyte, William H. ***The Social Life of Small Urban Spaces.*** New York: Project for Public Spaces, 1980.

Wilson, Ben. ***Metropolis: A History of the City, Humankind's Greatest Invention.*** New York: Doubleday, 2020.

Wilson, Ben. ***Urban Jungle: The History and Future of Nature in the City.*** New York: Doubleday, 2023.

Wolfe, Tom. ***From Bauhaus to Our House.*** New York: Farrar, Straus and Giroux, 1981.

Yeang, Ken, and Arthur Spector, eds. ***Green Design - From Theory to Practice.*** London: Black Dog Publishing, 2011.

Yin, Jordan. ***Urban Planning for Dummies.*** Mississauga, Ontario, Canada: John Wiley & Sons Canada, Ltd., 2012.

Websites

Berlage Institute. http://www.berlage-institute.nl/

Bing Maps. http://www.bing.com/maps/

Center for Land Use Interpretation. http://www.clui.org/

Centre for Landscape Research. http://www.clr.utoronto.ca/about.htm

City of Nanjing. http://english.nanjing.gov.cn/

City of Somerville. http://www.somervillema.gov/

Florida, Richard. ***The Fading Differentiation Between City and Suburb***, Urban Land Magazine, urbanland.uli.org, January 1, 2013, https://urbanland.uli.org/economy-markets-trends/the-fading-differentiation-between-city-and-suburb

Grand Paris. http://www.legrandparis.net/

MIT SENSEable City Lab. http://senseable.mit.edu/

MVRDV. http://www.mvrdv.nl/#/projects

TU Delft Bouwkunde. http://bk.home.tudelft.nl/en/

U.N.: ***World Population Increasingly Urban***, The Associated Press, CBSNews.com, February 26, 2008, https://www.cbsnews.com/news/un-world-population-increasingly-urban/

Urban Land Institute. http://www.uli.org/ResearchAndPublications/Reports/Infrastructure.asp

West 8. http://www.west8.nl/projects/

Singapore, Republic of Singapore
Bing, © Harris Corp, Earthstar Geographics LLC;
© 2011 Microsoft Corporation.

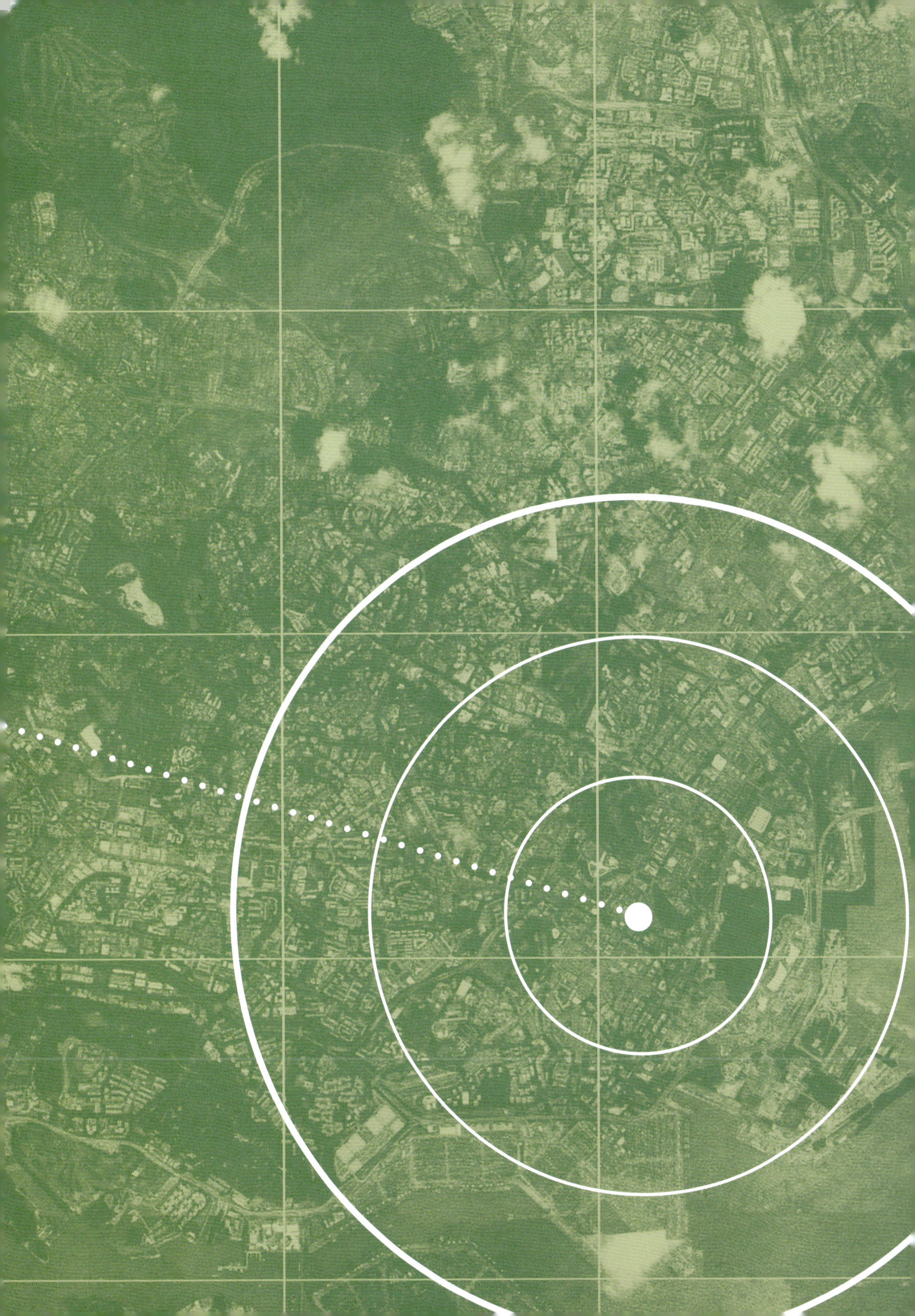

Appendix

7.5

Interpretive Mid-Polis maps

The Appendix contains detailed satellite images of international metropoleis ranging from 100,000 to 15 million in population. These maps are overlaid with diagrams illustrating the approximate location of the (1) city center, (2) outer perimeter of the metropolis, and (3) location of a mid-polis. These maps provide a range of mid-poleis for study, reminding us that, while the mid-polis is specific to location, its types vary depending on many local and regional characteristics. While its variations are many, mid-poleis share certain common attributes across the globe. The following diagrams are a first attempt to define mid-polis characteristics, thus serving as a reference guide to the mid-polis.

These interpretative maps were rendered by Jing Cai from Paul Lukez Architecture. Jing Cai overlaid layers of grids, linework, colors, and filters on top of the base satellite maps so as to highlight unique relationships among the mid-polis, its host city's core, and its outer edge. Each square in the grid is 2.5km (or 1.6 miles), providing easy reference to scale when comparing different cities. The copyright of the base maps belongs to Bing, © Harris Corp, Earthstar Geographics LLC; © 2011 Microsoft Corporation.

1 Amsterdam, the Netherlands
2 Barcelona, Spain
3 Beijing, China
4 Berlin, Germany
5 Boston, Massachusetts
6 Columbia, Maryland
7 Columbus, Ohio
8 Copenhagen, Denmark
9 Denver, Colorado
10 Dubai, United Arab Emirates
11 Düsseldorf, Germany
12 Hangzhou, China
13 Hong Kong, China
14 Istanbul, Türkiye
15 Jerusalem
16 Johannesburg, South Africa
17 Lagos, Nigeria
18 Los Angeles, California
19 Melbourne, Australia
20 Mumbai, India
21 Nanjing, China
22 New York City, New York
23 Paris, France
24 Rome, Italy
25 Rotterdam, the Netherlands
26 São Paulo, Brazil
27 Shanghai, China
28 Shenzhen, China
29 Singapore, Republic of Singapore
30 Suzhou, China
31 Valparaíso, Chile
32 Washington, District of Columbia
33 Zürich, Switzerland

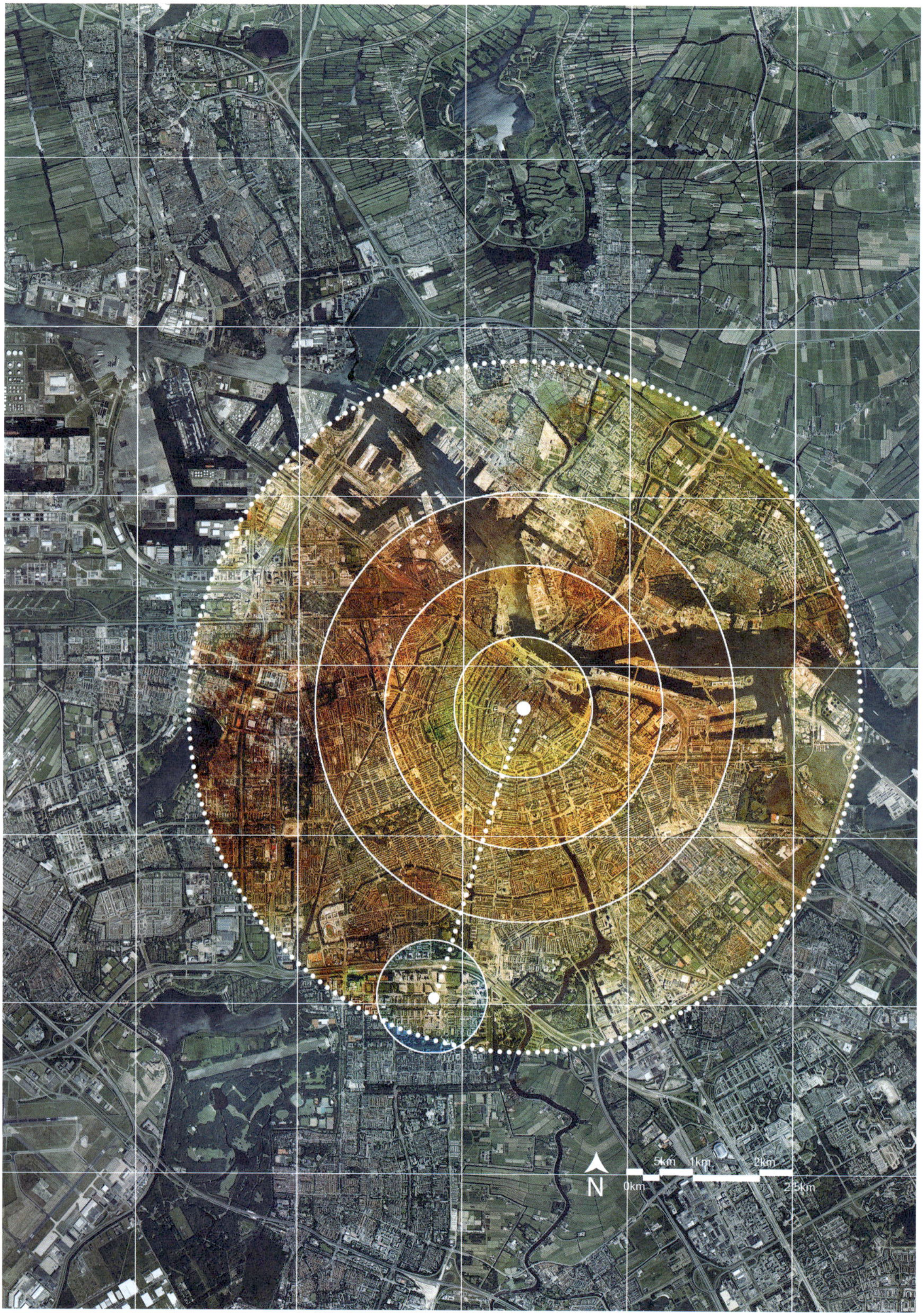

1. Amsterdam, the Netherlands

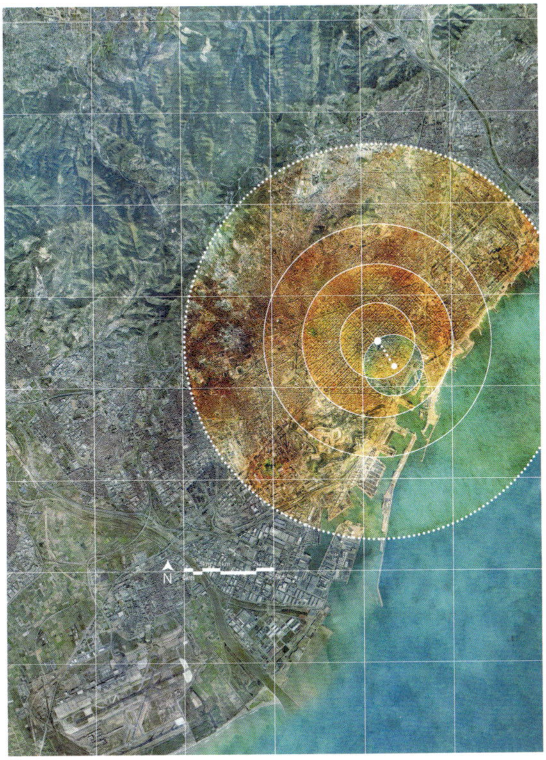

2. Barcelona, Spain

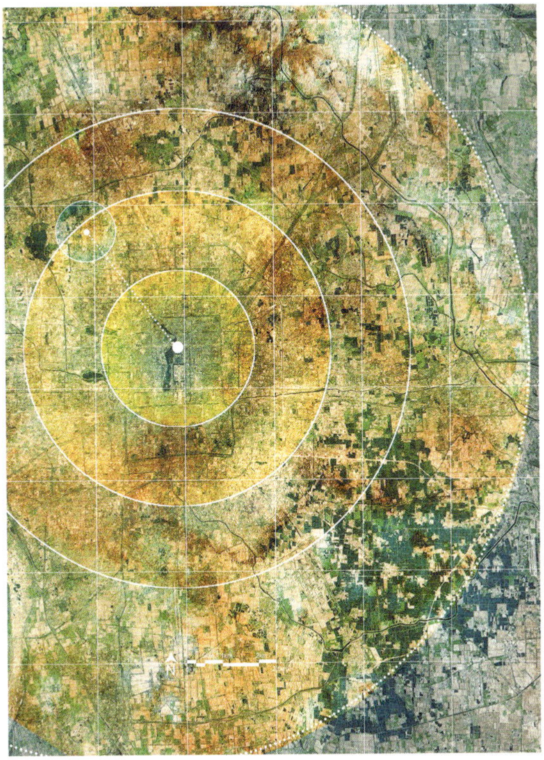

3. Beijing, China

4. Berlin, Germany

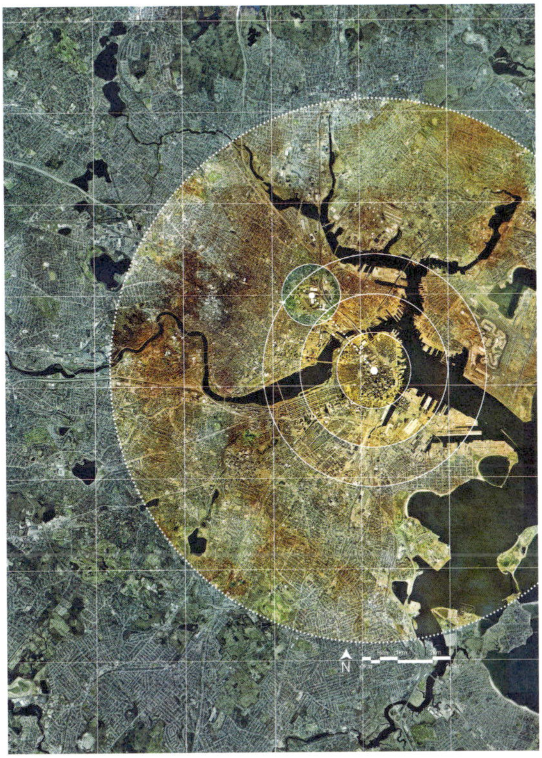

5. Boston, Massachusetts

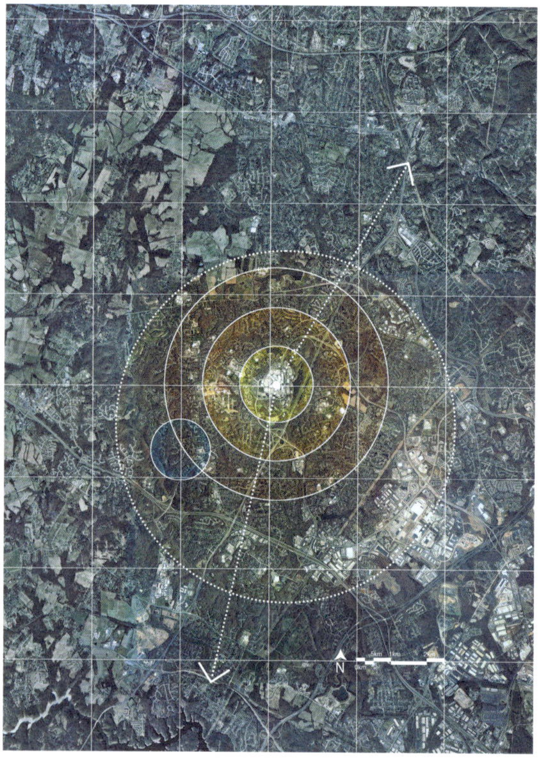

6. Columbia, Maryland

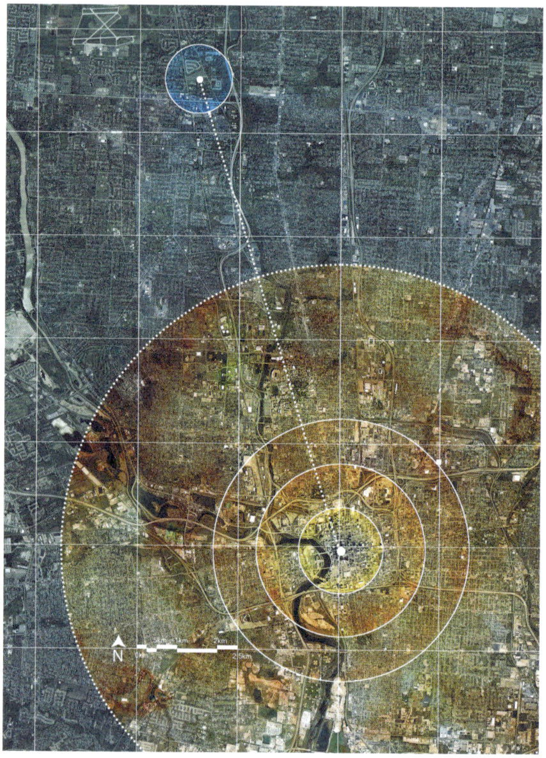

7. Columbus, Ohio

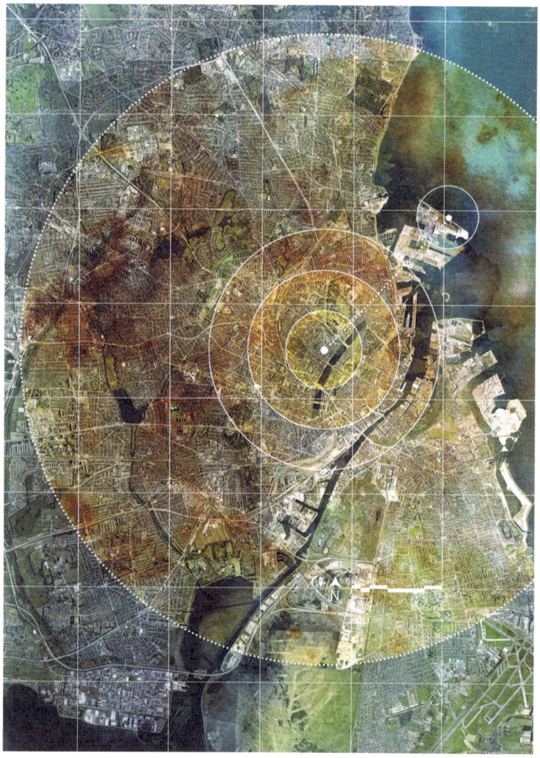

8. Copenhagen, Denmark

9. Denver, Colorado

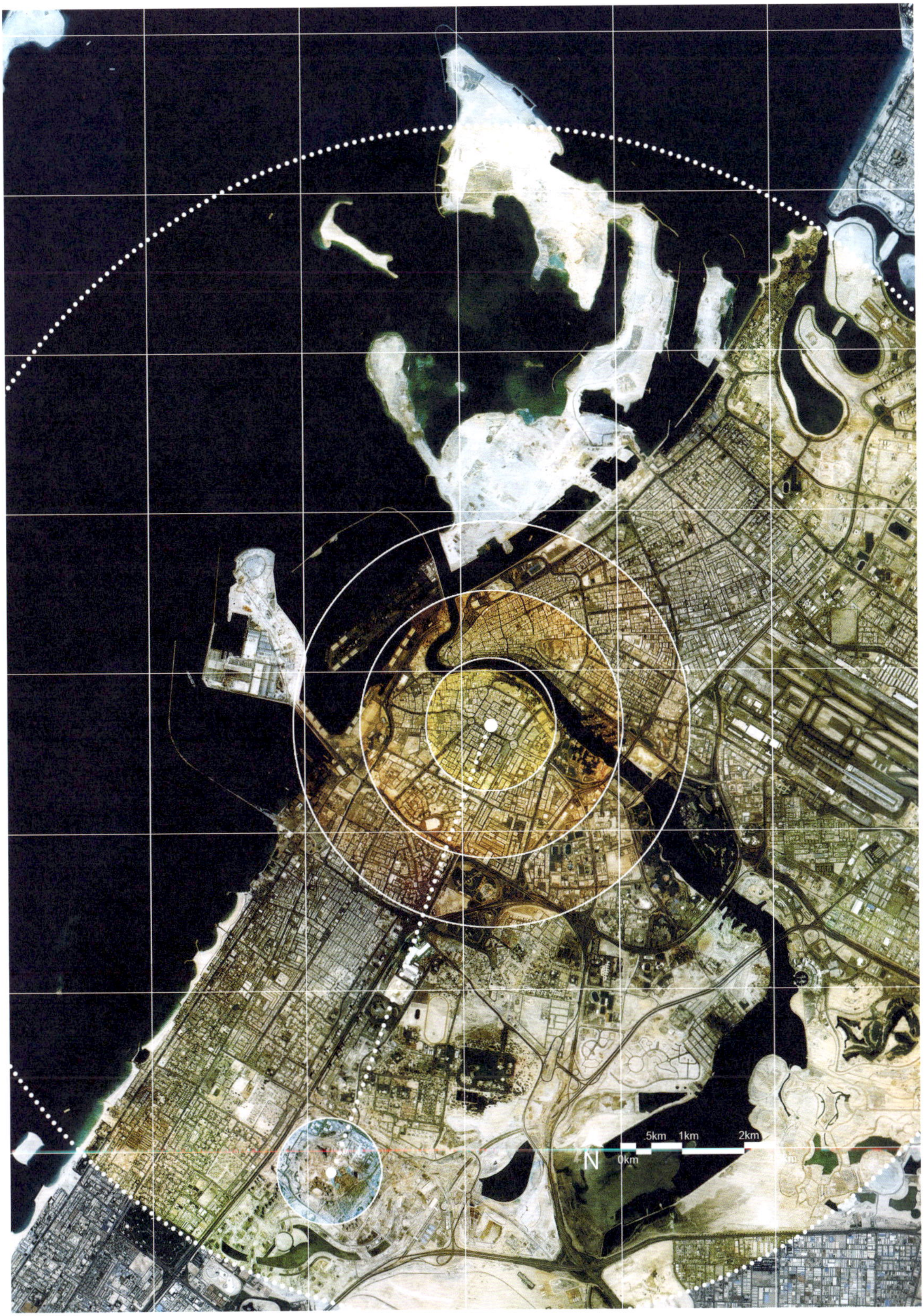

10. Dubai, United Arab Emirates

11. Düsseldorf, Germany

12. Hangzhou, China

13. Hong Kong, China

14. Istanbul, Türkiye

15. Jerusalem

16. Johannesburg, South Africa

17. Lagos, Nigeria

18. Los Angeles, California

19. Melbourne, Australia

20. Mumbai, India

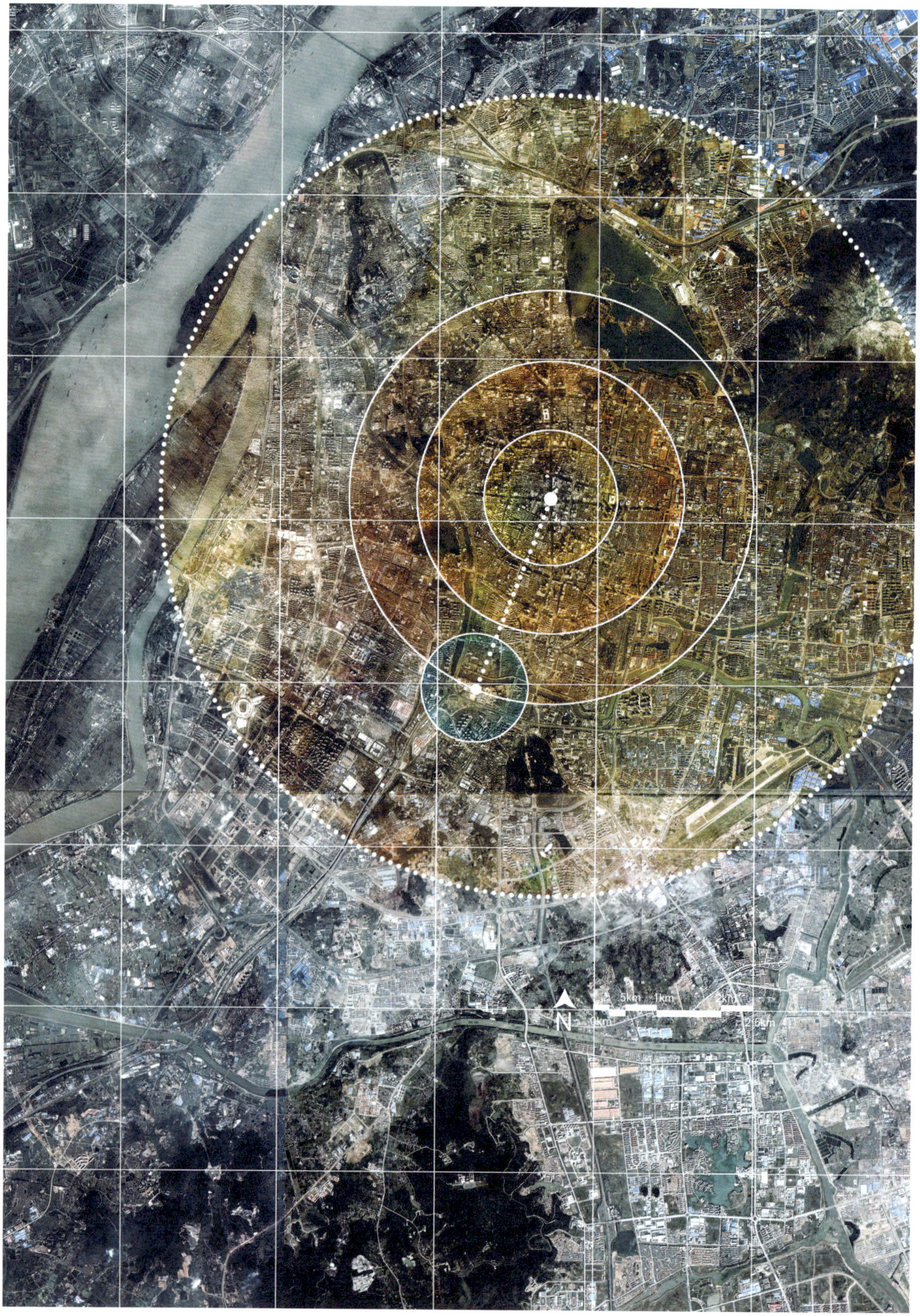

21. Nanjing, China

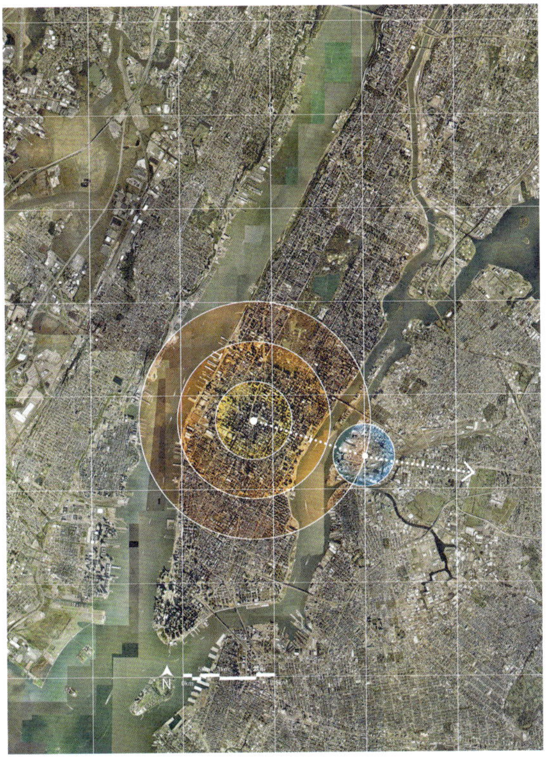

22. New York City, New York

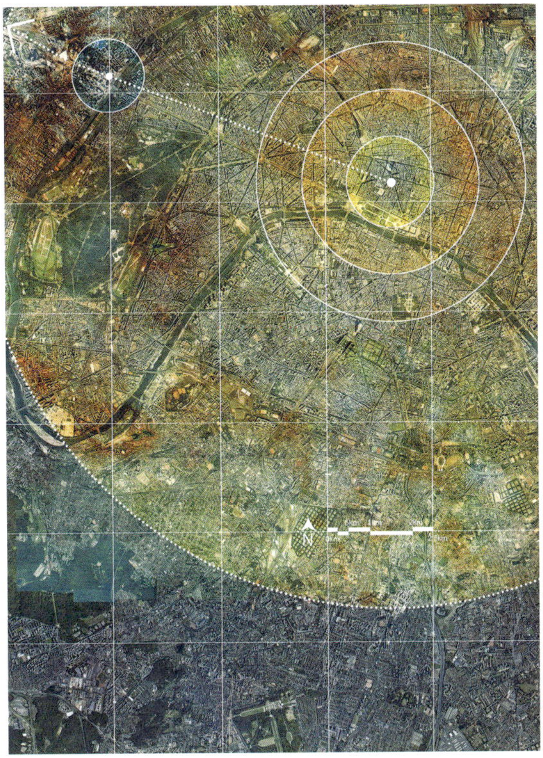

23. Paris, France

24. Rome, Italy

25. Rotterdam, the Netherlands

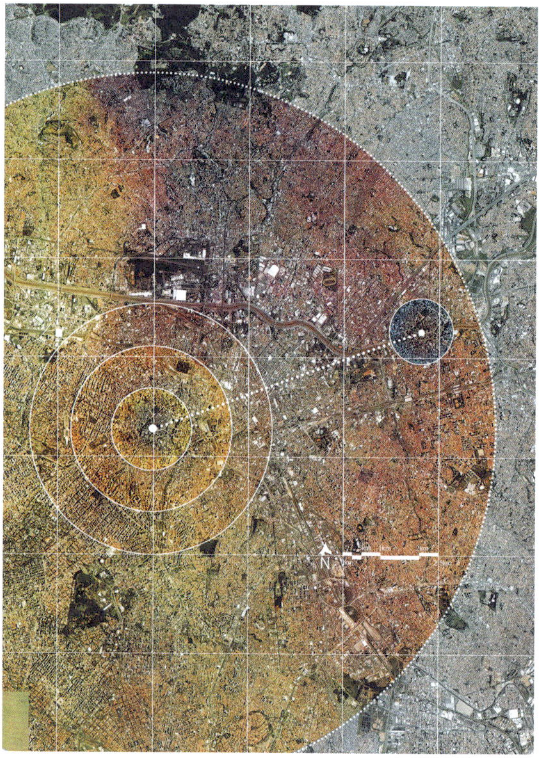

26. São Paulo, Brazil

27. Shanghai, China

28. Shenzhen, China

29. Singapore, Republic of Singapore

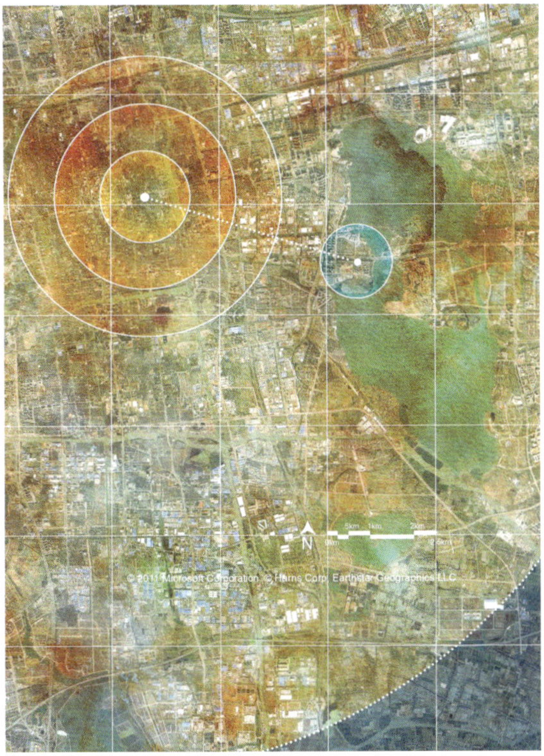

30. Suzhou, China

31. Valparaíso, Chile

32. Washington, District of Columbia

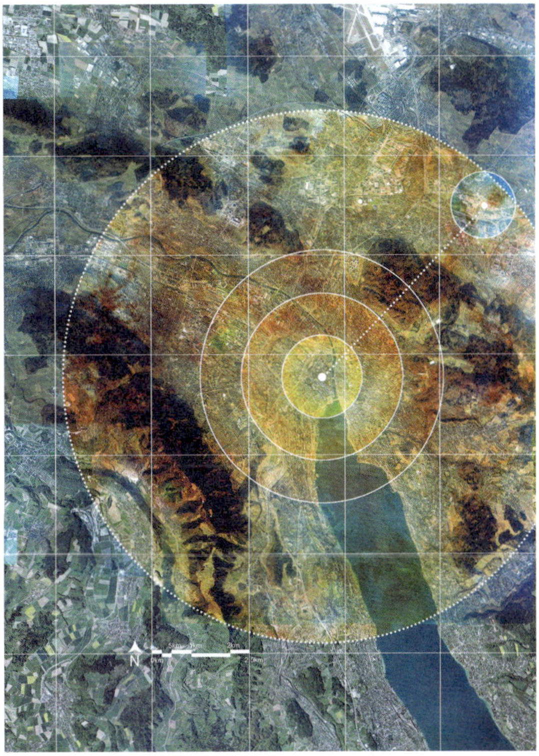

33. Zürich, Switzerland

Book Credits

Graphic Design: Florencia Damilano
Editorial Director: Caroline Kipling
Art Direction: Oscar Riera Ojeda
Copy Editing: Kit Maude

This book originated from a design studio initiated by Professor Bruce Lindsey, then Dean of the Sam Fox School of Design and Visual Arts at Washington University in St. Louis. The book would not be the same without the contributions of a diverse group of international academics and practicing architects who generously shared their work and perspectives. No reproduction of this material is permitted without written consent from the editor and contributors.

General Images — All images belong to the sub-chapter's author unless otherwise noted.

Mid-Polis Aerial Maps — Interpretative maps rendered by Jing Cai of Paul Lukez Architecture. Copyright of base maps: Bing, © Harris Corp, Earthstar Geographics LLC; © 2011 Microsoft Corporation.

Cover Image — "Burlington Re-Visited," a mid-polis "Traces," image by Paul Lukez and Patrick Zhang

OSCAR RIERA OJEDA
PUBLISHERS

ISBN 978-1-964490-22-9
Published by Oscar Riera Ojeda Publishers Limited
Printed in China

Oscar Riera Ojeda Publishers Limited
Unit 1331, Beverley Commercial Centre,
87-105 Chatham Road South, Tsim Sha Tsui, Kowloon, Hong Kong

Production Offices
Suit 19, Shenyun Road,
Nanshan District, Shenzhen 518055, China

International Customer Service & Editorial Questions: +1-484-502-5400

www.oropublishers.com | www.oscarrieraojeda.com
oscar@oscarrieraojeda.com